Cold War Mary

COLD WAR MARY

PETER JAN **MARGRY** ed.

Ideologies • Politics • Marian Devotional Culture

LEUVEN UNIVERSITY PRESS

This book appears in the peer-reviewed series
KADOC Studies on Religion, Culture & Society

Cover: Cover of pamphlet no 39 of *Colección popular. Fomento Social*: Fátima y Rusia (1947) by the Spanish Jesuit Felipe Solanes, published in Barcelona by Editorial Vicente Ferrer.
[Collection of William A. Christian Jr.]

ISBN 978 94 6270 251 6
eISBN 978 94 6166 356 6
D/2020/1869/74
https://doi.org/10.11116/9789461663566
NUR: 704

GPRC
Guaranteed
Peer Reviewed
Content
www.gprc.be

CONTENTS

1
ENVISIONING AND EXPLORING MARY'S THEATER OF WAR*

PETER JAN MARGRY

"Satanic ambushes"

In a smoothly orchestrated campaign, Catholic presses across Europe and North America brought popular, translated editions of Pope Pius XI's encyclical on "Atheistic Communism" to the market directly after it was published on March 19, 1937.[1] His words were delivered as an urgent message to be absorbed and internalized by the Catholic community worldwide. The encyclical contained a vigorous warning against the threat of "Bolshevistic and atheistic Communism" with its perceived intention to overthrow society and, in particular, "Christian civilization."[2]

This letter was far from being the Vatican's first condemnation. Ever since 1846, Pius IX had acted as a "cold warrior" *avant la lettre*, setting out a policy of anti-materialism in which Marxism and socialism (next to liberalism) were staged as world's major evils (Kent 2002: 11). However, *Divini Redemptoris*, to call Pius XI's new encyclical by its Latin title, was the most explicit and

* I would like to thank my colleagues and friends Charles Caspers, Brian Heffernan, Daniel Wojcik, Sandra Zimdars-Swartz and the three anonymous reviewers for their useful comments and suggestions on earlier versions of this introduction. Brian Heffernan edited the English of this introduction.

1 For example in the Netherlands: Pius XI 1937: 36-37, nos. 57 and 58. The encyclical was published in the Netherlands in various editions, including a cheap edition with a large print run for the Catholic Action movement.

2 See the official English translation: <https://w2.vatican.va/content/pius-xi/en/encyclicals/documents/hf_p-xi_enc_19370319_divini-redemptoris.html>.

combative of them all.[3] This doctrinal letter was published nine days after its 'twin', *Mit brennender Sorge*, an equally polemic work directed against German National Socialism. Together these letters represented Pius XI's double strategy of waging battle against the atheistic ideologies of the inter-war years.

It was during the 1930s that the Vatican became fully aware that communism was the more radical and militant form of socialism, an ideology that actually called for revolution and rejected religion (Spinka 1936; Kent 2002: 11-18). An early source for Pius XI's anticommunism was his experience of Russia and the Red Army during the Polish-Soviet war of 1919-1920. As nuncio in Warsaw, Achille Ratti witnessed the defeat of the Russians on August 15, 1920. The advance of their anti-Christian ideology had been halted, allegedly through the intervention of the Virgin Mary (the "Miracle on the Vistula").[4]

To communicate the urgency of the threat and to underline the message, Pius XI incorporated Catholicism's 'classic' dualism between good and evil into *Divini Redemptoris*, in a renewed attempt to convince the world of the fatal dangers of communism (Ramet 1990: 28-36). In this text, Pius XI addressed the 'malicious' ideology and methods of, and the 'false' propaganda employed by communism. In his conclusion, he called his fellow priests and bishops to action, encouraging them to start fighting the "satanic ambushes" of communism and its "plot to kill God". The latter referred not only to the closure of churches and the dismantling of the Orthodox Church, but also to (failed) secularization experiments, the attempts to purge the human psyche of beliefs in the supernatural and of everyday religious faith and to create an atheist alternative (Froese 2008: 1-3; Peris 1998).

Around the same time, the Hungarian-British writer Arthur Koestler published his novel *Darkness at Noon* – a terrifying book which is examined in chapter 6. In the context of Stalin's great purge and the show trials of the 1930s, Koestler revealed the dangers of Soviet Communism to the West from the perspective of a secular insider, familiar with communist ideologies and politics. Pius XI and Koestler were not the only ones to offer a severe critique, and many others over the following decade brought similarly grim messages and warnings to inoculate the public mind against communism.[5] The eschatological prophecy and warning about three days of darkness to come that Koestler referred to (re-)appeared in twentieth-century (Marian) visions and prophecies.[6]

3 Kent 2002: 11, called him the first "Cold Warrior" due to his rhetoric of anti-communism.

4 A website such as <https://justice4poland.com/2016/06/20/the-vistula-miracle-in-1920/> shows how the intervention story is being inscribed into Polish collective memory.

5 There were alternative (Catholic) voices, like French pleas for collaboration between Christians and communists: Thorez 1938: 3, 8.

6 This is a reference to Exodus 10,22; cf. Grabinski 1956; Speckbacher 1989; <https://en.wikipedia.org/wiki/Three_Days_of_Darkness>.

1.1 "All united against communism, as the battle is hopeless on its own". With hammer and sickle Stalin and his cohorts break into a Catholic home". Cartoon by Frans Van Immerseel, published in the Belgian weekly *Elckerlyc*, September 5, 1936.
[Leuven, KADOC: KYC3]

In his letter, Pius XI not only asked his fellow bishops to embrace modern methods of the apostolate, but, warning that "our country is in danger", also exhorted the Catholic community to urgent action to help "save the foundations of the faith and of Christian civilization."[7] In issuing this dictate, the pope not only addressed the universal Catholic hierarchy and the nation states that embraced a Christian culture, but also specifically the flock as a whole, all the Catholic laity who formed the basis of every parish in Catholicism. For the practical mobilization of the faithful, the pope reverted to the organization of Catholic Action. This was the Church's political mass lay campaign begun in the late nineteenth century as an instrument to counteract anti-clericalism in various countries, a goal that was particularly suited to the Church's rigidly anticommunist stance (Christian 1984: 244-245; Hanson 1987: 56-57). The pope envisioned Catholics in general, and Catholic Action members in particular, as his "auxiliary troops" in the fight.[8] This backdrop proved to be fertile ground for a postwar mobilization of the faithful around the Virgin Mary.

The Cold War, the Church, and the Virgin Mary

The Cold War, a period of high political, strategic, military, economic and social tensions in the world in the direct aftermath of the 'hot' Second World War, is at the heart of this volume and at the same time forms its backdrop. The postwar machinations of the Soviet Union created a division in Europe, to which Western Europe responded with political and military restraint (less so the United States). The Cold War became known as new phenomenon throughout the world through an article of the American author Walter Lippmann, published in September 1947 (Lippmann 1947).[9]

Although it is an important epoch in contemporary history, the Cold War and its periodization are not easy to define; they have regularly been the subject of scholarly debates, reinterpretations and redefinitions (Westad 2000). The Cold War as a historical era is usually dated from 1945 to 1989/1991. The traditional view of the Cold War as a single struggle of the West against communism is now seen as obsolete, among other things because it is based on a one-sided, West-centered perspective. Recent research has shifted from the idea of the Cold War as a conflict between the two superpowers, the United States and the USSR, to that of a conflict between two ideological worldviews: capitalism versus socialism (Saull 2007; Leffler & Westad 2010; Westad 2017). Nor was the Cold War just about the two seemingly obvious protagonists, but

7 Pius XI 1937: 39, no. 62.

8 Pius XI 1937: 40-41, 43-44, nos. 64-67, 73-74.

9 <https://www.politico.com/story/2010/04/bernard-baruch-coins-term-cold-war-april-16-1947-035862>; although George Orwell used it once before, in October 1945: Reynolds 1994: 1.

it also involved many other states and social and economic as well as political and military aspects. The ideological confrontation assumed global dimensions with various actors involved on all continents. The desire, particularly on the part of the United States, to suppress revolutionary and communist movements elsewhere in the world often led to domestic transformations that created new international crises. New contributions to Cold War history must thus take into account its omnipresence and pluriformity, and the changes it underwent as the decades progressed.

A focus on ideas and beliefs is relatively new to Cold War research. One of the beliefs in question is the role of religion. The significance of religion and of the churches within the Cold War paradigm has received little interest from researchers compared to strategic, military, and political aspects. Over the past few years, however, scholars have pointed out the importance of religion, which played "a crucial role in the unfolding of the Cold War" (Wallace 2013: 179). The subsequent publication of a number of studies shows that the neglected religious perspective has gained currency in Cold War research (see for instance Lahr 2007; Herzog 2011; Muehlenbeck 2012; Kirby 2013; Wallace 2013). Dianne Kirby has called the Cold War with its conflicting worldviews one of history's great religious wars, due to the imperial ambitions of the opposing superpowers and their vast realms of influence which defined this war and were based on their Christian and communist societies respectively (Kirby 2013: 1). The Christian churches, and in particular the Catholic Church, played a substantial role in the battle. Vatican diplomacy had an evident impact on the development of the Cold War, and even played a key role in the beginning and ending of the conflict (Winter 1972: 262-267; Coppa 2010: 342).

However, more recently interest in the role of religion or the churches in Cold War research seems to have begun to wane, as a number of handbooks or syntheses show (Leffler & Westad 2010; Harper 2011; Westad 2017). The redefining of the Cold War as an international system struggle between capitalism and socialism possibly reduced attention for the importance of religion, concentrating instead on global socioeconomic aspects. This book is intended to redirect the focus again to the dynamics of religion within the Cold War paradigm, breaking ground for the study of a hardly known but fascinating aspect involving the instrumentalization of the supernatural. This book shows how, across the world, Catholics fashioned local responses to the perceived threat of atheism in the context of the struggle over world communism. The rise of atheist totalitarian regimes was regarded by the Christian community as an existential threat. That feeling reached a high point directly after the Second World War, when communism became the leading ideology in the Eastern power bloc of states, in opposition to the Christian Democratic world.

The various chapters in this volume therefore take not a centralist-institutional perspective, but a popular or grassroots point of view. Instead of focusing exclusively on the pope and the Vatican, this volume looks at the global Catholic community and its religious and devotional actions and practices, and at the Marian politics and prophecies that emerged in relation to the developments and tensions of the Cold War.

Central to this perspective is the position and role of the Catholic figure of the Virgin Mary (Warner 1976; Rubin 2009). The contributions explore how, under the aegis and with the help of Mary, through her personal interventions on earth, initiatives were taken and strategies shaped to oppose and curb atheism, secularism, and materialism, and the volume thus provides new insights into the history of politics and piety. The roles that Mary and Catholicism[10] played in the Cold War were mainly limited to anticommunism and anti-atheism, the ideologies which were programmatically and inherently anti-religious.

This last aspect may explain why right-wing regimes were not or hardly attacked by Mary and her devotees during the Cold War period. Such regimes had not been set up to eradicate religion. They usually regarded religion as a strategic, stabilizing element of society (cf. Perry and Echeverría 1988: 210-227, 281-286). The apparitions of the 1930s in Belgium were initially been linked to the rise of Hitler, Nazism and Belgian Rexism because of their vague warnings, but they were reinterpreted later as anticommunist (ch. 5). The messages of Kérizinen (ch. 3) rejected the German occupation in 1940, but their content likewise transformed into anticommunism in 1942. During the Second World War, Nazi Germany acted against Catholicism, but despite the 1937 encyclical, it never became the object of a comparable Catholic movement to the anticommunist movement during the Cold War. The apparitions that took place during the war were more or less overlooked due to the circumstances of the time (Oddone 1944). The fact that the Nazi policy on the repression of Christianity was never set out as systematically and programmatically as its communist counterpart can perhaps account for this, and also explains the reorientation of Fátima during the war.

At the end of the Cold War, in 1983-1988, when fears of nuclear war were still very much alive in Chilean society, the Marian apparitions at Peñablanca and their apocalyptic content did not address the right-wing Pinochet regime. In fact, quite the contrary, they were possibly manipulated by the regime to support the dictatorship (Grasmück 2009: 153-161; 409-456).

The problems in the postwar Middle-East never became a serious battlefield for Mary. The apparitions in the Zeitoun district in Cairo in 1968-1971 were witnessed by Muslims – including President Nasser – and Coptic Christians alike. Yet after some years the apparition became linked to the persecution

10 Catholicism was multiform and not only communism, but also 'left Catholicism', with its priest-workers and the *nouvelle théologie*, part of an inner church battle of directions, were in the context of anticommunism and Maria, to a certain extent suppressed.

of Christian minorities in the country. At the end of the Cold War a certain interest in addressing new opponents was perceptible due to a new Russian expansion, the rise of Islamic radicalism, and the development of Western society itself, with its consumerism and secularism (cf. ch. 14).

The focus in this book is on the figure of Mary, the Mother of Jesus. Mary was to the fore during the Cold War as a militant saint. It is this context that has given rise to the book's title: *Cold War Mary*. She was the upgraded saintly intercessor to play a combatant role against the hegemonic struggle waged by communism. But why was Mary chosen to be deployed to the frontline so prominently by the Church? Was Christ (God) himself not the savior according to theology? Although the concepts of the Sacred Heart of Jesus and Christ the King had some militant traits, their instrumentalization against atheism in the nineteenth and twentieth centuries proved not very successful. The building of the Sacré Cœur was in a way the best visible material success of that policy; a symbol of atonement for the secular-socialist *Commune* uprising in Paris of 1871. But, despite this edifice's imposing aspect, the widely disseminated notion of the Sacred Heart remained too abstract to become an appealing and effective devotional means for the average Catholic around the globe (cf. Jonas 2000).

Mary had been the principal, most important intercessor with God from the beginning of Catholicism, and she was therefore a logical choice for the large-scale mobilization of Catholics. Firstly because of her direct influence with God himself, and because Catholics were already used to direct their prayers to God through Mary. Her gender is also relevant, as Mary was felt to be not only the mother of God, but also a mother for the whole faith community, to whom Catholics could relate easily and in whom they could find comfort (Zimdars-Swartz 1991).

Secondly, Mary's biblical background was crucial for her role in the Cold War period. The Bible begins and ends – Genesis and the Book of Revelation – with Mary as the warrior against Satan par excellence.[11] According to the later Catholic exegetical tradition, she is described in Genesis as the mother of God who protects her children by crushing the head of the serpent. In Revelation she is depicted victoriously in the midst of a battle against the satanic dragon. Catholic history subsequently showed that her power was indeed invincible. During the famous naval battle near the Greek town of Lepanto in 1571, 'Our Lady of Victory' interceded with God, thus saving – so it was claimed – Europe from the Muslim Ottomans.[12] For long, her power remained the most appealing

11 See Genesis 3,15 and Revelation 12,13. The other major warrior figures in the Bible, Saint Michael and his angels, who are also mentioned in the book of Revelation in the context of a battle against evil/dragon, belonged to a lesser category of saints.

12 In the Catholic calendar, five of the nine feasts that have some relation with war are feasts of Mary (Huf 1916).

1.2 Photographic collage representing a military aircraft flown by Pascual Arias, an anticommunist philanthropist based in Madrid, who distributed thousands of images of the Virgin of Fátima. The illustration symbolizes 'bombarding' communism and secularism out of the people with Fátima statues. Published in *Iris de Paz*, no. 2266, May 16, 1950, 162-163.
[Collection of William A. Christian Jr.]

bulwark against the attack on Christendom by other beliefs or ideologies. The use of the rosary as an additional spiritual weapon to implore her intercessory power has since become a recurring feature. The rosary would later also play a central role in the Fátima apparitions and in its apparitional offshoots. This background can help explain why in 1945, when the threat of communism mounted, Catholics looked once more to Mary to fulfill her trusted role as the militant defender of the faith.

Investment in Mary and her Cold War role was also clearly to the fore in the epoch-making definition of a new Marian dogma in 1950 and in the first Marian Holy Year of 1954, both confirmations of her increasing importance during the Cold War era. These proclamations provided even greater stimulus for Marian initiatives, ranging from rosary crusades and rallies to the erection of Marian statues and grottoes (Fuller 2002: 24-28; Roschini 1958).

It was not just the 'generic' Mary who played an important role during the Cold War: for the most part, it was a very specific version of Mary: Our Lady of Fátima. In this particular guise she became the symbol and patroness of anticommunism. The refashioning of Our Lady of Fátima in 1943 – which will be discussed extensively in the section on Fátima – constituted a crucial political intervention by the Vatican, which turned her into the anticommunist Madonna par excellence. This development, as well as the subsequent worldwide tours of her statue, allowed Our Lady of Fátima to surpass all other instantiations of Mary, even Our Lady of Lourdes and the Immaculate Conception or the patron saint of America, Our Lady of Guadelupe. The cult of the latter remained a typically ethnic devotion until she was adopted in the 1970s, particularly in the United States, first for protests related to the social situation of migrant workers and, since the 1990s, by the Pro-Life movement as the patron saint of unborn children (Hall 2016).

Since the Second World War, across the world, dozens of other new Marys were discovered or appeared before the eyes of visionaries, communicating messages of warning. Some of these became important in their own right – Our Lady of Syracuse, the Lady of All Nations (Amsterdam) – but none of them was able to dethrone Fátima, the militant Cold War Mary. Many of the newly received messages were, however, indebted to her because they repeated or rephrased the words from Fátima.

Historiography and research

Scholars such as William Christian Jr., Thomas Kselman, and Sandra Zimdars-Swartz (1991) have already opened up important areas of research at the intersection of visionary culture, religion, and politics. Christian (1984) and Kselman (1982, 1986) pioneered research on the role of local religion, Marian apparitions and devotionalism during the Cold War era. An early book that attempted to trace the theme of Mary's militancy across several centuries and geographical areas was *Under the Heel of Mary.* Although many scholars now consider it to lack balance and display bias in both approach and content, the authors Nicholas Perry and Loreto Echeverria (1988) did provide impetus to investigating the appropriation of the Virgin Mary for political causes and to addressing her militant aspects. Attention was drawn in these studies to the specific instrumentalization of Mary and the ways in which Marian apparitional culture became a focal point for the convergence of lived religion and secular political agendas. This volume brings together not only pivotal early scholars who offer us fresh views, but also new scholars who have distinguished themselves in the field of research of the interaction between the Virgin Mary and Cold War ideologies and politics.

This book project originates from two panels at conferences held in Europe and the United States, in which some of the contributors participated, as

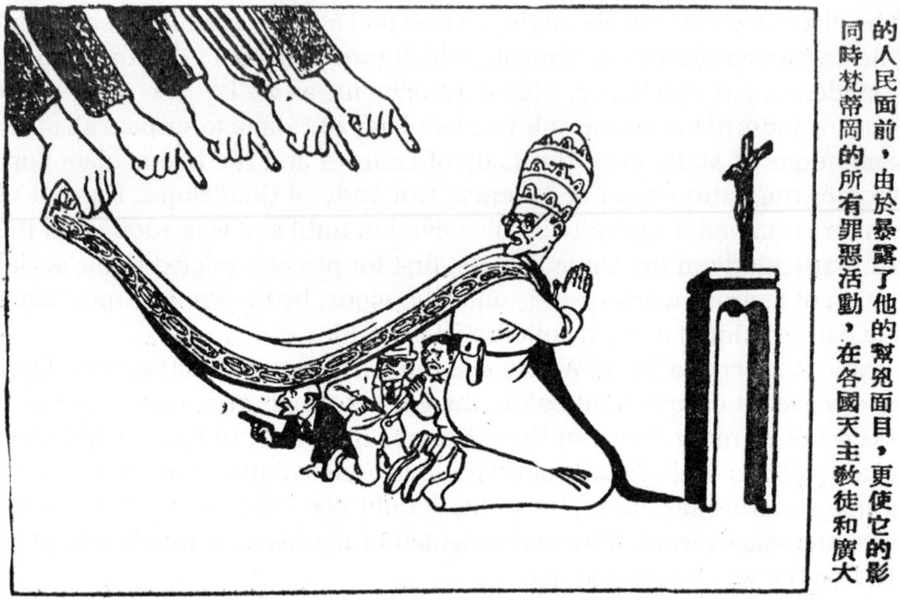

1.3 Chinese cartoon with the text "the Catholics and all countries increasingly look to the pope as the man who can aid Capitalist scoundrels". Reprinted in the Montfortian Marian journal *In Slagorde*, 1947, 46.
[Valkenburg, Archive Dutch Provincialate SMM]

well as from subsequent collegial discussions.[13] The participants of those panels and the authors of this volume are scholars with backgrounds in the fields of (Cultural) History, Ethnology/Anthropology and Religion/Theology. In their work and research most of them show an interdisciplinary approach. They break new ground in relation to religious grassroots Cold War politics, whether or not in connection to the Church and devotional history. The specific point of view 'from below' required new sources and has yielded new results, which can be taken as additional building blocks for the full history of the Cold War. Although Mary's Cold War, too, was a global one, and this volume includes studies that explore both sides of the Iron Curtain as well as non-aligned areas, it has not been possible to represent all regions and periods here.[14]

Various chapters have adopted gender and age perspectives (cf. Westad 2000: 2); women and children were regular local protagonists. Women first

13 Thematic panels on Mary and the Cold War were organized at the annual Meeting of the American Folklore Society in Santa Fe on November 8, 2014 and at the 12th International SIEF Congress in Zagreb on June 22, 2015.

14 Unfortunately, it was not possible to address all of these areas in the current volume; the situation in countries such as Cuba, Korea, Vietnam, China etc. remains to be explored; for the geographical dimensions and borders of the Cold War and religion, see the special issue of *The Journal of Religion* 99,1 (2019) 1-97.

and foremost fulfilled an important role as mediators of visions and of messages. Chapter 12 shows how schoolchildren were systematically infused with an anticommunist mindset by clerics, while elsewhere many non-communist youth movements, student organizations and religious organizations in the free world received payments from the United States (CIA) to help keep out Russian infiltration.[15]

New methodologies and approaches have yielded new results on the neglected theme of Mary and the Cold War. New data and sources required research, especially local details, to explain how Catholic grassroots anticommunism worked in practice. Various types of archives that had rarely been used in Cold War research were therefore consulted for the case studies. Multi-archival and media sources were used, including various "gray sources", booklets, pamphlets etc. often printed locally, but rarely catalogued or acquired by libraries (cf. Zimdars-Swartz, ch. 3; Wojcik ch. 9; Agnew, ch. 14). Visionary culture often exists in a gray area between the official and unofficial realms, and therefore often lacks sufficient archival material. Personal sources easily disappear, while institutions such as the Church usually sidestep this aspect due to their reluctance to give visionaries 'official' sanction. Instead, newspapers, magazines, police reports, visionary writings, leaflets, etcetera, but also websites are important sources. It means also that authors were sometimes dependent on just a few or even a single source. The authors also encountered a discrepancy between local/regional and national sources. For example, contemporary voices outside Italy complained that the successful *Peregrinatio Mariae* (ch. 11 and 12) was regionally well reported, but nearly fully overlooked by national media, or at least that the latter were not paying sufficient attention to it. De la Cruz (ch. 13) points at the heuristic problem that Filippino mainstream and vernacular newspapers offered diverging discourses on the apparitional events, the former discussing them in connection with the Cold War, and the latter more in connection with other, vernacular issues. This again highlights the necessity of consulting local sources to better understand geographical and cultural differences. In relation to this, Christian and Beltran (ch. 6) make a case for the importance of visual culture. (Press) photographs and postcards are essential for a better interpretation of the individual forms that massive mobilization takes within apparitional culture.[16]

15 For example the Swiss-based international lay Catholic movement of Pax Romana (Kotek 2003; Bolton 2011: 151-168) or the clandestine US 'Buddhist policy' in Southeast Asia where religion was used as an instrument of national stability to counter the communist advance (Ford 2017).

16 Various illustrations of this kind make their relevance in this book clear. Many of these rare visuals were collected by William Christian who gave us the free opportunity to make use of them.

Varieties are also evident in the formally 'uniform' sacred materiality of the Marian statues involved. Morgan (ch. 4) explains the relevance of the incongruity between them. A methodological issue of a different kind is the lack of documentation. Situations and issues, particularly in the domain of the Cold War or Church, were sometimes so delicate that related documents were not archived or not even created at all. Former communist Europe apparently has a distinct lack of sources for the topic discussed here (Halemba & Siekierski, ch. 7). Moreover, it is also clear that attempts were made to destroy archival traces of certain specific initiatives. A Dutch Catholic Cold War project was nearly erased from collective memory when the Church itself ordered all related documents to be eradicated. The previously hidden world of that project could only be retrieved and described through a lucky antiquarian find (ch. 12).

Focusing on practices and initiatives at the local level also raises questions about how relations within the Catholic world were shaped. Was there any kind of orchestration from the Vatican in Marian anticommunist action, and what was the relationship between local events or movements and centralist Rome? And, to mention the secular aspect: to what extent did Catholic grassroots initiatives receive support from or connect with governments or national politics? To what extent were there discrepancies between organizers, leaders, and their followings at a local level? From a historical-anthropological perspective, the essays explore often neglected elements such as sacred symbols, images, and devotional practices which further help to explain why the instrumentalization of Mary was so appealing and successful.

Not all contributors specifically address all of these questions, as each author has his own research aims, but an effort has been made at the end of the volume to formulate some general themes and conclusions by way of a synthesis. The remainder of this introduction will explore a number of defining elements and phenomena related to Mary and the Cold War in greater depth, explaining the ways in which Mary became connected to the Cold War and how this relates to the subsequent chapters.

In the following sections, the content of the corresponding three sections of the book will be placed in a wider context, showing how the topics discussed in the chapters relate to the greater and institutional framework of Catholic anticommunism during the Cold War and the role of Mary in particular. Section I of the book consists of chapters that provide broad surveys on the Vatican and the central protagonist of the book, Our Lady of Fátima. Section II deals with country-specific case studies of visionary culture and the local devotional practices and expressions of anticommunism. Section III focuses specifically on the organizational potential within Catholicism for mobilizing groups or masses of people to protest, pray or wage spiritual battle against the threat of communism, and also, in the post-Cold War era, against their own once cherished but now decayed Western culture.

Organizing a volume of contributions into sections provides structure, but also raises questions about overlap, as subtopics treated in a particular chapter may also speak to subjects covered in the other sections. Wherever this is the case, cross-references have been made so as to show the connections in content.

Church and ideologies

This part of the introduction offers a discussion of the context of the section Churches and Ideologies. It deals with the position of the Church and its general views, ideas and politics on how to relate to communism, and the role and position of Mary and her popular devotion.

As early as 1933, interdenominational Christian initiatives like "Pro Deo" were initiated to protect the faith. This was a Genevan international initiative against the increasing persecution of the churches. In 1948 for example a fundamentalist Christian network, the International Council of Christian Churches was founded in Amsterdam to support Christians on the other side of the Iron Curtain and to oppose communism (Ruotsila 2014), while Protestant organizations were also engaged in smaller campaigns such as bible smuggling to Eastern Europe (Boel 2014). But it was the Catholic Church, or rather Catholicism in general, that played the biggest role on the ideological battle field of the Cold War field as *ecclesia militans*. Not only did it have a universal religious-ideological agenda, it also had an active political agenda, which could be used to appeal to various (Catholic) nationalisms in the world. The Vatican's international status as a political power had been enhanced by the Lateran Treaty of 1929 and it wished to capitalize on this. Its politics concentrated especially on diplomacy and were generally marked by caution. As early as the 1930s, for example, Pius XI held back from launching a papal prayer campaign against Russia to save civilization (Winter 1972: 125-130). During the Second World War, President Roosevelt urged the pope to moderate his anti-communist stance even more (Coppa 2010: 342) vis-à-vis his wartime ally.

This caution is one reason why the Catholic Church made use of symbols or metaphors in its mission against communism. The conflict was often cast in terms of "God and Anti-God" (or Antichrist) or of a struggle between "light and darkness," and of waging a "just" war against atheism and religious persecution in communist territories. It was in fact a confrontation between two types of totalitarianism, albeit of a totally different nature. This confrontation became evident when the Russians, in response, also started a campaign, as they viewed Catholicism as an enemy and a threat to stability east of the Iron Curtain, especially since Mary had begun to appear in a number of Eastern Bloc countries and Marian devotion proved to be a strong binding force for nationalism.

Although political leaders in the United States were initially not convinced that the Soviet Union formed a serious threat, most of them soon embraced Pius XII's stance in early 1947, alarmed by what was happening in Eastern Europe. To a certain extent, the United States and the Vatican even became allies in this war, especially after Pius XII abandoned the Holy See's neutrality by approving NATO. Stalin regarded the Church with its presumed lies and slander as the source of many problems in the world and resented its "alliance" with Washington (Zugger 2001: 384-415; Coppa 2010: 343, 345).

Both the United States and Catholic clergy around the world recognized the necessity of anticommunism, including a central role for papal leadership. While the pope did not hesitate to exercise direct influence on the 'national', Italian, level to avert the communist threat, he had to be much more prudent on the international level. Despite the harsh words he spoke or wrote, the pope was usually prudent in his actions, reluctant as he was to jeopardize the interests of his flock in Russia and its satellite states. During the twentieth century the Church's modern means of exercising power took the exclusive form of politics and diplomacy, intelligence or dedicated mass activism. The pope also regularly attempted to mediate in international crises; increasingly by signing concordats and by taking diplomatic initiatives.

Its default diplomatic stance did not imply, however, that the Church or its members espoused pacifist views as such.[17] In the heat of the Italian election of 1948, it was discussed for example whether Pope Pius XII would approve the use of guns and the deployment of armed (secret) movements (such as the *Avanguardia Cattolica Italiana*) to prevent communism from gaining power in Italy. Although the Irish ambassador to the Vatican described the pope as a "great warrior," and although he had the impression that Pius XII "intends to fight," the pope in fact stuck to his spiritual arsenal (Keogh 1991: 937). Pius XII tried to remain as neutral as possible, strongly relying on diplomacy. His successor John XXIII would ultimately even mediate between Khrushchev and Kennedy about arms control issues in the nuclear age (Hanson 1987: 56, 281-322). Apart from diplomacy and intelligence, the other weapons for battling communism that Catholicism possessed belonged either to the genre of general admonitions or to a broad spiritual and devotional arsenal, whether or not of an activist kind. These tactics of the Church were even supported by world leaders such as Eisenhower – "When God comes in, communism has to go" –

17 The stance of the fervent and influential American anticommunist Jesuit Edmund Walsh – who advocated the nuclear "first strike" principle – is a case in point. Walsh was the best-known Catholic anticommunist in the United States and regarded the Soviets as inherently immoral. Basing himself on Christian theology (Thomas Aquinas) and natural law, he argued that man had the right to attack as a self-defense measure (McNamara 2005: 152-154). Walsh also tried to introduce Catholic principles into the field of international relations: McNamara 2005: 168; cf. Gorry 2013 on the nuclear taboo and the (divided) role of the Christians in it.

or Adenauer, who also regarded spiritual weapons such as prayer as crucial in the fight against communism (Wallace 2013: 168; Scheer 2012: 130).

During the first intense phase of the Cold War, a six-year span from the proclamation of the Truman Doctrine in March 1947 to the death of Joseph Stalin in March 1953, the pope worried about the outcome of the Italian elections. But in Belgium and France, too, communist parties had achieved electoral successes. Their increased popularity was due to the Soviets' successful participation in the war against Nazi Germany, to the role played by communists in resistance movements in occupied territories, and possibly also to the fact that these national communist parties had abandoned their initial revolutionary strategy and opted for a more parliamentary policy (Boxhoorn 1993: 1-4).

The Church proclaimed in strong terms that a vote for communism was a vote for the Antichrist, an act that could imperil the eternal salvation of the voter (Ventrone 1996: 267). Robert Ventresca (ch. 2) analyzes the crisis situation in Italy from 1947 to 1949, which was perceived as an existential threat to the Christian nation and to the Vatican, but was seen at the same time as a wake-up call for the Western allies. Ventresca demonstrates how these crucial years form a window on Italian and Cold War history, in which the apparitions and miraculous signs shed light on collective Catholic *political* responses to two simultaneous processes: on the one hand the changes to domestic and international politics brought about by the start of the Cold War, and on the other the institutional and cultural evolution of Italy's post-Fascist, democratic republic. This not only encouraged the pope to adopt a more activist stance but also reflects a broad grassroots awareness of the situation, leading to a response in the form of a steep rise in Marian apparitions.

The peril of communism was felt so deeply that people began to speculate about the evacuation of the pope from Italy, possibly to Ireland. In its deep loyalty to the pope, the Irish government in fact envisaged a role for itself in the crisis, and an opportunity to help influence the Italian elections, although without much success (Keogh 1991: 935). The Irish bishops supported the beleaguered pontiff and sent funds to the Holy See to finance its push-back against the inroads of communism (Keogh 1991: 949). But this was small beer compared to the millions of dollars that the American government, at Pius XII's request, sent through the CIA to the Vatican's political arm, Catholic Action, to influence the elections at the level of individual voters (Wallace 2013: 166).

Shortly after the election – which did not result in a majority for the communists – in July 1949, the Vatican issued the papal decree *Responsa ad dubia de communismo*. This left no space for doubts. It was the strongest admonition by the Church to its flock during the Cold War, a crucial tipping point.[18]

18 Decree of July 1, 1949, in *Acta Apostolicae Sedis* 1949, 334; English version: <http://www.montfort.org.br/eng/documentos/decretos/anticomunismo/>.

1.4 VW-van propagating the devotion and messages of Our Lady of Fátima, in front of the church Santa Maria deli Angeli in Assisi, where in 1948 an apparition of a sighing Maria was seen. Photo, ca. 1963.
[Collection Peter Jan Margry]

The decree warned Catholics worldwide – which applied to every individual Catholic in East and West – that it was not permitted to sympathize with communism or to defend or spread communist ideas, that reconciliation was impossible, and that doing so would expose Catholics to ecclesiastical penalties and excommunication (Dunn 1977: 171-179). The decree was intended to warn Catholics against the attractions of communism, while trying to imbue the Catholic mind with vigorous anticommunism. As Dennis Dunn has put it, in publishing this decree just one month before the first Soviet nuclear detonation, it was the Vatican that "dropped its atomic bomb" (Dunn 1977: 173, 178).

The papal threat conversely resulted in Eastern Bloc governments adopting a repressive policy which tried to subject the Church to state control to limit the impact of the decree. The communist leadership was nervous about the Church's hold over Catholic nationalities like the Croats or the Poles, fearing that its influence might cause national discontent. Active Catholicism was felt to be a potential threat to the stability of Eastern Europe, and indeed the later Solidarity movement in Poland would prove to be a fine example of just that (Coppa 2010: 348). But on the local scale, too, dissidence exercised a certain influence, as the Catholic underground churches in Slovakia (Doellinger 2013) show. For a long time, it was absolutely forbidden in those countries to mention miracles and apparitions – in particular Fátima – which were seen as thermometers of social unrest east of the Iron Curtain (Zugger, 2001: 102-103). The last thing party leaders wanted was another Fátima in their backyard.

In his book on Pope Pius XII, Peter Kent has credited the Holy See with offering consistent ideological rhetoric and leadership against communism. In a way, the Vatican had little choice: wherever communism appeared, the Church was usually the first victim (Kent 2002: 3). Moreover, it was Stalin's intention to destroy the Vatican and Latin Catholicism. Within his sphere of power he nationalized all Church property while imprisoning large numbers of Catholics. The years between 1945 and 1953 were characterized by Soviet disinformation (including framing Pius XII as a Nazi collaborator: "Hitler's Pope"), and vicious espionage and infiltration in the Church and among Catholics in the West.

Apart from the alliance between the United States and the Holy See in the run-up to the Italian elections, the pope had to fight his own "lonely" religious cold war. The Vatican was more or less the only pan-European institution which actively tried to protect Europe from destabilization by militant atheism. It had only a few political weapons at its disposal to realize this goal, of which the excommunication decree mentioned above was the most powerful; the decree was repeated by some national hierarchies (Kent 2002: 5). The Vatican received most of its backing from within the Catholic world community, as contributions in this volume will show. Influenced by the rhetoric on the satanic aspects of Russia's communism, Catholics were anxious about the consequences of their opposition to communism but were at the same time loyal to their Church. However, the distinctive personal forms in which they expressed their support were not always appreciated by Rome, which also regularly rejected these. Marian apparitions were only welcomed and recognized by the Church in exceptional, well-chosen cases, because often the accompanying heavenly messages conflicted with the Church's policy (cf. ch. 8 and 9).

Support for and confidence in the effectiveness of spiritual warfare through prayer and apparitions among ordinary Catholics was founded on their own faith, the rhetorical discourse that the Church had created, and frequent heavenly interventions. It was also stimulated by new narratives about the indoctrination of people in communist countries with the help of psychological manipulation of the masses. It was believed that such totalitarian means could manipulate people's minds, as Joost Meerlo described for example in his *The Rape of the Mind* (1956). For Catholics, this 'menticide', a kind of spell, could be broken by the power of religion, in particular with the help of prayer and the supernatural influence of the Virgin Mary. And, of course, they believed that such influence could conversely also be applied apotropaically to communism. The lay initiative of the Fátima-inspired meditative ritual of the Block Rosary of 1951, for example, performed with a "sense of the supernatural," was an attempt to combat the threat of the atomic bomb (Kane 2004: 102).

Stalin's death in March 1953 prompted a détente, a "cold peace," and after decades of closed gates, the Soviet Union began to open up. Symbolic proof of this came when the famed French photographer Henri Cartier-Bresson was allowed to portray the Soviet Union. His pictures presented the readers of the world's major illustrated magazines such as *Life Magazine* and *Paris Match* with a psychologically 'comforting' view of the enigmatic red state that did not, after all, appear very disturbing when viewed under the aspect of its everyday life.[19]

When speaking about popular visualizations, it is important to mention that this era of Marianization and anticommunism also produced cultural products. One cultural spin-off was the alignment of the motion pictures industry with anticommunism. This had started as early as December 1947 with a declaration made by movie industry executives in the Waldorf Astoria Hotel in New York. They subsequently produced a variety of Marian and anticommunist films, some of them related to Mary's earthly presence in the past or the present, as in Lourdes and Fátima. Christian and Beltran (ch. 6) describe the influence of such movies on the perception of local apparitional events. Sometimes these films proved to be an inspiration for new visionaries (Scheer

19 Like other Western magazines, the Dutch *Katholieke Illustratie* acquired the right to publish these revealing photos in a series of issues: 89 (1955): 433-445, 504-511, 552-559, 600-607, 626-633, 726-731, 789-791, 918-920.

1.5 Poster published by the Bonden van het Heilig Hart [Societies of the Sacred Heart], with the text "The communist world revolution must be thwarted" and an appeal to pray for Christian life in Madagascar, 1959.
[Leuven, KADOC: KCA2263]

2012: 138). Apart from illustrated magazines, radio and later also television, books were a major medium for disseminating views to big audiences. For example, books like *The God That Failed* in 1949, with confessions by six prominent ex-communists who left their former deity (communism), had an impact on Catholics, and appealed to the minds as well the hearts of many Western people in general.

In the meantime, the atomic arms race triggered ever stronger fears of a nuclear holocaust. This new threat caused the pope to call for a Cold War cease fire in 1955. The next year, in his Christmas message of peace entitled *The Fundamental Contradiction of Our Time,* Pius XII took a first step by promising not to launch any further Christian or Marian crusades against the Soviet regime, a pledge that first and foremost concerned Vatican initiatives. His successor, John XXIII, endeavored to further improve relations with Moscow. In response, Khrushchev released Catholics from prison, and even sent the Soviet Union's first-ever Christmas message to the pope in the aftermath of the Cuba crisis (Coppa 2010: 346-347). Despite this mild détente, it remained unclear for Fátima devotees at the time whether the 1952 consecration of the peoples of Russia had been effective, as no signs of their mass conversion appeared evident – although Stalin's death in 1953 could be ascribed to it – and whether the *Götterdämmerung* of communism was indeed imminent (Höcht 1957: 352-356).

After several years of détente, Cold War tensions flared up again in 1958, lasting until the Second Vatican Council reduced tensions between the Church and Eastern Bloc regimes. Although new communist infiltration was feared in Asia and Africa, the 1960s showed a certain decline of anticommunism in many Western countries as well as in the Vatican. The pontificate of John XXIII represented another Church that stood in a new and different relationship to the world. His encyclical *Mater et Magistra* (1961) focused on the importance of the demise of colonialism and of helping the Global South, while communism hardly featured anymore.[20] The Church renewal project was difficult to combine with militant Marianism. This became even more apparent after the renewal brought by the Second Vatican Council, which actually called for a dialog between Marxists and Christians.[21] Such dialog took place in the context of the theology of liberation, which was very successful in Latin America and in some countries in the Global South as it advocated concern for the poor and the oppressed. While in the United States liberation theology was rejected – claims of KGB involvement were made – and the Church was in part critical, in Western European society it blurred the fight of communism, as well as did the rise of anti-American and anti-capitalist sentiments there.

20 Encyclical of May 15, 1961, cf. point 34 "On Socialism", at <http://w2.vatican.va/content/john-xxiii/en/encyclicals/documents/hf_j-xxiii_enc_15051961_mater.html>.

21 On the later relations between the Soviet Union and the United States with the Catholic Church see: Hanson 1987: 323-353.

1.6 Marian medal inspired by President Eisenhower's "Atoms for Peace" speech to the United Nations on December 8, 1953. Depicting an "O Mary" prayer for protection. She appears from an atomic cloud protecting the earth upon which is engraved the word "Pax". The reverse presents the angel warrior St. Michael, engaged in successful battle against the devil.
[Amsterdam, Meertens Institute]

For Paul VI and his *Ostpolitik* the precarious position of Christians in the Eastern Bloc continued to form an obstacle to dialog with communist regimes, as the regimes there regarded the Fátima apparitions and the resulting movements as a dishonest anticommunist ploy on the part of the Church (cf. Haffert 1982: 160-162). But new developments were underway behind the Iron Curtain. In Catholic countries such as Poland and Hungary, or in East Germany with its Evangelical Church, new strategies of cooperation and accommodation removed the urgency of a continued hardline anticommunist policy (Doellinger 2013). The role of Pope John Paul II in relation to the demise of communism is also well known.

The end of the Cold War is usually dated either to the iconic year of 1989, the fall of the Berlin Wall, or to the dissolution of the Soviet Union on Christmas Day 1991, even though some scholars argue that the Cold War never actually ended at all. This latter view has gained traction since 2014, as a revived or new Cold War situation has reappeared according to some media commentators.[22] It reflects the new geopolitical tensions related to Russia's aggressive policy, including espionage, new nuclear weapons, cyber warfare, and territorial usurpations across its borders (Eastern Ukraine, Crimea). The Crimean crisis has given a new lease of life to devotees and Marian conspiracy thinkers who contend that the Fátima prophecies have not yet been fully fulfilled. They believe there is still an active role to play for Mary, as Michael Agnew argues in the last chapter.

Our Lady of Fátima occupies a central position in this study. The introduction and section I therefore give extra attention to her. Sandra Zimdars-Swartz (ch. 3) looks at the resources that were at the disposal of Mary of Fátima and her role in the start of the Cold War. The origin of her specific role lies in the inter-war years, when Mary began to influence Catholic lay persons like the French visionary of Kérizinen. The apocalyptic messages this visionary had been receiving since 1938 initially also addressed the German occupation, but after 1942 acquired an anticommunist tone and advocated the rosary prayer. Kérizinen served as a resource for the Cold War, in particular in France which seemed to be drifting away from the faith and which was in need of conversion and of being rescued from Russian invasion by Mary. The texts of the messages only became public in 1947, when they acquired a more nationalist tone in response to the influence of communism in France, and started to focus on the re-Christianization of France in relation to the *Grand Retour* movement (cf. the last section of this introduction).[23]

Given the importance of the visual aspect in apparitional culture and the popularity and proliferation of the image of Our Lady of Fátima, David Morgan in chapter 4 examines the history, proliferation and uses of the imagery and iconography of Our Lady of Fátima in the context of modern apparitional visual culture, and more particularly of Cold War America. He explores its uses and devotional and political programming, and the way in which it functioned through a variety of visual devices, as emblem, icon, advertisement logo, and totem. In this way the iconography of Fátima can be better situated within the history of modern apparitional imagery, making it possible to trace Fátima's emergence as a visual presence in twentieth-century Catholic devotional cul-

22 The expansion of NATO in 1999 can also be seen as a first restart of the Cold War.

23 A similar belated publicizing of messages happened in the case of the Amsterdam apparitions of the Lady of All Nations. Messages started there in 1945, and they reflected rising political tensions in becoming increasingly anticommunist, but the content was not publicly known until after 1951. *Messages*, 35: in 1946 the Lady spoke about "a fight all over Europe and beyond." She referred to a spiritual or ideological battle, in which the Christian cross was threatened by other crosses or symbols of Nazism and communism. Her later messages became explicitly anticommunist in tone, each time referencing topical issues such as the upcoming Italian elections or Russian nuclear detonations. Cf. Margry 2009.

ture, and to map the commercial production of her imagery in the second half of the twentieth century.

In addition to these two chapters, the remainder of this section will now provide relevant context information by addressing the strongly debated construction of the messages and secrets of Fátima.

Fátima

A major shift in the ideological position of the Catholic Church that was communicated to the Catholic faithful is the refashioning of Our Lady of Fátima into a Cold War warrior. In the small Portuguese village of Fátima, three children saw Mary on a little cloud atop a holm oak tree in 1917 (Freire 1992; Bennett 2012: 69-123). There was nothing unusual about this in the world of visions and apparitions, but after about two decades, Fátima started to grow from being an average rural apparition site, and then a Portuguese national cult, into a central revelation for modern times, including major secrets in relation to the preservation of Catholicism and its supreme pontiff. Because of its paramount importance for the battle against atheism and the controversy surrounding the messages, a deeper discussion of the complicated politics involved in "Fátima" will now be attempted, as this is relevant for the entire volume. The question is: how was it possible that this local cult came to occupy a place at the very heart of Catholic anticommunist world politics and practices.

The pope, out of a general concern for the faith, wanted to protect the faithful in Christ's global realm against the Soviet ideology of dialectical materialism. As a true devotee of the Virgin Mary, Pius XII fashioned a Mary entirely dedicated to that single goal. Due to a variety of peculiar circumstances he was able reshape Our Lady of Fátima into a global symbol of religious anticommunism. During the Second World War, her original messages were molded and extended into a new ideological frame under the influence of, and to suit this goal. From 1942 onwards, he fully embraced the help of this anticommunist Mother of God, or, as one priest of the Company of Mary called her, the true "Missionary of God" (Jongen 1944).

It is difficult to overestimate the importance of Fátima in the context of this volume. This is not only reflected in the chapters in this section dedicated to Fátima, by Zimdars-Swartz and Morgan, but also in nearly all the other chapters in which her cult features as a major agent of power. In analyzing the construction, distribution, and reception of the messages and stories of Fátima, two successive and substantially different narratives need to be identified.

The initial, formal Fátima narrative arose from the recognition of the authenticity of the apparitions by the local bishop of Leiria in 1930. At the end of the 1920s, Fátima was attracting great numbers of pilgrims, although it was still a typically Portuguese shrine.[24] Until the Second World War, Fátima was not widely known outside Portugal.[25] One early external source for these years is the account of the Bamberg church historian Professor Ludwig Fischer, who visited the shrine on the feast of Our Lady of Fátima on May 13, 1929 (Moreira & Cristino 2010: 176-177). Fischer wrote a lively and detailed report of his visit, seen from both a theological and an anthropological perspective. He was the first to identify an important clue for the explanation of Fátima's future anticommunist success. He wrote "[Fátima] ist das Antwort des Himmels auf die Revolution." To be clear, he was referring to the Catholic "taming" of the Portuguese revolution of 1910, the overthrow of the monarchy and anticlericalism, and certainly not to the Russian revolution of 1917, with which Fátima was only associated after 1942 (Fischer 1930: 35; cf. Bennett 2012).

The bishop's authentication of the apparition in 1930 turned the pit-shaped field at Fátima into an official shrine, and this new formal status called for publications passed by the ecclesiastical censor which needed to be translated, as an international audience was slowly beginning to discover the existence of Fátima. The books and brochures published in the 1930s (re)told the story of the apparitions, but did not contain any anti-revolutionary, anti-atheist or anticommunist discourse in relation to the messages.[26]

This narrative began to shift in August 1941, when the only surviving Fátima visionary, Lúcia dos Santos, who was living in monastic isolation in the Spanish municipality of Tuy where she had kept silent about the apparitions for nearly twenty years, began to remember, as she claimed, new details of and secrets from her 1917 experience. Lúcia explained that she had always kept these secrets of Fátima to herself because of their unnerving content. Lúcia eventually wrote them down in a letter as late as August 31, 1941. Remarkably, she not only remembered more about 1917 at that time than she had previously, but it also transpired for the first time that she had received follow-up apparitions of Our Lady of Fátima in 1925 and 1929.

Various reasons caused her to conclude that the time had come to reveal all this new information. The publication of *Divini Redemptoris* in 1937 had disseminated an anticommunist feeling and a hostile image of communism among Catholics, including Lucía, contending that Catholicism was inherently anticommunist. A combination of triggers – *Divini Redemptoris*, the experi-

24 The notion that Fátima was a specifically Portuguese shrine was still very prevalent in 1951, and Portuguese people also explicitly made this claim; foreign pilgrims did not feel part of it, as pilgrim Nico Adema expressed: see *Standaard van Maria* 28 (1952): 45-47.

25 In Germany and the Netherlands for example, it was not before 1929 that the press (and that year's Baedeker on Spain and Portugal) mentioned the apparitions of Fátima for the first time (Fischer 1930: 9). *L'Osservatore Romano* carried a short article on the pilgrimage to Fátima on June 3, 1928. For the 1930s see Dhanis 1945: 7.

26 Thus neither Vanden Vijvere's nor Pizarro's booklets on Fátima contained any mention of communism or of a battle against it.

1.7 Bishop José Alves Correia da Silva of Leiria shows the sealed envelope containing the Third Secret of Fátima. Some of the prophecies written in 1925/1929 were revealed in 1942, while the last had to remain secret until 1960 (the term was later extended to 2000). Photo published in *Katholieke Illustratie* 83 (1949), 549.
[Leuven, KADOC: KYC195]

ence of the 1938 aurora borealis,[27] the outbreak of the Second World War, and the upcoming 25th anniversary of the apparitions – inspired Lúcia to share her knowledge of the additional messages and two of the three secrets with the public (Jongen 1944: 76-81). The secrets were special messages that Our Lady of Fátima had supposedly already revealed to her in 1917. However, Mary's additional message of 1929 proved to be the most important one in the context of the Cold War, as it linked Fátima to Russia and atheism for the first time. After writing it all down, Lúcia sent her final letters or memoirs to the bishop of Leiria and to the pope, who published the content for the first time in 1942 (Zimdars-Swartz 2016 and ch. 3).

The original messages of Fátima, initially revealed in 1917, essentially deal with penitence, prayer (rosary), and conversion, in line with earlier nineteenth-century Marian apparitions. Decades later, having been stimulated to expand on her visionary memories, the first secret that Lúcia added to this existing repertoire of messages contains an apocalyptic, hellish vision of a

27 A blue light, an extraordinary manifestation of the northern lights, was visible even in southern Europe in 1938. Lúcia interpreted this as part of the Fátima prophecy which stated that when the night would be lit up in an extraordinary way, this was a sign from God that he was about to punish the world for its crimes (war, hunger, and persecution of the Church), Zugger 2001: 276.

possible future filled with war and horror for sinful humankind. These torments awaited all sinners and non-believers who would "burn like pieces of wood in the fire." Visions of hell of course were nothing new, but this one was considered more severe and explicit. The second secret offered a solution that could prevent the terrors of the first secret from coming to pass. The apparition stressed the crucial importance to conversion of devotion to the Immaculate Heart of Mary. This devotion is analogous to that to the Sacred Heart of Jesus. By imitating her virtues and uniting themselves with her sinless Heart, believers could foster greater love for Jesus and reconcile and unite humankind to God. The Virgin also desired that the world should be consecrated to her Heart, and that Catholics should perform a monthly Act or Communion of Reparation.[28] This would secure for the world the end of the First World War and the reconversion of Russia to Christianity.[29] The third secret would only be revealed in 2000.

All this implies that 24 years after 1917, a new link was forged between Fátima and a prophesied victory over Russian communism. At a time of war, this introduced a topical new interpretation of the Fátima message, giving it much greater importance and universal relevance. This redefining of Fátima joined together the practice of Marian devotion, the consecration and conversion of Russia, and the destiny of nations and the Catholic Church in what Zimdars-Swartz has called a "divine drama" (2016: 182).

The role of Mary in the later Cold War and the Fátima apparitions were unexpectedly and inescapably connected with each other. Until 1942, there was no indication that Our Lady of Fátima had the potential of becoming the Queen of Anticommunism. But on October 31, 1942, Pope Pius XII broadcast a wartime radio message in the presence of members of the Portuguese community in Rome, in which he spoke for the first time of Mary's predilection for Portugal, and in response to her request, announced the consecration of the world to the Immaculate Heart of Mary.[30] His message was repeated in a more generic way on December 8 in a message to all the bishops of the world, with the instruction to repeat the consecration for their respective dioceses. The message only contained a diplomatic, implicit reference to communism in the form of a call for freedom of religion and an end to the deluge of materialism.

28 The idea of reparation was important as it had a connection with concrete daily life; it meant that Catholics could work to amend the insults inflicted on Christ by others (communists); it is a religious act that is performed for other than personal reasons.

29 See for the official translation in English: <http://www.vatican.va/roman_curia/congregations/cfaith/documents/rc_con_cfaith_doc_20000626_message-Fátima_en.html>. During the war and immediately afterwards, for diplomatic reasons a slightly modified text was used by the Vatican, in which it was not Russia, but the whole world that was consecrated, but this was later corrected again.

30 *Acta Apostolicae Sedis*, 34 (1942): 313-325; <http://www.vatican.va/archive/aas/documents/AAS-34-1942-ocr.pdf>; "Cronaca Contemporanea", in: *La Civiltà Cattolica* 93 (4) (1942): 193-197, 256.

Shortly after Lúcia completed her memoir in August 1941, a handful of clerical authors from the circle around her obtained access to the new secrets and started to rewrite their existing books on Fátima to reflect the new discourse: Galamba de Oliveira 1942, Moresco 1942 and Barthas & Da Fonseca 1943. This was followed by a series of new Fátima publications by international authors, who directly used the new narrative in their work (Lebrun 1942; Zaffonato 1943; Jongen 1944). The new anticommunist message from the Portuguese Madonna spread throughout the world in a very short time.

However, the new narrative immediately faced a fundamental critique from within the Church. Édouard Dhanis, a professor at the renowned Leuven Faculty of Theology (and later at the Gregorian University), responded in 1943 with a critical study of the inconsistencies in Lúcia's new memoirs.[31] He contended that the narratives they contained were at variance with each other and he deplored the uncritical attitude of the authors who had just rewritten the Fátima story. Dhanis characterized the 1925 and 1929 visions, including the secrets, as "heterogeneous," composed differently to those of 1917. "The problem of Fátima," he argued, was that the core of the visions was sound, but that Fátima had acquired "a crust of later elements." He found aspects that had been antedated and even questioned their supernatural origin: the consecration to the Immaculate Heart, the conversion of Russia, and the notion that the Second World War had occurred as the result of Russian atheism (Dhanis 1945: 87-89, 95; cf. Barreto 2016: 405-406). In implicit acknowledgement of his charge, although without directly engaging his criticism, Lúcia's last memoirs were later labelled "Fátima II" as opposed to the 'first' texts of 1917, which came to be known as "Fátima I" (Laurentin & Sbalchiero 2007: 327-337; cf. Maunder 2016: 33-34). For a long time, Dhanis remained a lone critical voice within the Catholic Church, a voice that was disregarded.[32]

The new meaning superposed upon Fátima was further enhanced by the suggestion of various external issues which seemed to endorse it. As it happened, the 1917 apparitions took place more or less during the period between the February and October revolutions in Russia. It is quite customary that visionary experiences are interpreted in hindsight as reactions to societal issues or unrest, and here, too, subsequent clerical commentators easily made the connection between Fátima, the Russian revolution and the rise of Bolshevism. Another element that helped to ascribe prophetic force to Fátima was the political and religious situation in Portugal itself, where the suppression of the communist party in 1926 and the re-establishment of state Catholicism

31 First published in the Flemish Jesuit journal *Streven* in 1944, but a year later in an enhanced book publication: Dhanis 1945. Barthas & da Fonseca 1942, the latter book is an expanded version of Da Fonseca 1931.

32 It is only recently that his criticism is being acknowledged to a certain extent within the Church, see: Laurentin & Sbalchiero 2007: 327-337; from a scholarly perspective, see Maunder 2016: 33-34; Barreto 2016.

by the new right-wing regime in 1933 were seen as a restoration of the faithful nation after political and social upheaval, and were also attributed to Mary's intervention, as Fischer had observed in 1929 (Bennett 2012; Fischer 1930). Perhaps the most important factor in affirming the new role of Fátima was the fact that the reigning pope, Pius XII, had been consecrated a bishop on the very day of the first Fátima apparition, May 13, 1917. He was therefore strongly personally committed to the mission of Fátima. Again, in apparitional culture, the simultaneous occurrence of events on the same date is usually interpreted as something that is extremely meaningful, with the events in question mutually affirming each other. This fact deeply shaped Pius's life, convincing the Marian pope of the truth of Fátima, of the role of Mary as protector, and of the missionary task bestowed upon him by heaven (Maron 1972: 301; cf. Höcht 1957). Later in life, close to the day of the proclamation of the new dogma of the Assumption of Mary, which confirmed her 'divine' status, on November 1, 1950, the Vatican became a sort of "Fátima redux," as Pius XII himself experienced a four-day repetition of the Fátima miracle of the sun in the Vatican gardens (Goubert & Cristiani 1952: 225; Höcht 1957: 285-290; Laurentin & Sbalchiero 2007: 344). This was seen as yet another divine endorsement of the truth of his Fátima mission.

It is clear that the newly scripted narrative brought Fátima into perfect conformity with *Divini Redemptoris* and the Church's anticommunist mission. Henceforth, Mary, in her guise as Our Lady of Fátima, became the central protagonist in anticommunist Catholicism, and she would remain inseparable from it, as she had prophesied the victory of the Christian faith over atheism.

The consequence was that the newly extended '1917' narrative became the basis for the popularity of Fátima and for the more general "Fátimization" of revelational and apparitional culture since the Second World War.[33] It gave an impetus to the renewal and stimulation of Marian cults and Marian devotion across the world, and echoes of Fátima could be found everywhere, especially in the voices of new visionaries associated with conservative Catholicism (cf. Haffert 1950: 137; Margry 2019). An extensive stemma of connected apparitional cults emerged, from Ghiaie di Bonate, Italy (1944), Amsterdam, the Netherlands (1945), La Codosera, Spain (1945), Montichiari, Italy (1946), Lipa, the Philippines (1948), Necedah, Wisconsin, USA (1950), Bayside, New York, USA (1970), Medjugorje, Bosnia-Herzegovina (1981), and Kibeho, Rwanda (1981) to San Nicolás, Argentina (1983), to name but a few major ones (Laurentin & Sbalchiero 2007; Zimdars-Swartz 2016: 183-188). Our Lady of the Ukraine, who appeared in Hrushiv above the cupula of a church in 1987, also

33 This development in fact created two more or less separate 'Fátima' devotional spheres: on the one hand the locally embedded Portuguese national shrine for healing, penitence, and identity, and on the other Fátima as the global symbol against atheism and as movement for prayer (rosary), atonement and conversion.

1.8 Cover of the *Almanaque Apostólico de Fátima* (Pamplona, 1960), which depicts Pius XII's alleged Fátimist visions in the Vatican gardens with a repetition of the sun miracle, on October 31 and November 1 and 8, 1950.
[Collection of William A. Christian Jr.]

fitted the pattern. Her messages, couched in the Fátima tradition, claimed that the apocalyptic Chernobyl disaster of the previous year and Ukraine's martyrs of the faith were signs to the world that the conversion of Russia was underway (Petrisko 2002).[34]

During the Cold War, Lourdes was definitely replaced by Fátima as the primary point of reference in global Marian devotion. However, the fall of the Soviet Union in 1991 caused Fátima to lose some of its relevance, and it was itself partly replaced by new apparitions of the Queen of Peace in Medjugorje in Herzegovina (Laurentin & Sbalchiero 2007: 1195-1224). Although Fátima was mentioned only once in the Medjugorje messages, a few months before the collapse of the Soviet Union, Medjugorje is regarded, without any specific base, by devotees as the fulfillment of Fátima, itself the herald of the fall of communism (Varghese 2000: 189).[35]

Nevertheless, Fátima retained its power to attract attention. The consecration of the world to Our Lady of Fátima and her Immaculate Heart, which she had requested to bring about the collapse of communism, was still a burning issue. The question was whether this had been done properly (or not) by the pope – the conversion of Russia depended on it. Several popes performed the consecration but, due to reasons of diplomatic prudence, never exactly in accordance with the letter of the demand in the secret of Fátima. In 1982 the consecration was again repeated by John Paul II, this time in Fátima itself.[36] It took place a year after the assassination attempt – possibly commissioned by Iran and/or the KGB – on himself on May 13, 1981 (Koehler 2009).[37] That this attempted assassination took place on the feast of Our Lady of Fátima was a providential fact in John Paul II's eyes: to him it meant that Our Lady of Fátima had saved him, despite the fact that the third Secret of Fátima, which was revealed years later, supposedly prophesied his *death* rather than his survival (Congregazione 2000: 21). One of the bullets that had struck him was encased in the crown of the statue: a symbolic gesture to stress Mary's protective power, in particular against the machinations of Russia. Further consecrations followed in 1983 and 1984 during the extraordinary Holy Year of the Redemption, when the original statue of Fátima was placed in Saint Peter's Basilica. It was

34 <http://www.divinemysteries.info/our-lady-of-the-ukraine-hrushiv-ukraine-1914-and-1987/>; about the name link: <http://unveilingtheapocalypse.blogspot.com/2012/01/wormwood-chernobyl-and-hrushiv.html>, accessed October 31, 2018.

35 On August 25, 1991 the Gospa (Mary) demanded a nine-day fast and added, "everything I wanted to realize through the secrets I began in Fatima may be fulfilled."

36 See text: <http://www.ewtn.com/library/papaldoc/consecra.htm#JP2a>. The pope then asked for protection against (nuclear) war, but remarkably no longer explicitly referred to communism, instead making the following oblique reference: "From attempts to stifle in human hearts the very truth of God."

37 Despite various conspiracy theories, a connection between the assassination attempt and the Soviet Union has never been established. This attempt was allegedly foretold in the Third Secret of Fátima.

all just a few years ahead of 1989/1991, foreshadowing, finally, what in the eyes of some Catholics was the victory of the Christian faith over communism.

Fátima is still a source of inspiration for Catholics worldwide, as the example of Catholics in Benin City shows. After the re-consecration of Nigeria to the Immaculate Heart, on October 13, 2017, many inhabitants witnessed an endorsing Fátima-like sun miracle.[38]

Politico-devotional realms

In the summer of 1945, soon after peace had been established in May and the Russians were hailed as brave allies in Europe, this picture began to tilt: a geo-political rearrangement of Europe was becoming evident as Western leaders watched how the Soviet Union established regimes in the occupied countries, laying the foundations for a Soviet-style socialist order. The global campaign initiated by Pope Pius XII returned to the theme of *Divini Redemptoris*. He urged the whole Catholic flock to resist atheist socialism and communism. Along with prominent Catholic lay people and conservative movements he also marshaled the support of various Catholic groups and religious orders for a spiritual holy war which would ultimately draw on the energies of the hundreds of thousands of Catholics who were attracted by and devoted to Mary and her prophetic apparitions. And apparitions there were, dozens of them, and not only, as demonstrated in chapter 2, in the Church's heartland of Italy.

This second part of the volume addresses the ways in which Mary subsequently became instrumentalized in individual countries in Western and Eastern Europe, the United States, and Australia. It sheds light on the attitudes and behaviors of actors mainly at the local level, from visionary experiences and messages, devotional practices of pilgrimage and rosary prayer to larger organized Marian events. This shift entails further reflection on Richard Powers's thesis on the plurality of anticommunism and "the myth of monolithic anticommunism" (Powers 1995: 426-427). Although Powers's analysis focused on American society, his thesis can be applied globally, enabling researchers to distinguish different motives and regional variety. The chapters thus add to our understanding of the plurality of Catholic anticommunisms.

Although the entire twentieth century was a period of intense Marian (apparitional) presence, this presence reached an apex during the Cold War. Moreover, the messages that were advanced increasingly became expressions of Marian interference in secular and religious politics. The significance of the apparitions lies in the fact itself that they occurred, serving as a way to flag tensions and anxieties, an observation by Ventresca in respect of Italy that

38 <https://catholiclinkonline.com/2017/10/31/miracle-of-the-sun-the-re-consecrated-of-nigeria-to-immaculate-heart-of-mary/>, accessed October 31, 2018.

is equally applicable to other countries. Catholics were infused by visionary culture which was popularized through visuals in newspaper articles, photos and movie pictures. This was mostly about ordinary believers, individuals, visionaries, who "acted as antennas", as Monique Scheer has aptly called them (2012: 142), for the widely felt fears of communism and secularization. These apparitional phenomena are viewed as expressions of socio-religious, political and cultural circumstances and tensions in this volume, and not as delusions, or fraudulent or deceitful behavior. For individual believers they represented ways, through supernatural communication, of generating influence in the Church, specifically over its theology and politics. They were a relevant form of leverage especially for those whose voice was not normally heard: women and children. Messages from heaven enabled believers to disseminate interpretations and warnings about the world and about humankind. In the troublesome and anxious postwar era, apparitions seemed to vie with each other in making predictions about the near future.

It was obvious also to the Church that times of social and political tension, upheaval or war were correlated to the ups and downs and cyclical movements in apparitions, as Ciuffa pointed out in his article on the First World War and related visions (Ciuffa 1915). The Second World War was no exception to this rule (Oddone 1944; Graham 1981), although many of the visionary claims of those years were forgotten due to the arduous circumstances during the war. However, this unprecedented apparitional boom became apparent soon after the war. Countries that were in political danger (Italy and France), that had direct and long borders with the communist world (Germany), or were being incorporated by Russia (Poland), proved to be the most fertile ground for apparitions. In each year of the postwar decade, there were at least 10 to 15 apparitions, with an outlier of 30 in the Marian year of 1954; totaling more than a hundred by that year (cf. Christian 1984: 241-243; Scheer 2009). Internationally the most famous event of those years was perhaps the tears shed by the Madonna of Syracuse in 1953. Although this was not technically an apparition, she wept because of widespread disrespect for her Immaculate Heart, and the event thus fit the anti-atheist narrative and the aim of bringing "withered souls back to life again".[39]

Differences of perception between the Church hierarchy and the faithful are clearly visible. In an analysis of the German apparitional wave after 1946, Scheer explains the occurrence of this wave on the basis of the fact that Germany was a direct neighbor of the Eastern Bloc and was also itself a divided country at the time (Scheer 2006a+b, 2009, 2012). German visionaries were constantly asked by local people: "are the Russians coming?" or "is the end of the world near?" But the apparitions were not taken seriously by the prudent local Church, which opposed them in a desire to curb "naïve" enthusiasm and

39 "Verdorde zielen bloeien op...," *Katholieke Illustratie* 88 (May 8, 1954): 871-875.

"superstitious" Marianism and to prevent provocation in a religiously mixed nation. The visionaries were depicted as psychologically disturbed (Scheer 2009: 195, 214; cf. O'Sullivan 2009). Nevertheless the extensive media coverage of the various events in Europe transmitted the content of the messages to the Catholic community at large.

This section begins chronologically with a contribution (ch. 5) by Tine Van Osselaer on prewar Belgium, where a national boom of approximately forty apparitions took place as early as the 1930s, featuring warnings about an undefined 'enemy' and an apocalyptic future, apparently aimed against upcoming right-wing movements or Nazism. However, as Van Osselaer shows, the major sites – Beauraing and Banneux – were only approved by the bishops after a long authentication process during which they were redefined within the new Fátima framework, giving them a new, anticommunist focus. Interestingly, this change in perspective occurred not only in the approved apparitions, but also in those which were not approved. This again manifests the autonomous role of the visionaries and their followings, who were eager to apply strategic re-interpretations.

William Christian and Marina Beltran (ch. 6) describe an early Cold War apparition. They explore how, immediately after the Second World War, even before the proper start of the Cold War, a series of public apparitions to children occurred in Spain, mobilizing immense masses of devotees in a dramatic setting, as their case study of the village of Cuevas de Vinromá shows. Given that Spain had been involved in a civil war with changing alliances between Catholics and communists since 1936, the authors conclude that the Cold War and its anticommunism started earlier in Spain than it did in most other European countries. Their use of special sources such as personal testimony, the regional press and cinema publicity confirms connections between Spanish postwar visions, the ideas of the global threat of communism and the role of the media.

Agnieszka Halemba and Konrad Siekierski focus on the 'other', eastern side of the Iron Curtain, addressing Marian interventions in the communist domain. In chapter 7 they describe how 'new Fátimas' tried to establish themselves in post-1949 Poland, leading to confrontations between Catholics and the state, while the higher clergy chose to collaborate with the communist regime. Both the state and the hierarchy denounced the faithful for their credulity, but the faithful regarded Marian apparitions as a means of creating hope and receiving divine instruction. Halemba and Siekierski focus on the ambivalent position of a number of apparitions that occurred under socialism within existing Church-State relations and on the significance of Fátima for religious life under socialism.

The 1950 apparition of the Virgin Mary to Mary Ann Van Hoof in Wisconsin, the cult of "Our Lady of Necedah", is the starting point for Thomas Ksel-

1.9 “Mary Save Us”, a brochure containing the story and prayers of four Lithuanian girls imprisoned in Northern Siberia. Published in 1961 by the organization Aid to the Church in Need. The cover shows the Russian journal *Pravda*, the ‘mask’ of world communism. A tear in the mask reveals blood and tears, and the cry of millions who call on Mary for help, as the text explains.
[Collection of Peter Jan Margry]

man’s analysis of the link between Marian devotions and the Cold War ideology that shaped American attitudes. Marian campaigns such as the Blue Army and the Block Rosary contributed to a political atmosphere marked by fear of communist infiltration. He explores the evolution of the cult in its Cold War context, with changing practices related to the Second Vatican Council and a fluctuating relationship between the United States and the Soviet Union.

Katharine Massam turns to the somewhat sectarian landscape of Catholic Australia where the threat of Protestantism was ultimately replaced by fear of communism. Prayer, and the rosary in particular, was understood as a vital weapon in the fight for “world peace” and against “atheistic materialism”. In Australia, too, 1942 was a turning point, as it marked the beginning of Catholic participation in the “crusade” for the conversion of Russia as part of a growing engagement with political life. Massam analyzes the significance of anticommunist Marian devotion as a dimension of Australian Catholic political involvement, using the Australian tour of the pilgrim statue of Our Lady of Fátima as a lens for her research.

The subject of Daniel Wojcik’s study in chapter 9 is situated at a later point in the Cold War time line. He addresses the severe warnings in the visions received by Mrs. Veronica Lueken that had been occurring since 1970 in Bayside, in the borough of Queens, New York City. This conservative cult arose after the Second Vatican Council, which toned down the role of Mary as protectress of the faith against communism and formed the backdrop to the Church's courting of Marxism and socialism. The Church's urgent drive to modernize was not well received in traditional and conservative Catholic circles. In pursuing a program of modernization, the Church laid itself open to the suspicion that it was being infiltrated. This idea ignited another wave of Marian apparitions addressing communism, secularism and, increasingly, criticism of the renewed Catholic Church. San Damiano (1961), Garabandal (1961), and Bohan-Mortsel (1967) are well-known early examples of such sites (cf. Zimdars-Swartz 1991: 245-270; Margry 2019). Some were in touch with Michel Collin, antipope Clement XV, who claimed that Satan had entered the Vatican and that Pope Paul VI ("Paolo 666") was a member of the Italian communist party. To the protagonists of this apparitional culture this kind of knowledge was all part of the Fátima prophesies. They stated, "The Vatican deceived the whole world by disobeying Our Lady of La Salette and Our Lady of Fátima (...) and by condemning [the new] apparitions."[40] The Baysiders stand in this line of conservative religious movements. For Wojcik, Bayside represents the most apocalyptic of American Marian apparitions. The messages show an intensification of the eschatological and anticommunist themes of the Cold War Marian worldview expressed in the United States. He analyzes the anticommunist and apocalyptic themes that pervade the Bayside apparitions and the practices of devotees within the context of the politics and tensions of broader Cold War culture. Despite the end of the Cold War, Baysiders hold firm to their belief that communism remains the primary threat to the future of humanity. The movement also reflects involvement in a revival of pre-Vatican II rituals and a nativist return to traditionalist beliefs.

This line-up of devotional events, initiatives and practices shows the influence of local events in a number of countries. The fear of socialism or communism and subsequent Catholic or Marian responses was present throughout Europe, but surprisingly absent in Catholic Ireland. This island on the outer fringe of Europe whose Catholics always professed their full loyalty to the pope, was seen as the world's most Catholic country. Frank Duff's international Legion of Mary (see the next section) from Dublin was one of the devotional expressions of that culture. Although a minor and short-lived Red Scare occurred in Ireland fueled by pre-existing fears, there was in fact very little communism in the country and it therefore never became a real issue (Delaney 2011: 901-903). Moreover, Ireland congratulated itself on the fact that its workers had not fallen prey to "false ideologies"; in contrast to con-

40 Archive of the Collegio Pontificio Olandese in Rome: Antipope Clement XV (Michel Collin) files, 1968-1972.

tinental Europe, it remained shielded from modern influences (Fuller 2002: 28-29). Although communism hardly existed in Ireland, bishops' Lenten pastorals spoke at length about the menace of communism, thus creating a generic fear for the rest of Europe (Fuller 2002: 76-71). There was indeed strong awareness of the European election issues in 1947-1948 as potential dangers. The anticommunist statements made in countries with few communists like Ireland must be understood in this wider European context, including that of Pius XII's all-consuming struggle against communism, which meant that similar rhetoric was used everywhere.

Rhetoric and metaphors were utilized especially for the mobilization and organization of Catholics in groups and mass associations, as a means to fight atheism and communism. The next part will introduce this aspect of Cold War Mary.

Armies and crusades

Whereas nation states are able to deploy military force using physical arms to achieve their goals, this was no longer a serious option for the Catholic Church after the conquest of the Papal States in 1870 and the Lateran treaty of 1929. Joseph Stalin referred to this fact in 1935 in the famous response ascribed to him when the French foreign minister Pierre Laval asked him to improve the situation of Catholics in his country to reduce tensions with the Vatican. Stalin mocked the pope's power saying: "Oho! The pope? How many divisions has *he* got" (Churchill 1955: 121).

This third section addresses the ways in which initiatives were taken within the Catholic world to create and organize armies, under the aegis of Mary, to fight atheist ideologies. These modern faith crusades were simultaneously aimed at conversion, at opposing tepid faith and apostasy, and at preventing Catholics from defecting to such ideologies. And indeed, at the level of the Church's hierarchy, Stalin was right: apart from his ceremonial Swiss Guard, the pope did not have any divisions at his disposal. However, at the local or diocesan level, Catholicism was able to field many ranks of militant and missionary faithful. The rise of socialism and secularism since 1945 occasioned a new crusading era which developed its own elaborate idiom, with Catholics across the world grouped into a panoply of armies, legions, acies, guards, and militia. In their language and propaganda texts they used a prolific, militaristic mimesis which was widely metaphorically practiced. Of course, these groups did not have real soldiers or arms, but they used weapons of a spiritual, missionary, diplomatic and political kind. They assembled in small or large gatherings or even in mass meetings, and often organized militant marches or pilgrimages as a means to manifest their concerns and views publicly and collectively. A wide array of lay as well as clerical initiatives emerged.

The idea of opposing hostility to the faith and of fighting to achieve spiritual goals is inherent in Christianity. The phenomenon can in part be explained from the history of the Church, which had a strong tradition of crusading against infidels or enemies of the faith. When Islam conquered the Holy Land, or when the Ottomans threatened Christian Europe in the sixteenth century, it led to the creation of military expeditions under the sign of the cross, like the Crusades and the Christian Holy League at Lepanto. They were based on the idea of "just war" or the right of war ("jus ad bellum"), a tradition developed in interaction between holy war and jihad from early times up to the present (Hashmi 2012).

As a prefiguration of later Cold War views, after the fall of the Vatican state in 1870 concerned nineteenth-century European Catholics started a 'Black International', a secret militant movement to mobilize the Catholic masses and counteract the 'red' socialist International to fight socialism and support the Holy See (Lamberts 2002). Protection of the orthodox faith at the time also led to a Church-internal countermovement, the Eucharistic Crusade. This was launched to control and overshadow popular Marian devotions, which in the eyes of the hierarchy had become Mariolatry (Maron 1972: 300).[41] But these attempts to reform popular devotion could not prevent a victory for Mary, as Marian devotion remained the preferred devotion of the faithful and subsequently also of the pope in his struggle against communism.

The militaristic rhetoric of this period is partly connected to the pacifist stance of the modern Church and the need to adopt inspiring symbols to stimulate collective action. Faced with a new, aggressive generic enemy, the Catholic community needed a different stance than the devotional one practiced by pious sodalities and prayer groups.[42] The communist threat was presented as a fundamental struggle in which it was necessary to involve militant grassroots Catholic action. It is here that Cold War Mary was 'at her best', as an instrument used in collective forms and expressions. This was not only the case for the Marian legions and armies, but also for the dynamics of the hundreds of thousands of Catholics who came together at public sites to see and experience the Virgin Mary and her warnings, as section II demonstrates.

The spiritual armory used for this in practice usually consisted of liturgical and devotional exercises such as mass, prayer, rituals, the invocation of the supernatural – God and his saints – and, of course, the mass manifestation of the faith and the faithful as forms of more or less implicit protest and militancy. To create mass impact, the spiritual arsenal at the time was increasingly deployed via newly created organizations and Catholic Action

41 In Belgium a children's Eucharistic Crusade was set up in the 1920s, of hybrid character, as one of its devotional focuses was also on Mary and the rosary.

42 The danger for Catholicism was considered to be so great, that some of them advocated a deterrence strategy with the possible use of nuclear weapons (Gorry 2013, 1-5, 171-184).

groups, often initiated by lay persons, whether or not with the help of clerics or religious orders. Four chapters in section III analyze such collective initiatives. Scheer and Margry address the success of the new and appealing international and diocesan marches or pilgrimages which involved implicit protest against communism, and in the case of the latter, also the thwarted attempt to create a Marian underground movement to support Mary's defense ministry in the world (ch. 12). The idea was to mobilize the faithful and to create a mindset of Marian maximalism: Mary as protectrix and mediatrix of all graces. From young schoolchildren to the elderly, Mary was presented as a central figure for all groups in whom they could place their hope. The popularity of the idea of Mary as co-redemptrix increased in this era.

This phenomenon of diocesan, national or international marches gained popularity after it became more widely known that just before and during the Second World War, from 1943 to 1948, *Grand Retour* pilgrimages – a big return to God from error – had been held in France with a statue of Our Lady. These pilgrimages took the form of an itinerant mission which ultimately visited more than 12,000 French parishes in 1947 in order to avert the dangers of mass apostasy and rising French communism, revive communal religion, stimulate private devotion, and connect people with Mary's Immaculate Heart, to which France was consecrated in 1943 (Perouas 1983). In fact, more than ten million French Catholics dedicated themselves to the Immaculate Heart as propagated in Fátima, and to the rosary. The result was that after the war, a new Marian way of fighting communism and secularism emerged in the form of collective public tours and pilgrimages, often called *Peregrinatio Mariae*, a pilgrimage led by Mary, preferably Our Lady of Fátima. By carrying her statue through Europe, large masses of Catholics were able to encounter and find inspiration in a triumphant Mary (Maron 1972: 300-301). The pilgrimages always had a local origin, but were eventually generally approved by Pius XII, who qualified them as 'rescuing crusades' (Polman 1956: 124).

In May 1946, during the international Youth Congress in Fátima, the local bishop declared that Fátima, in its newly created anticommunist version, should become a shrine of global appeal. At the meeting, the delegates embraced the idea of starting a world pilgrimage with the statue, visiting all countries of the world: a statue as a missionary instrument to spread the anticommunist message. For the purposes of this plan, two new traveling statues of Our Lady of Fátima were crafted. They were created by the same sculptor, José Thedim, and were more or less exact copies of the original statue of the apparition (Haffert 1982: 39-40). Such apparitional representations are always interpretations and usually show a certain degree of variation, as Monique Scheer (2014) has demonstrated.

One of these two itinerant Fátima statues started its pilgrimage north- and eastward, with the international Marian congress in Maastricht in the

Netherlands as its first formal destination. Groups of boy scouts and volunteers carried the statue through Spain, France and Belgium and they were welcomed to Maastricht (Netherlands) in September 1947 (see Van Osselaer, ch. 5 and Margry, ch. 12). It was the first stage of a longer itinerary in Our Lady of Fátima's anticommunist mission or campaign, and the statue ultimately visited 53 countries.[43] In 1949, Mary's statue crossed the Mediterranean to visit Africa and it even traversed a number of Muslim countries. Before arriving at its final destination in the Vatican, the tour took an adventurous turn with a secret visit to Moscow in 1950, where the statue was enthroned in a church with diplomatic status. These tours also met another need, as Fátima was at that time still difficult to reach and could not accommodate large groups.[44]

The second statue went westward, first to the United States and to Canada, where devotional attention had begun to be focused on Fátima since 1945 (Haffert 1982: 42-43). In the United States, the tour was organized by the Blue Army of Mary from 1947 on, and it included the mass practice of Catholics taking pledges and making donations. The tours were announced as a form of redemption through permanent pilgrimage and millions of Americans came to gaze at the statue with feelings of devotion along the route. Spontaneous healings and conversions occurred, while tears were sometimes seen glistening in the eyes of the passing statue, while reprises of the sun miracle were witnessed. Massam describes in chapter 10 how the statue was received and instrumentalized in Australia in 1951.

The idea that atheism could be fought through *pilgrimage* retained its force throughout the 1950s in Europe and elsewhere. It inspired several dioceses to organize comparable tours. In their respective chapters, Scheer (ch. 11) and Margry (ch. 12) show in some detail how these statue-centered pilgrimages were conceived as collective anti-atheist rituals in dioceses in Germany and the Netherlands. They were often performed with Fátima statues, as part of the world tour, whether or not in combination or alternation with local or national traditions and regional traveling statues in order to enhance the commitment of the local population and their traditions.

During the year 1949 the Vatican journal *Osservatore Romano* listed a *Peregrinatio Mariae*, accompanied by bishops and cardinals, for every Italian diocese. It was also meant as a prelude to the 1950 "Anno Santo del Gran Ritorno," a title that referred to the earlier 1943 French pilgrimage. In Castelgandolfo, Pius XII himself joined in by attending the tour of the 'Roman' Our Lady of Divino Amore (Polman 1956: 129). In Belgium, the statue was initially carried in a joint procession with Our Lady of Beauraing in 1947, and the same happened in 1949 in Banneux (see Van Osselaer, ch. 5). In 1951, the "Fatimized" statue

43 For a more detailed travel scheme see Moreira & Cristino 2010: 541-545; on Spain and Italy see Christian 1984: 247-249.

44 Morgan has qualified the mission as an inversion of pilgrimage, because it brought the statue to the faithful instead of vice versa, see Morgan 2009.

of Our Lady of Banneux made a full tour along the parishes of the Belgian diocese of Liège, and similar marches with Our Lady of Fátima passed through the German dioceses of Münster and Cologne in 1953 and 1954. The following year a tour was held in the Dutch diocese of Breda (Polman 1956: 16-17). Belgium and the Netherlands were strongholds of the Montfortan Company of Mary, and this order played a crucial role there in organizing the tours and marches and in making propaganda for them.

These are just a few examples of a broad repertoire of such pilgrimages led by Mary, which brought Marian devotion to a highpoint, while pressing home the gravity of the threat of atheism. From the late 1950s onward up to the 1970s, more itinerant Fátima statues were made and sent around the world. Due to this proliferation and the longer distances, foot pilgrimages were partly replaced by peace rides and flights, even to communist countries. The statues were often accompanied by the bishop of Leiria or by ambassadors of the Blue Army (Anon. 1975: 325-351; Haffert 1950: 198-217, 242-264). These pilgrimages continued to be held after 1991, especially in the former states of the Soviet Union, but also in the United States, for instance in Indiana, where the International Pilgrim Virgin Statue Foundation is still an active organization (Morgan 2009: 49-50, 58-59).

Anticommunist meetings, marches, and campaigns may have taken place more often in the West, but Catholics east of the Iron Curtain also organized protests, more or less explicitly, with and for Mary's help. In Poland, the Catholic hierarchy drew inspiration from the *Grand Retour*, as well as from the Fátima pilgrimages. In 1957, after his release from three years of detention, Cardinal Stefan Wyszyński, a national hero due to his personal resistance against totalitarianism, ordered a copy of the icon of Our Lady of Częstochowa to be made. This famed Polish national image stands in a tradition of protective icons that have assured the "miraculous defense" of Christians against barbarians and pagans (Niedźwiedź 2010: 89-94). The prototype of its devotional narrative also goes back to the story of the naval battle of Lepanto, which was won through invocation of Our Lady by praying the rosary. When the copy was ready, Wyszyński had it blessed by Pius XII in Rome. Upon its return in August 1957, the painting as 'Queen of Poland' was brought on a similar protective anticommunist tour that visited every single parish church in the country (Niedźwiedź 2010: 162-163). Unsurprisingly, this grassroots action was regarded as a provocation by the authorities and at some point they stopped the tour and confiscated the painting. The Catholics continued the tour using the symbolically empty frame instead (Niedźwiedź 2010: 121).

The phenomenon of traveling statues was influential in the Eastern Bloc and it even had a "counterrevolutionary" effect. An article in the 1967 issue of a journal of the Russian Communist Party retrospectively acknowledged that the *Peregrinatio Mariae* had indeed had this effect. Twenty years into the pilgrimage, which was usually organized by the Blue Army, the anonymous author criticized the "fanatics" of this army who traveled the world with an endless stock of copies, giving inspiration to anti-Soviet and anticommunist provocations and counterrevolutionary acts.[45] The author was glad that the problem had been solved after 1960, when, he contended, the Cold War had ended with the downfall of the colonial system and the introduction of the peaceful system of socialism, as well as the Catholic Church's shift to "realism".

Marian armies and legions have been criticized for reviving the offensive medieval crusade concept. It has been said that their crusading activities inspired people to fight real wars against socialism and to stage Cold War-related uprisings in countries such as Korea, Hungary, Vietnam, Cuba, Angola, and Mozambique, although no clear evidence is available for such claims.

The Blue Army[46] mentioned above was the group that organized many of the described *pilgrimages*. The Army was an early Cold War foundation that called on Mary to realize a collective fight against communism. After becoming aware of the crimes of the Soviet Union and its Red Army, the American priest Harold Colgan, together with the Carmelite friar John M. Haffert, started this successful Marian movement under the aegis of Our Lady of Fátima in 1947. He envisaged the organization as spiritual militia that would oppose the Red Army, and therefore named it the Blue Army. The idea behind it was to help rescue humanity from prophesied catastrophe, while simultaneously spreading the message of Fátima to the rest of the world (Kohle 1997: 74-76; Haffert 1982: 320-326). Its members accepted the obligation to help the organization fulfil that goal. In May 1947, Colgan swiftly received papal recognition for the Blue Army after a visit to Pope Pius XII. From 1951 onward, the Army's headquarters were based in Fátima itself.

As early as 1950, the Blue Army numbered one million soldier-devotees, a figure that is said to have multiplied in the following years.[47] Jeffrey Bennett has explained the mass appeal of the Army in the United States by pointing to the fertile ground that existed at the time for the Army's "paranoid" ideas: since 1949, the Army increasingly tried to connect and reduce all wars in the world to a supposed cosmic battle between Satan and Mary (Bennett 2015: 263-272). This was a message that found many supporters during the equally paranoid political Red Scare – McCarthyism in the United States – and which

45 Article in the October issue 1967 of the journal *Science and Religion* of the Communist Party, a translation can be found in Haffert 1982: 334-340.

46 Not to be confused with the Army of Mary, a Canadian schismatic Marian group founded in 1971 related to the Canadian visionary Marie-Paule Giguère, see: <https://wrldrels.org/2016/10/08/army-of-mary/>.

47 These figures include both people who sent a signed pledge, donated, and recited the rosary prayer, and people who participated in Blue Army prayer groups, which was "quite a small percentage" of the former group, which comprised millions (Haffert 1982: 28).

also fed into anxieties surrounding the fear of global nuclear war. In this context, the Army functioned as an undercover force whose perfected propaganda techniques showed how Catholic action in the world could be a legitimate expression of spirituality (Anon. 1975: 2; Massam 1991). To what extent it was effective in other parts of the world is still not fully clear. The movement never gained much of a foothold in Europe, while it remained quite a loose group in Australia, where its captivating name was its most important asset, as Massam (1991) shows in her discussion in chapter 10. Once its prime target had disappeared after the collapse of the Soviet Union in 1991, the Blue Army went into decline (Agnew 2010: 59).

The Legion of Mary was a somewhat older Marian anticommunist pressure group. It was founded before the start of the Cold War, in 1921, by Frank Duff, an Irishman who was struck at a young age by Grignion de Montfort's book on Mary, *True Devotion*. In this work, Montfort advocated a central role for Mary in Christian life (Kennedy 2011: 58). On this basis, Duff created a new original movement "under the powerful leadership of Mary Immaculate," one that arguably became the most successful lay apostolate organization in the world. The Legion was essentially an international form of Catholic Action against secularization and atheism as Pius XI wanted it. Its handbook stated that the movement consisted of lay Catholics "for service in the warfare which is perpetually waged by the Church against the world and its evil powers," and described its goal as "crushing the head of the serpent and advancing the reign of Christ" (Anon. 1993: 9, 11). The Legion was clearly activist and militant. Until approximately 1940, it was mainly a Commonwealth phenomenon, but after the outbreak of the Second World War and the beginning of the Cold War the movement slowly began to spread throughout the European continent, obtaining a foothold in a majority of Catholic parishes.[48]

In his theology of the world apostolate of the *Legio Mariae*, the later Belgian Cardinal Suenens asked whether it was possible that the Antichrist – the Army of Satan – might prevail in the present world (1951), given Cold War power relations as they were (Suenens 1951: 191-193). He hoped that the members of the *Legio* would fight effectively as warriors in the service of Mary. The name of the group was changed at an early stage from *Militia Mariae* into *Legio Mariae*, a name derived from the organization of the ancient Roman legions. The movement was set up with the assistance of the Dublin Company of Mary (Montfort Missionaries) as an instrument at the service of the Church hier-

48 In 1939 the Legion was preparing for a wider launch in the world (cf. O'Connor 1939) and had translations made of its handbook for members in various languages. This plan had to be delayed due to the Second World War. French, Italian, and Dutch language editions of the handbook were actually published in 1939, but the establishment of *praesidia* began later: in the Netherlands in 1942; in France probably between 1942 and 1945; in Italy in 1944; in Belgium in 1946; in China in 1948, in Austria in 1949; in Germany in 1955; and in Russia in 1965.

archy. Its members were required to participate actively in the work of Mary, as happened for instance in the Low Countries, where the legion acquired an early foothold on the continent (cf. ch. 12). The purpose of its members was to identify "problems" at the local level that imperiled the saving of souls from atheism, and to try to foster conversion and, ultimately, the return of humankind to the faith. It envisaged the creation of an empire of Mary, in which the rosary was the central prayer practice.

In the same year that the Blue Army was founded, another important anticommunist Fátima movement came into being in the United States. In 1947, Patrick Peyton, a priest of Irish descent who was a member of the Congregation of the Holy Cross, started the Family Rosary Crusade in Albany, New York. Peyton was inspired both by the defeat of the Muslims through the rosary at Lepanto and by Fátima's anticommunist message. He found a new mission or crusade in life: to encourage families to pray the rosary, as the fundamental Marian prayer, as a permanent collective action of evangelization and struggle against atheism and the prevention of communism. With the help of the early and effective use of mass media such as radio and television, the movement rapidly gained momentum and expanded into mass diocesan rosary rallies. The goal was to have rosary rallies in every diocese in the world. The first one was held in Canada in 1947, but this was soon followed by other events throughout the United States, Australia, and later, in 1959 and 1962, also in the Philippines, as De la Cruz describes in chapter 13.

In her contribution, De la Cruz evaluates to what extent anticommunism was disseminated locally and nationally through two major Marian dynamics in the Philippines: the Family Rosary Crusade and the Lipa apparitions. De la Cruz shows that the apostolate that originated in the United States mobilized millions in mass rallies, for which Peyton was even flown in, but that the influence of the universal message was not as stridently anticommunist there as it was in North America, but was instead related more to domestic and family issues. Lipa was framed as an 'Asian Fátima' and connected to the Cold War in the discourse of mainstream English language media. In the United States, Lipa was used to define the Cold War as a global one. But Marian anticommunism hardly featured at all in the vernacular media. Her research also stresses the importance of researching global movements at the various local levels, and of examining the differences between general movements and their ideas and how these are practiced on the ground.

Popular slogans like "The Family That Prays Together Stays Together" and "A World at Prayer is a World at Peace" also to a limited extent entered Filipino collective memory. During the time of the heightened threat of nuclear warfare, Peyton also presented the world with a suggestive choice: "Beads or Bombs?" When the atomic threat ultimately receded, the Family Rosary Crusade similarly started to crumble, although it still exists on a much-reduced scale. The decline of the Crusade was partly caused by a split in the movement in 1978. This divide has a connection with chapter 14, by Michael Agnew, which deals with the role that this part of the Crusade played in relation to Russia and Crimea.

The background of the split in the Rosary Crusade can be traced back to the idiosyncratic activities of Father Nicholas Gruner, who started the international Fatima Center in Canada in 1978. He asked to be given charge of the Rosary Crusade in North America. After he visited Fátima he became even more fascinated by its message, and henceforth connected all significant political and religious events in the world with Fátima. He revived touring with one of the Fátima pilgrimage statues and initiated the *International Fatima Rosary Crusader* magazine. This publication gave an enormous boost to Fátima devotion in North America, and acquired global reach with 400,000 subscribers (Kane 2004: 120-121). Gruner then became obsessed by one of the conspiracy theories surrounding Fátima, the idea that all previous papal consecrations of Russia to the Immaculate Heart had been invalid. When the Soviet Union collapsed in 1991, he could not accept the widely-held belief among Catholics that this was the fulfillment of the Fátima prophecies. He then turned his magazine into a mouthpiece for the presumed hidden truth about Fátima and for the message that there were certain conspiracies that were thwarting a valid consecration. His Fatima Crusade became an institutionalized counter-Church structure which opposed the hierarchy mainly on this issue (Agnew 2010: 14-15).

Gruner strongly believed that the increasing military power of Russia and the alleged deceitfulness of the Vatican's *Ostpolitik* was proof that he was right. For the Blue Army, the main competitor to Gruner's Fatima Crusade in Northern America, the collapse of the Soviet Union in 1991 necessitated a re-evaluation of its worldview. The Blue Army began to regard these events as proof that the consecration of Russia by John Paul II had indeed been valid and that the peace that Mary had promised was in the process of being realized. In contrast, Gruner denied this possibility, stating that "nothing had changed, only different uniforms." For him Russia remained an apocalyptic and anti-Christian force. Like many before him during the height of the Cold War, he regarded his crusade as a cosmic battle between good and evil: Christian democracy and atheist communism (Agnew 2010: 27). After his suspension by the Church in 2001 he became marginalized within the Marian movement (Cuneo 1997: 137-152). To dissociate the Fatima Crusade from its disgraced former leader of the Fatima Center, the organization in 2005 changed its name to World Apostolate of Fatima. The updated twenty-first-century World Apostolate is now organizing new crusades for the conversion of the United States, and more generally against secularization and moral decay in the (Western) world.

The 9/11 attacks and the 2014 Crimea crisis brought new opportunities for Gruner's movement. In his chapter, Michael Agnew analyzes how the Fatima Center, as a conservative organization on the fringe of the Catholic Church, instrumentalized the attacks and the annexation by Russia, again insisting that the Virgin's demand had not been fulfilled, of which these recent events and threats and accompanying dangers offered further confirmation. The Center adapted its policy to the changed geopolitical circumstances and began to apply "pro-Russian apologetics." It argued that Russia had been isolated and provoked by the United States, NATO, and the Ukraine. The Center even began to defend some of Russia's policies against the decadence of the West, thus adapting its mission to the broader societal concerns of Christian conservatives and traditionalists. In the context of extended Cold War geopolitics, it can be concluded that Mary is again being utilized for the protection of the Catholic faith and of Christian values.

As has been seen, the third section of the volume looks at strategic initiatives for mass mobilization in which the Virgin Mary was used for politico-religious goals within the global power arena of early Cold War politics. She was used against atheist ideologies and regimes, but there were also interpretations of a new crusade, this time oriented against secularization and the moral 'evils' that are supposedly particularly present within Western Catholicism.

Readers of this volume are invited to submerge themselves in the fascinating theater of the personifications of Cold War Mary as described in the case studies presented here. Certain commonalities and provocative themes emerge, and the final chapter will bring the various threads together in a conclusion.

BIBLIOGRAPHY

Anon. 1931. "Portogallo: la Madonna di Fàtima." *La Civiltà Cattolica* 82 (3): 377.

Anon. 1948. *Verslagboek van het Maria-Congres gehouden te Maastricht op 3, 4, 5, 6 en 7 september 1947*. Maastricht: Bestuur Maria-Congres.

Anon. 1975. *"There is nothing more." Our Lady's Last Words at Fátima. The Blue Army Pledge to Our Lady of Fátima*. Washington, N.J.: AMI International Press.

Anon. 1993. *The Official Handbook of the Legion of Mary*. Dublin: Concilium Legionis Mariae / De Montfort House.

Agnew, Michael. 2010. *"Russia will be converted": The Fátima Crusade's Marian Apocalyptic Discourse during and after the Cold War*. MA Thesis McMaster University Hamilton, Ontario.

Barreto, José. 2016. "I messaggi di Fátima tra anticommunismo, religiositá populare e riconquista cattolica." *Memoria e Ricerca* 53: 395-420.

Barthas, Casimir, and Luís Gonzaga da Fonseca. 1942. *Fatima merveille inouïe*. Toulouse: Apostolat de la Prière.

Bennett, Jeffrey S. 2012. *When the Sun Danced: Myths, Miracles and Modernity in Early Twentieth-Century Portugal*. Charlottesville: University of Virginia Press.

Bennett, Jeffrey S. 2015. "The Blue Army and the Red Scare: Politics, Religion, and Cold War Paranoia." *Politics, Religion & Ideology* 16: 263-281.

Blumenau, Bernhard, Jussi M. Hanhimäki and Barbara Zanchetta. 2018. *New Perspectives on the End of the Cold War: Unexpected Transformations?* New York: Routledge.

Boel, Bent. 2014. "Bible Smuggling and Human Rights in the Cold War." In *Transnational Anti-Communism and the Cold War: Agents, Activities, and Networks*, edited by Luc van Dongen, Stéphanie Roulin and Giles Scott-Smith, 263-275. Basingstoke: Palgrave.

Bolton, Kerry R. 2011. *Revolution from Above: Manufacturing 'dissent' in the New World Order*. London: Arktos.

Boxhoorn, Abraham. 1993. *The Cold War and the Rift in the Governments of National Unity. Belgium, France and Italy in the Spring of 1947: A Comparison*. Amsterdam: University of Amsterdam.

Castelbranco, José. 1939 [1943²]. *Le miracle inouï de Fátima*. Paris: H. Sudour.

Chadwick, Owen. 1993. *The Christian Church in the Cold War*. London: Penguin Books.

Christian Jr, William A. 1984. "Religious Apparitions and the Cold War in Southern Europe." In *Religion, Power and Protest in Local Communities: The Northern Shore of the Mediterranean*, edited by Eric R. Wolf, 239-266. Berlin: Mouton.

Churchill, Winston S. 1955. *The Second World War*. Vol. 1: *The Gathering Storm*. London: Cassell & Co.

Ciuffa, Giuseppe. 1915. *La guerra europea e le profezie*. Rome: Desclée.

Clay, J. Eugene. 2017. "Marian Revelations in the Russian Context: The Cosmopolitics of Blessed John." *Nova Religio* 21 (2): 26-42.

Congregazione per la Dottrina della Fede. 2000. *Il Messaggio di Fátima*. Vatican City: Libreria Editrice Vaticana.

Coppa, Frank J. 2010. "Cold War and the Papacy." In *New Catholic Encyclopedia Supplement*, vol. 1, 342-349. Farmington Hills, MI: Gale.

Crossman, Richard (ed.). 1949. *The God That Failed: A Confession*. New York: Harper Row.

Cuneo, Michael W. 1997. *The Smoke of Satan: Conservative and Traditionalist Dissent in Contemporary American Catholicism*. New York: Oxford University Press.

Delaney, Enda. 2011. "Anti-communism in Mid-Twentieth-Century Ireland." *English Historical Review* 126: 878-903.

Dhanis, Édouard. 1945. *Bij de Verschijningen en het Geheim van Fátima. Een critische Bijdrage*. Bruges: De Kinkhoren.

Doellinger, David. 2013. *Turning Prayers into Protests: Religious-based Activism and its Challenge to State Power in Socialist Slovakia and East-Germany*. Budapest: Central European University Press.

Dunn, Dennis J. 1977. *The Catholic Church and the Soviet Government, 1939-1949*. Boulder Co. / New York: East-European Quarterly / Columbia University Press.

Ernst, Robert. 1959. *Maria redet zu uns. Marienerscheinungen seit 1830*. Eupen: Markus-Verlag.

Evans, Hilary, and Robert E. Bartholomew. 2009. *Outbreak! The Encyclopedia of Extraordinary Social Behaviour*. San Antonio: Anomalist Books.

Fischer, Ludwig. 1930. *Fatima, das portugiesische Lourdes. Reiseeindrücke*. Kirnach-Villingen, Baden: Verlag der Schulbrüder.

Ford, Eugene. 2017. *Cold War Monks: Buddhism and America's Secret Strategy in Southeast Asia*. New Haven: Yale University Press.

Frank, Robert L. 1992. "Prelude to Cold War: American Catholics and Communism." *Journal of Church and State* 34 (1): 39-56.

Freire, José Geraldes. 1992. *Documentaçáo crítica de Fátima. 1. Interrogatórios aos videntes 1917*. Fátima: Santuário de Fátima.

Froese, Paul. 2008. *The Plot to Kill God: Findings from the Soviet Experiment in Secularization*. Berkeley: University of California Press.

Fuller, Louise. 2002. *Irish Catholicism since 1950: The Undoing of a Culture*. Dublin: Gill & Macmillan.

Gorry, Jonathan. 2013. *Cold War Christians and the Spectre of Nuclear Deterrence, 1945-1959*. Basingstoke: Palgrave Macmillan.

Goubert, Joseph, and L. Cristiani. 1952. *Apparitions et messages de la Sainte Vierge de 1830 à nos jours*. Paris: La Colombe.

Grabinski, Bruno, 1956. *Flammende Zeichen der Zeit. Offenbarungen, Prophezeiungen, Erscheinungen, Mystik und Pseudomystik in der Gegenwart. Ist der Antichrist schon geboren? Steht die Welt am Vorabend einer neuen Menschheitskatastrophe? Leben wir bereits in der Endzeit?* Wiesbaden: Max Schacke Verlag.

Graham, Robert A. 1981. "Profezie di Guerra: Fátima e la Russia nella propaganda dei belligeranti dopo il 1942." *La Civiltà Cattolica* 132: 15-26.

Grasmück, Oliver. 2009. *Eine Marienerscheinung in Zeiten der Diktatur. Der Konflikt um Peñablanca, Chile: Religion und Manipulation unter Pinochet*. Berlin: Walter de Gruyter.

Haffert, John M. 1950. *Russia Will Be Converted*. Washington, NJ: AMI International Press.

Haffert, John M. 1982. *Dear Bishop! Memoirs of the Author Concerning the History of the Blue Army*. Washington, NJ: AMI International Press.

Hall, Linda B. 2016. "The Virgin of Guadalupe and the Americas: Migration and Movement." In *Marian Devotions, Political Mobilization, and Nationalism in Europe and America*, edited by Roberto Di Stefano and Francisco J. Ramón Solans, 233-252. London: Palgrave MacMillan.

Hanson, Eric O. 1987. *The Catholic Church in World Politics*. Princeton, NJ: Princeton University Press.

Harper, John Lamberton. 2011. *The Cold War*. Oxford: Oxford University Press.

Hashmi, Sohail H. (ed.). 2012. *Just Wars, Holy Wars, and Jihads: Christian, Jewish, and Muslim Encounters and Exchanges*. Oxford: Oxford Univeristy Press.

Herzog, Jonathan P. 2011. *The Spiritual-industrial Complex: America's Religious Battle Against Communism in the Early Cold War*. Oxford: Oxford University Press.

Höcht, Johannes Maria. 1957. *Fatima und Pius XII. Maria Schützerin des Abendlandes. Der Kampf um Rußland und die Abwendung des dritten Weltkrieges*. Wiesbaden: Credo Verlag.

Holstein, Henri. 1958. "Les apparitions mariales." In *Maria, études sur la Sainte Vierge*, vol. 5, edited by Hubert du Manoir, 755-778. Paris: Beauchesne.

Huf, Oscar. 1916. *Oorlogsfeesten. Studiën op den liturgischen feestkalender*. Bussum: Paul Brand.

Jonas, Raymond. 2000. *France and the Cult on the Sacred Heart: An Epic Tale for Modern Times*. Berkeley: University of California Press.

Jongen, Hub. 1944. *O.L. Vrouw van Fatima. Missionaris van God!* Leuven: Secretariaat O.L.V. Middelares.

Juergensmeyer, Mark. 1993. *The New Cold War? Religious Nationalism Confronts the Secular State*. Berkeley: University of California Press.

Kane, Paula M. 2004. "Marian Devotion since 1940. Continuity of Casualty?" In *Habits of Devotion: Catholic Religious Practice in Twentieth-Century America*, edited by James M. O'Toole, 89-129. Ithaca: Cornell University Press.

Kennedy, Finola. 2011. *Frank Duff: A Life Story*. London: Burns & Oates.

Kent, Peter C. 2002. *The Lonely Cold War of Pope Pius XII: The Roman Catholic Church and the Division of Europe, 1943-1950*. Montreal: McGill-Queen's University Press.

Keogh, Dermot. 1991. "Ireland, the Vatican and the Cold War: the Case of Italy, 1948." *The Historical Journal* 34: 931-952.

Kirby, Dianne (ed.). 2013 [2002]. *Religion and the Cold War*. Basingstoke: Palgrave Macmillan.

Koehler, John. 2009. *Spies in the Vatican: The Soviet Union's Cold War Against the Catholic Church*. New York: Pegasus Books.

Kohle, Hubert. 1997. "Fundamentalistische Marienbewegungen." In *Handbuch der Marienkunde*, vol. 2, edited by Wolfgang Beinert and Heinrich Petri, 60-106. Regensburg: F. Pustet.

Kosicki, Piotr H. 2014. "The Catholic Church and the Cold War." In *The Routledge Handbook of the Cold War*, edited by Artemy M. Kalinovsky and Craig Daigle, 259-271. London: Routledge/ Taylor & Francis Group.

Kotek, Joël. 2003. "Youth Organizations as a Battlefield in the Cold War." *Intelligence and National Security* 18 (2): 168-191.

Kselman, Thomas. 1982. *Our Lady of Necedah: Marian Piety and the Cold War*. Notre Dame: University Press of Notre Dame.

Kselman, Thomas, and Steven Avella. 1986. "Marian Piety and the Cold War in the United States." *The Catholic Historical Review* 72: 403-424.

Lahr, Angela M. 2007. *Millennial Dreams and Apocalyptic Nightmares: The Cold War Origins of Political Evangelicalism*. New York: Oxford University Press.

Lamberts, Emiel (ed.). 2002. *The Black International, 1870-1878: The Holy See and Militant Catholicism in Europe*. Leuven: Leuven University Press.

Laurentin, René, and Patrick Sbalchiero. 2007. *Dictionnaire des 'apparitions' de la Vierge Marie. Inventaire des orgines à nos jours. Méthodologie, bilan interdisciplinaires, prospective*. Paris: Fayard.

Leffler, Melvyn P., and Odd Arne Westad (eds.). 2010. *The Cambridge History of the Cold War*. 3 vol. Cambridge: Cambridge University Press.

Lippmann, Walter. 1947. *The Cold War: A Study in U.S. Foreign Policy*. New York: Harper & Brothers Publishers.

Margry, Peter Jan. 2009. "Paradoxes of Marian Apparitional Contestation: Networks, Ideology, Gender, and The Lady of All Nations." In *Moved by Mary: The Power of Pilgrimage in the Modern World*, edited by Anna-Karina Hermkens, Willy Jansen and Catrien Notermans, 182-199. Aldershot: Ashgate.

Margry, Peter Jan. 2019. "The Global Network of Deviant Revelatory Marian Movements." In *The Oxford Handbook of Mary*, edited by Chris Maunder, 662-683. Oxford: Oxford University Press.

Maron, Gottfried. 1972. *Die Römisch-Katholische Kirche von 1870 bis 1970*. Göttingen: Vandenhoeck & Ruprecht.
Massam, Katharine. 1991. "The Blue Army and the Cold War: Anti-communist Devotion to the Blessed Virgin Mary in Australia." *Australian Historical Studies* 24 (97): 420-428.
Maunder, Chris. 2016. *Our Lady of the Nations: Apparitions of Mary in 20th Century Catholic Europe*. Oxford University Press.
McNamara, Patrick. 2005. *A Catholic Cold War: Edmund A. Walsh, S.J., and the Politics of American Anticommunism*. New York: Fordham University Press.
Meerloo, Joost A.M. 1956. *The Rape of the Mind: The Psychology of Thought Control, Menticide, and Brainwashing*. Cleveland NY: World Publishing Company.
Messages of the Lady of All Nations: The New Edition. 1999. Amsterdam: The Lady of All Nations Foundation.
Moreira Azevedo, Carlos A., and Luciano Cristino (eds.). 2010. *Enciclopedia di Fatima*. Siena: Cantagalli.
Morgan, David. 2009. "Aura and the Inversion Marian Pilgrimage: Fátima and Her Statues." In *Moved by Mary: The Power of Pilgrimage in the Modern World*, edited by Anna-Karina Hermkens, Willy Jansen and Catrien Notermans, 49-65. Aldershot: Ashgate.
Muehlenbeck, Philip E. 2012. *Religion and the Cold War. A Global Perspective*. Nashville: Vanderbilt University Press.
Niedźwiedź, Anna. 2010. *The Image and the Figure: Our Lady of Częstochowa in Polish Culture and Popular Religion*. Cracow: Jagiellonian University Press.
O'Connor, John. 1939. "The Legion of Mary Enlists for World Conquest." *America* 61: 61.
Oddone, A. 1944. "Profezie di Guerra." *La Civiltà Cattolica*: 201-210.
O'Sullivan, Michael E. 2009. "West German Miracles, Catholic Mystics, Church Hierarchy, and Postwar Popular Culture." *Zeithistorische Forschungen/Studies in Contemporary History* 6: 11-34.
Peris, Daniel. 1998. *Storming the Heavens: The Soviet League of the Militant Godless*. Ithaca, NY: Cornell University Press.
Perouas, Louis. 1983. "Le Grand Retour de Notre-Dame de Boulogne à travers la France (1943-1948). Essai d'interprétation." *Archives de sciences sociales des religions* 56 (1): 37-53.
Perry, Nicholas, and Loreto Echeverría. 1988. *Under the Heel of Mary*. London: Routledge.
Petrisko, Thomas W. 2002. *The Fátima Prophecies: At the Doorstep of the World*. McKees Rocks, PA: St. Andrew's Productions.
Pius XI. 1937. *Divini Redemptoris. Over het goddeloze communisme*. Utrecht: Het Spectrum.
Pius XII. 1942. "Santa Sede. Radiomessaggio del Santo Padre per il XXV delle apparizioni di Fàtima, 1942." *La Civiltà Cattolica* 93: 256.
Pius XII. 1943. "Radiomessaggio al Portogallo. La consacrazione della Chiesa e del genere umano al Cuore Immacolato di Maria, del 31-10-1942." In *Atti e discorsi di Pio XII*, vol. 4, 263-272. Rome: Istituto Missionario Pia Società San Paolo (and in *La Civiltà Cattolica* 93 (1942): 193-197).
Polman, H.J.M. 1956. "Z.H. Paus Pius XII en de 'Peregrinatio Mariae'." *Standaard van Maria* 32: 124-132.
Powers, Richard Gid. 1995. *Not Without Honor: The History of American Anticommunism*. New York: The Free Press.
Ramet, Pedro (ed). 1990. *Catholicism and Politics in Communist Societies*. Durham: Duke University Press.
Reynolds, David (ed). 1994. *The Origins of the Cold War in Europe: International Perspectives*. New Haven: Yale University Press.
Rhodes, Anthony. 1992. *The Vatican in the Age of the Cold War*. Wilby Hall: Michael Russel.
Roschini, G.M. et al. 1958. *L'Anno Mariano 1954 nell'Urbe e nell'Orbe*. Cronistoria. Vatican City: Tipografia Poliglotta.
Rubin, Miri. 2009. *Mother of God: A History of the Virgin Mary*. New Haven: Yale University Press.
Ruotsila, Markku. 2014. "Transnational Fundamentalist Anti-Communism: The International Council of Christian Churches." In *Transnational Anti-Communism and the Cold War: Agents, Activities, and Networks*, edited by Luc van Dongen, Stéphanie Roulin and Giles Scott-Smith, 235-250. Basingstoke: Palgrave.
Sampaio Barbosa, David et al. 2013. *Documentação Crítica de Fátima. Seleção de documentos (1917-1930)*. Fátima: Santuário de Fátima.
Saull, Richard. 2007. *The Cold War and After: Capitalism, Revolution and Superpower Politics*. London: Pluto Press.
Scheer, Monique. 2006a. *Rosenkranz und Kriegsvisionen. Marienerscheinungskulte im 20. Jahrhundert*. Tübingen: Tübinger Verein für Volkskunde.

Scheer, Monique. 2006b. "Rettet Maria Deutschland? Die Diskussion um eine nationale Marienweihe nach dem Zweiten Weltkrieg." In *Alliierte im Himmel. Populare Religiosität und Kriegserfahrung*, edited by Gottfried Korff, 141-156. Tübingen: Tübinger Verein für Volkskunde.

Scheer, Monique. 2009. "Taking Shelter under Mary's Mantle: Marian Apparitions in the Early Cold War Years." In *The "Vision Thing": Studying Divine Intervention*, edited by Gabor Klaniczay and William A. Christian Jr., 195-218. Budapest: Collegium Budapest.

Scheer, Monique. 2012. "Catholic Piety in the Early Cold War Years or: How the Virgin Mary Protected the West from Communism." In *Cold War Cultures: Perspectives on Eastern and Western European Societies*, edited by Annette Vowinckel, Marcus M. Payk and Thomas Lindenberger, 129-151. New York: Berghahn Books.

Scheer, Monique. 2014. "Die Madonnen von Medjugorje. Zum Verhältnis zwischen Bild und Vision bei Marienerscheinungen in der modernen Epoche." In *Maria in der Krise. Kultpraxis zwischen Konfession und Politik in Ostmitteleuropa*, edited by Agnieszka Gasior, 51-75. Cologne: Böhlau.

Scheffczyk, Leo. 2002. "Kennzeichen und Gestaltkräfte des 'Marianischen Zeitalters'." In *Das Marianische Zeitalter. Enstehung – Gehalt – bleibende Bedeutung*, edited by Anton Ziegenaus, 179-200. Regensburg: Pustet.

Speckbacher, Franz. 1989. "Die vorhergesagte Weltkatastrophe der 'Drei Tage der Dunkelheit'." *Ave-Kurier. Monatszeitschrift im Dienste der Verehrung Marien* (May/June).

Spinka, Matthew. 1936. *Christianity Confronts Communism*. New York: Harper & Brothers.

Suenens, Leo J. 1951. *Theologie van het Apostolaat van het Maria-Legioen*. Antwerp: Zuid-Nederlandse Uitgeverij.

Varghese, Roy A. 2000. *God-Sent: A History of the Accredited Apparitions of Mary*. New York: Crossroad Publishing Company.

Ventrone, Angelo. 1996. *La Cittadinaza Repubblicana: Forma-Partito e Identita Nazionale alle origini della Democrazia Italia, 1943-1948*. Bologna: Il Mulino.

Vowinckel, Annette, Marcus M. Payk and Thomas Lindenberger (eds.). 2012. *Cold War Cultures: Perspectives on Eastern and Western European Societies*. New York: Berghahn.

Wallace, James C. 2013. "A Religious War? The Cold War and Religion." *Journal of Cold War Studies* 15: 162-180.

Warner, Marina. 1976. *Alone of All her Sex: The Myth and the Cult of the Virgin Mary*. London: Weidenfeld and Nicolson.

Westad, Odd Arne (ed.). 2000. *Reviewing the Cold War: Approaches, Interpretations, Theory*. London: Frank Cass.

Westad, Odd Arne. 2017. *The Cold War: A World History*. New York: Basic Books.

Winter, Eduard. 1972. *Die Sowjetunion und der Vatikan*. Berlin: Akademie Verlag.

Wojcik, Daniel. 1997. *The End of the World As We Know It*. New York: New York University Press.

Zimdars-Swartz, Sandra L. 1991. *Encountering Mary: Visions of Mary from La Salette to Medjugorje*. Princeton: Princeton University Press.

Zimdars-Swartz, Sandra L. 2016. "Fátima and the Politics of Devotion." In *Marian Devotions, Political Mobilization, and Nationalism in Europe and America*, edited by Roberto Di Stefano and Francisco J. Ramón Solans, 169-199. London: Palgrave Macmillan.

Zugger, Christopher Lawrence. 2010. *The Forgotten: Catholics of the Soviet Empire from Lenin through Stalin*. Syracuse, NY: Syracuse University Press.

CHURCH AND IDEOLOGIES

2
THE VIRGIN MARY AND COLD WAR POLITICS
POPE, CHURCH, AND DEVOTEES IN THE CONTEXT OF POSTWAR ITALY*

ROBERT VENTRESCA

> I shall come to ask for the consecration of Russia to my Immaculate Heart (...) If my requests are heeded, Russia will be converted, and there will be peace; if not, she will spread her errors throughout the world, causing wars and persecution of the Church. The good will be martyred; the Holy Father will have to much suffer; various nations will be annihilated. In the end, my Immaculate Heart will triumph.
>
> Message of Our Lady of Fátima, 1917[1]

On April 18, 1948, after two decades of fascist dictatorship, Italians went to the polls to elect the first parliament of the Republic inaugurated at the start of that year. The election was essentially a contest between the governing Christian Democrats, and the Popular Front, a coalition led by the Italian communists and revolutionary socialists. The election was not so much about "issues" as it was about "ideology," a clash between two competing versions of Italian society – a conservative Catholic, capitalist Italy envisioned by Christian Democracy, versus a revolutionary, secular, socialist Italy envisioned by the Popular Front. The fundamental clash of visions left pre-

* A previous version of this article originally appeared under the title "The Virgin and the Bear: Religion, Society and the Cold War in Italy," *Journal of Social History* 37.2 (2003): 439-456.

1 The message from Our Lady of Fátima to the three peasant children Lucia, Jacinta and Francisco in Portugal, 1917. The message was kept secret until 1941, when Lucia, the sole surviving of the three seers, divulged the secret in one of her four memoirs of the apparitions. See Zimdars-Swartz 1991: 198-206, and infra, chapter 3.

carious little room for any middle ground as Italy's revolutionary Left made a strong bid to seize power at the ballot box.

The Vatican made no secret of how the Church fathers expected the faithful to vote. Well over a year before the election, Pope Pius XII declared from the balcony of St. Peter's that the political decision Italians faced could be reduced to the following choice: "essere con Cristo o contro Cristo: é tutta la questione," to be either with Christ or against Christ (Ventrone 1996: 267). For Italian voters, then, unlike voters in traditional democracies, the choice was not between political parties or philosophies, but between heaven and hell. That was the implication of Pius XII's admonition, and in an overwhelmingly Catholic country, the pontiff's intervention was bound to influence the vote of many devout Italian Catholics.

The pope's declaration marked the start of a concerted, controversial, inventive campaign on the part of Italian Catholicism to reverse the seemingly inexorable trend toward communist victory at the ballot box. At the behest of the highest authorities in Vatican City, the Church employed its capillary network of parishes and lay organizations and experimented with new forms of mass mobilization to defend Catholicism as a central institution in the temporal and spiritual life of Italy. And, yet, for all the seeming novelty of these efforts, in the end, it fell to a most ancient and sacred devotional figure, the Blessed Virgin Mary, to help Italian Catholics fight what they would say was the "good fight" for God and country against a foreign, menacing presence.

But clerical intervention of an organized, almost official sort – as with the grand Marian pilgrimages of 1947-1948 – is only one side of the equation, one dimension of Catholic responses to the political crisis created by the Popular Front's drive for power. For we still have to account for popular responses among the Catholic masses to the political events of the early Cold War. In such an atmosphere of public devotion promoted by the Marian pilgrimages, and given the deep-seated faith in Mary's exceptional powers to save individuals and communities from danger, popular mobilization around the image of Mary spawned a wave of apparitions and miraculous cures. The Virgin was everywhere to be seen in the weeks preceding the 1948 election. She appeared in the most unlikely places: high atop churches, in caves, and even, we shall see, several meters underground. Officially, the Church urged caution and restricted public veneration of the unsubstantiated apparitions of the pre-election period. Some apparitions were actually publicly dismissed by high-ranking clergy as something other than celestial just days before the April vote.

The compelling question for historians is not whether the apparitions were true or not – something science can never fully disprove, and faith necessarily believes is possible; rather, for historians, the question is why did scores of Italians claim to experience apparitions and miracles in the weeks before the votes? Why did so many of those who did not see or hear or feel a supernatural sign, still believe the claims to be true? How was it that even the mainstream national media, from newspapers to the public radio, reported on the visions and miracles as fact, throwing caution and skepticism to the wind?

For many years, scholars have dismissed these questions as interesting, but ultimately historically inconsequential. Secular scholars and other commentators have usually dismissed popular devotion to apparitions as the product of a sincere but misguided adherence to a manipulative Church hierarchy, as the irrational reaction on the part of ignorant and impressionable Catholic masses. This was how Émile Zola and other secular critics characterized the intensity of popular devotion at Lourdes in the nineteenth century. In her compelling study of French Catholicism's most enduring Marian shrine, the historian Ruth Harris observes that Zola's basic assumption about Lourdes has become a kind of template for historians of the nineteenth century. Where medievalists revel in accounts of supernatural phenomena, treasuring them as invaluable insights into the mentality of the so-called "early modern" world, historians of the modern era are rather "ill at ease with, if not actually repelled by," modern variants of the same supernatural phenomena. "The magical incantations of the peasant world," writes Harris, "the pious murmurings of female devotees of the Sacred Heart (...) let alone miraculous cures, are usually seen as little more than superstitious remnants on the road to extinction" (Harris 1999: 12).

The critics of the Italian apparitions of the early Cold War have not strayed very far from this approach (Ginzburg 1989b: 672-673). What follows below argues just the opposite – such phenomena of a seemingly inconsequential, irrational, trivial nature may actually permit, as Carlo Ginzburg puts it, "the comprehension of a deeper, otherwise unattainable reality" (Ginzburg 1989a: 101). Writing about nineteenth-century Italian art expert Giovanni Morelli – who developed a new method to ascertain the authorship of paintings attributed to the old masters by paying close attention not to the most obvious characteristics of a subject of art, but to seemingly trivial details, such as earlobes, fingernails, fingers, and toes – Ginzburg notes that even Freud accorded the morellian technique of studying marginal or trivial data a privileged position in psychoanalysis. Freud himself reasoned that psychoanalysis owed much to the morellian interpretative method, since psychology too was "accustomed to divine secret and concealed things from unconsidered or unnoticed details, from the rubbish heap, as it were, of our observations" (Freud 1959: 270-271, quoted in Ginzburg 1989a: 99).

It is not my intention to submit the Italian election of 1948 to psychoanalysis, even less to a careful examination, figuratively speaking, of earlobes, fingernails and other such "trifle" matters. Still, by examining the use that was made of sacred images and devotional practices of Italian Catholicism during the 1948 campaign, I want to draw the reader's attention to seemingly minor details in order to arrive at what Ginzburg describes as "a more profound, less obvious type of history" (Ginzburg 1999: 15).

In so doing, I want to widen the notion of what is "political"; to weave together the broad political narrative of 1948 with the social and psychological dimensions that determined how the election was experienced at the grassroots; to understand how factors such as popular piety and gender, for instance, conditioned the conduct of the campaign, as well as its outcome. Like Ruth Harris, I want to employ a more "sympathetic approach," a different approach from that of so-called mainstream historians, to arrive at a deeper understanding of the Italian apparitions of the late 1940s (Harris 1999: 13). In some respects, this approach is more anthropology than history, in that it seeks to suspend preconceived notions of individual or collective behavior, and so assess the apparitions on their own terms. Such an approach begins from the basic assumption that, whatever their scientific veracity or theological credibility, apparitions are genuine spiritual experiences for the faithful involved, either as participants or observers. In fact, a more "sympathetic" approach may bring us close as we can come to being participant-observers of the events in question. This, in turn, can help us to render a more profound history both of the nature of the phenomena, and of the early Cold War in Italy.

The Marian apparitions that spread across Italy in the weeks leading up to the April 1948 election tell us much about the ways in which cultural, social, even psychological factors determined and conditioned how ordinary Italians, their political leaders, as well as foreign policymakers acted in the heady climate of 1947-1948. The wave of apparitions on the eve of the 1948 election reflected both an individual and collective search for meaning, order and protection on the part of ordinary Italians who worried about the implications for the faith and for the country of the Popular Front's bid for power. This was evidence of the extent to which the cult of Mary had moved from fighting secularization – the *bête noire* of the Church in the nineteenth century – to fighting the spread of Soviet Communism.

That the Madonna was effective in the campaign to defeat communism in 1948, to the extent this was the case, tells us something about the way in which Italian Catholics defined, articulated and defended their interests and that of their faith in the face of danger, real or perceived. The nature of the 1948 campaign and its outcome, for one, can best be explained in terms of Italy's unique position as the seat of the universal Roman Church, and by the age-old intersection between the civic and the religious in daily live and in official public discourse. Inconsequential and irrational though they may seem, I argue that the apparitions and miracles of the pre-election period were but a recent manifestation of the deep-seated tendencies and tensions of Italy's uneasy history as seat of two institutions, one temporal, and the other religious.

For centuries, Italians had turned to the Virgin Mary in times of individual or collective trouble to ask for salvation or deliverance. For centuries, Italians had been building churches, both immense and ornate sanctuaries, and tiny rural stone chapels that bore the name of the mother of Jesus. For centuries, Italian artists, from the geniuses of the Renaissance to anonymous and mediocre village artists and artisans had poured their artistic energy into rendering homage to the Virgin Mary. In towns and cities throughout the country, street-side frescoes, mosaics and tiny niches bearing the image of some Marian entity abounded. Borrowing from the historian Mario Isnenghi, I consider this intersection of political and religious symbols and discourse a constant in Italian history. As Isnenghi observes, the religious manifestations of the 1948 campaign, "come from far back" (Isnenghi 1977: 209-210).

The prospect of a Marxist victory at the polls in April 1948 and the rise to power of an atheistic, anti-clerical government in Rome; the specter of civil unrest or insurrectionary violence; or even the faint but frightening prospect of armed military invasion from behind the Iron Curtain; these were real threats to Italian Catholics in 1948. They did not need to hear it from the Church fathers to understand that Italy would be a very different place should the communists seize power at the dawn of the republican era. And so, like bread rioters or the crowds that flocked to apparition sites in the nineteenth century, Italian Catholics took to the streets and piazzas of their towns and villages, brandishing the symbols and practices of popular religiosity. The moving statues, the weeping icons, the throngs of the devotees who crowded around Marian statues or venerated her at one of the many apparition sites, chanting, singing, reciting the rosary en masse – these were to Italian Catholics in 1948 what Garibaldi, Gramsci, the hammer and sickle and the *Internationale* were to the Popular Front: tools with which to fight the good fight, for God and country.

Until recently, historians of modern Europe have dismissed apparitions as an illegitimate field of historical analysis believing, as Zola did, that apparitions belong to the realm of superstition and irrationality, not scholarly enquiry. Many scholars prefer to consider the phenomena of apparitions and miracles as merely the product of individual and at times collective delusion, deserving of our derision, not serious study (Carroll 1986 and 1992; Tavard 1996). To the extent scholars have paid attention to apparitions, we have seen, it has been to document and usually denounce the apparitions and their official promotion as evidence of the Catholic hierarchy's efforts to cultivate a direct relationship with the masses, and thereby preserve and promote Church power and influence in an increasingly secular age.

Other scholars who bother with the subject of apparitions seek refuge in the illusory explanatory certitude offered by Freud and psychoanalysis. Trying to account for the greater propensity of Italian Catholics to experience Marian apparitions, Michael Carroll reduces apparition experiences to a basic human need for parental protection from imminent danger. "The adult seeks protection from current danger," observes Carroll, "from a god or gods modeled upon (...) parental memories." And so, the argument goes, it is an easy step for the mind to take, from seeking protection in the memory of one's own mother, to seeking protection from the mother of all mothers; from the quintessential maternal figure, Mary, the Mother of God (Carroll, 1992: 52).

In recent years, however, historians have paid closer attention to popular culture, especially non-religious manifestations of popular culture, such as working-class movements. This emphasis on non-religious popular culture is understandable, writes historian David Blackbourn, "only if one accepts that this was a predominantly secular age." Writing on apparitions in nineteenth-century Germany, Blackbourn flatly dismisses the assumption that the modern era has been a largely secular age, and the same could be said about the twentieth century. Despite creeping secularization over the past two centuries or so, the fact remains that, even in so-called "secular" Europe of the nineteenth and twentieth centuries, most people professed one form of Christian faith or another. Indeed, Blackbourn carries his reasoning a step further – he considers the behavior of apparition crowds as a "window on forms of collective Catholic action," that merit the attention of historians as much as, say, the collective action of working-class movements. In a nineteenth-century world defined by secularization and the emergence of modern nation-states, the Virgin Mary proved a potent weapon for Catholics in their struggle against both secularization and the hostility of the nascent nation-states of Europe to Church temporal power and influence. "The pilgrimage badges, Marian hymns and miraculous spring-waters of the apparition crowds," Blackbourn argues, "were a rival set of emblems," to the flags, anthems and monuments of the modern nation-state (Blackbourn 1995: 27).

The appeal to the Virgin Mary for protection in a time of perceived crisis and uncertainty was by no means novel to popular Catholicism, in Italy or elsewhere. Indeed, since at least the twelfth century, Western Christian tradition considered Mary to possess a special ability and inclination to protect those who were loyal to her and showed their loyalty through prayer and patronage of religious sites (Zimdars-Swartz 1991: 6). This faith in the Virgin's exceptional intercessionary powers in troubled times has historically found its greatest expression in Marian apparitions. This explains, in part, why Marian apparitions have traditionally been most diffuse and attracted the most widespread appeal in times of political and social tumult. In Southern Europe especially, apparitions and weeping or moving statues, were most acute and pronounced during times of crisis, war or disease (Apolito 1990: 16). Over the centuries, religious figures – statues and icons – often wept during times of crisis. In seventeenth-century Spain, for example, bleeding and weeping religious icons were in vogue during moments of acute regional or national trouble. Similar movements and Marian apparitions were witnessed in Italy, in particular in the area of the Papal States, at the time of Napoleon's incursions in the 1790s. Indeed, it is no coincidence that the first great wave of Marian apparitions in the modern era came just after the French Revolution. Many more apparitions were reported in the latter half of the nineteenth century, to coincide with the political turmoil caused by the emergence of new states in Italy and Germany. The wars for Italian unification in the nineteenth century spawned yet another wave of Marian apparitions and moving statues. Among the more notable was the report of a moving statue in Soriano (Calabria) in 1870, at the time the armies of Victor Emanuel invaded the Papal States, and a similar case was witnessed in Rome in 1871 (Christian 1984: 257; Blackbourn 1995: 19-27).

In the twentieth century, communism replaced anticlerical liberalism, secularization and nation building as the principle cause of political and social unrest (Blackbourn 1995: 20-22). Not for nothing was the early Cold War era the most intense period of Marian apparitions in modern history. The years 1947, 1948 and 1954 stand out in particular both for the number of Marian apparitions and for their widespread popular appeal, especially in Southern Europe. In all, between 1947 and 1954, there were some 112 Marian apparitions reported, an average of 14 per year.[2]

Italy was a prominent apparition country in the early Cold War era. Tellingly, the year 1948 stands out for the number of Italian Marian apparitions reported. In fact, so widespread were these reports in the weeks before the election, that one student of the period refers to the phenomenon as a veritable "miracle boom" (De Lutiis 1973: 37-48).

Doubtless, the most celebrated of the 1948 apparitions was at Assisi, the tranquil Umbrian town in Central Italy, birthplace of Saint Francis, Italy's patron saint. On February 10, a woman reported seeing a statue of the Virgin Mary, perched high above the Church of Santa Maria degli Angeli, move her head and chest. According to the seer, whose name was never divulged to the public, it was as if the Virgin was breathing heavily, as if she were sighing.[3] Expectedly, word of the vision spread quickly through town, and before long people began arriving at the church from neighboring towns and villages. The next day, a local radio station announced, without a hint of caution or skepticism, that the Madonna had moved her head from side to side, and sighed heavily "as if She were in deep pain" (De Lutiis 1973: 48). The vision of a Ma-

2 As William Christian observes, there were approximately four times as many visions per year in the 1947-1945 period as in all the years from 1930 to 1975. After 1954, the number of apparitions in Southern Europe declined, though they maintained a regularity not apparent before the Second World War. See Christian 1984: 241-242.

3 "La Madonna degli Angeli meta di continui pellegrinaggi," *Il Messaggero*, February 13, 1948.

donna that visibly suffered, was sad or wept, was presumed to represent celestial displeasure at the course of events on earth. Within days, a stream of faithful devotees and the merely curious began arriving at Assisi from far away as Rome and the Marche region several hundred kilometers east of Assisi.

Almost immediately, one person's claim to have seen a celestial sign was transformed into a mass phenomenon as many of those who came to see what the fuss was about soon claimed that they too saw the Virgin move. The power of suggestion was so strong that it promoted a kind of chain-reaction of visions: when one person cried out, "She breathes!" another responded in agreement, "She breathes, her chest, her chest!" Yet another person suggested that the statue was actually moving its lips and opening its hands as if to salute the throng of onlookers below.[4] One man spent seven days with his eyes transfixed on the statue without seeing it move when suddenly, on the seventh day, he saw the Virgin move. "Now," he told an incredulous reporter from the communist daily *l'Unita*, "I see her move at once. In fact, I see her now. I don't even have to try. All I do is raise my eyes".[5]

To be sure, there was a fair share of skeptics at Assisi, but the skeptical and the non-believers spoke their mind at considerable personal risk. One young man, for instance, dared to voice his doubts while standing in front of Santa Maria deli Angeli, an act of temerity for which, as *Il Messaggero* reported, "he literally risked being lynched." In the end, only the intervention of an anonymous third party saved the man from harm at the hands of the impassioned crowd.[6] So great was the resolve of the believers to suppress all skepticism, that in the early days of the visions the crowds even refused to let an expert from the nearby University of Perugia conduct the analysis of the statue as ordered by ecclesiastic officials. The believers, most of who could not and would not claim to have actually seen the statue atop the church move, resented those who admitted aloud what many of them were probably thinking. One individual, frustrated at not having seen the statue move as he expected asked, "oh, why doesn't She ever move her leg?" A young girl next to him, bothered by this hint of doubt, quipped angrily "Why don't you go and tell her so yourself?"[7]

While a small chorus of voices expressed doubt about the celestial nature of the Assisi phenomenon, many others enthusiastically reported that

4 *Ibid.*; Gerardo Guerrieri, "Il caffettiere 'miracolato' ha incassato mezzo milione: si muove o non si muove la Madonna di Assisi?" *L'Unita*, February 24, 1948.

5 Gerardo Guerrieri, "Il caffettiere 'miracolato' ha incassato mezzo milione: si muove o non si muove la Madonna di Assisi?" *L'Unita*, February 24, 1948.

6 "La Madonna degli Angeli meta di continui pellegrinaggi," *Il Messaggero*, February 13, 1948.

7 Gerardo Guerrieri, "Il caffettiere 'miracolato' ha incassato mezzo milione: si muove o non si muove la Madonna di Assisi?" *L'Unita*, February 24, 1948.

2.1 Postcard of the large crowd watching Angela Volpini, enlarged by an inset, at her "appointment" with the Madonna on the Casanova Staffora hillside, March 4, 1947.
[Collection of William A. Christian Jr.]

the Madonna of Santa Maria degli Angeli had actually cured them of illness.[8] Arguably the most compelling case was that of Filide Gori, a 48-year-old woman who was taken to Assisi by her doctor, Francesco Lomi, to venerate the moving Madonna. According to Lomi's testimony, Gori suffered from various problems, which made it difficult for her to stand on her own. For some three years, Gori was treated exhaustively with standard medical treatments, but to no avail; hence the desperate decision to go to Santa Maria degli Angeli and pray for the impossible. The trip to Assisi was taxing, and Gori required several injections of camphor to ease the pain and discomfort. Having venerated the statue atop the church, Lomi recalled, Gori went back to the car where, according to Lomi, "praying fervently, she noticed a change in her condition." Gori proceeded to get out of the car on her own, "smiling". According to her doctor's testimony, the disease that had ravaged Gori's body for years had disappeared completely.[9]

These were but a few of the more celebrated miracles attributed directly to the Madonna of Santa Maria degli Angeli in 1948. But elsewhere in the country, similar reports of miracle cures and apparitions made their way into the local and national press. Apparitions were reported at the Tre Fontane grotto in Rome, in Gimigliano, Marta, Ponsacco, Frascati, Lucca, Liceta, Nocera Superiore and elsewhere, from north to south, both before and after the April election.[10] Already in 1947, in the run up to the elections, apparitions became more frequent. Cowherd Angela Volpini started to see the Madonna from June 1947 on. She was told to pray for which Maria would save the country,

8 Vittorio Di Giacomo, "Movimento di Fede attorno alla Madonna," *L'Osservatore Romano della Domenica*, April 25, 1948.

9 *Ibid.*

10 An informal list of the 1948 apparitions with brief details is provided in Falconi 1956. Sicily, too, witnessed what one observer called a "wind of miracles" on the eve of the election. See the writer Leonardo Sciascia's *Le parrocchie di Regalpetra*, 94-95, quoted by Christian 1984: 248-249.

2.2 The Tre Fontane grotto in Rome. Ed. A. T. Roma. [Collection of William A. Christian Jr.]

in reference to a possible breakthrough of the communists in the elections. It resulted in mass gatherings of thousands of devotees on the mountain slopes in the hope to experience the Marian protectrix.

In Montopoli Sabina (Lazio), near Rome, the brothers Fulvio and Oreste Antonini, blind since birth, regained their sight while praying at a grotto in the village of San Giovannone, at the spot where since December 1947 the Virgin Mary appeared in a series of dreams to Annunziata Gentili, a 43-year-old peasant woman.[11] In these dreams, Gentili could make out an image of the Madonna on the walls of the grotto of San Giovannone, where she lived. As Gentili described it, the image had a sad expression and was covered in rivulets of water, and surrounded by small rocks and patches of wild grass. In the first dream, Mary asked Gentili to go and look for her. "The water is deep," Mary said, "and in those days they spoke in Latin!" In the second dream, the Virgin appeared dressed in black, with a pained look on her face. Again, she exhorted Gentili to go and find her "before it is too late." Here, again, was the similar motif of the suffering Madonna with the 'pained' expression and clad in black as if in mourning. In the third dream, the Virgin's tone was more urgent, even

11 "Due bimbi ciechi miracolati dalla Madonna dell'Acqua a Montoboli" and "Visioni o allucinazioni?", both in *L'Osservatore Romano della Domenica*, February 10 and 22, 1948.

desperate. “Hurry,” she implored, “before extraordinary events occur. The water is deep and I have been sleeping here for centuries!”

The urgency of the Virgin’s pleas convinced Gentili to let her neighbors know about her dreams, and that the Madonna was asking to be found. The townsfolk wasted no time in organizing a search for what everyone assumed was a Marian statue or chapel of some sort. No one was quite sure what to look for. The digging began at the spot that corresponded to the directions Gentili received in her dream. This was on December 8, 1947, the Feast of the Immaculate Conception. The following evening, Mary appeared yet again to Gentili in a dream saying, “I am here. Proceed!” The night of January 9, Gentili told of having dreamed Mary a fifth time. “You have found me,” the Madonna had told her, “but you must dig a bit deeper.” The very next morning, the dig was halted: Gentili’s directions had yielded an object that appeared at first nothing more than a block of stone. The object was just that: a stone carving, eroded by water, but with a discernible figure of a woman holding something in her arms. For Gentili and the devout people of the area, there was little doubt but that the image was of the Virgin Mary holding the baby Jesus. Despite the remarkable discovery, Gentili continued to see the Virgin in her dreams, and the good people of San Giovannone and the surrounding area continued to dig in search of some other, even more spectacular celestial sign buried deep beneath the ground. All the while, pilgrims arrived in ever-greater numbers to stand before the grotto of San Giovannone and venerated the Virgin who, they believed, had come to earth to be with them in such a literal way.[12]

Similar stories of apparitions and other supernatural signs captured the attention of even the national media in the weeks leading up to the April vote. In early April, for example, Vittoria Casotti, a mother of four, reported seeing an image of Our Lady of Lourdes weeping at Borgo a Mozzano.[13] In the town of San Angelo dei Lombardi, near Naples, a farmer dreamt of a statue that was buried somewhere on the land he worked every day. As at San Giovannone, a dig was organized and a statue of the Virgin Mary thought to be from the early fourteenth century was discovered. As always, word of the unlikely discovery spread quickly, and attracted a steady flow of pilgrims and curious onlookers from surrounding areas.[14] By far the strangest report of a celestial sign came from Maria Gobbi of Ancona, on the Adriatic coast. Gobbi reported seeing a cross appear at the bottom of a basin where she kept olives to ferment. The cross was approximately 20 centimeters in height, and 15 centimeters wide and appeared to be crowned with the Holy Eucharist. Despite the unlikely location of the image, dozens of nearby residents flocked to the Gobbi home to

12 Corrado Calvo, “Un’altare nella cava,” *Il Messaggero*, January 22, 1948.

13 “La Madonna piange’ ha esclamato la folla,” *La Nazione*, April 6, 1948.

14 “Una Madonna apparsa in sogno rinvenuta scavando un podere,” *Il Messaggero*, March 30, 1948.

ILLUSTRAZIONE DEL POPOLO

ABBONAMENTI ITALIA: Anno L. 1.100 - Semestre L. 570 - Trimestre L. 290
ESTERO: Anno L. 1.450 - Semestre L. 750 - Trimestre L. 380
(Versare l'importo sul nostro conto corrente postale 2/6540)
Direzione ed Amministrazione: Corso Valdocco, 2 - Torino

Supplemento della Nuova Gazzetta del Popolo
PUBBLICAZIONE SETTIMANALE - SPEDIZIONE IN ABBONAMENTO POSTALE 2° GRUPPO

PER LA PUBBLICITÀ
rivolgersi alla Società Italiana Pubblicità S. I. P. R. A. Via Arsenale, 33 - Torino, tel. 52-521 - 41-172 - 52-389, oppure all'Amministrazione del Giornale - Corso Valdocco, 2 - Torino.

Anno 28° - Numero 12 21 Marzo 1948 Lire 25 —

PARLA CON LA MADONNA. — Il 4 marzo su una montagna presso Casanova Staffora (Varzi), per la decima volta la bambina Angela Volpini ha avuto un colloquio con la Madonna — visibile a lei sola — davanti ad una folla strabocchevole. L'autorità ecclesiastica mantiene il più stretto riserbo sul « caso ».
(*Leggere la notizia a pag. 2*).

Disegno di Mario D'Antona

dentatura sana e bianca dentifricio Alba Rumianca

2.3 Newspaper front page with a drawing of the visionary communication between Mary and Angela Volpini on March 4, 1948.
[Collection of William A. Christian Jr.]

catch a glimpse, and a respectable national newspaper such as *Il Messaggero* thought the incident newsworthy.[15]

Predictably, the Left denounced these stories as, at best, a case of collective hallucination, at worst, the deliberate machinations of the clergy to influence the outcome of the pending national election. The Church had masterfully orchestrated the Assisi visions, indeed all the visions and miracles reported in the weeks before voting day, the Left reasoned, in order to frighten Catholics into voting en masse against the Popular Front.[16]

In reality, it was impossible to substantiate the claim that the Church had deliberately orchestrated visions and miracles for electoral purposes. There were a few isolated reports, albeit from questionable sources like the extreme wing of the communist party, which told fantastic tales of priests who had reported seeing the Virgin Mary in a vision. In one such vision, the Virgin reportedly urged the faithful through the local priest to vote for the Christian Democrats or face excommunication. In another instance, a local priest told the wife of a well-known communist activist that the Virgin Mary had appeared to him in a dream and foretold the death of the couple's young daughter if her husband insisted on voting for the Popular Front.[17]

But reports such as these were relatively few, and serious ecclesiastic authorities sought to distance themselves from such improbable tales of celestial intervention in the election campaign. In reality, the Church reacted with its usual reserve and even outright skepticism to the "wind of miracles" which blew over the peninsula in the weeks leading up to the 1948 vote.[18] As early as the summer of 1947, in fact, powerful members of the Italian Church, such as Cardinal Dalla Costa, archbishop of Florence, warned that there were too many miracles going around, most of which could easily be explained as natural not supernatural phenomena.[19] What is more, was it not the case, the Catholic press persuasively argued in defense against the charge of electoral manipulation, that the Church had seized the initiative in declaring the

15 "Strana apparizione di una croce ad Ancona," *Il Messaggero*, April 2, 1948.

16 See "La Madonna di Assisi non si è affatto apparsa"; "Passati il 18 Aprile a che servono piú I miracoli?"in *Avanti!*, July 2, 1948; "Gli anticlericali e le 'apparizioni'," *Rabarbaro*, June 27, 1948; "La grotta dei miracoli chiusa dal Vicariato," *Il Paese*, July 20, 1948.

17 "Il 'pianto del parrocco' scomuniche e ricatti armi democristiane nella campagna elettorale," *L'Unitá*, April 27, 1948. See also the Archives of the Italian Communist Party at the Gramsci Institute, Rome, hereafter APC, FDP, MF 186 (here MF 186, 0936-55). The series FDP, MF 186 contains all the material related to the Popular Front of 1948, and to the election itself.

18 For a brief overview of the Church's official approach to apparitions and miracles, with specific references to the 1947-1948 period, see Oddone 1948b: 364-375. Not everyone believed in the sincerity of the Church's public disavowal of the apparitions. Consider, for instance, the skeptical perspective of the Catholic writer and eye-witness of the events Falconi 1956.

19 "Troppi miracoli in giro," *Rabarbaro*, July 20, 1947.

celebrated Assisi vision an optical illusion? To say nothing of the case of the "sweating" Madonna in San Felice, near Bologna, in February 1948. In that instance, it was in early April, just days before the election, that the local priest publicly expressed doubts about the supernatural quality of the liquid emitted by the icon of the Virgin Mary. The likely explanation, the priest reasoned, was humidity.[20]

In the case of the most celebrated and controversial vision at Assisi, the bishop of the diocese – the ecclesiastic authority of first recourse in these matters – promptly ordered the standard scientific examination of the statue atop the church to ascertain whether the reported movements had any substance to them. Mindful of the need to protect its credibility, the Church pronounced its negative judgement weeks before the scientific findings of the team of experts from the University of Perugia were published. Sensitive to the charge of electoral manipulation, the bishop of the diocese declared just one month after the first movements of the statue were reported that the visions were nothing more than an optical illusion. When the scientific results were made public, they merely confirmed what the Church had been saying almost from the start.[21]

The cautious response of the Church to the 1948 wave of visions and miracles was consistent with the centuries-old prudence and reserve with which the ecclesiastic order has approached the question of the supernatural. At heart, this prudence reflects the somber admission that visions and miracles may very well be either a hoax, innocent illusion, the result of psychological illness or even, as the Church would have it, "pre-natural interventions," which is to say the work of the devil.[22] The official promotion of an apparition site that was subsequently proved to be something other than of a supernatural nature would not only embarrass Church officials, but also seriously undermine the theological credibility of Church doctrine.

There is another factor just as important, which has tempered the Church's attitude towards the supernatural over the centuries. Apparitions, the Church has long realized, challenged not merely the authority but the very purpose of the clergy, by establishing a direct, immediate rapport between the Virgin Mary and the so-called "ordinary folk" – usually peasants, children, women – who have claimed to see her. "The authority of the parish priest in the confessional and even the solemnity of his celebration of the Mass before the local altar," observes the historian Jaroslav Pelikan, "seemed to pale into insignificance when compared with the dramatic appeal of a personal

20 "Gli anticlericali e le 'apparizioni'," *Rabarbaro*, June 27, 1948.

21 See, for instance, Gerardo Guerrieri, "Il caffettiere 'miracolato' ha incassato mezzo milione: si muove o non si muove la Madonna di Assisi?" *L'Unita*, February 24, 1948; "Il miracolo elettorale," *Rabarbaro*, March 14, 1948; "La Madonna di Assisi non si è affatto mossa," *L'Unita*, March 4, 1948.

22 "Gli anticlericali e le 'apparizioni'," *Rabarbaro*, June 27, 1948; Oddone 1948b.

appearance by none less than the Mother of God" (Pelikan 1998: 184). And so, while the Church has rightly seen in such apparitions a potent ally to defend its interest and promote its doctrine, it has also understood the need to direct public veneration in such a way as to bolster the Church's authority, not undermine it. In the end, none of the apparitions and miracles reported on the eve of the election received the Church's official stamp of approval, though a few cases are still undecided.[23]

It is clear, therefore, that the "wind of miracles" and the apparitions which swept through Italy on the eve of the 1948 election were not deliberately orchestrated by the Church to influence the outcome of the vote, save for a few instances of over-exuberance on the part of some parish priests. That the visions and miracles were the product of something other than overt clerical manipulation can also be seen in the fact that the apparitions had begun well before 1948, and many more visions were reported after the April election than in the weeks and months preceding it.[24] This is not to say, however, that the apparitions of 1948 can be easily dismissed as inconsequential, as the product of individual and at times collective delusion. Nor is this to suggest that the supernatural happenings on the eve of the vote did not have a political content or purpose. The compelling question, therefore, is why did so many people claim to see or have been cured by the Virgin Mary? Why did so many of those who did not see or hear or feel any sort of supernatural sign in 1948, still believe the claims to be true? How was it that even the mainstream national media, from newspapers to public radio, reported on the visions and miracles as fact, throwing caution and skepticism out the window? To borrow from William Christian, what was it in the 1948 visions that spoke to the historical moment of the 1948 election campaign (Christian 1984: 232)?

For many Italian Catholics, and indeed much of the Western world, the notion that the Vatican might soon find itself in the heart in a country governed by Stalin's close friend Palmiro Togliatti and the other Marxist leaders was simply unthinkable. It is true that a communist victory in Italy in the 1948 election would have represented, as the papal historian Andrea Riccardi observes, "a hard blow for the central government of the Church, from both a concrete and symbolic point of view" (Riccardi 1993: 90). From a symbolic point of view, the advance of communism into devout Catholic countries such as Poland and Croatia was bad enough, but the mere thought, however implausible, of the Red Army at the gates of the Eternal City was enough to send chills down the spine of any Catholic. At a concrete level, a Marxist victory at the polls in Italy threatened to spell the end of the centuries-long influence the

23 For a brief discussion of the official treatment of apparitions by the Church, beginning with Benedict XIV's treatise *De servorum dei beatificatione*, see Zimdars-Swartz 1991: 9.

24 On the post-election apparitions, see, for instance, "La Vergine appare ad una bimba di Frascati," *Il Messaggero*, May 22, 1948, and "Una ragazza invasata salvata da S. Rita da Cascia," *Il Messaggero*, May 26, 1948.

Church enjoyed in the daily life of Italians. The unified Italian State may have destroyed, nominally, the temporal power of the papacy, but it had allowed the Church to maintain its role in such critical areas of Italian society as the schools and hospitals.

It is also the case that Italian Catholics faced the postwar era with a renewed sense of unity, purpose and direction. This was due in no small measure to the cadre of lay Catholics, individuals with organizational and leadership abilities acquired through involvement in unions, political parties or other Catholic civic associations before and during Fascism (Pierscostante 1948: 56). Indeed, as Victoria De Grazia observes, Catholic civic organizations "thrived" under Fascism, riding the crest of popular reaction – among the urban middle and working classes especially – against both liberalism and modernity that underlay the rise of Fascism itself. The richness of Catholic civic culture in the 1920s and 1930s, De Grazia writes, reflected a "catholicization" of Italian life after decades of progressive secularization following unification.

When papal Rome fell into secular hands in 1870, Catholics went on the offensive. They did so, however, by appearing to do just the opposite. After losing its temporal power, the Holy See ordered Catholics to abstain from Italian political life – and that meant foregoing the right to vote, to hold office and even civil service jobs, as a way of denying the legitimacy of the newly unified Italian state. Indeed, after unification, Catholics turned inward, refusing to take part in the social, cultural and economic life of the secular Italian state. Many Catholics refused to send their children to non-Catholic state schools, for instance, and they snubbed recreational and cultural organizations that were not exclusively of, by and for Catholics. Catholics turned inward even in areas – the economy and the workplace – where religion seemed to have no place at all. Catholics established their own savings banks and cooperatives, for instance, and confessional unions were established in many factories to keep Catholic workers from falling into the hands of socialist organizers and trade unions. Guiding this Catholic impulse to stick with their own in the decades after 1870 was what the historian Arturo Carlo Jemolo called a "cult of organization" that anticipated by several decades the mass-based politics of the twentieth century; and this in an age before the major Italian political parties had given much thought to the need to organize the masses, let alone to the effective means of doing so (Jemolo 1977: 53-54). "By the 1920s," Victoria De Grazia writes, "Catholics associations were thus well-armed to launch a veritable counter-reformation" (De Grazia 1992: 243-244).

The end of the Second World War and the spread of Soviet Communism westward after 1945 tested the ability of the Catholic Church to effectively articulate and defend the interests of the faith and, by extension, the country; this, at the start of a new era in domestic and international affairs. The most pervasive image of the pope's postwar role is that of Pius XII as the veritable 'cold warrior' – a histrionic, frightened and isolated figure closed behind the Vatican's walls, growing ever-more suspicious of nefarious communist subterfuge at play in Europe and around the world. Indeed, the depiction by Wladimir d'Ormesson, French ambassador to the Holy See, of Pius XII as "obsessed" with the communist threat, has become axiomatic among scholars.[25] Yet, I would caution against exaggerating the point, lest our understanding of Pius XII's anticommunism degenerate into a kind of caricature of papal policy which, for its inveterate opposition to communism, always displayed the pragmatism and prudence that were the hallmarks of Pacelli's diplomatic style. In fact, pragmatism impelled Pius XII to find concrete strategies to actualize doctrinal-discursive tropes of democratization and anticommunism. In a previous study of Italy's democratic transition after Fascism, I argued that one of the practical effects of the 1948 campaign was that the Holy See came to "embrace" democratic politics to an extent that would have been unthinkable a generation earlier. Leaning on the authoritative work of Robert Leonardi (Leonardi 1991), I affirmed the view that this fundamental change was best demonstrated by Pius XII's conversion from hostile skeptic to "convinced democrat" (Ventresca 2003: 270-217).

I no longer believe this to be true. Or better yet, I now would say that such a bald assertion is inadequate insofar as it is imprecise and goes too far, or conversely does not say enough, to describe Pius XII's elusive and vague views on democracy and democratization on the eve of the Cold War. I believe that the broader point remains valid: that is, by 1948, in part because of the intense electoral competition that pitted primarily the Christian Democrats against the Popular Front, a powerful communist-socialist electoral alliance, Pius XII had emerged as the chief promoter of a kind of 'civic Catholicism' which contributed both to an evolving if contested discourse on democracy, as well as to practicable expressions of civic engagement during Italy's democratic transition.[26] But as to the argument that in the course of promoting civic Catholicism, Pius XII underwent something of a political conversion and became a "convinced democrat," that is another matter.

It is true that the Vatican worried that an emerging discourse of democracy and democratization might, in the face of postwar institutional and social dislocation, be exploited to fuel the spread of communism, especially domestic communist movements in the would-be Catholic heartland of Central and Western Europe. It is also the case that Pius XII continued to encourage a strain of doctrinal development that sought to reconcile the Church – its political the-

25 Wladimir d'Ormesson is quoted by Riccardi 1993: 89. See also Chadwick 1993, and Kirby's instructive review essay, "History Memory and the Living Witness" (2011), especially 112-113. See also the competing interpretations of Kent 2002 and Coppa 2002.

26 I have adapted the concept of "civic Catholicism" from the work of Forment (2004) on Catholicism in Latin America, which in turn draws from his monograph *Democracy in Latin America* (2003).

ology as well as its institutional and associational life – with the modern, liberal secular state. This was evident by the late stages of the Second World War when in 1944 Pius XII used the traditional Christmas Eve papal message to address directly the "problem of democracy" (Radiomessaggio 1961: 235-251).

By his own admission, Pius XII was motivated to broach the subject considering what he discerned to be a "democratic tendency" that was spreading rapidly and gaining a consensus among peoples everywhere. He was building on a theme broached in a radio address from a few months earlier, at the start of September 1944, on the fifth anniversary of the start of the war.

It is clear from both speeches that Pius XII's mind already was turning to the question of the postwar ordering or reordering of society. Mindful, of course, that representatives of the major powers were gathering at the time at Dumbarton Oaks to discuss the future of international relations, Pius XII wanted to add his own authoritative voice by acknowledging that an "old world" was passing away and that peoples everywhere longed for "*un nuovo mondo*," a new world, to rise from its ashes. Addressing the architects of this new world order, Pius XII insisted that whatever its structures and processes, the new world had to be "more sound, legally better organized, and in greater harmony with the demands of human nature." Otherwise, he said, the painful mistakes of the past would give way to new and equally destructive mistakes, leaving the world oscillating from one extreme to another. It was, in effect, a timely restatement – an *aggiornamento* one might say – of the corporatist ideals espoused authoritative in Leo XIII's *Rerum Novarum* and Pius XI's *Quadragesimo Anno*. These included a defense of the principle of private property, a living wage and workers' right to humane working conditions, the right to free association, and the limited authority of the state to preserve and promote the common good.[27]

It was no secret that Pius XII was especially worried about the communist threat, in Italy and well beyond. On the eve of the pope's 1944 Christmas speech, American representative Myron C. Taylor told F.D. Roosevelt that the spread of communism in Italy was Pius XII's greatest fear. The presence in the governing antifascist coalition of the PCI, whose leader Palmiro Togliatti was known to have close ties to Moscow, did little to inspire the pope's confidence in the democratization of Italian politics promised by the antifascist coalition. As Pius XII confided to Myron Taylor's assistant Harold Tittmann a year after his 1944 Christmas address, Italy's political situation remained "confused" and with elections planned for June 1946 to elect the Constituent Assembly and decide on the fate of the monarchy, Pius XII had doubts that the vote would be either free or fair. For one, the communist-socialist parties were well-organized, cohesive, militant and well-financed (presumably from Moscow). Moreover, they were not above using violence and intimidation –

27 From Pius XII's speech of September 1, 1944 reproduced in *Discorsi e Radiomessaggi* 1961: 121-132.

the pope referred to "terroristic tactics" to influence voters. He maintained that they were being helped by an influx of disgruntled ex-fascists who were welcomed into the parties of the Left and shared their "totalitarian mentality." Pius XII warned ominously that such developments presaged the ascent to power of a "dictatorship of the Left," with popular assent.[28]

All of this to say that we must read Pius XII's pronouncements on democracy with a view to understanding that they were meant to appropriate what the pope correctly discerned as a spreading discourse of democratization; to christianize it, as it were, so that as the postwar transition evolved, the democratization of politics and society would unfold in a way that was consistent with the doctrinal principles and political interests of the Church. And the political interests of the Church were foremost to defend the spiritual autonomy of the Church in temporal affairs and, by extension, the cultural and ethical force of Catholicism as an active agent in civil society.

It is possible to discern in Pius XII's teaching here an *implicit* preference for democratic forms of government, especially when we consider that he draws an *explicit* link between the reawakening of peoples and growing popular demands for, as he put it, "a system of government that is more compatible with the dignity of the freedom of citizens." Indeed, if *popoli* everywhere were awakening from what he called "a long torpor," it was precisely because of their "bitter experience" with "monopolies of dictatorial power." The "democratic tendency" that Pius XII discerned was born of the widespread sense that war itself results when it is impossible to "question and to correct the activity of public powers." To avoid yet another catastrophe, Pius XII concluded, it was necessary to create "effective guarantees" within and between states. One such guarantee was for more meaningful popular involvement in civic life. In his regard, Pius XII could be seen to reconcile the democratic tendency of his day with a line of Catholic thought with roots in Augustine's foundational doctrine of the "two cities." Such a view accepted the limited autonomy and authority of the secular temporal order, while rejecting the prevailing claims of the state to ultimate, absolute authority over the lives of individuals and communities.

In contrast to the profiteers of false democracy, Pius XII offered the normative model of democratically-elected legislators of "solid Christian conviction" as ideal rulers of a true democracy, whether constitutional monarchy or republic. While acknowledging the duties of various branches of government in democratic regimes – legislative, executive and judicial – Pius XII singles out the legislative branch as being especially important to the proper func-

28 Taylor to Roosevelt, Vatican City, December 13, 1944, document number 205 in Di Nolfo 1978: 403-404. The original is in the Franklin D. Roosevelt Library, Hyde Park, President's Secretary's File, box 72; Tittimann to Byrnes, Vatican City, December 14, 1945, document no. 256 in Di Nolfo 1978: 476.

tioning of true democracy. Referring to the legislative power as the "center of gravity" in representative democracies, from which policies emanate and descend into the public square, Pius XII calls attention to the "moral" standing and the "intellectual capacity" of parliamentarians. The question of the character of its elected officials, then, was a matter of "life and death" for democracies. This was especially true in difficult periods of transition – and here he almost certainly was thinking of Italy's own travailed transition. In such febrile circumstances, Pius XII insisted, it was more essential for a state to be governed by good Christian men – men of sound doctrine and clear ideas; of good sense and fairness; of personal and political coherence and consistency. In the absence of such men, capable of moderating and mediating the competing passions, opinions and policies of a pluralistic polity, the pope warned, other men come in their place. These, in contrast to the legislator of solid Christian conviction, played at politics for pure ambition, to advance their own interests along with the interests of their "caste or their class," to the detriment of the common good.

The Marian apparitions of the early Cold War offer us a window in at least *three* defining features of Marian devotion and Cold War politics in Italy. First, the apparitions can be viewed as a microcosm of popular Catholicism in the modern era, with its enduring beliefs – modernity notwithstanding – about supernatural beings and their powers to intercede before God on behalf of the faithful. Second, the apparitions are a window on the interaction between "official" Catholicism and "popular" religion, on the internal dynamic of Italian Catholicism, in the midst of massive social, cultural and political change, at home and abroad. Third, the apparitions serve as a window on collective Catholic responses to two simultaneous processes: the changes to domestic and international politics wrought by the start of the Cold War; and the institutional and cultural evolution of Italy's post-Fascist, democratic Republic. Whereas in the nineteenth century, the state-building process took place largely in opposition to the Church, in particular in opposition to the continued temporal powers of the papacy, Italy's postwar reality reflected what De Grazia refers to above as the "Catholicization" of Italian society in the decades after unification. Far from being outside the process of rebuilding and democratizing post-Fascist Italy, much less opposed to it, the Church used its influence on the ruling Christian Democrats and its direct control of Catholic lay associations, to defend the space it had carved for itself in the decades after unification destroyed, ostensibly, the temporal power of the papacy.

This underscores a basic point: popular responses to the cult of the Madonna in Cold War Italy, to borrow from David Blackbourn, carried a "political logic" of their own. What Blackbourn says about the behavior of apparition crowds or even bread rioters in the nineteenth century seems applicable to the apparition crowds in Italy in 1948 – far from being manipulated by Church officials or simply delusional mobs, Marian devotees "acted with an eye to logistic practicality and the symbolic importance of public space" (Blackbourn 1995: 27). Put another way, Marian devotees were sending a political message, as much as a religious one.

Popular devotion at the Assisi visions or at many of the other apparitions and miracles reported on the eve of the 1948 vote was neither the product of individual or collective delusion, nor the deliberate invention of the Church fathers for electoral purposes. More to the point, the wave of apparitions and movements in Italy on the eve of the 1948 vote, one might argue, reflected an individual and collective search for meaning, order and protection on the part of ordinary Italians who feared the fate that awaited them should the Popular Front win the April election. The anxiety created by the rise of communism and the possibility of a Left victory at the polls in April help to explain why so many people in every corner of Italy reported seeing visions. Just as important, it helps to explain why so many who did not see the Virgin appear or a statue move or an icon cry in 1948, still believed in the divine nature of the phenomena. One journalist put it well when he described the 1948 wave of apparitions and movements as "this need for the supernatural, this thirst for God, the God of which some would like to deprive the most Christian, the most Catholic, the most sensitive nation, the Italian people."[29]

Marian apparitions and other supernatural events, we have seen, have long been associated with political, social or economic upheaval. Modernity and secularization notwithstanding, the association between Marian apparitions and war and political turmoil continued unabated in the twentieth century as well. The anthropologist William Christian has documented the case of Marian apparitions to several people in the Basque town of Ezkioga over a period of several months in 1931. The Basque visions and other seemingly supernatural events, like moving crucifixes, Christian observes, reflect how "individual seers respond to general anxieties with what they say were God's instructions." But, adds Christian, however sincerely the seers believed what they saw and heard, the broader significance ascribed to the celestial signs "were as much a consensual product of the desires of the followers and the wider society as of the leaders, the prophets or the saints" (Christian 1996: 40).

Put another way, the visions at Ezkioga were a response to a clear and immediate political threat to the religious and social fabric, as well as the political autonomy of rural, Catholic, Basque society. The secular Second Spanish Republic, inaugurated in April 1931 following the collapse of General Miguel Primo de Rivera's seven-year military dictatorship, launched a campaign of secularization throughout Spain, challenging the authority of the Church. The new republican order went so far as to order the removal of all crucifixes from classrooms, hospitals and other public officers. The Second Republic of 1931

29 "Miracoli," *Il Gazzettino di Venezia*, March 10, 1948.

was, as Christian puts it, "totally outside the lines of authority that ran from God to bishop to priest to male head of household, with ancillary lines for civil and industrial authorities" (Christian 1996: 38-39). The overt political attack against the heart of Basque customs and traditions coincided with the inexorable secularization of a once devout Catholic region, a process that was in turn the product of profound social and economic changes in the region and the nation as a whole. The fall of the monarchy, for one, shook Spanish society to its core and, writes Christian, "opened the door to changes in relations between women and men, workers and employees, laity and priests, children and parents" (Christian, 1996: 14). Urbanization, the shift from an agrarian to an industrial economy meant greater mobility and rural depopulation which, in turn, meant greater sexual freedom, especially for women, and declining church attendance – all of which challenged the old order of rural dwellers in the Basque country. In short, the Catholics of northern Spain, the Basques in particular, looked around and saw their unified, ordered world collapsing under what they saw as an external enemy, the government in Madrid. It was this perception of attack from without, Christian concludes, which determined to some extent "the way Basque Catholics tapped, defined, and interpreted the new devotional powers" spawned by the apparitions at Ezkioga (Christian 1996: 39).

The significance of the Marian visions in Cold War Italy, in other words, lay not in whether they were true or not – not even the Church demanded that Catholics believe in the literal truth of apparitions which received ecclesiastic approval – but in the fact that they had occurred at all. More important is the fact that the apparition stories were listened to and widely believed, and reported to a national and an international audience. Even those Catholics who doubted the veracity of the visions still considered the phenomenon a legitimate response on the part of those who feared for the fate of the Church should communists seize power in, as many described it, the most Catholic country in the world. As *Il Gazzettino di Venezia* put it, the real miracle at work in Italy on the eve of the 1948 election was the frequency and consistency of the seeming miracles, spawned, it was argued, by popular desire for Devine protection form temporal events beyond their control. The Italian people, the *Gazzettino* said, could not live without the "spiritual food" represented by Faith. And when the source of this *cibo spirituale* was threatened, when the people found it wanting, as in 1948, the *Gazzettino* concluded, they moved to provide it themselves.[30]

Put another way, the miracle boom of 1948 in which the apparitions of Mary figured so prominently was to Italians what Lourdes had been to French Catholics in the mid-nineteenth century, or what the apparitions at Marpingen, Germany had been to German Catholics in the 1870s, or what the Ezkioga visions of 1931 had been to Catholics of Northern Spain: a form of collective action against hostile elements that threatened to undermine the fundamental

30 "Miracoli," *Il Gazzettino di Venezia*, March 10, 1948.

basis of local and national religious authority (Blackbourn 1995: 27). True, the 1948 visions occurred in very different circumstances than other celebrated apparitions of the modern era. In Italy, for one, Catholics were the overwhelming majority of voters, and a Catholic party was in power and had been since the end of the war. What is more, the Church enjoyed a preponderant influence in the daily lives of Italians, literally from the cradle to the grave. While this had been so for close to two thousand years, this did not diminish the genuine fear among Catholics that the Church was gravely threatened by the prospect of communists and socialists coming to power, through legal or illegal means in April 1948. This threat was no less real to Italian Catholics in 1948 than, say, the threat of secularization and anti-clericalism that haunted Catholics elsewhere in Europe in the nineteenth and twentieth centuries. And, like Catholics in a different time and place, Italian Catholics in 1948 defended their faith and its institutions in the best way they knew how – by summoning the Virgin Mary to lead them in a struggle they believed they could not afford to lose.

If the Italian apparitions in the early Cold War were neither instances of collective delusion on the part of ignorant and impressionable masses, nor willful manipulations of a shrewd Church hierarchy, then what were they? As stated at the outset, the important question for historians is not whether the apparitions were true or not, since that is something that we can never fully disprove, yet which the believer necessarily believes is always *possible*, though not probable. Why, then, is the story of the apparitions worth telling? And if the story is worth telling, then what, precisely, does it show us about religion and society in Cold War Italy?

First, the story of the apparitions is worth telling because they happened at all. The mere fact that hundreds, even thousands of people from all segments of society, flocked to the sight of an alleged miracle or apparition in an age that knew the radio, air travel and the atom bomb suggests that our comfortable divisions between the "modern" and "pre-modern" world – the former rational, secular, scientific, the latter irrational, confessional, superstitious – can no longer hold. Whatever our assumptions about the meaning and consequences of "modernity," the fact remains that popular Catholicism in the modern era clung to its traditional beliefs about supernatural beings and their powers to intercede before God on behalf of his people. That Italian Catholics did so with fervor, emotion, imagination, and with a clear *political* logic, compels us to rethink commonplace assumptions about peasant belief and popular engagement in the political life of the secular Italian state. Whatever one might think of them, the beliefs and practices of popular Catholicism demonstrated an enduring vitality and universality, and Italian Catholics manifested a steely resolve to bring these resources to bear in the political debate over the future of Italy's nascent Republic.

At the same time, the Italian apparitions of the late 1940s suggest that modern Catholicism was not a reactionary monolith trumpeting what has been described as the "triumph of the Counter Reformation," characteristic of Pius XII's papacy (Tavard 1996: 198). However many critics at the time, or commentators since, have wanted to explain away the apparitions as either collective hallucination, or more likely, the product of deliberate machinations of the Church hierarchy to influence the outcome of the crucial 1948 election, the cautious, even skeptical, reaction of "official" Catholicism to the apparitions refutes facile accusations that Church leaders purposefully exploited popular piety for political ends. By the same token, one can discern the continued appeal of miraculous phenomena among ordinary Catholics, evidence of the resilience and enduring relevance of popular devotion in the lives of modern men and women, to say nothing of the stubborn independence of popular piety and its somewhat contested relationship with the "official" Church.

Finally, the Italian apparitions of the early Cold War speak to the enduring relevance of modern Catholicism in the life of the modern secular state and in the arena of international politics. As we saw above, in the nineteenth century, the state-building process in Italy came about largely in opposition to the Church, in particular in opposition to the enduring temporal power of the pope. But things had changed by the start of the Cold War. Italy's postwar reality reflected what has been referred to as the "Catholicization" of Italian society in the decades after unification. Far from being outside the process of rebuilding Italy after Fascism, much less opposing it, as had been the case decades earlier, Italian Catholicism made its voice heard, loud and clear, as Italy's baby Republic was baptized into a Cold War world.

In the end, then, the Italian apparitions of the late 1940s serve as a window on Italian history in the twentieth century. The mingling of religious with civic traditions during the 1948 campaign is evidence of the degree to which Catholic culture in Italy had become inextricably engaged in and committed to democratic politics (Ventresca 2003). The integration of Catholic culture into the civic life of the country had been a long time in coming. Whether this was a good development or a negative one is ultimately more a matter of opinion. One thing is clear, though: the integration of Catholics into the civic life of the country – something that had not happened in the decades after unification – undoubtedly made for a healthier, sturdier, more representative democratic polity. Catholics were, after all, an overwhelming majority in Italian society, and their exclusion from the civic life of the nation-state rendered the post-unification parliamentary system weak and narrowly-based, and, therefore, that much more vulnerable to the rising tide of Fascism. Hence, the moving statues, the weeping icons, the throngs of devotees crowding around Marian statues – these were to Italian Catholics in 1948 truly the tools with which to fight the good fight, for God and country.

BIBLIOGRAPHY

Apolito, Paolo. 1990. *'Dice che hanno visto la Madonna': Un caso di apparizioni in Campania*. Bologna: Il Mulino.

Blackbourn, David. 1995. *Marpingen: Apparitions of the Virgin Mary in Nineteenth-Century Germany*. New York: Clarendon Press.

Carroll, Michael P. 1986. *The Cult of the Virgin Mary: Psychological Origins*. Princeton: Princeton University Press.

Carroll, Michael P. 1992. *Madonnas that Maim: Popular Catholicism in Italy Since the Fifteenth Century.* Baltimore: Johns Hopkins University Press.

Chadwick, Owen. 1993. *The Christian Church in the Cold War*. London: Penguin.

Christian, William A., Jr. 1984. "Religious Apparitions and the Cold War in Southern Europe." In *Religion, Power and Protest in Local Communities: The Northern Shore of the Mediterranean*, edited by Eric R. Wolf, 239-266. Berlin: Mouton Publishers.

Christian Jr., William A. 1996. *Visionaries: The Spanish Republic and the Reign of Christ*. Los Angeles: University of California Press.

Coppa, Frank. 2002. "Pope Pius XII and the Cold War: The Post-war Confrontation between Catholicism and Communism." In *Religion and the Cold War*, edited by Dianne Kirby, 50-76. Basingstoke: Palgrave Macmillan.

De Grazia, Victoria. 1992. *How Fascism Ruled Women: Italy, 1922-1945*. New York: University of California Press.

De Lutiis, Giuseppe. 1973. *L'industria del Santino.* Florence: Guaraldi.

Di Nolfo, Ennio. 1978. *Vaticano e Stati Uniti, 1932-1952: Dalle carte di Myron C. Taylor*. Milan: Franco Angeli.

Discorsi e Radiomessaggi di Sua Santità Pio XII. Sesto anno di Pontificato, 2 marzo 1944 – 1 marzo 1945. Vatican City: Tipografia Poliglotta Vaticana, 1961.

Falconi, Carlo. "La sete del prodigioso e le suggestione suprannaturali." In Carlo Falconi. *La Chiesa e le organizzazioni cattoliche in Italia (1945 1955)*, 115-116. Turin: Einaudi, 1956.

Forment, Carlo A. 2003. *Democracy in Latin America, 1760-1890: Civic Selfhood and Public Life in Mexico and Peru*. Chicago: University of Chicago Press.

Forment, Carlo A. 2004. "Civic Catholicism." *Italian Politics and Society: The Review of the Conference Group on Italian Politics and Society* 59: 12-20.

Freud, Sigmund. 1959. "The Moses of Michelangelo." In Sigmund Freud. *Collected Papers*. Vol. 4. New York: Basic Books.

Ginzberg, Carlo. 1989a. "Clues: Roots of an Evidential Paradigm." In Carlo Ginzberg. *Clues, Myths, and the Historical Method* (trans. John and Anne C. Tedeschi), 96-125. Baltimore-London: Johns Hopkins University Press.

Ginzburg, Carlo. 1989b. "Folklore, magia e religione." In *Storia d'Italia: I caratteri originali*, edited by Ruggiero Romano and Corrado Vivanti, vol. 2, 603-676. Turin: Einaudi.

Ginzburg, Carlo. 1999. *The Judge and the Historian: Marginal Notes on a late Twentieth-Century Miscarriage of Justice* (trans. Anthony Shugaar). London-New York: Verso.

Harris, Ruth. 1999. *Lourdes: Body and Spirit in the Secular Age*. London: Viking Adult.

Isnenghi, Mario. 1977. "Alle origini del 18 aprile: miti, riti, mass media." *Rivista di Storia Contemporanea*, April: 209-210.

Jemolo, Arturo Carlo. 1977. *Chiesa e Stato in Italia: Dalla unificazione agli anni settanta.* Turin: Einaudi.

Kent, Peter C. 2002. *The Lonely Cold War of Pope Pius XII: The Roman Catholic Church and the Division of Europe, 1943-1950*. Montreal: McGill-Queen's University Press.

Kirby, Dianne. 2011. "History Memory and the Living Witness: The Vatican, the Holocaust and the Cold War." *Intelligence and National Security* 26 (1): 106-113.

Leonardi, Robert. 1991. "The International Context of Democratic Transition in Postwar Italy: A Case of Penetration." In *Encouraging Democracy: The International Context of Regime Transition in Southern Europe*, edited by Geoffrey Pridham, 62-83. Leicester: Leicester University Press.

Oddone, A. 1948a. "Apparizioni e visioni." *La Civiltá Cattolica* 1: 359-370.

Oddone, A. 1948b. "Criteri per discernere le vere visioni e apparizioni soprannaturali." *La Civiltá Cattolica* 2: 364-375.

Pelikan, Jaroslav. 1998. *Mary Through the Centuries: Her Place in the History of Culture*. New Haven: Yale University Press.

Piercostante, Righini. 1948. "I Comitati Civici nelle prospettive del loro dirigenti." *Cronache Sociali*, July 15, 56.

"Radiomessaggio di Sua Santità Pio XII ai popoli del mondo intero," December 24, 1944. 1961. In *Discorsi e Radiomessaggi di Sua Santità Pio XII.* Vol. VI: *Sesto anno di Pontificato, 2 marzo 1944 – 1 marzo 1945*, 235-251. Vatican City: Tipografia Poliglotta Vaticana.

Riccardi, Andrea. 1993. *Il potere del papa. Da Pio XII a Giovanni Paolo II*. Rome-Bari: Laterza.

Tavard, George H. 1996. *Thousand Faces of the Virgin Mary*. Collegeville: The Liturgical Press.

Ventresca, Robert. 2003. *From Fascism to Democracy: Culture and Politics in the Italian Election of 1948*. Toronto: University of Toronto Press.

Ventrone, Angelo. 1996. *La Cittadinanza Repubblicana: Forma-Partito e Identita Nazionale alle origini della Democrazia Italia, 1943-1948*. Bologna: Il Mulino.

Zimdars-Swartz, Sandra. 1991. *Encountering Mary: From la Salette to Medjugorje*. Princeton: Princeton University Press.

3
FROM FÁTIMA TO KÉRIZINEN
DEVOTIONAL BACKGROUNDS AND RESOURCES FOR THE COLD WAR

SANDRA L. ZIMDARS-SWARTZ

In the 1930s, most Catholics understood Our Lady of Fátima primarily as the Patroness and Protector of Portugal. During this decade, Portuguese bishops had sought to enlist the help of their Patroness in warding off the threat of Bolshevism that they saw at work in neighboring Spain. Between 1935 and 1941, the sole surviving seer of the apparitions at Fátima, Lucia dos Santos, recalled and reconstructed the messages that she said the Virgin had delivered to her and her cousins in 1917. With the release of this material, beginning in 1942, suffering and anxiety-ridden Catholics in many nations, with the encouragement of high-profile Catholic officials and Catholic journalists, found in these messages some devotional resources that would allow them to join forces with the Virgin in defeating the evil powers then at work in the world and bring an end to the war.

In the years following the Second World War, Our Lady of Fátima came to be understood as a powerful force for Catholics in the Cold War struggle against Russia-inspired communism. At an apparition in Kérizinen in Brittany (1938-1965), for example, the Virgin's messages, reported by a devout Catholic woman in fragile health, included apocalyptic warnings about Russia and urgent calls to devotion that echoed material from Lucia's memoirs as reported in the popular press. In the early years of this apparition, these warnings, in combination with the Virgin's weaponizing of sacrifices and devotions like the rosary, constituted a discourse of militant religious nationalism ready to defeat the communist threats of the Cold War.

3.1 Cover of a booklet by John De Marchi on Our Lady of Fátima's crusade for peace and against communism (1964; 1st ed. 1947).
[Collection Peter Jan Margry]

Fátima from 1921 to 1936: Lucia's exile, mass pilgrimages, and the fear of communism

For the purposes of this study, little needs to be said about the events of 1917 and the three years immediately following. Lucia's two young cousins both died in these years, Francisco in 1919 and Jacinta in 1920, leaving Lucia herself as the only source of information about what the children heard and saw during the apparitions and the primary source of information about their activities before, during, and after those events. She was not only the oldest of the children, but she was apparently the only one to see, hear and speak to the Virgin. Jacinta (aged 7) saw and heard Mary but did not speak to her, while Francisco (aged 9) only saw her.[1]

In 1921, as the shrine at Fátima was taking shape, the recently-appointed bishop of Leiria, José Correia da Silva, arranged for Lucia, ostensibly to safeguard her and her knowledge, to be sent to live at the College of the Sisters of St. Dorothy at Vilar do Porto. To maintain her anonymity, she lived there as Maria dos Dores, and was expressly forbidden to discuss the apparition. In 1925 she decided to join the order, and in 1926 she was transferred to their convent in the city of Tuy in Spain (Zimdars-Swartz 1991: 194-201; Bennett 2012: 174-175; de Marchi 1950: 196-200).

While Lucia had virtually no contact with Fátima and no knowledge of what was going on there during the first two decades of her life in these convents, many things were taking place in Portugal in those years that would profoundly affect how the apparitions would be understood. As Jeffrey Bennett has observed, already in the midst of the great influenza epidemic of 1919, "hundreds of sick and dying people came to the apparition site seeking miraculous cures" (Bennett 2012: 167). However, anti-Catholicism was strong in these years of the First Republic, and in the spring of 1920, for example, when arrangements had been made for the installation of a small statue of the Virgin on the site, the ceremony was cancelled and the statue hidden out of fear of government reprisals (Bennett 2012: 169-171). Nevertheless, "tens of thousands of women and men trekked to Fátima before the collapse of the First Republic in 1926" (Bennett 2012: 2) and Fátima by then was well on its way to becoming a symbol, and Fátima pilgrimage a crucial focal point, of Portuguese Catholic identity.

On October 13, 1930, Bishop da Silva declared the Fátima apparitions worthy of belief and authorized devotions at the site. According to Bennett, this move was prompted in part by the fear of "bolshevik contamination" that swept through Portugal at that time. This fear was inspired by the anti-Catholic violence in Spain stemming from the establishment earlier that year of the Spanish Republic (Bennett 2012: 182). Bishop da Silva's declaration opened

1 For a discussion of the children's roles in the apparitions, see Zimdars-Swartz 1991: 68.

the way for the head of the Portuguese Church, the young Cardinal Manuel Gonçalves Cerejeira, to call for a national pilgrimage to Fátima on May 13, 1931. In his call for this pilgrimage, the cardinal said that Fátima had become "the new Bethlehem: the Mother of God has deigned to appear there [...] to give, by a certain particular grace, her Son Jesus to Our Portugal ravaged by an anti-Christian hurricane." The bishops would go there, he said, in thanks for her appearances and "to consecrate the country to her so that the Queen of Heaven would guard and protect her as her own" (Cerejeira 1943a: 305).

Perhaps as many as a million pilgrims made their way to Fátima for this 1931 national pilgrimage. Much of what Cardinal Cerejeira said at Fátima on that occasion was apparently a response to the already-mentioned fear of bolshevism. The cardinal entreated the Virgin to intercede for Portugal "at this very grave hour when from the East blow furious winds carrying cries of death against your Son and the civilizations based on his teachings." He spoke of Our Lady of Fátima, who had shown herself to the child visionaries "under the triple invocation of Our Lady of the Rosary, Our Lady of Sorrows, and Our Lady of Mount Carmel," and he then consecrated the Portuguese nation to her Immaculate Heart. The cardinal concluded his act of consecration by asking the Virgin of Fátima to remember what Portugal had done for her glory (Cerejeira 1943b: 306).

Five years later, in 1936, Portuguese Catholics' fear of atheistic communism was heightened by the outbreak of the Spanish Civil War. The Portuguese bishops, who were on retreat at Fátima in May of that year, renewed their appeal to the Virgin, promising that they would call for another national pilgrimage if she, as the protectress of Portugal, would protect the nation.

In 1932 Oliveira Salazar, a former seminarian said to be a good friend of Cardinal Cerejeira and a militant foe of communism, was appointed premier of Portugal, a position he would hold for thirty-six years until his death in 1968. When he assumed control of the government, according to Bennett, the public persona that Salazar presented to the Portuguese was "a monkish, celibate man of humble origins" who was a devotee of Fátima, a persona that, along with a number of other factors effected a merger of "the cult of the Virgin of Fatima" with this commonly described dictator's "cult-like New State" (Bennett 2012: 22). Elsewhere in Europe right-wing fascists and proto-fascists relied on the military to solidify their power, but Bennett notes that in Portugal at this time "it was a former seminarian rather than a soldier who commanded the devotion of the rural masses" (Bennett 2012: 22).

1935 to 1941: Lucia's devotional reconstructions of the children's experiences

In 1935, two closely-related events took place that would be especially important for the future of Fatima devotion, especially in relation to the Cold War. In that year the remains of Jacinta, whose holiness was already being celebrated by Fátima pilgrims, were transferred from a private tomb in Nova de Orem to the Fátima cemetery (Bennett 2012: 41), and Bishop da Silva asked Lucia, who was still in the convent of the Sisters of St. Dorothy in Tuy, Spain, to write a brief life of her young cousin, a work which became known as her *First Memoir*. In December of 1935, Lucia somewhat reluctantly took up her pen to write what was basically a hagiography of Jacinta, warning the bishop, however, that she would withhold some information about herself and Jacinta "that I would not wish to be read before I enter eternity" (Santos 1976b: 19).

After describing Jacinta's character through stories that emphasized her sensitive nature, her love for the Crucified Jesus, and her desire to see the Child Jesus in the Communion Host, Lucia recalled some important events in the years just before the apparitions. In 1915 she said that her mother decided she was old enough to be entrusted with the care of the family sheep. Her cousins who were already attached to her, begged their parents to let them accompany her, and received their permission (Santos 1976b: 27).[2] Lucia said that at first she and her cousins organized their time in the fields to maximize their leisure for play by abbreviating the prayers of the rosary that they had been instructed by their parents to pray after lunch (Santos 1976b: 28). But after the first apparition of the Virgin on May 13, 1917, in response to her request, they began to think about suffering and making sacrifices for the conversion of sinners (Santos 1976b: 30).

Looking for opportunities, then, to do what the Virgin had requested, they began giving their lunches to poor children that they encountered in the roads (Santos 1976b: 31). Lucia recalled that Jacinta began to eat bitter acorns or olives picked directly from the trees "for the conversion of sinners" (Santos 1976b: 31) and on hot summer days when there was no water to drink, the children offered their thirst "as a sacrifice for sinners" (Santos 1976b: 32). Lucia depicts Jacinta as persisting in her desire to suffer for sinners even in her final illness, recalling that in her last days, her little cousin offered all of her suffering, including thirst, homesickness, and loneliness, as sacrifices "for the conversion of many sinners" (Santos 1976b: 43-46).

Lucia wrote what became known as her *Second Memoir* two years later, in 1937, when the Spanish Civil War was still in progress but when Franco's anticommunist "National Catholicism" was well-established in those parts of

2 In her *Second Memoir*, Lucia says that at the age of seven, her mother gave her the choice between working in the fields or becoming a weaver or seamstress (Santos 1976c: 59).

Spain bordering Portugal. In this *Second Memoir*, in which the children's sacrifices were revisited and the descriptions more fully developed, Lucia said that the children's sacrifices began not after the first apparition in May of 1917, as indicated in her first memoir, but in 1916 – and that on three occasions in that year an angel had appeared to them.

On the first occasion, she said, the angel identified himself as "the Angel of Peace" and taught them to kneel with their heads touching the ground and to repeat the prayer, "My God, I believe, I adore, I hope and I love You! I ask pardon of You for those who do not believe, do not adore, do not hope and do not love You." From then on, according to Lucia, they would spend long hours prostrating themselves, as the angel had taught them, to the point of exhaustion (Santos 1976c: 62). On the second occasion the angel appeared to them as they were playing and asked them what they were doing. "Pray, pray very much," he said, for "the most holy Hearts of Jesus and Mary have designs of mercy on you. Offer prayers and sacrifices constantly to the Most High." When Lucia then asked how they were to make sacrifices, she said that he answered, "Make of everything you can a sacrifice and offer it to God as an act of reparation for the sins by which He is offended, and in supplication for the conversion of sinners. Thus you will draw down peace upon your country. I am its Angel Guardian, the Angel of Portugal. Above all, accept and bear with submission the suffering which the Lord will send you." (Santos 1976c: 62)

The angel's words here seem to anticipate a question that Lucia remembered the Virgin putting to the children in her first appearance on May 13 of the next year. Lucia recalled that Mary had said, "Are you willing to offer yourselves to God to bear all the suffering he wills to send you, as an act of reparation for the sins by which he is offended, and of supplication for the conversion of sinners?" (Santos 1976c: 66) Lucia responded that they were willing, and then the Virgin, after warning them that they would have much to suffer, reassured them that God would be their comfort (Santos 1976c: 67).

Lucia then described some additional practices of the children, "mortifications of the flesh" as they are called in the saints' lives, that she says they discovered "by accident" and then began to inflict on themselves. Sometime in mid-August 1917, for example, she says that she found a piece of rough rope and suggested to her cousins that they tie this around their waists and "offer this sacrifice to God" – and her cousins agreed (Santos 1976c: 75). Whether it was because the rope was thick and rough or simply tied too tightly, she recalled that "this instrument of penance caused us terrible suffering" (Santos 1976c: 76).

Late in 1941 Lucia, still in a convent in Tuy, completed work on her *Third* and *Fourth Memoirs*, both of which included material which would prove to be something like a lens through which Catholics would soon be able to see both Fátima itself and the difficult circumstances in which they were living in a new and significantly different way.[3] In her *Fourth Memoir*, Lucia introduced this material simply by saying that there were "some words" that the Virgin told her and Jacinta on July 13, 1917 that they were to tell no one besides Francisco (Santos 1976e: 162).[4] Lucia suggested that what the Virgin said to them, which many later Catholics have simply called "the secret," could be divided into three parts, only the first two of which she would reveal. The first part, simply stated, was a horrible vision of hell, and this was followed by a lengthy message, the basic elements of which are as follows: The Virgin said that the war would soon end,[5] but that if people did not cease to offend God, another worse war would soon break out.[6] She then said that she would come again to ask that Russia be consecrated to her Immaculate Heart, and that if this were not done, Russia would spread her errors throughout the world, "causing wars and persecution of the Church." Finally, the Virgin warned that "the good will be martyred, the Holy Father will have much to suffer, [and] various nations will be annihilated," but she also said that in the end, her Immaculate Heart would triumph, the Holy Father would consecrate Russia to her, that country would be converted, "and a period of peace will be granted to the world" (Santos 1976d: 104-105).[7]

In these memoirs, written over a five year period ten to fifteen years after she had joined the Sisters of Saint Dorothy in Tuy, Lucia has obviously reached back to some very personal memories from 1917 and the years immediately thereafter and recast this material in the form of some of the "saints' lives" with which she had been familiar even as a child and several of which were said to have been her favorite devotional readings during her years in the convent.[8] These hand-written devotional reconstructions of material from the time of the apparitions, formally addressed to the bishop of Leiria who re-

3 Lucia's *Third Memoir* was written in August, and her *Fourth Memoir* was written in November and December of 1941.

4 See also Lucia's first written account of the apparitions, on January 5, 1922, in Santos 2002: 255.

5 In 1917, this would, of course, have been the First World War.

6 This, in combination with other details in the message, is presumed by devotees to be the Virgin's prediction of the Second World War.

7 In her *Fourth Memoir*, Lucia adds at the end of the secret that "[i]n Portugal the dogma of the Faith will always be preserved" (Santos 1976e: 162). The third part of this secret was released by the Vatican in 2000. For the English translation of this Third Secret and other documents related to it, see website from the Congregation of the Doctrine of the Faith, "The Message of Fatima,<http://www.vatican.va/roman_curia/congregations/cfaith/documents/rc_con_cfaith_doc_20000626_message-fatima_en.html>.

8 According to William Thomas Walsh, Lucia read and reread the Portuguese translation of Thérèse of Lisieux's autobiography, *The History of a Soul* (Walsh 1947: 198). This devotional work was published the year after her death in 1898, and translated into six languages, including Portuguese by 1906 (Descouvemont 1998: 213).

quested them, were completed only shortly before the twenty-fifth anniversary of the Fátima apparitions in 1942.[9]

A jubilee and a divine plan for peace

The 25th anniversary of the Fátima apparitions was celebrated in 1942 with a jubilee which, like the apparitions themselves, began on May 13, and ran through the month of October. Several books that included material from Lucia's recently released memoirs were published in the months immediately preceding this jubilee, and some reviews of these books and of the jubilee's principal events in the French Catholic newspaper *La Croix* testify to an important shift in Catholic perceptions of Fátima that was beginning to take place at this time.[10]

Before 1942, while Fátima was not unknown to Catholics outside of the Iberian peninsula, it was seen primarily as a shrine where Portuguese and some Spanish Catholics came to be comforted, healed, and strengthened in their faith. But now, with the publication and widespread distribution of material from Lucia's first four memoirs including the so-called secret, Catholics throughout the world, with considerable assistance from some high-profile Catholic officials and Catholic journalists, began to see Fátima as part of a divine plan, announced and overseen by the Virgin, that would make use of sacrifices and devotions like the Rosary to bring an end to the war, to defeat the powers of evil at work in the world, and finally to bring about a lasting peace.

Especially important for bringing to public attention the material in Lucia's memoirs on which this plan was based was the publication in the spring of 1942 of a revised edition of Luis-Gonzaga da Fonseca's *La meraviglie de Fatima*, which was quickly followed by a French edition prepared with Canon Ca-

9 Lucia's *First Memoir* was completed in August 1935, the *Second Memoir* in November 1937, the *Third Memoir* in August 1941, and the *Fourth Memoir* in December 1941.

10 *La Croix* was founded in 1880 by RR. PP. Picard and Vincent de Paul Bailly of the Congregation of the Augustinians of the Assumption and the Count de la Epinois. First published monthly and then daily in Paris, it was part of the much larger publishing enterprise, Maison de la Bonne Press. Although it had competitors in the late nineteenth century, it quickly gained prominence and popularity. When the Germans invaded France, *La Croix* moved first to Bordeaux in June 1940 and after a few months to Limoges, where it continued publication until June 21, 1944 when it ceased publication, reappearing again in February 1945. For a history of this important Catholic newspaper, see Godfrin & Godfrin 1965. For a discussion of *La Croix* between 1940 and 1944, and insight into the censorship to which the paper was subject, see Massiani 1988: 301-321.

simir Barthas, *Fatima, merveille inouïe*, that appeared in April 1942.[11] J. Pélissier, in an article in the May 9-10, 1942 edition of *La Croix* announcing the impending celebrations of the Fátima Jubilee, spoke of the French edition of this work as "the most clear, most complete expose on the events of Fátima, the miracles, and the rapid development of the pilgrimage," and he said that all Catholics should own the book. "They will see there again," he said, "the expansion of the merciful love of Mary for her children and the conditions in which the world can be saved" (Pélissier 1942).

The most extensive coverage in *La Croix* of the Fátima Jubilee came from the pen of C. Martel, editor of the newspaper *Croix du Midi*, the author of an earlier book on Fátima, and perhaps the most important of the French journalists whose articles in these months would bring the basic parts of the Virgin's divine plan to the attention of Catholics who would not have access to Fonseca's book (Martel 1940).[12] In the first of his articles in *La Croix* entitled "Rome et Fatima: Nouveau sur le 'mystère' de Fatima," which appeared in the July 2, 1942 issue, Martel expressed his appreciation for Fonseca's recently published work. Like Pélissier, he saw it as very important, praising its comprehensive scope and taking the fact that it was published by the Vatican presses and bore the imprimatur of the vicar general of the Vatican to be a sign of the approval of the Holy See (Martel 1942c). He was especially impressed by its inclusion of information about the "mystical life" of the young visionaries and about the secret that he said had now been revealed "at the request of ecclesiastical authority and with the permission of Heaven" (Martel 1942c). Like other Catholics now who were aware of this secret, he understood it as prophecy, and he specifically noted some of its basic parts: the Virgin's assurance that the war would soon end and that people needed to stop offending God if the outbreak of another more terrible war was to be avoided; her assurance that if her requests were heeded the scourge would be delayed or weakened; and her statement that finally her Immaculate Heart would triumph.

Martel was aware, of course, that part of the secret had not yet been revealed, but he said that he was confident that the pope knew its content and that this would concern the good of souls and would be in harmony with the directives of the Church. When the whole of the secret is known, he said, one should not hesitate to think "that it is a question of the role of the Papacy in events which accompany or follow the end of the present conflict"(Martel 1942c).

11 Not long after Lucia had completed her *Third* and *Fourth Memoirs* in 1941, the bishop of Leiria had made available typed copies of these works to Fonseca, a Portuguese Jesuit teaching at the Biblical Institute in Rome. Fonseca then incorporated this material into the fourth edition of *La meraviglie de Fatima* (Fonseca 1942). Whereas earlier editions of Fonseca's work had been published by secular presses, this fourth edition was published by the Vatican presses. Barthas and Fonseca adapted the content of Fonseca's fourth edition for the French translation, published in Toulouse by the Apostolat de la Prière.

12 The book was reviewed by Delarnette in *La Croix* on January 30, 1941.

Martel then began an extensive sketch of what he called "the magnificent discourse" delivered at Fátima on May 13, at the opening ceremony of the Jubilee by the head of the Portuguese Church, Cardinal Cerejeira, who eleven years earlier had formally consecrated the Portuguese nation to Mary's Immaculate Heart. In his homily, according to Martel, the cardinal had emphasized hope and Portugal's role in bringing hope to a world in chaos. But he had also called attention to the fact that that day, May 13, 1942, was a *double jubilee*, celebrating not only the 25th anniversary of the first appearance at Fátima of Our Lady of the Rosary, but also the 25th anniversary of the reception of "the fullness of priesthood" by Monsignor Pacelli, who as Pope Pius XII would now be governing the Church in these "stormy times."[13] The cardinal called this "a providential coincidence," suggesting that it "opens luminous horizons of hope in the bloodied haze of the present." He was confident that by "the intercession of the Immaculate Heart of the One (...) whom we call the Mother of Mercy, God prepares great things for the world."

Cardinal Cerejeira said that for the past twenty-five years the protection of the Virgin had been a promise of what he and the bishops had only recently learned of the prayers and sacrifices of the humble, uneducated child visionaries, and the admonitions of the Guardian Angel of Portugal to them to pray much and offer prayers and sacrifices to the Most High. The "triple scourge of war, of sorrow, and of famine," he said, is the result of sin, and that to chase this scourge from the earth, people needed to heed Mary's recommendations of prayer and penitence. While he acknowledged that to speak of the terrible scourges of the present time might lead one to think about the end of the world, he suggested that "when one believes in Providence and in the maternal heart of the Immaculate Virgin, this is the painful birth-giving of a new world."

Martel concluded his article by noting that after the Pontifical Mass on that day the bishop of Leiria read a telegram from Pope Pius XII in which the pope exhorted the faithful "to a most solemn manifestation of faith and of active piety," and he asked "his beloved children for their prayers to the heavenly Queen." Martel lamented that difficulties in communication had kept the French from a timely knowledge of these events, commenting that the French had become increasingly interested in these Fátima events and especially "in the messages that Mary had transmitted there to the world for its salvation."

In an article published in *La Croix* on October 31, 1942, Martel reported on events in Portugal on the 13th of that month, the anniversary of the last of the apparitions, describing, first, a pilgrimage that had been called to commemorate that event. While transportation to Fátima was difficult, he said, an immense number of pilgrims had been able to come to the shrine, matching

13 The quotations in this and the next two paragraphs are taken from Martel 1942c. The translations are my own.

the numbers of the great national pilgrimages of earlier years. Again, Cardinal Cerejeira presided over the ceremonies, which were quite elaborate and which Martel described in some detail, before noting that the day was also observed in parishes throughout the nation. One of the most beautiful of those observances, he said, had taken place in Lisbon, where a candlelight procession through the streets had preceded ceremonies in the recently built church of Our Lady of Fátima. The day, he noted, had also been celebrated in Rome at the Church of Saint Anthony of Portugal and at the Portuguese College, with homilies being delivered by Fonseca, who taught in that city, and the Abbé Moresco, editor of *L'Osservatore Romano*, both of whom had written books on Fátima (Martel 1942a).

Martel made it clear in this article that even more important than these events on October 13, would be the closing ceremonies of the Jubilee on October 31, when the Sovereign Pontiff would broadcast a message to the Portuguese people and to the world. This message, he said, would be delivered in Portuguese, "the maternal language of the little seers of Fatima," an event that would be a singular honor for the nation (Martel 1942a).

While there was no extensive coverage in *La Croix* of the events of October 31, that Martel had anticipated in his article, on November 3, an article did appear in *La Croix* in which the newspaper's Rome correspondent summarized the pope's radio message. The pope, according to the author, had expressed his great interest in the homage that the Portuguese people from very early times had paid to the Virgin, who more recently had saved their country from what seemed to be an inevitable "shipwreck of an antinational and antichristian storm" ("Un message du Saint-Père" 1942). In an apparent reference to the Spanish Civil War, he noted that Portugal had escaped from "the red menace," and in an apparent reference to its neutrality in the present conflict, he said that, through the intercession of the Virgin of Fátima, it was now sheltered from the war. The pope then emphasized that, in the midst of these terrible manifestations of divine anger, the only way to obtain salvation was through penitence, after which he consecrated the entire world to Mary's Immaculate Heart. "Virgin of Mercy, Queen of Peace," he implored, "give us the peace of arms and of souls" so that the kingdom of God might prevail."[14]

In the weeks that followed, *La Croix* published two more articles responding to the pope's address. In the first, published on November 19, R. Fontenelle argued that Pius XII's consecration of the world to the Immaculate Heart of Mary was "a replica and a complement" to Pope Leo XIII's consecration of the

14 As quoted in "Un message du Saint-Père" 1942.

human race to the Sacred Heart of Jesus in 1899 (Fontenelle 1942).[15] In the second article, published on 1 December, Martel spoke of the Pope's address as the "realization of the desire expressed by Our Lady to the little seers of Fátima and renewed by the surviving Lucia of Jesus to see the Church and the world consecrated to her Immaculate Heart" (Martel 1942b: 2).

Kérizinen: the seer, her notebook, and the influence of Lucia's memoirs

Between 1938 and 1965, Jeanne-Louise Ramonet claimed that, on her farm in southwest Brittany, the Virgin Mary, sometimes accompanied by the Sacred Heart, appeared and spoke to her seventy-one times.[16] As she recalled some years later, the first of these apparitions apparently took place on September 15, 1938, a time when German troops were assembling on the French border. The second apparition occurred on October 7, 1939, and on that occasion the Virgin told her to convey an important message to her parish priest, which she did. Her priest, however, directed her to remain silent about her experiences, and in obedience to his directive, for the next eight years she told no one else about them (Auclair 1968: 21).

Jeanne-Louise's apparitions only became public knowledge in the fall of 1947 when a young girl heard her speaking about them in the confessional and then talked in school about what she had heard, after which word spread quickly, at first locally, and eventually throughout France (Auclair 1968: 21). By then the war had ended, but in France economic recovery and the rebuilding of infrastructure was painfully slow. And to judge from the Virgin's reported messages to Jeanne-Louise in these years, there was much fear of future conflicts, most of which was focused on communism.

Jeanne-Louise was born on October 7, 1910, the feast of the Holy Rosary, and grew up on a Breton farm consisting of a small field, a stable with two cows, and an adjoining one-room dwelling that was somehow able to accommodate a staunchly Catholic family of ten. Her earliest years were marked by delicate health and various disabilities, and she was only able to attend school

15 The French translation of the pope's homily was printed on page 3. After repeated requests by Sister Mary of the Divine Heart, mother superior of the convent of the Good Shepherd in Porto (Portugal), Leo XIII announced this consecration in his encyclical letter *Annum Sanctum* (May 25, 1899) which also authorized the First Friday devotions as well as the Prayer of Consecration to the Sacred Heart composed by Leo XIII. The consecration took place on June 11, 1899. The Portuguese text of the pope's radio address may be found on the Vatican website, <https://w2.vatican.va/content/pius-xii/en/speeches/1942.index.html>. An English translation may be found in Barthas & da Fonseca 1947: 215-220.

16 For an overview of the apparitions at Kérizinen, see Maunder 2016: 110-114. For two early devotional works, see Auclair 1968, and Le Rumeur 1970: 105-119. For a contemporary anthropological study of Kérizinen, see Badone 2007.

for a few years. By the time she was eighteen she had lost both of her parents and three of her seven siblings, and after the remaining siblings moved away, she was left to manage the small farm with the help of a few cousins. She had hoped to become a nun but was thwarted by her frail health. During some hospital visits that began in 1925, however, she learned some basic nursing skills and decided that, if she could not be a nun, she could at least be of assistance to the sick. For some years then, while her own health remained fragile, she found some joy and satisfaction in working as a volunteer nurse (Auclair 1968: 19).

In 1936, two years before her first reported encounter with the Virgin, Jeanne-Louise joined a group of sick and infirm parishioners on a pilgrimage to Lourdes, believing that she would be cured and would return home in good health. Upon returning home she apparently did think that she had been healed, but the cure, if it was that, was obviously incomplete (Auclair 1968: 20). Some of Jeanne-Louise's neighbors who were interviewed many years later, remembered her as being very devout and always reciting the rosary, and one of these persons remembered wondering if she had been "imitating Lourdes" and styling herself as a "second Bernadette" (Badone 2007: 459).

Unlike Lourdes and Fátima, where the Virgin requested her young visionaries to return to the apparition site on specific days, Jeanne-Louise's visions did not follow a predictable pattern.[17] Between 1938 and 1943, she reported nine visions, and in 1943 the priest recommended that Jeanne-Louise begin writing down the messages she said she received from the Virgin. That year she began recording them in a notebook, reconstructing the early and relatively short messages from memory. As the visions continued, the messages became longer and more apocalyptic in tone. Skeptics apparently questioned the reliability not only of Jeanne-Louise's reconstructed messages but the later, much longer messages as well, as sometimes days would elapse between her vision and her leisure to record the message.[18] During that interval, the visionary said, perhaps in response to such criticism, the words she heard

17 Bernadette was requested to return to the grotto at Lourdes for a fortnight; the three visionaries at Fátima were requested to return to the Cova da Iria on the 13th of each month through October. While in her first vision, Jeanne-Louise said that the Virgin indicated she would return "at different times in the years to come," no specific days or dates were specified, nor in subsequent appearances did the Virgin (or the Sacred Heart) indicate the date of the next appearance.

18 The lengthiest messages come in the late 1950s and 1960s. See, for example, the 49th apparition (April 26, 1961), in which Jeanne-Louise voices the complaint that the messages are too long, and the Virgin asks rhetorically, "Am I not free to speak openly, and as I wish to my children?"

would register in her memory and repeatedly turn over in her mind until she recorded them (Auclair 1968: 29).[19]

It is important to note that Jeanne-Louise began recording her messages in the year after the 1942 jubilee celebrations of the 25th Fátima anniversary. The publicity given to these celebrations in religious publications like *Le Croix* stimulated interest in the Portuguese apparition among French Marian devotees at this time, while the books and brochures about Fátima reviewed in these publications introduced the newly-released Fátima secret into Marian devotional discourses. Pius XII's address to the Portuguese people and his consecration of the world to the Immaculate Heart of Mary further raised the profile of Fátima and highlighted the importance of expressions of individual and national devotion in imploring the Virgin for the peace "of weapons and souls"[20] in times of social, political and spiritual crises (Pius XII 1942).

Content of the messages

From their onset, Jeanne-Louise's visions reflect a melding of the apparition of Lourdes with the more apocalyptic traditions of La Salette (1846) and Fátima. In her reconstruction of her first vision, the Breton peasant recalled that on September 15, 1938 she was alone in her pasture, watching her cows, when she saw a dazzling light a few meters above the ground, within which a woman was standing. Jeanne-Louise said that she was immediately thrown to her knees, and she knew instinctively that this was the Virgin Mary.[21] The Virgin, she said, reassured her that she meant her no harm, saying that she would return at different times in the coming years and would then identify herself and tell Jeanne-Louise what she wanted. The Virgin then said, "A new war is threatening Europe. I shall delay it for a few months because I cannot remain deaf to so many prayers that are being raised to Me for peace there at Lourdes."[22] The Virgin then disappeared "in a brilliant flash of light" (Auclair 1986: 98).

19 For Auclair, Jeanne-Louise's rudimentary education is an argument for the authenticity of the messages. Auclair maintains that Jeanne-Louise could not have composed herself "the sublime exhortations" that came from the Virgin and the Sacred Heart. She was thus limited to recording what she had heard, and even here the messages in her notebooks needed editing for punctuation and spelling. In the messages reconstructed from memory, he says, one finds some "hesitation" and "clumsiness" that must be attributed to the visionary herself, but in the long messages culminating the series of apparitions, "one feels the rectitude and harmony of the discourse flow from word to word."

20 The French translation is "des armes et des ames."

21 Jeanne-Louise described the Virgin as she appeared to her as about seventeen years of age with deep blue eyes. A white veil covered her hair, and she wore a blue dress with a white border, cinched at the waist with a double-white rope, and a white mantle that covered her shoulders and reached to her feet, which were covered by the dress.

22 Apparition 1 (September 15, 1938). Translation is my own.

Two things are especially worth noting in this report of her initial apparition. First, here, as in the Virgin's later messages, there is a blending of the apocalyptic themes of Fátima with the healing themes of Lourdes; and second, this experience reportedly took place on a day commemorating the Virgin's sorrow, a theme that would occupy an important place in the devotions that the Virgin would call for in her later appearances.

Jeanne-Louise said that her second encounter with the Virgin took place about a year later on October 7, 1939, the feast of Our Lady of the Holy Rosary and, perhaps not coincidently, the seer's birthday. On this occasion, when the war was well underway,[23] Jeanne-Louise said that the Virgin spoke about this terrible conflict, what had led to it, and what could be done about it. She recalled that Mary said, "The world continually offends God by very grave sins, especially sins of impurity, from which comes this war for its punishment." She added, however, that there was a way to bring peace more quickly and to achieve salvation, which was that people must "lead a life of prayer, sacrifice, and penance," and said that children should come together frequently to pray and to recite the Rosary, followed by the *Parce Domine* for sinners.[24] These warnings and instructions that Jeanne-Louise said were given to her by the Virgin would be repeated many times in her appearances through the remaining years of the war and well into the years of the Cold War.

A brief message that Jeanne Louise said the Virgin delivered in her third appearance two months later on December 7, 1939, a time when German troops were assembling on the French border, makes quite explicit the connection between bringing an end to the war and prayer and sacrifice. On this occasion, as Christmas was approaching, the Virgin told her to double the fervor of her prayers and sacrifices. "Arm yourselves therefore with prayer and sacrifice," she said, "while your soldiers use material arms. That is what is necessary to obtain a rapid victory." This was then followed by a prophecy: "If My requests are listened to, the war will end about mid-October 1940."[25]

Jeanne-Louise recalled that, late in the spring of 1940, when the German occupation of France was well underway, the Virgin spelled out some of the consequences of neglecting these devotions. On April 2, according to the seer, the Virgin complained that prayers then were less frequent than in the early months of the war, and she said that "This negligence will bring suffering for you all, but principally for your soldiers. Many of them will become prisoners,

23 On September 1, 1939, Germany invaded Poland, and on September 3, 1939 France and Great Britain declared war on Germany.

24 Quotations from Apparition 2 (October 7, 1939), translation my own. The *Parce Domine* is a Latin antiphon based on Joel 2:17: "Spare Lord, spare your people; do not be angry with us forever."

25 Apparition 3 (December 7, 1939).

and others will die from starvation and hardship on enemy soil."[26] Later that year on October 7, according to Jeanne-Louise, in another commemoration of the seer's birthday and the feast of the Holy Rosary, the Virgin explicitly identified herself as the "Mother of Christ" and said that she wished to be invoked at Kérizinen with the title "Our Lady of the Most Holy Rosary."[27]

A year then passed in which Jeanne-Louise reported no apparitions. But on May 5, 1942, Mary again appeared and spoke to her,[28] and what she reportedly said marks a shift from concern with the suffering occasioned by the German invasion and occupation to warnings about Russia and the dangers of communism. The Virgin now told her that Russia would soon "make a helpful contribution to the war" which would be a "shock to your enemies." But it would be necessary for Christians to pray a great deal since Russia was an enemy of the Church. She warned that, after the war, communists would seek to infiltrate every country, including France, and that the Church would be severely harassed. She exhorted people to "ask Jesus through My Immaculate Heart for the return of sinners and the conversion of Russia." Then she urged people to go to Communion as often as possible on the first Saturdays of every month in honor of her Immaculate Heart. She said she had asked for this practice for many years, but people had not heeded her request.[29]

In an apparition on February 2, 1944, the seer's account of which would presumably have been one of the first to have been entered in her notebook soon after the event, the Virgin repeated her warning that new chastisements awaited a world that did not do penance and her instruction that the Rosary was the key to peace. She then taught Jeanne-Louise a short, two-part prayer that she said should be repeated frequently: "O Jesus, I give myself to you, through the Sorrowful and Immaculate Heart of Mary, to be the consolation of Your Sacred Heart forever. Sacred Heart of Jesus, may your Kingdom come through the Sorrowful and Immaculate Heart of Mary."[30] This was the Virgin's first reference to these two hearts, the unity of which would become, for Kérizinen devotees, a central symbol and a major focus of devotion.

26 Apparition 5 (April 2, 1940). See also messages from Apparition 6 (May 1940). France formally accepted the German occupation of the country on 22 June 1940.

27 Apparition 7 (October 7, 1940).

28 Coincidentally, on May 5, 1942, *La Croix* published an article announcing Pius XII's request to Luigi Maglione, his Cardinal Secretary of State, requesting that during May (the month of Mary) he organize an "offensive of prayer" throughout the world. The author of the article notes that in preparing for the 25th anniversary of Fátima, the Portuguese bishops had issued a letter to the Portuguese people that echoed the voice of the pope in calling people to return to God.

29 Apparition 8 (May 5, 1942). According to Sister Lucia, the Virgin had appeared to her on December 10, 1925 and had requested that people take communion for five consecutive Saturdays. For a discussion of this practice and Sister Lucy's vision, Zimdars-Swartz 1991: 194-197.

30 Apparition 10 (February 2, 1944). Translation my own.

3.2 Kérizinen two-part panel drawing, according to the descriptions given by visionary Jeanne-Louise Ramonet on May 1, 1944, depicting on the left anti-religious communism, and on the right Mary protecting her devotees from communism. Drawing in *Kérizinen. Messages du Christ en de la Sainte Vierge, 1938-1965* (1981), 145.
[Collection Peter Jan Margry]

In her notebook, Jeanne-Louise reported that on May 1, 1944 she had a vision in which two different scenes were unfolding simultaneously as if on a two-part panel. On the left side of the panel, labeled "Image of Communism," the Virgin stood weeping while some men, urged on by a demon, tried to erect flags everywhere. The priests who were trying to stop them were threatened and injured. On the right side of the panel, labeled "Salvation of Communism" some young girls clothed in blue recited the Rosary.[31]

In the next year, 1945, Jeanne-Louise reported no visions or apparitions, but there is a report that on October 7, 1946 she had a vision of a rosary with white beads that was surrounded by the inscription, "Take courage, the faithful devotes of the Rosary will one day defeat communism through their perseverance."[32]

31 Apparition 11 (May 1, 1944) [including illustrations].
32 Apparition 12 (October 7, 1946).

Apocalyptic urgency and the role of France in world-renewal

In October of 1947 Jeanne-Louise's experiences finally came to public attention, and at about this time, as Kérizinen moved into the Cold War years, the Virgin began to speak specifically about Brittany and the French nation, and her messages became longer, more frequent, and increasingly apocalyptic. In these messages, Brittany would "re-Christianize" France, and France would assume a role similar to that assigned to Portugal in the divine drama sketched by persons such as Cardinal Cerejeira in the months of the Fátima Jubilee – that is, France would spread the devotions requested by the Virgin and would combat communism and bring salvation both to nations and individual souls.

In the message reported on December 27, 1947, for example, the Virgin, who on several previous occasions had expressed special concern for France, now said that France was beloved by her above all other nations, and that while the nation had remained deaf to her calls, she wished to save her. She said that there are ardent souls in France who would be the hope for her salvation, but the faults of the nation were so heavy, especially the sin of impurity, that it was necessary to "pray and pray ceaselessly without growing tired." Apostates, through their "lying propaganda," were conquering many souls, but they could be saved through the Rosary, which "is a terrible weapon against the enemy of your souls." While apostasy was spreading outside of Russia, according to the Virgin, within that country there were conversions and people were beginning to return to Christianity.[33]

On May 29, 1948, the Virgin spoke with still greater urgency, saying that a war, heavy with consequences, was imminent. She warned that France would be invaded and occupied by a Russian army and that the good would suffer persecution at the hands of atheists. She herself, however, had been appearing to raise up and save France, and it was through Brittany, which had remained the most faithful to her, that she wished to "re-Christianize" the nation.[34] Two months later, on July 17, 1948, Jeanne-Louise said that the Virgin issued a warning specifically to Brittany, saying that if it failed to fulfill her request the land would become "uninhabitable," but she promised that abundance would follow if the province became a "Breton Lourdes."[35]

The following year the Virgin began to suggest that she had chosen France to renew the world. On March 6, 1949, Mary again warned that a terrible tempest would break out over the world if people did not amend their lives, but she said that she had chosen the people of France to renew the "broken links between the world and God." At the end of her message on that day she promised to protect France from the Russians, but the latter, she said,

33 Apparition 15 (December 27, 1947).
34 Apparition 18 (May 29, 1948).
35 Apparition 19 (July 17, 948).

3.3 Pilgrims gather in front of the (first) chapel of Kérizinen, ca. 1967.
[Collection Peter Jan Margry]

would suddenly become enlightened and would "join in a new wisdom for the world."[36] Then on December 9, 1949, Jeanne-Louise said the Virgin again appeared to her and reassured her that, eventually, after suffering chastisements for its faults, France would recover her "true and bright appearance." She said that the Virgin then told her to take this message to the bishop,[37] asking him to authorize prayer and pilgrimages at the site of the apparitions to mitigate the coming chastisements and to ask that a chapel be built there.[38]

Two wounded hearts and a consecration to bring God's Kingdom

Jeanne-Louise reported no apparitions in the next four years, but when they resumed in 1954, the explicit references to Russia in the apocalyptic scenarios the Virgin had been sketching for several years were replaced by generic references to the sin of atheism and the abandonment of God. While those scenarios had very likely been inspired, at least indirectly, by the Fátima secret, the Virgin's messages now begin to return to the theme of the special prayer that she said the Virgin had taught her a decade earlier on February 2, 1944: that the Kingdom of the Sacred Heart of Jesus would arrive through the Sorrowful and Immaculate Heart of Mary.[39] Beginning at about this time, the Virgin

36 Apparition 21 (March 6, 1949).
37 The bishop of Quimper was Mgr. Fauvel.
38 Apparition 24 (December 9, 1949).
39 See Apparition 10 (February 2, 1944), and above.

3.4 Postcard of the image of the two Wounded Hearts of Mary and Jesus. [Collection of William A. Christian Jr.]

would often come accompanied by her Son, and there would be calls for a new consecration of the world to their combined, wounded hearts.

On March 5, 1955, for example, Jeanne-Louise reported a vision in which the Virgin was crying. Below her, she said, a picture was taking shape in which the world seemed to be in a state of indifference, and chastisements were threatening. Then, however, the Virgin began to speak, saying, first, that her heart was bleeding from human offenses, especially those of impurity, and that divine justice would soon be coming. But, she said, the Reign of God would also be coming, and to hasten that Reign, she again called for a chapel to be built at the apparition site. France, the Virgin said, as well as the other nations that had fought alongside her, and the Roman Catholic Church, would all emerge from their baptism of blood triumphant, renewed, and rejuvenated. And in place of the thrones of the impious, “there will stand two glorious thrones, one to the Sacred Heart of Jesus and the other, to My Immaculate Heart.”[40]

In two apparitions later that year, Jeanne-Louise recalled several messages delivered by the Virgin that speak of the power of these two hearts and of what could and would be accomplished by devotions built around them. On

40 Apparition 30 (March 5, 1955).

May 12, 1955, for example, Jeanne-Louise reported these words of the Virgin: "It is through my Sorrowful and Immaculate Heart that the Reign of the Sacred Heart, which is one of Justice and Love, will be established in the world. It is by our two Hearts, united in all things, riddled with the same wounds and continually martyred by the ingratitude of people, that the salvation of nations will be accomplished and that the Church will rise again, strong, united, triumphant."[41]

This message was followed by another message almost five months later, on October 1, 1955 that is again apocalyptic in tone. Here, nations and governments are said to be "united against God and Christ" and the world, trembling and cracking "like the mountain of Calvary in a paroxysm of agony." But, according to the Virgin, "these nations without foundation [and] these people in chaos" can still be saved – by an act of consecration. The power of this act of consecration may have to do with the peculiar image of unity that it invokes: "I ask that the world be consecrated, but this time to our two United Hearts. Let your families, your nations, the entire world be consecrated, but in the same consecration, to the Sacred and Merciful Heart of Jesus and to my Sorrowful and Immaculate Heart, to our two Hearts United in the Holy Spirit."[42]

The Virgin then explained that this consecration, performed in reparative love, would transform the wounds of their hearts into "sources of life," and would be a "harmonious voice that would fill the universe with a word of unconquerable hope for everyone," but this would be a "horrible trial" for Satan and his minions, as it would put an end to the reign of impiety. The world, the Virgin said, would be saved by the two United Hearts, for these two Hearts, "bound in the same sufferings, would triumph in the same Kingship." But this kingship would first need to be realized interiorly, in individual hearts and souls.[43]

Conclusion

The messages of Kérizinen were dominated by the theme of Mary's sorrow over sinful and suffering humanity, a theme that came to focus finally in the images of the two wounded and suffering hearts of Mary and Jesus, injured by human sin but offering mercy and redemption. During the Second World

41 Apparition 31 (May 12, 1955), translation my own.

42 Apparition 32 (October 1, 1955), translation my own. The two hearts in these messages would seem to be variations of Jesus' Sacred Heart as this was described and popularized in late-18th-century France by St. Marguerite-Mary Alacoque, and of Mary's Immaculate Heart, presumably as popularized internationally in the 1940s and 1950s in publications representing or promoting some form of Fátima devotion. Devotion to the Virgin's Sorrowful Heart was well-established in French Roman Catholicism before the 20th century.

43 Apparition 32 (October 1, 1955), translations my own.

War, these messages urged individual Catholics to offer sacrifices and prayers, making special efforts to recite the Rosary and to meditate on its mysteries. As France moved into the years of the Cold War, however, the Virgin's messages were characterized by a more militant religious nationalism in which re-Christianized France would take the lead in combatting Russia-inspired communism and atheism. In these years the emphasis shifted to official and corporate devotions, that is, the establishment of religious institutions dedicated to fulfilling Mary's requests. In these years, in the tradition of Pope Leo XIII's consecration of the human race to the Sacred Heart of Jesus and Pope Pius XII's consecration of the world to Mary's Immaculate Heart, the Virgin advocates the consecration of families, nations, and the world to the two United Hearts.

For the French devotees at Kérizinen who managed to endure both the traumas of the war and the fears and uncertainties of the Cold War, the sorrowful Virgin who appeared and spoke to Jeanne-Louise over those years offered both empathy for their suffering and agency through devotions that they believed would end war and bring peace. But the images of the wounded hearts of Jesus and Mary, their wounds transformed by consecrations into sources of life, have, for some French Catholics, apparently continued to give hope beyond those years. Despite four interdicts issued by the bishops of Quimper,[44] the shrine at Kérzinen has continued to attract devotees.

44 The interdicts were issued on October 12, 1956, March 24, 1961, May 20, 1973, July 12, 1975.

BIBLIOGRAPHY

Les Amis de Kérizinen. n.d. *Messages de Kérizinen.* Kérizinen: Association "Les Amis de Kérizinen."

Les Amis de Kérizinen. "Les Cahiers de Jeanne-Louise." <http://kerizinen.free.fr/message.htm>. Accessed June 11, 2018.

Les Amis de Kérizinen. "The Notebooks of Jeanne-Louise." <http://kerizinen.free.fr/messageap.htm>. Accessed June 11, 2018.

Auclair, Raoul. 1968. *Kérizinen: Apparitions en Bretagne?* Paris: Nouvelles Editions Latines.

Badone, Ellen. 2007. "Echoes from Kérizinen: Pilgrimage, Narrative, and the Construction of Sacred History at a Marian Shrine in Northwestern France." *Journal of the Royal Anthropological Institute* 13: 453-470.

Barthas, Casimir and Gonzaga da Fonseca. 1943. *Fatima, merveille inouïe: Les apparitions – Le Pèlerinage – Les Voyants – Des Miracles – Des Documents*, 2nd edition. Toulouse: Fatima-Éditions.

Barthas, Casimir and Gonzaga da Fonseca. 1947. *Our Lady of Light.* Milwaukee, WI: Bruce Publishing Company.

Bennett, Jeffrey. 2012. *When the Sun Danced: Myths, Miracles, and Modernity in Early Twentieth-Century Portugal.* Charlottesville, VA: University of Virginia Press.

Cerejeira, Manuel Gonçalves. 1943a. "Appel du Cardinal Patriarche pour le pèlerinage national du 13 May 1931." In Casimir Barthas and Gonzaga da Fonseca. *Fatima, merveille inouïe: Les apparitions - Le Pèlerinage – Les Voyants – Des Miracles – Des Documents*, 2nd edition, 305. Toulouse: Fatima-Éditions.

Cerejeira, Manuel Gonçalves. 1943b. "Acte de consecration du Portugal à Notre-Dame de Fatima." In Casimir Barthas and Gonzaga da Fonseca. *Fatima, merveille inouïe: Les apparitions - Le Pèlerinage* – Les *Voyants* – Des Miracles – Des Documents, 2nd edition, 306. Toulouse: Fatima-Éditions.

Christian, William Jr. 1984. "Religious Apparitions and the Cold War." In *Religious Power and Protest in Local Communities: The North Shore of the Mediterranean*, edited by Eric R. Wolf, 239-266. Berlin: Walter de Gruyter.

Congregation for the Doctrine of the Faith. 2000. "The Message of Fatima." <http://www.vatican.va/roman_curia/congregations/cfaith/documents/rc_con_cfaith_doc_20000626_message-fatima_en.html>. Accessed June 11, 2018.

"La consécration de la France au Cœur Immaculé de Marie." *La Croix*, March 30, 1943.

Delarnette. 1941. "Les Merveilles de Fatima." *La Croix*, January 30.

Descouvemont, Pierre. 1998. *Therese and Lisieux.* Translated by Salvatore Sciurba. Grand Rapids, MI: Eerdmans.

Fonseca, Gonzaga da, S.J. 1942. *La meraviglie de Fatima; Apparizioni – culto - miracoli della Madonna del Rosario di Fàtima.* Casalmontferrato: Propaganda Mariana.

Fontenelle, R. 1942. "Arore de Paix: La consécration du genre humain au Cœur Immaculé de Marie." *La Croix*, November 19.

Godfrin, Jacqueline and Philippe Godfrin. 1965. *Une Centrale de Press Catholique: La Maison de La Bonne Press et ses publications.* Paris: Presses Universitaires de France.

"Le 'grand retour' de Notre-Dame de Boulogne." *La Croix*, August 10, 1943.

"L'Heure d'Marie." *La Croix*, March 18, 1941.

Madigan, Leo. 2001. *A Pilgrim's Handbook to Fatima.* Bodmin, Great Britain: MPG Books.

Marchi, John de. 1950. *Fatima: The Facts.* Translated by I. M. Kingsbury. Cork: Mercier Press.

Maréchal, Hyacinthe. 1940. "Notre-Dame de la fin de la guerre." *La Croix*, 26 April.

Maréchal, Hyacinthe. 1941. "Promotion du people chrétien." *La Croix*, 8 May.

Maréchal, Hyacinthe. 1943. "A propos de la Consécration au Cœur Immaculé de Marie." *La Croix*. February 16.

Martel, C. 1940. *Les Merveilles de Fatima (Portugal): Les Apparitions et le Pèlerinage.* Toulouse: Éditions de l'Apostolat de la Prière.

Martel, C. 1942a. "Notules portugaises." *La Croix*, October 31.

Martel, C. 1942b. "Notules portugaises: La cloture du Jubilé Fatima." *La Croix*, December 1.

Martel, C. 1942c. "Rome et Fatima: Nouveau sur le 'mystère' de Fatima." *La Croix*, July 2.

Martins, Antonio Maria (ed.). 2002. *Documents on Fatima & the Memoirs of Sister Lucia.* White Park, MN: Park Press.

Massiani, Marie Geneviève. 1988. "*La Croix* sous Vichy." In *Cent ans d'histoire de "La Croix,"* edited by René Rémond and Émile Poulat, 301-321. Paris: Éditions du Centurion.

Maunder, Chris. 2016. *Our Lady of the Nations: Apparitions of Mary in 20th-Century Catholic Europe.* Oxford: Oxford University Press.

"Un message du Saint-Père du people portugais." *La Croix*, November 3, 1942.

Pélissier, Jean. 1942. "Fàtima, merveille inouïe: le 25th anniversaire des apparitions de Notre-Dame du Rosaire au Portugal." *La Croix*, May 9-10.

Pius XII. 1942. "Radiomensagem do Papa Pio XII aos fiéis portugueses por occasião da consagração da igreja e do género humano ao coração Imaculado de Maria." <https://w2.vatican.va/content/pius-xii/en/speeches/1942.index.html>. Accessed June 11, 2018.

Ramonet, Jeanne-Louise. "The Notebooks of Jeanne-Louise." <http://kerizinen.free.fr/messageap.htm>. Accessed June 11, 2018.

Rumeur, Guy le. 1970. *Apocalypse mariale: La Salette, Fatima, Kérizinen, Garabandal, San Damiano*. Argenton-l'Église.

Santos, Lucia dos. 1976a. *Fatima in Lucia's Own Words*. Edited by L. Kondor. Translated by Dominican Nuns of the Perpetual Rosary. Fátima: Postulation Center.

Santos, Lucia dos. 1976b. *First Memoir*. In Lucia dos Santos. *Fatima in Lucia's Own Words*, edited by L. Kondor, trans. Dominican nuns of the Perpetual Rosary. Fátima: Postulation Center.

Santos, Lucia dos. 1976c. *Second Memoir*. In Lucia dos Santos. *Fatima in Lucia's Own Words*, edited by L. Kondor, trans. Dominican nuns of the Perpetual Rosary. Fátima: Postulation Center.

Santos, Lucia dos. 1976d. *Third Memoir*. In Lucia dos Santos. *Fatima in Lucia's Own Words*, edited by L. Kondor, trans. Dominican nuns of the Perpetual Rosary. Fátima: Postulation Center.

Santos, Lucia dos. 1976e. *Fourth Memoir*. In: Lucia dos Santos. *Fatima in Lucia's Own Words*, edited by L. Kondor, trans. Dominican nuns of the Perpetual Rosary. Fátima: Postulation Center.

Santos, Lucia dos. 2002. "First Writings of the Seer about the Apparitions." In *Documents on Fatima & the Memoirs of Sister Lucia*, edited by Antonio Maria Martins, S.J., 255. White Park, MN: Park Press.

Walsh, William Thomas. 1947. *Our Lady of Fatima*. New York: Doubleday.

Zimdars-Swartz, Sandra L. 1991. *Encountering Mary: From La Salette to Medjugorje*. Princeton, NJ: Princeton University Press.

4
LIKENESS AND MESSAGE IN OUR LADY OF FÁTIMA FROM WORLD WAR TO COLD WAR

DAVID MORGAN

The cult of Fátima was virtually made to order for the era of the Cold War. The spread and appeal of the devotion were propelled in part by the secret that was eventually revealed concerning the conversion of Russia. And the medium of circulation and allure was a series of statues affirmed by Sister Lúcia, one of the seers, and consecrated by Church authorities from the bishop of Leiria to Pope Pius XII. Both endorsement and appeal were grounded in an older trajectory in which the likeness of the apparition and the message of Our Lady were worked out together. In this essay, I will trace the history of both from World War I to the height of the Cold War.

Early imagery

Just after the series of apparitions at the Cova da Iria ended on October 13, 1917, an image of Our Lady was placed on a table serving as an altar at the site. The image remains unidentified, but it is possible that it was a statue of Our Lady of the Rosary, who enjoyed local devotion.[1] On the night of October 23, the Portuguese newspaper *Diário de Notícias* reported republican detractors of the

1 Devotion to Our Lady of the Rosary is common among Carmelite convents and churches in Portugal such as Nossa Senhora do Carmo, the Carmelite church in Porto. We do know that one of the first images offered to occupy the small chapel built on the site of the apparitions depicted Our Lady of the Rosary, see De Marchi 1952: 227. For a study of the development of the iconography of Our Lady of Fátima, see Duarte 2010: 236-344; see also Duarte 2007.

new cult cut down what they took to be the oak tree where Our Lady had last appeared only ten days before, and removed the "table on which a modest altar had been arranged, and on which a religious image [of Our Lady] had been placed" (De Marchi 1952: 170). They took the items to nearby Santarém, where they created a mock display and procession. Reaction was immediate. One writer sent a letter to the government's minister of Interior, objecting to the profanation of "the image of the Virgin who has presided over our destinies in all periods of our history" (De Marchi 1952: 171). This sentiment illumines the earliest impulse behind the desire to place an image at the heart of devotion to Fátima: Our Lady was a national totem of Portugal and her apparition at the Cova da Iria was, from the beginning, taken as a favor to the nation in a day of national political turmoil. A secular republican government replaced the long tradition of Portuguese monarchy, with the assassination of King Carlos I and his heir, Luís Filipe, in Lisbon, in 1908, and a republican coup d'état in 1910. A period of considerable instability followed. As in contemporary Spain, the Church strongly sided with the monarchy, and met with a strong ally in the reactionary power that eventually emerged in the person of António de Oliveira Salazar, who steadily rose to power in the government that formed following a military coup in 1926.

Our Lady had told Lúcia in the apparition of August 13 and once again on October 13 to have a chapel built in her honor at the Cova da Iria, so local organizers wasted little time in making arrangements (Kondor 1976: 169 and 172). A woman named Maria dos Santos Carreira, better known as Maria da Capelinha (Maria of the Chapel), who was present at nearly all of the apparitions and was among the first to embrace the devotion, emerged as the organizer (De Marchi 1952: 60, 178-182). When she approached the local parish priest, Father Manuel Marques Ferreira, to ask permission to begin construction, Maria told him supporters of the venture "intended to put the statue of Our Lady in it" (De Marchi 1952: 181). A very small structure was begun in 1918 and completed in the following year. According to Father John De Marchi, an Italian Consolata priest and one of the authoritative biographers of Fátima, who interviewed Maria regarding the origin and construction of the first chapel, the first image of Our Lady of Fátima was a small stone statue that was first brought to display there on May 13, 1920, the third anniversary of the first apparition.[2] Lúcia, De Marchi tells us, was among those who welcomed the figure on that day (De Marchi 1952: 182).[3]

2 Giovanni (John) De Marchi was an Italian priest, assigned to Portugal and worked at Fátima, where he became an authority on the apparition during the 1940s. In 1950, he transferred to the US. He published several books on Fátima in Portuguese and English. For a brief biography, see Cristino 2007a.

3 See also the letter of Gilberto Santos, May 2, 1920, to the Rev. Dr. Manuel Formigão, which records Lúcia's response to the statue (Fox & Martins 1992: 203-204).

The statue was delivered in an ox cart, hidden beneath farm tools for fear that it would be confiscated by civil authorities or destroyed by the sort who had destroyed the altar at the site.[4] The patron of the statue was Gilberto Fernandes dos Santos of nearby Torres Novas, who came to Fátima and presented himself to Maria da Capelinha, volunteering to sponsor the creation of a statue (fig. 4.1). He visited Fátima several times with a sculptor, she recalled, "to question the children about how Our Lady had looked." On other occasions, Santos came to speak with Dr. Manuel Formigão, a seminary professor and priest who had conducted interviews with the children on several occasions during the period of the apparitions (De Marchi 1952: 227).[5] In these interviews, Formigão had asked the children specifically about the figure's appearance. From the beginning, then, a concern for the authentic appearance was to be captured in details of the image (see fig. 4.1). The completed image was secretly delivered to the parish church in Fátima and hidden there until May 13, 1920. Lúcia saw it at the church in Fátima and Santos recorded her response:

> She said it *was good*, that *it was quite a good likeness*, that it *was very well copied*, that the shape of the dress, the veil, the position of the hands, and the hanging beads, *everything was very well imitated but that Our Lady was much more beautiful still, for She was white, but a whiteness that gave off light.*
> *That the face of Our Lady was very beautiful! That they could hardly look at Her, for she gave off such a bright light that it was almost blinding! The beads were also white and gave off light. Her feet were also white and gave off light, and that for that reason she did not know if Our Lady was wearing shoes or was barefooted.* (Fox & Martins 1992: 203-204)

The emphasis was in the original, and clearly demonstrates how important to Santos it was to register the authenticity of the likeness in Lúcia's own words.

Opposition to the cult of Fátima intensified since its brand of conservative and popular Catholicism was the target of secular reformists. At first it was considered important to bring the statue to the chapel only on the thirteenth of each month, and return it that evening to safekeeping off-site. But this did not stop an enthusiastic popular response to the figure. Santos described cures and miracles that affirmed the authentic character of the statue. And he told the bishop of Leiria that, "in order to further spread the faith among the peo-

4 De Marchi 1952: 226-227 and 235-236, for an account of the first statue of the chapel. Several letters concerning the first statue are reproduced in Fox & Martins 1992: 200-211.

5 For the transcripts of Formigão's interviews, see Fox & Martins 1992: 143-166; the descriptions provided by the children to Formigão in September and October of 1917 are also reproduced in De Marchi 1952: 119-130. The source for both De Marchi and Fox & Martins is Formigão's 1921 pamphlet, *Os Episódos Maravilhosos de Fátima*. On Formigão, see Gomes 2007.

4.1 José Ferreira Thedim, Our Lady of Fátima, 1920, with crown installed in 1946. [Collection of David Morgan]

ple, I also had some thousands of holy pictures made [of the sculpture], which I distributed gratuitously to the people on May 13, June 13, and July 13 of this year [1920]" (Fox & Martins 1992: 209). When he placed the statue on a small table in front of the chapel on the afternoon of June 13, 1920, the response was immediate: "at that very moment the people fell to their knees shouting. They prayed in a loud voice. With upraised hands, they cried, imploring forgiveness, for they were witnessing the same solar phenomenon as that of October 13, 1917." Santos described a supernatural floodlight cast on the statue from heaven and he said the face of the figure "was completely transformed" (Fox & Martins 1992: 207). Maria da Capelinha told De Marchi that she later brought the statue home each night for safe-keeping. It was a prudent measure because on March 6, 1922, the chapel was damaged by bombs presumably placed there by republican sympathizers who regarded the emerging devotion as an ally of reactionary forces. Having eluded destruction, the statue returned to Cova da Iria in a large procession on June, 13. "We had no bier," Maria recalled, "but everyone wanted a turn at carrying it [the statue]" (De Marchi 1952: 235). The chapel was rebuilt and slightly enlarged and known thereafter as the Chapel of the Apparitions, and remains the site for displaying the statue to the present.

De Marchi indicates that the statue provided by Santos was made of stone. If that were true, then it could not be the famous figure that was produced by the young Portuguese sculptor, José Ferreira Thedim, which is carved from cedar and still displayed at the shrine (De Marchi 1952: 225).[6] But De Marchi likely conflated the stories of a small figure placed on site in 1917, possibly made of stone, with the 1920 figure that was sculpted by Thedim, which is commonly cited as "the first image of Our Lady of Fátima."[7] Thedim worked with the Casa Arte Sacra Fânzeres in the city of Braga that specialized in the production of church statuary and it was this firm that Gilberto dos Santos contacted in 1919 in his search for an image for the chapel at Cova da Iria. Thedim relied on catalog imagery of statuary models for ecclesiastical use, adapting one version that satisfied Gilberto as matching the descriptions provided to Formigão by

6 For a live video feed of Thedim's first image on the pedestal at the entrance of the Chapel of Apparitions (now reduced to an architectural outline) at Fátima, see <http://www.fatima.pt/pt/pages/transmissoes-online>.

7 "A primeira Imagem exculpida de Nossa Senhora de Fátima," 2011. The source of the piece is listed as Zacarias Thedim, nephew of the sculptor. McGlynn 2017: 42 wrote that José Thedim's figure was "the first statue ever made of Our Lady of Fátima. It has occupied the place of honor at Fátima since 1920." Thedim's figure measures one meter and ten millimeters in height, which comports closely with what we learn in a letter in which Santos indicates that the figure he commissioned was "one meter in height" (Fox & Martins 1992: 209). The date of Thedim's figure is sometimes incorrectly listed as 1929, see for example Rędzioch 1996: 39. Thedim produced a copy of the statue of Our Lady of Fatima for the Colégio Português in Rome, a work that was blessed by Pope Pius XI on December 6, 1929, see "Renacimiento de Portugal después Fátima (1)," 2006.

the children (Duarte 2010: 236-238). That meant removing features pictured in the catalog model (angels, a veil, and the Christ child) and inserting particular details such as a golden belt, tassel, stars, rosary on the right arm (Duarte 2010: 238). In spite of the descriptions of the apparition available to him, Thedim chose to keep features from the model such as the elaborate garments. The temptation to do so must have been considerable since the cult statue needed to reference the dense visual tradition of Mary's appearance. She was, after all, represented in virtually every church and shrine in Portugal with images grounded in centuries of pictorial precedent. If she appeared too different, she might not be recognized, or the new devotion would be ostracized as an innovation. Likeness meant affirmation of precedent but also the registration of the characteristic features of what the children reported. The ratio between the two was delicate. But tradition mattered. The last thing Santos would get from a conventional church statuary firm is novelty. Thedim knew the task at hand and provided an image made to order.

Although Santos recorded her approbation of the figure that she saw in 1920 when it was brought to Fátima, the adult Lúcia felt Thedim's figure was inaccurate in key features. Thedim's rendition of the Virgin's garments clashed with what Lúcia later remembered seeing. The figure wears a tunic, a second long-sleeved stole, and a mantle over everything that spreads outward as it descends to her feet, features which have been attributed to the sculptor's church goods catalog model. Thedim also decorated the hem of the mantle with golden, floral motifs, and he placed the figure on a cloud that Lúcia later said she never witnessed, although others reported having seen.[8] Lúcia's comments on what she saw could be vague, the result of translating childhood memories of visionary sensations to the solidity of sculptural media. Thus, for example, the golden border that Thedim used to delineate the edge of the mantle, Lúcia remembered as something like an aureole, "a ray of sunlight all around the mantle."[9]

The deviations from her adult memory bothered Lúcia sufficiently to move her to urge that they be corrected. One account reports that she told the bishop of Leiria that "it was indeed beautiful, but that if she were making such a statue, she would have excluded much of the ornamentation on the mantle, that there would only be a single mantle, and that she would change the tassel around her neck for a golden globe [hanging on a cord]" (Haffert 1982: 41). The bishop, we are told, then asked Thedim to produce another, rectified version of the figure, which he did in 1947. We will return to this version shortly for further discussion, but it will be helpful first to discuss the context of Thedim's

8 For more on Lúcia's criticisms of Thedim's 1920 figure, see Duarte 2010: 240-243.

9 Related by Lúcia to Fr. Thomas McGlynn, O.P., see McGlynn 2017: 65. The first edition of the book was published in Boston by Little, Brown and Company in 1948. McGlynn's conversation with Lúcia in February of 1947 is illuminating for the details it clarifies about Our Lady's appearance and the very nature of the vision, see McGlynn 2017: 61-68.

4.2 Cover of the pamphlet *Cruzados de Fátima* (Lisbon, 1934).
[Collection of David Morgan]

1920 version because it was this one that shaped national and international response to the cult of Fátima and informed popular imagination very powerfully about the appearance of Our Lady.

The political setting and the politics of Marian devotion

Local church authorities moved cautiously toward endorsing the apparitions. The parish priest of Fátima, Father Manuel Marques Ferreira, interviewed Lúcia in the summer of 1917 and concluded while he did not think there was any divine revelation at work, he worried the children might be deluded by Satan (De Marchi 1952: 68). Many clergy remained skeptical long after that, but Pope Benedict XV appointed the bishop of Leiria, José Alves Correia da Silva, to lead the diocese in 1921, and the bishop took up the task of officially assessing the apparitions, and became a defender of the apparitions early on.[10] He soon removed Lúcia from public access, assigned her a new name that would conceal her identity, and forbade her to speak about the apparitions. In

10 The bishop of Leiria issued a pastoral letter in 1922 that defends the supernatural reality of the solar prodigy of October 13, 1917 (De Marchi 1952: 150).

1930, after several years of investigation, the bishop officially proclaimed the apparitions worthy of belief. But pilgrims had been flocking to the Cova da Iria since 1917. The sculpture put in place in 1920 served as a vital focal point for the devotion. Figure 4.2 is the cover of a small pamphlet printed in 1934, promoting membership in the Devout Union of the Crusaders of Fátima (Pia União dos Cruzados de Fátima), an auxiliary association of the larger group, Portuguese Catholic Action (Acção Católica Portuguesa, or ACP).[11] The regional focus of the cult is very clear in the pamphlet. The purpose of the group was to petition Our Lady of Fátima regarding the needs of Catholic Action, especially in Portugal. The ACP was formed in 1933 as a national lay organization and apostolate that worked for the re-Christianization of Portugal. The political sentiment was counterrevolutionary, strongly opposed to the secular, republican government with its intensely anticlerical interest in limiting the Catholic Church's extensive influence in national life.[12] The ACP had a major ally in Antônio de Oliveira Salazar, a member of the ACP who had become prime minister of Portugal in 1932 and championed a strongly pro-Catholic nationalist, authoritarian ideology that was deeply suspicious of all aspects of modernism (from democracy to socialism), which had been excoriated by many popes since the nineteenth century.[13]

From the beginning, the ACP looked to Fátima as a special Marian endorsement of its effort to reclaim Portugal for the Catholic faith. The rightwing government under Salazar as prime minister regarded the Catholic faith as an essential feature of the nation's character and considered the apparition at Fátima to confirm heaven's will in the matter. The message of Fátima was deeply political: Our Lady is calling the nation to herself. The opposition of the mayor to the apparitions and his interference with the Virgin's scheduled appearance on August 13 certainly alerted the children to the deep ideological opposition between republic and Catholic views of the nation's purpose, if they had not noted it already, even at their young age. Although Lúcia did not reveal the matter of converting Russia until 1930,[14] and in writing with the publication of her third memoir, the political framework of the apparitions was already at work during their occurrence since Lúcia had reported in 1917 Our Lady's repeated reference to the end of the current war. The ACP was one of the many organizations in Portugal that associated Fátima with the culture war between the Church and republicanism, and the image of Our Lady (see

11 On the ACP and counterrevolutionary efforts by the Catholic Church, see Rao 1985. See also <http://entreostextosdamemoria.blogspot.com/2007/08/x.html>. On the Acção Católica, see Fontes 2007: 9-15.

12 A fine study of the apparitions in the context of Portuguese Catholicism, republican revolution and the following dictatorship is Bennett 2012; see also Sardica 2007: 190-199.

13 See for example Pius X 1907 and Pius XI 1937.

14 See Fox & Martins 1992: 244, 246, 339-340, 347-349 and 366-368, for Lúcia's discussions between 1930 and 1941 of the second secret - Russia's consecration and conversion.

fig. 4.1) was part of the organization's visual program for doing so. The physical appearance of Our Lady crystalized iconographically in 1920. Thedim's statue fixed in the devotional imagination how the apparition looked.

Eventual papal approval of the cult of Fátima inaugurated a series of official forms of recognition that brought Fátima out of Portugal and placed it on the world stage, and did so during the time of World War II. Until then, devotion to Fátima had been confined largely to Portugal itself.[15] But when Pius XII consecrated the world to the Immaculate Heart of Mary in 1942, and did so with reference to Fátima's express concern for the conversion of Russia, the devotion entered a new framework. The coronation of Our Lady of Fátima became a permanent feature of devotion to Fátima following the crowning of the statue of Our Lady at Fátima on May 13, 1946 by the papal legate, Cardinal Aloisi Masella, who was dispatched by Pius XII to crown the statue. He placed on Thedim's sculpture an elaborate crown that included gems and precious stones donated by the women of Portugal in gratitude to Our Lady for the nation's protection from the political upheaval and social turmoil of the Spanish Civil War and the Second World War (Johnston 1980: 124-125).[16] On the day before, an estimated 800,000 people gathered at the Cova da Iria to welcome the papal legate. At the ceremony of coronation, he conveyed to the Portuguese his "warmest wishes for the prosperity of your beloved country," but the event was not content to assign Fátima to a national setting alone. The crowning affirmed Portugal as the national polity favored by Our Lady's manifestation, but Pius XII had grander ambitions. In 1954, in the encyclical *Ad caeli reginam*, he proclaimed Mary "the Queen of all creatures, the Queen of the World, and the Ruler of all" (Pius XII 1954: para. 22). The idea of world monarch challenged the postwar logic of nation-states that was rapidly structuring in the East-West divide of alliances and spheres of influence. The Vatican certainly relied on the United States more than it ever had before, but it did not wish to become a satellite of Western capitalism nor to see the Christian faith identified with the United States, the new Protestant powerhouse of the postwar world. Fátima was ideally suited to the task of re-Christianizing the world, which meant both the conversion of atheist Russia and the curbing of Western materialism. The regional devotion was being re-scripted to an international scale.

The dual nature of the devotion was asserted by Pius XII himself on the occasion of the coronation in 1946. He told the crowd via a live radio address from Rome, invoking old rhetoric of the political vision of Roman Catholicism put to new purpose in the postwar world: "By crowning the Statue of Our Lady of Fátima, you signed, as it were, a document of faith in her supremacy, a loyal

15 For a review of major events that describe the arc of growing acceptance of Fátima in the diocese of Leiria and Portugal in the 1920s and 1930s, see De Marchi 1952: 251-254.

16 For a photograph of Cardinal Masella placing the crown on the figure of Our Lady, see Rędzioch 1996: 38.

4.3 Holy card Nossa Senhora de Fátima, Rainha na Paz, edited by the Centro do Apostolado do Coração de Maria (Lisbon, 1950).
[Collection of David Morgan]

submission to her authority, a filial and constant correspondence to her love. You did yet more; you enlisted as Crusaders in the conquest and re-conquest of her Kingdom which is the Kingdom of God."[17] The linkage of Fátima to the larger setting of Roman Catholicism during the pontificate of Pius XII is clear from a small holy card celebrating the 1950 Jubilee declared by Pius (fig. 4.3). Our Lady of Fátima and the (yet to be completed) Basilica of Fátima are paired with Pius XII and a view of Saint Peter's in Rome. Pius extended to Fátima during the Jubilee year the privilege of a special indulgence for pilgrims. In 1954, Pius XII recalled his 1946 radio message, delivered during the crowning of Our Lady of Fátima, as heralding the sovereignty of Mary (Pius XII 1954: para. 4).

Pius XII had begun this process with the consecration of 1942, and it continued significantly with the global attention focused on the devotion and its

17 Quoted in De Marchi 1952: 266.

focal object, the figure of Our Lady at Fátima. The ritual attention to the shrine and cult statue at Fátima helped to move the devotion to a larger stage because it gave the devotion a movable object. Now Our Lady could travel anywhere. And for this stage a new visual strategy was developed to take Fátima to the world. Public procession of the existing statue had already proved enormously effective. In April of 1942, the Girls' Catholic Youth movement had arranged for a procession of the statue from the Cova da Iria to Lisbon and back (Martindale 1950: 172). The crowning in 1946 was politically very significant because it celebrated the third centenary of King João IV's proclamation of Our Lady as Queen of Portugal. João had removed his crown to make the proclamation and no monarch since then had worn it. He vowed that he and his successors would defend the Immaculate Conception of Our Lady. Crowning Our Lady of Fátima therefore renewed the national tradition and updated it in veneration of Our Lady's condescension to favor Portugal with the apparitions of 1917. Having the legate of the Holy Father in Rome perform the coronation only underscored the very Catholic nature of the nation's honor.

To celebrate the crowning in December, the statue was once again taken on tour from the Chapel of the Apparitions at the Cova to Lisbon. On the way, crowds witnessed several doves perched themselves on the pedestal of the statue and remained there for several days, only leaving after the statue had visited Our Lady of Fátima church in Lisbon. The "miracle of the doves" affected devotional iconography of the image thereafter in the form of three doves sometimes pictured at the feet of Our Lady. The doves were taken as a providential sign of the peace promised to the world by Our Lady during the apparitions. One Portuguese devotee, Father José Galamba de Oliveira, a biographer of Jacinta, wrote his American friend, the fellow Fátima devotee John Haffert, a first-hand account of the miracle of the doves. Oliveira concluded his letter with the hope of the devotion's growth in the United States: "May these doves, which have flown in Lisbon, fly into American hearts, and from there be sent forth as carriers to bear the peace message of Our Lady of Fátima to the world under the protection of the American Eagle."[18] From early on, the relation of Fátima to the cultural politics of Europe and far beyond has been seamless.

Art and likeness in Fátima's statues

The portrayal of Our Lady of Fátima by artists is not arbitrary. The details of her costume, pose, and expression have since 1920 been taken as visual indication of her nature and her message. Her beauty, the brilliance of her man-

18 Father José Galamba de Oliveira, canon in the archdiocese of Leiria-Fátima, quoted in "Miraculous Fatima Statues." Galamba published his *Jacinta: episódos ineditos das aparições de Nossa Senhora* in 1941. For an account of the doves, see McGlynn 2017: 161-170.

tle, the gesture of prayer, the effulgent details of her tassel and pendant, the presence of crucifix and rosary - all merge form and content, appearance and message into a single visual impression. Yet, as pointed out above, the descriptions provided by the children were never more than minimal. Because of this, the images of Fátima were inevitably dependent on both the weight of tradition and the conception of the artists who conceived and produced them. The brother of José Thedim, Guilherme, also a sculptor, pointed out to the sculptor-priest Thomas McGlynn in 1947 that an artist exercised artistic license that did not diminish the authenticity of the imagery of Fátima that he created (McGlynn 2017: 80). But the global circulation of Thedim's statue (see fig. 4.1) and the many wonders and spiritual favors attributed to it from its earliest installation suggest that, for devotees of Fátima, what mattered was not artistic expression but seeing what the children saw, with the very important assumption that what they had seen was something as fixed and clear as the carved statue enshrined at the Cova da Iria.

The importance of Thedim's image only grew over time as pilgrims continued to come to the Cova da Iria. But its power to command enthusiastic crowds achieved a new level of intensity when the figure made the spectacular pilgrimage to Lisbon in December of 1946. Recognizing the importance of traveling the statue to generate popular response and encourage devotion to Fátima across Portugal, the bishop conferred with Sister Lúcia, who visited the Cova in early summer of 1946, asking her if the statue of Our Lady might be sent on additional pilgrimages. It was then that she registered her concerns with the bishop about the appearance of Thedim's original version, pointing out the inaccuracies in the clothing and accoutrements. Correcting José Thedim's original was impossible since it had found such a fond place in the hearts of millions of pilgrims.[19] The image had become a national icon in the Church's ongoing battle in Portugal and far beyond. So the bishop decided to ask the artist to produce another version, one that would be informed by Lúcia's recently published specifications. On May 13, 1947, the bishop consecrated the new statue and named it the Pilgrim Virgin Statue of Our Lady of Fátima (fig. 4.4).[20] A second, very similar International Pilgrim Virgin Statue was produced to focus on pilgrimage in the West (fig. 4.5). The differences between the two are minor, evident for instance in the shape of the mantle over the Virgin's face. Figure 4.4 shows two creases over her forehead while Figure 4.5 shows a single crease forming a single arching angle over her forehead. The first was to remain based at Fátima; the second eventually made its home in the United States in the care of the Blue Army. Given the global focus

19 The bishop of Leiria put it this way to Father McGlynn when he visited him in February of 1947 (McGlynn, 2017: 31).

20 "Our Lady of Fatima, Pilgrim Virgin Statue." The statue is one meter in height, carved from cedar, and weighs 33 pounds. For further discussion of the statue, see Morgan 2009: 49-65. For further discussion of the pilgrim virgin idea and imagery, see Cristino 2007b.

4.4 José Thedim, Pilgrim Virgin Statue, 1947.
[Basilica of Our Lady of Fátima]
4.5 José Thedim, International Pilgrim Virgin Statue, 1947.
[Collection of David Morgan]

of the cult and its embrace by the highest authority in the Church, Lúcia was doubtless pleased to have the more accurate portrayals of Our Lady going on pilgrimages around the globe.

The new figures are closer in appearance to what Lúcia reported. The golden floral tracery on the borders of the first Thedim image (see fig. 4.1) was removed from the mantle, and the Virgin's clothing simplified to two items: tunic and mantle. A single golden edge traces the margins of the mantle. This is the sculptor's new interpretation of what Lúcia described in September of 1917 as "two gold cords which fall from the neck and are joined at the waist by a tassel, also gold."[21] In 1942, in her fourth memoir, Lúcia described her memory as follows: "I remember a golden cord which, like a brilliant sunbeam, seemed to border her mantle. It was reflected in the space left by the mantle as it fell from the head to the shoulders, shimmering in the light which enveloped Our Lady's whole person in undulating variations." (Kondor 1976: 178). Clearly, this memory was preferred by Thedim in designing the Pilgrim Virgin statues (see figs. 4.4 & 4.5).[22]

In February of 1947, an American priest and sculptor, Father Thomas McGlynn, O.P., visited Portugal in order to show to Lúcia a small model of Our Lady of Fátima that he had crafted. His trip was underwritten by the DaPrato Statuary Company of Chicago, a producer of plaster copies of religious subjects for Catholic churches. The firm had commissioned McGlynn to produce three sculptures of religious subjects, one of which was to be Mary. A devotee of Fátima, Father McGlynn chose to portray Our Lady of Fátima, but determined that in order to assure the authenticity of the model he had produced, he should consult the person who saw her.[23] The particular conception that McGlynn had chosen to portray was Our Lady of the Immaculate Heart, who had revealed herself to the children at the Cova da Iria on June 13, 1917. Lúcia had indicated in her fourth memoir (1942) that Our Lady on that occasion had opened her hands, moving them from their usual gesture of prayer before her chest, to the position of the right hand raised, palm down, and the left hand at waist-level, palm facing upward (Kondor 1976: 165). McGlynn came to Portugal armed with a letter of introduction from New York's Francis Cardinal Spellman, addressed to the bishop of Lisbon, requesting access to Lúcia. "If permitted to see her," McGlynn later wrote in his book-length account of the trip, "I would show her this statue as the means of obtaining from her a complete description of the apparition." (McGlynn 2017: 4) He had confidently imagined that she "might suggest a few alterations in details of the statue, but I had little doubt of its meeting her general approval." (McGlynn

21 Lúcia's description, responding to Manuel Formigão's questioning, in De Marchi 1952: 122. She pointed out that Our Lady wore no belt or ribbon. Both Francisco and Jacinta described the manner of dress to Formigão with less detail. Francisco: "She has a long dress, and over it a mantle which covers her head and falls to the edge of her dress (...) It is white, and the dress has gold lines," De Marchi 1952: 120; Jacinta: "She has a white dress, decorated with gold, and on her head a mantle, also white," De Marchi 1952: 120.

22 The differences are the elimination of golden floral motifs on the cope of the 1920 statue, which are replaced by a simple golden hemline, and a simpler tunic and sleeves evident in the 1947 figures.

23 *Vision of Faith*, which McGlynn wrote immediately after his return from Portugal and published in 1948, details the journey and interaction with Lucia, the bishops of Lisbon and of Leiria, and Pope Pius XII, and conveys a number of aspects regarding the history of the apparitions that were not widely known in the United States at the time. On McGlynn's life see McAlister 1981. Father McGlynn's papers are at Providence College. A finding tool is available online at <http://digitalcommons.providence.edu/cgi/viewcontent.cgi?article=1011&context=spcol_findingaids>, accessed June 9, 2017.

2017: 13) Yet Father McGlynn's presumption soon faltered. His quest for "the whole, accurate picture of the vision of Our Lady of Fátima" collided with the insistent, lapidary succinctness of Sister Lúcia (McGlynn 2017: 14). He quickly determined to scrap his original model and begin again, with Lúcia at hand to correct and guide his efforts from start to finish.

Within five days, McGlynn had completed the new figure, had a local sculptor cast it in plaster, and then prepared to leave. On the eve of his departure, the mother provincial of the Dorothean community to which Lúcia belonged asked that he blessed the statue in the convent's chapel. The image was placed on the altar in the presence of all the sisters (McGlynn 2017: 116).[24] This act of consecration was the first of several ceremonial blessings and affirmations. Father McGlynn next went to show the figure to the bishop of Leiria, who liked the new figure more than the model that McGlynn had brought to Portugal. The bishop indicated he would like a copy of the new figure in a niche of the basilica at Fátima. Father McGlynn then took the figure to the Chapel of Apparitions, where he placed it on the column marking the very spot at which Our Lady had appeared to the children. The bishop came to the Cova da Iria while McGlynn was still there and informed him that he would in fact like a larger, marble version of the figure to be placed in the niche over the entrance to the basilica (McGlynn 2017: 122). The bishop blessed the statue while it rested on the column in front of the chapel. Stopping in Rome before returning to the United States, McGlynn was able to arrange a private audience with Pius XII, who also blessed the statue (McGlynn 2017: 193). Father McGlynn then returned to the United States, delivering the new model to the DaPrato Statuary Company in Chicago for the production of a larger version, five feet high, to fulfill his original commission for a design to be produced for sale by the company. The larger version then served as the model for the marble statue to be carved for the basilica (McGlynn 2017: 127, 201-202).[25] That sculpture, fifteen and one-half feet in height, was executed in Italy (fig. 4.6). The campaign to secure funds required a few years, but in 1956 McGlynn was able to travel to Pietrasanta, Italy, to begin work on the figure at the DaPrato studio there. The marble figure was completed in April 1958 and dedicated the following month on May 13 at the Cova da Iria. After the structure of the tower was reinforced to support the massive figure, the sculpture was hoisted into place over the main entrance of the basilica in 1959 (McAlister 1981: 67, 191-213).

24 For reproductions of the original model and the new one produced with Lúcia, see McAlister 1981: 192-193.

25 The five-feet tall plaster version produced by DaPrato from the smaller model that McGlynn brought with him from Portugal was installed at the Dominican church of St. Vincent Ferrer in New York City on May 11, 1947, where it is still to be found; for a reproduction, see McAlister 1981: 195. DaPrato Statuary Company still exists under the name DaPrato Rigali Studios, see <https://dapratorigali.com/>.

Fátima in the Cold War

Father McGlynn had gone to Portugal with an agenda: not only did he want to secure an authorized version of Our Lady of the Immaculate Heart of Fátima, he had chosen the very subject as a way of promoting the devotion in the United States. American Catholics paid for the figure, and its placement on the façade of the basilica served to link the devotion to America: the prominence of the figure at Fátima, paid for by Americans, assured American supporters of the devotion that they had an investment in the devotion that the Holy Father in Rome celebrated as Mary's mission in the modern world. Although he journeyed to Fátima in 1947 and published his account of the trip in the following year, McGlynn gives no evidence of a political engagement in Marian devotion. McGlynn's image stresses the continuity of Fátima within mainstream Marian tradition rather than the apocalyptic, secret-driven story that appealed to the zealous John Haffert. McGlynn's figure was neither conceived nor deployed with the sharp edge of Soviet containment and conversion. Father McGlynn was not interested in a traveling image, a processional figure that might command vast crowds. He wanted to produce a work of art that would help encourage the devotion to Fátima by linking individual parishes in the United States with the shrine at the Cova, vouching safe the authenticity of the apparitions as an affirmation of Our Lady's Immaculate Heart as revealed to modest children in a remote part of the world.

A different passion drove the efforts of other American devotees who came to Fátima. Many American contemporaries of McGlynn were drawn to Our Lady of Fátima for what Lúcia described as Our Lady's second secret: the need to convert Russia. This mission, shaped by what a shepherd girl may have heart about the Bolshevik Revolution in 1917, echoed the Church's opposition to communism, whose godless ideology of modern materialism fit the longstanding denunciation of modernism issuing from pope after pope since the nineteenth century, most passionately perhaps by Pius XI in the 1930s. The approach to Fátima corresponds to Our Lady's urgent message regarding the state of modernity: reparations are necessary since God is offended at human iniquity, especially from those who abuse the Sacred Hearts of Jesus and Mary. Opponents of the Church include both the atheism of Soviet ideology and the agnosticism of liberal theological understanding of religion per se. Pius X had outlined in his 1907 encyclical *Lamentabili sane* a syllabus of sixty-five errors of modernist thought commonly informing scholarship in biblical studies, which included many scholars who, Pius pointed out, were Catholic (Pius X 1907). Fátima likewise addressed modernity on two fronts: opposition from within and from without the Church. The message of Fátima became a firm affirmation of Church dogma as championed by Our Lady and a strong opposition to political ideologies that targeted the Church. Published in English

4.6 Thomas McGlynn, Our Lady of Fátima of the Immaculate Heart, 1956-58, marble, 15 ½ feet high. [Providence College, Phillips Memorial Library, Special and Archival Collections, Thomas M. McGlynn, O.P. papers]

translation in 1952, Father John De Marchi's assessment of Fátima spoke for official Catholicism in a resounding way. Referring to the meaning of the angel that appeared to the children in 1916, urging them to pray and affirming the Rosary, the Trinity, the divinity of Christ, the Real Presence of the Eucharist, and the infinite merits of the Sacred Heart of Jesus as delivered through the Immaculate Heart of Mary, De Marchi concluded:

> it seems here so entirely clear that the Angel, in addition to preparing the children for the spiritual privileges to come, undertook to demonstrate and underline for our theological health and guidance that the binding orthodoxies of the Church have not been vitiated by time or error. The centuries have left them undamaged (...) here, at Fatima, it does appear that an Angel has walked among us with a Catechism open in his hands. (De Marchi 1952: 42-43)

Catechism-toting supernatural beings continued to appear to Lúcia over the next decade and more. On October 13, 1917, the apparition of Our Lady was followed by a momentary succession of several figures – St. Joseph and the Christ Child, Our Lady of Sorrows, and Our Lady of Carmel, who seemed to hold scapular and rosary in either hand. It was likely this last figure that brought John Haffert to Fátima in 1946 to speak to Sister Lúcia. In contrast to McGlynn's pastoral view of Fátima and her image, Haffert embraced a zealous missionizing of the faith that saw in Fátima an apocalyptic prompt for global outreach that fit the Cold War's script of good versus evil. Since 1940, Haffert had been director of the Scapular Apostolate in New York City, a lay organization associated with the Carmelite Order. Haffert took along a few yards of brown wool that he had taken to England (where Our Lady had given the scapular to St. Simon Stock and pledged her aid to any who died wearing the device), then visited various Marian shrines with it and presented it to Pius XII in Rome for his blessing. He had gone to Fátima with the purpose of having Lúcia touch the cloth since he planned to make multiply blessed scapulars from the cloth. He handed it to her when he mentioned the apparition of Our Lady of Carmel. The conversation that ensued resulted in a pledge that Haffert wrote with the intention of conveying it to the membership of the Scapular Apostolate. The pledge is clearly imbricated on what Our Lady told the children at Fátima in successive apparitions, but with the deft addition of the scapular: "Pray the Rosary daily; Wear the Scapular as a sign of consecration to the Immaculate Heart; Offer up the sacrifices demanded by daily duty, extending our Morning Offering through the day." If followed, Lúcia assured him, according to Haffert, "these are the basic things which must be done in order to obtain the conversion of Russia" (Haffert 1982: 7). In 1950, he joined Father Harold V. Colgan's recently founded organization, The Blue Army, and put to work the pledge he had penned in Sister Lúcia's presence, calling the new pledge, "The Blue Army of Our Lady of Fatima."

Haffert and McGlynn represent two faces of American Catholicism that are worth limning a bit more clearly in order to understand the conflicting visualities of the faith in mid-century America.[26] It was Francis Cardinal Spellman of New York who dispatched his endorsement of the Dominican Father McGlynn when he went to Fátima to consult with Lúcia to craft his image of Fátima (see fig. 4.6). And it was Francis Cardinal Spellman who adamantly opposed the circulation of the International Virgin Pilgrim statue (see fig. 4.5) in the United States. Haffert had brought it to the United States in 1947 with the hope of enlisting the US Council of Bishops in sponsoring the procession of the statue in their dioceses. The bishop of Buffalo, John F. O'Hara, had agreed to coordinate reservations among bishops for the diocesan visit of the statue. But at a national meeting of the Council of Bishops, the powerful Cardinal Spellman objected, asserting, in Haffert's words, that "it was not fitting, in a country predominantly Protestant, to carry a statue of Our Lady in the streets and that he thought we should not become involved with the Pilgrim Virgin. As a result, not a single bishop answered the offer of Bishop O'Hara to arrange for the statue to come to their diocese." (Haffert 1982: 43) Spellman was an outspoken opponent of communism and no less an advocate of Americanism, having secretly collaborated with J. Edgar Hoover and the FBI for years on labor unions as targets of communist infiltration.[27] As America's most outspoken cardinal, he wielded unmatched power and exerted much of it to make the case that Catholicism was soundly at home within American democracy. Spellman may have seen Haffert's zealous Marian devotion, expressed in the Pilgrim Virgin statue, as compromising the effort. Yet, although Spellman had quelled any official vote in favor of circulating the statue, Haffert reported that individual bishops approached him after the meeting to arrange visits until eventually "virtually every bishop of America had received the statue and almost all of them had laid their croziers and mitres at Our Lady's feet." It is all the more noteworthy that Cardinal Spellman engineered the termination of Haffert as director of the Scapular Apostolate in July of 1948 (Haffert 1982: 18; McGrew 2009: 26).

Father McGlynn's contemporary account of his trip to Fátima, which appeared in 1948, drew a different portrait of the devotion. Aiming directly at Haffert, he noted that "there had been [recent] reports in the United States that the use of the scapular was part of the devotional message of the Blessed Virgin at Fátima. Lúcia and the bishop have both been quoted in support of this view. Were the reports accurate?" McGlynn quoted the blunt response

26 For historical studies of the reception of Fátima in the United States see Kselman & Avella 1986: 408-413, and Cadegan 2004.

27 On Spellman's Cold War career, see Cooney 1984: 146-168.

he received from the bishop: "I have never spoken of the scapular." Haffert, for his part, registered the doubts expressed by his detractors. In his autobiographical account of the Blue Army, he described his "misgivings as I sat there in the presence of Sr. Lúcia with the final draft version of the pledge on the table in front of me." Since Our Lady "had not mentioned the Scapular but had merely held it out from the sky in the final vision (...) would not everyone think that I had arbitrarily introduced this into the pledge?" (Haffert 1982: 36) He assured readers that the same bishop reviewed the pledge in Haffert's presence and then solemnly announced, "You may promulgate this as coming from me." (Haffert 1982: 38) The comments attributed to the bishop of Leiria by both McGlynn and Haffert dated to the same year, 1946.

Short of resolving the contradiction, we can certainly agree that the difference corresponds at the very least to the divided reception of Fátima among Catholics in the United States and elsewhere. But in the context of the Cold War spreading over the globe at mid-century, Haffert's version of Fátima was to take the more public stage and exert itself with greater volume than McGlynn's. Both were soundly Catholic in every official sense. But Haffert's Fátima became the more visible and assertive. And it represented a traditionalist notion of the faith, one that would be challenged by the Second Vatican Council and vigorously reasserted by John Paul II thereafter in his pilgrimage to the Basilica, where he deposited the bullet from his attempted assassination in 1981 in the crown of Thedim's statue and where he met with Sister Lúcia.

If affirmation of Catholic orthodoxy was the internal aspect of the "message of Fátima," the external aspect was served no less explicitly by the mission of the Blue Army. The Blue Army began as an apostolate seeking faithful Catholics who would dedicate themselves to honor Our Lady and oppose communism in doing so. Colgan urged members to wear blue at gatherings since this color was sacred to Our Lady and contrasted with the color of the godless Red Army. Colgan recognized an ally in the promotional and orthodox zeal of Haffert and embraced his pledge, making Fátima the totem of the Blue Army. This encouraged Haffert to move ahead with something he had been planning since 1947: a visual program that would deploy Our Lady of Fátima as traveling warrior in the Cold War.[28]

Haffert indicates that the bishop of Fátima entrusted two statues of Our Lady of Fátima to him. Both were blessed at Fátima on October 13, 1947. One was crowned and the other was to be crowned in the United States. At Haffert's request, a third copy of the figure was produced in order to be sent to Russia as part of the mission to realize the directive of Our Lady. It was flown to Helsinki in 1950, where it awaited the opportunity to continue to Moscow (Haffert 1982: 15, 42, 46). Eventually there were many, many more statues duplicat-

28 On the Blue Army, see Bennett 2015: 263-281; on Haffert: 266-272.

ing the International Virgin Pilgrim. In 1965, the International Virgin Pilgrim traveled to Vietnam, where it was warmly received and requested to remain. The Blue Army decided instead to produce dozens of "National Pilgrim Virgin" statues, have them blessed at Fátima (as it turned out, by Paul VI, who visited Fátima that year), then transported to nations around the world, where they would remain (Haffert 1982: 242-243). In 1967, the statues were delivered on a round-the-world voyage of an airplane dubbed "the peace flight," carrying 107 American members of the Blue Army and the bishop of Fátima (who became president of the Blue Army in that year). It was delayed by the Soviet controlled-government when it stopped in Prague, but succeeded in delivering its payload in twenty-four nations. In 1971, the Blue Army delivered seventy more statues to individual nations (Johnston 1980: 127).

The globe-trotting International Pilgrim Virgin statue became engaged in a long succession of annual trips, including a round-the-world tour in 1978 that began in the US, then went to Japan, Korea, Taiwan, Thailand, India, Egypt, Israel, Rome, Austria, Budapest, Hungary, several cities in Poland, Santiago, Spain, Berlin, and Lourdes, France. At each stop, the figure was the focal point of the Blue Army's program, "Our Lady of Fatima's Peace Plan from Heaven," which was distributed in a pamphlet that outlined her story and the vision that "foretells World War II and Communism" (Anon. 1950: 9). It was a message of good versus evil. Louis Kaczmarek, the statue's official escort from 1975 to 1993, framed devotion to Fátima in a lively demonology that infused the communist threat with an apocalypticism that featured Mary as God's principal instrument of redemption in the modern age (Kaczmarek 1986: 28-35). The dedication of the Pilgrim Virgin statue to fighting the satanically driven atheism of Soviet Russia was the Blue Army's interpretation of the message of Fátima.

The 1978 tour included a dramatic stop in Poland that allowed the Blue Army to stage an effective performance in which the statue played a crucial role. Upon arriving at the airport in Warsaw, the passengers of the "Queen of the World," as the airplane was named, were greeted by Russian military officers, who quickly determined that the statue would not be allowed to accompany the pilgrims. Locking it inside the airplane's cockpit, Kaczmarek and Haffert took the suggestion of a priest in the group to fabricate an actual size metal outline of the statue, which they would carry in procession in the Polish cities they had intended to visit with the statue (Kaczmarek 1986: 51). It is likely that the idea was inspired by a powerful episode in recent Polish history, when, in 1966, state officials would not allow a miracle-working copy of the icon of Our Lady of Częstchowa to go on procession in Poland. Devotees instead took an empty frame in processions until 1972, when the image itself was released from what devotees considered the "arrest" of the Virgin Mary (see Niedźwiedź 2010: 174-177). The Blue Army contingent took the wire-outline of the Pilgrim Virgin statue to Częstochowa and were able to set it directly in front of the Black Madonna, where they told what had happened at the airport. "Praise be the Mother of God!" was the spontaneous chant of the large crowd. "Long live Poland!" (Kaczmarek 1986: 53) In 1997, the statue made a five-day tour in Papua New Guinea and the nearby island of Bougainville.[29] On most trips Our Lady was reported to extend many spiritual favors to those who venerated the statue and on many occasions was seen to weep (see Kaczmarek 1986: 104-111; Johnston 1980: 130-131). The Blue Army continues to sponsor the travel of the International Pilgrim Virgin to this day. The figure's current custodian resides in Indiana, where the statue has been based for many years.[30]

In the wake of the Soviet Union's capitulation and the revelation of the third secret (in which the Holy Father and a host of bishops are executed), the devotion of Fátima has shifted to other passions gripping conservative Roman Catholicism. Islam, abortion, homosexuality, divorce, and a liberal theology and reformist spirit identified with the Second Vatican Council have occupied many devotees who have struggled to recode the devotion with a mission that salvages the "message of Fátima" as something still compelling and calling to pilgrims the world over. There is, of course, no shortage of causes. And the imagery remains to anchor the devotion to a continuity that transcends social change and the vicissitudes of history.

BIBLIOGRAPHY

Anon. 1950. *Our Lady of Fatima's "Peace Plan from Heaven."* St. Meinrad, Indiana: St. Meinrad's Press.

"A primeira Imagem exculpida de Nossa Senhora de Fátima." 14 May 2011. <https://virgemimaculada.wordpress.com/2011/05/14/a-primeira-imagem-esculpida-de-nossa-senhora-de-fatima/>. Accessed 11 June 2017.

Bennett, Jeffrey S. 2012. *When the Sun Danced: Myth, Miracles, and Modernity in Early Twentieth-Century Portugal.* Charlottesville: University of Virginia Press.

Bennett, Jeffrey S. 2015. "The Blue Army and the Red Scare: Politics, Religion, and Cold War Paranoia." *Politics, Religion & Ideology* 16 (2-3): 263-281.

Cadegan, Una M. 2004. "The Queen of Peace in the Shadow of War: Fatima and U.S. Catholic Anticommunism." *U.S. Catholic Historian* 22 (4): 1-15.

Chapel of the Apparitions, Fatima. <http://www.fatima.pt/pt/pages/transmissoes-online>. Accessed 9 June 2017.

Cooney, John. 1984. *The American Pope: The Life and Times of Francis Cardinal Spellman.* New York: Times Books.

Cristino, Luciano. 2007a. "De Marchi, Giovanni (1914-2003)." In *Enciclopédia de Fátima*, edited by Carlos A. Moreira Azevedo and Luciano Cristino, 175-177. Estoril, Portugal: Principia.

Cristino, Luciano. 2007b. "Virgem Peregrina." In *Enciclopédia de Fátima*, edited by Carlos A. Moreira Azevedo and Luciano Cristino, 605-609. Estoril, Portugal: Principia.

DaPrato Rigali Studios. <https://dapratorigali.com/>. Accessed 9 June 2017.

De Marchi, John, I.M.C. 1952. *The Immaculate Heart: The True Story of Our Lady of Fatima*, edited by William Fay. New York: Farrar, Straus and Young.

Duarte, Marco Daniel. 2007. "Iconografia." In *Enciclopédia de Fátima*, edited by Carlos A. Moreira Azevedo and Luciano Cristino, 252-257. Estoril, Portugal: Principia, 2007.

29 For an account of this visit, see Hermkens 2009.

30 <http://www.pilgrimvirginstatue.com/>; see also Morgan 2009: 49-65.

Duarte, Marco Daniel. 2010. “A iconografia da Senhora de Fátima: da criação ex nihilo às composições plásticas dos artistas.” *Cultura: Revista de História e Teoria das Ideias* 27: 235-270.

Entre os textos da memoria. <http://entreostextosdamemoria.blogspot.com/2007/08/x.html>. Accessed 5 June 2017.

Fontes, Paulo. 2007. “Acção Católica.” In: *Enciclopédia de Fátima* , edited by Carlos A. Moreira Azevedo and Luciano Cristino, 9-15. Estoril, Portugal: Principia.

Fox, Robert J. and Antonio Maria Martins (eds.). 1992. *Pictorial Documentary and Historical Update: Documents on Fatima and the Memoirs of Sister Lucia.* Alexandria, South Dakota: Fatima Family Apostolate.

Gomes, Jesué Pinharanda. 2007. “Formigão, Manuel Nunes (1883-1958).” In: *Enciclopédia de Fátima*, edited by Carlos A. Moreira Azevedo and Luciano Cristino, 232-237. Estoril, Portugal: Principia.

Haffert, John M. 1982. *Dear Bishop! Memoirs of the Author concerning the History of the Blue Army.* Washington, NJ: AMI International Press.

Hermkens, Anna-Karina. 2009. “Mary’s Journeys through the Warscape of Bougainville.” In *Moved by Mary: The Power of Pilgrimage in the Modern World*, edited by Anna-Karina Hermkens, Willy Jansen and Catrien Notermans, 69-85. Burlington, Vermont: Ashgate Publishing.

Johnston, Francis. 1980. *Fatima: The Great Sign.* Rockford, Illinois: TAN Books and Publishers.

Kaczmarek, Louis. 1986. *The Wonders She Performs.* Manassas, Virginia: Trinity Communications.

Kondor, Louis (ed.). 1976. *Fatima in Lucia’s Own Words: Sister Lucia’s Memoirs.* Trans. Dominican Nuns of Perpetual Rosary. Fatima, Portugal: Postulation Centre.

Kselman, Thomas A. and Steven Avella. 1986. “Marian Piety and the Cold War in the United States.” *The Catholic Historical Review* 72 (3): 403-424.

Martindale, C. C., S.J. 1950. *The Meaning of Fatima.* New York: P. J. Kennedy & Sons.

McAlister, Ambrose. 1981. *Thomas McGlynn: Priest and Sculptor.* Providence: Providence College Press.

McGlynn, Thomas. 2017. *Vision of Fatima.* Manchester, New Hampshire: Sophia Institute.

McGrew, Edna. 2009. *Herald of Fatima Apparitions: John M. Haffert.* West Conshohocken, Pennsylvania: Infinity Publishing Co.

“Miraculous Fatima Statues.” <http://www.unitypublishing.com/Newsletter/history-PilgrimStatue.html>. Accessed 4 June 2017.

Moreira Azevedo, Carlos A. and Luciano Cristino (eds.). 2007. *Encyclopédia de Fátima.* Estoril, Portugal: Principia.

Morgan, David. 2009. “Aura and the Inversion of Marian Pilgrimage: Fatima and Her Statues.” In *Moved by Mary: The Power of Pilgrimage in the Modern World*, edited by Anna-Karina Hermkens, Willy Jansen and Catrien Notermans, 49-65. Burlington, Vermont: Ashgate Publishing.

Niedźwiedź, Anna. 2010. *The Image and the Figure: Our Lady of Częstochova in Polish Culture and Popular Religion.* Cracow: Jagiellonian University Press.

“Our Lady of Fatima, Pilgrim Virgin Statue.” <http://www.pilgrimvirginstatue.com/history>. Accessed 4 June 2017.

Panorama Católico Internacional, 20 April 2006. <http://panoramacatolico.info/articulo/renacimiento-de-portugal-despues-de-fatima-I>. Accessed 11 June 2017.

Pilgrim Virgin Statue. <http://www.pilgrimvirginstatue.com/>. Accessed 6 June 2017.

Pius X. 1907. *Lamentabili sane. Syllabus Condemning the Errors of the Modernists*, 3 July. <http://www.papalencyclicals.net/Pius10/p10lamen.htm>. Accessed 10 June 2017.

Pius XI. 1937. *Divini Redemptoris. On Atheistic Communism*, 19 March. <http://www.papalencyclicals.net/pius11/p11divin.htm>. Accessed 5 June 2017.

Pius XII. 1954. *Ad Caeli Reginam*, 11 October. <http://www.papalencyclicals.net/Pius12/>. Accessed 5 June 2017.

Rao, John C. 1985. “Portugal, Austria, and Counterrevolution in Interwar Europe.” *Faith and Reason*, Spring: 1-25. <http://jcrao.freeshell.org/Portugal,Austria.html>. Accessed 5 June 2017.

Rędzioch, Włodzimierz. 1996. *Our Lady of Fatima.* Narni, Italy: Plurigraf.

“Renacimiento de Portugal después Fátima (1).” 2006. *Panorama Católico Internacional*, 20 April. <http://panoramacatolico.info/articulo/renacimiento-de-portugal-despues-de-fatima-I>. Accessed 11 June 2017.

Sardica, José Miguel. 2007. “Estado e Fátima.” In *Enciclopédia de Fátima*, edited by Carlos A. Moreira Azevedo and Luciano Cristino, 190-199. Estoril, Portugal: Principia, 2007.

POLITICO-DEVOTIONAL REALMS

5
THE CHANGING FACE OF THE ENEMY

THE BELGIAN APPARITION SITES IN THE 1940S

TINE VAN OSSELAER

> And finally, that terrible prophesy concerning atheist Communism (...) Whilst the Holy Virgin pronounced those words, Communism grew ... today it suffices to take note, looking at the map of the world, of the number of countries that have been communized or are under the yoke of atheist Communism, so many priests, bishops even, so many Christians martyred or in prison ... and one might say that the progression of that terrible tide continues.

In 1966, Abbé Aneuse, curé of Wancennes and longtime promotor of the series of Belgian apparitions in the 1930s, thus reflected on the prophecies of Fátima and, more specifically, on the threat of communism, in his memoirs on the Belgian apparition site of Beauraing. As the original message of the Beauraing apparitions was not laden with this political meaning and every resemblance to the Fátima apparitions was initially minimized, the references are more surprising than one might first think.[1] This article will address the link between the Beauraing site, the Portuguese apparitions and the Commu-

1 "Et enfin cette terrible prophétie au sujet du communisme athée (...) Lorsque la Ste Vierge prononçait ses paroles, le Communisme naissait ... aujourd'hui il suffit de se rendre compte, en regardant la carte du monde, du nombre de pays communisés, ou pour le moins sous le joug du communisme athée, que de prêtres, d'évêques même, que de chrétiens martyrisés ou dans les prisons ... et peut-on dire l'avance de ce terrible fleau continue (...)." Archives of the diocese of Namur (ADN), L.2. Faits surnaturels & apparitions. Commission diocésaine pour la reconnaissance des apparitions de Beauraing. Oppositions: J. Aneuse, "Les souvenirs d'un témoin. Les oppositions à Notre Dame de Beauraing." Dactylographie, 1966, 101.

nist threat that, if not entirely new, had certainly intensified during the 1940s. Rather than focusing on the link between anticommunism and post-World War II apparitions, as other scholars have done, the focus here is on the reinterpretation of the Belgian apparitions of the 1930s, and the use of this redefinition in the campaigns for their approval.[2]

Apart from Beauraing, the Belgian apparition series included events in Banneux, as well as approximately 40 lesser known sites such as Onkerzele, Etikhove and Lokeren (Van Osselaer 2012). The Belgian wave of apparitions has primarily been linked to the rise of Nazism and related Rexism (a Belgian right-wing movement) and the fear of Hitler, with the vague warnings about the undefined 'enemy' that pervaded some of the discourses primarily interpreted from this perspective. However, as it would take more than ten years for the two initial sites of Beauraing and Banneux to be recognized by the bishops, the initial enemy had by then long been defeated. In the intermediate period, the two sites were caught up in anticommunist propaganda and were more intimately linked to the cult and discourses surrounding the Fátima apparitions. This article focuses on these years, leading up to the final selection of the two apparition sites, showing the shifts in emphasis at both the approved and non-approved sites.

1930s: a series of Marian apparitions

From late 1932 until 1935, a series of Marian apparitions swept across Belgium. The series started with reports on apparitions in Beauraing (November 1932 - January 1933) and Banneux (January-March 1933). These events, involving child visionaries, have been described as similar to the Lourdes apparitions of Bernadette Soubirous in tone, setting and message. At the Belgian locations, the Virgin admonished the whole of humankind, with only a few secrets for the individual seers. The Jesuit Herbert Thurston summarized the messages of Beauraing a year later: "The apparition has declared that she wants a chapel built there, but beyond an avowal of her identity and an exhortation to the children to be very good (...) no communication was made which seems proportionate to so strange an occurrence or to the interest it has excited" (Thurston 1934: 4). As the eldest girl had also seen a golden heart on the chest of the Virgin, the supporters of the site linked the apparitions to the devotion of the Immaculate Heart of Mary, but also saw similarities with the Lourdes apparitions.

2 On the multivalent meaning of the Virgin and her apparitions, see e.g., Blackbourn 1991: 788 (Mary stands for peace and justice but also for anticommunism); and Orsi 2005: 61. On the use of apparitions and pilgrimage sites for political causes, see Scheer 2014.

In its sober messages, rural setting and child visionaries, Beauraing was indeed similar to the Pyrenean apparitions and quite different from the more exuberant Belgian series of apparitions that followed. However, Banneux seems to have been even more Lourdes-like, as it also included a local source. In Banneux, Mary called herself the Virgin of the Poor, who came to ease the suffering and singled out the local source "for all nations" and "to relieve the sick" (Maunder 2016: 85, 87-88).[3] The apparitions in Beauraing and Banneux were indeed extensively covered in the press and well attended by devotees. The two initial events were followed by a series of apparitions and diverse mystical epiphenomena, including stigmatization, celestial signs (e.g., changing color of the sun) and miraculous cures. Apparitions were reported at almost 40 locations and hundreds of visionaries were involved.[4] Many of these new sites also drew the attention of the faithful and curious.

The series clearly seemed to fit a pattern, as the 1930 commentators also noted. The Catholic author Louis Wilmet, for example, during a presentation held in Brussels, observed that the Virgin had first appeared in Belgium while the nation was in the midst of an electoral contest (the national parliamentary elections were held on November 27, 1932).[5] He already observed that Mary frequently appeared in politically uncertain situations, as had been the case for the Marian apparitions in Paris, La Salette, Lourdes, Pontmain and Fátima. On these occasions, the Virgin had warned the people against political upheaval and urged them to pray and repent.[6]

The reception of the apparitions in Belgium was not only colored by national politics, as the impact of the economic depression could also be perceived (Blackbourn 1993: 361). After the crisis of 1929, the number of unemployed in Belgium rose, from 76,000 in 1930 to 400,000 in 1934. Salaries also dropped and there was an overproduction of coal. In late December 1932, special powers that the government had been granted by the parliament resulted in a "black fortnight" ("quinzaine noire") of reductions in salaries and social welfare. In the midst of this economic turbulence, the message of Our Lady of Banneux, who introduced herself as "the Virgin of the poor," sounded particularly soothing. As Jean-Pierre Delville summarized the historical context for

3 On the parallels with Lourdes see also, Zumholz 2008: 217.

4 For a first overview, see Van Osselaer 2010.

5 In the parliamentary elections of November 27, 1932, Catholics did better than they had done at the local elections of October 9, 1932 (when the Catholics had lost seats to the Liberals and the BWP). On December 17, 1932, the new cabinet, led by De Broqueville, was sworn in (Gerard 2006: 1049-1050). On the conjuncture of wonders in times of crisis and "Aufbruchszeiten," see: Geppert & Kössler 2011: 45.

6 Archives of the Sanctuary of Beauraing (ASBg), Archives Comité Pro Maria, Dossiers Mr. Pierroux: Conférence donnée à Bruxelles le 25 janvier 1933 par Monsieur Louis Wilmet sur Beauraing, après La Salette, Lourdes, Fátima.

5.1 Membership card of the International Union of Prayers (Banneux, 1935). [Antwerp, Library of the Ruusbroec Institute]

the Banneux apparitions: “Mary appeared thus at the most tragic moment of the crisis in Belgium” (Delville 2012: 92).[7]

Political developments on the international level only increased the sense of unease. Stalin’s five-year plan to eradicate religion (including the destruction of churches and the incarceration of the clergy) incited a distrust of communism, while the rise of Hitler and Nazism cast long, dark shadows. Tellingly, it was the publishing house Rex – led by Léon Degrelle, a future Nazi collaborationist – that took a leading role in the promotion of the Beauraing apparitions. Rex published several very successful booklets on the topic. At the time, Rex was still the publishing house of the Catholic Youth Action Movement and had not developed into the right-wing political movement it would become. Nonetheless, the link between Beauraing and Rex reflected badly on the apparition site when Degrelle’s political position became more outspoken. Eventually, it was publicly rejected by the Catholic Church. Some contemporaries even suggested that Degrelle had invented Beauraing (Perry &

7 “Marie apparaît donc au moment le plus tragique de la crise en Belgique.” See also, Van Osselaer 2009: 381.

Echeverria 1988: 165; Van den Steen, 1992).[8] Within this context of exalted nationalism, Mary's message in Banneux – that she came to bring "relief to those who are ill" and set a local spring apart as "for all nations, for the sick" (Thurston 1934: 35) – was particularly striking. This unusual message (and mission) was later strengthened by the creation of the Union Internationale de Prière in 1934, an international prayer society linked to the apparitions of Banneux (Delville 2012: 99). Those who joined up promised to pray the Rosary each night (in unison with the Rosary prayed in Banneux) for the poor, sick and suffering, and for peace among the nations (Deneweth 1993: 25-26).

The series of apparitions that occurred in the aftermath of those in Beauraing and Banneux had a format that was quite different from the original two. Nevertheless, the political and economic uncertainty left similar marks in the discourses concerning them. Several of these apparitions fit into the type of public apocalyptic vision described by Sandra Zimdars-Swartz as religious experiences "in which the Virgin Mary appears to one or more individuals to commission them to warn the world that a divine chastisement is imminent unless people repent and do penance for their sins" (Zimdars-Swartz 1989: 37). The form of chastisement – the notion of an imminent threat – was often not specified, but when we study the discourses of the various Belgian sites, it becomes clear that the fear of an invader echoes through several of these.

One of the most popular visionaries of the later series was 58-year-old Tilman Côme from Pontaury-Mettet. He claimed to have been miraculously cured of spondylitis and osteitis by the Virgin in Beauraing on June 11, 1933, and attracted thousands of people to the site to witness a series of apparitions. The apparition he announced for August 5, 1933 in Beauraing was one of the best attended of the entire series, with no less than 150,000 people present (Billet 1973: 26; Toussaint & Joset 1981: 115-118). Tilman Côme claimed to see the Virgin, who told him: "I have come here for the glory of Belgium and to preserve this land from the invader. You make haste" (Thurston, 1934: 27).[9] The invader was generally interpreted to be the German army, and in that context Côme's insistence on calling Mary "Our Lady of Boring" ("Notre Dame de Boring") rather than "Beauraing," inspired mockery for its very "Germanist" ("germanique") spelling.[10]

8 The publications included *Que se passe-t-il à Beauraing?* and *Les dernières apparitions à Beauraing* (also a success in France), an article in *Rex*, a special issue of *Soirées* (July 28, 1933) on the apparitions, and the book by Roger Saussus, *Le scandale de Beauraing*.

9 Or "Je préserverai ce pays des envahisseurs." Or, in another version: "Je suis venue en ce lieu pour le gloire de la Belgique et pour préserver ce sol de l'Envahisseur!" Archives of the Archdiocese of Mechelen (AAM), Processus circa assertas apparitiones et revelationes BMV in Belgio 1935-1938. B.XII.3. Documenta G Varia, Annexe Onkerzele. Dossier Wilmet "Notes Thérèse Neumann."

10 "Du nouveau à Beauraing," *Le Peuple*, June 18, 1933, 1.

5.2 Devotional card referring to Tilman Côme's description of the Virgin's apparition: "I have come here for the glory of Belgium and to preserve this land from the invader" ("Je suis venue pour la gloire de la Belgique et pour préserver cette terre de l'envahisseur.")
[Antwerp, Library of the Ruusbroec Institute]

Echoes of this warning could also be found at other apparition sites. In July 1935, in Gentbrugge and Bergenkruis, the Flemish visionary Jules D.V. warned of an "invader," "a man of anger, of the division of the people, an usurper." He reported visions of the archangel Michael destroying flags with the swastika on them, and divine messages on how Catholic Austria was being tested by evil Germany. On October 1, 1935, in a chapel in Onkerzele, Jules reported that he had seen Saint Joseph appear with two flags, the Belgian flag and a yellow flag with a black lion, and in between a large shield. Saint Joseph allegedly said to him: "I will save your land of Belgians."[11] Similarly, the messages of the apparitions in Chaineux were, according to some contemporaries,

11 Archives of the Diocese of Ghent (ADG), Onkerzele, File Onkerzele: "Geval J. De Vuyst tot 24 November 1935": "boven zijn hoofd twee gekruiste vaandels: de Belgische driekleur en een gele vlag met zwarte leeuw, er tusschen een groot wapenschild. De H. Jozef zegde: 'Ik zal uw Belgenland sparen.'" January 1, 1935.

"nothing more than a mind informed about events might predict: 'a menace coming from Germany and the German clergy persecuted.'"[12]

Fear of emerging communism also permeated the reports on the apparition series, although it cannot be called a dominant theme. Sometimes this fear of communists was expressed in general descriptions within the apparition messages (e.g., Bolshevism and communism as the "race of Satan," 1934) or "bad priests as the precursors of communism." Other visionaries claimed to have received more detailed messages, for example, about how the Russian and French communists would come to the aid of the Spanish communists and how this would give Germany the opportunity to invade France (1938).[13]

In other words, in Belgium, as at other European apparition sites, the Marian apparitions made sense within the given political and economic setting. As Bennett has phrased it so eloquently in relation to the Portuguese apparitions, "to say that the Virgin may have actually appeared to the children was also to say that she had good reasons to appear to them, and those reasons were rooted in the perceived necessity of turning the tides in the ongoing struggle between good and evil in both Portugal and the wider world" (Bennett 2012: 140). The success of the apparitions lay precisely in this intervention aspect, as David Blackbourn noted, "many achieved their large followings because they were perceived as intercessions in favor of the downtrodden, the neglected, and the ill-used" (Blackbourn 1991: 788).

As the Belgian series continued, the bishops decided to respond to the enthusiasm they seemed to inspire. On October 30, 1933, they circulated a statement that "the said apparitions, visions, communications, or revelations" can in no way be "said or considered to have been, either directly or indirectly, approved, or recommended as true and genuine by ecclesiastical authority."[14] While this was not exactly a condemnation of the diverse manifestations and new pilgrimage sites that had developed in their aftermath, the text does show that the bishops were "alive to the dangers of illusion and of an enthusiasm which flatters national feeling" (Thurston 1934: 21).

12 ADN, L.42. Wilmet: Circulaire au collaborateurs des Annales (in pencil: "Princesse de Croy, Juillet 1934").

13 ASBg, Récit des Apparitions. Divers témoins, "Août 1934, Cahier Gilles Carlsbourg"; ADG, Onkerzele: Report on Jules De Vuyst, September 15, 1936: "Bid veel voor de priesters. Want slechte priesters zijn voorboden van het communisme."; Decanal archive of Geraardsbergen, Parish archives Onkerzele (DAG), 36, III. B. Verslagen over verschijningen. Nationaal 4: Jules De Vuyst about August 5, 1937 in Beauraing, August 8, 1937 in Sint-Amandsberg.

14 Translation by Thurston 1934: 21.

1940s: Changes? Authorized and unofficial sites

Ten years later, the cards had shifted and only a few of the original sites still drew the attention of the faithful. Beauraing and Banneux continued to attract pilgrims and were among the few apparition sites to gain episcopal approval in the midst of what might be called a worldwide conjuncture of Marian apparitions (Scheer 2006: 29; Zumholz 2004: 11). It is important to note that this decision was primarily the bishops' choice (in whose power the decision lay), rather than that of the advisory commissions or the Vatican (Zumholz 2004: 565 and 13). For both apparition sites, it was a two-step process: first the cults that had developed at the sites were approved in the midst of the war (Banneux in 1942 and Beauraing in 1943) and second, in 1949, the supernatural character of the phenomena that had inspired the cults was also recognized (Delville 2012: 89; Kerkhofs 1959: 42-45).

The first initiatives to have the apparitions approved had already started in 1935 (with the creation of several commissions), but the campaigns received new impetus in the summer of 1939 when Mgr. Kerkhofs (the bishop of Liège) wrote an elaborate report to the archbishop of Mechelen listing his personal reasons for believing in the apparitions of Banneux.[15] In his opinion, the name Mary assumed on the occasion and her choice of apparition site and visionary (a young girl from a working-class background) were no coincidence: "The working class is certainly the most numerous and also the most endangered in its Christian life by socialism and communism (...)."[16] A few weeks later, in September 1939, he also wrote to the pope. In his opinion, a positive message would be most welcome to the public in the "darkness of the hour" ("la gravité de l'heure"), with the nations rising against each other "today as evil and suffering without end are being prepared, why do we not grasp the opportunity and urgency of the message of Banneux?"[17] As for the apparitions in Beauraing, in 1940, Mgr. Heylen (the bishop of Namur) admitted to a group of pilgrims that he daily invoked Our Lady of Beauraing, and a year later he allowed thousands of people to gather there, at which they prayed for peace (Maunder 2016: 95). In these years of pleading and lobbying for the approval of Beauraing and Banneux, the Belgian sites were increasingly linked to Fátima. The Portuguese cult itself had undergone a shift in emphasis and not only

15 There had been more indirect signs of approval as well: Mgr. Heylen visited the Beauraing site in June 1933 and allowed the chapel to be built a month before Mgr. Kerkhofs had authorized the construction of a chapel in Banneux. Maunder 2016: 89.

16 "(...) La classe ouvrière est certes la plus nombreuse, et aussi la plus menacée dans sa vie chrétienne par le socialisme et le communisme (...)." Archives of the sanctuary of Banneux Notre Dame (ASBN), 2 C 3 XV 6: Démarches à Rome, August 19, 1939.

17 "(...) aujourd'hui où des maux et des souffrances sans fin se préparent ne saisisons-nous pas l'opportunité et l'urgence du message de Banneux?" Archives of the diocese of Liège (ADL), Kerkhofs, D/IC, 30. Banneux: Copy letter Kerkhofs to the pope, September 4, 1939.

exhibited the Catholic Church's anti-modernism but also its growing anticommunism (Scheer 2006: 22, 63, 69, 107; Bennett 2012: 126, 184).[18]

Two statues of the Virgin: Fátima and the Belgian apparitions

In the initial years after the apparitions in Beauraing and Banneux, references and comparisons with Fátima seem to have been limited to the bare minimum to avoid creating the impression that the Portuguese events had inspired the apparitions of the child visionaries. The fear of imitation can be heard in the interrogations of the five Beauraing children in the first diocesan commission of Beauraing. One of the basic questions every visionary had to answer was whether or not he or she knew about Fátima before their own apparitions started. While the children all responded in the negative, some witnesses called to testify before the same commission (1935) stated how booklets about Fátima were sold at the site.[19]

Other witnesses insisted that La Salette (1846), Pontmain (1871) and Fátima (1917) were hardly known at the time.[20] These sources confirm what scholars working on the Fátima apparitions and their reception have noted: that up until the 1940s, knowledge of the apparitions was primarily limited to Portugal (although the cult of Our Lady of Fátima was officially approved in 1930) (Zimdars-Swartz, 1991: 190). Nevertheless, when the pope consecrated humanity to the Heart of Mary on October 31, 1942, this echoed the Fátima messages (25 years earlier), although this is not mentioned in the official documents (Heinz 2008: 70).

After World War II, interest in the apocalyptic messages of the Portuguese apparitions increased, as they were linked to anticommunism (and an anti-Soviet campaign) (Zimdars-Swartz 1991: 53; Perry & Echeverria 1988: 166; Margry 2009: 246). This included a rescripting of the message, encouraging the faithful to "compensate God for the offense caused by sin." According to David Morgan, the nature of the offense changed "in step with Sister Lucia's ongoing writings." In a Cold War setting, this meant interpreting the offense as communism and unbelief, while promises of world peace inspired practices of reparation (Morgan, 2009: 53).[21] Emphasis was placed on the second of the three secrets communicated in Fátima, which was related to the need to convert Russia and its consecration to the Immaculate Heart of Mary, for "if not,

18 For the anticommunism of the Belgian bishops see e.g. their pastoral letter of 1936 in which they presented the Catholic party and social movements as a bulwark against communism. Gerard 1988: 165. See also Gevers 2009: 215 and 224.

19 Rome, 116-119, 141-142, 151-153.

20 See testimony of Sr. Théophile (July 5, 1935), Rome, 122; ADN, L.2: Notes Pierroux, réflexions sur De Greef, March 13, 1936.

21 See also Zimdars-Swartz 1991: 190-219.

she will spread her errors throughout the world, causing wars and persecutions against the Church. The good will be martyred, the Holy Father will have much to suffer, various nations will be annihilated."[22] This was a universal message of a looming apocalypse with an impact far beyond the confinements of a local shrine – the message was to travel the world (Morgan 2009: 53).

The moment Rome started to support the Fátima apparitions more publicly (e.g. in a radio broadcast of 1942, the dedication of the world to the Heart of Mary on May 1, 1948, and on July 7, 1952, the consecration of Russia to the Heart of Mary through an apostolic text) (Imorde 2011: 135), the Belgian bishops started to refer to the Fátima apparitions more explicitly when writing about the Belgian sites.[23] In the early 1940s, the Virgin with the Golden Heart from the Beauraing apparitions was explicitly linked to Fátima and its emphasis on the Immaculate Heart of Mary. A telling example is the letter by Mgr. Charue (the bishop of Namur) of March 1943 on the Virgin and "our time," which was added to the decree that approved the cult of Notre Dame de Beauraing. In this letter, he referred to the consecration of humankind to the Immaculate Heart of Mary (as requested at Fátima) and her proclamation as Regina Mundi. He added: "Isn't this also what is taught in Beauraing, where the visionaries depicted her crowned with her glorious diadem and calling herself the Mother of God and the Queen of Heaven?" (Monin 1949: 199).[24]

Thus, in the bishop's opinion, in essence, the message of Beauraing was similar to that of the apparitions in Fátima, Lourdes and other such sites: "conversion and penitence, prayer and return to Jesus-Eucharist" (Monin 1949: 199).[25] He thereby quoted the call of Pius XII, echoing the message of Fátima, "to do penance; to change one's life and flee sin, the principal cause of the great chastisements with which eternal justice pains the world."[26] In his episcopal letter of October 30, 1943, Mgr. Charue explicitly compared the two apparitions: "For, my dear brothers, the lesson of Beauraing surprisingly reproduced – and it is only today that we realize it – the lesson of Fátima that

22 English translation of text in Sister Lucy, "Fourth Memoir," in *Fatima in Lucia's Own Words* 1976: 162.

23 Monique Scheer notes that the German Amtskirche was only willing to receive the Fátima cult more willingly after the pope started to support it so publicly in 1942. Scheer 2006: 107.

24 "N'est-ce pas aussi ce qui est inculqué à Beauraing, où les voyants la représentent couronnée de son Glorieux diadème et se nommant la Mère de Dieu et la Reine des cieux?"

25 "conversion et pénitence, prière et retour à Jésus-Eucharistie."

26 " (...) de faire pénitence; de changer de vie et de fuir le péché, cause principale des grands châtiments dont la justice éternelle afflige le monde (...)." *Acta Apost. Sedis*, November 23, 1942, 316.

5.3 Devotional card of the Virgin of Beauraing.
[Library of the Ruusbroec Institute]

has inspired the solemn act via which the Pope consecrated the Church and the whole of humanity to the Immaculate Heart of the Queen of the world."[27]

The link between the two apparition sites became almost palpable on August 22, 1947 (Feast of the Immaculate Heart of Mary), when two statues of the Virgin Mary were carried in procession through the streets of Beauraing. The first was the statue of the Virgin of Fátima that was on a European pilgrimage.[28] The second statue was the Virgin with the Golden Heart, the form in which Mary was said to have appeared to the child visionaries (solemnly blessed in the sanctuary exactly one year earlier) (Monin 1949: 168). The whole procession was fitting to the global mission of this International Pilgrimage of the Virgin Statue of Our Lady of Fátima. Conceived in 1947, it intended to in-

27 "Car, nos très chers frères, la leçon de Beauraing reproduit étonnamment, - et c'est maintenant seulement qu'on s'en rend compte, la leçon de Fatima, celle qui a inspiré l'acte solennel par lequel le Pape consacrait l'Église et toute l'humanité au Cœur Immaculé de la Reine du monde." Charue, "Fatima et Beauraing. Lettre Pastorale," October 30, 1943, in: Charue 1946: 19-20.

28 First on its way to the Maastricht Marian congress (cf. Margry's chapter 12) and to be continued to the Vatican.

form people about the apparitions and their apocalyptic messages and inspire them to atone for their sins (Morgan 2009: 53). For Mgr. Charue, the tour of the Fátima statue was an opportunity to emphasize once more the parallels between Beauraing and Fátima, including these two sites in a trio with Lourdes. In his letter announcing the visit of the Portuguese statue of July 25, 1947, he wrote that it "gives us the opportunity to note once more the doctrinal parallel between the great Marian apparitions of recent times. Lourdes, Fátima, Beauraing form an admirable Marian trilogy, in which the precious revelations converge in that comforting image of the Immaculate Heart, motherly in a tender way and all mighty, of the blessed Virgin who is the Mother of God, the Queen of the Heavens and the Mediatrix of all graces."[29]

The Fátima statue also passed through Banneux. On the feast day of the Immaculate Heart of Mary in 1949, Mgr. Kerkhofs referred to similar links between this new sanctuary dedicated to the Queen of the Nations (a reference to her calling the Banneux a source "for all nations") and the consecration of the world to Mary's heart:

> By dedicating the future sanctuary to the Queen of the Nations, we want to answer the message and desire of our honored visitor, honor her Royalty and underline the link between her visit and the consecration of the world to her Immaculate Heart. Moreover, is it not in the interest of all the people, so justly preoccupied with their future and security, to direct their regard and their heart toward Her who is the Queen of the Nations and the Queen of Peace? (Kerkhofs 1950: 190)

A converted communist and the Marian Leagues

The Fátima connotations were not the only way in which anticommunist rhetoric pervaded the discourse on the Belgian apparitions, as a story of a communist who had converted in Beauraing and ultimately created the Belgian Legion of Mary was also used in the promotional campaign for the initial apparitions of the child seers.

On September 26, 1948, *The Standard* went with the headline, "Ex-Communist leads the Legion in Belgium." The newspaper article referred to a speech by the auxiliary bishop of Malines, Mgr. Suenens, who was visiting the headquarters of the Legion, an apostolic lay movement, in Dublin (on September 19, 1948). He narrated how he had received a letter from a "converted

29 "(...) nous donne l'occasion de noter une fois de plus le parallèle doctrinal entre les grandes apparitions mariales des derniers temps. Lourdes, Fatima, Beauraing forment une admirable trilogie mariale, dont les précieuses révélations convergent en ce signe réconfortant du Cœur Immaculé, tendrement maternel et tout puissant de la Vierge bénie qui est la Mère de Dieu, la Reine des Cieux et la Médiatrice de toutes les graces." The day after (August 22) the benediction of the first stone of the sanctuary (Joset 1981: 132, 141: picture).

communist (...) asking to be allowed to attempt to start the Legion." The writer of the letter had turned out to be the previous editor of the *Drapeau Rouge*, the newspaper of the communist party. He had converted after a pilgrimage to Beauraing and two periods of war captivity, during which he believed he received the help of Our Lady of Beauraing (Perry & Echeverria 1988: 202; Toussaint & Joset 1981: 172). Suenens later commented on the newspaper coverage of his presentation (April 1949). In his opinion, the journalist had focused too much on this one paragraph, using it for the headline, but he also realized that this was how journalism worked. It was indeed a catchy headline. The historical reality – as he admitted – was slightly different. The Legion already existed in Liège even before "our friend" appeared on the stage and instigated the expansion of the movement in Belgium.[30] It was, of course, a more compelling tale to claim that a vibrant new and key Catholic movement owed its existence to a former communist.[31]

Suenens himself had initially thought the whole story to be more like a "golden legend."[32] Nevertheless, he liked referring to the tale and documented the case in his correspondence. A typed copy of the famous first letter that the convert sent to Malines on May 29, 1946 was among Suenens' letters to the diocese of Namur on the matter.[33] In this letter, the convert described the history of his conversion, concluding by saying that Jesus' "Gospel is the only viable 'communism' and also the only road that leads to peace, that total peace that the world needs so badly. It is the only means to break the chains of the vicious circle that hate creates."[34]

The case of the communist convert was to become prototypical. The diocesan commission responsible for the evaluation of the Beauraing apparitions knew about the conversion and wanted to present it in their files as a "typical case" ("cas typique"). To this end, Mgr. Charue contacted Mgr. Suenens, sending him a draft version of their narration of the events and asking for his opinion on it and on its potential use. He also said it would be acceptable for him to change a word or two if he thought that, in spite of the vague descriptions, the convert might still be recognized. In the short summary that they suggested, the convert is described as a man "who no longer had faith and was even a militant of the antireligious battle" ("qui n'avait plus la foi et s'était

30 ASBg, 44. Guérisons et faveurs diverses, file "Beauraing conversion": Cutting from *The Standard*, "Ex-Communist leads the Legion in Belgium," September 26, 1948.

31 *Ibid.*: Letter of Mgr. Suenens, April 1, 1949.

32 *Ibid.*: Letter of Mgr. Suenens to Charue, June 30, 1947.

33 *Ibid.*: Letter of Mgr. Suenens to Charue and copy of the letter of the convert, June 30, 1947.

34 "(Son) Evangile, qui est le seul 'communisme' viable, et aussi le seul chemin qui conduise à la Paix, cette Paix totale dont le monde a tant besoin. C'est le seul moyen de brise les chaines du cercle vicieux que la haine engendre." ASBg, 44. Guérisons et faveurs diverses, file "Beauraing conversion": Letter of Mgr. Suenens to Charue and copy of the letter of the convert (May 29, 1946), June 30, 1947.

même fait militant de la lutte antireligieuse").[35] Suenens responded favorably on September 30, 1948, as the person in question had explicitly given him permission to use his testimony, and the text in question was perfectly discrete about his identity. Suenens had only changed a few elements, indicating that the convert had already been a communist before the war and that during the war it was primarily the anti-German battle that he fought. As he had just given a speech in Dublin and an Irish newspaper had picked up on the story, he promised to keep the report, in case the file ever needed support, in Rome for example.[36]

It seems, furthermore, that the story of the convert (whose name was often left unmentioned or abbreviated to 'H.') was double-checked. The same file holds the report by the curé of Beausaint of November 28, 1948, who apparently knew 'H.' personally. He had always been impressed by his Marian doctrine and his zeal, which he called beyond normal, and which had made him believe that he might indeed be facing a real convert. However, he had also asked himself whether the story was not a little too good to be true. In order to test his sincerity and teach others a lesson, he had asked him to give a public presentation about his life as a militant communist, as well as *Drapeau Rouge* during the war, his captivity and conversion. At one point during his speech, he burst into tears, but it was not – as the writer believed at the time – because he was so moved by his own story, but because he knew that some of the "fortes têtes" among the local youth had come to "hiss him down." They were there "against him and against Her" (the Virgin) ("contre lui et contre Elle"). For the curé, the fact that he gave the speech was sufficient proof of the truth of his convictions.[37] Another curé (from Aye) had been convinced after hearing that the convert had joined the third order of the Dominicans and had to fight his family members, who wished to hinder him from attending mass. In the curé's opinion, the family's maneuvers were "diabolical," and he concluded that he wished that his "best Catholics might have his faith and energy."[38]

The Belgian bishops Charue and Suenens (auxiliary bishop of Malines at the time), as mentioned, liked to refer to this story. Suenens, as noted, mentioned it in his speech in Dublin, where it was picked up and slightly mispresented. Mgr. Charue used it in his opening sermon of the Année sociale (December 8, 1948).[39] In a 1949 book by Arthur Monin (who had been a

35 ASBg, 44. Guérisons et faveurs diverses; file "Beauraing conversion": Letter of Mgr. Charue, September 26, 1948 (?).

36 *Ibid.*: Letter of Mgr. Suenens to Charue, September 30, 1948.

37 "Mais je me demandais aussi si ce n'était pas trop beau pour être 'vrai.'" ASBg, 44. Guérisons et faveurs diverses, file "Beauraing conversion": Letter curé of Beausaint to Monseigneur, November 28, 1948.

38 "Je souhaiterais que mes meilleurs catholiques aient sa foi et son allant." ASBg, 44. Guérisons et faveurs diverses, file "Beauraing conversion": Letter curé of Aye, March 11,1948.

member of the diocesan commission) on the Beauraing apparitions, the story featured under the heading, "The signs of the supernatural, conversions and healings" ("Les signes du surnaturel. Conversions et guérisons"). The convert is described as someone who "had lost his faith and had given his body and soul to the most subversive and antichristian ideologies." In the footnote that follows two pages later, however, there are references to the press coverage of Suenens' speech and the description of the "converted communist."[40]

Suenens once again reflected on the story in an article on the link between Beauraing and the Legion of Mary in a special Beauraing issue of the Canadian journal *Marie* in autumn 1956. In his opinion, both were part of the spiritual renewal that characterized his time and represented the Marian revival and need for the apostolate of every layman: "To be able to fulfil her promise and convert the sinners, the Virgin calls upon the help of all. The legionaries are happy to offer her their exhaustion and sufferings for her to turn into instruments of redemption and salvation."[41] While Beauraing had already been linked to the anticommunist message of Fátima, the Belgian site itself now became an important means in the battle against the threat of communist thought and militancy.

Anticommunism and other apparitions

Apart from Beauraing and Banneux, only a few of the numerous apparition sites and visionaries survived the initial interest. Tilman Côme, for example, continued to attract the attention of a small group of followers (organizing an annual pilgrimage), while his original messages received a new meaning. According to the visionary, Mary had told him that she would protect his country against "the invader" ("envahisseur"). In the first months and years after this apparition, the "invader" was interpreted as the German army, as Hitler had just become the German chancellor and his political and military moves were regarded with mistrust. In his memoires, Abbé Aneuse commented on Tilman's popularity and the interpretation of the message he claimed to have received. He noted that if Côme had been asked at the time whom he meant by "envahisseur," he would have said the merchants of religious medals who had installed themselves at the apparition site in Beauraing. However, the press

39 Mgr. A.-M. Charue, "Sermon de l'Inauguration de l'Année sociale", December 8, 1948, in: *Bulletin Mensuel du diocèse de Namur*, December 1948, 188-193. The text is cited in Monin 1949: 131-132.

40 "Perdu la foi et s'était donné corps et âme aux idéologies les plus subversives et les plus antichrétiennes." Monin 1949: 133, footnote 1.

41 "Pour pouvoir accomplir sa promesse de convertir les pécheurs, la T.S. Vierge fait appel au concours de tous. Les légionnaires sont heureux de lui offrir leurs fatigues et leurs peines pour qu'elle en fasse des instruments de rédemption et de salut." Suenens 1956: 98-99.

interpreted the invaders as the armies that had occupied the country in 1914. They knew that the German army had started preparations and there were numerous rumors about war, and now the Virgin was going to save them. The following events countered the prediction, even though Côme's supporters would blame this invasion on those who had opposed his apparitions.[42]

Côme not only warned about an invader, he also requested that an annual pilgrimage, in honor of Our Lady of "Boring", to take place on May 18. In 1940, the ecclesiastical authorities pushed the date of that pilgrimage forward to May 13 (as the committee promoting the other Beauraing apparitions had planned a pilgrimage on that day – it was of course also the anniversary of the Fátima apparitions). As that was the date on which the Germans had arrived in Beauraing, it would seem like a celestial sign and a divine confirmation of the truth of what Côme had been saying.[43] Nevertheless, Côme's warnings were vague enough to leave room for a reinterpretation, and they were eagerly reused by his followers. As Belgium was invaded, the meaning attached to this word slowly changed to mean the communist threat and, in the years after World War II, Côme's supporters could still claim that the Virgin had indeed saved Belgium from the "invader," this time defined as the communists. In a text of 1961, called "Tilman Côme and ... I," the author explicitly writes how Côme had told him twice that he thought "envahisseur" meant "communism," and added that protection against communism had proven to be true.[44]

Epilogue

The changing interpretations of the 'open' messages to Tilman Côme perfectly document evolving fears in Belgium and Mary's role in controlling them.[45] Warnings about an undefined 'enemy' and an apocalyptic future pervaded reports on the apparitions, which inspired and stimulated fear and uncertainty. While the communist threat was not absent in the initial reports on the Bel-

42 ADN, L.2. Faits surnaturels & apparitions. Commission diocésaine pour la reconnaissance des apparitions de Beauraing. Oppositions: J. Aneuse, "Les souvenirs d'un témoin. Les oppositions à Notre Dame de Beauraing." Dactylographie, 1966, 77.

43 ASBg, 37. Apparitions diverses diocèse Namur, E.2: Letter of Leon Jourdain (May 24, 1941) to the dean of Beauraing; letter of Guibert Naniot, Maredsous, December 12, 1942 to 'Excellence' (Bg, 60); ADL, Fund Kerkhofs, D IV Culte mariale, 30. Banneux, II. Tilman Côme, Onkerzele: Leo Van Winkel, "Quelques réflexions au sujet des apparitions à Tilman Côme en 1933," 1940, 1.

44 ADL, Fund Kerkhofs D/IV Marian cult, 30. Banneux, II. Tilman Côme: "Tilman Côme en ... ik" (1961).

45 ASBg, 37. Diverse apparitions in the diocese of Namur, E.2. Tilman Côme: Letter of Guibert Naniot (Maredsous), December 12, 1942; ADL, Fund Kerkhofs D/IV Marian cult, 30. Banneux: Letter of Leon Van Winkel, 1940; *Ibid.*: text 1961. Matter 2012: 128: the messages of the Virgin became more political in the twentieth century.

gian apparitions, the anticommunist stance and the link with the Fátima apparitions became more explicit in the 1940s, and especially after World War II. The meaning of Mary's apparitions was multivalent (Blackbourn 1991), and it is interesting to see that in their promotion of the apparitions of Beauraing and Banneux in the 1930s, the Belgian bishops actively contributed to these shifts in emphasis by linking the events to the Fátima apparitions and consecration to the Immaculate Heart of Mary. The previous fear of similarities between the Belgian and Portuguese sites had evaporated.

As Côme's case illustrates, the messages could be reinterpreted and readjusted to a changing political context (Boniface 2005: 57). The vagueness of his messages might help to explain the loyalty of his devotees, which persisted decades after the initial interpretation and failure of his warnings, as the Cômistes kept returning to Beauraing on the day he had chosen. In those years of political tension, it was not hard to think of a new enemy – a potential invader – from which one needed to be saved.

BIBLIOGRAPHY

Bennett, Jeffrey S. 2012. *When the Sun Danced: Myth, Miracles, and Modernity in Early Twentieth-Century Portugal.* Charlottesville: University of Virginia Press.

Billet, Bernard. 1973. "Les faits des apparitions non reconnues par l'église." In *Vraies et fausses apparitions dans l'Église*, edited by Joaquin-Maria Alonso et al., 5-54. Paris: Lethielleux.

Blackbourn, David. 1991. "The Catholic Church in Europe since the French Revolution." *Comparative Studies in Society and History* 33 (4): 778-790.

Blackbourn, David. 1993. *Marpingen: Apparitions of the Virgin Mary in Bismarkian Germany*. Oxford: Clarendon Press.

Boniface, Xavier. 2005. "Le culte marial au XXe siècle." In *Mille ans de dévotion mariale de l'an mil à nos jours*, edited by Bruno Béthouart and Alain Lottin, 51-65. Arras: Artois Presses université.

Charue, André-Marie. 1946. *Documents Épiscopaux*. Beauraing: Pro Maria.

Delville, Jean-Pierre. 2012. "Marie apparue à Banneux (1933): figures et réceptions économiques, politiques et écologiques." In *Marie, figures et réceptions: Enjeux historiques et théologiques*, edited by Jean-Pierre Delville, Joseph Famerée and Marie-Elisabeth Henneau, 83-100. Paris: Desclée-Mame.

Deneweth, Herman. 1993. *Kroniek van 50 jaar Brugge-Banneux*. Beernem: Depré-Printing.

Fatima in Lucia's Own Words: Sister Lucia's Memoirs. 1976. Edited by Louis Kondor; translated by Dominican nuns of Perpetual Rosary. Fátima: Postulation Centre. <http://www.fatima.org/essentials/message/tspart2.asp>. Consulted November 23, 2017.

Geppert, Alexander and Till Kössler. 2011. "Einleitung: Wunder der Zeitgeschichte." In *Wunder: Poetik und Politik des Staunens im 20. Jahrhundert*, edited by Alexander Geppert and Till Kössler, 9-49. Berlin: Suhrkamp.

Gerard, Emmanuel. 1988. "Grondlijnen van de katholieke verzuiling tussen 1914 en 1945." In *Tussen bescherming en verovering. Sociologen en historici over zuilvorming*, edited by Jaak Billiet, 135-169. Leuven: Universitaire Pers.

Gerard, Emmanuel. 2006. "De democratie gedroomd, begrensd en ondermijnd, 1918-1939." In *Nieuwe geschiedenis van België. 2: 1905-1950*, edited by Michel Dumoulin, Emmanuel Gerard, Vincent Dujardin and Mark Van den Wijngaert, 869-1099. Tielt: Lannoo.

Gevers, Lieve. 2009. "Hoogtepunt en einde van een tijdperk. Het aartsbisdom onder kardinaal Van Roey (1926-1961)." In *Het aartsbisdom Mechelen-Brussel 450 jaar geschiedenis. Deel II: 1802-2009*, 173-253. Antwerp: Halewijn.

Heinz, Andreas. 2008. "Maria in Liturgie und Frömmigkeit des Marianischen Jahrhunderts." In *Maria und Lourdes. Wunder und Marienerscheinungen in theologischer und kulturwissenschaftlicher Perspektive*, edited by Bernhard Schneider, 56-85. Münster: Aschendorff.

Imorde, Joseph. 2011. "Tränen aus Gips. Zur politischen Dimension eines Marianischen Bildwunders in Syrakus." In *Wunder: Poetik und Politik des Staunens im 20. Jahrhundert*, edited by Alexander Geppert and Till Kössler, 126-145. Berlin: Suhrkamp.

Joset, Camille-Jean. 1981. *Dossiers de Beauraing.* Vol. 2: *André Marie Charue reconnaît les apparitions*. Namur/Beauraing: Facultés universitaires Notre-Dame de la Paix.

Kerkhofs, Louis Joseph. 1950. *Notre-Dame de Banneux. Études et documents*, vol. 1. Liège: H. Dessain.

Kerkhofs, Louis Joseph. 1959. *Notre-Dame de Banneux. Études et documents*, vol. 3. Liège: H. Dessain.

Margry, Peter Jan. 2009. "Marian Interventions in the Wars of Ideology: The Elastic Politics of the Roman Catholic Church on Modern Apparitions." *History and Anthropology* 20 (3): 243-263.

Maunder, Chris. 1991. *Apparitions of the Virgin Mary in Modern European Roman Catholicism.* PhD dissertation University of Leeds, Department of Theology and Religious Studies.

Maunder, Chris. 2016. *Our Lady of the Nations: Apparitions of Mary in Twentieth-Century Catholic Europe*. Oxford: Oxford University Press.

Monin, Arthur. 1949. *Notre Dame de Beauraing* Bruges: Desclée de Brouwer/Beauraing: Pro Maria.

Morgan, David. 2009. "Aura and the inversion of Marian pilgrimage: Fatima and her statues." In *Moved by Mary: The Power of Pilgrimage in the Modern World*, edited by Anna-Karina Hermkens, Willy Jansen and Catrien Notermans, 49-65. Burlington: Ashgate.

Orsi, Robert. 2005. *Between Heaven and Earth: The Religious Worlds People Make and the Scholars who Study Them*. Princeton: Princeton University Press.

Perry Nicholas and Loreto, Echeverría. 1988. *Under the Heel of Mary*. London-New York: Routledge.

Scheer, Monique. 2006. *Rosenkranz und Kriegsvisionen. Marienerscheinungskulte im 20. Jahrhundert*. Tübingen: Tübinger Vereinigung für Volkskunde.

Scheer, Monique. 2014. "Die Madonnen von Međugorje. Zum Verhältnis zwischen Bild und Vision bei Marienerscheinungen in der modernen Epoche." In *Maria in der Krise. Gesellschaftspolitische Instrumentalisierung einer religiösen Symbolfigur*, edited by Agnieszka Gąsior, 51-75. Cologne: Böhlau.

Suenens, Léon. 1956. "Notre-Dame de Beauraing et la Légion de Marie." *Marie. Revue Canadiene*, September-October 1956: 98-99.

Thurston, Herbert. 1934. *Beauraing and Other Apparitions: An Account of Some Borderland Cases in the Psychology of Mysticism*. London: Burns Oates and Washbourne.

Toussaint, Fernand and Camille-Jean Joset. 1981. *Beauraing, les apparitions: le livre du cinquantenaire*. Paris: Desclée De Brouwer.

Van den Steen, Christian. 1992. "Les apparitions de la Vierge à Beauraing, un jalon dans l'aventure Rexiste?" *Beauraing et sa région: archéologie, histoire et folklore* 4: 44-57.

Van den Steen, Christian. 1996. "Tilman Côme dit Côme Tilman ou l'aventure beaurinoise sans lendemain d'un 'miraculé-mystificateur'." *Beauraing et sa région: archéologie, histoire et folklore* 12: 22-36.

Van Osselaer, Tine. 2009. "Christening Masculinity? Catholic Action and Men in Interwar Belgium." *Gender & History* 21 (2): 380-401.

Van Osselaer, Tine. 2010. "Mystics of a Modern Time? Public Mystical Experiences in Belgium in the 1930s." *Revue Belge de Philologie et d'Histoire* 88: 1171-1189.

Zimdars-Swartz, Sandra. 1989. "Religious Experience and the Public Cult: The Case of Mary Ann Van Hoof." *The Journal of Religion and Health* 28 (4): 36-57.

Zimdars-Swartz, Sandra. 1991. *Encountering Mary. From La Salette to Medjugorge*. Princeton: Princeton University Press.

Zumholz, Maria Anna. 2004. *Volksfrömmigkeit und katholisches Milieu. Marienerscheinungen in Heede 1937-1949*. Cloppenburg: Runge.

Zumholz, Maria Anna. 2008. "Volksfrömmigkeit und totalitäres NS-Regime: Marienerscheinungen in Heede/Emsland 1937 bis 1940." In *Maria und Lourdes. Wunder und Marienerscheinungen in theologischer und kulturwissenschaftlicher Perspektive*, edited by Bernhard Schneider, 198-223. Münster: Aschendorff.

6
DARKNESS AT NOON
THE VISIONS AT CUEVAS DE VINROMÁ IN 1947 IN A DIVIDED SPAIN DURING THE COLD WAR

WILLIAM A. CHRISTIAN JR. & MARINA SANAHUJA BELTRAN

Cuevas de Vinromá and the visions of 1947

In mid-November 1947, a ten-year-old girl in Cuevas de Vinromá announced that the Virgin Mary had told her that on December 1 at noon the sky would go dark and a cross of stars surrounded by angels would appear to all who were present, and that persons who were sick should come.[1] This was one of a series of religious visions in the 1940s and 1950s in Spain, and like many of them, it was to a child from a family on the Republican side of the Spanish Civil War of 1936-1939 (Christian 1999). Her announcement, spread by word of mouth, telephone switchboard operators, newspaper articles, and episcopal press releases that warned people not to attend, provoked what was perhaps the greatest concentration of persons anywhere in postwar Spain.

Seventy years later, our research about the events was stimulated by a remarkable series of photographs of the event, along with a short film, which captured the magnitude of an event that attracted several hundreds of thousands of spectators. Our discovery of these images provided the occasion for

1 *Las Provincias* (Valencia), November 25, 1947, 4 and *Diario Español*, Tarragona, November 28, 1947.

revisiting “El Milacre” with the town’s citizens.[2] The photographs, the film, and the testimonies add context, detail and color to contemporary reports by the psychiatrist F. Marco Merenciano (1949)[3] and the provincial head of Public Health José Jimenez, in addition to a well-documented book by the journalist José Calvo Segarra (2015: 114-117), himself present as a child on the Miracle day.

Les Coves de Vinromà, as it is known now, is an agricultural town of about 2000 inhabitants in the province of Castelló. Like other towns in the region it had a core of shopkeepers, professionals and landowners who with jobs, loans, and sharecropping contracts maintained political control over a population largely consisting of peasants and laborers, some of whom held ideas of unions and revolution. The blessing of the town banner of the government-sponsored upper-class militia, the Somatén, on May 31, 1926, provided an occasion for enunciating in the town the notions of order promoted by Spain’s military government of Miguel Primo de Rivera. The speakers warned of “conspirers and agitators of the masses” and “the constant menace of anarchy” (Anon. 1926). Under the Spanish Republic from 1931 to 1936, the town had center-left governments, with members of Izquierda Republicana and the Radical Republicano parties.[4]

The Franco rebellion on July 18, 1936 galvanized the town, and effective power in September shifted from the town council to the anarchist-oriented *comité*, whose leaders came from the El Matutino Workers’ Center. In coordination with the *comités* of neighboring towns, activists burned statues and furniture of the town’s churches and chapels in a pyre outside the town.[5] Land that had belonged to large estates was confiscated, and by October 1936 two hundred families were farming it as an anarchist collective, storing produce

2 The research reported here developed over four decades, with preliminary visits by Christian to Les Coves in 1977 and 1980, the location starting in 2009 of the Calafell photographs, first through sellers on the collection website Todocolección (in particular Ramón Pla) and then through Àngels Calafell. Sanahuja conducted interviews in Les Coves and its zone in January 2017, and then again with Christian in July and August 2017. Àngels Calafell and her daughters, along with the authors, showed the photographs and the film in Les Coves on December 2, 2017, and the authors followed up by research in newspaper archives of Castellón and Tarragona online and in the Hemeroteca Municipal de Madrid. We are deeply grateful to Àngels Calafell and her sisters for permission to publish their father’s photos here, to the mayor and the town council of Les Coves de Vinromà, to Laura Villaplana and Vicent Rocher of *Tossal Gros*, to José Calvo, Odette Covelli, Javi Bueso, Cinta Moliner and Vicente Villaplana, to Monique Scheer, Amira Mittermaier and Peter Jan Margry for their comments, and above all to the many people who shared their recollections.

3 The Cuevas de Vinromá chapter consisted of three articles first published in *Levante* (Valencia) December 14, 16 and 18, 1947.

4 Causa General Legajo 1404 Exp. 5, 14 “en su mayoría simpatizantes del famoso frente Popular” and Legajo 1401 Exp 18, 81.

5 Causa General Legajo 1404 Exp. 5 and Legajo 1401 Exp. 18, passim.

in the chapel dedicated to Saint Vincent Ferrer for barter with other villages.[6] A socialist collective was set up in December. The *comité* confiscated property documents and account books of loans and mortgages, and controlled prices for goods. The wealthy were pressured to make substantial cash contributions for the benefit of the poor.[7]

Throughout Spain, for any given location the number of persons killed in the Civil War is a good indication of the subsequent degree of division. In this respect Cuevas de Vinromá was not unusual for the province (Porcar 2016; Bueso Boira 2019). During the two years between the start of the war and the town's capture by Nationalist troops, about twenty-one persons were killed in the town, whether directly by villagers, by squads from neighboring towns or Barcelona, or by soldiers. Some nine of those killed were from the town and killed in the town,[8] some twelve were from elsewhere, including three clerics and a nun, killed in the town.[9] Others from the town were taken elsewhere and killed, and members of the town's *comité* were also accused of aiding in killings in neighboring towns of rightists there. Fourteen townspeople were held in Republican prisons, first in Castellón, 50 km to the south, then in Valencia.

Three months after the arrival of Franco troops on June 11, 1938, the victors drew up a list of those who had been killed, another list of forty victims of confiscations and monetary demands, and a third list of sixty persons suspected of doing the killings and the confiscations.[10] Virtually all of the persons on this longer list had departed before the arrival of the enemy troops. Several were subsequently captured and imprisoned, and at least six (some say nine) were executed. All of these events left the village deeply divided in the postwar period, with a reputation for religious and political recalcitrance. In Cuevas de Vinromá a minority was firmly in control, and the majority was in submission.[11] There was at the end of the Civil War a nationwide purge of Republican schoolteachers, including several from Cuevas de Vinromá, as well as other government employees.

The visions of the girl began in March of 1947[12] in her house in the village, attracting the interest of her mother (who was devout), the parish priest, and her schoolmates, but not her father, who was skeptical of the visions. He had been a telegraph operator in a village in Cuenca, but was removed for being

6 "Le travail positif du peuple laborieux" (about Cuevas de Vinromá) in *L'Espagne Antifasciste*, November 11, 1936, 2.

7 Causa General Legajo 1401 Exp. 18, 8.

8 Causa General Legajo 1404 Exp. 5 Estado N°. 1, dated September 28, 1938, Legajo 1401 Exp. 18, 4-5.

9 Causa General Legajo 1404 Exp. 5 Estado N°. 2, Legajo 1401 Exp. 18, 6.

10 Causa General Legajo 1404 Exp. 5, 3-8.

11 The Guardia Civil reported that at when the town was taken by the Nationalists "the majority, which was leftist, went on towards Valencia." Legajo 1401 Exp. 18, 84.

12 *Las Provincias* (Valencia), November 25, 1947, 4 and (with slight variations) *Diario Español*, November 28, 1947.

a Republican, and the family ended up in Cuevas de Vinromá, where his brother was a schoolteacher. Those in the town with access to agriculture had enough to eat, despite the poverty and autarchy of post Civil War Spain. But the girl's family did not have access to land, and all who remember them told us that the family had a rough time. The division in the girl's family between a Catholic mother and a Republican father mirrored a division in the village, the province and in Spain as a whole between those who had supported the Republican government and those who supported the Franco uprising in the Civil War. Some townspeople remember that the girl told her father, "You, father, even though you don't want to, will also fall on your knees [before the Virgin]."[13]

It was in this ambiance that the girl's visions began. The word quickly spread among her schoolmates, to whom the girl reported the different forms of Mary and the Saints she had seen. It is clear from our interviews that the children at that time were imbued with and took for granted a series of devotions including the Sacred Heart of Jesus and Thérèse of Lisieux. Already in this early phase, the girl performed services for her playmates, announcing that the Virgin could bless medals for them. Rosa Sales, for instance, remembers giving a medal of the Immaculate Conception to the girl's 13-year-old sister, and the sister brought it back blessed.[14] The girl also had visions in the parish church, where she was granted a special place to sit.[15] For the adults the girl provided information of another kind, observing angels or devils behind them when they received communion (Marco Merenciano 1949: 155).

At some point the girl began to have her visions a fifteen-minute walk away from town at La Morería, the cliff-face pocked with the caves that gives the town its name. It is an iconic location in view of most of the town, where children still play and townspeople go for walks. There the visions took place at the base of one particularly imposing grotto-like opening, known as La Campana (The Bell). It looks out over a valley and the confluence of two streams, with the garden zone of the town visible to the left. Directly facing the caves were a series of steep hillsides, with the ridgeline of the town and its church in the background. One boy the same age as the seer girl recounted playing tag and being surprised that the girl did not react to being tagged as she was absorbed in a vision.[16] As time went by, her visions would start during the litanies of the Rosary. One of her playmates imitated for us how the girl would go still for a while, then snap out of this state and explain in a chipper and nonchalant matter what she had seen and heard.[17] Miguel Prats remem-

13 Interview Senior Day Center, August, 3, 2017. "Tu, padre, aunque no quieras, también te arrodillarás [ante la Virgen]."

14 Rosa Sales, b. 1934, July 31, 2017.

15 José Calvo, July 29, 2018, Anroig (Xert).

16 Tomás Barreda Prades (Bosa), b. 1940, December 2, 2017.

17 Rosa Sales, July 31, 2017.

bered that in the fall of 1947 a female and a male schoolteacher walked their classes in formation to the Morería to attend the girl's visions. Once, after the girl went still, a bird (a "*cuablanca*" or "whitetail") flew up and hovered in the cave, and the male teacher explained that was a sign that the girl was seeing the Virgin Mary. Prats told us, "We prayed with the teachers, all together, inside the cave."[18]

By all accounts, then, in this early, more local phase of the visions, the girl's mother, her slightly older sister, the parish priest, and at least two of the town's schoolteachers, in addition to the children who were the girl's contemporaries, took the girl's visions seriously. In this phase the townspeople who attended tended to be those more devout.[19] But they also included families in the area like that of Vicente Bort, age 14, who came with a sick relative from Villanueva de Alcolea, twelve kilometers to the south.

> I didn't go just once, I went about twenty times. Before the Miracle. Because Uncle Guillermo's sister had tuberculosis and we accompanied her. And we went on foot. That was months before.
> [The visionary girl] saw the Mother of God. And spoke with her. But somebody made her see [the Mother of God]. The little girl was not lying. Or maybe the Mother of God was really there.[20]

By mid-October 1947 word of the visions had spread to the wider region, reaching Valencia, and the civil governor ordered the mayor, the parish priest and the town doctor to come to Castellon for an exchange of views on the matter.[21] By mid-November 1947 the girl had made more specific her revelations. The Virgin had told her, she said, that she should say the Rosary daily at the cave for the following fifteen days, and she did so at noon to growing crowds, becoming abstracted in vision during the litanies. She said that on November 30 there would occur the darkness and the cross of stars, and the sick should come for that. When someone objected that November 30 was a Sunday, and the apparition would conflict with attendance at mass, the girl consulted with the Virgin, who changed the date to December 1. People

18 "Resavem amb los mestres, tots juntets, dins la cova." Miguel Prats, b. 1937, August 4, 2017.

19 "Ixa era gent del poble molt beatos"; "Mosatros teníem faena. I no podíem anar. I a demés, no erem creients." (witnesses from Les Coves de Vinromà).

20 "Jo no vaig anar una vegada, jo vaig anar com unes 20 vegades. Antes del miracle. Perquè na germana del tio Guillermo també estava tísica i l'acompanyavem. I anàvem a peu. Això mesos antes. ... Ella la veia a la mare de Deu. I parlava amb ella. Però li ho feien vore. La xiqueta no en va dir cap de mentida. O és veritat que estava la Mare de Déu." Vicente Bort, b. 1933, January 1, 2017, Vilanova d'Alcolea.

21 Ayuntamiento de Las Cuevas de Vinromá, Libro de Actas de la Comisión Permanente, May 18, 1947-March 25, 1949, session of October 25, 1947, the only direct mention of the visions.

noticed that on the leaves of the blackberry brambles near the Morería there were marks resembling Ms or Vs, and they saved the leaves as sacred tokens.

On December 1 an immense crowd of hundreds of thousands of persons (estimates ranged from 250,000 to 500,000, larger than at any other single-day apparition event in Spanish history) blanketed the slopes facing the cave, as can be seen from photographs. Many pilgrims were ill or disabled, including large contingents of the blind. They came from an extensive zone that included the regions of Aragon, Catalonia and Valencia by train, truck, horse cart, bicycle, and on foot, despite recommendations from bishops not to attend and roadblocks set up by civil guards.

Many people took pictures of the event, but perhaps none so extensively as Jaume Calafell i Pifarré (Cruañas i Tor 1991; Barnadas Rodriguez 2017), an inventive and enterprising young photographer from the town of Tárrega in the province of Lérida, 100 km to the north, who came with his brother and a helper, at least two still cameras and a movie camera.

December 1, 1947 was a bitter cold day. During the Rosary led by the girl at noon, the sky did not go dark, and a cross of stars surrounded by angels did not appear. When a *cuablanca* flew up in the cave, people cried out, "Now the Mother of God has come!,"[22] and took this to be a sign, and the sick, the halt and the blind washed themselves and drank the water from the river, which gave the impression of cresting. "For when they said, 'Now!,' everyone who was on the hillside brruum...all went in an avalanche toward the river."[23]

Some people claimed to be cured and were taken to Red Cross first aid tents. And there are still people in the region who say they were healed. But in general the reaction, especially because there was no darkness, was disappointment. A truck driver who took pilgrims from the province of Tarragona remembers that on the way people were excited and called out phrases such as, "Virgin Mary, have pity on this poor sinner!" and "Praise be to God our Lord, who will heal me!"; but the return trip was made in total silence (Escoi & Panadés 2014: 24).[24] The provincial health authority after a few days released a report saying that no true cures could be verified (Calvo Segarra 2015: 108-118). We were told that the girl had to leave the village, and her family eventually moved away.

Asking people to remember national and international contextual aspects of the visions for a period 70 years ago when they were children is asking too much. But one way to approach the matter is to ask in what frame of mind they went to the grand finale of the visions on December 1, 1947.

22 "I la gent quan van dir que salió el pajaro, 'Ya està allà la mare de deu,' uns ho van vore, i al dir uns 'ja està! ja està!'" Vicente Beltrán, b. 1929, July 31, 2017, Xert.

23 "Perquè quan va dir 'Ahora' tota la gent que estava a la muntanya brrruuum... tots en avalanxa cap al riu." Vicente Bort, b 1933, January 1, 2017, Vilanova d'Alcolea.

24 "Verge Maria, tin compassió d'este pobre pecador," "Alabat sia Déu Nostre Senyor, que em curarà!" recalled by Josep Curto.

6.1 La Morería, Cuevas de Vinromá, December 1947, with the Cueva la Campana to the left. [Photo by Jaume Calafell, all rights reserved]

Preliminary indications are that for those who were older teenagers (in 2017 in their late eighties and early nineties), what they expected depended on the political history of their family. Rosita Denia, then age 18, is an extreme case. Her father was a leader in the *comité* during the civil war and had been executed in Castellón de la Plana on January 25, 1947. For this reason Rosita was wearing mourning when she went to the visions, where she expected nothing to happen. When she was there she had her picture taken with two friends from a neighboring town in front of the cave by an itinerant photographer. In her photograph album the picture is emphatically labeled, "The Miracle that wasn't!" ("so my children will always know," she told us at the town senior center, "that, whatever people say, nothing happened here").[25]

Similarly Carmen Ferrando, age 21, whose father was a Republican soldier jailed after the war, and who went with a boyfriend who had also been a Republican soldier, expected nothing to happen, and thus was not disappointed when it did not.

Others had low expectations because of the skepticism of their priests. When Cuevas de Vinromá was evacuated in the war, Ferrando's family had been taken in Carlet, 150 km to the south, by a family who were members of Catholic Action, and thus close to the clergy. Women from that family came on November 30, 1947, for the final vision, and seventy years later Ferrando still recalled her conversation with one of them.

25 Rosita Denia, b. 1929, August 3 and 4, 2017.

6.2 Part of the crowd along the river, Cuevas de Vinromá, December 1, 1947. [Photo by Jaume Calafell, all rights reserved]

6.3 Another section of the crowd, December 1, 1947, with Cuevas de Vinromá in the background. [Photo by Jaume Calafell, all rights reserved]

6.4 People by the river during the visions, December 1, 1947.
[Photo by Jaume Calafell, all rights reserved]

> She said to me, "Carmen, what do you think?"
> And I said to her, "What did your priest say to you?"
> She said, "He told us we wouldn't see anything.'
> I said, 'Well... that sums it up."[26]

Note that the woman from Carlet came nevertheless, in spite of her low expectations.

Others who came despite the opposition of their priests did so with hopes of something big. Vicente Beltrán, an altar boy age 18 from Chert (now Xert), walked five hours with three other altar boys. Their parish priest feared the event would end up discrediting true and recognized miracles, like those in the Bible. He advised them not to go, but they went nevertheless: "We went to see if we could see the Virgin. We waited for Her, for something to happen with the sun or things never seen before. And we saw nothing. We expected to see something very big, and there was nothing! The miracle was that we got back home safe and sound."[27]

26 "El dia antes van vindre unes de Carlet (que matros havíem estat evaquats allà) i eren de l'Acció Catòlica. I aquella me va dir: 'Carmen, a tu que te pareix?' I jo li vaig dir 'A vatros lo capellà que vos ha dit?' Diu 'Mos han dit que no vorem res.' Jo dic 'Pos... ja no cal parlar més.'" Carmen Ferrando Agut, b. 1926, August 3, 2017.

27 "a ver si veiamos la Virgen! La esperàvem allà que s'haguere fet un sol o coses que no s'han vist mai. I no es va vore res... Esperábamos ver una cosa muy grande y no salió nada!... El miracle va ser que tornarem a casa i bé." Vicente Beltrán, b. 1929, July 31, 2017, Xert.

6.5 "1-12-1947 18 years old. Day of the miracle that nothing appeared", in Rosita Denia's photo album. [Les Coves de Vinromá, by permission]

Many were more puzzled than dismissive about what had happened; there were those who were simply curious; and there were townspeople, like an atheist Republican café owner, who had simply refused to go.[28] This wide spectrum of opinion and attitude was reflected in a somewhat contentious session when we showed photographs of the visions at the Senior Day Center in July 2017. In 1947 it was not infrequent for this diversity of expectations to exist within a family or a couple. Sara Barrera Garcia was twenty-one at the time and went in the family's covered wagon from their farm outside of town with her grandmother, who was extremely devout, and her grandfather, "who blasphemed about everything."

Those we talked to who were slightly younger and who had been brought up under the Franco regime, however, were generally hopeful and like Beltrán went with excitement and a certain dread. Miguel Prats, age 10, fearful that something bad would happen, stayed home and watched with his grandparents from his rooftop. His father, mother and sister went. "We were all worried, believing," he said.[29] Symptomatic of this worry about what might happen was the experience of one girl, who was fourteen. She had climbed up on top a large boulder to get a better view, but people told her to get down in case there was an earthquake.[30]

The local reaction to the girl's visions certainly had a component of explication that was personal and local: for many people we talked to, the girl was convincing and consistent, or at least plausible, and her family was known and respected; her playmates had no reason to doubt her.

But the astounding echo she found on a multi-regional scale, despite Church and government discouragement, is another matter. Only the larger socio-political context can help us to address the central issue: what could lead hundreds of thousands of people, many from far away, to overcome harsh weather, police roadblocks, episcopal opposition and clerical discouragement to go to Cuevas de Vinromá on foot, bicycle or mule-cart simply on the say-so of a 10-year-old girl they did not know and had never seen or heard, and whose visions were reported with the barest of details?

The fact is that the visions occurred in a region that was deeply divided, with fault lines regarding religion running through families and couples. In one Benicasim family we spoke to, a mother with a son with a birth defect had gone to the final vision hoping the son would be cured. She did not tell her atheist husband, who was firmly opposed to her going, nor her brother, who was a seminarian in Tortosa and would not have approved. As a heavenly intervention by means of a child of a Republican, the presence of the Virgin at Cuevas de Vinromá may have been seen as a way to transcend the divisions

28 Vicente Rocher Leche, August 2, 2017.

29 Miguel Prats, b. 1937, August 4, 2017. "Estavem tots pensatius, creguts."

30 Pepita Zaragoza Prats, b. 1933, August 3, 2017.

of the society, and provide a grace and a healing power for everyone, losers as well as winners.

The Cold War as seen from Castellón

Severely limited in its freedom to write about domestic issues aside from sports and praise for the regime, much of the reporting and opinion in Spanish newspapers under Franco (and generally most of the front and back pages), were dedicated to international news, which was intended to keep its readers satisfied with their government.

During the Civil War, in the adversarial imaginary of the Nationalist press the emphasis was on an enemy that was foreign and directed from Moscow. This imagery was informed by the long confrontation of Spanish Catholicism and its political representatives, on the one hand, and the communist regime of Russia and the Soviet Union, on the other. For both sides the Cold War, in this sense, was a hot one and had been ongoing since 1917.[31] There was a seamless continuity of anticommunist rhetoric from the Franco side and regime from the civil war through the 1960s. The different components of the Spanish Republic (socialists, republicans, anarchists) were conflated as generic "*rojos*"(reds) and thereby in essence non-Spanish. With the enemy identified as Russia, Russia's enemies were considered Spain's natural friends ("The attitude of the Axis powers, in the face of the Soviet expansion, encounters an ardent sympathy in the combative Spanish spirit of the Falange"[32]). German pilots and planes, and Italian troops, of course, had fought on the Franco side in the Civil War.

The Foreign Minister Serrano Suñer's speech, "Russia is to blame," on July 25, 1941,[33] was followed by coordinated anti-Soviet demonstrations in cities throughout Spain. In Castellón, the provincial capital, Falangists carried Spanish, German swastika and Italian flags, and placards praising Franco, Hitler and Mussolini. As elsewhere, at the end of the demonstration the local Falangist leader roused enthusiasm for a Spanish volunteer force to fight against the Russians ("Crusade against Communism").[34] Recruitment began in major Spanish cities the following day.

By mid 1941, then, Spain was, once more, effectively at war with Russia, and for the next two years the Castellón Falangist newspaper *Mediterráneo* carried periodic reports of Spanish contingents leaving for or returning from Russia, interviews with local soldiers about their Russian experience, and ar-

31 See for instance the anticommunist interpretations of the visions of the Christ of Limpias in 1919 and the Virgin of Ezkioga in 1931 (Christian 1992: 19, 104; Christian 1996: 370-372).

32 *Mediterráneo* (Castellón), June 25, 1941, 1.

33 *Ibid.*, June 26, 1941, 1.

34 *Ibid.*, June 27, 1941, 2.

ticles honoring the dead.[35] In June 1942 the city named a street for a Castellón commander killed in Russia.[36]

By the summer of 1943 the tide turned in the war, and despite optimistic reports of German victories and Russian losses, by the end of the year *Mediterráneo* headlines began to reflect a worry about what North Africa and Europe would look like after an Allied victory, with headlines like "A Communist republic 100 kms from Alicante,"[37] "Russia will dominate the Baltic States, the Balkans, Poland, Germany and France," "Great Britain's mission will be to combat Communism,"[38] and "The shadow of Communism continues to hang over Europe."[39] These worries were often quoted from statements by foreign political leaders, like Republican senators in the United States, British Conservatives, or Pius XII. For while the European left continued to shun Franco's regime as a fellow-traveler of the Axis, the Right in Europe and the United States began to see it, as they did Salazar's Portugal, as a solid ally in the ongoing realignment of nations for or against the Soviet Union.

The Falangist press in August and September 1945 recognized that the stakes in this conflict had been raised with America's use of the atomic bomb in Japan. *Mediterráneo*'s headlines cite Clement Atlee (who worries the bomb will "unleash chaos"),[40] the United Nations ("a mortal danger to civilization"),[41] and Stafford Cripps ("a sword of Damocles").[42] With the end of the war in the Pacific the global realignment is made explicit in the headlines, which cite Pius XII ("The gap that divides the world into two halves is made deeper and wider each day"),[43] Indalecio Prieto (who "sees very clearly the reality of the communist danger and declares that the Catholic Church is the only force able to stop it"),[44] and Oliveira Salazar ("onto the smoking ruins of Europe slinks the new communist order").[45] Headlines take note of the persecution of priests and bishops as more and more Eastern European nations come under Soviet control, and warn of communist infiltration in France and Italy. In the context

35 *Ibid.*, February 27, 1942, 3; January 8, 1943, 3; January 22, 1943, 2; March 12, 1943, 3; September 16, 1943, 3. *Mediterráneo* was the regime-oriented newspaper of the city of Castellón de la Plana, the provincial capital, and was distributed throughout the province. It produced local news and sports, and printed occasional reports from village correspondents. Its national and international news depended on wire services. Like other Spanish newspapers during the early Franco period, it gave ample coverage to sermons, missions, and other religious events.

36 *Mediterráneo*, June 26, 1942, 5.

37 *Ibid.*, December 31, 1943, 4.

38 *Ibid.*, January 4, 1944, 1.

39 *Ibid.*, December 31, 1944, 3.

40 *Ibid.*, August 7, 1945, 1.

41 *Ibid.*, September 8, 1945, 1.

42 *Ibid.*, September 26, 1945, 1.

43 *Ibid.*, October 30, 1945, 1.

44 *Ibid.*, November 7, 1945, 1.

45 *Ibid.*, November 10, 1946, 1.

of a world menaced by reds, *Mediterráneo* follows the American media in paying close attention to whether the Soviet Union has obtained the A-bomb,[46] and reports rumors of Russian missiles overflying Sweden and Finland.[47] While in 1946 the main international antagonist to Russia is the Vatican, with protests against persecution of Catholics in Yugoslavia and the Baltic states, in 1947 the center of attention widens to the United States ("The cold war between the United States and Russia heats up day by day").[48] In American anticommunist Republicans and churchmen like Cardinal Spellman, the Franco regime recognized kindred spirits and a hope for an end to Spain's diplomatic isolation.

In *Mediterráneo*, as in the Spanish press in general, the conflict with communism, then, was understood as a constant that morphed from hot war to cold war and from one set of allies to another: from Germany and Italy in the Spanish Civil War; to Germany against the Soviet Union in 1942; to the Vatican against Russia as the Axis waned and lost; and to Portugal, the Vatican, the US and the UK against communist dominance in Europe, in what became known as the Cold War.

During the campaign for a yes vote in a referendum, in July 1947, the regime tried to bring home the implication for Spain of all this news about international communism with pointed reminders of the killing of fellow-citizens in the Civil War. In its front page *Mediterráneo* carried a list of victims in Castellón with the headlines, "Who and why did they assassinate our martyrs?" and "Spain, a Russian satellite (It is not today, thanks to FRANCO)."[49] The next day the list was followed up by the headlines, "For those who did not consider themselves referred to yesterday" (addressed to those who considered themselves neutral or apolitical) and "The forces of evil made a very bloody experiment in our homeland in order to flatten the banners of Catholicism." The articles were illustrated by a pair of photographs headed "Peace and happiness in Spain and sorrow in the rest of Europe." The photo captions read, "This is what Franco won for us. While thousands of Europeans suffer in concentration camps [showing people lined up in rows], Spaniards live happily in peace enjoying their typical fiestas [showing a family having a picnic]. Think seriously about this."[50]

This constant diet of confrontation with Soviet Communism was communicated as well by the government No-Do newsreels obligatory for every cinema session. How it had affected the people who came to the visions of Cuevas de Vinromá is challenging to measure but impossible to ignore. Certainly as

46 *Mediterráneo* (Castellón), January 9, 1946, 1; March 9, 1946, 1; August 14, 1946, 4; November 7, 8, 1947, 1.

47 *Ibid.*, June 22, 1946, 4.

48 *Ibid.*, November 14, 1947, 3.

49 *Ibid.*, July 3, 1947, 1.

50 *Ibid.*, July 4, 1947, 1.

the Franco regime was challenged by the Allies and Russia in early 1946, the town council of Cuevas de Vinromá followed its peers by sending a telegram supporting the government.[51] As in other towns, periodic religious-patriotic celebrations, paid for by the town government, reminded the citizens who was in charge on the national level, including: April 1, Victory Day with a Te Deum mass and the requirement that all houses hang decorations; June 11, the town's Liberation Day, which included a mass and the reenactment of the arrival of Franco's troops; a mass on August 17 during the town Fiesta Mayor "for the town's dead and those who fell in the Holy Crusade"; and October 1, the Day of the Caudillo, with a Te Deum mass of thanks.[52]

Consecrations to the Immaculate Heart of Mary

The series of consecrations of dioceses and then cities to the Immaculate Heart of Mary, initiated by Pius XII in 1942 following divine revelation of a nun, were a top-down procedure throughout Europe that sensitized the church hierarchy and militant Catholics to the geopolitical importance of Mary in the struggle against Soviet Communism. They point up the extent to which the highest levels of the Church were just as attentive to heavenly signs, if not more so, as the everyday Catholic laypeople that paid attention to child visionaries. For theologians, bishops and popes were trained to be alert for visions and revelations as guides for what they should do. As a Spanish Jesuit (Bover 1943: 5) explained in his book on the consecrations, "The Catholic theologian, not content with studying ancient documents of Christianity, keeps an eye open for divine events, the supernatural interventions of divine Providence in the history, past and present, of the Church."

In Spain the active participation of the Claretians (Missionaries of the Immaculate Heart of Mary) sharpened the effect of these consecrations and associated them directly with the apparitions of Fátima.

Members of religious orders often hold deep spiritual attachments to the order's particular patron saints and advocations (named varieties of holy figures, like the Sacred Heart of Jesus, or Our Lady of Sorrows), which are the focus of prayers for help, the source of consolation and the objects of affection. These attachments are instilled in school or seminary, or sometimes earlier as family or lineage devotions that led to joining the order in the first place. In the worldwide economy of divine helpers, members of religious orders and enthusiastic secular priests or laypersons proselytize in favor of "their" saints. Their efforts have taken various forms, including making feast dates official, or obligatory, or higher in rank, or the approval of specific liturgies.

51 Libro de Actas de la Comision Permanente, Cuevas de Vinromá, January 6, 1946-May 18, 1947; session of January 6, 1946, in favor of the government's statement of December 28, 1945. See *Mediterráneo*, December 29, 1945, 1 and 3 and January 5, 1946, 1.

52 *Ibid.*, sessions of March 31, June 2, August 4, and September 29, 1946.

In exceptional instances saints or advocations are the protagonists of solemn consecrations of individuals, organizations, parishes towns, dioceses, provinces, nations, or humanity. Consecration, in this usage, means committing persons, places, or institutions to be devoted to the divine figure in exchange for this divine figure's protection. As an article in *La Vanguardia* of Barcelona explained it, "The Consecration is a complete surrender of ourselves and all that we have to the Immaculate Heart of Mary, in recognition of her supreme and universal dominion and in redress for the sins that so offend God and Her. (...) She, in exchange, promises salvation and peace. What a favorable arrangement it is for us!"[53]

One of the devotional agendas at play in the postwar context of visions in Spain was the long-term campaign of the Claretian Fathers to promote the cult of the Immaculate Heart of Mary.[54] In this respect it followed the model of devotion to the Sacred Heart of Jesus, promoted by the seventeenth-century mystic Marguerite-Marie Alacoque, by the Jesuits (who adopted the devotion as their own), and by the Peruvian Mateo Crawley-Boevey, of the Fathers of the Sacred Hearts, (who persuaded Alfonso XIII to consecrate Spain to the Sacred Heart in 1919). It was a German, Maria Droste zu Vischering, the superior of a convent near Oporto, who persuaded Pope Leo XIII in 1899 that she had had a revelation that the entire world should be consecrated to the Sacred Heart of Jesus. This he duly did on June 11 of that year, composing a prayer for people to say on the night of December 31, 1899. By the 1930s devotion to the Sacred Heart of Jesus was fully consolidated, with statues in most churches, the feast day celebrated in all parishes, images installed in devout households, in Catholic factories, and for Catholic countries in many public institutions. In many predominantly Catholic areas larger than life statues were erected strategically overlooking towns and cities.

As a recently ordained 24-year-old priest at the turn of the century, Eugenio Pacelli attended in person Leon XIII's consecration of humanity to the Sacred Heart of Jesus. In 1942, as Pius XII, he, as Leo XIII before him, received revelations from Portugal to consecrate humanity, this time to the Immaculate Heart of Mary. He made the consecration first in a radio address to the Portuguese people on October 31, 1942, and again, more formally on December 8 of the same year, with the request that bishops throughout the world consecrate their dioceses to the Immaculate Heart of Mary as well.

The Vatican website in 2004 insisted that the revelations in question came from a bedridden Portuguese woman, Alexandrina Maria da Costa.[55] But in

53 *La Vanguardia*, May 21, 1943, 6. For a contemporary theology of the consecrations, Bover 1943: 22-52.

54 The order was founded by the Catalan Antonio María Claret in 1849 in Vic, and was especially strong in Catalonia. It specialized in education and parish missions.

55 <http://www.vatican.va/news_services/liturgy/saints/ns_lit_doc_20040425_da-costa_it.html>, as of February 18, 2018. On Alexandrina see Marques 2017.

1942 and 1943 the Claretians, and through them the Spanish press and clerical establishment (José de Castro 1943: 251), took it for granted that the revelations came from the seer of Fátima, Lucia dos Santos, then a nun in Spain ("'I have come to ask for the Consecration of the World to my Immaculate Heart' (The Most Holy Virgin in her message at Fátima, June 1, 1917").[56] Pius XII himself was extremely attentive to the Fátima visions, and 1942, the year of his consecration to the Immaculate Heart of Mary, as the Madrid newspaper *ABC* pointed out, coincided with the 25th anniversary of the Fátima visions.[57] The Fátima visions, then, provided a kind of semi-hidden transcript for the consecrations.

At any rate the Claretians, in Spain and in Rome, went into high gear promoting devotion to the Immaculate Heart and the visions of Fátima, publishing holy cards, books for children and adults, booklets on how to consecrate individuals, parishes and schools, and explanations of the connection between the consecration, the Fátima visions, and the conversion of Russia. A Claretian historian (Pujadas 1981: 247) writes, "In Rome the Claretians of Via Giulia converted their residence into a prestigious center for propaganda and information, frequented by bishops, news agencies, writers, lecturers, historians, religious orders, pious associations etc." Within the order a place of honor is accorded to a Spanish Claretian, Juan Postius, a practiced organizer and indefatigable promoter of the cult, who maneuvered in the Vatican for the promotion of the Marian Heart liturgy.

In May 1943 Claretian fathers explained in a Marian Congress in Seville the Consecration and its Fátima connection, and the order placed inserts in diocesan bulletins advertising to parish priests their Immaculate Heart and Fátima literature and holy cards. There was a clear demand throughout the country as bishops scrambled to organize consecrations, not only of dioceses, but also of cities and towns. By the end of 1943 least 45 of the 60 dioceses in Spain had been consecrated to the Immaculate Heart of Mary.[58] In some dioceses the consecration was combined with another religious event, as if this procedure, ordained by Rome, did not in fact respond to a particularly popular demand or necessity. In this matter much depended on the proclivities of the bishop in question. There was special interest in the dioceses bordering on Portugal (Coria, Badajoz, Astorga and Seville were among the first), and in the dioceses of Catalonia, where the Claretians were influential, especially Barcelona and Tarragona. For the zone around Cuevas de Vinromá, the archdiocese of Valencia was consecrated in February, and the diocese of Tortosa in May.

56 *La Vanguardia*, Barcelona, May 21, 1943, 6, with a message first communicated by Lucia dos Santos in 1930. Dates given here and below for Lucia's piecemeal release of Marian messages regarding Russia, First Saturdays, and the consecration to the Heart of Mary are from Barreto (2016).

57 *ABC*, May 29, 1943, 10.

58 See *Iris de Paz* passim 1943, Zurdo 1943, and Anon. 1944. Five bishoprics were vacant in 1943.

As with the First Friday devotions promoted by the Jesuits to the Sacred Heart of Jesus, so the Claretians, following the subsequent piecemeal revelations of Lucia, promoted First Saturday devotions to the Immaculate Heart of Mary, setting up prayer groups and publishing prayer booklets. As there were promises of the Sacred Heart to Marguerite Mary Alacoque and to the Spanish Jesuit Bernardo de Hoyos, so the Claretians promoted The Great Promise of the Heart of Mary (of eternal salvation for praying the first Saturdays), based on visions of Lucia dos Santos in 1925 and 1930, made known in 1937.[59]

The Spanish pious literature in 1943 linked the visions of children in Fátima, the Immaculate Heart of Mary, the First Saturdays and consecrations in Spain to the end of the war and the conversion of Russia. Their main source was the July 13, 1917, Fátima message, as elaborated in successive versions by Lucia in 1938, 1940, 1941 and 1942. This message is a crucial element in the visionary expectations of postwar Europe.

Perhaps the most extensive text of this message published in Spain was furnished by the Claretian Gonzalo Torres (1943: 62-63):[60]

> You have seen hell, where the souls of the poor sinners go. In order to save them God wants to establish the devotion to my Immaculate Heart in the world. If what I tell you is done, many souls will be saved and there you will have peace.
> The war will end; but if they do not stop offending God, another worse one will begin.
> When you see a night lit up by an unknown light, know that this is the great sign God gives that he will punish the world with war for its great crimes with hunger and with persecution of the church and the Holy Father. To prevent it I will come to ask for the consecration of Russia to my Immaculate Heart and for the reparatory communion of the First Saturdays.
> If they accede to my request, Russia will be converted and you will have peace. If not, it will spread its errors throughout the world, causing wars and persecution of the Church: good people will be martyred, the Holy Father will have to suffer greatly, and a number of nations will be annihilated.
> Finally, my Immaculate Heart will prevail. The Holy Father will consecrate to me Russia, which will convert, and the world will be granted a period of peace.

59 The First Saturdays devotion was widely promoted in Spanish newspapers in 1943 and 1944 by, in addition to the Claretians, a pious organization, Los Caballeros Comendadores de Santa Teresita del Niño Jesús y la Santa Faz.

60 The preface is dated April, 1943. For an abridged version of the message see Bover 1943. Some works on Fátima published by Jesuits in Spain tended to downplay the role of the Immaculate Heart of Mary, emphasizing, as had the Dominicans in the 1930s, the advocation of Our Lady of the Rosary. See other early Claretian Fátima booklets by Gr. Martínez de Antoñana (1943) and Luis Ribera (one printing of Ribera's 1943 *Fatima y el Corazón de María* has the Barcelona Consecration poster on the cover). See also Solanes (n.d.) for the connection of Fátima and Russia.

Lourdes and Fátima in cinema

The massive response to the visions of a young girl in Cuevas de Vinromá was likely primed by the socio-religious context of the aftermath of the Spanish Civil War, the international tensions in post-World War II Europe, and the consecrations to the Immaculate Heart of Mary. It was most certainly primed by the widespread knowledge in the general public of the apparitions to other young girls at Lourdes and Fátima.

Cuevas de Vinromá fell within the Mediterranean corridor extending to Valencia of pilgrimages by train to Lourdes, although the number of persons who had actually gone to Lourdes on organized pilgrimages from the Valencian region was limited (fourteen thousand from 1868 to 1936), and generally from devout and more prosperous Catholic households (Christian 1992: 15, 150). In addition a number of people we talked to had stopped off at Lourdes when going to or coming from France for seasonal agricultural work or more long-term jobs. Many fewer would be those who by 1947 had been to Fátima.[61]

The cinema was a more accessible way to know about these shrines. Like the consecrations, the movie industry spread the model of child visions beyond national borders and made them worldwide phenomena. In post-civil war Spain the movie theater was one of the few ways to leave the country, as well as to escape from daily life. *Mediterráneo* calculated in 1945 that in the city of Castellón the equivalent of half of the population attended one of the six movie theaters every week.[62] Symptomatic of the enhanced place of cinema in daily life is this headline in 1948: "Dies age 104, never saw a movie." The woman (in Essex, UK) had never seen the ocean either, but only the movies made the headline.[63]

The Lourdes story had reached many of the people of the region in the form of a popular 20th Century Fox movie. *Canción de Bernadette* (*Song of Bernadette* [1943]), directed by Henry Wing, was 20th Century Fox's featured

61 There were annual pilgrimages to Fátima organized by Dominicans from Barcelona, geared to prosperous clients, with multiple stops including Madrid, Toledo, Guadalupe, and Lisbon. See *La Vanguardia*, Barcelona, November 17, 1943, 5; *Diario Español*, February 19, 1946, 3, about lecture in Tarragona with slides by Dominican pilgrimage leader; *Diario Español*, April 10, 1946, 7; and the prospectus, distributed in Tarragona, "VII Peregrinación al Santuario de Nuestra Señora del Rosario de Fátima del 6 al 22 de junio de 1947. Organizada por los RR. PP. Dominicos y la Junta Diocesana de Peregrinaciones de Barcelona, Dirección Técnica de los servicios en España, Viajes 'Internacional Expreso,' Viajes en Autocars Pullman." Collection of authors.

62 *Mediterráneo*, December 2, 1945, 4.

63 *Ibid.*, January 24, 1948, 4.

offering in its Spanish 1946-1947 catalogue of over 50 films, and its high rental fee testified to its drawing power.[64]

In Spain it was released by September 1946,[65] and was extremely successful. In Castellón it showed at Ciné Capitol in October.[66] In Cuevas de Vinromá it was shown in the cinema by the Quatre Cantons on March 12, 1947, during the first postwar pastoral visit by the bishop of Tortosa. It was in this month, according to the girl, that her visions began.[67]

As an American film geared to a worldwide, pluralistic, and multidenominational audience, *Song of Bernadette* was pro-religion without being sectarian (Kane 2008; Scheer 2009; Scheer 2012). The advertising slogans on the handbills given out at Spanish movie theaters were those suggested by the studio, and centered on the skill of the acting and the profound emotion the film evoked. The cover picture of the handbill distributed with the film was based on a painting by Norman Rockwell showing Bernadette with a cloth over her head looking up in vision, her hand to her chest, against a dark background with rays of light coming from above. Cinemas at the time often had the backs of handbills printed locally with dates, times and film publicity. They were given out freely before the arrival of a film and during its stay. The back side of the Castellón handbill uses set phrases, follows the general thrust of the studio's publicity, and emphasizes its appropriateness for children: **"A miracle of cinematographic art and science.** Grandeur..., Marvel..., Majesty.... A film that human words cannot describe, but the heart can feel. **No one will neglect to see this marvel, and they will recommend it to others with special affection. PERMITTED FOR MINORS.**"[68]

Some scenes in the film prefigured directly the scenes at the visions of Cuevas de Vinromá: a poor girl with visions in a grotto, large numbers of people coming to be cured, the use of water in healing, and skepticism from the authorities and the Church.

64 Catalogue, Collection of authors. Rental for one day was 750 pesetas, as opposed to 250 pesetas for a documentary about Pope Pius XII, *Pastor Angelicus* (Escoi 1991: 27). Prior to the Civil War, at least three films about Lourdes, made in France, had circulated in Spain: *El milagro de Lourdes* (1925), *La maravillosa tragedia de Lourdes* (1933) and *La Virgen de la Roca* (1935).

65 Bilbao playbill, <www.todocoleccion.com>.

66 Playbill, <www.todocoleccion.com>.

67 *Mediterráneo*, March 30, 1947, 2; Agustí Escoi rented the film for the town in Valencia (Escoi 1991: 27; Calvo 2015: 51-53).

68 Playbill, Collection of authors: "**CAPITOL Teléfono 2018 Castellón, Lunes 21 de Octubre 1946,** Sesiones NUMERADAS a las 6'45 tarde y 10'15 noche, Imágenes n. 68. **Un milagro del arte y la ciencia cinematográfica. La Canción de Bernadette**. Grandeza... Maravilla... Majestad... Una película que la palabra humana no puede describir...pero el corazón puede sentir. **Nadie dejará de ver esta maravilla y la recomendarán con especial cariño. TOLERADA MENORES**. La película empezará a las 7 tarde y 10'30 noche. **La Canción de Bernadette** no será exhibida en ningún local de Castellón y provincia, hasta seis meses después de su salida de cartel de este Salón."

Canción de Bernadette was not advertised as a way to convert unbelievers, and in fact the accompanying 70-page booklet rather rejected this idea, as it had as its first sentence Cardinal Newman's phrase, "For those who believe in God, no explanation is necessary; for those who do not believe in God, no explanation is possible" (Ediciones Bistagne 1946: 3). But in fact the plot involves a fairytale-like series of obstacles in which parents, priests, civil authorities and mother superiors are convinced by a child.

Another film, two years earlier, however, had addressed directly the issue of unbelievers, so pertinent to the region's postwar situation, including the element of couples divided by faith. *El Milagro de Fátima* was first released in Portugal in 1943. It was shown in 1945 in Castellón de la Plana, as well as in Tortosa, the diocesan seat.[69] Designed for a Portuguese and then a Spanish and European Catholic audience, it centered on faith and disbelief, in particular on an atheist doctor in Coimbra, separated from his family and upset by his daughter's decision to enter a convent. When his older son is mortally ill he refuses to let his wife take the boy to Fátima, and the boy dies. His younger son is then injured in a horse-riding accident. As the second boy is dying in a hospital, a nun counsels the father on the meaning of faith. The doctor's conversion then occurs in the corridor of the hospital as he remembers his wife's earlier plea for his older son and hears a heavenly choir singing and a bell tolling. The second son is then healed in his arms by intercession of the Virgin of Fátima, for the day of the conversion and healing coincides with the national pilgrimage. The film ends with 20,000 pilgrims singing the Ave Maria and waving white handkerchiefs. The handbill shows the distraught doctor holding his injured boy, in front of a bell bearing the name of the Virgin of Fátima, with a doctor lower left scrutinizing an x-ray.

The Spanish publicity sheet is a folio sized poster with on the back the synopsis of the plot, a list of quotes from reviews in Portuguese newspapers, and four suggested phrases for publicity. Two of these centered on men without faith: "The spiritual crisis of a man without faith, reflected wonderfully in images of the finest cinematographic production." "The moving setting of the pilgrimage to Our Lady of Fátima frames the most compelling intimate drama of a man without faith."[70] These phases were sometimes supplemented with what seem to be local additions. A small town cinema in Valencia urged, "Do not fail to see this wonderful film in which faith and reason clash, with victory for the former..."[71] A cinema in Asturias proclaimed, "It serves a doctrine, the

69 Playbill, Collection of authors. Plaza de Toros Cine de Verano, Castellón, Martes 12, Miércoles 13 y Jueves 14 de Junio de 1945, "Un film que conmueve profundamente a las multitudes." In Tortosa it was already news when the film was first released in Portugal, in 1943, see "Una película sobre Fatima" in *Reparación*, September 1943, 238: 417.

70 21x27.8 cm poster / publicity sheet for *El Milagro de Fátima* issued by the Spanish distributor, Cyre Films. Collection of authors.

71 Cine Jardín Eslava, Algemesí, undated handbill. Collection of authors.

NATION, a belief, THAT OF CHRIST, an idea, THE FAMILY."[72] Cine Perelló in Melilla, for a showing in 1951, claimed that the film "would enlighten those who have sight and make those who were blind of heart see."[73]

Conversion, of atheist Portuguese and atheistic Russia, was at the heart of the visions of Fátima in the form they became known in the early 1940s. And as the prospect of communism became more and more conceivable in Western Europe given the defeat of the Axis, the visions of Fátima became more and more attractive for anticommunist governments, and more and more urgent for the Catholic hierarchy. As we have seen, the dedication of the world to the Immaculate Heart of Mary by Pius XII in 1943 was one example, and it whetted the appetite for films like this one.

While the international Cold War enemies of Russia and communism are not named in these cinema advertisements, nor, at least explicitly, in the publicity material for *Milagro de Fátima* or *Song of Bernadette*, we have seen from the daily headlines in Spain's national and provincial newspapers that the Franco regime in these years was making every effort to keep international communism front and center in the minds of the population.

Parish missions and sermons

Newspapers also provide accounts of parish missions and sermons, which can bring us one step closer to the voices these people heard and pressure they felt. The missions, led by preachers of religious orders brought in from the cities, were concentrated efforts to bring inhabitants to repent, sector by sector (boys, girls, male and female youths, women, men). In the municipalities of the Valencia region, where so much of the population had sympathized with the Republic and where killings had taken place on both sides, the missionaries placed a special emphasis on forgiveness and reconciliation.

In Burriana, a town of 20,000 on the coast, the mission led by Jesuits in November 1940 included a cumulative Via-Crucis in which people from fourteen streets gradually joined the procession with their crosses after each prayer-stop, gathering the barrios of the town with their images to form a community enactment of penance. The town correspondent of *Mediterráneo* referred to "the thousands of sinners" who needed and were able to find Christ's forgiveness "to repair their disordered past." The newspaper report paid special attention to the child procession, "a fantastic spectacle, filling the air with their singing, and happily waving little flags, signs, and banners

72 Teatro Casino, Navia, May 9-10, 1945.
73 Cine Perelló, Melilla, January 25, 1951. <www.todocoleccion.com>.

6.6 Snapshot of boys with *peana* in mission procession in the barrio of Patraix, Valencia, February 10, 1955.
[Collection of William A. Christian Jr.]

of a thousand shapes and colors, carrying on their shoulders more than thirty hand-carried floats [*peanas*]."[74]

A photograph of boys, perhaps accompanied by their teacher, carrying one of these *peanas* in Patraix (a district of the city of Valencia) in 1955 gives us an idea what these small floats were like. It shows a kind of religious scene in which an image is inserted into a miniature landscape. It is not difficult to imagine that such scenes could include depictions of visions like those of Lourdes and Fátima.

Among the many ceremonies of the week-long mission led in October 1943 by Capuchins in the Castellón city parish of the Most Holy Blood, *Mediterráneo* chose two to describe in detail. The first was the procession of children, accompanied by the municipal band, with over sixty *peanas* the children had constructed, which ended with the distribution to the children of 1500 snacks of bread and chocolate contributed by the provincial governor. The second was a "moving Forgiveness of Enemies," which took place on a Friday night.

> (...) the church was not big enough for the crowd, which occupied a large part of the square as well. In the silence of the night the Missionary preached charity with one's enemies that should go so far as to pardon them, and in the midst of the sermon ordered the host to be exposed and

74 *Mediterráneo*, November 28, 1940, 3.

> then commanded the parish priest to ask forgiveness of his parishioners. With great emotion the priest climbed to the pulpit and with great simplicity and emotion said, "Brothers, I have been ordered to forgive and to ask for your forgiveness, and I, as a priest and as a Christian cannot fail to fulfill this obligation. In the name of Jesus Christ I forgive all who have offended me, and I ask all of my parishioners for the love of God that they forgive the offenses I have done to them. Do you truly forgive me?"[75]

Chodos (now Xodos) is a small village in the Maestrazgo mountains, 50 kilometers southwest of Cuevas de Vinromá. *Mediterráneo* reports a mission there by two Vincentian fathers in October 1944. Again the peak emotional moment was a forgiveness ceremony on the final day, this one including forgiveness between children and parents. It would have been especially poignant in the postwar context in which parents may have been irreligious and children were being schooled in Catholicism. By the same token the parish priest asking forgiveness was an eloquent role reversal in a province in which scores of parish priests had been killed and virtually all churches profaned.

> When the time came to hand out the Bread of Heaven, the missionary Father aroused the faithful with a beautiful homily about forgiveness. He began by asking offspring to forgive parents and vice-versa, a moment of indescribable emotion that the pen neither dares nor is able to transcribe. He asked the parish priest to beg forgiveness of his parishioners, and tears and emotions took over all hearts, and sobs filled the parish church (...)[76]

In Cuevas de Vinromá too there was a mission, announced in *Mediterráneo* for February 23 to March 5, 1944 as an exercise in repentance:

> Divine Providence will call at the door of our conscience seeking that from all the hearts of the sons of Cuevas will flow streams of water of repentance that coming from the springs of their eyes will erase the ugliness of their sins, thereby sending his abundant grace, beautifying our souls with rays of holiness, peace and perfection.

The town correspondent hoped that as a result "in our town a new era will begin of social, moral, and religious elevation, of peace and true dignity (...)."[77]

Every day at noon there was a child mission session, with one of the Claretian missionaries "explaining the children the fundamental points of the Faith, and doing so in a manner most attractive with a multitude of stories

75 *Mediterráneo*, November 5, 1943, 2.

76 *Ibid.*, November 3, 1944, 3 (final day, October 29). The Chodos church was used as a sheep corral, and the parish priest was killed elsewhere, in Almazora (Causa General Legajo 1404 Exp. 32, 1401, Exp. 23).

77 *Mediterráneo*, January 30, 1944, 2.

and songs." Given the preoccupations of the order, it is likely that the stories in question included accounts of the visions of Fátima.[78] These sessions culminated on March 2 with a mass for all the children of the town and the outlying farms. It was followed in the afternoon by a procession of the children with their little banners, presided by the Immaculate Conception and the child Jesus, and ending in the church with loud responses to the Vivas led by a missionary.

Friday March 3 was the traditional feast day of Saint Michael, which the missionaries marked with a ceremony that linked personal penance with the nation's welfare:

> In the afternoon there was the traditional petitionary procession with a special aspect this year - carrying heavy wooden crosses crowned with crowns of thorns and some wearing penitential robes joined the procession praying not only for the general purpose, but especially that the Lord bless Spain, keeping it out of the war, and praying so fervently that without doubt the Lord will listen to those innocents.

The reference to those carrying the crosses as "innocents" indicates that those given the crosses to carry were children, in a calculated effort to affect their parents and adults in general.

The following day a large procession with town authorities, musicians, and with children bearing flowers accompanied a priest with the host to the homes of eighteen sick people. This procession to "impedidos" had deep roots in early modern Spain (Del Río 2002, 2010: 73-75) and was an indication of the place of the sick in the general imaginary and the sacred nature of their care. We see this attention again as an aspect of the visions three years later.

The climactic final day included long and numerous confessions by many priests from neighboring towns, a great number of communions, and twenty-five first communions that had been "delayed by the revolution." It was followed by a large and enthusiastic Eucharistic procession to outdoor altars at the four points of the town, "which gave the lie to the general idea that people have about Cuevas and what some people had predicted [about a boycott of the mission]."[79] In the ceremonies people asked Christ for "mercy, forgiveness and grace." In conclusion the image of the Christ of the Calvary, which had presided the mission, was returned to its chapel, watched by the

78 Indeed the choice of the parish priest, the Escolapian Francisco Escorihuela, to invite Claretians for the mission would have been in line with his subsequent encouragement of the visionary girl.

79 This telling phrase indicates the reputation for revolution and disbelief of Cuevas de Vinromá in the region, which may have enhanced the attraction for the visions there three years later as a sign of conversion.

townspeople, in the words of the enthusiastic village reporter, whose "eyes were bathed in tears of repentance, of love, of hope and of happiness."[80]

Not all the sermons reported in *Mediterráneo* so emphasized forgiveness; others reminded their listeners of chastisements. Oropesa del Mar was a coastal town of 1000 inhabitants. In June 1944 a new statue of the Sacred Heart of Jesus unexpectedly arrived by train, the gift of anonymous donors. A Capuchin was called in from Castellón to preach at the welcoming mass. He "emphasized how men, ungrateful for the Sacred Heart's love, violate the Commandments of God's Law, and wallow in the mud of passions. And the entire world suffers punished by war, which is heaven's chastisement, the result of the world's prevarications. And from that terrible destruction will emerge triumphant the glorious refuge of Christ's Cross and Charity and the Love of his Divine Heart."[81] Chastisement, in addition to penance, forgiveness and healing of the sick, was also on the minds of some of those who attended the subsequent visions at Cuevas de Vinromá.

The religious revival in these towns was such that in August 1944, writing about Albocacer's reception of the new image of its patron, Our Lady of the Assumption, the local correspondent could write, "the spiritual resurgence of our towns after the terrible shock of the last few years is a palpable and pleasing reality."[82] There are additional indications in the accounts of pastoral visits by its bishop. On March 12 and 13, 1947, the bishop of Tortosa, Manuel Moll Salord, came to Cuevas de Vinromá. The *Mediterráneo* report gives a precious glimpse of the religious organization of the town and its children in the period when the girl there was beginning to tell of visions. The town prepared for the visit by erecting ceremonial arches and hanging draperies from balconies. The bishop on arrival was greeted by municipal and Falange authorities, religious sodalities, the town in general, and children waving little flags. In the church he urged people to prepare themselves for communion the next day. That night there was a showing of the "magnificent" film *Canción de Bernadette* to benefit the diocesan seminary under construction. The girl, her mother, her aunt, his sister and her cousin attended the showing (Calvo 2015: 53, citing the girl's cousin).

The next day after a mass in which "close to a thousand" hosts were distributed, the bishop administered the sacrament of confirmation to a substantial backlog of persons, dating from before the Civil War, consisting in 268 men and 308 women, with the mayor and his wife acting as godparents. That afternoon in the school there was a performance in which the children recited poems, performed dances, and sang religious songs, and on behalf of all the

80 *Mediterráneo*, March 16, 1944, 1, 3.

81 *Ibid.*, June 28, 1944, 2.

82 *Ibid.*, August 18, 1944, 2.

children two girls presented the bishop with an album and a contribution for the seminary.

What we see from these reports, then, seems to be a post Civil War religious recuperation, with the determined collaboration of the government, in which penance and forgiveness are emphasized, a backlog of persons are confirmed, and children are accorded a central dramatic role, surely in part as a way of engaging their parents. Here again we recall of the phrase supposedly addressed by the girl seer to her father, "You, father, even though you don't want to, will also fall on your knees," where the operant metaphor is conversion or persuasion by means of a child, as with the atheist doctor in the film *The Miracle of Fatima*, and the many persons convinced by Bernadette, beginning with her parents and including the parish priest, the bishop, the emperor, and Sister Vauzous in *Song of Bernadette*.

In the diocese of Tortosa, as throughout what was Republican territory in the Civil War, there was a slow process of restoring churches, replacing images, and replacing as well the decimated clergy. For Spain as a whole, the entire media apparatus of the regime, with its monopoly on information and education, was mobilized to promote the satisfaction of the population with the regime and a general disqualification of the outside world with the exception of Portugal, the Vatican, Argentina, and anticommunist conservatives in the United States and the United Kingdom. This world was threatened by Russia, a Russia that, in the view promoted by the regime, had occupied through its proxies the minds and the territory of the region before and during the recent Civil War. And it should be added that the rural inhabitants of the provinces of Castellón, Tarragona and Teruel were intensely aware of the "reds" in a way not covered in the press, the hundreds of Republican guerrilla fighters in the hills, infiltrated from France (González Devis 2016). Just five months after the visions, these fighters raided the flour mill at Cuevas de Vinromá, and in the aftermath at least seventeen townspeople were rounded up and jailed accused of collaboration with the guerrillas (Bueso Boira 2019).

Neither in our interviews, nor in most newspaper articles about the Cuevas de Vinromá visions, did anyone relate the visions to Russia or indeed to the Civil War. There is one exception, and a telling one, in the articles by the psychiatrist Marco Merenciano (1949: 173, orig. pub. in *Levante*, 6, December 18, 1947). After describing his visit with the girl, laying out the incongruity of her visions, noting their models in the visions of Lourdes and Fátima, a explaining the girl's visions as a child's game in which adults eagerly joined in, he concludes by pointing out how Spanish and how orthodox the visions were. The crowd itself was, in his view, an admirable demonstration of faith in a world in which there were clear alternatives.

> The people - hundreds of thousands of them - heard the call of the girl because they believed that the Virgin Mary could perform the miracle; it was the Virgin who was the miraculous one, the Mother of Christ, and not Stalin or Mohammed. The cry had gone out from the most heartwarming aspect of Christianity, and had touched the souls of many who had even forgotten they were Christians.

Note the two alternatives to Mary. One was Stalin, but the other Mohammed, the ultimate, age-old antithesis to Christianity in Spain, and more particularly in Mediterranean Spain, an alternative other whose memory survived in vocabulary, agricultural practices and was commemorated in festive reenactments and confronted in the nations across the inland sea.

The vision outbreak in Spain

What we have, then, seems to be a context that throughout Spain stimulated miraculous events, for which Lourdes and Fátima, with their child protagonists, their healing miracles and their divine visions served as models. Newspapers are sown with these kinds of miraculous items, which, far from threatening the regime, confirmed by analogy its providential nature, and indeed providence in general as a solution to human problems. In both *Mediterráneo* of Castellón de la Plana and *Diario Español* of Tarragona, these reports accumulate in late 1946 and 1947. Neither includes what appears to be the first of the Spanish post Civil War vision series, the visions of Marcelina Barroso, age 10, and others in La Codosera beginning in late May, 1945. This series was reported extensively in the Madrid newspaper *Informaciones*, with at least one report in *ABC* (also in Madrid).[83] But both the Castellón and the Tarragona newspapers report apparitions and cures in the northern Portuguese village of Vilarchao, where 30,000 persons gathered October 11, 1946. And while the Cuevas de Vinromá girl was having her visions unreported in the press between March and mid-November 1947, two other girls and a young woman, in Extremadura and Andalusia, were having visions as well. *Mediterráneo* carried on May 7 news of the visions of Mercedes Trejo, age 7, in Aldeamoret, a company town adjacent to Cáceres. As in Cuevas de Vinromà seven months later, and following the model of Fátima, the visions at Aldeamoret were supposed to culminate in a great miracle related to the sun. Both newspapers reported the visions of Ginesa Simón Casanova, age 14, in rural Almería between August and October. And on November 2 the Tarragona newspaper car-

83 *ABC*, June 19, 1945. José de la Cueva, articles in *Informaciones* (Madrid), June 19, 27 and 30, July 2, 4, 7, 11, 16, 21, September 7, 10, 14, 20, December 4, 1945; November 21, 1946; May 28 and July 18, 1947. De la Cuevas's 1945 articles were published as a booklet.

ried the story of a mute woman, Asunción Claret, age 28, who regained her speech upon having a vision of the Virgin of Fátima in a church in Cádiz. In this same period the first of the Fátima image visits, which would be so dramatic throughout Spain and Catholic Europe in subsequent years, occurred in Badajoz, coming across the border from a circuit in Portugal on October 26, 1947, to great enthusiasm and fervor.

A learned young Dominican theologian who had studied and taught in Rome, Emilio Sauras García,[84] writing in the Valencian newspaper *Levante*, noted that the visions of Cuevas de Vinromá were one of several, including those mentioned above, and, in the past, those of Lourdes, Fátima, and the visions of Ezquioga in the Basque country in the early 1930s (Sauras 1947: 4). His article was published November 15, 1947, and was, we think, the first to take notice of the enthusiasm the visions had aroused. It is written in the form of a letter to someone intending to go to Cuevas de Vinromá, counseling caution, and noting that, in addition to the vast majority of people who are simply curious, those who attend would include vision aficionados who flock from one site to another with little critical sensibility.

> Today extraordinary manifestations abound everywhere. We breathe an atmosphere of spectacular supernaturalism. Apparitions and messages follow one after another, as if in competition. Some become well known, like La Codosera, in Badajoz; El Cerrico, in Almería; Cádiz, and this one you want to witness. And some are unpublicized, and are or could be in every Spanish city, town or village. You know this atmosphere, you breathe it, and you spread it.

Sauras allows that there have been true apparitions, like Lourdes and Fátima, then so much on people's minds, and suggests their stories have stimulated the new visions.

> The Fátima story is on everyone's lips, as is that of Lourdes, recently recalled on the screens of movie theaters. The two girls are charming, speaking with the Virgin about serious matters and asking the world to do penance. And don't you think that constantly hearing about little Jacinta and Bernadette could excite the imagination of other girls who until now had seen nothing and now begin to see and hear what those girls saw and heard? And also, and I do not speak idly, of other girls who until now saw at night a bogeyman who frightened them, and now no longer see the face of this fellow, but rather the attractive face of the smiling Virgin?
>
> You, my friend, know the stories of many apparitions, and you know that for every authentic Jacinta and Bernadette there are ninety-nine false Ja-

84 Sauras went on to a distinguished career as a teacher in Valencia and Salamanca; he was a consultant for the Second Vatican Council.

> cintas and Bernadettes; and that for each Fátima and Lourdes there are ninety-nine big or little Ezquiogas.

It seems, then, that in many parts of Spain the period from 1945 to 1947 was the beginning of what the French historian Claude Langlois (2000), referring to the Restoration in France in the early part of the nineteenth century, terms a "conjunction miraculaire," a conjuncture of miraculousness. In his article Sauras thinks out loud why it is happening:

> The postwar world is out of whack (desquiciado). It was men who unhinged it, and they should be the ones who fix it (...). And the law of least effort makes us hope for exceptional means by which God comes to fix what we ourselves have broken. Consciously or unconsciously, there is this underlying laziness or cowardice in the atmosphere of excited supernaturalism that surrounds us, and in the facility with which we desire it and assimilate it.

As it turned out, the visions of 1945-1947 were only the beginning of this conjunction in Spain. Subsequently, coinciding with the circulation of Fátima statues and the sharpening of Cold War tensions, this spontaneous eruption of visions would include many more examples. This multiplication was spurred on by two additional Fátima films, in both of which the international aspect was emphasized. The Spanish production of 1951, *La Señora de Fátima*, starring Inés Orsini, was designated by the Franco government as being "in the national interest." It depicts the visions of Lucia and her cousins in the context of an alcoholic father and an anticlerical judge. In the film the Virgin foretells in minute detail of the next war and "the anguish of the nations dominated by Russia, the hatred and persecution of the Church, and the danger of the Sovietization of the world." Devotion to Fátima is cast as a confrontation between Portugal's devout peasantry and its radical revolutionary government. The ongoing presence of unbelievers is acknowledged, and one of the suggested publicity phrases is "If you believe, you should see *La Señora de Fátima*. If you do not believe, there is even more reason to see it." (Suevia Films 1951: [2], [4]).

The Miracle of Our Lady of Fatima, a Hollywood version of the Fátima story, was released by Warner Brothers in the United States in 1952, and in Spain as *El Mensaje de Fátima* a year later. The studio spared no effort with the publicity in Spain, and issued for cinema owners a luxurious 14 page glossy guide with 13 large production stills. The plot, which begins with the proclamation of a Socialist Republic in Lisbon in 1910 that persecutes the clergy, includes as a central character an agnostic adult male friend of the child seers. Among other things, the Virgin asks for "The consecration of Russia to her Immaculate Heart, and announces that if this is done Russia will convert and there will be peace. If not, its errors will be spread through the world, causing wars and persecution of the Church. Good people will be martyred and a number of nations destroyed." (Warner Brothers 1952: [5]) After the miracle of the sun on October 13, 1917 and the conversion of the agnostic, the scene shifts to 1951, the 35th anniversary of the miracle, with the convert and the seer Lucia visiting the graves of the other seers.

Among the production anecdotes recounted in the guide was the conversion to Catholicism of the director, John Brahm, a few weeks after the filming. The brochure introduction, addressed to theater owners, is quite explicit about the film's relevance for the Cold War.

> Although the Miracle occurred in 1917 in Fátima, the story is now as fresh as it was then. Our Lady prophesized the circumstances that keep us now divided into two worlds, one on each side of the iron curtain, and the film shows, without useless verbosity, the only solution for achieving the so desired 'Peace on earth for men of goodwill.' (Warner Brothers 1952: [1])

Emilio Sauras's article on Cuevas de Vinromá in *Levante* about this "voracious desire for the spectacular" shows how in 1947 (and indeed, subsequently in the 1950s) the various visionaries, if they were indeed ignorant of one another, could not remain so for long. For, as in the 1930s, persons like the one who had asked Sauras for advice would be traveling serially from vision site to vision site, unwittingly spreading and unifying messages, liturgies and procedures by the news they bear and the questions and petitions they pose to the seers.[85] Sauras warns his correspondent about them, "persons who follow after anything new, as long as it is religious. You will see: they will come from Madrid, from Barcelona, from Zaragoza and even from Cáceres and Soria. They are like aficionados who trail all over Spain to see their favorite bullfighter (...). Years ago one saw them in Ezquioga, last year, in La Codosera, this summer in El Cerrico... I know some of them, that is, I know some from Valencia who will be part of this group."

This same kind of enthusiast Sauras describes was indeed present at the Ezquioga visions. One of them, Father Amado de Cristo Burguera from Sueca, went to speak to the Cuevas de Vinromá girl in Picasent after her visions were over.[86] And we know that some of the Ezquioga enthusiasts remained active in the 1940s and 1950s, always ready to charge off to the latest vision site (Christian 1996: 396-398).

85 One can see how this process could take place in the short film Jaume Calafell made of the visions, as prior to a vision session a man in a suit, tie and trench-coat gives two holy cards to the seer girl, who quickly puts them away (undistributed footage, courtesy Àngels Calafell).

86 Interview with Burguera's disciple, Juan Castells, Sueca, December 6, 1983, who said that Burguera found it unlikely that the Virgin would have adjusted the date of the miracle.

Through the visionaries this kind of self-made expert would ask the Virgin to confirm the validity of the previous seers they had visited, read about, or heard about. These aficionados, then were circulating among the rural miracle sites, connecting them and giving a physical and informational substance to the "conjuncture." Note that Sauras's questioner, who lived presumably in Valencia or the zone in which *Las Provincias* was circulated, already knew, prior to November 15 and this first newspaper article, about the visions and about something special announced to happen. This person was therefore part of a word-of-mouth circuit of information independent of the press, or as Sauras put it, "I know that your sources of information are the street, the conversation group, the patio, the neighbor."

These aficionados, true experts in their way, not only linked the contemporary seers to each other, unwittingly unifying messages, liturgies and language, they also connected them to their predecessors in previous decades, providing a bridge from conjuncture to conjuncture since the same persons lived through one and the other. Perhaps it is not a coincidence that Felix Bilbao, the bishop of Tortosa from 1925 to 1943, and Prudencio Melo y Alcalde, archbishop of Valencia from 1923 to 1945, were both particularly assiduous visitors at Lourdes (Christian 1992: 151).

Sauras himself is part of another systemic dynamic, the antibodies, as it were, to the visions, who also, through personal experience or acquired wisdom, were wary of visions and enthusiasm for miracles. For Valencia, and in particular the Dominicans there led by Sauras' teacher Luis Urbano (Forcada Comins 1997: 31-32), writing in the journals *Rosas y Espinas* and *Contemporánea*, had been on the forefront of this skepticism for thirty years. They were acquainted with the fraudulent bleeding of a crucifix in Gandía in 1918, then the visions of the Christ of Limpias starting in 1919 (Christian 1992: 19-28, 77-78, 99) and then the visions at Ezquioga starting in 1931 (Christian 1996: 501). The equivalent of Sauras for Castellón was the Discalced Carmelite Fray Rigoberto de la Trinidad who, without mentioning Cuevas de Vinromá, published an article in *Mediterráneo* on November 23, 1947, a week before the announced miracle, with the severe warnings against visions by San Juan de la Cruz. We saw a similar attitude in the parish priest of Chert, who feared that failed miracles would discredit true ones.[87]

87 "He didn't want to go, because he said if it fails, then all miracles will be considered lies." (Ell no va voler vindre perquè va dir, si fracassa tots los miracles seran mentirà. Si fracassa allò... y ya no quiso venir. Como si no lo creiera con eso.) Vicente Beltrán, b. 1929, July 31, 2017, Xert. Calvo (2015: 64) reports, however, that a number of priests were sympathetic, and we were told that some of them were present on the final day in civilian garb.

Darkness at noon

In November 1947 the girl of Cuevas de Vinromá, according to a Valencia newspaper, announced that the sky would go dark and a cross of stars would emerge accompanied by angels.[88]

> She says that after praying the Rosary every day, on December first will occur an event of a universal nature: at noon it will become night completely dark in the entire world, and visible to those who are in the town will appear a monumental luminous cross formed by stars and surrounded with angels; she adds that the Virgin has advised that the sick should come to be present for this marvelous event.

For the people of the region the prospect of the darkness, as we have heard from witnesses present on the dramatic day, was in turn fascinating, exhilarating, and disquieting. On that day, at noon, at least some people in the city of Castellon went out on their balconies with lighted candles (Ballester Querol 1997: 34). What the girl announced had deep roots and recent analogies and parallels, in addition to the collective memories or theoretical knowledge of eclipses.

Celestial signs had special meaning to the many people in postwar Spain versed in the visions of Fátima. They knew about the sun spinning and falling from the sky, and they knew from the later revelations of Lucia that an unknown light in a dark sky would be a sign of a coming war. They also knew that parish missionaries sometimes erected luminous crosses (with candles or with electric lights) in the final ceremony of parish missions. These signs were in turn part of a long history of crosses in the sky, like the famous cross formed by stars in the sky of Migné, near Tours during a mission sermon in 1826 (Anon. 1827; Delcourt 1830; Langlois 2000), or the cloud formations seen in El Bonillo (Albacete) in 1638 (Christian 2017: 37), and in Buendía (Cuenca) in 1555, whose meaning, positive or negative, had to be discerned.[89] A kind of ur-model was the cross of Constantine, a sign (like perhaps that of Cuevas de Vinromá) meant to convert.

But in any case the notion of strange and dangerous material in the sky was very much in the air in postwar Europe. *Mediterráneo*, like newspapers throughout Spain, amply covered the A-bombs of Hiroshima and Nagasaki, the new danger they represented for mankind, and the fears that the Russians could be making them. While these fears and this coverage by no means reached the intensity and levels of those in the United States, they were

88 *Las Provincias*, Valencia, November 25 1947, 4, and, with small variants, *Diario Español*, Tarragona, November 28, 1947, 7.

89 Archivo Diocesano de Cuenca Inquisición, Legajo 202, Exp. 2292: "Toca a la cruz que dizen que vieron en el cielo" (About the cross they say they saw in the sky).

manifest in other news as well. During the wars, V-2 rockets, referred to in the Spanish press as "flying bombs," cropped up in reports of presumably Russian rockets being seen overflying Switzerland, Sweden and Finland. These reports, in turn fed into the small notices mentioning flying saucers that appeared, almost incidentally, in *Mediterráneo* starting in 1947. Symptomatic is a humorous notice in *Mediterráneo* about "Voices from the sky" in Waukesha, Wisconsin, describing the town's disquiet when an airplane with a powerful loudspeaker was the source of a public announcement.[90]

Arthur Koestler's *Darkness at Noon* (English edition 1940, Spanish edition 1947), from which we have borrowed the English title, was perhaps the most widely read novel about totalitarianism. The title made reference to passages in Matthew (27:45) and Luke (23:44) of a darkness that came over the land during the crucifixion. This darkness, for Koestler and his readers, became a metaphor of the shadow of totalitarianism (not only of the Soviet Union, but of Fascism as well) over Europe. On a different level it addresses many of the issues present in the massive response to the visions of the girl of Cuevas de Vinromá.

Armed Truce, the classic history of the beginnings of Cold War by Hugh Thomas, has no entries in its extensive index for Portugal, Spain, the Vatican, Pius XII or Fátima. In its southern European and Catholic form, the Cold War began earlier than it is generally supposed, and included a surprising protagonism of children. The elicitation of personal testimony and a review of the regional press and cinema publicity reaffirms the plausibility of connections between the child visions of postwar Spain, the division of Spain as evidenced by the Civil War, a postwar spiritual reexamination and revival, and the wider projection of the global danger of international communism.

90 *Mediterráneo*, September 17, 1947, 2.

BIBLIOGRAPHY

Anon. 1827. *Rapports sur l'apparition d'une croix dans la paroisse de Migné, présentés à monseigneur l'Evêque de Poitiers et imprimés par son ordre*. Poitiers: Barbier.

Anon. 1926. "Cuevas de Vinromá. Bendición del Banderín del Somaten." *Boletín Oficial de los Somatenes Armados de la 5ª Región* (Zaragoza) 3 (20): 4-7.

Anon. 1944. "Casi todas las diócesis españolas están ya consagradas al Corazón de la Virgen." *Iris de Paz*, 2132: 322-324.

Ballester Querol, María Carmen. 1997. "Recuerdo de mis vivencias en el 'Miracle de Les Coves.'" *Tossal Gros* (Les Coves de Vinromà) 52: 34.

Barnadas Rodríguez, Ramón. 2017. *Jaume Calafell i Pifarré (1917-1986): mig secle de fotografia*. Tàrrega: Ajuntament de Tàrrega.

Barreto, José. 2016. "I messaggi di Fatima tra anticomunismo, religiosità popolare e riconquista cattolica." *Memoria e Ricerca* 53 (3): 395-420.

Bover, José María, SJ. 1943. *El mensaje de Fátima y la consagración al Inmaculado Corazón de María*. Barcelona: Balmesiana.

Bueso Boira, Javi. 2019. "II República: conflicte, revolució i Guerra Civil a les Coves de Vinromà, 1931-1938. Posguerra a Les Coves de Vinromà." [Comunicaciós Jornades Culturals a Les Coves de Vinromà, Octubre, 2018]. Les Coves de Vinromà: Associació Cultural Tossal Gros.

Calvo Segarra, José. 2015. *El misterio de El Miracle de Les Coves*. Vinaros: Antinea.

Castro, José de. 1943. *Apariciones de la Santísima Virgen en Fatima. Historia documentada, datos biográficos de los tres videntes Lucia de Jesús, Francisco y Jacinto Marto, y milagros ocurridos en la Cueva de Iria*. Sevilla: Editorial Católica Española.

Christian Jr., William A. 1992. *Moving Crucifixes in Modern Spain*. Princeton: Princeton University Press.

Christian Jr., William A. 1996. *Visionaries: The Spanish Republic and the Reign of Christ*. Berkeley: University of California Press.

Christian Jr., William A. 1999 [orig. 1984]. "Religious Apparitions and the Cold War in Southern Europe." In *Religión y símbolos*. Special issue *Zainak, Cuadernos de Antropologia-Etnografia*, edited by Roldán Jimeno Aranguren 18: 55-86 <www.euskomedia.org/PDFAnlt/zainak/18/18065086.pdf>.

Christian Jr., William A. 2017. *The Stranger, the Tears, the Photograph, the Touch: Divine Presence in Spain and Europe since 1500*. Budapest: Central European University Press.

Cruañas i Tor, Josep. 1991. "Fotografs: Jaume Calafell i Pifarré." *Capçalera, Revista del Col. legi de Periodistes de Catalunya* 20: 46-48.

Delcourt, Adolphe. 1830. *Voyage à Migné ou recueil de faits et de témoignages concernant l'apparition miraculeuse de la croix à Migné*. Lille: L. Lefort.

Del Río, María José. 2002. "Eucaristía y vecindad. Las procesiones parroquiales de Madrid en la Edad Moderna." In *Integrazione ed emarginazione. Circuiti e modelli: Italia e Spagna nei secoli xv-xviii*, edited by L. Barletta, 128-163. Naples: CUEN.

Del Río, María José. 2010. "Rituals of the Viaticum: Dynasty and Community in Habsburg Madrid." In *Exploring Cultural History: Essays in Honour of Peter Burke*, edited by M. Calaresu, F. De Vivo and J. P. Rubiés, 55-75. Aldershot: Ashgate.

Ediciones Bistagne. 1946. *La Canción de Bernadette: argumento de la película*. Barcelona: Ediciones Bistagne. Ediciones especiales cinematográficas.

Escoi Nos, Angelita and Antoni Panadés. 2014. "Mes sobre el miracle de les coves." *Tossal Gros* (Les Coves de Vinromà) 157: 23-25. (Orig. pub. in *Tot Parc*).

Forcada Comins, Vicente. 1997. *Biografia. Padre Emilio Sauras García*. Valencia: Provincia Dominicana de Aragón.

González Devis, Raúl. 2016. *Tragèdies silenciades: Repressió franqista i maquis a les comarques del nord del país valencià*. Valencia: Universitat Jaume I.

Kane, Paula M. 2008. "Jews and Catholics Converge: *The Song of Bernadette* (1943)." In *Catholics in the Movies*, edited by Colleen McDannell, 83-105. Oxford: Oxford University Press.

Koestler, Arthur. 1940. *Darkness at Noon* (trans. D. Hardy). London: Jonathan Cape.

Koestler, Arthur. 1947. *El cero y el infinito* (trans. E. Serrano Balanyà). Barcelona: Ediciones Destino.

Langlois, Claude. 2000. "La conjoncture mariale des années 'quarante.'" In *La Salette. Apocalypse, pèlerinage et littérature (1856-1996)*, edited by François Angelier and Claude Langlois, 21-38. Grenoble: Jérôme Millon.

Marco Merenciano, Francisco. 1949. *Tres ensayos psicológicos*. Valencia: Editorial Metis.

Marques, Tiago Pires. 2017. "Experiencing Religion and Medicine: Marian Apparition and Victim Souls in Portugal, 1910-1950." In *Sign or Symptom? Exceptional Corporeal Phenomena in Religion and Medicine in the Nineteenth and Twentieth Centuries*, edited by Tine Van Osselaer, Henk de Smaele and Kaat Wils, 141-162. Leuven: Leuven University Press.

Martínez de Antoñana, Gr., CMF. 1943. *El mensaje de Fátima y el culto al Corazón de Maria*. Madrid: Coculsa.

Martínez de Antoñana, Gr., CMF. 1947 [1st ed. 1943]. *La gran promesa de los primeros sábados del mes*. 7th ed. Madrid: Coculsa.

Porcar Orihuela, Juan Luis. 2016. *Un país en gris i negre. Memòria històrica i repressió franquista a Castelló*. 2nd ed. Castelló: Universitat Jaume I.

Pujadas, Tomás Luis, CMF. 1981. *El Padre Postius: un hombre para la iglesia*. Barcelona: Editorial Claret.

Ribera, Luis, CMF. 1943. *Fátima y el Corazón de María*. Barcelona: Gráficas Claret.

Rigoberto de la Trinidad. 1947. "San Juan de la Cruz y las visiones." *Mediterráneo*, November 23: 3.

Sauras, Emilio, OP. 1947. "Cuevas de Vinromá: Carta abierta a un posible testigo de cosas maravillosas." *Levante*, November 15: 4.

Scheer, Monique. 2009. "Taking Shelter under Mary's Mantle: Marian Apparitions in the Early Cold War Years, 1947-1953." In *The "Vision Thing": Studying Divine Intervention*, edited by William A. Christian Jr. and Gábor Klaniczay, 159-218. Budapest: Collegium Budapest Institute for Advanced Study.

Scheer, Monique. 2012. "Catholic Piety in the Early Cold War Years, or How the Virgin Mary Protected the West from Communism." In *Cold War Cultures: Perspectives on Eastern and Western European Societies*, edited by Annette Vowinckel, Marcus M. Payk and Thomas Lindenberger, 129-151. New York: Berghahn Books.

Solanes, Felipe SJ. n.d. (c. 1945). *Fátima y Rusia*. [Colección Popular Fomento Social, no. 39]. Barcelona: Edit. Vicente Ferrer.

Suevia Films. 1951. La Señora de Fátima [color publicity brochure]. N.p.: Suevia Films Cesareo González.

Thomas, Hugh. 1986. *Armed Truce: The Beginnings of the Cold War 1945-46*. London: Hamish Hamilton.

Torres, Gonzalo, CMF. 1943. *El milagro de Fátima: videntes, visiones y secretos*. Madrid: Coculsa.

Warner Brothers. 1952. *Warner Bros presenta El Mensaje de Fátima en Warnercolor*. N.p.: Warner Brothers.

Zurdo, Manuel, CMF. 1943. "Movimiento consagracionista de las diócesis españolas." *Iris de Paz* 2108: 242-247.

7 APPARITIONS OF THE MOTHER OF GOD IN SOCIALIST POLAND IN THE EARLY YEARS OF THE COLD WAR

AGNIESZKA HALEMBA & KONRAD SIEKIERSKI

This chapter concerns apparitional events in socialist Poland during the first decades of communist rule (1945-1960). It is conceived as an initial step towards analysis of such events in socialist countries, a task which up to now has not received much academic attention. As the very composition of this volume shows, more academic effort has been devoted to investigating apparitions of the Virgin Mary on the capitalist side of the Iron Curtain (see also Christian 1964; Margry 2009; Scheer 2006 and 2009). Polish scholars who have recently researched miracles in the Polish People's Republic, have likewise pointed to a shortage of studies on this topic (Bączek 2014: 279; Krzywosz 2016: 13).[1]

1 Only the miracle in Lublin in 1949 inspired a considerable number of studies (e.g. Krzywoń 2016, Magier 2016, Mazur 2005, Przytuła 1999, Szulc 2009, Ziółek & Przytuła 1999). As for other similar events, the pioneering work of Andrzej Hemka and Jacek Olędzki (1990) has been more recently followed by Hubert Czachowski's (2003) study on apparitions in Radymno, where Jadwiga Bartel was an active visionary from 1948 to 1993. Ariel Zieliński (2004) wrote a book on Kazimierz Domański in Oława, a man who received visions and messages from the Mother of God for almost twenty years starting in 1983. Maciej Krzywosz (2016) published a monograph on apparitions in Zabłudów in 1965, where the visionary was Jadwiga Jakubowska. These works are complemented by a few articles focused mainly on state policies towards miraculous events and based on the archives of the Institute of National Remembrance (e.g. Bączek 2014; Kaliski 2017; Sychowicz 2004). There are virtually no works on apparitions in the Polish People's Republic in languages other than Polish. To the best of our knowledge, a similar situation obtains for other former socialist countries, a least for literature published until 2017.

A variety of reasons can account for this situation. On the one hand, researchers in many post-socialist countries were only recently allowed access to communist archives. On the other, it could be assumed that atheistic regimes prevented such events from obtaining any broader social significance. Moreover, the apparitional and miraculous events that received wider publicity in the early years of socialist Poland usually did not result in such rich and politically charged visions or narratives as those on the capitalist side of the Iron Curtain. For example, Monique Scheer writes that at Heroldsbach in Western Germany in 1949 the seers "had visions of soldiers in close combat, the one side dressed in brown, the other in black. The men in brown went into the houses of the village and brought out the old people, the women and children, and shot them point blank" (Scheer 2009: 205; see also Scheer 2006 for detailed descriptions). In the visions of Mary Ann Van Hoof, which started in 1950 at Necedah, Wisconsin, the Virgin Mary showed her a "Brown Bear" (i.e. Russian) submarines along the American coast, and warned her of food, water, and soil poisoning that could have weakened the "minds and wills of the American people and made them amenable to the work of evil forces" (Zimdars-Swartz 1991: 261; see also Kselman, this volume). Researchers have interpreted such accounts as part of a "culture of fear", which characterized the early years of the Cold War in the West (Christian 1999; Scheer 2009: 201).

Similar cases in the postwar Soviet Bloc were rare. A few notable exceptions include the apparitions in Seredne (Ukraine) and Turzovka (Slovakia) in the 1950s. In Seredne, the messages of the Virgin Mary evoked apocalyptic images and militant rhetoric, which strongly criticized the Soviet regime as the personification of evil. This led to the creation of the *Pokutnyky* (Penitents) sect, which denounced both the Soviet and Catholic authorities, and awaited the end of the world (Hurkina 2014: 9; cf. Naumescu 2006; Prytula 2002). In Turzovka, the visionary Matúš Lašut saw a series of maps of the world that gradually changed color. These visions were interpreted as a presage of the further spread of communism.

Apparitional and miraculous events in the first two postwar decades of state socialism in Poland seem focused instead on the relations between various this-worldly powers – the socialist state, the Catholic Church, different factions of Catholic believers, and the general public. We do not claim that Polish visionaries did not receive any divine messages at all that played on emotions related to the political situation. Still the divinely induced content of most such events was quite simple: lights that formed a human silhouette, a few words of the Virgin Mary, a weeping image or figure, or a bleeding cross. Even when messages from the Mother of God were more complex – as in the case of the apparition in Mazury in 1949, which we will discuss in more detail below – their content was not the aspect that drew the most attention or that was most remembered. For pilgrims, anticipation of or curiosity about divine intervention served as an initial trigger to visit places where "the transcendent broke into time" (Orsi 2008: 12). Once they were there, the pilgrims' main focus of interest quickly shifted to the tensions that were playing out between the state apparatus, the Catholic Church, and believers. Consequently, the "Brown Bears" and the soldiers in the visions on the Western side of the Iron Curtain were seen in real life by pilgrims on the Soviet side. They were the actual actors in the confrontations that took place on the streets and in the fields around the apparition sites and in the narratives that were developed afterwards.

During the period of late socialism (from the late 1960s onwards, according to Yurchak 2005), and especially since the beginning of the 1980s, visions and messages of the Virgin Mary became more intricate on the socialist side of the Iron Curtain. Researchers have thus far focused on the apparitions in Medjugorje in Bosnia-Herzegovina, which started in 1981 and continue to this day (Barbato et al. 2012; Claverie 2003; Jurkovich & Gesler 1997; Skrbiš 2005, 2007; Vukonić 1992; Zimdars-Swartz 1991). In Poland, the best-known apparitions of this period began in 1983 in Oława and were followed by events in Chotyniec, Okonin, and Wykrot, which coincided with the collapse of the Soviet Bloc (Czachowski 2003; Krzywosz 2016: 121ff; Zieliński 2004). Maciej Krzywosz has underlined, however, that even in Oława, where the visionary received many detailed messages, there is hardly any politically charged content, other than the Virgin Mary's simple statement that she was not calling upon people to fight the regime. In his opinion, the apparitions in Oława were not perceived as being directly linked to the socio-political situation. Instead, pilgrims focused on miraculous healings and on miracles such as bleeding crosses or light phenomena, which had much more profound social significance than the content of the apparitional messages (Krzywosz 2016: 122).

In this chapter, we focus on the apparitions that took place during the first fifteen years of communist rule in Poland, with special attention to the events in Lublin in 1949, Mazury in 1949, and Warsaw in 1959. Drawing on the latter example, we argue that the apparitions and miracles only in recent years have become part of the dominant historical discourse of "opposition to communism". This is followed by an analysis of the apparition in Mazury, the first one to trigger a full-scale prevention campaign by the communist authorities.[2] In the last section, based on the example of the Lublin miracle, we analyze the attitudes of the Catholic Church in Poland towards miraculous events in the early years of communist rule.

2 Bączek (2014: 248) lists this prevention campaign as the chronologically first one in his study of apparitions in Poland between 1946 and 1953, based on archival materials from the Institute of National Remembrance (IPN). According to oral materials collected by Siekierski, a similar campaign was also launched in reaction to a miracle in nearby Lipnica, which started right before the events in Mazury.

Apparitions in socialist Poland and the discourse of "opposition to communism"

On September 21, 2017, the Polish Radio Channel 1 broadcasted a radio drama called "Miracle at Nowolipki".[3] Based on witness accounts and archival materials, the play starts with the sound of a typewriter in the background and a voice which tells the listener that fourteen years after the end of the Second World War, six years after the death of Stalin, and three years after the 1956 mass protests, the year 1959 was relatively uneventful. However, the situation changed dramatically on October 7, when a Marian silhouette appeared on the roof of the bell tower of St. Augustine's church on Nowolipki Street in Warsaw. This apparition attracted thousands of people who besieged the church for around two weeks. The main protagonists of the radio play are Krystyna, who is five months pregnant, her mother, and Krystyna's husband Wiktor – an employee of the internal Security Service (*Służba Bezpieczeństwa*).[4] Krystyna's mother is not pleased with a son-in-law who reads and reports on other people's mail for a living, and who did not marry her daughter in church. In the opening dialogue, the mother tells Krystyna about the Marian apparition at Nowolipki and about the news circulating in the city that crowds of people are praying while the police (MO, *Milicja Obywatelska*) are trying to decide whether to join the praying or follow orders to disperse the crowds. While mother and daughter talk, Wiktor sits in his office and writes reports on the letters that people send to their families and friends all over Poland, spreading the news about the miracle.[5] The play then turns to the Security Service's negotiations with the parish priest and the repeated attempts of state functionaries to paint over the church roof so as to prevent any further light phenomena. In the final scenes, Krystyna accompanies her mother to see the miracle with her own eyes, but she gets caught up in the tumult caused by the police and ends up in hospital. When she wakes up, her husband tells her that he has decided to give up his job at the Security Service, and that he is going to ask a priest to marry them and baptize their children. Krystyna says that even if for some people the silhouette on the church tower was just a reflection of the sun, for her the miracle has happened on this day.

3 "Cud na Nowolipkach," <https://www.polskieradio.pl/7/5609/Artykul/1767326,Cud-na-Nowolipkach-Premiera-w-Jedynce>, directed by Andrzej Mastalerz, accessed on December 7, 2017.

4 In 1956, the Office of Security (UB, *Urząd Bezpieczeństwa*) was restructured and received the name of Security Service (SB, *Służba Bezpieczeństwa*). As this change is not crucial for our argument, we have used the name SB throughout our chapter.

5 Such reports can be found in the archives of the National Institute of Remembrance. For example, in a secret report dated October 13, 1959, the SB summarized the content of 320 letters, and in a secret report from October 16, 1959 – 262 letters mentioning the miracle in Nowolipki ("Opracowania Biura "C" Ministerstwa SW dotyczące cudów w latach 1945-1963", file: IPN BU 01283/527/J, microfilm signature: V14-14A-3).

"Miracle at Nowolipki" serves here not only to illustrate the miraculous appearance that happened in 1959. Aired in 2017 it indicates that apparitions and other miracles, which took place under socialism, have gained an important position in discourses on the memory of communism in present Poland (e.g. Chełmiński 2014; Dąbrowski 2012; Nesterowicz 2014; Reszka & Bielesz 2015 [2009]; Szczesiak 1998). We argue that apparitions and other miraculous events have become in present Poland a part of the memorialization of socialist rule as a time of widespread "opposition to communism"; a narrative, which presents the opposition between the Polish people (*naród*) and the state apparatus as the basic characteristic of life under state socialism.

Agnieszka Pasieka (2015) has noted that since the mid-1980s, "resistance" and "subversion" have become critical axes of analysis within the social sciences in general. She has pointed out that scholars have played an important role in romanticizing, idealizing, or even crafting forms of resistance, seeing them in practically every action, from participating in manifestations, to going to work or to the hairdresser's (Pasieka 2015: 7-8). According to Pasieka, this approach oversimplifies and distorts the past. Instead, our understanding of events under communism "has to be based on unearthing and analyzing complex or even disquieting dependencies between discourses and practices of 'dominating' and 'dominated'" (Pasieka 2015: 8).

At first glance, there are many good reasons to analyze apparitional events in terms of subversive practices. Clashes between police, other agents of the state, and pilgrims, as well as the arrests of visionaries and the destruction of sacred sites constructed around the place where the miracle happened, are the main focus of archival materials and publications to date. Yet it is important to remember that archival materials are mostly composed of reports by state security agents, whose main task was to establish control over the events. Both popular and academic publications produced in recent years were equally focused on the socialist state's attempts to suppress the events and on the believers' efforts to keep them alive. There is a specific mutual reinforcement of the available materials and the kind of interpretations they have received in post-1989 Poland (e.g. Dąbrowski 2012; Krzywosz 2016).

As Czesław Robotycki wrote in his essay on the memory of the Polish People's Republic, "black-white schemes are not enough here to understand the country's fate and the motivations of its inhabitants" (2003: 66).[6] It is true that the communist regime rejected and suppressed events that countered its secular or even atheist ideology. Consequently, participation in Marian apparitions could be dangerous and pilgrims had to take into consideration possible po-

6 At present, in Polish historiography one observes a beginning of an important debate concerning the sociological aspects of the introduction of the communist rule, in which this dominant narrative on the basic opposition between the communists (who are usually presented as agents of foreign, namely Soviet, power and almost never called "Polish") and the Polish society, is challenged. See, for example: Fidelis 2015; Leder 2014; Zaremba 2012.

lice violence. It is also true that state attempts to reject and ridicule miraculous events at times produced exactly the opposite effect. This was the case, for instance, in Olsztyn in 1956, when an irreverent press article entitled "Only for Fools" (*Tylko dla głupców*) about a girl who was paralyzed after removing a cross from a wall, was taken seriously and sparked great interest among believers (Dziurok 2007: 37-38). In a similar vein, the apparitions in Oława received much more publicity after they were criticized by Wojciech Jaruzelski, the then leader of the communist government. However this does not mean that people were motivated to visit sites of apparitions because they opposed communism. Rather, the fact that authorities challenged and rejected miraculous events was interpreted by some as an indication that "something was actually going on."

As Bartosz Kaliski wrote in his insightful article on the 1959 events in Warsaw, the gatherings at apparition sites "were extraordinarily pluralistic: there were the sceptics interested in the natural source of the phenomenon, the onlookers, who did not offer any judgement or opinion, and the devoted pilgrims, convinced that, although they could not see the Virgin Mary, the light was surely a sign from Her" (2017: 45). Thus, to analyze these gatherings simply as cases of subversion to communist rule, or as "weapons of the weak," in James Scott's (1985) terms, would be to greatly reduce the variety of participants' attitudes and motivations. Furthermore, even if we use a broad definition of opposition and resistance, the apparitional events under communism cannot be described as Scott's "weapons of the weak" because they were not part of everyday life. Miracles were extraordinary events, which suddenly appeared in public space, triggering violent reactions from the state apparatus. As we show in the section on the role of the Catholic Church in apparitions, they can be understood as emerging from below. During these events, negotiations concerning the role of religion in socialist Poland took place between at least three parties: the state apparatus, the believers, and the organisational Church, none of which was a monolith.

Useful clues for alternative interpretations can be found, for example, in the works of Angie Heo (2012) and Galina Lindquist (2000). Heo, who has investigated apparitions of the Virgin Mary in predominantly Muslim cities in Egypt, has interpreted them as intercessory images, which bring particular issues to the fore. We refer to her work because of her focus on apparitions as time-spaces where particular groups and problems are made visible through simple images, without explicit ideological messages conveyed in words or complex visions. The apparitions Heo has analyzed took the form of figures of light that appeared above church buildings. They made the presence of Coptic Christianity visible. They also created spaces for negotiation between members of various ethnic and religious communities, whose attitudes towards these events cannot be seen as a simple function of various group identities.

Lindquist has analyzed the activities of so-called *magi* and other kinds of clairvoyants in post-Soviet Russia in terms of hope, which she has defined as "ungrounded faith in good outcomes" (2000: 317). Lindquist's clairvoyants strove to help their clients find orientation in an environment they perceived as unpredictable, where trust was difficult to establish. In this case, the relationship between an aspiring business(wo)man and a magus was not conceived as a way to change circumstances, to secure a desired outcome, or to allow for establishing trust, which Lindquist has defined as a strong conviction that there are people and/or institutions upon whom or which one can rely (2000: 318-319). Rather, according to Lindquist, people had recoursed to magi because the latter gave their clients a shimmer of hope that they would be fine in the complex and dangerous environment of free market reality in Russia, which its participants experienced as unknown, strange, and new. Contact with magi did not necessarily cause people to act differently, or to break with their usual way of dealing with life; instead, it helped people to feel differently. The magi gave people the hope that, despite difficult circumstances, they would be fine in those fields of life that were important to them.

These kinds of analysis provide an alternative way of interpreting apparitional events in the early years of socialist Poland. These early events can be seen as one way of dealing with and functioning in an environment that was new, that altered the familiar way of life, and that seemed potentially dangerous, but also potentially empowering. If we approach miracles and apparitions from this perspective, they resemble sparks of hope, not in the sense of an escape into the religious to avoid the dangers and challenges of life (see Jastrząb 1998, as quoted in Kaliski 2017: 30), but in the sense of creating a space in which ways of relating to a new reality can be renegotiated.

Apparition sites tended to be spaces of interaction: every action of one of the parties involved generated a response from another group. People could walk through forests when roads were blocked, secretly dig out holy wells previously destroyed by state functionaries, ignore calls to disperse and return home, or even clash with police. Parish priests could follow the orders of state organs to deny the supernatural character of the events, or keep silent. Often, the most dramatic events associated with the apparitions were not the ones evoked in visions, but those that actually took place around the apparition sites. The radio play about the apparition at Nowolipki supports this proposition. In the end, Wiktor quits his job at the State Security service and goes to see the priest because of what happened to his wife as a result of police provocation when she wanted to witness the miracle.

Apparition in Mazury, 1949

The events in Mazury and Lublin are important as they are part of the largest wave of apparitions in communist Poland in 1949-1950. SB registered 280 such events during this period. In comparison, only 20 apparitions were registered in the year before (1948) and 15 in the year after (1951) (Bączek 2014: 280).[7] Moreover, to quote the words used in the ministerial report, the apparitions of 1949 were characterized by a high level "of mass participation and militancy" (Bączek 2014: 280). Thus it would not be an exaggeration to call 1949-1950 "the time of apparitions". The apparitions included instances where the Mother of God appeared herself, where her image materialized on windows, roofs or trees, and where already existing images wept (at times tears of blood) or showed other "signs of life".[8] In the SB's documents any such event, regardless of its specific form, was classified as "alleged miracle" (*rzekomy cud*) or simply "miracle" ("*cud*", with quotation marks).

In this section, we offer a detailed discussion of the June 1949 apparition near the village of Mazury in what was then the Rzeszów voivodeship.[9] In contrast to the miracles in Lublin in 1949 and Warsaw in 1959, the apparition in Mazury has not been described in earlier scholarly literature on miraculous events in communist Poland, with the exception of a brief mention in Bączek's article (2014: 284).[10] Furthermore, this apparition is a telling case for at least three reasons. For a start, it was among the first events of this kind in com-

7 Despite these numbers, no reliable statistics exist today regarding either the total number of such events in communist Poland or the frequency of their different forms. The scale of the problem is well exemplified by the fact that whereas the central state administration registered 280 'miracles' for 1949-1950 in the entire country (Bączek 2014: 280), the Provincial Office of Public Security in Lublin qualified as such more than a hundred events in a single voivodeship in July 1949 alone (Bączek 2014: 288). Another illustrative case is that of the ministerial statistics for the years 1964-1970, which contain twenty records, but exclude, for example, the miracle in Lubenia in 1969, which produced hundreds of pages of reports, letters and other documents on the level of the provincial administration of the Rzeszów voivodeship.

8 The events recorded by the SB also include miracles related to other figures venerated by the Catholic Church, but it is safe to say that an overwhelming majority of them were apparitions of the Mother of God.

9 Currently Podkarpacie voivodeship.

10 Our account is based on interviews with relatives of the visionary, witnesses of the apparition, and current guardians of the apparition site. These interviews were conducted by Konrad Siekierski in 2015-2017 as a part of the research project "Multisensory Religious Imageries in Selected Catholic Shrines in South-Eastern Poland," headed by Dr. Magdalena Lubańska and financed by the National Science Centre (decision no. DEC-2013/11/B/HS3/01443). These oral materials were backed by a series of articles in the local press written by a resident of Mazury, Benedykt Popek (1999a, 1999b, 1999c, 1999d, 2009), the unpublished notes of Jan Boguń (an uncle of the visionary), and archival materials from the Institute of National Remembrance and the Voivodeship Archive in Rzeszów, studied as part of the same research project.

7.1 Visionary Maria Boguń, having fallen upon the ground, communicating with the Virgin Mary during an apparition in Mazury, June 1949.
[Photo from a local information board; photographer unknown]

munist Poland to occasion decisive countermeasures by the state. Second, it offers an illustrative example of the specific interplay between the divine and anti-religious authorities. Third, unlike most other early apparitions in socialist Poland, the visionary in Mazury actually received detailed messages from the Mother of God, but these were largely lost amid the state authorities' suppressive actions and the Church's negative stance.

On June 6, 1949, the feast of Pentecost, 14-years old Maria Boguń went on a pilgrimage from Mazury to Leżajsk, the main regional Marian shrine. She got lost in the crowd, and was brought back to her companions by a woman who told her, "Tomorrow, I will come to you." The next day, in a village pasture, the same woman appeared before Maria and introduced herself as the Mother of God. During the next ten days, at around 6 p.m., Maria would make the sign of the cross, fall back on the ground, her eyes wide open, and speak with someone in Latin for about an hour. News of these encounters spread fast, and each day more people came to see the visionary. On June 15, Maria Boguń was taken to the police station for interrogation. Before 6 p.m. she was brought back to the pasture, where a crowd of some 5,000 people awaited her. Immediately after the vision, many people saw the "miracle of the sun", resembling the famous miracle in Fátima where the sun swirled and shined in different colors. The police, alarmed by the excited crowd, left the visionary and fled from the apparition site. The following day, according to the police report,

> some ten thousand people gathered in a pasture and the girl performed her tricks as before. Fr. Gołdasz from Ranižów also came to the place of the alleged miracle, and after watching the girl and her deeds asked her what

7.2 The visionary from Mazury, fourteen-years old Maria Boguń (the tall girl in the bright coat) on the spot of the apparitions, together with nine younger village girls in a posture of prayer. A mass of devotees and pilgrims waits in the background. June 1949.
[Photo from a local information board; photographer unknown]

> she saw and what she was talking about. She answered that she saw the mother of god[11] who talked to her in Latin, but she could not repeat what she said (...) Fr. Gołdasz turned to the people and told them to go back to work, because there was no miracle and the girl made it up. The people gathered did not believe him and started to flock around the girl (...) (Sprawozdanie 1949).

On June 17, before dawn, Maria Boguń was arrested. She was released only two days later after signing a statement drawn up by the Security Service saying that she would not go to the pasture anymore. As a result, pilgrims started to gather at her home. The apparitions did not continue there, but the visionary retained the gift of prophecy and answered pilgrims' questions.

While she was at home, the visionary received a visit by another priest, who came to examine the apparitions. After a few questions, he dismissed the Virgin Mary's messages that the visionary revealed to him and destroyed his notes. Due to this rejection, the only written testimony of these messages was a short note made twenty years later by Jan Boguń:

> (...) the first change will be in celebrations of the Holy Week, the second change will be shortening the fast before receiving the Eucharist from midnight of the previous day to one hour before, and, finally, the mass will be celebrated in the vernacular, here in Poland, in Polish. And she talked about many things and foretold many events which were fulfilled in the future, and then she called the nation to prayer, penance and love of one's

11 A reference almost always written with small initial letters in this kind of report.

> neighbor, and said that if the nation does not follow, it would be punished in a horrible way (...)[12]

Some other messages that the Mother of God delivered to the visionary spread by word of mouth, most were forgotten. However, witnesses remembered the prophecy that the Mother of God would come to earth and visit every home, but that some people would not accept her. Later this message was interpreted as a prophecy of the attitude of some people towards the pilgrimage of the copy of the icon of the Mother of God of Częstochowa, which was supposed to visit all the parishes in Poland between 1957 and 1980 (Popek 1999d). This tour of the best known image of the Mother of God in Poland was the stage of repeated clashes between the faithful and state authorities (Niedźwiedź 2005).

In the meantime, another miraculous event took place in the pasture in Mazury: overnight, a myrtle bush grew on the site of the apparition. While the pilgrims were gathered in the village church for the feast of the local patron saint, the Security Service came and burned the bush. Subsequently, Maria announced that everyone should take a handful of the ashes that remained from the bush and scatter them over their houses and fields for protection. A great number of people followed her advice and within a short time they dug a deep hole, from which there emerged a spring. The spring was immediately recognized as being endowed with healing powers. Beside it, the pilgrims erected two crosses. These new events brought the Security Service back to Mazury. They spread stories that Maria was mentally ill and that her family had invented the whole event to earn money. From the beginning of July, armed patrols came daily to the pasture, dispersing and threatening those who gathered there. Towards the end of the summer of 1949, the Security Service ordered the crosses removed from the apparition site. The persons who carried out this order were later said to have been suddenly struck dead. Nevertheless, as a result of these actions, and because of the absence of new apparitions, people gradually stopped visiting the site.

As we already have mentioned, the apparition in Mazury was among the first apparitions to trigger serious countermeasures by the State Security forces. These included a wide range of strategies and actions: the blockade of access to the apparition site and its destruction, the use of physical force against believers, arrests, interrogation, threats and administrative persecutions of the visionary and the supporters of the miracle, and finally, the use of pro-

12 Excerpt from a notebook of Jan Boguń, written around 1970. He was an uncle of the visionary, who lived with him at the time of apparition. For several decades after the events of 1949, he was also a guardian of the apparition site. This rough translation of a text, which was not written in grammatically or orthographically correct Polish, is our own. Starting from the late 1980s, a more detailed account of the messages delivered to Maria Boguń was created by Benedykt Popek, who interviewed many eyewitnesses of the apparitions, including Jan Boguń (Popek 1999a,b,c,d).

paganda to ridicule and discredit the event. While before 1949 state functionaries monitored and documented similar events but took only limited action against them (Bączek 2014: 281), the methods tested and proved in Mazury were later used against most of the miraculous events that attracted the attention of the state authorities.

It is also important to note a kind of interplay that developed at Mazury between the divine and believers on the one hand, and the state authorities on the other. A whole chain of actions and responses can be observed: Maria receives visions in the pasture – Maria is not allowed to go there – a myrtle bush grows on the place of the apparition – the myrtle bush is burned – ashes are endowed with power to protect homes, and a healing spring emerges where the myrtle bush used to grow – religious symbols are removed from around the spring – those who remove them receive divine punishment. Another example of such interplay can be identified at Nowolipki in Warsaw, where Hemka and Olędzki noted the following remark by one of the believers: "Today, the Mother of God is dressed in dark, because more of them [police forces] have come here" (Hemka & Olędzki 1990: 10). When the authorities ordered to cover the church tower with black paint, "on the next day [the paint] was washed off by the rain. Needless to say, this occurrence only enhanced people's faith in the divine power that protects the church and precludes the actions of the State Security" (Chełmiński 2014). These examples show that at least some of the miraculous events in the early years of socialist Poland followed a kind of dialectic in which successive sacralizations and desacralizations of space served as tools to negotiate not only the future of a given apparition site, but also a place of religious practice under socialism in general.

Finally, in contrast to most other similar events in the early years of communist Poland, the apparitions in Mazury contained rather detailed and elaborate messages from the Mother of God. However, they did not include any direct political messages related to the rise of communist power. Moreover, they were not written down until many years later, since state repression precluded any group of supporters of the visionary to emerge that could have freely disseminated these messages among believers. There was also a lack of interest on the part of the Church hierarchy. As a result, little importance was given to the messages delivered to Maria Boguń and their content has been largely lost. This example points once again to the fact that in the early years of communist Poland, the tensions that apparitions produced between the faithful, the Church, and the state, that were apparent through the repeated erection and damaging of sacred sites, the closing and opening of churches, the arrival and dispersal of pilgrims, prevailed over the significance of the content of the visions themselves.

The Catholic Church in the Polish People's Republic and the apparitional events

Relations between the Catholic Church on various levels (laity, clergy, hierarchy) and the socialist state were by no means straightforward – depending on the particular issue at hand, the Church was treated by the state apparatus as an enemy, as a nuisance, but also as a potential ally (Dudek & Gryz 2006; Żaryn 2005). Moreover, various factions within the Church, understood both as a religious organization and as a community of believers, had varied attitudes vis-à-vis the socialist state.

In 1949, the socialist state undertook serious steps towards the subjugation of the Catholic Church to the new political order. On March 14, the Polish government released a statement, published widely in the media, accusing the Church of anti-state activities in favor of "Anglo-American imperialism" (Poksiński 1992). This was the beginning of a formidable anti-clerical campaign by the government, which included attempts to divide the Church from within. The government supported the activities of so-called "patriotic priests", who accepted the new communist powers and declared loyalty to the socialist state. Gradually, many Catholic organizations were taken over by such priests, while legal charges were filed against other members of the clergy. The situation further deteriorated when on July 1 the Vatican Congregation of the Holy Office published its *Decree against Communism*, which declared that Catholics who professed communist doctrines were excommunicated as apostates from the Christian faith.

Yet as soon as 1950, an agreement was reached between the Polish episcopate and the socialist authorities in which the Church condemned all kinds of anti-state activity and the underground anticommunist movement, in exchange for leaving religious education in schools untouched, the right to organize pilgrimages, and other privileges (Musiał n.d.). Neither side respected the agreement wholeheartedly; thus in the same year the state confiscated monastic property, and religious education in schools was abolished a decade later. Moreover, part of the clergy accused Stefan Wyszyński, the Polish Primate from 1948 to 1981, of signing a "shameful and unrealistic" document. Nevertheless, both communist authorities and the Church were avoiding open confrontations. In Jan Żaryń's words, "The Polish Church hierarchy (...) looked upon priests who got involved in contacts with the authorities with disapproval, but it was also very skeptical about priests who were close to placing the interest of the widely understood political, legal and underground opposition above that of the Church" (2005: 34).

These complex relations between the Church and the state were also visible in responses to the apparitions. Krzywosz has claimed that "in order to survive communist times," the Church "relied on popular religiosity, the dominating element of which was and is a devotion to the Mother of God" (2016: 95). At the same time, however, the Church did not support Marian apparitions, which were an important feature of this devotion. In turn, during the first years of the communist regime, the state authorities regarded miraculous events as "a form of the hostile activities of clergy" (quoted from Bączek 2014: 280), by means of which the Church tried to defend its position. In the post-Stalinist era (from the mid-1950s onwards), the SB's approach became more nuanced: while its functionaries continued to investigate the priests' engagement in apparitions, they accepted the possibility that miraculous events could appear without the inspiration or participation of the clergy.[13] Moreover, they expected and urged Church representatives to publicly dismiss such events in order to calm believers.

An illustrative case is the miracle in Lublin (*cud lubelski*) in 1949, which "for years defined the fears of the Church regarding similar events" (Krzywosz 2016: 96). On July 3, a copy of the icon of the Mother of God of Częstochowa in the cathedral church of Lublin began to weep tears of blood. The miracle occurred just before the fifth anniversary of the proclamation of the Polish Committee for National Liberation, which was celebrated in socialist Poland as the beginning of communist rule. This miracle attracted mass attention, and after a week the cathedral square was packed with twenty thousand people, who waited for hours to approach the icon. Stories of miraculous healings and conversions ignited a general religious exaltation that for a while could not be controlled either by the state authorities or by the clergy. But the events soon triggered a massive response from the communist authorities: the blockade of transportation routes, a propaganda campaign, and the arrest and trial of the believers.

According to Krzywosz, the events in Lublin were met with ambivalence by the representatives of the Church. Some of them saw the tears of the Virgin Mary as "a sharp, tangible supernal sign, giving fortitude for further resistance and strengthening the faith" (Krzywosz 2016: 109). Others, however, feared the negative consequences this event might have for the Church. Local bishops established a commission, which declared that the supernatural character of the event could not be confirmed. In a letter dated July 10, they called on the faithful to refrain from visiting the place. This and subsequent calls did not produce any results, so finally, on August 8, the bishops ordered the closure of the cathedral. Soon after, the tears disappeared from the icon and the situation in Lublin calmed down (Bączek 2014; Krzywosz 2016; Mazur 2005; Przytuła 1999).

The 2017 radio play, which we described above, also provides an interesting example of the relations between communist authorities and representa-

13 For instance, one of the SB's early reports on the apparition in Zabłudów in 1965 states that "there are no signs of inspiration from the local priesthood" (Sychowicz 2004: 61).

7.3 A demonstration organized by communist authorities in July 1949 after the miracle in Lublin. The banners read: "Lublin will not be a backwater!", "We will not allow abuse of faith for political ends!", and "Down with politicians in cassocks".
[Photo by Karol Szczeciński/EAST NEWS]

tives of the Church. The dialogue featured in the play between the police functionary and the parish priest of St. Augustine's church in Warsaw can be read as an indication of the ongoing re-evaluation of the position of the Catholic Church under the communist regime in academic literature – from a vision of the Church as the most stable space of freedom and opposition under state socialist rule (Kubik 1994), to the Church as skillful negotiator interested chiefly in its own organizational survival (Pasieka 2015). The police officer in the play secretly requests that the priest should help to "end the miracle". He is asked to provide access to the roof so that it can be investigated and painted black. He is also asked to tell the people that there is no miracle, to forbid them from gathering around the church, and to close the area at 10 p.m. every day. The priest responds that he has to ask his superiors first.

The play ends there, but we know what happened next from other sources. On October 15, the Archdiocese of Warsaw issued the following statement, which was to be read in all Warsaw parishes on the following Sunday:

> After consultation with the clergy of St. Augustine's parish in Warsaw, the Metropolitan Curia declares that the light phenomena occurring in recent days on the tower of St. Augustine's Church in Nowolipki in Warsaw can be explained by natural causes. The Metropolitan Curia therefore asks that all believers keep calm, gather for religious services in their parish churches,

> and refrain from frequenting St. Augustine's Church en masse, as this disturbs the normal pastoral service there (quoted from Kaliski 2017: 40).

Still, this statement did not satisfy the state authorities, and the reaction of the Church hierarchy was judged to be too mild. On the other hand, according to Kaliski, the parish priest of St. Augustine's church, who featured in the radio play talking to the functionary, was left "without [the] support of the Curia during these days" (2017: 41). This situation shows that apparitional events presented an extremely complex situation for local clergy. At times, they may have felt abandoned amid the turmoil, with contradictory expectations and accusations coming from all sides – the Church hierarchy, the state, and the believers. In the worst-case scenario, the same priest might come under pressure from the SB for not doing enough to discredit an apparition, while at the same time being called a "communist" and an "atheist" (*bezbożnik*) by the miracle's proponents for not doing enough to support it.

A few years after the 1959 miracle at Nowolipki, the approach of the state apparatus towards apparitions was explained in a series of publications by the Ministry of Internal Affairs. These internal publications summarized the experience gained thus far by the SB in "suppressing miracles" (*zlikwidować cud*, this was the phrase used in state jargon) and provided a set of instructions concerning future similar events (Sałkowski 1970; Siemaszkiewicz & Wójcicki 1965, 1971; Zakrzewska 1966). For example, Siemaszkiewicz and Wójcicki's report praised the SB for having "strived and undertaken efforts, in all activities so far, to include clergy in the process of relieving the tensions (...). This experience shows that the appropriate engagement of the clergy in the process of denying [the miracles] plays a crucial role in bringing the situation under control" (Siemaszkiewicz & Wójcicki 1965: 13-14).

In the context of miracles and apparitions in communist Poland, little attention has been paid so far to the often reluctant and suspicious attitude of the Catholic Church towards apparitions and other miraculous events in general. Clearly, the vehemence and spontaneity characteristic of such events can undermine the authority of an organization such as the Church (cf. Halemba 2015). As a result, it has gone largely unnoticed that the conditions under which the Catholic Church operated in the Polish People's Republic created certain opportunities for dealing with unwanted apparitions which were no longer available after the fall of the communist regime, when the Church had to directly face and respond to people's yearning for the extraordinary.

A good illustration of this phenomenon is the history of the visionary Kazimierz Domański from Oława. Although his visions were rejected by the Church as early as 1986, three years after the first apparition took place, Domański continued his prophetic activities, which attracted thousands of followers up to 1999, when the local bishop imposed an interdict upon him and his supporters. This decision almost led to a schism, which was avoided mainly due to the visionary's illness and death in 2002 (Zieliński 2004). As Hubert Czachowski (2003: 10) has observed, cases like this lead "to a situation in which thousands of Polish Catholics [operate] on the verge of heresy. [...] Nonetheless, the hierarchy of the Catholic Church offers no solution to this problem." In communist times, the solution was, in a way, offered by the state, which (at least until the 1980s) took all possible steps to immediately "suppress miracles", thus to some extent relieving the Church from the obligation to take action. It is true that the Church often found itself in a difficult position between the expectations of the communist regime on the one hand, and the desires of its faithful on the other. At the same time, however, the Church could, with some maneuvering, dismiss events which the believers perceived to be miraculous without being seen by them as their main opponent, this role being reserved for the communist authorities instead.

It is telling that recent scholarly publications on Church and state relations in communist Poland often contain assertions like the following: "[The bishop's] letter [on the miracle in Lublin] has to be understood in the context of intensive pressure from the authorities on the Catholic Church" (Bączek 2014: 285), or "the Church, as if sensing that the miracle in Lublin might be instrumentalized in the fight against religion, decided to limit its scope" (Krzywosz 2016: 102). Such statements do not take into account that the Church could be genuinely unconvinced that a given event was a miracle. This kind of argumentation vindicates what might otherwise be seen as the Church's excessively careful position, suggesting that without state pressure, the Church would have acted differently with respect to the apparition in question. As such, it points to the larger social phenomenon of justifying the actions of the Catholic Church during communist times, which ultimately helped this organization build a very strong position in Polish society.

The observation that the Church's reluctance towards miracles was not only the result of pressure exerted by the communist authorities (though, surely, many decisions were influenced by them), but also reflected its own stance on apparitions is supported by the fact that the Church in post-communist Poland has continued to show little enthusiasm for such events, or for the people who try to make past apparitions a part of their religious lives today. For instance, recent attempts by a group of lay believers to revive the apparition site in Mazury have been ill-received by the local diocese, which refuses to investigate the events of 1949 and bans public liturgies at this site (Siekierski 2018: 139-140). It is also telling that the only apparition in the Polish People's Republic to be officially acknowledged and promoted by the Church in post-communist Poland is the miracle in Lublin. In 1988, the icon in Lublin cathedral was crowned, and the annual day of pardon dedicated to the Weeping Blessed Virgin Mary (*Najświętsza Maryja Panna Płacząca)* has been celebrated there on July 3 every year since 2014. Apparently, this appreciation of the miracle in Lublin was encouraged by the fact that it was the most 'ecclesiastical' apparition in communist Poland: it took place inside a cathedral, was first seen by a nun and a priest, and the tears appeared on a copy of the most venerated icon in Poland, an image of the Mother of God of Częstochowa (Niedźwiedź 2005).

Conclusions

While there was a remarkable rise on the capitalist side of the Iron Curtain of religiously inspired rhetoric against what was characterized as "godless communism", in the Soviet Bloc the situation as presented in literature seemed much quieter. In fact, it was no less intense. It certainly differed across the various countries of the region and changed overtime. There are many important threads, and this article could not unravel all of them. For example, we did not address the question of symbolic interconnections between apparitions in socialist countries and the anticommunist message of Fátima. Halemba's previous research on the underground (delegalized) activities of Greek Catholic priests in Ukraine indicates that they were important agents in spreading devotion to the Virgin of Fátima during Soviet times (Halemba 2015). Further scholarly investigation could focus on how Orthodoxy and Eastern Catholicism, which were dominant in many parts of the socialist world, shaped apparitional experiences. Eugene Clay (2017) has shown that while Marian apparitions are mainly examined in their Catholic context, the Virgin Mary also appeared in Russia and Ukraine during the October Revolution and in the period of late socialism. He has contended that Marian apparitions "naturally became an expression of opposition to a secular, atheistic political order" (Clay 2017: 29).

This article has focused on the initial years of the Cold War period in socialist Poland, where from 1949 onwards the sites of apparitions and miracles became places of direct physical confrontation between representatives of the state apparatus and believers. Yet interpreting these events simply as acts of resistance to the communist regime would subordinate our analysis to the dominant narrative of mass "opposition to communism", and ignore recent debates in anthropology concerning the concepts of resistance and subversion as analytical tools. More importantly, it would fail to take into account the specific position of apparitions and miracles in the Catholic Church. Although they are an important part of Catholic devotion, at the same time they represent both a challenge to, and an opportunity for the Church as an organization. They challenge the Church's status as the guardian of the faith and the only legitimate channel of divine intervention. Simultaneously, they provide an opportunity for religious vitalization and the development of new forms of religious devotion (Halemba 2017).

Both the Catholic hierarchy and the socialist state at times looked at such events as a stage for the credulous and the naïve, who should be managed and brought back into line. It is not surprising therefore that state agents sought – and sometimes found – help in suppressing apparitional events from the higher levels of the Church's hierarchy. There is no doubt that the Catholic Church was persecuted during socialist times, with varying force and fervor. Consequently, one could argue that the Church was impotent to support apparition events. However the Catholic Church in Poland did manage to successfully negotiate with the socialist government on several other issues. This suggests that the hierarchy's reluctance vis-à-vis apparitions and miracles was rather due to its unwillingness to intervene on behalf of the people involved.

For the pilgrims and visionaries, and for those local priests who supported the apparitions, such sites can be considered spaces where their relations with the hierarchy of the Church and the state authorities were negotiated. The apparitions created the opportunity for different forms of religiosity and religious sentiment to become visible in the public arena of a communist country. They revealed the presence of religious communities beyond the organizational Church (Heo 2012). By creating temporary spaces, apparition events to some extent made it possible to negotiate and shift certain dimensions of communist ideology, particularly its "godless" attitude. They also enabled people to feel hopeful and protected by the divine in a new and trying situation (Lindquist 2000). Finally, miraculous and apparitional events provide insight into how Christianity was practiced under socialism beyond the usual attention that is given to relations between the socialist states and the Churches as organizations.

BIBLIOGRAPHY

Barbato, Mariano, Chiara de Franco and Brigitte Le Normand. 2012. "Is There a Specific Ambivalence of the Sacred? Illustrations from the Apparition of Medjugorje and the Movement of Sant'Egidio." *Politics, Religion & Ideology* 13 (1): 53-73.

Bączek, Piotr. 2014. "Działania komunistycznego aparatu bezpieczeństwa w odpowiedzi na wydarzenia uznawane za cuda w latach 1946-1953." *Saeculum Christianum* 21: 279-290.

Chełmiński, Jakub. 2014. "Cud na Nowolipkach." Wyborcza.pl <http://wyborcza.pl/alehistoria/1,121681,15856720,Cud_na_Nowolipkach.html>.

Christian, William A. 1964. "Religious Apparitions and the Cold War in Southern Europe." In *Religion, Power and Protest in Local Communities*, edited by Eric Wolf and Herbert Lehmann, 239-266. Berlin: Mouton Publishers.

Claverie, Elisabeth. 2003. *Les guerres de lka Vierge: Une anthropologie des apparitions.* NRF Essais. Paris: Gallimard.

Clay, Eugene. 2017. "Marian Revelations in the Russian Context: The Cosmopolitics of Blessed John." *Nova Religio: The Journal of Alternative and Emergent Religions* 21 (2): 26-42.

Czachowski, Hubert. 2003. *Cuda, wizjonerzy i pielgrzymi: studium religijności mirakularnej końca XX wieku w Polsce*. Warsaw: Oficyna Naukowa.

Dąbrowski, Witold. 2012. *Cud na Nowolipkach. Objawienia w kościele św. Augustyna w 1959 roku w Warszawie*. Warsaw: Witold Dąbrowski.

Dudek, Antoni, and Ryszard Gryz. 2006. *Komuniści i Kościół w Polsce (1945-1989)*. Cracow: Wydawnictwo Znak.

Dziurok, Adam. 2007. "Meldunek 'z frontu z walki z klerem.'" *Biuletyn Instytutu Pamięci Narodowej* 4 (75): 34-39.

Fidelis, Małgorzata. 2015. *Kobiety, komunizm i industrializacja w powojennej Polsce*. Warsaw: W.A.B.

Halemba, Agnieszka. 2015. *Negotiating Marian Apparitions: The Politics of Religion in Transcarpathian Ukraine*. Budapest: CEU Press.

Halemba, Agnieszka. 2017. "Apparitional Movements as Sites of Religious Experimentation: A Case Study from Transcarpathian Ukraine." *Nova Religio. Journal of Alternative and Emergent Religions* 21 (2): 43-58.

Hemka, Andrzej, and Jacek Olędzki. 1990. "Wrażliwość mirakularna". *Polska Sztuka Ludowa* 44 (1): 8-14.

Heo, Angie. 2012. "The Virgin Made Visible: Intercessory Images of Church Territory in Egypt." *Comparative Studies in Society and History* 54 (2): 361-391.

Hurkina, Svitlana. 2014. "The Response of Ukrainian Greek-Catholics to the Soviet State's Liquidation and Persecution of their Church: 1945-1989." *Occasional Papers on Religion in Eastern Europe*, 34 (4). <http://digitalcommons.georgefox.edu/ree/vol34/iss4/1>.

Jurkovich, James M., and Wilbert M. Gesler. 1997. "Medjugorje: Finding Peace at the Heart of Conflict." *Geographical Review* 87 (4): 447-467.

Kaliski, Bartosz. 2017. "Nowolipki AD 1959, czyli cud w komunistycznej Warszawie." *Pamięć i Sprawiedliwość* 1 (29): 25-49.

Krzywosz, Maciej. 2016. *Cuda w Polsce Ludowej. Studium przypadku prywatnego objawienia maryjnego w Zabłudowie*. Białystok: Instytut Pamięci Narodowej.

Kubik, Jan. 1994. *The Power of Symbols against the Symbols of Power: The Rise of Solidarity and the Fall of State Socialism in Poland*. University Park: Pennsylvania State University Press, 1994.

Leder, Andrzej. 2014. *Prześniona rewolucja. Ćwiczenie z logiki historycznej.* Warsaw: Krytyka Polityczna.

Lindquist, Galina. 2000. "In Search of the Magic Flow: Magic and Market in Contemporary Russia." *Urban Anthropology* 29 (4): 315-357.

Magier, Dariusz. 2016. "Wokół Cudu Lubelskiego. Dwie relacje o 'jaśniejących' obrazach w powiecie radzyńskiem w lecie 1949." *Wschodni Rocznik Humanistyczny* 13: 399-412.

Margry, Peter Jan. 2009. "Marian Interventions in the Wars of Ideology: The Elastic Politics of the Roman Catholic Church on Modern Apparitions." *History & Anthropology* 20 (3): 243-263.

Mazur, Mariusz. 2005. "'Cud' lubelski na łamach prasy." *Annales Universitatis Mariae Curie-Skłodowska*, Sectio F, Historia, 60: 335-351.

Musiał, Filip. (N.d.). "Realizm Kościoła katolickiego w czasach PRL-u." *Ośrodek Myśli Politycznej*. <http://www.omp.org.pl/artykul.php?artykul=164>.

Naumescu, Vlad. 2006. *Modes of Religiosity in Eastern Christianity: Religious Processes and Social Change in Ukraine*. Münster: LIT Verlag.

Nesterowicz, Piotr. 2014. *Cudowna*. Warsaw: Dowody na Istnienie.

Niedźwiedź, Anna. 2005. *Obraz i postać. Znaczenia wizerunku Matki Boskiej Częstochowskiej*. Cracow: Wydawnictwo Uniwersytetu Jagiellońskiego.

Orsi, Robert. 2008. "Abundant History: Marian Apparitions as Alternative Modernity." *Historically Speaking* 9 (7): 12-16, 24-26.

Pasieka, Agnieszka. 2015. *Hierarchy and Pluralism: Living Religious Difference in Catholic Poland*. Basingstoke: Palgrave Macmillan.

Poksiński, Jerzy. 1992. "Przeciw Kościołowi." *Karta* 9: 137-139.

Popek, Benedykt. 1999a. "Mała Fatima Rzeszowszczyzny (cz. I.)." *Ziemia Kolbuszowska* 2 (43): 18-19.

Popek, Benedykt. 1999b. "Mała Fatima Rzeszowszczyzny (cz. II.)." *Ziemia Kolbuszowska* 3 (44): 16-17.

Popek, Benedykt. 1999c. "Mała Fatima Rzeszowszczyzny (cz. III.)." *Ziemia Kolbuszowska* 4 (45): 18-19.

Popek, Benedykt. 1999d. "Mała Fatima Rzeszowszczyzny (cz. IV.)." *Ziemia Kolbuszowska* 5 (46): 20-21.

Popek, Benedykt. 2009. "Rocznica mazurskich objawień." *Wieści Ranizowskie* 148: 14-15.

Prytula, Volodymyr. 2002. *Pokutnitskii rukh v Ukraini*. Thesis. L'viv: L'viv Theological Seminary.

Przytuła, Agnieszka. 1999. *Cud lubelski 1949: łzy, nadzieje, represje*. Lublin: Abakus.

Reszka, Paweł, and Marcin Bielesz. 2017. "Cud w Lublinie, władze zamykają miasto. Matka Boska Płacze." *Wyborcza.pl*. <http://lublin.wyborcza.pl/lublin/56,48724,20349674,cud-w-lublinie-wladze-zamykaja-miasto-matka-boska-placze-reportaz.html?disableRedirects=true>.

Robotycki, Czesław. 2003. "*Pamięć PRL*, antropolog wobec doświadczenia wlasnej kultury." *Polska Sztuka Ludowa - Konteksty* 57 (3-4): 66-70.

Sałkowski, M. 1970. *Problematyka nielegalnego budownictwa sakralnego i "cudów" oraz metod przeciwdziałania zagrożeniom występującym na tym tle w świetle Zarządzenia Ministra SW nr 0077/70 z dnia 30-07-1970 r.* Olsztyn: Komenda Wojewódzka MO, 1970, IPN BU 01522/449.

Scheer, Monique. 2006. *Rosenkranz und Kriegsvisionen: Marienerscheinungskulte im 20. Jahr--hundert*. Tübingen: Tübinger Vereinigung für Volkskunde.

Scheer, Monique. 2009. "Taking Shelter under Mary's Mantle: Marian Apparitions in the Early Cold War years, 1947-1953." In *The "Vision Thing": Studying Divine Intervention*, edited by William Christian and Gabor Klaniczay, 159-218. Budapest: Collegium Budapest.

Scott, James. 1985. *Weapons of the Weak: Everyday Forms of Peasant Resistance*. New Haven: Yale University Press.

Siekierski, Konrad. 2018. "Charismatic Renewal and Miracular Sensitivity at a Catholic Marian Apparition Site in Poland." *Catholics & Cultures: Journal of Global Catholicism* 2 (2): 124-146.

Siemaszkiewicz, Józefa, and Ryszard Wójcicki. 1965. *O niektórych problemach związanycyh z występowaniem 'cudów' i zasadach organizacji pracy operacyjnej w tego typu wydarzeniach*. IPN BU 01283/525/J, syg, mikrofilmu: V14-14A-1, Materiały Wydziału IV Departamentu Ministerstwa Spraw Wewnętrznych dotyczące cudów w latach 1964-1970.

Siemaszkiewicz, Józefa, and Ryszard Wójcicki. 1971. *Niektóre Elementy organizacji współdziałania MO i SB w zakresie zapobiegania zagrożeniom lub naruszeniom porządku publicznego wywoływanym działalnością hierarchii kościelnej i kleru*. Warsaw: Departament Szkolenia i Wydawnictw MSW, IPN Rz 0232/12/1 S.

Skrbiš, Zlatko. 2005. "The Apparitions of the Virgin Mary of Medjugorje: The Convergence of Croatian Nationalism and Her Apparitions." *Nations & Nationalism* 11 (3): 443-461.

Skrbiš, Zlatko. 2007. "From Migrants to Pilgrim Tourists: Diasporic Imagining and Visits to Medjugorje." *Journal of Ethnic & Migration Studies* 33 (2): 313–329.

Sprawozdanie. 1949. *Sprawozdanie z przebiegu rzekomego cudu w miejscowości Mazury na pastwisku*. Raniżów, 15 lipca, IPN BU 01283/527/J, syg. mikr. V14-14A-3, Opracowania Biura "C" Ministerstwa SW dotyczące cudów w latach 1945-1963.

Sychowicz, Krzysztof. 2004. "Żadnych cudów." *Biuletyn Instytutu Pamięci Narodowej* 10 (45): 60-66.

Szczesiak, Edmund. 1998. *Oni uzdrawiają. Reportaże z miejsc najgłośniejszych cudów w Polsce*. Gdańsk: Oficyna Pomorska.

Szulc, Paweł. 2009. "Jak 'cud lubelski' przyjęto na Pomorzu Zachodnim?" In *Trzebiatów – spotkania pomorskie 2008*, edited by J. Kochanowska. Pruszcz Gdański: Wydawnictwo Jasne - Trzebiatów: Trzebiatowski Ośrodek Kultury.

Vukonić, Boris. 1992. "Medjugorje's Religion and Tourism Connection." *Annals of Tourism Research* 19 (1): 79-91.

Yurchak, Alexei. 2005. *Everything Was Forever, Until It Was No More: The Last Soviet Generation*. Princeton: Princeton University Press.

Zakrzewska, A. (ed.). 1966. "(Niektóre) Problemy pracy-polityczno-operacyjnej związanej z występowaniem rzekomych cudów." *Problemy pracy polityczno-operacyjnej Ministerstwa Spraw Wewnętrznych*. Warsaw: Departament Kadr i Szkolenia, IPN BU 0423/8831 8832 8833.

Zaremba, Marcin. 2012. *Wielka Trwoga. Polska 1944-1947. Ludowa reakcja na kryzys*. Warsaw: Znak.

Żaryn, Jan. 2005. "Kościół katolicki w PRL – wybrane zagadnienia, hipotezy, prowokacje." *Pamięć i Sprawiedliwość* 1 (7): 11-34.

Zieliński, Ariel. 2004. *Na straży prawdziwej wiary. Zjawiska cudowne w polskim katolicyzmie ludowym*. Cracow: Nomos.

Zimdars-Swartz, Sandra. 1991. *Encountering Mary: From La Salette to Medjugorje*. Princeton, NJ: Princeton University Press.

Ziółek, Jan, and Agnieszka Przytuła. 1999. *Represje wobec uczestników wydarzeń w Katedrze Lubelskiej w 1949 roku*. Lublin: Towarzystwo Naukowe KUL.

8
MARIAN PIETY AND THE COLD WAR IN THE UNITED STATES

THOMAS KSELMAN

On May 28, 2017, a small crowd gathered in the small town of Necedah, Wisconsin, at the shrine of the Queen of the Holy Rosary, Mediatrix between God and Man. About fifty devotees observed a procession of forty or so, who walked through the shrine grounds to a small outdoor chapel situated in front of a large and unfinished house of prayer. After the crowd gathered around a statue of the Virgin at the center of the chapel, four young girls dressed in white became the center of attention. As the congregation sang the Marian hymn "Bring Flowers of the Rarest," one of the girls mounted a ladder to crown the statue. The crowning was followed by a prayer vigil including the recitation of the rosary and the saying of prayers, some of them written by Mary Ann Van Hoof, whose visions of Mary are the basis of the shrine.[1]

The vigil of 2017 was a distant echo of more momentous days at the shrine, when in 1950 it became a focal point for Marian devotion and Cold War patriotism. Mary Ann Van Hoof claimed she first saw the Virgin in November of 1949, followed by a series of other visions, news of which spread throughout the Midwest and beyond. A climactic moment was reached on August 15, 1950, when a crowd of 100,000 assembled at the farm of Fred and Mary Ann Van Hoof, hoping to witness a miracle that would confirm rumors and press reports that Mary had been appearing there regularly over the previous months.

1 Observation based on a visit by the author to the shrine on May 28, 2017. I would like to thank Father Joseph Redfern, pastor of St. Francis of Assisi in Necedah for the dossier he provided me on the cult. This essay incorporates material originally published in Avella & Kselman 1986.

Just before noon Mrs. Van Hoof left her house and knelt before a statue of Our Lady of Fátima erected as an improvised shrine. After a few minutes of prayer she turned to the crowd and delivered a message she had just received from the Virgin, who warned of Satanic forces threatening America, both at home and from abroad.

> The time has come, dear children of God! (...) You must all remember your Commandments, the Rosary, the Way of the Cross, for the enemy of God is all over America. You'd be surprised if the sheep's clothing were taken off – and how they'd spring up all around you – which would be the enemy of God. (...) The black clouds are coming over, not to Europe, Asia, Australia, Africa, but to America – South and North America. Alaska is the first stepping stone. (...) We have no time to lose. We must carry out now, at once, for prayer only will save us (Van Hoof 1971: 12-13).

The August pilgrimage to Necedah received national attention during the next few days. *Life* magazine published three pages of photos featuring Mrs. Van Hoof, the shrine, and the crowd of August 15 in a lead article. In *Life*, and in stories published in *Newsweek* and *The New York Times*, journalists stressed the size of the crowd, but kept their distance from assertions about supernatural events, with the *Times* commenting that "the Roman Catholic Church has officially cast doubt on the claims of the farm wife and frowned on today's demonstration."[2] Many in the crowd that day were hoping for a miracle that would confirm Mary's visits to Mrs. Van Hoof, having in mind reports of a spinning sun that some observers claim to have witnessed at Fátima, Portugal, in 1917. Although the sun kept its place, the news reports suggest that the crowd was consoled and edified by the message from Mary, which resembled similar warnings conveyed in previous apparitions to Mrs. Van Hoof. Mary made a final visit on October 7, a day that drew a smaller but still substantial crowd of 30,000. Clouds blocked the sun for much of the morning, but at noon it burst through. Heeding a call from the loudspeaker to "look at the sun," many people claimed it spun in the sky, approached the earth, and changed color (*Testimonials* 1966). This "miracle of the sun," along with numerous accounts of miraculous healings and of rosaries turning to gold convinced supporters that Mary had indeed appeared to Mrs. Van Hoof, and that her calls to prayer must be heard if the United States and the world were to avert a catastrophe.

The events at Necedah constitute what the journalist Mark Garvey has called America's "most historically significant apparition series" (Garvey 1998: 204). Although shaped by the American political and religious environment, the apparitions at Necedah in 1950 also form a link in the chain of apparitions that are central to the revival of Marian devotions in the nineteenth and twentieth centuries (Kselman 1983; Zimdars-Swartz 1991; Christian 1996;

2 "100,000 in Wisconsin Watch Virgin's 'Visit'," *New York Times*, August 16, 1950, 19.

8.1 An aerial photo of the crowd who went by bus, car and special train to the farm of Mary Ann Van Hoof in Necedah in Wisconsin to witness her Marian vision on August 15, 1950. Estimations of the crowd varied from 35,000 to 100,000.
[Collection of William A. Christian Jr.]

Harris 1999; Maunder 2016). In the United States they set the stage for series of post-World War II apparitions at Conyers (Georgia), Scottsdale (Arizona), and Bayside (Queens, New York), to mention the most prominent sites where Mary renewed her call for prayer, especially the rosary, as the only means of countering the Soviet Union, and preventing an apocalyptic outcome of the Cold War. Mary Ann Van Hoof's visions mark a moment in which Marian piety generated complex responses in American Catholics, anxious to assert both their American identity and their loyalty to the devotional traditions of the Church. For some this meant embracing Mrs. Van Hoof as a visionary in the tradition of Bernadette of Lourdes and the three children of Fátima, a saintly figure worthy of respect and even veneration for her courageous call to prayer and penitence. For others, and especially for the ecclesiastical leadership, Necedah was a disruptive force, the site of a spurious claim of supernatural intervention that opened the Church to ridicule from non-Catholics, and divided the Catholic community at a moment when it was entering the mainstream of American society. Within a year of the apparitions of 1950 ecclesiastical officials had clearly sided with the critics. The local bishop, John Treacy of the diocese of La Crosse, demanded that the statue of Our Lady of Fátima at the shrine be removed from public view. Msgr. Alfredo Ottaviani, assistant secretary of the Congregation of the Holy Office, included Necedah in his warning against a series of alleged miracles that showed signs of "frivolity and unhealthy eccentricity."[3] Despite such criticisms, a core of believers continued to support Mrs. Van Hoof, and began an argument with the Catholic Church that led to decades of public controversy. Although its numbers have declined over the past several years, the cult of Our Lady of Necedah has endured to the present, echoing but also amending the fearsome messages of 1950.

Marian Piety in post-World War II America

The cult at Necedah borrowed directly from the tradition of Marian devotion that was a central element in the parish churches and schools that were at the heart of the Catholic culture of the United States in the first half of the twentieth century. Catholics recited the rosary, assisted at May crownings, and celebrated the Virgin's feast days with processions that were major communal events (Dolan 1985; Orsi 2002; Matovina 2005). The shrine at Lourdes, France, commemorating the apparitions to Bernadette Soubirous in 1858, was of particular importance to American Catholics, who visited Lourdes as a national group in 1874. By the 1950s there were at least 127 parishes named for Our Lady of Lourdes in the United States, and hundreds of replicas of the famous grotto where Bernadette had seen the Virgin. These replica shrines could draw large crowds, with over 300,000 pilgrims visiting the "Lourdes of the West" at Altadena, California in 1939. At the grotto at the University of Notre Dame, over one-quarter of the male students prayed at the shrine daily from the 1930s to the 1950s (McGreevy 2000: 415-418).

The appeal of Our Lady of Lourdes reached a climactic moment during World War II with the success of Franz Werfel's novel, *The Song of Bernadette* (1942), turned into an academy award winning film in 1943. The novel and the film, which Mary Ann Van Hoof recalled seeing in 1944, brought Lourdes to an audience beyond the Catholic community, creating connections across confessional borders that Mary had previously had helped to defend (Van Hoof 1959: 177). From the film Mary Ann Van Hoof would have learned of Bernadette's struggle to gain a hearing from both civil and religious officials, all of whom treated her accounts of the apparitions with skepticism. In the end, however, the healing miracles at the grotto and the obedient and pious character of Bernadette convinced the bishop to approve the devotion to Our Lady of Lourdes.

3 "Vatican Condemns Alleged Miracles," *New York Times*, February 4, 1951, 76.

8.2. Mass crowd for the Bronx miracle, November 12, 1945. Up to 25,000 devotees gathered that evening. In the foreground, nine-year old visionary Joseph Vitolo, seeing "Our Lady of the Universe", prays before a statue of Mary.
[Collection of William A. Christian Jr.]

The popularity of Our Lady of Lourdes forms an important part of the background for the Marian apparitions in the United States, which began in Bronx, New York, just after the conclusion of World War II. In October of 1945 Joseph Vitolo (1936-2014), a nine-year old boy living in the Bronx told his family that he had seen the Virgin on a rocky ledge overlooking the Grand Concourse, and that she had asked him to return to the site over a sixteen-day period. By November 17, the last day of the apparitions, between 25,000 and 30,000 people had gathered to watch Joseph carried by his family to the new shrine. A hundred police kept order while the crowd sang hymns and prayed the rosary, led by an unidentified priest. But no miracle was observed and Mary, although she called for prayers and for peace, issued no warnings about Satan or the Soviet Union (McGreevy 2000: 405-412). Church officials did not endorse the apparitions, which came to be known as the "Bronx miracle," but neither did they condemn them, or try to suppress the devotees who continued to come and pray at the site. Joseph attended a seminary for a time, hoping to become a Catholic priest. Although he was never ordained, he remained a Catholic in good standing until his death. A small shrine commemorating Joseph's visions still exists at 3091 Grand Concourse.[4]

The history of the "Bronx Miracle" offers a striking contrast to the events that followed the apparitions at Necedah in 1950. In Wisconsin Mary abandoned the reticent manner she had assumed five years earlier in the Bronx and engaged volubly and extensively with current events, a pattern that would continue in the private revelations that Mrs. Van Hoof received until her death in 1984. At Necedah, and in her subsequent apparitions in the United States, Mary took on the role of a Cold Warrior, responding to the frightening course of events that had occurred in the aftermath of World War II. During this period the Soviet Union expanded into Eastern Europe, where Communist regimes took aim at the Catholic churches, drawing the attention of the American press. The Polish government broke off relations with the Vatican in 1945; the communist regime in Yugoslavia arrested Archbishop Stepinac for treason in 1946; in Hungary Cardinal Mindszenty was put on trial for treason in 1949. Fears of Soviet military power led to the organization of NATO in 1949, an alliance in which thousands of American soldiers were stationed in Europe, facing what was understood to be a powerful and determined enemy on the other side of the "Iron Curtain." When the Soviet Union successfully tested a nuclear weapon in 1949 it added an apocalyptic dimension to the conflict, as Americans were now forced to imagine a war in which bombs like those that had destroyed Hiroshima and Nagasaki would fall on their own cities (Kirby 2003).

In the context of the early Cold War, Our Lady of Fátima emerged as a rival to Our Lady of Lourdes as the focus of Marian devotions in the United States. The devotion to Fátima derived from a series of apparitions that took place in 1917 in the village of Fátima. Portugal, which had recently entered World War I, was governed by a Republic that had taken a number of anticlerical measures after replacing the monarchy in 1910. The Republic separated Church from State, banned religious orders, expelled the papal nuncio, seized church property, and severely restricted public worship (Bennett 2012: 47). In her messages to the visionaries Mary called for the daily recitation of the rosary as a way to obtain world peace and convert sinners. Following a pattern established at Lourdes, the visions of Fátima provoked a hostile response from government officials, and at first skepticism from the local clergy. Public opinion began to shift in favor of the cult in response to harsh government tactics, including the arrest and intimidation of the children by a local administrator. During the summer of 1917 the apparitions at Fátima were incorporated into stories in the Catholic press, and associated with opposition to the anti-clerical policies of the Republic. As word spread in the region, large crowds began to assemble on the thirteenth of every month, the days on which Mary an-

4 <https://www.roadsideamerica.com/story/48451> (accessed December 29, 2017).

nounced she would return. On October 13, 1917, 70,000 pilgrims were present for the last of the apparitions; many of them claimed to have seen the sun spin in the sky and then plunge toward the earth, a miracle that confirmed for them the truth of the children's story. The popular and political appeal of the apparitions was a factor in the successful military coup of Sidónio Pais in December 1917, inaugurating a period when the regime pulled away from its anti-clerical policies (Livermore 1947: 450-460). An investigation by the Catholic Church led to official approval of the shrine by the bishop of Leiria-Fátima in 1930, but in its early years the cult was a Portuguese affair, and received little international attention.

American Catholics received scattered and occasional reports about Our Lady of Fátima throughout the 1930s, but at this point the cult was not explicitly tied to a geopolitical conflict pitting the Soviet Union against a free world. To judge by the Catholic press, Lourdes received most of the attention given to Marian shrines during the period until the late 1940s. The Catholic Periodical Index lists 43 articles on Lourdes between 1935 and 1944, compared to 10 on Fátima. This balance shifted dramatically over the next decade (1945-1954), when the Index lists 30 entries for Lourdes and 86 for Fátima. Una Cadegan reports that of the 356 pamphlets on Fátima in the database at the Marian Library of the University of Dayton, only one was published in English before 1940 (Cadegan 2004: 3). American Catholics began to learn more about Fátima following Pope Pius XII's radio broadcast on the cult in 1942, to celebrate the twenty-fifth anniversary of the apparitions. In his address Pius attributed the restoration of Catholicism in Portugal and the defeat of communism in Spain to the devotional response to the apparitions at Fátima; he concluded with a prayer asking for Mary to intercede in history, and bring an end to the war (Scheer 2012: 137). By the conclusion of World War II Our Lady of Fátima was beginning to draw an international audience, and her opposition to communism had been announced, setting the stage for her wholehearted engagement in the Cold War.

The weaponization of the rosary

Our Lady of Fátima's status as Cold Warrior in the aftermath of World War II was based first of all on the anticommunist political messages that Sister Lucia, a Carmelite nun and the only surviving visionary, began to produce in the 1930s (Zimdars-Swartz 1991: 198-202). In the context of the Spanish Civil War, Sister Lucia recalled that in 1917 Mary had asked for the consecration of Russia to her Immaculate Heart, and for Catholics to receive Communion on the first Saturday of five consecutive months. Fulfilling these requests would lead to the conversion of Russia and world peace, while ignoring them would result in war, hunger, and the persecution of the Church. During the late 1940s, in the context of fears about the spread of communism in Europe, the cult of Fátima assumed a prominent role in American Catholic devotional life, aggressively promoted in the Catholic press. Jeffrey Bennett has documented the role of the Blue Army of Fátima, whose magazine *Soul* reached a circulation of 70,000 in 1951, and had five million members by 1953 (Bennett 2015). The Blue Army was joined in its promotion of Fátima by the Militia of the Immaculata, an organization founded by the Polish Franciscan Maximilian Kolbe in 1917 dedicated to the conversion of sinners through the intercession of Mary. In 1950 a group of Franciscan friars associated with the Militia and located in Kenosha, Wisconsin, began publishing *Immaculata*, which had an audience of 20,000 readers in 1954 for its message in which Mary led the battle against communism (Davis 2007: 147-190). The devotion to the Sorrowful Mother run by the Servites of Chicago offered another means for American Catholics to view Mary as a Cold Warrior. The devotion first achieved a wide following during World War II, when Catholics prayed to her for the safe return of family members fighting overseas, and for the end of the war. In 1946 the devotion's weekly publication *Novena Notes*, which reached 200,000 Catholics in 1951, began providing details on the Fátima devotion, and organized a prayer crusade for the conversion of Russia (Huels 1976). A similar shift in focus from World War II to the Cold War occurred in the organization dedicated to the Block Rosary. In 1944 Mary Hall, a Detroit housewife, received an apparition while praying for the safety of her brother, fighting in the Pacific. Mary asked Mrs. Hall to organize neighborhood groups to pray the rosary as a way of protecting their homes and families. With the support of the clergy the devotion spread rapidly in the United States, and under the patronage of Nicholas Schorn, a Detroit businessman, made the conversion of Russia through the devotion to Fátima a major goal of it program (Orsi 2016: 83-86, 93-102).

The burst of Catholic publicity for Our Lady of Fátima in the late 1940s was accompanied by a direct link to the shrine through the Pilgrim Virgin, a statue representing Mary as she appeared in Fátima, which toured the United States in the 1940s. The statue was produced in Portugal at the special request of John Haffert, one of the founders of the Blue Army (see chapter 4 by David Morgan). After receiving an episcopal blessing in Fátima the statue reached the United States on December 8, 1947. By the end of 1948 over three million people had viewed the Pilgrim Virgin, which was on tour in Wisconsin in 1950, when the Necedah apparitions took place (Oraze 1948; Tansey 1950).

Marian devotions and their links to the Cold War were promoted by the Catholic press and Catholic parishes, but were sanctioned as well by Monsignor Fulton Sheen, the most prominent and popular spokesman for American Catholicism in this period. In 1947, after describing the apparitions and warnings of Our Lady of Fátima to a national radio audience, Sheen made the following assertion: “We are not concerned about proving the authenticity of these phenomena at Fátima, for those who believe in the realm of Spirit and the Mother of God need no proof, and those who reject the Spirit would not accept it anyway” (Blanshard 1951: 228). Sheen also dedicated the final chapter of his 1948 book, *Communism and the Conscience of the West* to Our Lady of Fátima, explicitly linking American military history with the Blessed Virgin.

> As Americans we cannot be unmindful of the relation of this country to the Woman to whom God gave the power of crushing the head of the serpent. (...) It was on December 8, 1941, the feast of the Immaculate Conception, that the United States went to war with Japan. (...) It was on August 15, 1945, the Feast of the Assumption of Our Blessed Mother, that victory came to us in the war with Japan. It was the nineteenth of August, 1945, that the United States declared official V-J Day and this happened to be the anniversary of one of the appearances of Our Lady of Fatima (Sheen 1948: 216).

For Monsignor Sheen, the coincidence of Marian feast days with key events in America’s participation in World War II suggested that Mary had played a role in the victory of the United States, and would continue to intervene on its side in the battle against communism.

Bishop Sheen’s embrace of Fátima was echoed on a local level by pastors throughout the country. Father Urban, a Catholic pastor in a Southern city, urged his parishioners to respond to Our Lady of Fátima by praying the rosary as she had requested, using language similar to that of Mary Ann Van Hoof.

> Friends, say the Rosary every day. Our Mother of Fatima has promised that Russia will be converted, and that there will be peace in the world. Let us prolong the peace and not let them break it up. That’s possible, you know. Only prayer can save the world – and anyhow, don’t you need the assistance of the Blessed Virgin yourself? (Fichter 1951)

The chaplains at the University of Notre Dame were less equivocal than Father Urban in their invocation of Our Lady of Fátima. In October 1951 their religious bulletin put the issue to students in blunt terms.

> Our Lady has told us at Fatima “we must pray the Rosary.” Will any student ignore her outright command? She promised world peace if we said the Rosary. Does any student want another world war? She promised the conversion of Russia if we said the Rosary. Will any student belittle the Russian threat?[5]

5 *University of Notre Dame Religious Bulletin*, October 6, 1951.

The pastoral message conveyed by these rhetorical questions is clear and coercive: a failure to respond to Our Lady of Fátima's requests meant accepting the responsibility for another war and the victory of communism.

In the period immediately following World War II American Catholics were familiar with and favorably disposed toward major European apparitions of Mary at Lourdes and Fátima. In the context of the Cold War the warnings about communism associated with Our Lady of Fátima took on enormous significance, and provided the setting for the apparitions and messages at Necedah at the end of 1949. Mary Ann Van Hoof and her followers might reasonably have expected that the Church, after some initial hesitancy, would look favorably on the new cult. In the devotional and political context of the late 1940s, Catholics in the Midwest and beyond were able to imagine that Necedah could become a new Fátima, establishing an important outpost in the United States for Mary's war against communism.

Necedah was a small town in 1949, with a population of about 900, but not immune from the social, political, and religious tensions of the period. An influx of Catholics, associated with dam construction on the Wisconsin River, provided a boost to the local parish, led by Father Sigismund Lengowski, responsible for converting an old mansion into a convent and home for elderly women, and for a new parish hall. This activity led to Protestant fears that Necedah was turning into a Catholic town (Frakes 1950: 1020). Catholic-Protestant tension was also fed by the controversial senator from Appleton, Wisconsin, Joseph McCarthy. A declared Catholic who was educated at Marquette University, McCarthy's speech in February 1950, in which he accused the State Department of being infested with communists, attracted enormous public attention, adding to the fears of anticommunism. Although not all Catholics approved of McCarthy's tactics, even those who criticized him accepted the need for Catholics to endorse his message of anticommunism (Crosby 1978). McCarthy, like other Irish Catholics, looked back on a history in which American Protestants were convinced that Irish politicians were inevitably corrupt. Anticommunism might have seemed a path towards Catholic assimilation, but Protestant suspicion of Catholicism was in fact fueled by McCarthyism, to judge by the influential work of Paul Blanshard, the most prominent critic of Catholicism in postwar America. In 1949 Blanshard's collected essays, originally published in *Nation*, became a best-seller when published as *American Freedom and Catholic Power* (McGreevy 2003: 166-168). For Blanshard, McCarthyism represented the illiberal tendency of Catholicism, on display in the Church's sympathy for fascist regimes in Spain and Italy, and in the racist polemics of Father Charles Coughlin, whose radio broadcasts won wide attention in the 1930s (Blanshard 1949). Blanshard's views were shared by others, including the prominent sociologist Seymour Martin Lipset, who saw McCarthyism as an indication of the links between Catholic culture and political authoritarianism (McGreevy 2003: 180-181). The anticommunism that Mary preached at Necedah may have been designed to encourage Catholic assimilation into American democracy, but the tactics of McCarthy could also work in the opposite direction. Blanshard's assault on Catholicism included a swipe at Marian devotions, and in particular at the apparitions to Joseph Vitolo in the Bronx, an example of the superstitious and irrational tendencies of Catholics which made them a threat to American freedom. Although it is highly unlikely that Mary Ann Van Hoof knew of the controversy surrounding Blanshard's work, the call for Christian unity she attributed to Mary can be read as a response to the continuing anxiety of Catholics about their acceptance and status in America. More generally, the apparitions at Necedah, and the divergent reactions to them among both laity and clergy, can be seen as a reflection of the complex and shifting status of Catholic culture in the United States as it moved into the Cold War.

Our Lady of Necedah

Mary Ann Van Hoof was born Anna Maria Bieber in Philadelphia in 1909, where she received an eighth-grade education. Her family was poor, and although we lack details, she and her six siblings apparently suffered from an abusive father (Zimdars-Swartz 1989). In 1934 Mary Ann married Fred Van Hoof, responding to an advertisement he placed in the *Wisconsin Farmer and Agriculturalist*.[6] After several years of sharecropping in the Southwest the Van Hoof family returned to Wisconsin in the early 1940s, eventually settling on their farm in Necedah in 1944. Elizabeth Bieber, Mary Ann's mother, accompanied her daughter to the Southwest and then back to Wisconsin, and was living in Kenosha, not far from Necedah, at the time of the apparitions. Mary Ann Van Hoof had been baptized as a Catholic, but only began to practice her religion under the influence of her husband, with whom she was raising their seven children in 1950. Elizabeth Bieber also played a role in shaping the religious sensibility of Mary Ann, through her association with Spiritualism. From 1945 to 1948 Mrs. Bieber was vice-president of the Kenosha Assembly of Spiritualists, and although Mary Ann Van Hoof would later deny any belief in Spiritualism, she seems to have participated in her mother's assemblies in the late 1940s. As we will see, some of the experiences of Mrs. Van Hoof's followers in the 1970s suggest the enduring presence of Spiritualist practices in the cult of Our Lady of Necedah.

6 For a useful timeline and overview of the cult see Joseph Laycock, "Necedah Shrine," an entry on the World Religions and Spirituality Project website: <https://wrldrels.org/2016/10/08/necedah-shrine/> (accessed December 29, 2017).

Although her testimony needs to be evaluated cautiously, Mary Ann Van Hoof's account of the early days of the cult of Necedah generally conforms to journalistic reports, and placed alongside evidence from the press and from Catholic officials, allows us to see the excitement, confusion, and controversy that developed in and around Necedah in 1950 (Van Hoof 1959). Mary first appeared at the "Sacred Spot" over four ash trees on the Van Hoof farm on May 28, and then again on May 30. The local pastor of St. Francis parish, Fr. Stanley Lengowski, was ill when Mary Ann and Fred first tried to tell him of the apparition on May 29, but he was handed a written version of the message by his sister and mother, who lived with him in the rectory. By May 31, Fr. Lengowski was well enough to visit the Van Hoof farm, where he blessed the Sacred Spot, decorated with a bouquet brought by his mother. Over the next two weeks small crowds began to gather at the farm, as word spread through the family network of the Van Hoofs that Mary would return on June 16. On June 15 a delegation of priests led by Fr. Anthony Wagener, the director of the diocesan press, arrived at the Van Hoof farm and questioned Mary Ann about her visions, and the messages delivered by Mary. Over 1,000 people were present for the June 16 apparition, and the presence of the clergy, along with Fr. Lengowski's initial favorable response, suggests why Catholics in the region were open to the possibility that Necedah might become another Fátima. The first official response from the Church, in a June 19 press release from the Chancery of the diocese of La Crosse, announced that no judgment would be made until church officials had completed a thorough investigation.

> It has been our wish to exclude all sensationalism which such incidents invariably provoke, and for all to maintain a devotional attitude concerning these seemingly unaccountable occurrences. We realize that in past Church-approved earthly appearances of the Mother of God her messages to mankind in a dark hour have been the same – namely, a plea for immediate personal penance and prayer, particularly the Rosary. The happenings in Necedah should be approached in the same spirit of prayer and penance by everyone.[7]

In the two months that followed the June 16 apparition, word of the Necedah miracles began to spread beyond the local area. Catholics from Necedah and Appleton, led by Henry Swan, the president of the Necedah Chamber of Commerce, began distributing pamphlets and buying time on local radio stations reporting the messages of Mary to Mrs. Van Hoof and advertising the August 15 apparition.[8] Stories of rosaries that miraculously changed color at the shrine circulated widely, and would continue to be a common theme for believers

7 National Catholic Welfare Conference (hereafter NCWC) press release, June 19, 1950.

8 According to the *La Crosse Tribune*, August 15, 1950, 2, 176,000 pieces of literature on the visions were distributed between June 16 and August 15.

over the next years and decades. The activity of the Necedah Committee organized by Henry Swan prior to August 15 threatened to create a cult that would escape the control of the ecclesiastical hierarchy. Bishop John Patrick Treacy opened an official investigation, but it would take months if not years to reach a decision, leaving church officials in a difficult position. In late July the Chancery of La Crosse began to release statements critical of some of the activity surrounding the apparitions. Some of the literature distributed by the Necedah Committee was labelled "spurious and regrettable," but the Church stopped short of issuing an outright condemnation, declaring that "for the present the Church is not in a position to make any pronouncement."[9] By early August the publicity campaign of the Necedah Committee was having a major impact on Catholics throughout the Midwest. Special trains were organized to bring pilgrims from Milwaukee, Chicago, and St. Paul, and chartered buses came from as far away as Pittsburgh. The Necedah Committee hired a Milwaukee food service to feed the crowd anticipated for the August 15 apparition; hotel rooms within a fifty-mile radius of Necedah were booked for the event. Increasingly fearful that events in Necedah were proceeding outside of clerical control, the diocesan paper hardened its stand, declaring on August 9 that the apparitions were "highly questionable," and calling on Catholics to "stay at home and pray the rosary there" on August 15. Conscious of the ways that the apparition might feed anti-Catholic sentiment, the paper warned that the credulity on display at Necedah "can result in real harm and ridicule to our holy religion and to legitimate devotion to Our Blessed Mother."[10] In an attempt to keep pilgrims away Bishop Treacy prohibited an open-air Mass at the shrine, and announced that only the two regular Sunday masses at St. Francis parish would be permitted. This decision put thousands of Catholics who planned to come to Necedah at risk of falling into mortal sin for missing Mass on August 15, the Feast of the Assumption and a holy day of obligation. Despite episcopal warnings, it was clear by August 14 that an enormous crowd would be present at the "Sacred Spot" on the Van Hoof farm on the following day, even at the risk of missing Mass. Bishop Treacy, facing a serious pastoral problem, retreated, and allowed Masses to be said every half-hour at St. Francis parish, starting at four in the morning (Frick 1950: 3). By the middle of August 1950 the shrine at Necedah had clearly established itself as a powerful influence on Catholics and a threat to the authority of the ecclesiastical hierarchy.

On the morning of August 15 what has been called "the largest assembly in rural Wisconsin's history" took place in the front yard of the Van Hoof farm. Some sense of the crowd can be gained from a short film that shows the crowd, hundreds of cars, and one of the special trains reserved for pilgrims (Frakes

9 NCWC press release, July 25, 1950.
10 Editorial reprinted in the *Brooklyn Tablet*, August 12, 1950, 4.

1950).[11] The rosary was recited continually over loudspeakers as the crowd gathered in the morning. Despite episcopal warnings that the clergy stay away at least sixty priests and thirty nuns were present, lending an air of orthodoxy to the pilgrimage. At 10:30 Steve Breen, a Catholic journalist and devotee of Fátima, later to be the editor of *Scapular magazine*, addressed the crowd and referred to the anticommunist campaign of Senator McCarthy: "People say it cannot happen here. I say to you it is happening. Look at the State Department! Look at Acheson!" (Frakes 1950) The climax of the day came with Mary Ann Van Hoof announcing to the crowd the message she had just received from the Blessed Virgin.

Why did people go to Necedah? Some pilgrims went to the shrine in the hope of a miraculous cure. Busloads of the sick were given prominent places near the shrine, and the *Life* photos from August 15 include several of cripples seeking relief. As early as June, one woman claimed that she had been cured of her asthma by visiting the shrine, and healing powers were attributed to rosaries blessed by Mrs. Van Hoof (Van Hoof 1959: 1-3). But the thaumaturgic aspect of the cult, though important, was not the primary attraction for most pilgrims. It was the religiously infused political message that drew the crowds to Necedah, where Mary and Mrs. Van Hoof addressed the Cold War anxieties of Americans and reassured them about their ability to master the current crisis. Fear of communist Russia and internal subversion were the most important themes addressed by Mary, prominent in Catholic culture, and endorsed by Mary in her appearances at Fátima (Crosby 1978; DeSantis 1965; Blanshard 1949: 258-265). But despite the hopes of the circle of believers around Mrs. Van Hoof, the shrine at Necedah never became an American Fátima. The suspicion of church officials expressed in the early days of the cult grew over the years, leading to a rejection of any claims that Mary had appeared to Mrs. Van Hoof, and eventually to an interdict which denied the leaders of the cult access to the Catholic sacraments.

The chancellor of the La Crosse diocese, Monsignor Hammes, explained the Church's opposition on the grounds that Mrs. Van Hoof's apparitions failed to meet two fundamental criteria: "First, innocence and integrity of life. Secondly, amenability and submission to the divinely established authority of the Church."[12] Hammes saw Mrs. Van Hoof's visions as "nothing more than a sad rehash of Fátima," supplemented by "silly personal remarks about people" that would never have been spoken by the Blessed Virgin. He was particularly critical of Mrs. Van Hoof for claiming that Mary had announced to her that she and her family had no knowledge of the apparitions at Fátima and Lipa. News of Marian apparitions at Lipa, in the Philippines, starting in 1948, had reached Necedah by 1949, and pamphlets describing the cult were dis-

11 <https://www.youtube.com/watch?v=L83PNkEqiv8> (accessed December 29, 2017).

12 Copy of Hammes' letter, October 26, 1950; Necedah dossier, St. Francis parish.

tributed at the August 15, 1950 pilgrimage (Zimdars-Swartz 2017). According to Msgr. Hammes, reliable witnesses testified that they had shared information on these cults prior to Mary's comment. For Hammes, the case was clear: "Either Mrs. Van Hoof or the Blessed Mother is a liar. You can take your choice." In addition to skepticism about the apparitions, Hammes was concerned that Mrs. Van Hoof "has become increasingly arrogant in her attitude in general and even towards the local Church authorities." Hammes was puzzled about the origins of these sentiments, and in a comment that reflects the same atmosphere that produced the apparitions, speculated that they might be the result of "communistic activity" and were being used "as a front to divide the lay people from their Bishops."

Mary Ann Van Hoof's religious experiences did not end with the apparition of October 7, 1950. In the period after this last public apparition she continued to have revelations in private, and claimed to endure terrible suffering that mirrored the agonies of Christ on certain days, such as Fridays in Advent and Lent. In order to investigate these stories Bishop Treacy had Mrs. Van Hoof observed during a hospital stay of five days in April 1952, which resulted in a decision that there was nothing supernatural in her experiences, although this was not released as a public statement (Zimdars-Swartz 1989: 44). Apparently hoping that the cult would fade away Bishop Treacy avoided making any definitive judgment until 1955, when he issued a statement declaring "that all claims regarding supernatural revelations and visions made by (...) Mrs. Van Hoof are false."[13] Despite this forthright announcement, Mrs. Van Hoof continued to have revelations, at least until 1980 (Van Hoof 1971; typescripts of revelations, 1971-1980, Necedah dossier).

The skepticism expressed by the Chancery of La Crosse grew over the next years, marked by a series of increasingly severe sanctions directed at the cult, culminating in an interdict that separated seven leaders of the cult from the sacraments in 1975. Despite this hostility, however, the shrine at Necedah continued to attract adherents, creating a small but significant insular community that created tension in the region. Until her death in 1984 Mrs. Van Hoof continued to have visions, not only of the Blessed Virgin, but of a pantheon of saints, including Joan of Arc, Thérèse of Lisieux, and of political figures, including George Washington and Abraham Lincoln. In the 1950s the Cold War continued to be a central theme in the revelations, as Mrs. Van Hoof described Russian submarines and missiles that she had personally witnessed, as she was transported to their bases while she remained invisible (Swann 1959: 201-218). By the 1970s, however, Mary and other saints, including Joseph, Benedict, Anthony Claret, and the lay visionary Ann-Catherine Emmerich were concerned with a number of other topics as well: the corruption of youth by

13 The original 1955 statement is included in a press release from Michael Mertens, chancellor of the diocese of La Crosse, July 19, 1968; Necedah dossier.

drugs and music, evil films that preached impurity and violence, toxic chemicals introduced into the food chain, abortion, disloyal clergy. This list suggests a narrowing of the geographic field of concern, as Mrs. Van Hoof and her followers sought to improve the moral atmosphere in and around Necedah. During this period the enemy was reconfigured as well, with the threat coming not so much from the Soviet Union, as from a mysterious group of 30,000 led by a Grand Master, all of them under the influence of Satan and aiming to bring the United States under the control of the United Nations. Racist and antisemitic elements find their way into these messages, echoing conspiracy theories that date from the nineteenth century (Swan 1959: 153-155). Over the course of the 1970s Cold War themes faded in the messages attributed to Mary and the other 'Celestials' who communicated with Mrs. Van Hoof. The threat of a devastating war remained, but the direction from which the attack would come grew vague. The vast majority of the clergy were condemned for surrendering to the corruption of morals that threatened to destroy American society. In the messages of the late 1970s the 'Celestials' became increasingly preoccupied with the personalities of the immediate circle around Mrs. Van Hoof, offering praise and blame over the administration of the shrine, the relationships between individual members, and the construction of the House of Prayer.[14] By the time of the last recorded messages in 1980 the shrine at Necedah had become an insular cult disassociated with the Catholic Church.

The evolution of the cult at Necedah was the result of internal developments, centered on the voluminous and heterodoxical messages of Mrs. Van Hoof. But its marginalization from the institutional Church was due as well to series of episcopal decisions, beginning with the suspicious response to the initial apparitions in 1950, and the decree of 1955 prohibiting public and private worship at the shrine. This pressure, however, was ineffective in preventing Mrs. Van Hoof and her followers, led by Henry Swan, from continuing to promote the cult. Until his death in 1964 Bishop Treacy opted for a relatively tolerant policy in which the devotees at Necedah were still able to participate in the life of St. Francis parish. Bishop Frederick Freking took a harder line when he became bishop in 1964, reiterating the decree of 1955, and noting that the followers of Mrs. Van Hoof had openly flouted it by maintaining and publicizing the shrine.[15] A new committee formed to investigate the cult produced a report in 1970 which unequivocally condemned it based on the character of Mrs. Van Hoof and the content of her revelations. Mrs. Van Hoof was criticized for violating "the basic dignity and freedom of individuals," and for showing "a notable absence of justice and charity." The committee likely had in mind the strict control that Mrs. Van Hoof and her immediate circle sought to exercise over their followers, restricted from travel more than thirty miles

14 Typescript of 1980 messages; Necedah dossier.
15 Letter of July 19, 1968, Office of the Chancellor, Diocese of Lacrosse; Necedah dossier.

away from the "Sacred Spot." The messages were interpreted as advocating "some basic Christian values, but on the whole manifest a spirit antithetical to Christianity. The messages contain for the most part questionable accusations about leaders in Church and State. The messages also contain general admonitions and threatening statements that seem to prey on the troubled times in which we live."[16]

This episcopal criticism was as ineffective as the previous attempts to shut down the shrine. Bishop Freking's frustration with the failure of the leaders to comply with orders to remove statues and stop publicizing the apparitions and their messages shows in a letter he wrote to Mrs. Van Hoof in 1972, where he noted that "directives have been increasingly ignored and even greater efforts have been, and are being made, to promote the so-called 'Queen of the Holy Rosary Mediatrix of Peace Shrine' and the alleged 'revelations' and 'apparitions' of Mrs. Mary Ann Van Hoof."[17] Bishop Freking's concern with the cult was based on the formation of a community of several hundred in Necedah, drawn there by Mrs. Van Hoof's revelations. Shrine activities expanded beyond the prayer vigils that marked important dates in the history of the cult to include a home for infants, and a school that eventually enrolled as many as eighty students. In conjunction of Father James Barney, the pastor of St. Francis parish, the bishop acted forcefully, insisting that the shrine be closed in 1972. The refusal to comply with this order led eventually to an interdict directed against seven of the leaders in 1975, which forbade them from receiving the sacraments.

The tougher line adopted by Bishop Freking was no more successful than the tolerant policy of Bishop Treacy in repressing the cult at Necedah. Devotees managed to find clergy who claimed the canonical status that would allow them to offer mass and administer the sacraments at the shrine, leading to continued controversy over its activities. The ability of the cult to attract several hundred adherents to the area around the shrine also created tension in Necedah, as devotees voted as a bloc in local elections and expanded their real estate holdings around the shrine. The suicide of over 900 people in Jonestown Guyana in 1978 sparked an investigation by *The Capital Times*, the principal newspaper in Madison, which published a series of damning articles in February 1980 (Fixmer & Allegretti 1980). The stories documented caches of weapons held by devotees, a suspicious shooting death, illegal practices at the home for infants, and strategic voting in local elections. In the 1970s the revelations to Mrs. Van Hoof also took on a different character, as she claimed communication with the dead, including Henry Swan, and reported out of body experiences in which she was transported to alien space ships, which

16 Report of the Necedah Investigating Committee, August 4, 1970; Necedah dossier.

17 Letter of Bishop Freking to Mrs. Van Hoof, May 26, 1972; Necedah dossier.

would save the inner circle of the cult prior to an imminent apocalypse.[18] Rumors of these sessions, which moved completely outside of orthodox Catholic tradition, created internal tension among the devotees, which was compounded with Father DiBenedetto, who had administered to the community since 1980, abandoned the shrine in 1983, reconciled with the Catholic Church, and in a farewell sermon, claimed that the recent history of the cult had been tainted by Satanism.[19] After the death of Mary Ann Van Hoof in 1984 the cult continued to fracture, as some of the most loyal members, including Ray Hirt, who had married Mary Ann Van Hoof in 1978, were reconciled with the Church, while others maintained a separatist posture. Attempts at reconciliation continued in 1995, when Bishop Raymond Burke met with members of the cult, hoping to persuade devotees to accept diocesan authority.[20] Despite all these efforts the shrine continues to operate, claiming a Catholic identity that is contested by the bishop and Father Redfer, the current pastor of St. Francis parish. Anyone interested in Our Lady of Necedah can consult the internet site devoted to Mary "Queen of the Holy Rosary, Mediatrix between God and Man," where they will find links to the newsletter, which still appears regularly, and to a wide range of publications, including collections of the revelations and messages to Mrs. Van Hoof.[21]

The staff at the Necedah bookstore today offers a friendly welcome to visitors, and will admit that over the past few years the shrine has "gone down," with fewer participants at the vigils held to mark the days when Mary appeared to Mrs. Van Hoof. The death of Mrs. Van Hoof in 1984, along with the interdict of 1975 and turmoil resulting from the departure of Father DiBenedetto have posed challenges to the cult, which nonetheless continues to be an active presence in Necedah. The messages given to Mrs. Van Hoof, and her personal experience of conflict with Church authorities, have had an impact beyond the cult at Necedah, exercising considerable influence on the cult of "Our Lady of the Roses" inspired by the visions and messages of Veronica Lueken, which began in 1970 in New York City (Laycock 2015: 22-28, 34-35; see chapter 9 by Wojcik). Unlike the cults of Our Lady of All Nations in Amsterdam and the Queen of Peace at Medjugorje studied by Peter Jan Margry, the Catholic hierarchy was successful in marginalizing Our Lady of Necedah, without being able to repress it entirely (Margry 2009). The early history of Necedah allows us to capture a moment in which devotional Catholicism and militant patriotism came together, revealing the depth of Marian piety and its identification with Cold War politics. The subsequent history of Our Lady of Necedah reveals a fissure between laity who claim authority through direct access to the super-

18 Interviews with former devotees; Necedah dossier.

19 Farewell Speech of Most Rev. Francis DiBenedetto, May 29, 1983; Necedah dossier.

20 Meeting with persons associated with the 'Shrine' at Necedah, held at Saints Peter and Paul Church, Wisconsin Rapids, May 25, 1995; Necedah dossier.

21 <http://www.queenoftheholyrosaryshrine.com/> (accessed December 29, 2017).

natural, and the Church hierarchy anxious to maintain control over a cult that compromised clerical authority and risked being the source of criticism and ridicule from non-Catholics. Visiting the shrine today evokes a strange combination of reactions, surprise about the endurance of the shrine, anxiety about the sustained power the cult exercises over its devotees, fascination over its history that melds traditional Catholicism, militant patriotism, and a variety of occult belief-systems. The ability of the cult to survive, if not to flourish, suggests the sustained appeal of messages that reveal the evil conspirators responsible for the world's ills. The shrine at Necedah may not look ahead to a brilliant future, but its devotees do not seem entirely out of place in today's world.

BIBLIOGRAPHY

Avella, Steven and Thomas Kselman. 1986. "Marian Piety and the Cold War in the United States." *Catholic Historical Review* 72: 403-424.

Bennett, Jeffrey S. 2012. *When the Sun Danced: Myth, Miracles, and Modernity in Early Twentieth-Century Portugal*. Charlottesville: University of Virginia.

Bennett, Jeffrey S. 2015. "The Blue Army and the Red Scare: Politics, Religion, and Cold War Paranoia." *Politics, Religion and Ideology* 16: 263-281.

Blanshard, Paul. 1949. *American Freedom and Catholic Power*. Boston: Free Press.

Cadegan, Una. 2004. "The Queen of Peace in the Shadow of War: Fatima and U.S. Catholic Anticommunism." *U.S. Catholic Historian* 22: 1-15.

Christian, William Jr. 1996. *Visionaries: The Spanish Republic and the Reign of Christ*. Berkeley: University of California Press.

Crosby, Donald F., SJ. 1978. *God, Church, and Flag: Senator Joseph R. McCarthy and the Catholic Church, 1950-1957*. Chapel Hill: University of North Carolina Press, 1978.

Davis, Maryellen. 2007. *Mary as Media Icon: The Madonna in Twentieth-Century American Catholic Devotional Cultures*. PhD thesis, Department of Religious Studies, University of North Carolina, Chapel Hill.

De la Cruz, Deirdre. 2015. *Mother Figures: Marian Apparitions and the Making of a Filipino Universal*. Chicago: University of Chicago Press.

DeSantis, Vincent. 1965. "The Catholic Bishops and McCarthyism." *Catholic Historical Review* 51: 1-30.

Dolan, Jay. 1985. *The American Catholic Experience*. New York: Doubleday.

Fichter, Joseph. 1951. *Southern Parish: Dynamics of a City Church*. Chicago: University of Chicago Press.

Fixmer, Rob and Dan Allegretti. 1980. *The Necedah Cult: Praise the Lord and Pass the Ammo*. Madison, WI: The Capital Times.

Frakes, Margaret. 1950. "Setting for a Miracle." *Christian Century*, August 30: 1019-1021.

Frick, Ann. 1950. "Catholics Jam 'Vision' Rites." *Milwaukee Journal*, August 15.

Garvey, Mark. 1998. *Searching for Mary: An Exploration of Marian Apparitions Across the U.S.* New York: Plume.

Harris, Ruth. 1999. *Lourdes: Body and Spirit in a Secular Age*. New York: Viking.

Huels, John. 1976. "The Popular Appeal of the Sorrowful Mother Novena." *Marianum* 38: 191-199.

Kane, Paula. 2008. "Jews and Catholics Converge: The Song of Bernadette (1943)." In *Catholics in the Movies*, edited by Colleen McDannell, 83-105. New York: Oxford University Press.

Kirby, Dianne (ed.). 2003. *Religion and the Cold War*. New York: Palgrave Macmillan.

Kselman, Thomas. 1983. *Miracles and Prophecies in Nineteenth-Century France*. New Brunswick, NJ: Rutgers University Press.

Laycock, Joseph P. 2015. *The Seer of Bayside: Veronica Lueken and the Struggle to Define Catholicism*. New York: Oxford University Press.

Livermore, Harold. 1947. *A History of Portugal*. Cambridge: Cambridge University Press.

Margry, Peter Jan. 2009. "Marian Interventions in the Wars of Ideology: The Elastic Politics of the Roman Catholic Church on Modern Apparitions." *History and Anthropology* 20: 243-263.

Matovina, Timothy. 2005. *Guadalupe and her Faithful: Latino Catholics in San Antonio, from Colonial Origins to the Present*. Baltimore: Johns Hopkins University Press.

Maunder, Chris. 2016. *Our Lady of the Nations: Apparitions of Mary in Twentieth-Century Europe*. Oxford: Oxford University Press.

McGreevy, John T. 2000. "Bronx Miracle." *American Quarterly* 52: 405-443.

McGreevy, John T. 2003. *Catholicism and American Freedom*. New York: Norton.

Oraze, Stephen. 1948. "Our Lady Tours the United States." *Our Lady's Digest* 3: 97-99.

Orsi, Robert. 2002. *The Madonna of 115th Street: Faith and Community in Italian Harlem, 1880-1950*. New Haven: Yale University Press.

Orsi, Robert. 2016. *History and Presence*. Cambridge: Harvard University Press.

"Pray and Pray Hard." 1950. *Newsweek*, August 28, 81-82.

Scheer, Monique. 2012. "Catholic Piety in the Early Cold War Years, or How the Virgin Mary Protected the West from Communism." In *Cold War Cultures: Perspectives on Eastern and Western European Societies*, edited by Annette Vowinckel, Marcus Payk and Thomas Lindenberger, 129-151. New York: Berghahn.

Sheen, Fulton. 1948. *Communism and the Conscience of the West*. New York: Bobbs-Merrill.

Swan, Henry. 1959. *My Work with Necedah*. Vol. 4 (2nd ed. 1976). Necedah, WI: For My God and Country.

Tansey, Anne. 1950. "Tale of the Pilgrim Virgin." *Action Now*, May, 9-12.

Testimonials of Pilgrims – Queen of the Holy Rosary Mediatrix of Peace Shrine. Volume 1, 1950 to 1966. [ca. 1969]. Necedah, WI: For My God and Country.

"The Vision of Necedah." 1950. *Life*, August 28, 21-23.

Van Hoof, Mary Ann. 1959. *Mary Ann Van Hoof's Own Story of the Apparitions of the Blessed Virgin Mary*. Vol. 1 of Henry Swan. *My Work with Necedah*. Necedah, WI: For My God and Country, 1959.

Van Hoof, Mary Ann. 1971. *Revelations and Messages as Given Through Mary Ann Van Hoof*. Necedah, WI: For My God and Country.

"Vatican Condemns Alleged Miracles." 1951. *New York Times*, February 4, 76.

Zimdars-Swartz, Sandra L. 1989. "Religious Experience and the Public Cult: The Case of Mary Ann Van Hoof." *Journal of Health and Religion* 28: 36-57.

Zimdars-Swartz, Sandra L. 1991. *Encountering Mary: From La Salette to Medjugorje*. Princeton: Princeton University Press.

Zimdars-Swartz, Sandra L. 2017. "Lipa Comes to Necedah: Personal Experiences, Signs, and a Confluence of Imagery at an American Cold War Apparition." *Nova Religio: The Journal of Alternative and Emergent Religions* 21: 100-110.

9
THE VIRGIN AND THE BOMB
THE BAYSIDE APPARITIONS, COLD WAR ANXIETIES, AND MARIAN ANTICOMMUNISM

DANIEL WOJCIK

> O My children of the United States, do you not understand what is ahead for you? Your country, the United States, has not known what it is to suffer through destructive forces. My children, you shall not escape the destruction that the Bear of communism has set upon many countries in Europe and the world. You cannot compromise your Faith to save what there is left, for everything upon earth shall fall as rubble with the Chastisement. A ball of fire, a chastisement, a baptism of fire, is heading for mankind. Can you not understand?
>
> Message from the Virgin Mary delivered to Veronica Lueken, November 20, 1978.

The Bayside apparitions of Veronica Lueken that began in 1970 in the borough of Queens, New York City, are perhaps the most apocalyptic of American Marian visitations, and represent an intensification of the anticommunist and eschatological themes that became central to Marian apparitional culture during the Cold War. For more than twenty years, until her death in 1995, Lueken communicated end times prophecies to humanity from the Virgin Mary, Jesus, and numerous saints. The shrine as well as the visitations from the Virgin Mary are referred to as "Our Lady of the Roses" and "Our Lady of Bayside." The number of devotees who have participated in the Bayside movement over the years is difficult to estimate. Throughout the 1980s and the 1990s, the shrine's mailing list was said to consist of roughly 55,000 names worldwide; the shrine's own past publications claim that there are more than 40,000 Baysiders throughout the world. During the height of the

Bayside movement in the 1980s, there were as many as 15,000 pilgrims reported to have gathered at the apparition site for the yearly events that celebrated the anniversary of Lueken's visions.

Although initially the attendees at the apparitions were from the New York area, the movement expanded into an international phenomenon, with devotees and financial support from around the world. Lueken's private revelations began in 1968, with her first public vigils at the apparition site occurring in the summer of 1970, and these were attended by a small group of followers. In 1973, Lueken received significant institutional support from a conservative Catholic group from Quebec known as The Pilgrims of St. Michael, which seemed to influence the content of her prophecies while definitely increasing participation and pilgrimages to the apparition site (Laycock 2015: 51-54). Organizers of the Bayside movement promoted the apparitions through radio and television programs, advertisements, public presentations, and a network of shrine coordinators in the United States and abroad who tapped into the broader Marian movement and traditionalist Catholic subcultures, gaining a large number of devotees not only from Canada but also in Latin America, Africa, Europe, the Philippines, India, and Malaysia, among other places.[1]

Lueken's apparitions address an enormous range of topics, but the most prominent are the demonic threat of communism, anti-Christian super-conspiracies, the evils of contemporary society, corruption within the Catholic Church and the Vatican itself (including the assertion that Paul VI was replaced by a satanic imposter pope who was a communist agent), the urgent need for worldwide atonement, and especially, the approach of an apocalyptic scenario. The apparitions assert that "a worldwide Warning, Miracle, and fiery Chastisement in the form of a 'Ball of Redemption' – a comet which will strike the earth, and along with World War III and other disasters, will remove three-quarters of mankind – are very near at hand" (*OLR Booklet*, n.d.: i). The coming worldwide cataclysm, or what Baysiders refer to as the "Great Chastisement," may be averted through the defeat of communistic world atheism, praying the rosary, the conversion of Russia to Mary's Immaculate Heart, and a return to pre-Vatican II traditional Catholic teachings.

The Bayside prophecies have direct antecedents in previous Marian apparitions and reflect aspects of the broader institutional anticommunist rhetoric of the Roman Catholic Church. Lueken's messages are elaborations and amplifications of familiar Cold War apparitional tropes, and offer insights into widespread American fears of World War III, nuclear annihilation, and the "disease" of atheistic communism that many believed had infected not only the United States but that threatened the future of humanity. In the context

1 See Laycock (2015: 137-165) for the growth of the Bayside movement, and Margry (2004a; 2019) for a discussion of the global network of Marian devotion.

of such anxieties, the religious commitment of Marian devotees as "God-fearing" Christians became directly linked to American national identity during the Cold War period, as an explicit expression of one's anticommunist stance and as protection against accusations of un-American subversive behavior (Scheer 2012: 129). For American Catholics in particular, whose religious faith had been historically marginalized or maligned in relation to the more privileged Protestant traditions in the United States, a vehemently anticommunist religious identity assumed a powerful patriotic significance in the Cold War context.

Fátima and Cold War prophecies

After World War II, apparitions of the Virgin Mary not only became increasingly apocalyptic, but repeatedly identified communism as the "serpent," the "beast," and the "red dragon" referred to in the Book of Revelation, with Mary appearing as the "woman clothed with the sun," an apocalyptic prophetess and warrior who promised protection and victory over a perceived communist assault in the last days. According to such messages, familiar to millions of Catholics globally, the conflict of ideologies between democracy and what was referred to as "godless communism" was a cosmic battle between Satan and God, a holy war to be fought in a world seething in sin and teetering on the edge of annihilation.

The anticommunist and apocalyptic themes of Cold War apparitions may be traced to the Fátima messages of 1917. Two of so-called "secrets" associated with these apparitions were later revealed by the only surviving visionary, Lucia dos Santos in 1941. Particular emphasis was given to the second part of the Virgin Mary's message which was said to communicate her desire for the consecration of Russia to her Immaculate Heart and for the conversion of Russia. Fulfilling Mary's requests in the message would prevent future wars and disasters, and bring about peace on earth. But the message also warned that if Mary's requests were neglected, Russia would "spread her errors throughout the world, causing wars and persecution of the Church" (Zimdars-Swartz 1991: 197-200).

The veneration of Mary was the antidote to a world gone astray, a devotional weapon that could defeat the spread of communism and prevent worldly cataclysm in the nuclear era. The Fátima apparition cult and praying the rosary not only assumed a political role as religious weaponry that could conquer communism, but also were embraced as apotropaic devotions to protect the faithful against the ever-present threat of communist contamination. The Fátima apparitions served as the template and anchoring framework for the Marian visitations during the Cold War. As the Cold War heated up in the

1950s, the intensification of devotion to Mary coincided with the apocalyptic anxieties of the nuclear era, and the Fátima-inspired Marian revival attracted millions of Roman Catholics worldwide and was endorsed by prominent figures in the Catholic hierarchy, including Pope Pius XII, the American Archbishop and Cardinal Francis Joseph Spellman, and the influential American Archbishop Fulton Sheen, known for his popular radio and television broadcasts (Herzog 2012: 48-48; Kselman & Avella 1986: 411-412).

The Bayside prophecies, Cold War anxieties, and nuclear apocalypse

Before analyzing specific aspects of the Bayside apparitions in the context of the Cold War, some background information about Lueken's visions and their development is necessary. The Bayside movement began on June 5, 1968, the day that New York senator Robert F. Kennedy was assassinated. At that time, Lueken was a housewife and mother of five children from Queens, New York. On the day of the assassination, as she prayed for the dying senator, she experienced a perfume of roses in her car. Soon afterwards, Lueken had a vision of St. Thérèse of Lisieux, who later gave her sacred writings and poems by dictation. On April 7, 1970, the Virgin Mary appeared to Lueken in her home and told her to establish a shrine on the grounds of the St. Robert Bellarmine Roman Catholic church which was Lueken's parish church in Bayside, New York. The Virgin Mary told Lueken that she would appear at the site if rosary prayer vigils were held there on June 18, 1970. Mary also promised to return and speak through Lueken (who would act as a "voice box" repeating words from heaven) in the evenings of all the great feast days of the Catholic Church, if vigils were faithfully kept on those days. The shrine was to be named "Our Lady of the Roses, Mary Help of Mothers," in accordance with Mary's desire to provide help to "all mothers who weep for their children" – those children who have gone astray in an evil world. Lueken also had experiences of a perfume of roses when she prayed, and Mary told her that she would appear when the roses bloom; references to roses abound in Lueken's locutions, which include a vision of Mary dispensing miraculous rose petals from heaven that offered conversion and healing, inspiring the practice of distributing blessed rose petals as sacramental objects at the apparition site.[2]

More than three hundred messages were transmitted by Lueken until her death on August 3, 1995, and her missives are among the most voluminous and discursive of any Marian visionary. The number of pages in the devo-

2 Lueken (1998-2003, vol. 1: xiii–xx); "The Construction of an Oasis." Our Lady of the Roses, Mary Help of Mothers Shrine website: <http://www.ourladyoftheroses.org/ourladyoftheroses/index.php/welcome/welcome-to-the-shrine> (accessed November 11, 2017).

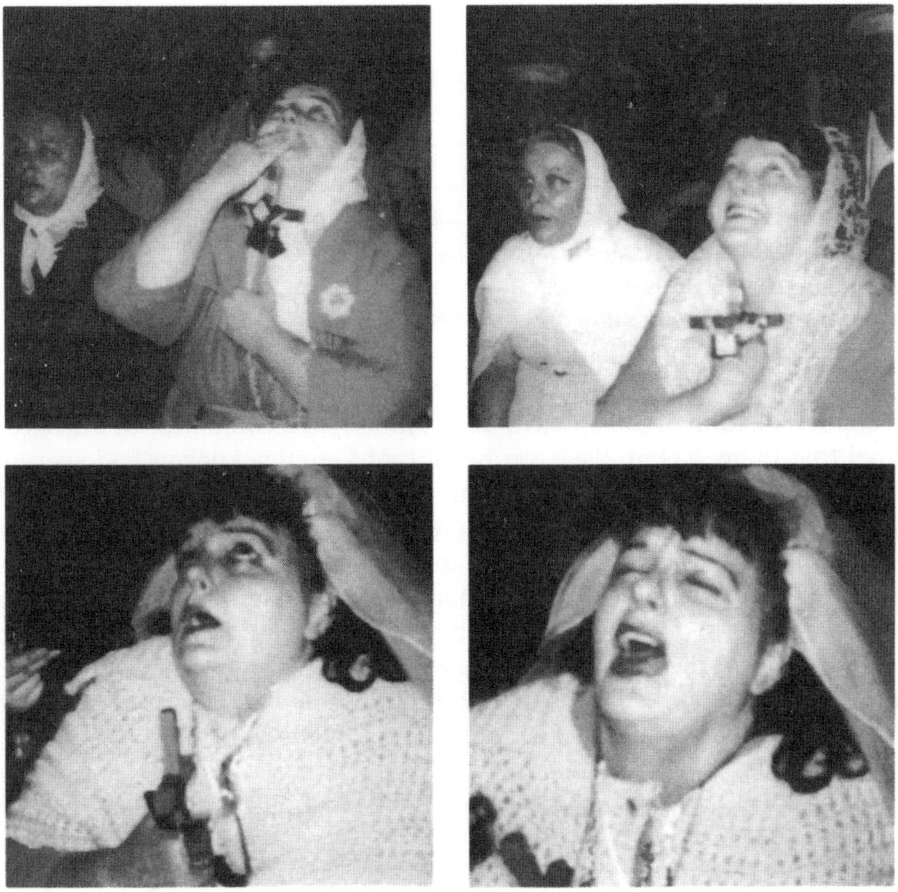

9.1 Photographs of seer Veronica Lueken during her visions: in the first photograph she sends a kiss to the Virgin Mary, the second shows her in ecstasy, and the last two images document her response to a vision of hell.
[From a booklet published by the Apostles of Our Lady]

tional books that record Lueken's prophecies vary from approximately 1,030 pages in the oversized two-volume *Roses from Heaven* collection (no date), to 3,800 pages in the compact six-volume collection entitled *Virgin Mary's Bayside Prophecies: A Gift of Love* (Lueken 1998-2003), which includes occasional commentary and photographs. Lueken said that she repeated these messages from the Virgin Mary (and those of Jesus and other holy personages) word-for-word, although often she would add her own elaborate accounts of what she saw in her visions, such as detailed descriptions of the outfits that Our Lady of

Bayside wore when she appeared or the effect of the weather conditions in the sky on her appearance.[3]

Initially, the Bayside vigils were held on the property of the St. Bellarmine church, after Mary's first appearance there in June 1970. By 1973, the disruptive nature of the vigils created a crisis on church grounds and in the neighborhood, as busloads of pilgrims arrived at the site and participated in loud prayer services that lasted until midnight and were amplified by microphones. Local homeowners became upset with the onslaught of believers, the traffic, the noise, the appearance of vendors selling hotdogs and ice cream, Baysiders urinating on their lawns (the vigils were three-to-four hours long with no bathroom facilities) and other conflicts.[4] As tensions escalated between community members and the Baysiders, the Diocese of Brooklyn called for an investigation of the apparitions. In June 1973 a committee of priests declared that there was no basis for belief that Veronica Lueken had seen the Virgin Mary.[5] In 1975, the Supreme Court of New York issued an injunction that banned Lueken from continuing the vigils in Bayside. Lueken then received a vision from Our Lady informing her to relocate the vigils to Flushing Meadows-Corona Park, specifically to a concrete exedra monument that commemorates the location of the former Vatican Pavilion that was constructed for the 1964-1965 New York World's Fair. Today this largely forgotten site consists of a modest granite marker and bench, but during the Fair it housed Michelangelo's famous *Pietà* sculpture, which was sent by the Vatican from St. Peter's Basilica for display at the Pavilion.

3 Each time Lueken had a vision at the apparition site, she was apparently recorded on audio tape. The messages were then transcribed and printed by the Our Lady of the Roses Shrine and other organizations. In addition to the shrine publications with specific authors cited in this essay, the following works which list no apparent author were consulted and are cited within the text with the following abbreviations: *Our Lady of the Roses, Mary Help of Mothers: An Introductory Booklet on the Apparitions of Bayside* (referred to as *OLR Booklet*); *Our Lady of the Roses, Mary Help of Mothers "Blue Book"* (referred to as *OLR Book*); *Roses from Heaven, Jesus and Mary Speak to the World* (referred to as *Roses Book*). There are also numerous other publications and websites that promote the Bayside prophecies, as well as assorted websites that selectively embrace some of Lueken's messages. Lueken's detractors, some of whom are apostate Baysiders, have accused her of being a charlatan, an occultist, a paranoid psychotic, and a tool of demonic forces (see Cuneo 1997: 163-168; Laycock 2015: 156-160), and numerous websites condemn her apparitions as false, against Church authority, or as satanic manifestations.

4 Phone conversation with Kevin Farrelly, January 5, 2011; Laycock (2015: 52-54, 72-97).

5 In 1986, the Diocese of Brooklyn issued a similar declaration which stated that "a thorough investigation revealed the alleged 'visions of Bayside' completely lacked authenticity (...) [and] are contrary to the teachings of the Catholic Church." The declaration advised the faithful to "refrain from participating in the 'vigils' and from disseminating any propaganda related to the 'Bayside apparitions'" (Mugavero 1989: 209-211). For further discussion of the Bayside movement, see Cuneo (1997: 152-177), Wojcik (1997: 60-96), and Laycock's insightful book-length study (2015).

For Baysiders, the move to this new apparition site, sanctioned by Lueken's messages from Mary, has a symbolic connection to the Vatican, and devotees ritually sanctify the space by constructing a temporary shrine here for every vigil and Holy Hour event. To do so, Baysiders transport a statue of the Virgin Mary to the site and place it at the center of the exedra monument, and then adorn and surround the statue with sacred and revered items, including devotional lanterns and candles; crucifixes, roses, and religious statuary; images of Padre Pio and other saints; the American flag and the flag of Vatican City; and since Lueken's death, photographs depicting her. Shrine organizers also sprinkle holy water around the monument to consecrate it. Although this second *loca sacra* for Lueken's apparitions was moved five miles down the road to Flushing Meadows Park from the original site in Bayside, the visions are still referred to as the "Bayside apparitions" and devotees continue to call themselves "Baysiders," believing that someday they will be allowed to return to the original location, where a basilica will be built, a miraculous spring of curative waters will appear, and the shrine will be recognized as "The Lourdes of America."

The Bayside phenomenon exhibits the familiar features of previous apparitions and Lueken's messages elaborate upon the primary themes of the Cold War Marian apparitional worldview, with condemnations of communism, secularism, modernity, and the liberalizing changes implemented by the Second Vatican Council. The messages convey traditionalist apprehensions that also occur in other apparitions, such as pronouncements by the Virgin Mary on homosexuality, abortion, societal decay, apostasy, and corruption in the Vatican. In addition, Lueken's missives also include some unconventional aspects that express ideas associated with the occultic milieu, such as conspiracy theories about an imposter pope and the Illuminati, and warnings about vampires, demonic UFOs, the evils of television, and the sinister nature of rock and roll music, among other things. While the content of some of Lueken's messages may be idiosyncratic, or even phantasmagoric for some critics, taken as a whole her prophecies reflect many of the fears and vernacular preoccupations inherent in traditionalist Catholic and American Cold War culture. The Bayside prophecies not only have clear antecedents in the Fátima messages but also in the ecclesiastically unsanctioned apparitions at San Sebastian de Garabandal, Spain (1960-1965), and Necedah, Wisconsin (during the 1950s), which have explicitly apocalyptic themes and warn of imminent divine punishments to be unleashed because of the spread of communism, secularism, and the rejection of God. Like the Garabandal apparitions, the scenario described by Lueken includes a supernatural "world-wide warning" (which will reveal the spiritual condition of one's soul and a realization of one's sins), followed by a "great miracle" (perhaps in correlation with the Fátima miracle) and then, if people do not convert and change their lives, a horrible and punishing "great chastisement" sent by God.[6] Historian of religion Sandra Zimdars-Swartz refers to this popular eschatological worldview that arose in the Cold War era as a transcultural apocalyptic ideology, and asserts that Marian devotees regard the Virgin's recent appearances as part of a pattern of end times warnings revealing an "all-encompassing divine plan" occurring at the end of history before the return of Christ (1991: 246). In this role, Mary appears as intercessor and nurturing mother, a representation of divine mercy warning of impending divine chastisements to be unleashed because of the sins of the world, intervening on behalf of her children to rescue them from the apocalyptic punishments of an angry God.[7]

Of the apocalyptic messages that pervaded Cold War Catholic culture, the most widely known and influential was the "third secret of Fátima" which was rumored to predict a catastrophic nuclear scenario. According to popular speculation, the third message communicated by the Virgin Mary to Lucia dos Santos in 1917 was delivered in a sealed envelope decades later to the Vatican and was to be revealed to the world by the pope in 1960. When the message was not revealed, legends and beliefs circulated about its contents, which included predictions of a fiery apocalypse during the term of the fifth pope after the letter was unsealed, crises in the Roman Catholic Church, the spread of communism and its infiltration of the Church, and other cataclysms. When the third secret finally was disclosed in the year 2000 with no mention of apocalypse or communism, many devotees of the Marian apparitional subculture refused to believe that the secret had been revealed in its entirety. The possibility of global nuclear war and the danger of communist subversion so pervaded Cold War Marian consciousness and lore that such concerns could not be easily forgotten, and speculation about the third secret embodied the very real fears of communist menace and thermonuclear apocalypse.

As numerous commentators have observed, the dropping of atomic bombs on Hiroshima and Nagasaki in August, 1945, fundamentally altered contemporary culture and thought. The Soviet Union's first atomic bomb test in 1949 and the ensuing proliferation of nuclear weapons in the following decades fueled fears of global annihilation and widespread feelings of societal crisis and imminent doom (Boyer 1985; Lifton & Falk 1982; Weart 1988). E. P. Thompson asserts that the self-identities of many Americans were conditioned by the tensions of the Cold War (1982: 171), while Robert Jay Lifton claims that the threat of nuclear warfare formed the context of life during the Cold War period, with the image of the bomb casting an ominous shadow that intruded

6 For a discussion of the end times scenario presented in the Garabandal apparitions, see Zimdars-Swartz (1991: 225-233).

7 The apocalyptic themes of Marian pilgrimages and apparitions have been discussed by the Turners (1978), Christian (1984, 1996), Claverie (2003); Cuneo (1997), Kselman & Avella (1986), Apolito (1998, 2005), Matter (2001), Margry (2004b, 2009), Wojcik (1997, 2019), and Zimdars-Swartz (1991), among others.

upon American culture and consciousness (Lifton & Falk 1982: 3). The pervasive fears associated with nuclear warfare during the Cold War were characterized by a sense of helplessness and fatalism, with nuclear cataclysm often viewed as uncontrollable and inevitable, an ever present reality that evoked images of imminent death and the death of all humanity (Anders 1962; Boyer 1985: 278-281; Lifton 1987: 10-27; Wojcik 1997: 133-147).

In the context of Marian piety, these anxieties about nuclear apocalypse were initially reflected in beliefs about the third secret of Fátima, which reverberated throughout Cold War apparitional culture. Although nuclear cataclysm often was predicted to be imminent in Marian messages, a crucial component in such apparitions is the role of the Virgin Mary as an intercessor who can avert nuclear annihilation if human beings follow her decrees. Unlike other manifestations of Cold War apocalypticism, such as Protestant premillennial dispensationalism, which asserts that apocalypse is inevitable and part of God's divine plan (an expression of *catastrophic millennialism*), the messages of Cold War Catholic visionaries express a form of *avertive apocalypticism*, emphasizing Mary's role as mediatrix who may intervene and prevent nuclear war if people change their ways and adhere to her redemptive mandates (Wojcik 2011). Because of the emphasis on Mary as mediator between God and the faithful on earth (the doctrine of the communion of saints), in which Mary can petition God and intercede on behalf of the faithful in times of crisis, Marian apparitions offered the promise that cataclysms and societal evils could be prevented, providing hope amid widespread feelings of doom and fatalism about the future of humankind in the nuclear age.

The Bayside prophecies exemplify the avertive apocalyptic aspects of the broader Marian apparition worldview and reflect the terror of nuclear warfare that gripped much of the American populace at the height of the Cold War. Lueken's messages vacillate between graphic predictions of impending nuclear destruction and the slender hope of preventing doomsday if humanity abides by Mary's directives from heaven. As noted, the apocalyptic scenario prophesied in the Bayside apparitions describes a "Chastisement" that will destroy three-fourths of humanity and that will consist of two parts. First, there will be World War III, and then a God-sent "Fireball of Redemption." Prior to the Chastisement, a great Warning will be sent to humanity that has the features of an atomic blast:

> There will be a tremendous explosion and the sky shall roll back like a scroll. This force shall go within the very core of the human (...) buildings shall disappear from their moorings; the atmosphere shall spell forth currents of great heat; a darkness of spirit and a darkness of atmosphere shall settle in a deadly quiet upon mankind. As the day follows night, so shall this warning follow soon. Beware of the sunrise! Do not look up to the sky,

> the flash! Close your windows! Draw your shades! Remain inside! Do not venture outside your door, or you will not return! (*OLR Book* 1986: 44-45).

Lueken's prophecies of a Warning and Chastisement replicate the end times scenario presented in the Garabandal apparitions (with the Warning as a burning and painful revelation of one's sins), combined with apocalyptic predictions presented at Fátima, but include more detailed descriptions, with the Warning seeming to resemble a divinely-sent nuclear explosion, although its apocalyptic consequences are not exactly clear. While other Marian apparitions foretell of such cataclysmic events, Lueken's visions expound on the destructive nature of these events, emphasizing the devastation and violence that will occur in the end times.

In an elaboration upon the Garabandal messages, Lueken's prophecies proclaim that after the Warning there will be a "Great Miracle" that will appear in the sky, which will occur through the intercession of the Virgin Mary. Its purpose is to encourage humanity to amend its sinful behavior, but agents of Satan will attempt to disprove its divine nature (*OLR Book* 1986: 45). If humanity does not change after this supernatural spectacle, the Chastisement will follow, and unlike the Garabandal messages, Lueken's prophecies are explicit about the first portion of the Chastisement involving nuclear war: "A war far greater than any war fought in the history of creation shall come upon mankind soon. Flames shall engulf many nations, burning the skin from bones, and the skin shall dry up and blow away as if it had never been!" (*Roses Book*, vol. 2: 149). In another apparition, Lueken has a vision of a nuclear explosion, "Oh, I see a great horrible war. I see (...) it looks like a mushroom. A tremendous explosion and everything is gone! Oh! [The Virgin Mary then says:] 'Satan, My child, shall have his hand upon the button'" (Skovmand 1993: 86). In the next part of the message, Lueken speaks of uniformed soldiers with "red stars on their hats," and identifies the aggressor in this third world war as Russia, and concludes with a command from the Virgin Mary to pray for the conversion of Russia in order to avert nuclear catastrophe. In the Bayside messages, as in other Cold War apparitions, communism and Satan are one in the same, part of the all-encompassing plot to destroy the world and Christianity.

Lueken's prophecies are replete with extensive descriptions of the Fireball Chastisement which is predicted to follow the nuclear Chastisement, with visions of bodies that have been incinerated and cities flattened and "knocked over, like a stack of cards" (*OLR Book* 1986: 46). Although Lueken makes a distinction between the nuclear Chastisement and the comet Chastisement hurled by an angry God, one cannot help but consider the Fireball in terms of the imagery of nuclear conflagration. Lueken's accounts of bodies burnt black and cities completely leveled evoke the images of the destruction of Hiroshima and Nagasaki by nuclear bombs and the blackened bodies amid the ruins.

Visions of a fiery apocalypse and its aftermath, whether by means of nuclear weaponry or divine fireball, are easy to imagine in the nuclear age and imbue Lueken's prophecies with a disturbing visual power.

The visions of apocalyptic annihilation and communist invasion that are consistently repeated throughout Lueken prophecies also are conveyed through the illustrations in the shrine's publications. For example, on one page of the shrine's "Blue Book" is an illustration of a communist demon emerging from Russia with blood dripping from its fingers, alongside a quote from the Virgin Mary: "Communism (...) the scourge of mankind"; beneath this is another illustration of a cemetery filled with crosses and then a photograph of a mushroom cloud, with a description of World War III "that will almost exterminate the earth" (*OLR Book* 1986: 49). Such recurring descriptions and imagery that emphasize nuclear annihilation in the Bayside literature present a vision of the nuclear threat as a menacing presence looming over all humanity, an event that human beings are powerless to prevent. Like other Cold War era prophecy interpretations, the Bayside apparitions portray the proliferation and use of nuclear weapons as inevitable, and any human effort to bring about peace and disarmament is viewed as hopeless: "My children, all of the cries of peace that go out throughout your world cannot prevent the explosion of nuclear warfare upon mankind! The hand of God that withheld this punishment upon mankind is being withdrawn!" (Skovmand 1993: 87). In this view, human beings are helpless in the face of overwhelming nuclear and communist threats, and the destiny of the world can only be altered by following Mary's interdictions from Fátima, which are consistently reaffirmed in the Bayside messages: "I warned you in Fátima that, unless you prayed and did penance, Russia and the agents of the sickle and the hammer would go throughout the world cutting down nations and bringing death, destruction, and slavery" (Skovmand 1993: 86).

The anticommunist themes that characterize other Cold War apparitions are reiterated and amplified in Lueken's prophecies, which predict a Russian invasion of the United States, a "master plan of takeover" that involves ships and submarines, with the enemy surrounding the entire country and assaulting the nation on its borders and secretly from within: "Russia, My children, is not entering where you can see them. They are infiltrating now into every side of your nation: north, south, east, and west – on the outer fringes and the inner fringes" (*Roses Book*, vol. 2: 447). In other messages, Lueken foresees streets "running with blood," an invasion by Chinese communists, and the presence of "enemies all around you, waiting. They plan to move upon you from within" (*Roses Book*, vol. 2: 400-411).

Such predictions of a communist invasion of the United States, as well as communist infiltration of American institutions and society in general, pervade the Bayside prophecies, echoing ongoing Red Scare anxieties that arose after World War II, and reflecting the conspiratorial "paranoid style" that came to the fore during the Cold War.[8] For many Americans, the widespread fear of communism existed as a foreign apocalyptic threat but also as a creeping, sinister presence that lurked around every corner, and these domestic and alien threats coupled together became a defining feature of the Cold War. As historians James Gilbert and Peter Kuznick argue, the Cold War convinced millions of Americans to "interpret their world in terms of insidious enemies at home and abroad who threatened them with nuclear and other forms of annihilation" (Gilbert & Kuznick 2001: 11).

This fear of communism grew during the 1940s and 1950s, as J. Edgar Hoover, the director of the Federal Bureau of Investigation, created a network of surveillance to monitor the activities of potential communist subversives. From 1947 to 1958, the House Committee on Un-American Activities obsessively investigated alleged communist subversion in the film industry, resulting in the "blacklisting" of roughly 2,000 individuals, a process that garnered extensive media coverage and further publicized concerns about communist infiltration. Most famously, the fervent and sensationalistic anticommunist activities of Wisconsin Senator Joseph McCarthy from 1950-1954 further fueled fears of communist subversion and espionage, as he claimed that communist spies had "infested" the U.S. State Department as well as universities, labor unions, Hollywood, and other American institutions, in what he referred to as the most evil and massive conspiracy in the history of the world. McCarthy was a Catholic, and while anticommunist attitudes were already prevalent among many American Catholics, his views about the infiltration of evil communist enemies were embraced by influential members of the Catholic community and promoted in Catholic publications and the popular media, and Catholics remained at the forefront of the anticommunist movement during the McCarthy era (Crosby 1978; Perry & Echeverria 1988: 248-253).

In the 1950s, Cold War McCarthyism found full expression in the apparitions experienced by Mary Ann Van Hoof in the town of Necedah in rural Wisconsin, which communicated apocalyptic, conspiratorial, and adamant anticommunist themes. Van Hoof's visions received extensive media coverage at the time, especially after approximately 100,000 people journeyed to her farm to witness her converse with the Virgin Mary on August 15, 1950 (Zimdars-Swartz 1991: 259). Like the Bayside apparitions, the earlier Van Hoof messages are lengthy and discursive, and restate the key components of the Fátima messages, with condemnations of atheistic communism, the need for devotion to Mary's Immaculate Heart, penance, rosary prayers for the consecration and conversion of Russia, and the encroaching Russian threat. Warnings about the Soviet infiltration of American society were transmitted as well, reaffirm-

8 For an analysis of the conspiratorial mindset in American history and its emergence during the Cold War, see Hofstadter (1967).

ing McCarthy's pronouncement in 1950 about communist infiltration of the government. Van Hoof in fact asked devotees to pray for McCarthy, who she portrays as somewhat of an American saint in her messages (Zimdars-Swartz 1991: 261). Much like Lueken's locutions, Van Hoof's prophecies also contain graphic descriptions of the horrors of nuclear war, warnings about a coming Chastisement, information about Soviet invasion plans, satanic-communist super-conspiracies, references to spaceships, and a preoccupation with the location of Soviet submarines off the coastline.[9]

Lueken was aware of Van Hoof's apparitions and communicated with her at least once and perhaps numerous times, with one source asserting that Van Hoof had to change her telephone number because Lueken began calling her so often in the middle of the night.[10] The possibility that Lueken imitated the Necedah messages has been noted by several observers, who see similarities in the language, topics, and style used by both visionaries (Carroll 1986: 138-140; Cuneo 1997:167-168; Laycock 2015: 22-23). While the correlations between Lueken's messages and those of Van Hoof deserve further analysis, Lueken's apparitions also clearly incorporate aspects of previous Marian visitations (not only Fátima and Garabandal, but La Salette, Lourdes, Pontmain, Beauraing) as well as themes present in the millennialist Marian writings of St. Louis-Marie Grignion de Montfort (1673-1716), the anticommunist prophecies of Sister Elena Aiello (1895-1961), the writings of Father Nicholas Gruner (1942-2015; publisher of *The Fatima Crusader* magazine), and the conspiratorial views of The Pilgrims of St. Michael group from Quebec that began to support Lueken's visions in 1973.

In the context of American Cold War culture, the Bayside phenomenon emerged in 1970, the same year that the Necedah apparitions were condemned a second time by church officials and interest in them had diminished. The Bayside movement thus filled a void in American apparitional culture, with its overt hints of Necedah, a seer with similar attributes, and the reiteration of other familiar prophecies as well as new messages from heaven that addressed current concerns. Interest in Lueken's apparitions grew in popularity throughout the 1970s and 1980s and the movement superceded Necedah as a nexus for the devotional desire for an apparitional cultus that channeled the apocalyptic fears and anticommunist fervor that existed among Marian devotees in the United States. Although such anxieties ebbed and flowed during the Cold War, they were ever-present for many in American culture, and intensified during the 1980s when U.S. President Ronald Reagan characterized the

9 The Necedah apparitions have been discussed by Kselman & Avella (1986), Zimdars-Swartz (1989, 1991: 259-267), and Kselman (this volume).

10 "My Memories of Veronica Lueken by Mrs. Ann Ferguson." These Last Days Ministries website: <http://www.tldm.org/news4/memoriesofveronica.htm>; "Bayside, New York." Unity Publishing Inc. website: <http://www.unitypublishing.com/Apparitions/Bayside.htm>l (both accessed December 5, 2017).

Soviet Union as an "evil empire" and asked for prayers for those who lived under communist oppression; he also advocated for a build-up of the U.S. nuclear arsenal and described nuclear warfare with the Soviets as a manifestation of the ageless battle between good and evil (Goodnight 1986). The popularity of Lueken's prophecies peaked in the mid-1980s, in accordance with escalating Cold War apprehensions, in the same way that Van Hoof's messages had a popular appeal during the height of the anticommunist McCarthy era.

Importantly, the apparitions of both seers clearly repeat the core elements of Fátima messages, and illustrate the enduring influence of Fátima in the context of the Marian subculture in the United States. In addition to the familiar themes of impending apocalypse, communist menace, and the conversion of Russia, the Necedah and Bayside apparitions both condemn the liberalizing changes in Church doctrine and policy implemented by the Second Vatican Council (1962-1965), and reflect the broader Roman Catholic traditionalist movement that arose in response to Vatican II. Although most Catholics embraced the Council's *aggiornamento* ("updating"), a small segment regarded the changes as a betrayal of the faith and the abandonment of a rich heritage of sacred traditions. As Margry notes, "since the 1960s the modernization of the Roman Church has in practice increasingly taken on the nature of a cultural war between the large group of mainstream Catholics who have accepted the modernization, and smaller groups of conservative Catholics who wish to remain traditional (...) the messages [from Mary] with their opposition to the new course of the faith, are literally a gift from heaven" (Margry 2009: 245).

Like other Marian apparitions with traditionalist ideologies, the Bayside prophecies depict Vatican II and the renewal of the Church as heretical and the result of a vast conspiracy perpetrated by communists, Freemasons, the "Illuminati," and other satanic infiltrators. Lueken's messages, for example, condemn the administration of Pope Paul VI (1963-1978), who endorsed the reforms of Vatican II, and they assert that the authentic Paul VI was poisoned, held captive, and replaced by an imposter who had undergone plastic surgery to resemble the real pope (*OLR Book* 1986: 118-124). This doppelgänger "Antipope," a communist agent who was aided by his satanic allies, then implemented the modernist changes in the Church. Thus, Baysiders believe that they do not oppose the authority of Pope Paul VI, because they maintain that he had nothing to do with the progressive reforms of Vatican II, and they assert their identities as true and righteous Catholic devotees who are upholding the faith during a time of evil conspiracies and demonic assaults on the Church.

Conspiracy theories about the changes instituted by the Second Vatican Council are not unique to the Baysiders, but are associated with other ecclesiastically unsanctioned Marian apparitions, existing as a persistent feature of the traditionalist Catholic belief that the enemies of Christ created Vatican II in their effort to destroy the Church. In the Bayside prophecies, the connection between Vatican II and the satanic infiltration of the Church is allegedly contained in the third secret of Fátima, which Mary reveals to Lueken: "How I warned and warned that satan would enter into the highest realms of the hierarchy in Rome. The third Secret, My child, is that satan would enter into My Son's Church" (*Roses Book*, vol. 2: 146). In this locution, Lueken asserts that the disclosure of the third secret of Fátima in 1960 would have warned the faithful of the takeover of the Church, and prevented the liberalizing changes; when the third secret was finally revealed in the year 2000 and there was no mention of this plot, Baysiders predictably rejected the contents of the message as fraudulent. Like other traditionalists, for Baysiders the loss of traditional Catholic doctrines and rites remains a conflict between good and evil, an eschatological battle between the righteous army of Christ and a horde of communists, atheists, and other sinister minions of Satan.

Similar to previous fundamentalist and nativistic movements, the emphasis on the restoration of traditions that characterizes the Bayside phenomenon and other post-Vatican II Marian apparitional movements is a reaction to a sense of religious and cultural crisis, and a loss of one's religious heritage and identity. Lueken's jeremiads about societal decay and corruption specifically condemn the ways that traditional Catholic attitudes about God, morality, family, sexuality, and the roles of women and men, among other things, are being destroyed. As a direct response to the liberalizing changes in the Church as well as the threat of secularization and modernist tendencies in general, the Bayside messages not only depict the end of the world, but portray the end of pre-Vatican II Catholicism as an apocalyptic assault. Lueken's prophecies abound with descriptions of societal upheaval, inexplicable change, and cultural crisis, which are the recognizable features that have given rise to apocalyptic movements in general, and express a similar sense of overwhelming chaos, lawlessness, and uncontrollable societal disintegration (Cohn 1970; Barkun 1974: 44-45; Wojcik 1997: 133-147).

While this apocalyptic perception of contemporary society as overwhelmingly evil conceivably might lead to fatalism and resignation about the state of a doomed and irredeemable world, the Bayside prophecies, like other Fátima-inspired apparitions, and the Catholic traditionalist movement in general, are characterized by a militant rhetoric that positions devotees as spiritual warriors and members of Mary's army who are actively fighting modernist threats and current evils.[11] In the context of the Cold War, the target of this spiritual militancy was obvious, as atheistic communism assumed the role of primary enemy, "the evil other" that threatened tradition and the faith that necessitated the Virgin Mary's intercession and divine directives for protecting Christianity and averting societal destruction. Marian devotion thus became both a weapon and a form of armor, and praying the rosary as well as

11 For a discussion of this militant aspect of Catholic traditionalism, see Dinges (1991).

9.2. Baysiders kneel and pray the rosary during an evening vigil at the apparition site. [Photograph by Daniel Wojcik, 1990]

performing novenas and utilizing decorated statues of Mary not only provided personal protection but had the political and militant meanings of fighting communism and saving the world. Although the messages and practices associated with the Virgin Mary had humble origins, they gained enormous political power throughout the Cold War era. Her prophecies were circulated and elaborated upon throughout the vast network of Marian veneration, reflecting local and national concerns and contexts, affecting the lives of millions of people and influencing popular attitudes and politics in ways that have been ignored or underestimated by most scholars of the Cold War.

The practices by the Baysiders at the apparition site in Flushing Meadows Park express the widespread notions of Marian piety as protection and religious weaponry, with Mary's instructions to Lueken often functioning as strategic communiqués and spiritual maneuvers in the battle against communism and other perceived evils. Aligned with Lueken's prophecies, the prayers and practices of Baysiders enact a form of spiritual warfare in a world they believe is pervaded by evil forces, demons, and Satan in physical form.[12] The temporary shrine that Baysiders construct for their vigils at the apparition site is a primary way to combat such wickedness, as devotees ritually transform a secular place in the park into a sacred space of divine power where Mary appears as warrior, protectress, and spiritual military advisor, delivering heavenly directives. The apparition site becomes a spiritually-charged focal point for the salvation of the world, and Baysiders believe their prayerful efforts are especially amplified at this sacralized place, comparable to a devotional missile-base, where their prayers are launched in the fight against evil.

Of the various practices at the vigils, of particular relevance to Cold War concerns are the incorporation of additional prayers into the Baysiders' version of the rosary, specifically the Fátima Prayer and the Prayer to Saint Michael. The Fátima Prayer was communicated to the seer Lucia dos Santos by the Virgin Mary in her appearances at Fátima, and Mary apparently told Lucia to add it to the rosary. Because of Mary's other well-known request at Fátima for Russia to be consecrated to her Immaculate Heart, the Fátima Prayer is believed by some to combat the atheistic threat of Russia and facilitate its conversion. The Prayer to Saint Michael that the Baysiders recite dates from 1886, when it was added by Pope Leo XIII to the "Leonine Prayers." These prayers were later specified by Pope Pius XI in 1930 to be recited with the intention of granting tranquility and freedom of religion "to the afflicted people of Russia."[13] After Vatican II, the recitation of the Prayer to Saint Michael and the other Leonine Prayers that were said after mass were officially suppressed by the Church and no longer included in services. At the Bayside vigils, the inclusion of the Fátima Prayer and the Prayer to Saint Michael into the recitation of the rosary thus invokes the messages of Fátima about converting Russia while also reviving officially suppressed pre-Vatican II prayers, as one of the many lost traditions that Baysiders and other traditionalist Catholics want reinstated. The Saint Michael prayer has special significance in the context of apocalyptic fears and the Baysiders' battle against communism, as Michael the Archangel is the commander of the army of God who defeats Satan and the forces of evil in the apocalyptic war in heaven at the end of the world, as described in the Book of Revelation.

12 One of Lueken's frequently cited messages, for instance, asserts that Satan entered into the priesthood in 1971, while another message states that "Satan – not the lesser demons of hell, but Satan himself – now walks your earth. Earth-year 1940 was his beginning. He entered your country (the U.S.A.) in 1970" (*OLR Book* 1986: 96).

13 *Allocution Indictam ante*, June 30, 1930, in *Acta Apostolicae Sedis* 22 (1930): 301; Laycock 2015: 129-130.

For Baysiders, their rosary prayers also are believed to offer protection from imminent nuclear war and ongoing evil assaults. The following narrative is included in the Bayside literature as proof of the power of rosary prayers as a shield from a nuclear attack:

> When Hiroshima was 'annihilated' by the first atomic bomb, one household was singularly spared. To this day, all 16 members of that household are alive while every other person within an area of one mile of the center of that explosion is dead (...) there was only one thing that was found to be different: In that house, the family rosary was said every day! In that house they were living the message of Fatima! (*OLR Book* 1986: 48).

Although rosary prayers serve as the primary spiritual artillery and protective practice utilized during the vigils, Baysiders also emphasize the wearing of sacramentals and the use of other holy objects as auxiliary fortification to protect against evil forces and future catastrophes. Lueken's messages from Mary instruct Baysiders to store food, nail crucifixes to their doors, pray, and protect themselves with their "spiritual armor," such as the brown scapular, rosaries, religious medals, saint's statues, and the shrine's miraculous rose petals believed to be blessed by Mary and Jesus at the apparition site. The importance of these spiritual objects is continually stressed in the prophecies: "Both front and back doors must have a crucifix. I say this to you because there will be carnage within your areas, and this will pass you by if you keep your crucifix upon your doors" (*OLR Booklet* n.d.: 11). The brown scapular (the Scapular of Our Lady of Mt. Carmel) is especially emphasized, as Baysiders believe that wearing it expresses one's consecration to the Virgin Mary, and in return they receive her divine protection and are promised salvation. The wearing of the brown scapular, popularized in the Middle Ages, also was promoted by the Fátima seer Lucia, who said that the Virgin Mary wanted her devotees to wear it, a request that was interpreted by some to imply its power to defend against communist assaults. Like the Fátima messages, Lueken's prophecies reiterate that the two most powerful devotions to protect against evil are the rosary and the scapular:

> My child, this is your armor and the armor for all mankind. With these sacramentals, We will withstand the onslaughts of satan and his agents. (...) you will make it known to the world that the rosary of prayer and the scapular for protection shall be the major instruments from Heaven to safeguard mankind in the days ahead.[14]

14 "The Rosary and the Brown Scapular." Our Lady of the Roses, Mary Help of Mothers Shrine website: <http://www.ourladyoftheroses.org/ourladyoftheroses/images/The_Messages/VigilMessages/THE%20ROSARY%20AND%20THE%20BROWN%20SCAPULAR.pdf> (accessed October 20, 2017).

Another important tradition developed by Baysiders that pertains to Cold War anxieties involves the ritual use of cameras as divinatory devices to document supernatural phenomena at the apparition site. Referred to as "miracle photos" or "miraculous Polaroids," the photographs taken by devotees are regarded as divine communications that offer prophetic and personal insights, with some of the photos believed to contain end times signs, communist imagery, and allegorical symbols that reveal the redemptive role of the Virgin Mary in the last days. The use of Polaroid cameras to document miraculous phenomena emerged as a tradition during the early years of the Bayside apparitions and continues today at the site, with some devotees still preferring to use old Polaroid SX-70 cameras rather than digital cameras. Although this practice might appear idiosyncratic, the use of miraculous photography is not unique to the Baysiders, as the devotional use of cameras is now an established feature of Marian visionary culture (see Apolito 2005: 101-121; Christian 2001; Margry 2004b).[15]

In my visits to the apparition site over the past three decades, Baysiders were observed taking photographs for the duration of the three-hour evening vigils, although most began snapping pictures once Lueken began receiving messages from Mary and other divine beings, with some individuals wandering around the site with their cameras in hand in search of supernatural manifestations. The symbols and figures on the photos include streaks and swirls of light; images representing Mary, Jesus, various saints, angels, and demons; and dotted lines and beads of light that are said to be the Baysiders' rosary prayers ascending to heaven. Perhaps the most well-known Bayside photograph is the "Jacinta 1972" Polaroid image, taken in 1971, which is believed to be a direct communication from Jacinta Marto, one of the Fátima seers, who appeared to Lueken in a vision and confirmed that she had inscribed the message on the Polaroid. This photograph is variously interpreted to reveal the exact date and hour of the coming Chastisement, the year that Satan and the Antichrist entered the Vatican (said to be 1972), or facts about the true third secret of Fátima that have not yet been disclosed.

After the introduction of the popular Polaroid SX-70 camera in the early 1970s, hundreds of miraculous photographs were produced by Baysiders depicting the apocalyptic scenarios described by Lueken in her prophecies, with

15 Margry (2019) traces the practice of using photography to document miraculous phenomena to the apparitions at San Damiano, Italy (1964-1981) where it developed into a widespread devotional tradition. Previous examples of miracle photography occurred on occasion at other apparition sites, such as Necedah (Zimdars-Swartz 1991: 299, n. 74), while the belief in the camera's ability to document the supernatural emerged soon after the development of photography in the nineteenth century and is intertwined with the perceived apparitional abilities of the photographic process (Wojcik 2009). The availability of affordable Polaroid cameras in the 1970s coincided with the appearance of the Bayside apparitions and Baysiders popularized the tradition of instantaneous miracle documentation, with the sharing and interpretation of miraculous Polaroids at the apparition site.

photos revealing the Ball of Redemption, a comet striking the planet Earth, the Warning, and "Exterminatus" (an apocalyptic angel of death), as well as the imposter pope, corruption in the Vatican, and communist threats. A famous photograph taken on May 7, 1976 exposes the communist menace, depicting two statues of the Virgin Mary and an ominous communist image that affirms the Fátima messages: "looming between the two statues of Our Lady appears a large reddish-brown head of a bear. What does this bear represent? Russia, communist Russia. Our Lady is calling to mind the messages She gave us at Fatima in which Our Lady told us that if Her requests for prayer, for penance, for amendment of life were not heeded, that Russia would be the scourge of mankind."[16] Another well-known photograph reveals the "red hammer and sickle and the clenched fist of communism symbols," which are interpreted as communist forces infiltrating the Vatican.[17] These and other miracle photographs thus provide visual proofs that confirm the anticommunist and apocalyptic messages of the Bayside apparitions, while the practice of taking such photos at the site allows devotees to directly experience heavenly presence and receive tangible materializations of the supernatural.

Although the Baysiders' practice of miraculous photography, their use of sacred objects for spiritual protection, and their praying of the rosary as a devotional weapon clearly express anticommunist anxieties and apocalyptic themes, not everyone who participates in the apparitional events in Flushing Meadows Park necessarily embraces every aspect of Lueken's Cold War-infused prophecies. Devotees attend the vigils for deeply personal reasons, such as the need for healing, the renewal of faith, protection, heavenly graces, or asking for divine intercession for loved ones. Others are attracted to the vigils because of the expression of traditionalist practices de-emphasized after Vatican II, and the Baysiders' emphasis on direct revelation, miraculous phenomena, healing, and prophecies advocate a return to a form of religiosity characterized by the belief in miracles and tangible divine presence. Ultimately, in the midst of perceived apocalyptic and evil threats, and personal suffering and individual concerns, Our Lady of Bayside is embraced by devotees as the compassionate and loving Mother, the Mother who nurtures all, who suffers and weeps over her children, and who intercedes and offers protection in the modern world.

16 "Miraculous Photographs taken at Our Lady of the Roses Shrine Gallery #1." These Last Days Ministries website: <http://www.tldm.org/photos/f4jp.htm> (accessed October 21, 2017).

17 "Roses from Heaven, March 24, 1973." These Last Days Ministries website: <http://www.rosesfromheaven.com/1973/730324.html> (accessed October 21, 2017).

The end of the Cold War and the future of the Bayside movement

With the end of the Cold War and the collapse of the Soviet Union in 1991, many of the themes and anxieties expressed in the Bayside prophecies suddenly seemed in question. Previous predictions about Soviet invasion and mass infiltration of American society by communists that may have resonated with Marian devotees in decades past would appear to have lost their credibility. Furthermore, Lueken's locutions about Russian death rays, UFOs from hell, an imposter pope, demonic vampires, and the machinations of the Illuminati might seem to situate the movement on the religio-cultural fringe. Yet in response to the changing political and cultural contexts, Baysiders have selectively highlighted certain prophecies and de-emphasized others, modifying and adapting their interpretations of Lueken's predictions to correspond with current events and dominating concerns.

Nonetheless, a significant proportion of the Bayside messages are clearly frozen in the Cold War context and cannot be simply ignored, such as the notion of Russia as a godless communist menace. As previously discussed, the peril of atheistic communism has been a central component of Marian apparitional culture since the revealing of the Fátima messages, and the fear of a Soviet global takeover helped fuel the Marian revival during the Cold War. While the collapse of communism in the Soviet Union and the Eastern bloc might be viewed by Marian devotees as a direct result of Mary's intervention and the fulfillment of her directives presented at Fátima, Lueken and her followers have steadfastly denied that the Russian and communist threat has ended. Like other apocalyptic prophecy interpreters who have assigned the Soviet Union an essential role in the last days, the end of the Cold War is regarded by Baysiders as a temporary "false peace" that may have even brought the world closer to Armageddon. This view also is expressed, for instance, by televangelist Pat Robertson, who claimed that the collapse of the Soviet Union was a devious ploy and that Russia will revert to its Cold War and communist ideology after rebuilding itself with economic assistance from the United States and European nations (Robertson 1991: xiv-xvi).[18]

The Bayside apparitions express similar ideas about Russian deception and the persistence of the communist threat, with Lueken's messages reasserting the anticommunist warnings common in the Cold War era. For example, after Lueken finished reading a newspaper article in 1991 about the demise of communism in the Soviet Union, the Virgin Mary appeared and delivered a desperate message: "Do not be deceived. Their father is the father of all liars: satan. Their master plan is in motion. Pray for the light. Minds are clouded.

18 In this regard, also see Lindsey (1994) for discussions of continuing nuclear apocalyptic threats and the prophetic role of Russia in the post-Cold War era.

I repeat: it is a ruse. Wake up America or you will suffer much" (*Directives from Heaven* 2 (10), January 24, 1992). Other Bayside messages also warn of imminent Soviet attack, with condemnations of Mikhail Gorbachev and Boris Yeltsin as agents of Satan, and emphasizing that the democratic reforms in the Soviet Union are part of a demonic communist strategy: "Russia is perpetuating one of the cruelest hoaxes in history (i.e., the so-called failure and death of communism with the replacement of a free and democratic government) with its objectives remaining, as always, the same: communist enslavement of the world."[19] The miraculous photographs taken by Baysiders at the apparition site are believed to further confirm such assertions. A well-known image taken at a vigil in 2003 is said to depict a "large red sickle," and this photo is equated with news reports of Russia supplying Iraq with military equipment for use against the United States, and the related commentary makes clear the continuing Russian threat: "Our Lady has warned us for years that Russia is not converted – atheistic communism still rules in the Kremlin – but is perpetrating a diabolical ruse as a means to achieve their longtime stated objective of worldwide communist domination."[20]

In the same way that the belief in the unending evil of communism is inextricably woven into the Bayside prophecies, so too is the assertion that Russia is stockpiling nuclear weapons in preparation for an apocalyptic attack on the United States: "For it is their plan to subdue you, once they get the billions that they need in aid, to bring up the economy and buy more armaments. They have not disposed of their armaments, My child and My children. They store them in other nations. They have the same goals as their forefathers" (*Directives from Heaven* 3 (57), November 12, 1993: 1). Current Bayside publications and the various websites devoted to Lueken's prophecies continue to emphasize the imminence of the Chastisement, World War III, and a nuclear conflagration with Russia, as this scenario is relentlessly expressed in the majority of Lueken's messages delivered from the early 1970s until her death. Fears of nuclear catastrophe may have decreased in secular culture in the decades after the end of the Cold War, but the inevitable role of nuclear weapons in the last days remains deeply embedded in the Baysider worldview, just as the notion of communist ideology as an apocalyptic adversary in the end times is thoroughly ingrained in Marian prophecy culture, reflecting a belief tradition that has existed for three-quarters of a century. As theorists of religion have observed, when long-standing and deeply held prophecy beliefs are disconfirmed or challenged, devotees do not necessarily abandon them but often assert their beliefs with greater intensity, finding ways to rationalize and

19 *Directives from Heaven* 4 (63), February 4, 1994: 2; Lueken 1998, vol. 6: 467-469.

20 "More Miraculous Photos from August '02 to August '03." St. Michael's World Apostolate website: <http://www.smwa.org/documents/miraculous_photos/More_mps_8-02_8-03/Document_More_Mirac_photos_8-02--8-03.htm> (accessed October 23, 2017).

ST. MICHAEL GUARDIAN OF THE FAITH

ROSES

REDEMPTION GRACE PEACE

BAYSIDE, "THE LOURDES OF AMERICA"

Our Lady of the Roses, Mary Help of Mothers Shrine
Box 52, Bayside, New York 11361-0052

MESSAGE OF OUR LADY AND OUR LORD TO VERONICA LUEKEN

VATICAN PAVILION SITE, FLUSHING MEADOW PARK

March 26, 1983 — Eve of Palm Sunday

"Russia plans to invade the United States with missiles" —Jesus

★ Warhead In Abandoned N.Y. Subway Tunnel ★

BACKGROUND STORY

Veronica Lueken, the seer of Bayside, is a wife and mother of five children. She is in her late fifties and lives on Long Island, New York. The story of her heavenly visitations goes back to the year 1968 when St. Theresa started appearing to her and giving her poems and sacred writings by dictation. Prior to this, Veronica had not received any manifestations from Heaven.

Our Lady Herself appeared to Veronica in her home on April 7, 1970, informing her that She would appear on the grounds of the old St. Robert Bellarmine Church in Bayside on June 18, 1970, that vigils of prayer be held there, and that full directions be given to the clergy of the parish to prepare for Our Lady's first visit there. Our Lady also requested that a Shrine and Basilica be erected on this Her chosen Sacred Site, which is to be named "Our Lady of the Roses, Mary, Help of Mothers". She promised to come on the eve of the great feast days of the Church, which dates would be given to Veronica beforehand. The Blessed Mother also instructed Veronica to disseminate the Messages given to her throughout the whole world.

Our Lady has requested that the Rosary be recited aloud by the crowd during the whole of the Vigil. All are requested to kneel in the presence of Jesus. The Message is repeated word for word by Veronica. Veronica also describes what she sees. All is recorded by tape.

Veronica—I was startled to see the lights, the blue lights, coming out from among the trees. And there are two—you could explain them as being, like ball in shape; it is very difficult...round. And these lights—in human language I would find it very difficult to explain to you the beauty of them and where they came from.

Veronica in ecstasy at this same Vigil of March 26, 1983.

standing at Our Lady's left side; Our Lady's now by His right side. And Our Lady is looking up. And Jesus now is looking all about Him. He has on His burgundy cape. And it's down from His back—I can see Jesus' hair—and the cape is extending down to His footsteps, down to His feet.

Now, Jesus is now taking His hand out, like this, and making the sign of the cross: In the name of the Father, and of the Son, and of the Holy Ghost. Now Jesus also is turning to His left, our right side, and making the sign of the cross: In the name of the Father, and of the Son, and of the Holy Ghost.

Now He's moved over. He's floated over a bit to the uppermost branch on our right side of the trees. And now He's turning and going back to standing next to Our Lady—oh, about—now They're about—I can't judge the distance through the sky, but I would say They're standing about sixteen feet above Our Lady's statue.

Now Jesus is taking His first finger and placing it to His mouth; that means to listen and repeat.

Jesus—"My child, I will not continue the discourse at this time over the matter of obedience, charity, and other virtues that have dimmed the working force within the circle. You

9.3. Front page of a Baysider religious tract (dated March 26, 1983) with a headline that conveys heavenly warnings about a nuclear attack on the United States and imminent communist Russian invasion. After the end of the Cold War, this message was reinterpreted to refer to portable nuclear devices that are now in the hands of terrorist organizations planning to attack the United States.
[From a newsletter distributed by St. Paul's Guild]

reaffirm ostensibly failed prophecies (see Festinger et al. 1956; Dawson 1999). For Baysiders, the collapse of the Soviet Union and the *seeming* end of the Cold War do not disprove Lueken's apparitions, but are interpreted as further confirmation of her predictions of a conspiratorial communist master plan, in an evil world on the verge of destruction that can only be saved by increased devotion to Mary.

Although belief in communist attacks and a nuclear war with Russia remain central to the Baysider worldview, after the terrorist attacks of September 11, 2001, a number of subsequent interpretations of Lueken's prophecies include Islamic terrorists as agents of future assaults on the United States. For example, Lueken's proclamation in 1983 that "Russia plans to invade the United States with missiles!" has been retroactively interpreted to refer to portable nuclear devices and "suitcase nukes" that are now believed to be in the hands of terrorist organizations. These transportable bombs are said to have been acquired either directly from Russia or that somehow "disappeared" during the chaos of the collapse of the Soviet Union and are currently the property of hostile organizations, perhaps already smuggled into the United States.[21] Similarly, Lueken's prophecies about the upcoming carnage, "mass and slaughter death," and streets "running with blood" to be experienced in the United States – originally delivered in the context of her predictions of nuclear war, communist aggressions, or strife in the American government – have now been recontextualized in terms possible future terrorists attacks, with commentary and links to supporting "news stories."[22] One of Lueken's visions from December, 1979, has received particular attention, as she describes a cross in the sky with a handle resembling an Arabian "dagger-like saber, with a cross on a handle"; this vague reference culled from hundreds of messages has served as a springboard for post-Cold War discussions of Islamic terrorism, the "Islamic hatred for the cross," Islamic infiltrators wearing the cross as camouflage, terrorist sleeper cells in major American cities, and an assortment of other discussions and diatribes.[23] With the apparent lack of explicit references to Islamic terrorism in Lueken's lengthy locutions, believers in the Bayside apparitions have attempted to uncover new prophetic meanings, sometimes in the most obscure detail, in their interpretative acrobatics.

The terrorist destruction of the World Trade Center in 2001 also provided a significant opportunity for a confirmation of Lueken's prophecies of imminent apocalypse. Over the years, Lueken repeatedly predicted various destructive assaults on New York City, as a center of sin and a target of God's wrath. In some apparitions she communicated vague and generalized prophecies, but on other occasions she specified the locations and details of these attacks, which include the Statue of Liberty and the Empire State Building. She also was told by Jesus that a nuclear warhead would be placed in an abandoned subway station and that there would be a submachine gun massacre on the

21 "Russia plans to invade the United States with missiles!" These Last Days Ministries website: <http://www.tldm.org/news2/missiles.htm> (accessed December 16, 2017).

22 "Secret Report: Terrorists Running Wild Within US Borders," These Last Days Ministries website: <http://www.tldm.org/news31/terrorists-running-wild-within-us-borders.htm> (accessed December 18, 2017).

23 "Here's Everything You Need to Know about Islamic Hatred for the Christian Cross." These Last Days Ministries website: <http://www.tldm.org/News26/heres-everything-you-need-to-know-about-islamic-hate-for-the-christian-cross.htm>; "Muslims May Wear and Pray to the Cross to Deceive Christians." These Last Days Ministries website; <http://www.tldm.org/news32/muslims-may-wear-and-pray-to-the-cross-to-deceive-christians-says-muslim-cleric.htm> (accessed December 18, 2017).

streets of Manhattan by members of a communist nation. Although none of these events have transpired, after the terrorist attacks of September 11, it was revealed that the Virgin Mary purportedly told Lueken about an attack "on the state building" eleven years earlier in a "private locution" that Lueken shared by telephone with the shrine director Michael Mangan. In the search to find updated meaning in Lueken's prophecies, this alleged reference was equated with the World Trade Center, and Mangan confirmed that the attacks were divine punishment for ignoring the Bayside prophecies during a "time of Armageddon" and for the ongoing sins of abortion, homosexuality, blasphemy, pornography, and the loss of religious faith, among many other societal evils.[24]

In addition to the post-Cold War interpretations of Lueken's prophecies mentioned above, her predictions have been applied by prophecy enthusiasts to hundreds of topics and contemporary events, in a process of apocalyptic semiotic arousal that sees the signs of the end times everywhere, including the financial collapse of 2008, tensions in the Middle East, a Chinese communist threat, natural disasters, plagues of locusts, clergy sexual abuse scandals, escalating tensions between Russia and the West, the development of nuclear capabilities by North Korea, and further indicated by legalized abortion, homosexuality, secularism, liberalism, and the loss of pre-Vatican II traditions, among other traditionalist concerns and condemnations. In 2017-2019, for example, the accusations and evidence of Russian interference in the politics and policies of other nations, including alleged criminal activities and cyberwarfare, added renewed verification of Lueken's prophecies for Baysiders. In early 2020, as awareness of the coronavirus (COVID-19) crisis increased, websites promoting Lueken's messages began to underscore her prophecies from the 1970s that refer to a coming plague. Initially, when less information was available about the virus, Lueken's numerous predictions about an imminent "Children's Plague" were highlighted, which asserted that "Many children will die in this cleansing. Young souls rescued from the contamination of a world that has given itself to Satan!"[25] A month later, after researchers of infectious diseases revealed that children are at a relatively low risk of becoming seriously ill from COVID-19, the postings on websites shifted emphasis away from prophecies of a children's plague to Lueken's more vague messages about chastising plagues and pestilence; other recurring themes reframed in

24 For the context of the prophecies related to 9/11 and their varied interpretations, see Laycock (2015: 180); "Our Lady of the Roses Predicted 9-11 Attack Exactly Eleven Years Before to the Day," These Last Days Ministries website: < http://www.tldm.org/news3/terrorism1.htm>: "New York City Targeted for Destruction," St. Michael's World Apostolate website: <http://www.smwa.org/Message/Text/1980_1989/88_01_10.htm>; and "Armageddon Rages," St. Michael's World Apostolate website: <http://www.smwa.org/Golden_Warrior/Index_Golden_Warrior.htm> (accessed December 19, 2017).

25 "Directives from Heaven #576–Children's Plague," These Last Days Ministries website: <https://www.tldm.org/Directives/d576.htm> (accessed April 7, 2020).

the context of the coronavirus pandemic include a world monetary crash and "global meltdown," the rise of a one world government, the implementation of the mark of the beast 666 to track people, and predictably, the pandemic considered as a "sinister communist plot to destabilize and spread fear."[26]

Despite these continuing attempts to reassert the prophetic relevance of Lueken's messages in times of crisis, the Bayside movement lost momentum after the end of the Cold War and especially after Lueken's death in 1995. Overall interest and participation in the movement declined further in the late 1990s when a schism in 1997 split the Baysiders into two opposing factions: Our Lady of the Roses Shrine (led by Lueken's husband, Arthur, until his death in 2002), and Saint Michael's World Apostolate (led by Michael Mangan, a former shrine director and workshop coordinator). The two groups have fought over the use of the apparition site, shrine assets, control of the Bayside shrine facilities, the shrine statue of the Virgin Mary, ownership of miraculous photos, and have even disputed the meanings and authenticity of some of Lueken's messages. Both groups seem to agree, however, that the schism is part of a communist-satanic plot to discredit the Bayside prophecies and demoralize Baysiders. Unlike the crowds of thousands of devotees that participated in the apparitional events at the height of the movement in the 1970s and 1980s, the number of people I have observed at the vigils and holy hour events in recent years has varied from less than ten to approximately fifty individuals, with somewhat larger attendance at the yearly anniversary celebration of Lueken's visions held each June.

The future of the Bayside movement is uncertain, as the turnout at prayer services and vigils has dwindled, organizers of the movement have aged or died, and twenty-five years after Lueken death, the bulk of her messages may seem frozen in another era. The entrenched Cold War tone of the apparitions no longer resonates for most Catholics, although Baysiders' efforts to update the prophecies and interpret them in terms of current crises may sustain the relevancy of Lueken's predictions for some. Apocalyptic fears and a sense of overwhelming evil in the world persist for many in American society, and globally as well, and the Bayside apparitions address those fears. In any case, the Bayside phenomenon presumably will continue as an online presence, subsumed within the broader Internet discourses involving Marian apparitions, apocalyptic belief, conspiracy theories, vernacular spirituality (or "conspiri-

26 "The Bayside Prophecies in the News," These Last Days Ministries website: <https://www.tldm.org/> (accessed April 7, 2020); "Coronavirus: Apocalyptic Pestilence? Sinister Communist Plot to Destabilize and Spread Fear?"; St. Michael's World Apostolate website: <https://www.youtube.com/watch?v=33rXgStjh4Y&feature=youtu.be> (accessed April 8, 2020).

tuality"), Catholic traditionalism, and in the cyber-cultic milieu of stigmatized knowledge.[27]

While the Bayside movement might appear to be in its last days in Flushing Meadows Park, a remnant of Baysiders most likely will survive, as devotees have endured for nearly fifty years, holding their vigils on a regular basis in veneration of Lueken's apparitions. Regardless of its future, the Bayside movement should not be dismissed as an anomalous religious occurrence or a manifestation of non-normative Catholicism. As an expression of grassroots religiosity, with its roots in the broader Marian apparition network and influenced by post-Vatican II Catholic traditionalism, the messages of Our Lady of Bayside reveal the dominating concerns and existential anxieties of the Cold War era, reflecting widespread apocalyptic angst, the fear of communism and other political concerns, as well as the revitalistic search for meaning among estranged Catholics in response to the loss of traditions post-Vatican II. In retrospect, Lueken's visions gave birth to one of the more significant Marian movements in American history, an extensive and largely unexplored elaboration upon the notions of Mary as a militant Cold War warrior, as a devotional weapon, and as a compassionate divine intercessor who could save humanity from nuclear annihilation. The Bayside movement may not have had an observable effect on Church politics in the United States, but its emphasis on communist, apocalyptic, and secularist threats expressed common concerns among the laity and within the Catholic hierarchy, while its insistence on a return to pre-Vatican II traditions intersected with the larger traditionalist Catholic movement, giving voice to the dissatisfaction with the post-conciliar reforms that disturbed many Catholics after Vatican II.

In a world believed by many to be increasingly out of control, Lueken's prophecies have offered explanations of crises and the promise that by following the Virgin Mary's directives, cataclysms could be averted, suffering and evil could be eliminated, and worldly salvation could be obtained. Although the Bayside movement now may be a shadow of its former self, its history offers insights into an important moment in American religious culture when the ideological aspects of Marian devotion converged with nuclear fears and anticommunist anxieties, revealing the political persona of Cold War Mary and the dynamics of vernacular religious piety.

27 See Barkun (2013), Apolito (2005), and Partridge (2005) for discussions of discourses of belief on the Internet, conspiracy subcultures, occulture, and stigmatized knowledge.

BIBLIOGRAPHY

Anders, Gunther. 1962. "Reflections on the H Bomb." In *Man Alone*, edited by Eric and Mary Josephson, 288-298. New York: Dell Publishing Company.

Apolito, Paolo. 1998. *Apparitions of the Madonna at Oliveto Citra: Local Visions and Cosmic Drama*, trans. William A. Christian, Jr. University Park: The Pennsylvania State University Press.

Apolito, Paolo. 2005. *The Internet and the Madonna: Religious Visionary Experiences on the Web*, trans. Anthony Shugar. Chicago-London: The University of Chicago Press.

Barkun, Michael. 1974. *Disaster and the Millennium*. New Haven, CT: Yale University Press.

Barkun, Michael. 2013 [2003]. *A Culture of Conspiracy: Apocalyptic Visions in Contemporary America*. Berkeley-Los Angeles: University of California Press.

Bennett, Jeffrey S. 2012. *When the Sun Danced: Myth, Miracles, and Modernity in Early Twentieth-Century Portugal*. Charlottesville-London: University of Virginia Press.

Boyer, Paul. 1985. *By the Bomb's Early Light: American Thought and Culture at the Dawn of the Atomic Age*. New York: Pantheon Books.

Boyer, Paul. 1992. *When Time Shall Be No More: Prophecy Belief in Modern American Culture*. Cambridge, MA: Belknap Press of Harvard University Press.

Bromley, David and Rachel S. Bobbitt. 2011. "Visions of the Virgin Mary: The Organizational Development of Marian Apparition Movements." *Nova Religio: The Journal of Alternative and Emergent Religions* 14 (3): 5-41.

Carroll, Michael P. 1986. *The Cult of the Virgin Mary: Psychological Origins*. Princeton, NJ: Princeton University Press.

Christian, William A., Jr. 1984. "Religious Apparitions and the Cold War in Southern Europe." In *Religion, Power and Protest in Local Communities: The Northern Shore of the Mediterranean*, edited by Eric R. Wolf, 239-266. Berlin: Mouton Publishers.

Christian, William A., Jr. 1996. *Visionaries: The Spanish Republic and the Reign of Christ*. Berkeley-Los Angeles: University of California Press.

Christian, William A., Jr. 1999. "Religious Apparitions and the Cold War in Southern Europe." (An updated version of 1984 article). In *Religión y símbolos*, edited by Roldán Jimeno Aranguren, 55–86, Zainak, Cuadernos de Antropologia-Etnografia 18 (Donostia: Eusko Ikaskuntza).

Claverie, Elisabeth. 2003. *Les guerres de la Vierge. Une anthropologie des apparitions*. Paris: Gallimard.

Cohn, Norman. 1970. *The Pursuit of the Millennium: Revolutionary Millenarians and Mystical Anarchists of the Middle Ages*. Revised and expanded edition. New York: Oxford University Press.

Crosby, Donald F. 1978. *God, Church, and Flag: Senator Joseph R. McCarthy and the Catholic Church, 1950-1957*. Chapel Hill: University of North Carolina Press.

Cuneo, Michael W. 1997. *The Smoke of Satan: Conservative and Traditionalist Dissent in Contemporary American Catholicism*. New York: Oxford University Press.

Dawson, Lorne. 1999. "When Prophecy Fails and Faith Persists: A Theoretical Overview." *Nova Religio* 3 (1): 60-82.

De la Cruz, Deirdre. 2015. *Mother Figured: Marian Apparitions and the Making of a Filipino Universal*. Chicago: University of Chicago Press.

Dinges, William D. 1991. "Roman Catholic Traditionalism." In *Fundamentalisms Observed*, edited by Martin E. Marty and R. Scott Appleby, 66-101. Chicago: The University of Chicago Press.

Festinger, Leon, Henry W. Riecken and Stanley Schachter. 1956. *When Prophecy Fails: A Social and Psychological Study of a Modern Group that Predicted the Destruction of the World*. New York: Harper & Row, Publishers, Inc.

Gilbert, James and Peter J. Kuznick (eds.). 2001. *Rethinking Cold War Culture*. Washington: Smithsonian Institution Press.

Goodnight, G. Thomas. 1986. "Ronald Reagan's Re-formulation of the Rhetoric of War: Analysis of the 'Zero Option,' 'Evil Empire,' and 'Star Wars' Addresses." *Quarterly Journal of Speech* 72 (4): 390-414.

Herzog, Jonathan P. 2012. "From Sermon to Strategy: Religious Influence on the Formation and Implementation of US Foreign Policy in the Early Cold War." In *Religion and the Cold War*, edited by Philip E. Muehlenbeck, 44-64. Nashville, TN: Vanderbilt University Press.

Hofstadter, Richard. 1967. *The Paranoid Style in American Politics and Other Essays*. New York: Vintage Books.
Kirby, Dianne, ed. 2003. *Religion and the Cold War*. New York: Palgrave Macmillan.
Kirby, Dianne. 2013. "The Religious Cold War." In *The Oxford Handbook of the Cold War*, edited by Richard H. Immerman and Petra Goedde, 540-564. New York: Oxford University Press.
Kselman, Thomas and Steven Avella. 1986. "Marian Piety and the Cold War in the United States." *The Catholic Historical Review* 72 (July): 403-424.
Laycock, Joseph P. 2015. *The Seer of Bayside: Veronica Lueken and the Struggle to Define Catholicism*. New York: Oxford University Press.
Lifton, Robert Jay. 1987. *The Future of Immortality and Other Essays for a Nuclear Age*. New York: Basic Books.
Lifton, Robert Jay and Richard Falk. 1982. *Indefensible Weapons: The Political and Psychological Case against Nuclearism*. New York: Basic Books.
Lindsey, Hal. 1994. *Planet Earth - 2000 A.D.: Will Mankind Survive?* Palos Verdes, CA: Western Front, Ltd.
Lueken, Veronica. 1998-2003. *Virgin Mary's Bayside Prophecies: A Gift of Love*, vol. 1-6. Lowell, MI: These Last Days Ministries.
Margry, Peter Jan. 2004a. "Global Network of Divergent Marian Devotion." In *Encyclopedia of New Religions: New Religious Movements, Sects and Alternative Spiritualities*, edited by Christopher Partridge, 98-102. Oxford: Lion Publishing.
Margry, Peter Jan. 2004b. "New Transnational Religious Cultures: The Networks and Strategies of Modern Devotions in Contemporary Europe." In *Times, Places, Passages: Ethnological Approaches in the New Millennium*, edited by Attila Paládi-Kovács, 205-213. Budapest: Akadémiai Kiadó.
Margry, Peter Jan. 2009. "Marian Interventions in the Wars of Ideology: The Elastic Politics of the Roman Catholic Church on Modern Apparitions." *History and Anthropology* 20 (3): 243-263.
Margry, Peter Jan. 2019. "The Global Network of Deviant Revelatory Marian Movements." In *The Oxford Handbook of Mary*, edited by Chris Maunder, 664-685. Oxford: Oxford University Press.
Massam, Katharine. 1991. "The Blue Army and the Cold War: Anti-Communist Devotion to the Blessed Virgin Mary in Australia." *Australian Historical Studies* 24 (97): 420-428.
Matter, Ann. 2001. "Apparitions of the Virgin Mary in the Late 20th Century." *Religion* 31 (2): 125-153.
Maunder, Chris. 2016. *Our Lady of the Nations: Apparitions of Mary in Twentieth-Century Catholic Europe*. Oxford: Oxford University Press.
Morgan, David. 2009. "Aura and the Inversion of Marian Pilgrimage: Fatima and Her Statues." In *Moved by Mary: The Power of Pilgrimage in the Modern World*, edited by Anna-Karina Hermkens, Willy Jansen and Catrien Notermans, 49-65. Farnham, UK: Ashgate.
Mugavero, Bishop Francis. 1989. "Declaration Concerning the 'Bayside Movement.'" In *Cults, Sects, and the New Age*, edited by James J. LeBar, 209-211. Huntington, IN: Our Sunday Visitor Publishing Division.
Our Lady of the Roses, Mary, Help of Mothers: An Introductory Booklet on the Apparitions of Bayside. No date. Bayside, NY: Our Lady of the Roses, Mary, Help of Mothers Shrine.
Our Lady of the Roses, Mary, Help of Mothers: A Book about the Heavenly Apparitions to Veronica Lueken at Bayside, New York. 1986 [1981]. Lansing, MI: Apostles of Our Lady, Inc.
Partridge, Christopher. 2005. *The Re-Enchantment of the West: Alternative Spiritualities, Sacralization, Popular Culture, and Occulture*, vol. 2. London: T & T Clark International.
Perry, Nicholas and Loreto Echeverria. 1988. *Under the Heel of Mary*. London-New York: Routledge.
Robertson, Pat. 1991. *The New World Order*. Dallas: Word Publishing.
Roses from Heaven, Jesus and Mary Speak to the World – 1970-1976 (no date). Vol. 1, compiled by 'Children of Mary'. Orange, TX: Children of Mary.
Roses from Heaven, Jesus and Mary Speak to the World – 1977-1986 (no date). Vol. 2, compiled by 'Children of Mary'. Orange, TX: Children of Mary.
Scheer, Monique. 2012. "Catholic Piety in the Early Cold War Years or: How the Virgin Mary Protected the West from Communism." In *Cold War Cultures: Perspectives on Eastern and Western European Societies*, edited by Annette Vowinckel, Marcus M. Payk, and Thomas Lindenberger, 129-151. New York: Berghahn.

Skovmand, David Clyde. 1993. *The End Days: Breakdown of the Apocalypse*. Oakland, CA: Our Lady's Worker of Northern California.
Thompson, E. P. 1982. *Beyond the Cold War: A New Approach to the Arms Race and Nuclear Annihilation*. New York: Pantheon Books.
Turner, Victor W. and Edith Turner. 1978. *Image and Pilgrimage in Christian Culture: Anthropological Perspectives*. New York: Columbia University Press.
Ventresca, Robert. 2003. "The Virgin and the Bear: Religion, Society and the Cold War in Italy." *Journal of Social History* 37 (2): 439-456.
Weart, Spencer R. 1988. *Nuclear Fear: A History of Images*. Cambridge, MA: Harvard University Press.
Wojcik, Daniel. 1997. *The End of the World As We Know It: Faith, Fatalism, and Apocalypse in America*. New York-London: New York University Press.
Wojcik, Daniel. 2009. "Spirits, Apparitions, and Traditions of Supernatural Photography." *Visual Resources: An International Journal of Documentation* 25 (1-2): 109-136.
Wojcik, Daniel. 2011. "Avertive Apocalypticism." In *The Oxford Handbook of Millennialism*, edited by Catherine Wessinger, 66-88. London: Oxford University Press.
Wojcik, Daniel. 2019. "Marian Apocalypticism." In *The Oxford Handbook of Mary*, edited by Chris Maunder, 648-663. London: Oxford University Press.
Zimdars-Swartz, Sandra L. 1989. "Religious Experience and Public Cult: The Case of Mary Ann Van Hoof." *Journal of Religion and Health* 28 (Spring): 36-57.
Zimdars-Swartz, Sandra L. 1991. *Encountering Mary: From La Salette to Medjugorje*. Princeton, NJ: Princeton University Press.

10
"WEARING UNEASILY THE MANTLE OF PEACE"
MARIAN DEVOTION AND THE POLITICS OF FEAR IN COLD WAR AUSTRALIA

KATHARINE MASSAM

> During Lent I rode my bike to Mass every morning. I did the nine First Fridays to ensure I would not die without making my final confession and the five First Saturdays to Our Lady of Fatima to save the world from communism (...) None of this religious activity was extraordinary. Most of my peers followed the same pattern. It is arguable that never before, and never since, did the Catholic church in Australia have such a devoted and loyal group of young people as those growing up in the 1950s.
>
> Kevin Peoples, *Santamaria's Salesman*, 14.

As the Cold War cut anxious furrows into Australian domestic politics through the 1950s, fear also haunted Catholic piety. Warned from pulpits and in the press of the "real and present danger" of an armed conflict that would be divine retribution if evil were left unchecked, Australian Catholics appealed to Mary as a mother who could be trusted to appease the wrath of her wronged and suffering Son. Idealistic young Catholics, like Kevin Peoples quoted above, held, in roughly equal parts, an eagerness for a better world and a sense of separation from broader society. Like their elders, who were even more bruised by sectarian conflict and memories of Ireland, they understood prayer to be a weapon and the Blessed Virgin Mary, Our Lady, to be their particular advocate and heavenly ally. Formally, in devotional associations like the Blue Army of Fatima and the Family Rosary Crusade, both founded from the USA in the 1950s, and informally from the 1930s, Australian Catholics wielded acts of piety to defend the nation.

Spiritually, the battle was to enlist Mary's help against "atheistic materialism" in public life thereby also protecting families from government coercion and moral collapse in the private realm. Australian Catholics had invoked Mary as Our Lady Help of Christians since pioneering bishops petitioned Rome to appoint her patroness of Australia under that title in 1844.[1] "Help of Christians" foregrounded the rosary that was the mainstay of Catholic life in colonial Australia where priests and sacraments were rare, and recalled the Battle of Lepanto in 1517 when Christians across Europe had prayed the rosary for protection against Islamic forces. It intertwined powerfully with devotion to Mary as Our Lady, Queen of Peace and Our Lady of Victories, as well as blending easily with the apparitions at Fátima that also promised security and conversion of enemies through the rosary. As "Queen of Peace", Mother of the Prince of Peace, Mary's additional title itself evoked a battle. Theology might have been clear that victory was assured, but popular piety underlined the dangers of defeat as the political met the personal and the mystical: "We receive the Prince of Peace from her on Christmas morn," the *Australian Voice of Fatima* told its readers in December 1951, "and peace will descend upon us to the extent to which we have made room for peace in our own souls."[2] The gift was contingent on the faithful being prepared.

Politically, the clandestine Catholic Social Studies Movement had been founded by B.A. (Bob) Santamaria in 1941 to combat communist influence in the trade unions (and hence in the Australian Labor Party). In September 1945 Santamaria reported to an extraordinary meeting of the Australian Catholic bishops on the communist threat in Australia. In response the bishops created a committee of three of their members to oversee the Movement's "policy and finance" directly (Ormonde 1972: 3). Santamaria remained the day-to-day leader of the Movement alongside his role as deputy director of the Church's Australian National Secretariat for Catholic Action (ANSCA), and continued in the position when he became ANSCA's sole director in 1946. The Movement's secret harnessing of official Catholic Action to party politics was ultimately condemned by the Vatican in 1958 as a flagrant distortion of Catholic teaching on the relationship between Church and State (Duncan 2001b: 88-90), but not before it had precipitated a bitter split in the Australian Labor Party (Ormond 1972; Fitzgerald 2003). Catholics who questioned its strategies or its zeal found themselves ostracized and their faith questioned (Charlesworth 1972: xiv-xv; Buckley 1983: 111-112). The Movement remains a textbook example of religious influence in Australian political life (Warhurst 1979; Strangio 2017).

I have argued elsewhere that Catholic anticommunism was not simply political but woven together with devotion in the fabric of popular spirituality

1 *Morning Chronicle*, Sydney, September 28, 1844, 2.

2 *Australian Voice of Fatima*, December 4, 1951, 1. Family Rosary Crusade Box, Melbourne Diocesan Historical Commission.

(Massam 1991; Massam 1998). Anticommunism was the litmus test of sincere Catholicism in most Australian parishes in the 1940s and 50s. Political organization and covert trade union activism was one expression of anticommunist religious conviction, and, as public pledges during parish campaigns attested, commitment to the prayer of the rosary for the conversion of Russia and the safeguarding of the world was another.

As an upwardly mobile and increasingly confident Church took Catholicism into the streets to demonstrate their commitment and call for conversion, Our Lady of Fátima was a particular focus for public devotion. The dynamics of fear on the one hand, matched with recourse to a powerful protector on the other, played out in both Church and politics. The threat in both cases was communism, or "atheistic materialism," understood to augur the consequent collapse of the moral order through the impersonal power of the state. This chapter explores the balance between personal piety and collective solidarity in the fear-driven Australian battle for the common good and against "the World Crisis" of communism.[3]

In the public realm, democracy was barely trusted as sufficient defense against "the disorders of our age".[4] There was a long history of political anxiety among ordinary citizens who feared they were, or would be, powerless to order their own lives. Former Prime Minister Robert Menzies addressed the "forgotten people" of Australia's war-time middle class from the political wilderness in May 1942. He identified himself as the champion of independent Australian families standing against increasing bureaucracy and government control especially of state education (a longstanding Catholic grievance) and seeking bulwarks of enterprise to safeguard society from the danger of class warfare (Brett 2007: 36-51).[5] Through the 1940s, internal and external threats of the "Red Menace" had fueled anxiety in Australia. Long-standing fear of Asian "invasion" of the sparsely settled continent shored up discriminatory immigration policies to maintain a "White Australia" (Walker 2012). Internally, there was "unprecedented growth" of the Australian Communist Party (ACP) to a peak of 23,000 (in a population of just over 7 million people; 0.3%) in 1943 and increasing influence of the ACP and their "sympathizers" in Australian trade unions (Duncan 2001a: 57). Beyond the national border there was the growth of networks to Australia from Europe and, in the neighboring "near north" of Asia, the creation of communist republics in North Korea in 1948 and China in 1949 (Love 2001: 13-15). As European empires contracted, Australia welcomed the expansion of Western powers into the Pacific to counter the Sino-Soviet bloc. Australia saw itself, in the words of R.G. Casey, the country's

3 "Fatima and the World Crisis," Editorial, *Advocate (Melbourne)*, May 11, 1950, 6.

4 *Ibid.*

5 "The Forgotten People – a speech by Robert Menzies on 22 May 1942," <http://www.liberals.net/theforgottenpeople.htm>, July 11, 2018.

longest serving minister for External Affairs, as "a lone outpost of democracy" (Casey 1954: 3), at risk through communist expansion in the north and dependent on the USA and Britain for security (Meaney 1995; McLean 2001). White Australia's entrenched fear of Asia combined with the domino theory to fuel a sense of threat.

The "forgotten people," surely a group that sectarianism marked out for Catholics as their own, swept Menzies back to government at the head of the Liberal-Country Party coalition in December 1949. Cold War fears secured his position, especially among women voters and not least through an eighteen-month campaign to ban the Australian Communist Party, a "shamelessly engineered, persistent and inflamed (...) exemplar of a democratic polity in crisis" (Hocking 2001: 48). Assisted by Catholic voting preferences, Menzies remained prime minister until 1966 and his conservative party governed continuously until 1972 (Warhurst 1979 and 2005).

Fear also pervaded the realm of faith. For many Catholics the political tensions were linked to a spiritual crisis and God's mercy seemed contingent on concerted prayerful effort and the intercession of Mary as Our Lady of Fátima, Queen of Peace. By appealing to Mary and following her clear directions to the child visionaries at Fátima in Portugal in 1917 (to pray the rosary, fast in reparation, keep the first Saturdays of the month in her honor, and consecrate homes, dioceses and the nation to her Immaculate Heart) the conversion of Russia would be secured and the collapse of the West could be averted. Fear suffused both politics and piety as Australian Catholics joined a cosmic battle for the future.

Prayer as a civic duty bridged the traditional division between the private realm of religion and the public world of politics (Massam 1996: 91-97, 192-196). The Catholic press took the social implications of keeping the devotion for granted. A parish reminder to members of the Catholic Young Men's Society at St Ambrose's parish in Melbourne's working-class suburb of Brunswick was typical. This was the parish that had nurtured Bob Santamaria. Warnings against communism and the action that should follow were as regular and unremarkable in the *Ambrosian*, the eight and sometimes twelve-page monthly parish newspaper, as the listing of parish activities on page one, the promotion of the Santamaria family grocery business above snippets gathered from other periodicals on page three, and advertisements for films at the Empire Theatre opposite the church on the final page. As the first Saturday of May 1947 approached, the parish reminded its young men that choice was clear:

> Will it be said that we in Australia, especially in Brunswick, are too slow-witted and spiritually dull to perceive the blessing and the favour that is offered to us[?] Accept what Our Blessed Mother has offered us and we

> have a divine assurance of a new foundation for a better world. Resist it and we plunge headlong into the deeper chasms of uncontrollable chaos.[6]

Ahead of notices about their sports clubs (cricket, tennis and football) and a thriving schedule of social events (a fancy dress ball as well as a monthly parish dance and a country weekend away), the announcement on the "Crusade for the Conversion of Russia" had pride of place. Anyone who had not already begun their crusade was urged to make May 3 the first of five consecutive Saturdays at Mass and Holy Communion. The *Ambrosian* gave a simple diagnosis, cut down from a longer article where it announced the Fátima promises a year earlier: "The world today is wearing uneasily the mantle of peace faced with the curse of Communism and the challenge of the Mother of God".[7] The familiar choice was for consecration to Mary against the threat of Russia.

The politics of devotion were unquestioned. By the time a small pilgrim statue of Our Lady of Fátima touched down by plane from Europe, Africa and Asia on the Australian leg of a world tour in January 1951, the Menzies government was defending its bill to outlaw the CPA in the High Court of Australia and planning was underway for a national Marian Congress in October 1951 to coincide with the first anniversary of the dogmatic definition of the Assumption. As the statue made its way to Catholic parishes around the country the full court of judges, six to one, struck down the Communist Party Dissolution Bill as unconstitutional in peacetime, and undeterred, the government called for even more sweeping powers in a referendum campaign to change the constitution itself (Love 2001: 11-22; Hocking 2001: 48-49; Curthoys & Damousi 2013: 3-4). As the referendum campaign raged through August and September 1951, the Blue Army of Our Lady of Fatima was instituted in Australia, and quickly enrolled 10,000 members.[8] Its founder, Father Harold Colgan of New Jersey USA, was quoted in the Catholic press assuring the Australian promoter, Father Geoghegan of Ivanhoe in Melbourne, that "Everywhere the movement is going like wildfire and only Our Lady herself could be behind it."[9] At rallies in parishes around Melbourne, Geoghegan told prospective recruits that the prayers of the Army would secure the conversion of Russia.[10]

The Marian congress to honor Mary as "Mother of God and Mother of Men" brought Catholics onto the streets of Adelaide in late October 1951, a bare month after the narrow defeat of the referendum, praying the rosary in languages from across Europe and astounding their neighbors with their numbers and their fervor in the most staunchly Protestant of Australian cities

6 *Ambrosian: Official Organ of St Ambrose's Parish*, May 1947, 9.

7 *Ibid.* The same question and warning formed part of a two page article on "'Fatima': the Undying Challenge," *Ambrosian*, August 1946, 8-9.

8 *Advocate*, August 16, 1951, 18 and October 25, 1951, 18.

9 *Catholic Weekly*, August 16, 1951, 5.

10 *Ibid.*, December 20, 1951, 2; *Advocate*, September 6, 1951, 7.

(Hilliard 1991: 401; Massam 1998: 236-237). Weeks later Father Patrick Peyton CSC, the American "Pied Piper of Prayer", preached to a crowd of 80,000 who had rallied at the Melbourne Cricket Ground as part of his international Family Rosary Crusade. It was the Catholic contribution to celebrations for the centenary of the state of Victoria, a diocesan precursor to Peyton's national tour two years later, and deemed the conclusion of "An Amazing Marian Year (...) remarkable in Australia for what appears to be a spontaneous upsurge of devotion to Our Lady."[11] Embracing the public realm in specialist Catholic Action groups, as well as in traditional pilgrimages, processions, congresses and in print the Catholic faithful of the Australian Cold War sought the security of the nation, fighting with confidence on an eschatological horizon. The message of Fátima bridged the notional divide between private devotion and public demonstration of faith.

A long history of fear and resistance: Fátima, Spain and the "Red Menace"

Fear of persecution haunted the predominantly Irish Catholicism of Australia and laid a deep foundation for Cold War piety. Diocesan papers around the country were quick to see the threat of hostile regimes and vigilant in reporting the danger that "atheistic materialism" in particular posed for the Church. From heralding Pope Leo XIII's 1891 encyclical supporting workers against "avaricious and grasping men [of free enterprise or government] (...) able to impose a yoke almost of slavery on an infinite number of people,"[12] through warning against the new Soviet allies in 1941 that "the Red leopard hasn't changed his spots,"[13] and enlisting the rosary to protect Australian Catholics from "the strange alliance [that] (...) may bring disaster hardly less than defeat",[14] a potential crisis of freedom of religion always loomed. As a hallmark of Catholic faith, the public expression of devotion to Mary signaled the independence of the Church within the secular state, and proved especially resonant when Our Lady of Fátima was the focus. As the Cold War deepened and galvanized Australian Catholics through the 1950s, commitment to Mary and

11 *Australian Voice of Fatima*, December 4, 1951.

12 "Leo: the friend of workers," *Catholic Press*, Sydney, August 17, 1901, 9; see also coverage when *Rerum Novarum* was issued: "The Pope and the Labour Problem," *Freeman's Journal*, May 16, 1891, 18; "A Papal Encyclical: Capital and Labour," *Advocate*, May 23, 1891, 6.

13 "Radio Review," *Advocate*, November 20, 1941, 9; also "Guns not 'Butter' for Soviet Russia," *Advocate*, July 10, 1941, 8.

14 "Our Lady's Secret Weapon," Editorial, *Advocate*, October 7, 1943, 8.

the rosary became ever more clearly linked to "peace in the home, in industry and the nation".[15]

Readers of the Australian Catholic press had seen reports of the "recent" apparitions at Fátima in the south of Portugal since at least 1922.[16] From the outset the accounts included notes of resistance to the prevailing order – the processions or pilgrimages to the shrine were not sanctioned by local bishops and had been prohibited by a government (mistakenly identified in one sub-heading as "Spanish") that was hostile to the Church. "The only result," Melbourne's Catholic weekly, the *Advocate*, announced, "was that last month fifty thousand people flocked there in one day."[17] Australian readers heard that a cautious hierarchy had also established the customary commission to investigate the visionaries' claims; the article's tone was for popular devotion that would not be denied. Within the decade the apparitions were at the heart of reports of a reversal of the fortunes of Catholic Portugal: diplomatic relations had been restored with Rome in 1918, a military coup had overthrown the ruling "Masonic clique" in 1926,[18] and the Church was flourishing under the new regime as members of government pledged to "moralise society according to the eternal Christian principals" and joined 150,000 people in pilgrimage to Fátima in 1931.[19] The move to the political right was presented as a move away from anti-clericalism. The regime's support for the Fátima devotion was also synonymous with support for Catholicism. While there was no coverage of a message against Russian Bolshevism at this stage, Fátima had secured a new "depth and fervour of Portuguese piety."[20] If early reports in Australia had initially confused the national borders on the Iberian peninsula, the outbreak of civil war in Spain in 1936 brought both geography and the potential peril of Catholics into focus.

Fear of a communist uprising in Australia deepened from July 1936 as the conflict of the Spanish Civil War filled the columns of devotional magazines and diocesan newspapers. Awareness of international anxiety was heightened after the publication of the anticommunist encyclical *Divini Redemptoris* in March 1937. Catholic support for General Franco's Nationalist "uprising" against "Red" Republican and anti-clerical forces was all but unquestioning, especially when a joint pastoral letter of the Spanish bishops identified the conflict as a "crusade" for the Church (Perez-Molina 2000). The brutal deaths of monks and nuns were all of a piece with the more familiar stories of the Soviet state. The *Madonna*, a monthly magazine published by the Society of

15 "The Message of Fatima: Peace in the home, in industry, in the nation," *Southern Cross* (Adelaide), November 2, 1951, 10.

16 "A Vision of Our Lady," *Advocate*, September 14, 1922, 9.

17 *Ibid.*

18 "Remarkable Catholic Revival in Portugal," *Advocate*, May 14, 1931, 10.

19 "Religious Revival in Portugal," *Southern Cross*, April 24, 1931, 14.

20 "Remarkable Catholic Revival in Portugal," *Advocate*, May 14, 1931, 10.

Jesus in Australia to support and promote the sodality of the Children of Mary and their Apostleship of Prayer, reported in May 1936 that persecution of the Church in Russia was "growing more bitter" with 2 million people persevering without the sacraments. The magazine predicted that "the objective of militant atheists that all churches would be destroyed or converted to other uses" was likely to be achieved soon.[21] The implication was that the weakening of public prayer would undermine the social fabric as well as jeopardize the sacramental system linked to personal salvation.

The undercurrent of alarm for souls imperiled by the state continued in November 1936 when the magazine carried a full-page photograph of Pope Pius XI receiving refugees "saved from the satanic fury in Spain."[22] The editor aligned the readers with the grieving pontiff. Mary was interwoven with Christ and his Church as a focus for prayer:

> What sorrow fills his heart! All Australasian Sodalists will offer Masses, Communions, prayers for the triumph of the Church and in reparation for insults and outrages against Our Divine Lord and His Holy Mother and their devoted servants.[23]

Their sodality slogan "Communion not Communism" coupled the personal and the political. Members would combat the "god of the State" by receiving the sacrament to underline the "supernatural dignity of each person [with the] coming of Jesus Our Lord and God into each soul." Meditation after communion would shed light on "the World's great problem: the subjecting of the individual's interest to those of the Community without violating the individual's personal rights."[24] The call to the Eucharist linked Marian devotion and Christology: as Mary had brought Jesus to the world so should each communicant.

In the same issue, the Melbourne Jesuit priest John Nerney drew a local analogy: communism loomed as surely as bushfires at the opening of the southern summer. He recorded his unstinting admiration for the professional men in his apologetics group who were keen to hear more theology, even at 10.15 pm after long days in the city. He urged others to follow their example of preparation in the dangerous season as conflagration threatened:

> If a bush-fire were sweeping across the country, you would not remain idle. You would fight back the flames. You would remove all inflammable material. Communistic philosophy is like a large bush-fire. It finds lots of ready material owing to the utter failure of the non-Catholic Church bodies and

21 *Madonna*, May 1936, 132, 227.
22 *Ibid.*, November 1936, 323.
23 *Ibid.*, November 1936, 323.
24 *Ibid.*, November 1936, 322.

> our State systems of secularised education. Stop this bush-fire of Communism from spreading.[25]

The Church was vulnerable and needed to act quickly against a hostile environment to avoid devastation. Significantly, among professional men in the 1930s it was familiarity with Catholic teaching and prayer, rather than Marian devotion in particular, that would clear the dangerous undergrowth.

In the same month the *Madonna*'s companion publication the *Australian Messenger of the Sacred Heart* mobilized younger "crusaders" of that devotion to Jesus. The *Messenger* reminded readers of a prayer invoking Australia's patron Our Lady Help of Christians alongside the missionary sponsor Francis Xavier:

> Are you remembering to pray for the conversion of our dear country? Little children can fight Communism with prayer. Be a good Australian! In Spain, Mexico, Germany and Russia the Church is persecuted. Pray that the Church may be safe in Australia.[26]

Mary's importance was clear: "May Our Lady make you and her other Australasian Sodalists efficient and fearless in the defence of Christ's Kingdom."[27] Efficiency and fearlessness were not standard virtues associated with Marian devotion but Crusader groups were promoted especially among Catholic schoolboys in parishes around the country.

The Australian Catholic press continued to warn against the menace of communism through the 1940s. The news that Russia had taken up arms against Hitler did not deter Australian Catholics from prayer for the collapse of Soviet rule, warning that "soon or late, their weapons will be once more turned against us [for] (...) the establishment by civil war of a society from which religion and human freedom are alike excluded."[28] Dr Leslie Rumble, the "Radio Priest" whose answers to written questions were broadcast on 2SM in Sydney and then syndicated through the diocesan papers, kept his focus firmly on lack of freedom of religion in the Soviet bloc.[29] In December 1942 he responded to the 'pink' Anglican bishop of Goulbourn who had argued that communism put into practice what Christianity espoused (Hempenstall 1993). Rumble's full page rebuttal was headed "Stalin would not agree with Bishop Burgmann," and warned against "misguided Christians who profess such profound reverence for Communism fail to remember that Communism as no

25 *Ibid.*, November 1936, 322.
26 "With the Little Ones," *Australian Messenger of the Sacred Heart*, November 1936, 671.
27 *Madonna*, November 1936, 322.
28 For example, *Advocate*, July 9, 1941, 8.
29 For example, *Catholic Weekly*, July 9, 1942, 13.

respect whatever for their religion."[30] There was speculation that Polish Catholics in exile in Russia might influence the "religion-starved Russians" and see the country "come back to Jesus and Mary (...) marching under the banner of the Legion of Mary"[31] (also active in Australia since 1932 (O'Brien 2005: 11-12)), but if there were any deference to the Soviet Union as an ally restraint fell away entirely after August 1945: "The war being won, there is no longer need to pretend that there is freedom of religion in Russia," the *Ambrosian* remarked between a note on the local "Communist Railways Union boss" who had almost bought a ticket in a raffle organized by the Movement, and a report on Pius XII exhorting men and women to vote wisely.[32] As the Cold War deepened, an emphasis on a "manly tribute to Mary" from citizen voters increased within the Australian Church, and blurred the institution's feminine, otherworldly stereotype (Massam 1996; 1998). The political implications of Fátima, explained at the Marian Congress of 1950 as a devotion that would truly unite nations where "the great men of the world have (...) failed because they have relied too heavily on worldly things, such as statesmanship, speeches, press publicity, radio propaganda,"[33] underlined the significance of devotion for political realities in this world, not only for personal salvation in the next.

Australia's devotional magazines saw themselves correcting an anti-Catholic bias in the secular press and making space to acknowledge divine realities in the public realm. They argued that undiscerning coverage was propaganda in the guise of journalism, preparing the way for revolution.

> Take for instance, Spain. Read our dailies. How little of truth! How much of lying propaganda! (...) Sympathy for Reds whose atrocities overwhelm the imagination and fill us with horror; on the contrary, coldness, even hatred for patriots who are making every sacrifice to save their country for God.[34]

They wanted to see faith, including devotion to Mary, acknowledged as a dimension of world events. In the case of the Spanish civil war battle for Toledo (1936) for example, the *Madonna* magazine was at pains to point out that General Moscardó and the troops that defended the fortress of the Alcázar for seventy days had prayed the rosary continually; furthermore, they were members of the same Sodality of Our Lady as the *Madonna*'s Australian readers. As the world had "thrilled" to the news that Moscardó had commended his son to God rather than surrender the stronghold to save him from execution, so Aus-

30 *Catholic Weekly*, December 10, 1942, 12.
31 *Southern Cross*, December 11, 1942, 4.
32 *Ambrosian*, December 1947, 3.
33 *Mother of God and Mother of Men*, 10.
34 *Madonna*, January 1937, 209.

tralian and all sodalists should stand firm under "their Captain, Our Lady".[35] The military title was masculine, fitting for the devotion of soldiers.

Even Melbourne's *Catholic Worker* newspaper, the publication vehemently against the co-option of Catholic Action into the service of a party political anticommunist agenda, shared the broad trajectory of Marian piety. Founded by members of the university's Campion Society pledged to "study (…) of the Catholic outlook on problems of the modern world,"[36] and sharing a masthead with the New York paper of the same name produced by Catholic social activists Dorothy Day and Peter Maurin, Melbourne's *Catholic Worker* had launched in February 1936. Its opening manifesto positioned Catholicism as "the only organisation which has a revolutionary teaching" sufficient to address the equal evils of both capitalism and communism.

> We have come into existence because there is a solution which the Catholic Church alone can provide, and because there is a taunt to which the Church must reply (…) The new Communism is only the old Capitalism plus a little missionary fervour. Both are the illegitimate offspring of the same diseased materialism: both insult Man by rewarding him as the labour unit rather than as God's noblest creation; both regulate their behaviour by economic expediency rather than by considerations of justice.[37]

Marian devotion featured in the second issue. In an article picked up from its US prototype, the *Catholic Worker*'s Mary was a widowed working woman, her son "crucified this time on the bloody cross of modern industrialism."[38] In a hallmark challenge to piety that neglected hospitality readers were reminded the Madonna was among them if they cared to reach out.

> She didn't live far from you and you might have been there. But, of course, you weren't. You were reading a sweet spiritual book, and thinking of all the lovely things you would have done for her, had you met her on Calvary two thousand years ago.[39]

Contextualizing Mary's sanctity as well as the holiness expected of the readers, the *Catholic Worker* collapsed the boundary between the ordinary woman and the traditional queen of heaven. Mary was simultaneously intercessor, advocate and widowed neighbor in need.

35 *Ibid.*
36 *Advocate*, August 3, 1934, 17.
37 *Catholic Worker*, February 1, 1936, 1.
38 *Ibid.*, February 29, 1936, 4.
39 *Ibid.*, February 29, 1936, 4.

> [Her son] begs his Divine Prototype to let his mother find a friend and a home even here on earth, for the little time she has left. Perhaps she will, if His grace strikes your heart when it is soft. You will not lose, for some day you too will need a home – a home to house your immortal soul – and Mary will receive you into her resplendent one in the Holy City which "hath no need of sun" (...) But you'll have to drop that pretty spiritual book and get going for now "The Madonna is Dying."[40]

If the time for other-worldly devotion were passing away, salvation would be found securely in solidarity with the poor.

There was no mention of Fátima in the *Catholic Worker* for more than a decade. There was Marian devotion in striking woodcuts by the Australian artist Thelma Fisher as well as reprints of Ade Bethune's work from the US paper. By the late 1940s, a rising climate of anticommunism included cautions against "political racketeers" and reminders to campaigners that "[c]hecking the spread of truth and falsehood is important but it is even more important to say a rosary after tea."[41] Workers were urged towards the habit of "fitting in" a decade of the rosary on the train or at lunchtime but discretely: "there is no need to dangle your beads ostentatiously before all eyes."[42] Piety was to be undemonstrative. Similarly, the *Catholic Worker* recommended anticommunism tempered by friendship. Readers were warned against fanaticism and sectarian bigotry that flew the "flag of God" on each and every issue: "There have been cases where a political controversy so untheological as municipal drainage has been resolved on a sectarian basis," admonished the columnist in "Sermons to a Layman" in October 1947.[43] Rather than opposition for its own sake, the *Catholic Worker* urged practical love of neighbors including reaching out to "that fanatical Comm. who works with us (...) it's a sorry commentary on active Catholicism if he has to call a fellow comrade to help when there are men about allegedly flying the banner of Christ."[44] There was no doubt about the political threat or the need for a positive response. Reporting the revival of an international network of communist governments with expansionist ambitions as the front-page story for November 1947 with an accompanying photo of Stalin, the *Catholic Worker* urged readers to a social order of love:

> The Communists have made no secret of their aims and methods. There will be no excuse for Australia if they seize power here. It is however, no use just being anti-Communist. We must be pro-Christian. We must show that a Christian social order based on love of one's neighbour is better than

40 *Catholic Worker*, February 29, 1936, 4.
41 *Ibid.* 141, October 1947, 4.
42 *Ibid.* 147, April 1948, 4.
43 *Ibid.* 141, October 1947, 4.
44 *Ibid.* 141, October 1947, 4.

> social disorder based on hate. The Comintern is alive again. Is the Christian social order dead?[45]

Democracy, home ownership, worker co-operatives, effective trade unions, access to education and freedom of religion were touchstones in the *Catholic Worker*'s vision. Secure these, the message was, not necessarily without prayer but certainly by activism, in order to safeguard the nation.

The *Catholic Worker*'s relative distance from the fervor of anticommunist devotion to Mary ended suddenly in May 1948. "Prayer and Penance – Or Else": the banner headlines on page one announced that "rather belatedly the 'CW' ha[d] woken up (...) the message of Fatima is the only answer to the problems of mankind."[46] The editors answered the "Why now?" question they knew readers would be asking by pointing to four centuries of crisis since the Reformation. They heard a call to all Christians for a new social order; one that Catholics had a particular responsibility to enact through obedience to the instructions Mary had given at Fátima.

> Today Christendom is dying. The break in Christian unity at the time of the so-called Reformation was a terrible blow. Men's hearts and minds were turned from the primacy of spiritual ends to the primacy of national and material ends (...) Caesar has triumphed; God is denied or ignored; all things must be rendered to Caesar. Our Lady sees and knows all this. She is burning with love for God, and it grieves her that men reject Christ. That is why she keeps appearing. She is trying to save us from the wrath of God, and she says men will not be saved unless they repent and do penance.[47]

The time for complacency was over. The loss of spiritual fervor that triggered the Protestant Reformation was playing out as increased materialism and loyalty to worldly concerns ("Caesar") over God. The editorial team had consecrated their work of spreading Catholic social teaching to the Immaculate Heart of Mary at a Mass celebrated by Archbishop Mannix late in 1947; it had featured quietly in the paper with a photo at the time.[48] Now, in the traditional month of May they took the commitment further calling for "real hard penance," far beyond "an extra Hail Mary," to combat "militant atheism."[49] Not governments but ordinary Christians (the *Worker* included Protestants alongside Catholics) were to blame for the increasing crisis through lack of repentance for sin. Ordinary Christians also had the power to change the world through prayer and penance. Giving details of the Fátima apparitions, and accompanying articles with the history of other devotions and titles of Mary, they assured readers

45 *Ibid.* 142, November 1947, 1.
46 *Ibid.* 148, May 1948, 1.
47 *Ibid.* 148, May 1948, 2.
48 *Ibid.* 1947.
49 *Ibid.* 148, May 1948, 2.

10.1 The *Handbook for Priests* for Family Rosary Crusade. Publication by the Advocate Press in Melbourne, ca 1951.

they were not being "alarmist." Instead the *Catholic Worker* reiterated: "The Mother of God has spoken. It will be the height of folly to ignore her message."[50] They encouraged readers to initiate a Holy Hour in their parishes on first Saturdays, reporting good progress in the following months, and making a firm connection to the regular hour of reparation that had been established at St. Francis church in the city in April 1948.[51] The campaign for pledges to pray the rosary daily, and vigils of continuous devotion at St. Francis were spearheaded by Father Rosario Morin and linked to the international Reparation Society of the Immaculate Heart founded in Baltimore USA in 1945. By 1951, five thousand Catholics in Melbourne had signed a formal commitment to practices promoted at Fátima (Cash 2007: 158-159), and the devotional society of the Blue Army had attracted 10,000 in a few short months in the same year in Victoria alone.[52] When Father Patrick Peyton's Rosary Crusade visited Australia in 1951 and again 1953, outdoor displays in the capital cities saw thousands of schoolchildren, dressed in white with red, blue or yellow capes and hoods, form "living rosaries" while massed crowds recited the prayer

50 *Catholic Worker* 148, May 1948, 2.
51 *Ibid.* 159, July 1950, 4.
52 *Advocate*, October 25, 1951, 18.

in sports grounds or public arenas. The assembly of 150,000 to pray at Melbourne's Botanical Gardens in 1953 was perhaps a world record, and larger than any officially estimated crowd to that time.[53] The crusade slogan, "The family that prays together, stays together," had a domestic ring but connected directly with the wider campaign against the forces of atheistic materialism (Massam 1991; Fitzgerald 2003; Mason 2008). The Catholic press reported enrolments of 2,100 at a time in the Blue Army of Our Lady of Fátima alongside reports of the success of Father Peyton's family rosary crusade.[54]

Our Lady Help of Christians, patron of Australia, was traditionally associated with other crusades, specifically, readers of the *Catholic Worker* were told, with halting "Moslem Turks who sought to conquer Europe for Islam, much as Soviet Russia today seeks to convert the world to Communism." A woodcut image of Mary above a globe featuring the map of Australia set the struggle she championed firmly in the local context.[55]

Contextualizing Fátima: the cosmic battle fought at home

It was not only global connections but the cosmic implications of the Fátima devotion that most captured the imagination of the Australian Catholic community through these years – both in the threat of communism and in making the heavenly remedy to that threat present in their parishes, homes and streets. From suburb to suburb, city to city, public demonstrations of faith played out the connections between the apparition of Mary in Portugal, the local commitment to the prayer and fasting she had requested, and the consequences for world peace and eternal salvation. It was a heady mix.

Something like a glimpse into heaven was guaranteed by the resemblance between the images of Our Lady of Fátima and the apparition to the children in 1917. The pilgrim statue that arrived in Australia in January 1951, and other "Portugese-made" copies of the Fátima figure, came with the assurance of the surviving visionary, Sister Lucia, that "the crowned image [was] based on her recollections of the apparition."[56] Lucia was known to support public demonstrations but devotion involving Mary's image risked reinforcing stereotypes of Catholic superstition in Protestant Australia. The Melbourne *Advocate* was at pains to stymie accusations of idolatry and publicity stunts, asking that "Christian fellow-citizens" would not condemn the effort without taking time to understand the honor paid to the statue. There was no sense

53 *Ibid.*, December 10, 1952, 3.
54 *Catholic Weekly*, December 20, 1951, 2.
55 *Catholic Worker* 148, May 1948, 2.
56 *Advocate*, January 18, 1951, 6.

in which "the image is falsely deemed to have a magical life of its own"[57] but rather a conviction that the material world could point towards divinity and beauty could appropriately uplift the soul.[58] The image of the Blessed Virgin "from that favoured shrine of Fatima (...) will remind us of Our Lady's message and warning to cease offending God.[59] The danger posed by communism was a muted theme but present through the Marian congress of 1951 every time a preacher invoked Mary as "Lady of Victories and Queen of Peace" and the "forces of evil" ranged against Australia, and congregations "thundered forth" the Fátima hymn to the Immaculate Mother of Grace, naming her "hope of the human race."[60]

The strict theological conviction that the particular honor (*hyperdulia*) paid to Mary was distinct from the worship (*latria*) owed to God blurred in practice. That the public veneration of the figure of Mary was open to misinterpretation was borne out in the Australian secular press too. In the country town of Forbes the local newspaper announced that the council had granted permission for "Lady Fátima: Goddess of Peace Procession"[61], and the diocesan administrator wrote on behalf of the Catholic population to demand an apology for the "blasphemous parody of their religious beliefs."[62] The paper retracted immediately below the letter of protest, indicating there had been no intention to imply Catholics viewed Mary as a goddess, and giving the details of the procession planned in honor of "Our Lady of Fátima". The *Barrier Daily Truth* from the same area had an echo of Catholic apologetics as it put the view to "scoffers" that it was a good bet to respect the procession. Fátima was about more than private faith.

> If Catholics (or any Christian or religious person for that matter) think they can achieve something by prayers and they are wrong, what harm does it do? (...) If by praying Catholics can secure peace for the world, what is to be lost by their prayers? If God does not exist there has merely been a waste of the time taken in praying, but if God does exist, the odds are too good to miss for peace. A hard-boiled gambler could easily appreciate the odds offered were the best ever. If Fatima had no interest to the world at large quite apart from its religious significance we would not have brought it to your attention, but it is of interest – or should be – to everyone so that those who know nothing of it should at least be given some knowledge.[63]

57 *Advocate*, January 18, 1951, 6.
58 *Ibid.*
59 *Mother of God and Mother of Men*, 14.
60 *Ibid.*, 14, 53, 73.
61 *Forbes Advocate*, May 1, 1951, 2.
62 *Ibid.*, May 4, 1951, 1.
63 *Barrier Daily Truth*, May 2, 1951, 2.

Typically, the pilgrim statue was carried in procession on a platform attached to poles borne by a team of eight, sometimes young women from the Children of Mary, more often young men of the Holy Name [of Jesus] Society or another sodality. Just under 4 feet tall, head inclined forward and hands joined in prayer, veil and robe painted white and marked by one telling star, the image of Our Lady of Fátima was reserved and gentle. Her European features were young and serene, her bare feet rested on a cloud. There was no question of a continuous pilgrimage in a country whose far-flung cities of Brisbane in the east and Perth in the west were separated by more than the distance from Dublin to Moscow. Instead, the statue arrived by plane or train or car, and was installed in a central church before a procession through the streets the following day. The procession was usually accompanied by the singing of traditional hymns to Mary praising her purity, her maternal care, and the favored place she held in the heart of her son, and interspersed with the recitation of decades of the rosary recalling her life intertwined with the life of her son. Frequently, the procession would wind its way back to a different altar in the same church, or to an outside altar, or to a neighboring parish, where the occasion would end with a short homily advocating the rosary as "to implore the protection of the Mother of God against (…) all the furies of Satan," followed by Benediction.[64] Like the monstrance containing the consecrated host for veneration, but usually at a distance from it, the statue of Our Lady of Fátima was presented to the people in a place of honor decorated with flowers and candles. The statue itself stood in for the other-worldly presence of the Blessed Virgin as she had appeared at Fátima, and as she remained active in the lives of the Catholic faithful.

The sacralization of otherwise "hostile" public space was a major dimension of the Fátima pilgrimages. The account of one observer who witnessed the conclusion of Adelaide's Marian congress captured the pride in the Catholic witness as the supernatural forces of prayer cleansed the city streets and parks.

> As Mary's marchers moved down King William Street, the Rosary rolled with them, and rebounded from the T&G [Temperance and General Insurance Building] and was re-echoed from the Bank of New South Wales, and ran around the corners into Grenfell, Rundle and Hindley Streets; and when the Rosary temporarily halted, the songs of praise which rose up fairly inundated and enveloped the city of Adelaide. They swept around and through the business buildings so often associated with avarice and hu-

64 For example: "Fatima Statue installed at West Melbourne," *Advocate*, October 25, 1951, 18. See also *Record* (Emerald Hill), February 24, 1951, 7; *Barrier Truth*, May 7, 1951, 1; *Barrier Miner*, May 8, 1951, 3; *Northern Star* (Lismore), October 5, 1951, 4; *Advocate*, October 25, 1951, 2.

> man passions like a keen breeze – a refreshing and cleansing tide. The rolling Rosary and the rising hymns were washing Adelaide like a baptism.[65]

The pilgrimage or procession there featured "New Australians" arrived from Europe in the waves of postwar migration, in national dress, singing and praying in Italian, Polish, Hungarian, Slovak, Ukrainian, Maltese and German, sometimes with banners or statutes of their local Madonna. A large contingent of men "from the parishes" led other groups of nurses, university graduates were followed by the Children of Mary, robed and veiled leading the statue in a progress from the cathedral to the park beside the river.

> Now, Our Lady herself is here – moving slowly along, accompanied by a body of reverent, gentle, chivalrous and filial young men. It is scarcely credible that Our Lady is proceeding down the main street of Adelaide, hailed, accepted, loved![66]

The seminarians, clergy and the visiting bishops followed. The *Advertiser*, Adelaide's secular daily, estimated the 20,000 marchers took an hour and a quarter to pass.[67] There were cameras on the city buildings to capture the spectacle for news reels, teaching sisters in heavy habits watching from another balcony, and police on motorcycles kept an eye on barricades where onlookers prayed a "throbbing rhythm of the Hail Marys and the Holy Marys."[68] An eye-witness account in the diocesan weekly recalled that the words had been heard first in Nazareth and had echoed around Ephesus 1520 years before they rolled down King William Street and into Elder Park.[69] There was a long history being made present.

The interest shown by their neighbors from other Christian denominations was part of the victory that Catholics attributed to the prayer of the congress. The crowd gathered by the river to mark the end of the congress numbered 30,000 according to the *Advertiser*, and closer to 100,000 according to the writer of a congress souvenir who extrapolated from the crowds recorded at the annual Carols by Candlelight shared by the community at Christmas time. Both sources agreed "something like half" were not Catholic.[70] Cardinal Gilroy acknowledged the diversity and paid tribute to the engagement of the Protestants as he reminded the Catholics in the crowd: "You marched as an army of peace and goodwill. Your fellow citizens received you as such with all

65 *Mother of God and Mother of Men*, 78.
66 *Ibid.*
67 *Advertiser*, October 29, 1951, 3.
68 *Mother of God and Mother of Men*, 78.
69 *Ibid.*, 79.
70 *Advertiser*, October 19, 1951, 3; *Mother of God and Mother of Men*, 79.

the graciousness that is characteristic of this city and South Australia."[71] As he raised the monstrance in benediction over the "vast throng" gathered by the river, they sang together to honor "One greater than Mary (...) praising in the *O Salutaris* the Saving Victim (...) who opens the gates of heaven."[72] The town that had long thought of itself as the least Catholic and most English of Australia's cities had been astonished by the festival, caught up in its drama and the novelty of national groups parading in costumes and praying in their own languages, and perhaps, as the eye-witness reporter maintained, they had been moved by "God's gifts (...) the gifts of a Mother and a Baby."[73] Certainly Catholic Adelaide vowed it would never forget this opportunity to demonstrate faith in the streets.

Australian Catholics were "wearing uneasily the mantle of peace" because they saw a battle raging for the conversion of their own country as part of a conflict with the forces of atheism that would determine the future of the world. And yet, as the Fátima devotion rolled into the public spaces, there was exultation and hope that peace would prevail. The Adelaide reporter of the Marian congress echoed sentiment that followed the Queen of Peace through the parishes: "May it not just be for the day; may it not be only with our lips that she is accepted; may it be with our hearts – and proved by our lives."[74] From a foundation of personal prayer and private devotion Australian Catholics understood themselves as part of a divine drama that could still change the world.

"Citizen of the world, have you forgotten how to pray?"

When Father Patrick Peyton visited Australia for the first time in November 1951, Catholic Melbourne turned out in force to the city's hallowed sports ground. In perfect spring weather, the familiar parish devotion of rosary, sermon and benediction had played out on a grand scale, and after a statue of Our Lady of Fatima had been enthroned among flowers at the outdoor altar and honored by a choir of 1,200 schoolchildren who sang the canticle of the Magnificat, a modern morality play followed. Dialogue opened with a repeated question to the everyman character that recalled "Citizen" to prayer.

> *Angel*: Citizen of the world, have you forgotten how to pray?
> *Citizen*: What was that?
> *Satan*: Your flabby, worn-out conscience, ignore it.
> *Angel*: Citizen of the world, have you forgotten how to pray?[75]

71 *Advertiser*, October 29, 1951, 3.
72 *Mother of God and Mother of Men*, 79.
73 *Ibid.*
74 *Ibid.*, 78.
75 *Advocate*, November 22, 1951, 3.

The insistent exchanged summed up the dynamics of Cold War devotion to Mary in Australia. Written and produced in the crucible of Melbourne's Catholic Action groups, with a script by Ronald Conway of the Campions, performers drawn from the Cardijian Players of the Young Christian Workers, assisted by the diocesan drama club, the Therry Society, and young women trained by the Ladies of the Grail, it assumed private faith had social consequences and a civic dimension. Prayer was part of a Catholic commitment that required believers to engage as citizens of the world. It offered confident encouragement "to carry the challenge of living faith to the godless world outside [the arena]."[76] The morality play also modelled a blend of affective tradition with contemporary technology, as professional actors read the speaking parts over the public broadcast system. In common with other aspects of Australian Cold War devotion, the local intervention was triggered by connections from the global Church: a long familiarity with Marian devotion in the first instance, the observances promoted at Fátima in the more immediate sense, and then mobilized by American Catholicism that spoke in Irish cadences and challenged Australians to think as citizens of the world. This was a community that saw communism threatening their freedom in this world and their salvation in the next if it undermined the Church. Political organization was one response, already well underway as the pilgrim statue toured and parishes promoted Saturday devotions. When the crowds gathered in devotion, the *Catholic Worker* pointed to the pope "forming his divisions (...) not for war but for peace,"[77] and asking for trust that shared prayer and private conviction could indeed change the world.

BIBLIOGRAPHY

Brett, Judith. [1998] 2007. *Robert Menzies' Forgotten People*. Carlton: University of Melbourne Press.

Buckley, Vincent. 1983. *Cutting Green Hay: Friendships, Movements and Cultural Conflicts in Australia's Great Decades*. Ringwood, Victoria: Penguin Books.

Casey, R.G. 1954. *Friends and Neighbours: Australia and the World*. Melbourne: F. W. Cheshire.

Cash, Damien. 2007. *The Road to Emmaus: A History of the Blessed Sacrament Congregation in Australia*. Melbourne: Blessed Sacrament Congregation in Australia with David Lovell Publishing.

Charleswoth, M. J. 1972. "Foreword." In Paul Ormonde. *The Movement*. Melbourne: Nelson.

Curthoys, Ann and Joy Damousi. 2013. "Remembering the 1951 Referendum on the Banning of the Communist Party." *Australian Historical Studies* 44: 1-3. DOI: 10.1080/1031461X.2012.760638.

Duncan, Bruce. 2001a. *Crusade or Conspiracy? Catholics and the Anti-Communist Struggle in Australia*. Sydney: University of New South Wales Press.

Duncan, Bruce. 2001b. "The Role of the Catholic Church in the Cold War: The Conundrum of B.A. Santamaria." In *Arguing the Cold War*, edited by Peter Love and Paul Strangio, 85-90. Melbourne: Red Rag Publications.

Fitzgerald, Ross. 2003. *The Pope's Battalions: Santamaria, Catholicism and the Labor Split*. St Lucia: University of Queensland Press.

76 *Advocate*, November 22, 1951, 3.

77 *Catholic Worker* 190, November 1951, 1.

Hempenstall, Peter, 1993. *The Meddlesome Priest: A Life of Ernest Burgmann*. St Leonards, NSW: Allen and Unwin.

Hilliard, David. 1988. "Popular Religion in Australia in the 1950s: A Study of Adelaide and Brisbane." *Journal of Religious History* 16: 219-235.

Hilliard, David. 1991. "God in the Suburbs: The Religious Culture of Australian Cities in the 1950s." *Australian Historical Studies* 97: 399-419.

Hocking, Jenny. 2001. "Robert Menzies' 'Fundamental Authoritarianism': the 1951 Referendum." In *Arguing the Cold War*, edited by Peter Love and Paul Strangio, 47-59. Melbourne: Red Rag Publications.

Love, Peter. 2001. "Australia's Cold War." In *Arguing the Cold War*, edited by Peter Love and Paul Strangio, 11-22. Melbourne: Red Rag Publications.

Lowe, David. 1999. *Menzies and the Great World Struggle: Australia's Cold War 1948-1954*. Sydney: University of New South Wales Press.

Massam, Katharine. 1991. "The Blue Army and the Cold War: Anti-Communist Devotion to the Blessed Virgin Mary in Australia." *Australian Historical Studies* 97: 420-428.

Massam, Katharine. 1996. *Sacred Threads: Catholic Spirituality in Australia 1922-1962*. Sydney: University of New South Wales Press.

Massam, Katharine. 1998. "Representing Active Discipleship: Images of the Madonna in Twentieth-Century Australia." *Australian Feminist Studies* 13: 235-249.

Mason, Robert. 2008. "The Looming Battle: Our Lady of Fatima and Public Space in Cold War Queensland." *Journal of the Royal Australian Historical Society* 94: 57-74.

Mathews, Race. 2016. *Of Labour and Liberty: Distributism in Victoria 1932-1966*. Clayton: Monash University Press.

McLean, David. 2001. "Australia in the Cold War: A Historiographical Review." *The International History Review* 23 (2): 299-321. DOI: 10.1080/07075332.2001.9640932.

Meaney, Neville. 1995. "The end of 'white Australia' and Australia's changing perceptions of Asia." *Australian Journal of International Affairs* 49: 171-189. DOI: 10.1080/10357719508445155.

Mother of God and Mother of Men: Record of the Marian Congress Adelaide October 24-28, 1951. 1951. Adelaide: Catholic Education Office.

O'Brien, Joachim. 2005. *A Most Beautiful Story to Be Told: The Legion of Mary in Oceania, 1932-2005*. Melbourne: The Legion of Mary.

Ormonde, Paul. 1972. *The Movement*. Melbourne: Nelson.

Peoples, Kevin. 2012. *Santamaria's Salesman: Working for the National Catholic Rural Movement 1959-1961*. Edited by Maryna Mews. Mulgrave, Vic: John Garratt Publishing.

Perez-Molina, Isabel. 2000. "'Por Dios y Por La Patria': Francoism and the Spanish Benedictine Mission at New Norcia, Western Australia During the Spanish Civil War." *New Norcia Studies* 8. <https://www.academia.edu/545099/_Por_Dios_y_por_la_patria_Francoism_and_the_Spanish_Benedictine_Mission_at_New_Norcia_Western_Australia_during_the_Spanish_Civil_War>.

Strangio, Paul. 2017. "Australian politics explainer: the Labor Party split." *The Conversation*, 18 April. <https://theconversation.com/australian-politics-explainer-the-labor-party-split-74149>.

"The Forgotten People – a speech by Robert Menzies on 22 May 1942." <http://www.liberals.net/theforgottenpeople.htm>, July 11, 2018.

Walker, David. 2012. *Anxious Nation: Australia and the Rise of Asia 1850-1939*. Crawley, WA: UWA Publishing.

Warhurst, John. 1979. "Catholics, communism and the Australian party system: A study of the Menzies years." *Politics* 14 (2): 222-242. DOI: 10.1080/00323267908401710.

Warhurst, John. 2005. "Was the DLP a 'Church' Party?" In *The Great Labor Schism: A Retrospective*, edited by Brian Costar, Peter Love and Paul Strangio, 301-310. Melbourne: Scribe.

Periodicals

Advocate. Archdiocese of Melbourne, Victoria. <http://nla.gov.au/nla.news-title792>.

Ambrosian: Official Organ of St Ambrose Parish. [Brunswick, Victoria], January 1945-February 1948.

Australian Messenger of the Sacred Heart. Holdings of Jesuit Publications, Richmond, Victoria.

Australian Voice of Fatima, December 4, 1951. Family Rosary Crusade Box, Melbourne Diocesan Historical Commission, Victoria.

Barrier Daily Truth. Broken Hill, New South Wales.

Barrier Miner. Broken Hill, New South Wales.

Catholic Press. Sydney, New South Wales.

Catholic Worker. Campion Society, Melbourne, February 1936 – June 1958, University of Melbourne Archives, Parkville, Victoria.

Madonna: the Australasian Children of Mary's Home Magazine. Holdings of Jesuit Publications, Richmond, Victoria.

Morning Chronicle. Sydney, 1843-1844.

Northern Star. Lismore, New South Wales.

Record. Emerald Hill, Queensland.

Southern Cross. Archdiocese of Adelaide, South Australia. <http://nla.gov.au/nla.news-title826>.

ARMIES AND CRUSADES

11

MISSION AND PROTECTION

BRINGING FÁTIMA TO WEST GERMANY IN THE EARLY COLD WAR YEARS

MONIQUE SCHEER

When it comes to devotion to the Virgin Mary, it is difficult to clearly separate the high and the low, the elite from the popular. She has been the focus of prayers from popes and bishops no less than from the masses of the faithful, and each has had decisive influence on the other. Apparition cults which spring up in the remotest of villages reproduce and, in turn, contribute to imagery legitimated and disseminated by the Church, drawing on and transforming iconographies long enshrined in Catholic artwork in cathedrals all over Europe. In this chapter, I will explore this interplay from the perspective of the local clergy in the diocese of Cologne in the postwar period, focusing on the dynamics between priests and the diocesan leadership as they sought to take up initiatives coming from Rome, mobilize their parishioners, and increase church influence in society as a whole. The setting for this examination is Germany in the process of recuperating from the devastation wrought by fascist dictatorship and war and faced with its new position as a divided country on the frontline of a new conflict, the Cold War.

In this situation, the Catholic Church negotiated its new standing in postwar West Germany: No longer a religious minority in the newly drawn boundaries of the country, Catholics sought to position themselves as strong allies of the state in its struggle against communism. Some clergy saw the potential of Marian devotion, particularly in the form of the new Portuguese apparition cult in Fátima, to recruit the faithful in this struggle, and took measures to promote it in West Germany. However, they were confronted not only with vocal protest from Protestant quarters, but also from clergy sympathetic to the Liturgical Movement, a progressive group seeking to rid the Church of its ultramontane aesthetic and attitudes, including what they viewed as an overblown cult of Mary. Even those priests who promoted traditional Marian devotion in their parishes were reticent to lend their support to a newer apparition cult, particularly when, in the years 1949 to 1952, an unparalleled outbreak of Marian apparitions in West Germany took place that the Church felt it had to bring under control (Scheer 2006). These apparitions addressed Cold War anxieties among their followers very directly, and promoting the politicized, anticommunist Fátima message in the churches was feared to lend credence to such apparition activities.

Nevertheless, as the Marian Year of 1954 approached, plans were made to draw on devotional elements specifically targeting the threat presented by the Cold War in order to mobilize parishioners to participate in a 'Christian renewal' with a political message. This chapter will look at two of the most prominent events. First, the diocese of Cologne organized what they called a *Peregrinatio Mariae*, in a direct reference to the inversion of the pilgrimage paradigm as described by David Morgan (2009): Instead of taking parishioners to Fátima, a replica of the statue in Fátima was brought to Cologne and travelled through the diocese. Second, the bishop's conference agreed to a ritual consecration of the German nation by its episcopate to the Immaculate Heart of Mary – a devotion she is said to have explicitly requested at her appearances to the Fátima visionaries. Planned as the high point of the congress of Catholic laity in Fulda, it was ostensibly a special, festive activity intended only for the faithful. However, the location as well as the diction of the ceremony was overloaded with meaning: As a pilgrimage site to the remains of Saint Boniface, the "Apostle of Germania" credited with the conversion of the Germanic peoples in the eight century and thus a forerunner of the German nation, Fulda had been a diocesan seat since the eighteenth century and the meeting place of the German bishops' conference since the nineteenth century. In addition to this national symbolism, Fulda was near the militarily strategic area under special observation by the American occupation force, the "Fulda gap" through which Russian tanks were expected to attempt to break through in the event of an invasion. Thus, in the public eye, the event could not be treated as a mere inner-Catholic matter. The consecration of the nation in Fulda all too clearly transgressed the boundary between religion and politics in a situation in which the country was struggling to find its feet as a democratic society in defiance of its communist neighbor.[1]

1 Substantial material for this chapter is taken from my book, *Rosenkranz und Kriegsvisionen: Marienerscheinungskulte im 20. Jahrhundert* (2006, 144-168). Many thanks to Diana Madden for her translation of the original text for my use here.

Fátima and the religio-political climate in postwar Germany

Prepared by a 'Marian Century' from the declaration of the dogma of the Immaculate Conception in 1854 to that of the Assumption in 1950, devotion to the Virgin was promoted by the Church throughout both World Wars. In his declaration of 1950, Pope Pius XII noted that "piety toward the Virgin Mother of God is flourishing and daily growing more fervent." The hardship associated with wartime had caused the faithful to be more "vigorously aroused to a more assiduous consideration of [Mary's] prerogatives," and so the truth of her glorification had "shone forth more clearly" (Doheny & Kelly 1954: 221). Since the *Kulturkampf* of the 1870s that ensued after the unification of the nation under one Kaiser, German Catholics had been accustomed to viewing themselves as a religious minority in a Protestant empire, and thus only felt partial responsibility for the role of their country as aggressors in both World Wars (cf. Scheer 2012). Thus, the clergy emphasized an interpretation of the war as divine punishment – not for the crimes perpetrated by the Nazi regime per se, but more broadly on the German people for the sins of apostasy. The war was visited upon them, the bishop of Münster claimed in 1945 in a speech from the ruins of the city hall, because "wide sections of the German people have increasingly renounced the belief in God and in Christ, and have left the Church," getting caught up in "truly satanic entanglements" with the regime (cf. Damberg 1997: 107-108). From the Catholic point of view in Germany, Nazism had been the logical extreme of a generally anthropocentric trend that had begun with the Renaissance, or, at the latest, with the French Revolution – an interpretation of history included the *Kölner Leitsätze* (Guiding Principles of Cologne) in 1946, the party program of the newly formed Christian Democratic Union party (CDU; cf. Wolgast 2001: 129). As soon as the threat of the next World War became tangible, this interpretive scheme could be reapplied: If Europe did not entrust itself to God, another war would be initiated by an atheist regime as punishment: the Soviet Union. This was the message contained in the so-called 'secrets of Fátima' which had begun to make the rounds after the visionary's memoirs had been translated and published all over Europe in the early 1940s.[2]

One effect of these publications was a wave of Marian apparitions which swept across the European continent between 1947 and 1954, triple the num-

2 The Italian original from Luigi Gonzaga da Fonseca, *La Meraviglie de Fátima*, first published in Casale Monferrato in 1931, was revised and approved by the visionary and published in Rome in 1942. Casimir Barthas presented Fonseca's material in the French translation in the same year, and an English translation was prepared based on his book with the title *Our Lady of Light* (published in Dublin and Milwaukee in 1947). The book was published in a German translation in 1944 in Fribourg, Switzerland, under Fonseca's name with the title: *Maria spricht zur Welt! Geheimnis und weltgeschichtliche Sendung Fátimas.* On the "secrets" and their dissemination, see Zimdars-Swartz 1991: 201-219.

11.1 Postcard of the visionaries of Heroldsbach, standing before an open, make-shift chapel, where they saw on October 9, 1949 the Virgin Mary.
[Collection of William A. Christian Jr.]

ber in previous decades, with an average of thirteen to fourteen sightings reported to the diocesan authorities each year,[3] sometimes drawing crowds that numbered in the tens of thousands for weeks and months on end. Germany was no exception, with two large apparition events beginning in 1949, one near the border to France, in the village of Fehrbach, the other near the Czech border, in Heroldsbach-Thurn.[4] Church authorities seemed overwhelmed, viewing these events on the one hand as pious excess, superstition, and *Wundersucht* (literally: addiction to miracles, or 'apparition fever'). The "piety toward the Virgin Mother of God" which Pius XII had praised in November 1950 as "flourishing and daily growing more fervent" needed to be reined in, as Cardinal Ottaviani noted in *L'Osservatore romano* a few months later (February 4, 1951). What the clergy perceived as excess, however, was of their own making, as William Christian Jr. has argued, particularly because missionary activity in the postwar period drew strongly on the symbolic capital that Mary provided, including the belief in her appearances in places like Fátima (cf. Christian 1984).

3 In the decades before this period, from 1931 to 1946, the average number of apparitions reported in Europe was four per year; the decades following, from 1955 to 1975, saw an average of three per year. See the table in Christian 1984: 242, which builds on the statistics presented in 1971 to the Société française d'études mariales in Pontmain (cf. Billet 1976: 11-24).

4 The histories of these and two other apparition events are the subject of Scheer 2006.

The attention lavished on Fátima by Pope Pius XII was certainly decisive. In his address on Vatican radio on the twenty-fifth anniversary of the apparitions in October of 1942,[5] he attributed the successful aversion of the "red menace" in Spain during the mid-1930s to the tide of devotion stimulated by Mary's appearances in Fátima. The protection that she had provided Portugal was now needed elsewhere, moving the pope to close his speech with a prayer to Mary, consecrating not only the Church, but "the entire world torn by violent discord, scorched in a fire of hate, victim of its own iniquities" to her "Immaculate Heart" and asking for her aid and intercession to end World War II (cf. Doheny & Kelly 1954: 202-204). On the Feast of the Immaculate Conception, December 8, 1942, the pope renewed this consecration of the world in a ritual celebration in St. Peter's Basilica, as reported on the front page of *L'Osservatore Romano* the next day.[6] During the following year, Catholic bishops were requested by the curia to reiterate the ritual at the local level by consecrating their dioceses to Mary, triggering a wave of activities commemorating Fátima, even in the German dioceses whose activities were still suppressed by Nazi rule and wartime privations (cf. Scheer 2006: 124-127). After the war's end, on May 13, 1946, before a crowd of 600,000, papal emissary Cardinal Masella placed a crown on the Fátima statue made of the gold of jewelry donated by those who believed Mary had protected them in wartime (cf. *Bote von Fatima* 7 (82) 1949: 326-327). In 1952, ten years after his world consecration, Pope Pius XII issued an apostolic letter stating that he would now consecrate specifically the peoples of the Soviet Union to Mary's Immaculate Heart, thereby granting a request made in countless letters he had received in the last two years (cf. *Carissimis Russiae Populis* 1952, in Doheny & Kelly 1954: 249-251).[7]

Such letter-writing campaigns were among the instruments that the many Fátima-inspired organizations used to further their cause of "fulfilling the demands Mary made at Fátima." Perhaps the most high-profile of these organizations was the Blue Army of Fátima, founded in the United States in 1947 and boasting millions of members worldwide within a few years (cf. Kselman & Avella 1986: 409-410). The organization spread quickly throughout Europe, reaching West Germany in 1951 and – according to the organization's own historiography – inspiring 80,000 devotees to sign the pledge to fulfill

5 The salutation "Benedicite Deum" was printed in full on the front page of the Vatican newspaper the next day with the headline: "Il Radiomessagio del Sommo Pontefice al Portogallo: Il Supremo Pastore nella grave ora presente consacra il genere umano al Cuore Immacolato di Maria" (*L'Osservatore Romano* 1942: 1).

6 The headline read: "Il Sacro Rito Espiatorio e Impetratorio nella Basilica Vaticana: Il Sommo Pontefice in unione al Suo popolo rinnova la Consacrazione dell' umanità al Cuore Immacolato di Maria."

7 See also the Latin version (*Epistula Apostolica ad Universos Russiae Populos*) published on August 4, 1952 in *Acta Apostolicae Sedis* 44 (1952): 505-511.

Mary's wishes expressed at Fátima.[8] Its popularity is difficult to quantify, as the renewal of Marian devotion it represented did not conflict, in principle, with the organizations already present. The "message of Fátima" was integrated into the enormous infrastructure of Marian piety that had been built up in Europe since the mid-nineteenth century with its Marian congregations, sodalities, and brotherhoods. Organizations from the interwar period which emerged in tandem with Rome's hopes for a 'Catholic Action' movement also bore militaristic titles, such as the *Legio Mariae* and Rosary Crusades.[9]

The pope supported their activities by responding to their requests. The special situation of pastoral work in the postwar years, which, according to the opinion of prominent representatives of the Church, required a missionary stance, as well as in the interpretation of history contained in the Fátima message, increased the willingness of German pastors to use the symbol of "Maria Fátima" in their work.

The goal of this work was clear: Christian renewal, a return to the Church after years of Nazi party rule. The German clergy were heartened by the "religious spring" which took place directly after the war, in which mass attendance noticeably rose,[10] and by the rising influence of Catholicism in the smaller West Germany, particularly due to the immigration of millions of Catholic refugees from Eastern Europe. But this euphoria soon gave way to talk of Germany as a country in need of mission (*Missionsland*), a key word that the Jesuit priest and diplomat of the Vatican Ivo Zeiger (1898-1952) introduced in the Jesuit periodical *Stimmen der Zeit*[11] and at the 1948 *Katholikentag*, the national convention of Catholic laity (cf. Gotto 1983: 470). Within only a few years after the war's end, the focus shifted from rehabilitating Germans from former Nazi indoctrinations to combatting socialist ideologies as competitors for the hearts and minds of the people. Resistance against communism was as much a religious as a political issue. Ultimately, the Catholic Church (which formerly had its own political representation in the *Zentrum* party) accepted the CDU as representative of its interests in the Bundestag, not least because it took a hard anticommunist line (cf. Damberg 1997: 118-119). Its leader and West Germany's first chancellor, Konrad Adenauer, was key to this acceptance, as historian Anselm Doering-Manteuffel points out, since "in the eyes of the Church the chancellor appeared to be a guarantor of a politics that rested on a

8 <www.fatima-weltapostolat.de/historie.html>. This was well under 0.5 percent of West German Catholics.

9 See Scheer 2006: 96-108.

10 Cf. for instance the statistics for Münster in Damberg 1997: 109. On the "religous spring" see also Blessing 1988: 60-71.

11 "Seelsorge im Missionsland erfordert Missionsmethode (...). [Es geht um] Rettung und Wiedergewinnung unserer Gefährdeten oder Verlorenen" (Pastoral work in a mission country requires the methods of missionary work (...) [What is at stake] is the rescue and recovery of our vulnerable or lost). Zeiger 1947-1948: 250.

foundation of Christian and conservative values and that offered Catholicism both political and ideological safety from ideological opponents and plenty of room for its own social development" (Doering-Manteuffel 1982: 123). A Marian cult with an anticommunist charge like the one offered by Fátima was an appropriate religious expression of this coming together of the interests of Church and State, marked by Adenauer's acceptance of the Blue Army's first 'Peace Prize' in May 1954 (cf. Scheer 2006: 21).

The Madonna travels the Rhineland

Such was the religious and political atmosphere in West Germany, when in September of 1953, the papal encyclical *Fulgens corona* proclaimed 1954 a Marian Year in honor of the 100-year celebration of the dogmatization of the Immaculate Conception, which dioceses should celebrate with special devotions to the Virgin Mother. In his memoirs, the Archbishop of Cologne, Cardinal Josef Frings, writes of his own response to this call:

> The Pope proclaimed 1954 a Marian Year. The worship of the Mother of God of Fátima was also in full swing at the time. (...) In many countries, the custom had evolved of carrying a statue of Our Lady of Fátima through the parishes and dioceses in order to invoke the special protection of the Mother of God. I decided to carry out this custom in my diocese as well (Frings 1973: 166).

This is the full extent of Frings' remarks on his decision here; it is possible, however, that impressions from a trip he made to Fátima in the early summer of 1952, which he describes as thoroughly positive, played a role (cf. Frings 1973: 143-158). As he remarks, the idea of travelling an image of Mary of Fátima throughout a region had already been well-established in neighboring Catholic countries from the mid-1940s onward, building on the *Grand Retour* in France (1943-1948), which used the Notre Dame de Boulogne, but with an equally militant message. As Robert Ventresca points out, these revitalizations of much older practices of processing an image of the Virgin around a region in order to ward off disaster and protect the faithful were now linked to explicit missionary zeal: "The purpose of the *Grand Retour* was 're-evangelization.' It symbolized the 'return' of the Virgin to traditional devotion sites which, in turn, was meant to symbolize the wider 'return' of France to God."[12]

The records of the Office of Pastoral Care in the archives of the archdiocese give a more precise picture of the decision process. The *Peregrinatio Mariae* was discussed at the end of June in 1953, before the publication of

12 Ventresca 2004: 108-109. See also his discussion of the *Madonna Pellegrina* events in Italy 1947-1948, *Ibid.*: 108-117.

the *Fulgens corona*, and the archbishop, who was also the chairman of the German bishops' conference, wanted to organize it all over Germany. Wilhelm Heinen, the head of Cologne's Office of Pastoral Care, shared this in a letter to a staff member of their publication for local priests, *Seelsorgehilfe* (Pastoral Aid): "His eminence would like to try to win over all of the bishops of the Fulda conference to this plan. If he does not succeed, then Cologne will go ahead on its own."[13] The minutes from the meeting of the German bishops noted the formation of a committee to consider this question as well as other suitable possibilities for the celebration of the Marian Year.[14] Frings was perhaps the most popular bishop in postwar Germany, known for his 'folksy' and tolerant approach in those hard times, and as chairman of the episcopate certainly had a certain amount of sway, and yet he could not generate whole-hearted support for his plan.

As the publisher of *Seelsorgehilfe*, Heinen was charged with motivating the priests, and he, too, saw himself confronted with a problem: "A big difficulty for the realization of the plan lies with the clergy, who, out of an exaggerated liturgical stance, for the most part see no sense in Marian devotion." He planned a special issue of *Seelsorgehilfe* with articles designed to "relax the all-too rational piety of the Germans." Apparently, his own recent visit to an apparition site had inspired him to this step, as he adds: "That this is necessary became very apparent to me in Lourdes."[15] After its publication, Heinen expressed optimism in a letter to a colleague, again gesturing to the importance of supernatural aid: "One notices that the plan for the *Peregrinatio Mariae* continues to gain ground among us. The Mother of God makes sure of this. His Eminence has submitted the plan to the Bishops' Conference in Fulda and it has met with no objections. It could not yet be agreed, however, whether a statue from Fátima or a local image of Mary should be carried around."[16] In fact, interest among the German bishops seems to have actually been rather tepid. At the beginning of October 1953, the Bavarian episcopate decided at their meeting to leave the decision about a *Peregrinatio Mariae* up

13 Historisches Archiv des Erzbistums Köln (HAEK), Seelsorgeamt Heinen (erzbischöfliches Seelsorgeamt (archbishop's Office of Pastoral Care)), Abteilung Allgemeine Seelsorgefragen (Department of General Questions on Pastoral Care), Leader: Prelate Wilhelm Heinen), II. Einzelne Ereignisse im Erzbistum 1948-1955, 3. Marianisches Jahr 1954, Peregrinatio Mariae, 103 (Correspondence): Letter from Heinen to the university professor Dr. A. S. from June 30, 1953.

14 Archiv des Bistums Speyer (ABSp) BA A-II-26: Protokoll der Plenarkonferenz der Bischöfe der Diözesen Deutschlands in Fulda vom 18. bis 20. August 1953, 5.

15 HAEK Seelsorgeamt Heinen 103: Letter from Heinen to university professor Dr. A.S. from June 30, 1953.

16 ABSp BA A-I-32: Notes on the discussion of the Bavarian bishops at the Freising Conference, October 1-2, 1953, 3: Tagungsordnungspunkt 4 (Point 4): Das Marianische Jahr 1954 (The Marian Year 1954) (Presentation Augsburg).

to the individual bishops.[17] At the beginning of November, the West German bishops were also tentative, as they clearly could not count on cooperation from all quarters. Special religious events were often viewed as detrimental to the regular attendance of mass – and the popularity of local Marian apparition cults of the previous few years in spite of Church disapproval still stuck in the higher clergy's craw. Thus, they argued for tying the event to everyday pastoral work:

> We suggest a special evaluation of the potential of the Marian Year for *regular pastoral care as a form of inner renewal*. Guiding principles could be the content of the Fátima message: prayer, atonement, penance, a simple attitude toward life, a deepening of faith here among us, responsibility for the *East*. (...) The Peregrinatio Mariae as such is affirmed, but its performance is not recommended for all dioceses; rather, it should only be performed in those places where good preparation of both the priests' internal will and the external surroundings allow us to hope for a pastoral success. Whether a Fátima Madonna or another likeness of the Mother of God will be used for the Peregrinatio must be decided on a place-by-place basis.[18]

In the end, then, Cologne proceeded on its own.[19] There had been some similar activities spearheaded by the *Johannesbund* in Leutesdorf, headquarters of the German branch of the Blue Army.[20] They had already traveled a Fátima Madonna around West and East Berlin in September 1953[21] and offered this service to individual parishes in West Germany throughout the Marian Year.[22] But the *Peregrinatio Mariae* of the Archdiocese of Cologne enjoyed far more publicity. As an official church-run presentation of the Fátima devotion, the

17 *Ibid.*

18 ABSp BA A-I-32: Letter from Josef Cardinal Wendel, archbishop of Munich-Freising, from December 17, 1953 to the bishops of Bavaria. Attached: Excerpt from the Minutes of the Meeting of the West German Bishops on November 3-5, 1953, about the celebration of the Marian Year (emphasis in original).

19 HAEK Seelsorgeamt Heinen 102: Letter from Heinen to Bishöfliches Ordinariat Würzburg, November 21, 1953.

20 The same organization which is at the center of Morgan's examination of the Pilgrim Statue in Indiana (2009). The five-day travel of a Pilgrim Statue in Bougainville (Papua New Guinea) in 1997 described by Anna-Karina Hermkens (2012) was also organized by a lay organization with the help of the local priests, but without approval from the bishop.

21 "Die Statue Unserer Lieben Frau von Fatima auf Pilgerreise," *Maria siegt* 2 (10) (October 1953): 4 and "Unsere Liebe Frau von Fatima in Berlin," *Maria siegt* 12 (December 1953): 4.

22 The reports in the Blue Army's magazine, *Maria siegt* (Mary is victorious), suggest sporadic use in diverse parts of Germany, see the reports in numbers 1, 3 (Hünsruck), 4, 5 (Karlsruhe), 7 (Oldenburger Land and Niederbayern), 9 (Wolfsberg), and 12 (Hamburg) of Volume 3 of the periodical (1954). Closing report from Karl Pfister, M.S.J.: "Mit der Pilgermadonna quer durch Deutschland," *Maria siegt* 4 (2) (February 1955): 4. From November 1953 through December 1954, Fátima tridua were held in 135 parishes in 13 dioceses.

only one in Germany, with full support of the bishop, it covered double the number of parishes in half the time and was overall far more prestigious.

Frings first addressed his flock with thoughts on the Marian Year and his plans for the *Peregrinatio* in a pastoral letter from November 24, 1953. Taking his cue from the pope in *Fulgens Corona*, he linked the more controversial Fátima image to the more acceptable one from Lourdes, writing: "The images of the Virgin of Lourdes, who called herself the Immaculate Conception, deserve special notice this year. Over the course of the year, a Fátima Madonna will be displayed and venerated for a period of time in the main cathedral in Cologne and perhaps in some other churches of the archdiocese."[23] In February, Heinen sent out a bulletin to local clergy explaining the plan.[24] They should not think it was "propaganda in religious garments in the style of the parades so popular today in order to create excitement for an idea among the people," he warned, rather, it was motivated by "the events in Fátima, where the Mother of God once again appeared on the historical stage in order to bring a message to the people in these troubled times. The fate of the world and its individual peoples depends to a large extent on compliance with this message." In this letter, Heinen compared the event to evangelization (*Volksmission*) and described how it should be designed, with a celebratory entrance into the parish church and nightly vigils. In closing, the parish should be consecrated to the Immaculate Heart of Mary to ensure peace, as Mary of Fátima demanded. In words spiked with apocryphal metaphors and the rhetoric of religious war, Heinen encourages the clergy to take part:

> Structured in this way, conceived of with faith and performed with piety, the Peregrinatio would bring on just the Christian renewal that we, up until now, have not managed to bring about with the numerous methods employed by our pastors. Experience has shown over and over again that on her pilgrimage, the Mother of God pulls people out of religious indifference and sinful lives and guides them to Christ. We must have belief and faith in the power of the divine grace that is offered to us by the Mater gratiae in such difficult times! He who truly believes that God is the master of history and the people can see how appropriate it is that He sends us a signum elevatum in these times when the kingdoms of both God and Satan stand in sharp contrast to each other, a signum elevatum in which we can prevail.[25]

23 Pastoral Letter on the Marian Year from November 24, 1953 (to be read on the 2 Sunday of Advent [December 6]) in the ecclesiastical journal of the Archdiocese of Cologne 93 (508) (1953): 454-458, cited in Trippen 2003: 478.

24 HAEK Seelsorgeamt Heinen 104 (Reports and Correspondences about the preparation, performance, and effects): Letter from February 1, 1954 (manuscript). Published in its full length in *Maria Königin in Christi Reich* 6 (5) (May 1954): 1. Longer excerpts in *Maria siegt* 3 (3) (March 1954): 4. Reprint in *Bote von Fatima* 12 (136) (April 1954): 785-786.

25 *Ibid.*

Despite his rising worry that many of the clergy would see the *Peregrinatio* as overblown worship of Mary, Heinen received so many applications that not all of the willing parishes were given the chance to participate. He solved the problem by having each district kept the statue for three days, generally for one day each in a different church or for three days in one place.[26] In total, 300 churches were visited between May and December.[27] And as the records of the event show, it clearly took on a momentum of its own. If the local clergy had doubts, as Heinen feared, then the parishioners themselves did not, appearing in large numbers to witness the presence of Maria of Fátima in their local churches.

The diocese ordered a portable Madonna statue directly from the workshop in Fátima, Portugal, where the original was made.[28] It was blessed by the bishop of Leiría and transported to Germany free of charge by a Portuguese military aircraft (appropriately named the *Santa Maria*). On April 9, 1954, a delegation of 30 clergy and laypeople under the leadership of Auxiliary Bishop Wilhelm Cleven (1893-1983) from Cologne received the statue at the Frankfurt airport as if it were living notable on a state visit.[29] The newsletter *Maria Königin in Christi Reich* (Mary, Queen in Christ's Kingdom) published a photograph of the moment and wrote:

> After the "Salve Regina," sung by all of those present in the middle of the international airport with the drone of airplanes arriving from and departing to all the corners of the globe, Bishop Cleven held a short welcome speech for the reception of the Mother of God of Fátima in Germany.[30]

But in a report for the Office of Pastoral Care, the situation on the tarmac was described in more emotional terms:

> The moments in which the airplane arrived and the statue was brought out and removed from its packaging quite spontaneously became ones of deep religious devotion. All of those present, even those of a different faith, took

26 HAEK Seelsorgeamt Heinen 104: Letter from June 4, 1954: Die Peregrinatio Mariae in der Erzdiözese Köln. Kurze Hinweise für die Feierlichkeiten beim Besuch der Fatima-Madonna.

27 Here and in the following the representation is based on: Report on the development of the "Peregrinatio Mariae" in the archdiocese Cologne in Marian Year 1954. In: HAEK Seelsorgeamt Heinen 104.

28 Bill for statue, 120 cm high, 6,600 Escudos, in HAEK Seelsorgeamt Heinen 102. The Pilgrim Madonna is not identical to the original statue in Fátima; it is considered to be one of two "subtypes" made by the sculptor José Thedim, the other being the statue of the Immaculate Heart of Mary located at the Carmel of Saint Theresa in Coimbra where the seer Lucia dos Santos lived from 1948 until her death at age 97 in 2005. The main difference between the Pilgrim type and the original statue is the lack of ornamentation of the cloak as well as slightly different facial features and expression. See Duarte 2017, 36-39.

29 Images are original photographs from HAEK Seelsorgeamt Heinen, II.3. File 119.

30 *Maria Königin in Christi Reich* 6 (5) (May 1954): 1.

11.1 Women and children lined up along the streets watching the procession pass. [Historical Archive of the Archdiocese of Cologne]

> part. All agreed that it was a religious experience, which would remain unforgettable.[31]

The statue passed the following weeks with contemplative orders that were not allowed to participate in the public celebrations, ending at the Carmelite abbey in Cologne. From there, it was carried on the evening of April 30, in a procession of about 5,000 men carrying lights, praying, and singing to the Cologne cathedral. The newspapers described the procession through the dark streets of the city center: at the head came mounted policemen, followed by the Catholic societies and organizations in rows of six; in the center was the statue, carried by a group of Knights of the Holy Sepulcher and escorted by torch bearers. Behind the Madonna were the dignitaries, clergy, and members of the *Schützenverein* (marksmen's club). On the side of the road, thousands of women and girls were lined up to watch, and the houses were decorated with lights.[32] At the cathedral around 10 p.m., the statue was received by Archbishop Cardinal Frings and displayed in the crossing, which was decorated with flowers and candles. In front of around 8,000 people inside and in front of the cathedral, the archbishop gave a sermon that connected the traditional May Day celebrations of the Catholic workers with the Marian theme of the jubilee year. In it, he emphasized that humanity "does not want to recognize the grave nature of sin," neither under National Socialism nor in the libertinism of the postwar period.[33] The punishment for this sin now threatens Europe in the form of the Soviet Union, interpreting the Fátima message as a call to "pray for peace. May God protect people from the horrors of a new war, because human intentions and conferences alone are not adequate to turn this evil away from the world."[34]

The statue of the Madonna was kept in the cathedral for a week, and every day a celebratory mass was held in her honor.[35] The report in the diocesan archives records: "During these days, the number of believers visiting the cathedral rose by the hour. On one day, over 60,000 visitors were counted. The

31 HAEK Seelsorgeamt Heinen 104: Report on the development of the "Peregrinatio Mariae".

32 Description of the procession with a photo, in "Erhebende Lichterprozession mit Fatima-Madonna," in the daily newspaper *Kölnische Rundschau*, 9 (101) (May 1, 1954), 14.

33 "Botschaft von Fatima für Erzdiözese Köln," *Kölnische Rundschau*, 9 (101) (May 1, 1954), 2. The size of the crowd was almost the same as the May Day rally organized by the trade unions on the next day with good weather, where according to the same newspaper, about 10,000 were in attendance, see *Kölnische Rundschau*, 9 (102) (May 3, 1954), 3.

34 "Menschen- und Christenwürde achten. Kardinal Frings predigte über die Botschaft von Fatima," *Kölner Stadt-Anzeiger*, 102 (May 3, 1954) in HAEK Seelsorgeamt Heinen 105.

35 Monday was the day of the ill; Tuesday was the day of women with a devotion held by priests once imprisoned in concentration camps; Wednesday was the day of youth and nuns; Thursday was set aside for schoolchildren; on Friday, a devotion was held for the displaced. See: "Tausende verehren die Fatima-Madonna im Dom," *Kölnische Rundschau*, 105 (May 6, 1954), in HAEK Seelsorgeamt Heinen 105.

believers performed their worship with a very respectful attitude. It was generally thought that at no time before had there been so much and such pious prayer in the Cologne cathedral."[36] The unexpected success of the presence of the Fátima Madonna in Cologne prompted the archbishop to change the expected order of the festivities: the crowning of the statue of the Madonna in the name of the pope was now to take place after only one week. He asked the Holy See in Rome by telegram for a permission, which was immediately granted. The celebration of the crowning on the evening of May 8 in the presence of the Vatican nuncio "was without doubt the high point of the Peregrinatio Mariae in the Cologne Cathedral."[37]

The next day, the Madonna statue was sent on its journey through the archdiocese. In a procession of mounted police, bands, girls in white dresses, and the cathedral chapter, she was brought to the Rhine and loaded onto a steamship named *Frieden* (Peace),[38] every mention of the term being not only an affirmation of the end of the war just past, but another reminder of the threat of a new war. According to the guidelines, the statue was to be picked up at the border of each parish by a priest and a procession (with lights if at night). If two parishes were far apart, the statue was taken by car and received by a motorcade.[39] The streets were to be decorated with wreathes and lights. The onlookers were to greet the passing statue of the Madonna by "standing piously – bowing their heads – and participating in prayers and songs."[40]

Upon entering a church, a Marian song would be sung until the statue, which was 1.60 meters high and weighed 25 kg, had been unscrewed from the litter and placed "not too far away from the people, if possible visible to all, [with a] simple but tasteful flower arrangement and possibly illuminated by spotlights."[41] It was very important that, while the Fátima Madonna was present, services to honor her be held around the clock; the parishes must be prepared to sacrifice in order to receive her graces. At night, the men, in the morning, the women; during the day, the ill were taken to mass and blessed

36 HAEK Seelsorgeamt Heinen 104: "Bericht über den Verlauf der 'Peregrinatio Mariae.'"

37 *Ibid.* See also the announcement: "Krönung der Fatima-Madonna," *Kölnische Rundschau*, 9 (107) (May 8, 1954), 18.

38 See "Festlicher Abschluß der Fatima-Oktav," *Kölnische Rundschau*, 9 (108) (May 10, 1954), 4.

39 Cf. "Fatima-Statue traf ein," *Mettmanner Zeitung*, July 27, 1954, in HAEK Seelsorgeamt Heinen 105: "The statue was mounted on the roof of a car and illuminated with spotlights. The Mettmann delegation (...) took over the statue, and then the motorcade, which had at this point grown to about 60 cars, began to move again."

40 HAEK Seelsorgeamt Heinen 104: Letter, June 4, 1954: The Peregrinatio Mariae in the archdiocese of Cologne. Short notes for the celebrations at the visit of the Fatima Madonna, divided into 1. The Pilgrimage Plan; 2. The Statue in the Parishes: Reception and Hand Off at the Parish Border, Entry into the House of God (with nightly worship), Closing Celebration and Rites; 3. Concerns for the order members that accompany the statue; 4. Behavior of believers upon the passing of the statue.

41 *Ibid.*

individually, and in the early afternoon, the children were to be brought to the statue before the closing celebration was performed. The priests received support for the planning of the worship services and taking confessions on this day from missionary orders, Redemptorists, Jesuits and others.[42]

At the end of the seven months, the Office of Pastoral Care was enthusiastic about its success in its report, calling it a "continual triumph" because

> without exception, all of the parishes greeted the Mother of God with great joy. They took great pains to give joy to her during her stay through hours of prayer, night vigils, and numerous receptions of the holy sacraments. In many cities, the Peregrinatio was such a historic event that it gave character to the city for hours. During this time, the visit of the Madonna was the chief topic of conversation. (...) Many parishes remarked to us in their reports about the development of the Peregrinatio that their houses of God had never been so well-visited.[43]

In many cities and communities, reports appeared in the local newspapers – sometimes in a special large spread.[44] With photos of the processions and the silent worship and with headlines highlighting "peace" and "triumph" (and thus again linking the two in the face of an imminent Cold War threat) the newspapers consistently reported unusually high participation rates in the devotions. In Heinen's eyes, the *Peregrinatio* proved that Catholicism was still alive in the Rhineland:

> If one would like to formulate the fruits of the Pereginatio in religious life, one could say: *The piety of the people broke through.* Already at the cathedral anniversary festival in 1948, we were happy to see how strongly religion still lived in the people. This became even more visible during [the Marian Year]. It was time for this religiosity to get a special awakening, since religious feeling and religious understanding had actually threatened to die out in the countryside. It seemed as if modern man threatened to lose his religious capacity under the influence of the secular world and carried no sense of obedience to God and the Holy within himself.[45]

The key, in his view, was giving people a way to access religion less through reason and more through the eye and emotion, something that the apparition cults were achieving and which explained their success. Taking the opportunity to criticize the influence of the Liturgical Movement, he wrote:

42 HAEK Seelsorgeamt Heinen 104: "Bericht über den Verlauf der 'Peregrinatio Mariae.'" See also *Ibid.*: Letter, June 4, 1954.

43 "Bericht über den Verlauf der 'Peregrinatio Mariae,'" HAEK Seelsorgeamt Heinen 104.

44 Cf. the collection of around 50 newspaper clippings in HAEK Seelsorgeamt Heinen 105.

45 HAEK Seelsorgeamt Heinen 104: Letter "Früchte des marianischen Jahres und deren Erhaltung" (Fruits of the Marian Year and their preservation), n.d. (ca. October 1954) (emphasis in original).

> In the last decades, we priests have placed far too much trust in outer means to awaken the religious spirit – in organizational work, in lectures and conferences, in rational training through radio and press. None of this has brought about the desired results; we have completely forgotten the most important factor, and that is the grace of God, which we must ask for. Only those who have come to this realization find the correct understanding of those appearances of the Mother of God in which she announces a message to the modern world, which we have shaped into short phrases during the Peregrinatio Mariae: To Christ through Mary! Pray! Atone! Live in Christ![46]

Here, Heinen rejects the importance of religious education and valorizes the ritual efficacy of prayer and penance ("Pray! Atone!"). Not "rational training" but appealing to divine forces will not only convert the "secular world" (of which communism was only one, albeit the most aggressive, manifestation), but also protect the population by preventing a war. This was the "message to the modern world" the Mother of God was spreading. But when necessary, this pointedly Cold War agenda of mission linked to protection could be submerged under a more general and broadly accepted traditional Marian devotion. At the final triduum of the *Peregrinatio* and the Marian Year from the 9 to 11 of December 1954, the statue was once again displayed in the Cologne Cathedral, where Archbishop Cardinal Frings gave the closing sermon on the last evening.[47]

Even though the reports from the parishes largely confirm the image painted by Heinen of an enthusiastic reception of the Fátima Madonna, there are complaints about the transience of this excitement. One priest wrote, "As far as a deeper influence goes, unfortunately it is clear that attendance of daily mass has not risen in the least. This also applies to the receiving of communion on Sundays."[48] Enthusiasm for Fátima did not necessarily transfer to everyday religious practice. Another criticism was the style of preaching, perhaps more suited to the evangelizing than regular church service, using "every means possible to create fear and horror in the people, probably in an attempt to use shock value to make the parishioners receptive to the consecration."[49] Heinen

46 *Ibid.*

47 The statue was then brought to the town of Alzen (near Morsbach/Sieg) to stay in a newly built church consecrated to the Immaculate Heart of Mary in August 1954, where it still resides today. On the occasion of the 100-year anniversary of the Fátima apparitions, the parish processed with the statue and the archbishop of Cologne, Cardinal Rainer Maria Woelki, who officiated at the celebratory mass on October 13, 2017. See the report on the website of the parish with photos: <http://begegnung-im-netz.de/pages/st.-gertrud-morsbach/fatima-madonna.php>.

48 HAEK Seelsorgeamt Heinen 105: Letter from the priest from Leverkusen-Wiesdorf from August 24, 1954. Cited in Trippen 2003: 482.

49 HAEK Seelsorgeamt Heinen 102: Letter from priest from Flerzheim from October 2, 1954 to the Office of Pastoral Care.

even spoke of a “divide” among the clergy over the “tone” of the Marian Year, exacerbated by “a foreign theologian’s speech at the beginning of the Marian Year on Mariology and Marian devotion” since many listeners were not open to its focus on Mariological dogma, forcing him “to proceed with extreme caution.” He had apparently harbored hopes that the *Peregrinatio* would also convert the German clergy and “slowly guide those priests to us that up till then had taken an oppositional stance. This hope has, unfortunately, to this day been left unfulfilled.”[50] This was also apparent during the decision to consecrate the nation to Mary’s Immaculate Heart in September of the Marian Year.

The national consecration to the Virgin Mary

In spite of the consecration of the individual dioceses to the Immaculate Heart in 1943, a paper by an unknown author, likely intended for the first postwar bishop’s conference in Fulda, circulated three years later, claiming the pope’s consecration of the world to the Virgin Mary in 1942 in Fátima had remained “largely unnoticed, especially in Germany, because of the World War.”[51] Admittedly, it was not easy during the Third Reich to effectively reach an audience with information about the consecrations: by 1941, most Catholic periodicals had been forbidden. Still, attendance at worship services dedicated to the consecration of the Virgin Mary was estimated to be very high. What was missing was a nationwide publicity, which was hoped for after the war. Again, the response by the bishop’s conference was muted; no mention of a national consecration is made in the minutes of its first five meetings.[52] Laypeople in Marian organizations continued their efforts, sending, for instance, a petition to the archbishop of Cologne in 1950 that, making an explicit connection with the Marian apparition in Fátima, demanded the consecration of Germany at the *Katholikentag* that year in Passau in this “most difficult time,”[53] claiming it was a direct command from heaven and expressing their fear of a new war between the existing world powers. A monthly journal published by such a lay organization, the *Fatima Lesebogen*, warned on the first page of the June 1950 issue:

50 HAEK Seelsorgeamt Heinen 102: Letter Heinen to Prof. Pater Dr. Tiberius Gallus, S.J. in Messina, December 20, 1954.

51 Copies of this typewritten document are found with the documents on the Fulda bishops conference from August 20-22, 1946 in ABSp BA A-II-19, in Erzbischöfliches Archiv München, Nachlass (EAM NL) Faulhaber 6360 (Marian consecration) and in Diözesanarchiv Rottenburg (DAR), G1.1, D 17.1h (Materials on the Marian consecration).

52 ABSp BA A-II-18 to 22 (Fulda Bishops Conference 1945-1949).

53 HAEK, Generalia 29.4d (Maria et Mariana).

> If our people only knew what a modern war means, they would from this day forward get down on their knees and beg God to avert his tribunals. The messages from the Mother of God – beginning with those from Fátima – would be taken seriously. We ask: When is the consecration of Germany to the Immaculate Heart of Mary to come, the consecration through which alone we can erect a dam against Bolshevism?

Catholics also turned individually through letters to their spiritual leaders, for instance a teacher from Bergisch-Gladbach who wrote to Cardinal Faulhaber on August 20, 1950, referring to the recent apparition events in Germany:

> The Mother of God demands over and over again when she appears in different places and to visionaries that Germany be consecrated to her; then she will protect us from the worst of what might come. Thus, I am asking you, honorable Eminence, just as politely as urgently, to consecrate Germany to the Immaculate Heart of the Mother of God at the next opportunity, which is the *Katholikentag* in Passau (...) together with the other German bishops who are present there. While some bishops have already consecrated their diocese to the Mother of God, this is apparently not sufficient for her, "it should be all of Germany," including the Eastern zone. I hope, your Eminence, that I will not be met with a refusal, especially because the dangers of war and Bolshevism (...) are [becoming] ever more pressing and one can clearly say that it is 5 minutes before 12! If your Eminence perhaps does not believe in the individual Marian apparitions, please arrange for the consecration in any case as it is definitely something good (...), and you will not have to reproach yourself later for having refrained from doing something that serves to rescue our Fatherland.[54]

The commitment of Catholics who believed in apparitions to the German consecration complicated the matter for German bishops. In a time when, from the bishops' perspective, the faithful were afflicted with a veritable *Wundersucht*, the repetition of the consecration from 1942, which was expressly connected with a cult of apparition, could represent too high a risk now that there were active apparition cults taking place. On the other hand, the divine messages that were said to have been communicated in Fátima enjoyed high, church-sanctioned authority. Though the episcopate, under the leadership of Cardinal Frings, gave a hesitant signal of willingness to consecrate all German dioceses (the term "nation" was avoided) to the Immaculate Heart in connection with the declaration of the new Marian dogma in 1950,[55] in the end, none

54 EAM NL Faulhaber 5956 (Privatoffenbarungen).

55 ABSp BA A-II-23: Minutes of the plenary conference of the bishops of the dioceses of Germany in Fulda from the 22nd to the 24th of August 1950, 9 (emphasis in original).

transpired. It was not until the Marian Year that the bishops saw the appropriate opportunity, and again, the initiative came from the Rhine.[56]

On the penultimate evening of the *Katholikentag* in Fulda, the 4th of September, 1954, the ritual of consecration was performed in front of a gathering of 300,000 Catholic laypeople and pastorate, but its wording was different from that of the wartime diocesan consecration. In contrast to the papal example of 1942, the prayer was directed not to Mary but to God:

> To her, the refuge of human kind, we, the emissaries from all the tribes of our German people (...), raise up our souls full of trust. We consecrate ourselves to her immaculate heart, so that we love you, our master and God, as she loved you (...). We consecrate our families to her, we recommend her motherly protection to our people: our people with their sins and needs, with their hope and will.[57]

The relatively carefully worded prayer clearly takes the interdenominational tensions in Germany into consideration. It had been difficult enough to communicate the decision of the Vatican to announce the new Marian dogma in 1950 to Protestant compatriots,[58] and four years later, Protestant representatives were again aghast at the idea of a national consecration (cf. Trippen 2003: 483-487). The day before, the leading Protestant bishop in Germany, Hans Meiser, sent his colleague Frings a telegram in which he communicated that the Marian consecration was viewed with "deep discomfort" among Protestants. He took notice of the fact that the wording of the consecration only referenced "Catholic Germany," but he warned against "endangering the peace between the confessions."[59] Several statements by Catholic functionaries had led him to believe that they indeed intended to include Protestants in this act of consecration, an act deemed invasive and presumptuous.[60] Symbols and

56 When the conference of the Bavarian bishops in Freising was in session at the beginning of October 1953 in order to discuss the implementation of the *Fulgens Corona*, they noted no recommendations for a German consecration (ABSp BA A-I-32: Minutes of the conference of the Bavarian Bishops in Freising on October 1 and 2, 1953). In December, however, the Bavarian bishops were informed in a letter from Joseph Cardinal Wendel, archbishop of Munich-Freising, about the decision of the meeting of the West German bishops. Letter from Wendel from December 17, 1953 with attachment: Excerpt from the minutes of the conveniat of the West German bishops from November 3-5, 1953.

57 *Katholisches Sonntagsblatt*, 102 (37) (September 12, 1954), 669-670. See also: Zentralkomitee deutscher Katholiken (Central Committee of German Catholics) 1954: 454-455.

58 Cf. an exchange of letters between an evangelical and a Catholic theologian about Marian devotion at the forefront of dogmatization in: "Besinnung und Ausschau. Durch Maria zu Christus," *Benediktinische Monatschrift* 26 (1950): 233-246.

59 Original telegram in HAEK Gen II 8.3,3, cited in Trippen 2003: 484.

60 HAEK Gen II 3.8,3: "Erklärung des Leitenden Bischofs der Vereinigten Evangelisch-Lutherischen Kirche Deutschlands," Evangelischer Pressedienst, September 15, 1954 (Protest writings from individual people and from Evangelical groups against the national Marian consecration), cited in Trippen 2003: 485 f.

symbolic actions with political connotations ("national") that were clearly coded as Catholic could be disturbing in a time when, with the founding of the CDU, both of the large Christian denominations in Germany wanted to work together politically. With Catholics in key positions in the CDU, Protestants were already worried about the "denominational face" of the Federal Republic (cf. Trippen 2003: 550). Thus, the careful wording of the prayer, and the ritual iconography which also avoided referencing Fátima; instead, a medieval statue of Mary from a local monastery was used in the procession.[61] These details did not pass by the Marian-minded onlookers unnoticed. One Marian newsletter regretted that the consecration "did not seem to go beyond the scope of a normal Marian ceremony." It was supposed to be "a conscious dedication and a vow in order to make those attending the *Katholikentag* aware of the power of the intercession and the protection of Mary in the hideousness of the state of the world today (...) in the middle of the age of collectivism and the tremendous danger of nuclear weapons, both of which cast terrible shadows."[62]

Conclusion

The Marian Year in Cologne offers a concise example of how bishops took up impulses from the Vatican at the local level, negotiating their own wishes and those of some parishioners and adjusting them to the requirements of their local religious landscape. The consecration performed by the pope in 1942 provided powerful inspiration for those who saw it as indispensable help in times of war. His crowning of the Fátima image in 1946 and the proclamation of the dogma of the Assumption in 1950 were also linked to Mary's protection in wartime, and as Cold War tensions rose, so did fears of impending violence. The bishops had to manage the balancing act between using the dynamics of this piety, directing it in a way that was acceptable to the majority of church leaders, and staging it such that it would not offend non-Catholics in a sensitive bi-confessional political situation. They turned the Vatican's last large Marian event, the proclamation of the Marian Year 1954, as best they could to their own interests. Here they could finally embed the new apparition imagery

61 *Katholisches Sonntagsblatt*, 102 (37) (September 12, 1954), 669: The "400 Jahre alte Gnadenbild" (400 year-old holy image) came from the Franciscan monastery Frauenberg in Fulda. In the newspaper *Die katholische Frau*, 7 (9) [September 1954], 2, the image was described as a late Gothic *Schutzmantelmadonna* with a crescent moon under her feet – an iconography which nonetheless addresses the same issues that the Fátima devotion does: protection and apocalypticism. For links between late medieval iconography drawing on the imagery of the Woman of the Apocalypse and the modern apparition image, see Scheer 2006: 263-298.

62 "Fuldaer Marienweihe und was nun?" *Maria Königin in Christi Reich* 6 (10) (October 1954): 1.

provided by Fátima into a traditional Marian infrastructure, thereby also reining in the 'apparition fever' of the previous years. Thus, the bishop of Speyer was able to make the following closing assessment at the end of the Marian Year: "In contrast to an unhealthy, sensation-seeking Marian cult, the kind that appeared in connection with illegal places of apparition, the Marian year had a cleansing and clarifying effect on the mind and guided no small number of confused Marian worshipers back to the straight road of true Catholic piety."[63] Retrospectively, however, these events could be considered the final fanfare for the cult of Mary which had flourished in the culture of Ultramontanism from the mid-nineteenth to the mid-twentieth centuries. Wartime had done its part to provide one last upswing in the popularity of the Virgin as the protector of her devotees and mighty ally in the battle against anti-Christian, anti-Catholic forces. But with the death of Stalin in 1953, the successive relaxation of tensions between the blocs, and in Germany, the facilitation of communication between East and West in the 1970s, the Cold War impetus for Mary's protection was fading. With the introduction of Vatican II reforms, viewed as a victory of the more progressive Liturgical Movement, Marian devotion itself was dialed considerably back by the German clergy. Attention to the Fátima message was brought again after the assassination attempt on Pope John Paul II, which took place on May 13, 1981. Following this event, the pope paid considerable attention to the Fátima devotion (among devotees it is common knowledge that he was saved by the Virgin of Fátima since the shooting took place on the anniversary of the first apparition), but it was assiduously framed as a private devotion, his own personal preference, and not a message to the rest of the Catholic world. More widely, the enthusiasm for Fátima was waning and since 1989 has been associated with an older generation, if not in fact a politically reactionary and overly devout one with fundamentalist tendencies. Currently, there are no signs of its reactivation in the Catholic Church in Germany, neither from the clergy nor the laity. It would appear that Fátima's encoding as a Cold War devotion has made it too specific to be easily transformed for present-day Germany.

63 ABSp BA A-II-27: Fuldaer Bischofskonferenz 1954: Akte zum Marianischen Jahr.

BIBLIOGRAPHY

Billet, Bernard et al. (eds.). 1976. *Vraies et fausses apparitions dans l'Église*. 2nd ed. Paris: Lethielleux.

Blessing, Werner K. 1988. "'Deutschland in Not, wir im Glauben...' Kirche und Kirchenvolk in einer katholischen Region 1933-1949." In *Von Stalingrad zur Währungsreform. Zur Sozialgeschichte des Umbruchs in Deutschland*, edited by Martin Broszat, Klaus-Dietmar Henke and Hans Woller, 3-111. Munich: Oldenbourg.

Christian, William A. 1984. "Religious Apparitions and the Cold War in Southern Europe." In *Religion, Power, and Protest in Local Communities: The Northern Shore of the Mediterranean*, edited by Eric Wolf, 239-265. Berlin: Mouton.

Damberg, Wilhelm. 1997. *Abschied vom Milieu? Katholizismus im Bistum Münster und in den Niederlanden 1945-1980*. Paderborn: Schöningh.

Doering-Manteuffel, Anselm. 1982. "Kirche und Katholizismus in der Bundesrepublik der fünfziger Jahre." *Historisches Jahrbuch* 102: 113-134.

Doheny, William J. and Joseph P. Kelly. 1954. *Papal Documents on Mary*. Milwaukee: Bruce.

Duarte, Marco Daniel. 2017. "A escultura de Nossa Senhora do Rosário de Fátima: Estudo histórico-artístico deum dos mais importantes ícones do catolicismo contemporâneo." In *Estudo científico da Escultura de Nossa Senhora do Rosário de Fátima*, edited by João de Freitas Coroado and Marco Daniel Duarte, 13-45. Fátima: Santuario de Fátima.

Frings, Josef. 1973. *Für die Menschen bestellt. Erinnerungen des Alterzbischofs von Köln Josef Kardinal Frings*. Cologne: Bachem.

Gotto, Klaus. 1983. "Zum Selbstverständnis der katholisch Kirche im Jahre 1945." In *Politik und Konfession. Festschrift für Konrad Repgen zum 60. Geburtstag*, edited by Dieter Albrecht et al., 465-481. Berlin: Duncker & Humblot.

Hermkens, Anna-Karina. 2012. "Journeys of Resistance: Marian Pilgrimages During the Bougainville Crisis." In *Pilgrimage in the Age of Globalisation: Constructions of the Sacred and Secular in Late Modernity*, edited by Nelia Hyndman-Rizk, 58-78. Newcastle: Cambridge Scholars.

Kselman, Thomas and Steven Avella. 1986. "Marian Piety and the Cold War in the United States." *The Catholic Historical Review* 72: 403-424.

Morgan, David. 2009. "Aura and the Inversion of Marian Pilgrimage: Fatima and Her Statues." In *Moved by Mary: The Power of Pilgrimage in the Modern World*, edited by Anna-Karina Hermkens, Willy Jansen and Catrien Notermans, 49-65. Farnham, UK: Ashgate.

Scheer, Monique. 2006. *Rosenkranz und Kriegsvisionen: Marienerscheinungskulte im 20. Jahrhundert*. Tübingen: TVV.

Scheer, Monique. 2012. "How the Virgin Mary Protected the West from Communism." In *Cold War Cultures: Perspectives on Eastern and Western European Societies*, edited by Annette Vowinckel, Annette Payk and Thomas Lindenberger, 129-151. New York: Berghan Books.

Trippen, Norbert. 2003. *Josef Kardinal Frings (1887-1978)*. Vol. 1: *Sein Wirken für das Erzbistum Köln und für die Kirche in Deutschland*. Paderborn: Schoeningh.

Ventresca, Robert. 2004. *From Fascism to Democracy: Culture and Politics in the Italian Election of 1948*. Toronto: University of Toronto Press.

Wolgast, Eike. 2001. *Die Wahrnehmung des Dritten Reichs in der unmittelbaren Nachkriegszeit (1945/46)*. Heidelberg: C. Winter Universitätsverlag.

Zeiger, Ivo. 1947-1948. "Um die Zukunft der katholischen Kirche in Deutschland." *Stimmen der Zeit* 141: 241-252.

Zentralkomitee der deutschen Katholiken (eds.). 1954. *Ihr sollt mir Zeugen sein. Der 76. deutsche Katholikentag vom 31. August bis zum 5. September 1954 in Fulda*. Paderborn: Schoeningh.

Zimdars-Swartz, Sandra L. 1991. *Encountering Mary: From La Salette to Medjugorje*. Princeton: Princeton University Press.

12
CONTESTED COLD WAR MARIAN POLITICS
THE DUTCH PENTAGON AND THE EMPIRE OF MARY

PETER JAN MARGRY

Pope Pius XI's March 1937 *cri de cœur*, the encyclical *Divini Redemptoris* which called on Catholics to fight against atheism and communism, and to protect "Christian civilization" [1], fell on fertile ground in the Netherlands. Dutch Catholics, together with their Irish coreligionists, were often characterized as being among the most devout and Rome-oriented in the world, while at the same time the Dutch population was well aware of the threats of rising totalitarianism.[2] Living in a religiously mixed country with a history of suppression of Catholicism had turned Dutch Catholics into dedicated believers who were willing to profess a 'perfect' Catholicism as it was propagated by the Vatican. Their minority position under long-term Calvinist domination had molded them into a strongly coherent group, and at the end of the nineteenth century and the first half of the twentieth century this resulted in a Catholic 'pillar', the strongest societal community within an ideologically rigidly divided ('pillarized') Netherlands. They formed a diaspora among Protestant 'heretics', and this had given them an inherently missionary tradition. The missionary mentality of Dutch Catholics resulted in an even stronger attachment to the pope and the Vatican: it was a trope that Dutch Catholics were "more Catholic than the pope". Their *ultramontanist* orientation was revealed in strong Dutch participation in the papal army, and in the willingness

1 It was a 'twin' encyclical with *Mit brennender Sorge*, which was published nine days earlier, on March 10, 1937, and which was directed against German National Socialism.

2 The year before, in October 1936, the national Catholic anticommunistic initiative Action "For God" had started, Luykx 1978: 1-14, 183-198, 401.

of Dutch Zouaves to sacrifice themselves for the 'good' cause of protecting the Papal State in the 1860s. This ultramontane view remained a characteristic of Dutch Catholicism until the end of the Second Vatican Council, after which it suddenly became a trailblazer for 'liberalism'.

However, as early as the years immediately after the end of the Second World War, traditional Dutch denominational relations came under pressure to change, while the evolving geopolitical constellation and newly triumphant ideologies urged a reevaluation of international politics, construing a former ally, Russia, as the central new enemy. In the postwar setting these aspects – a highly organized Catholic population, a tradition of missionary work for the conversion of heretics and the Godless, and a changing political pattern – proved to be effective in shaping a specific Dutch contribution to Cold War politics. Even before the Second World War was fully over, rumors started to spread in the Netherlands about the advance of the Red Army and its ruthless soldiers, who were supposedly eager to reach the shores of the North Sea, implying an immanent new invasion of the nation. It was the first signal of growing fear of the new Soviet imperialist agenda. As we now know, this advance to the sea did not materialize. Instead, the reconstruction of Europe developed along the dividing lines set out at Yalta at the conference that had been held in this Crimean seaside town earlier in 1945.

When the last festivities to celebrate the peace had ended in 1947 and the trauma of the war was provisionally buried, European states looked once more to the future. But that very same year, not even five years after the great conflagration of the world war, news of a big new 'cold war' began to appear in the media.[3] In November of that year Dutch newspapers discovered the first articles written by the American journalist Walter Lippmann in the *New York Herald Tribune* about the United States' opposition to the expanding influence of the Soviet Union in Western Europe.[4]

Organized communism had been a feature of Dutch society since 1909, when a first national communist party was set up, but communists only gained a more substantial foothold in Dutch politics after the Russian Revolution of 1917 (Verrips 1995). However, the interwar edition of the Dutch *Catholic Encyclopedia* wrote confidently: "our national character does not seem propitious to Russian communism" (Sassen 1934: 762). Scholars have even qualified the Dutch nation at the time as "exceptionally strongly anticommunist" (Hellema 1995; cf. Christiaens 2015: 188). During the Second World War the communist party nonetheless played an important role in resistance against the German occupation, and it gained widespread sympathy among the population on account of this. The communists were consequently able to attract ten percent of

3 See a first mention in newspaper *De Tijd*, September 9, 1947; on the Dutch political position during the Cold War see: Wiebes & Zeeman 1994.

4 "Rusland heeft de 'koude oorlog' verloren," *De Tijd*, November 6, and November 14, 1947.

12.1 Election campaign poster of the Dutch RKSP (Roman Catholic Political Party) asking for votes to help protect Christendom against both communism and the Dutch pro-Nazi party NSB, 1937.
A blue colored Christian fist withholds a red colored Communist hand with a red dagger. Design by J.S.A.M. van Woerkom.
[Nijmegen, KDC]

Dutch votes in the first postwar elections. This popularity proved to be short-lived. Their criticism of the colonial war which the Netherlands was waging against Indonesia (in the "Dutch Indies") ensured that communists began to be seen as traitors, and as the early Cold War developed, they were increasingly perceived as a threat to the democratic nation state. This was fed by opinion makers like Jacques de Kadt, who professed in 1947 that through their will to power and their idealism, the Russians were called to rule the world and to turn that world into a communist one (De Kadt 1947: 31). Meanwhile the memoir *I Chose Freedom* of Victor Kravtchenko, a Soviet defector, pulverised the Russian myth of communism. As "the ultimate warning" against the Soviet aggression the Dutch translation of 1946, heavily propagated by the Jesuit anticommunistic weekly *De Linie*, had an immense influence on the public opinion (Ribbens 1992: 103-106). After the Czech coup of February 1948 reservists were called and the border with Germany stood under extra surveillance. A small-scale "red scare" took hold of the population, but Prime Minister Willem Drees estimated the risk of a Soviet attack as low. The greater danger, in his view, came from a fifth column within the country, given ongoing relations between the Dutch Communist Party and Russia (cf. Lippmann 1947: 40-41). Under the government's appropriately named Operation Freezer, lists were compiled of communists who would be arrested or even executed in case of an immediate threat of war (Traa 2009: 25-28). Improving welfare was considered the best antidote to the temptations of communism. However, the ruling Christian Democratic parties, as well as the Christian Churches, also believed that there was serious danger emanating directly from Moscow, especially after the detonation of first Russian atomic bomb in August 1949.

As a follow-up to Pope Pius XI's prewar anticommunist encyclical, the Holy Office issued a firm decree in July 1949 to the effect that people who adhered to communism were apostates in the eyes of the Church and that they risked excommunication.[5] It further stated that the influence of the Soviet Union had increased due to a "slackening of the anticommunist consciousness in Western Europe," making more evident the need for an anti-Russian front.[6] Within the relatively large Dutch Catholic minority – 40% of a total population of circa 10 million in 1947 – both the pope's call in *Divini Redemptoris* and this new decree were warmly received. Since the 1930s, Dutch Catholics with their longstanding tradition of grassroots lay devotional initiatives and self-organization, had become increasingly aware of the necessity to organize against communism.

5 The decree of July 1 was published in *L'Osservatore Romano* on July 16, 1949, and appeared in Dutch in *Katholiek Archief* 4 (1947-1950), k. 465.

6 *De Tijd*, November 14, 1947, which mentions growing Russian influence in Romania and Poland due to the "hardening of anticommunist feeling in Western Europe."

In this chapter I will describe and analyze a number of Dutch Catholic anticommunist initiatives; in particular I will focus on an ambitious idiosyncratic spiritual project that took its inspiration from symbols deriving both from the United States and the Soviet Union. This chapter is intended as a contribution to the historiography of the Netherlands during the Cold War, as it wants to show how actions were prepared and executed at the local level, and establish to what extent these were related to (inter)national Church politics and to the global stage on which the Cold War was performed (cf. Christiaens 2015: 187; Christiaens 2016).

Anticommunist Marian activism: missions, armies, and crusades

Dutch Catholic conversion politics and anti-atheism did not come out of the blue. As has been mentioned, the long-term suppression of Dutch Catholics by the Protestants establishment had created a mentality of which missionary activity and campaigns for the conversion of Protestants were an important part. Catholics could therefore fall back on a great number of devotional associations and missionary organizations dedicated to the conversion of pagans and non-Catholics, not just in distant countries but especially at home. As we will see, one important agent in this context was the Marian religious order called the Company of Mary or Montfort Missionaries (SMM). This congregation had been founded in France in 1705 as the *Compagnie de Marie* by the Mariologist Louis-Marie Grignion de Montfort (1673-1716). The Montfort Missionaries have always been strongly dedicated to Mary, and felt a particular vocation to specialize in Mariology. The SMM's spirituality and apostolate were programmatically laid out in the booklet *True Devotion to Mary* written by Montfort himself.[7] The book regained great popularity at the beginning of the Cold War, when Montfort was canonized (July 1947). At the time, the Montfort Missionaries had a strong foothold in the Netherlands, and they cherished a militant approach to conversion under the aegis of the Virgin Mary. During the interwar years, they began to stimulate Dutch Catholics to regard themselves as members of a "Church combatant" in which everyone had the duty to fight for the spread of the Kingdom of Christ (Frijns 1939).

It was pure coincidence that on the very day that the papal encyclical was published in 1937, the militant Society of St. Willibrord was founded in Teteringen, a village in the Catholic south of the Netherlands. This society was

7 Although the *Traité de la vraie dévotion à la Sainte Vierge* was written in 1712, it only gained popularity after its late publication in 1843; since his canonization in 1947 Montfort has been considered as one of the founding fathers of Mariology. Later in the 20th century, the popularity of his book received a major boost after Pope John Paul II, himself a fervent Marian devotee, began to use and propagate Monfort's work.

named after the intrepid early medieval missionary to whom the conversion of the Netherlands to Christianity was ascribed. Following in the footsteps of their patron, the members of the society had to vow to act and obtain "from God, at his [= Willibrord] intercession, the remorseful conversion of the godless and of communists," in line with what Pius XI called for in his encyclical.[8] The Dutch missionary landscape also counted various other organizations: the Lay Apostolate, the Mission Action, the Sodality of Our Lady, the Catholic Action and its "army"[9], and of course the militant movement of the Legion of Mary.[10] The spiritual father of this last movement was, again, Grignion de Montfort; and for this reason the Montfort Missionaries were the Legion of Mary's most enthusiastic propagandists. The Legion was seen as an instrument of the church hierarchy which required active participation in the work of Mary, to create an empire for her in which the rosary would take center stage, with lay Legionnaires as warriors in the service of Mary.

The Dutch branch of the Legion ("Legioen van Maria") was founded relatively late. The Legion, with its symbols and pyramidal structure reflective of ancient Roman military organization, set foot on Dutch ground in 1942, after two decades of successful growth in the Anglo-Saxon world.[11] After receiving strong support from the Dutch Mariolatric bishop Guillaume Lemmens the Marian association numbered dozens of departments, totaling about 1500 members in the early 1950s.[12] The Lay Apostolate, also supported by the Montfort Missionaries, called on Catholics to actively participate locally in the work of Mary and the Church, at the service of their bishop or parish priest, mostly with the goal of "crushing the snake" (atheism), and spreading the Kingdom of Christ. The Jesuits, in their turn, propagated the Dutch Marian Congregation, also called "Mary's Guard of Honor" (Noyons 1935: 7-8; Anon. 1939; Anon. 1946b). The Guardians focused on working for the salvation of non-Catholics through intense Marian devotion, and on helping protect the Church against the onslaught of atheism. No fewer than 1800 congregations were active in the

8 Statutes Willibrordvereniging: "om zoo door zijn voorspraak van God te verkrijgen (...) de rouwmoedige bekeering van godloozen en de communisten."

9 Catholic Action had a late (re)start after the war in the Netherlands. In a fundamental text drawn up in 1947, its lay members were supposed to unite as apostles and "create a large organized army for Christ"; it was not particularly Marian (Voets 1981: 309-317).

10 Non-Marian anticommunist organizations were also created, for example in 1936 the Action 'For God' (Luykx 1978: 183-198) and in 1950 the Roman Catholic Church Guard ("R.K. Kerkwacht in Nederland"), a lay initiative in reaction to the swift expansion of Russian and domestic communism, which wanted to build a dam to protect Christianity, even with the help of Protestant Christians see: Archive Archdiocese Utrecht, Bishops' conference: Letter of the board of the R.C. Church Guard to Cardinal De Jong, December 14, 1950.

11 The Legion started in 1942 in the town of Hoensbroek. Contact with Frank Duff in Dublin dates already from 1932, while in 1939 a Dutch translation of the handbook came on the market. The Legion started in Belgium in 1945/1946.

12 Valkenburg, Archive Provincialate Montfort Missionaries, box 21, no. 92. See for a history of the first ten years of the Dutch Legion: Robroek 1952.

Netherlands in the 1940s (Anon. 1946a: 553-554). There was, in sum, a comprehensive web of organizations. Clerics liked to characterize the Netherlands as "Maryland".[13] The size of the existing network seems to have precluded the Blue Army of Fátima, the archetypal Cold War anticommunist association that started in 1947, from gaining any serious presence in the Netherlands.[14]

A number of organizations focused on the rosary. A Dutch Apostolate of the Rosary was set up in 1936 by the Dominicans to organize collective prayer for the crisis of the time. In the later Cold War era the main goal became the organization of national Rosary Prayer Meetings. Brochures on the Dutch Catholic World Crusade were spread in large quantities among the population from 1949 onward. The foreword was written by Henri de Greeve, a famed media preacher, who was one of the first to take a stand against communism and materialism. He wanted to recruit "modern papal Zouaves, dressed in Gods armor," who, under God's command, would initiate a counterattack (Anon. 1949: 2, 34). Between 1951 and 1954, prayer meetings and light processions for peace, world improvement and re-Christianization took place in more than 42 Dutch shrines, attended by huge crowds.[15] Thus the Dutch Dominican Dalmatius Linnebank managed to mobilize some 200,000 Dutch people. The profile of the Catholic World Crusade was broadly ideological, as it fought the "degeneration" of society in general: indifference, demoralization, humanism, communism, materialism, defection from the faith, atheism – all seemingly symptoms of an imminent apocalypse. Its purpose was to create a single world army during the Holy Year 1950. It was seen as every Catholic's duty to support the Church, "like earlier against the Turks," and it was "God's will to make use of all permitted human means, within our abilities": the weapons of God: the rosary, Mass, and the communion of reparation, dedication to the Sacred Heart of Jesus and the Immaculate Heart of Mary, and even a Catholic moral protest at the United Nations.

The Dutch Discalced Carmelites of 's-Hertogenbosch, inspired by Fátima visionary and later Carmelite sister Lúcia, started the National Apostolate of the Immaculate Heart of Mary in 1948, which used more or less the same instruments and had the same goals. In 1950 the Apostolate already had more than 10,000 "apostles" who committed themselves to saving the world and keeping communism at bay by saying the rosary. As late as 1960, the Apostolate organized the Dutch participation in an international day of prayer and

13 A description used in an article that sums up the many Marian churches and patronages in the Netherlands: Polman 1948: 355; cf. Van Driel 1956.

14 The organization was refounded in 2005 under the name of World Apostolate of Fátima, with new statutes and goals.

15 *Wetenswaardigheden en richtlijnen voor de Nationale Rozenkrans-bedestonden te organiseren in het najaar 1954 op instigatie en onder auspiciën van Rozenkranskruistocht- en St. Willibrord-Apostolaat*, in the archive of the Montfort Missionaries; cf. D.A. Linnebank, "De Rozenkranskruistocht in Nederland," *Standaard van Maria* 32 (1956): 290-292.

penance against communism and materialism under the slogan of "Fatima calls!"[16]

The rosary crusade was supposed to be "the most powerful antidote against the evils that threaten human society," as Pope Pius XII said in respect of the international *Rosario* movement in 1952 (Tondini 1954: 705-709). An important stimulus for the rosary campaign came from the Fátima apparitions. Given their anticommunist significance, it must be asked when 'Fátima' actually reached the Netherlands, and what impact it had.

Reception of 'Fátima' in the Netherlands

The Dutch first heard about what had happened in Fátima halfway through the interwar years. The very first time the press mentioned it was on July 1, 1929 when the national Catholic newspaper *De Tijd* received a contribution from a Portuguese correspondent which referred to the victory of Fátima over the religious crisis and the country's forces of liberalism, which had resulted in a renaissance of Catholicism there.[17] Soon after the formal approval of the apparitions by the local bishop on October 13, 1930, Ludwig Fischer wrote a compelling first account of Fátima as the new Lourdes, a publication that mobilized a Dutch newspaper and the *Katholieke Illustratie*, a nation-wide Catholic illustrated magazine, to inform its readers about Fátima pilgrimage (Metz 1931).[18] Translations from Fischer's and other books appeared soon afterwards in the Low Countries (Van de Vijvere 1931; Pizarro 1931). They all described the apparitions and messages, but there was no anticommunist aspect to these articles, as that content of the revelations had then not yet been disclosed.

The reception of 'Fátima' in the Netherlands (and elsewhere) gathered steam in 1941 when visionary Lúcia declared that it was the wish of the apparition in Fátima to consecrate the world to Her Immaculate Heart, an act that the 'Marian Pope' Pius XII carried out twice, on October 31 and December 8, 1942 (Pius XII 1946). The Dutch Church repeated the consecration for the Netherlands on October 3, 1943. The most important news was that newly written memoires by Lúcia disclosed the previously unknown anticommunist content of the messages ("the conversion of Russia"), a disclosure that was well received by Pius XII as it fitted his own deep-felt hostility towards this ideology

16 Information kindly given by Brian Heffernan, from his forthcoming book on the Discalced Carmelite Nuns in the Netherlands.

17 "Wederopbloei van het Katholicisme in Portugal," *De Tijd*, July 1, 1929. Various other Dutch newspapers reprinted the article. Only one earlier reference to Fátima could be found, in *De Maasbode* of November 14, 1924, which briefly addressed the government's intervention forbidding a group pilgrimage to go from Lisbon to Fátima.

18 A full page article in *De Maasbode* of June 7, 1931, speaking about the Portuguese Lourdes, a text derived from Fischer's book.

(Chadwick 1993: 17). This sensational reinterpretation of the central Fátima message gave rise to a new stream of books in Dutch during the war (Gonzaga da Fonseca 1943; Bekkers 1944; Spauwen 1944; Van der Scheer 1944; Van Es 1944; Martel 1944; Barthas 1944; Herraets 1945; Coenen 1945).[19] The Montfort Missionaries in Leuven took it as a starting point for a whole new series of books on Fátima (Jongen 1944).

Inspired by these developments, the priest Hendrik Geertman went on a pilgrimage to Fátima in 1946. He wrote the first published witness account of the sanctuary from a Dutch perspective, and also brought a copy of the statue home (Geertman 1946).[20] He was one of a handful of Dutch people[21] who were there for the ceremony of the coronation of the statue on May 13, an event that was still without any explicit anticommunist meaning, as Geertman's elaborate report does not refer to any mention of this new content at the local shrine. But that would soon change. The persecution of clergy in Eastern Europe brought a popular booklet on the Dutch market containing the (new) message of Fátima and the fate of Cardinal Mindszenty in the battle against communism and the safeguarding of Catholicism. There were seven editions of this booklet up to the Hungarian revolution, and it compared the danger of communism to the 1940 invasion by the Nazis. It was a pamphlet against persecution of Catholic leaders, intended to rouse Dutch Catholics from their ignorance of and complacency towards the rise of communism. The archbishop of Utrecht spoke of "a darkness that has fallen over the whole world" (Van der Velden 1948: 4).

The Montfort Missionaries, who also had a house in Fátima, soon started to organize pilgrimages to the Portuguese shrine. In the Netherlands itself sanctuaries also began to think of links with the new Cold War situation, organizing one-off events and other initiatives to campaign or protest against communism. The management of the major Marian shrine of Heiloo passed into the hands of the Montfort Missionaries in 1946, and the new custodians frequently organized events or missions of an anticommunist character (Thiers 2005: 71). In Schiedam, home of the shrine of the famed medieval mystic Lidwina, this saint was invoked in 1948 to save the Netherlands from communist influence. Two years later devotees were instructed at Saint Gerard Majella's shrine in Weebosch to invoke his help for "the speedy extinction of

19 For example the booklets by a Missionary of the Company of Mary, H.J.M. Polman, *De eerste zaterdag O.L. Vrouw van Fatima een kwartier gezelschap houden door het overwegen der Rozenkransgeheimen* (1940) or the Jesuit Spauwen 1944; a first critical publication was by Dhanis who published in 1944 and 1945.

20 After his death in 1949, Geertman bequeathed the statue to his own church, the church of the Sacred Heart in Enschede.

21 Geertman was preceded by the Dutch anthropologist Paul Julien who went to Fátima directly after the war. The difficulty of getting there and finding accommodation made him skeptical that Dutch pilgrims would flock there in any great numbers: Julien 1945.

communism." In 1951 at the 'national' shrine of the Miracle in Amsterdam, pilgrims were warned against the danger of communism, an ideology that was said to have "already caught hold of hundreds of thousands" of Dutch people. In the following year the organization took as its prayer intention the slogan "Putting an end to the persecution of the Church in communist countries." Similarly, the Marian sanctuary of Amersfoort organized a procession to raise awareness of the "communist threat."

Marian wandering statues

Mary's title of Star of the Sea (Stella Maris) expresses Mary's role as a lodestar for Catholics. The town of Maastricht has a centuries-old shrine of the miraculous statue of Our Lady Star of the Sea ('Sterre der Zee'), a statue with a reputation for missionary peace work.[22] Just before the war, in 1938-1939, every deanery in the diocese of Roermond and the province (= diocese) of Limburg as a whole was consecrated to the Star of the Sea, a dedication which was supposed to conclude with a Marian congress, but this had to be postponed due to the beginning of the war.[23] During the war itself, Mary was often invoked, as were various other local miraculous Marys in the Netherlands, to save the country's inhabitants, push the German V2 rockets beyond the populated areas, and ultimately end the war. After May 5, 1945, the day the Netherlands was liberated, these Marys were praised and thanked. Elsewhere in Europe, the end of the war lead to similar expressions of gratitude to famed Marian statues for the peace brought or the protection given. In the context of the developing Cold War, people started to invoke Mary's protective power against new threats from the east. Again, Marian statues were used for symbolic and militant missions or pilgrimages in the world. The newly accredited anticommunist meaning of the Fátima apparitions made it obvious that Mary, and in particular Our Lady of Fátima, had a special role to fulfill.

The very first international pilgrimage of a copy of the Fátima statue crowned in May 1946 was a gift of the bishop of Leiria to Pius XII. But Our Lady of Fátima was first carried in a trans-European foot pilgrimage by groups of boy scouts to Maastricht, where the first postwar Marian Congress was held in September 1947. After a 100-day prayer march from Fátima, during which the unique replica was ostentatiously carried through Spain, France, and Bel-

22 The statue of Mary 'Star of the Sea' was part of a local tradition of protest and struggle. A peace procession was organized in 1918 in which the statue was carried along; the same happened in 1931 in processions against the anti-religious work of Dutch freethinkers' organizations and for reparation/atonement for blasphemy; in 1939 schoolchildren organized a procession to ask Our Lady Star of the Sea for peace.

23 See the proclamations in the diocesan bulletin *Mariaklok* of May 1938, July 1939, and January 1940.

gium,[24] the statue arrived to participate in the congress (Anon. 1948: 28-34, 268-270).[25] It was the first stage of a longer itinerary in an anticommunist pilgrimage visiting many countries before arriving in the Vatican.

The whole idea of an openly traveling Marian statue, a *Peregrinatio Mariae*, was taken from the Grand Retour pilgrimages that brought Our Lady of Boulogne to thousands of parishes in France between 1943 and 1948 (Perouas 1983).

Maastricht is in the diocese of Roermond, whose bishop, Guillaume Lemmens, was the co-organizer of the congress. He took direct inspiration from the cohabitation of the Star of the Sea with the Fátima statue. Lemmens was a fervent, fanatical Marian devotee whose somewhat naive ideas about Mary's intercessional powers would later cause him serious trouble. The goals of the congress were many, but the list that cataloged them ended with the meaning of Mary's protection against the "darkness that is embodied in godless communism" and its "poisonous breath" that will destroy all divine life.[26] For the time being, he regarded the instrumentalization of Mary as a major tool for the salvation of the world and arresting "the fatal attraction of latent paganism that runs through the world." With the help of both Marys, he called on the delegates of the congress to participate in a holy crusade and to work for "the expansion of the Empire of Mary" (Anon. 1948: 277-278).

Three years later, the idea of the 1947 international pilgrimage was transformed into a regional variant, to bring Mary to the people in materialistic times and get them spiritually mobilized. The idea was to fight like an army through collective prayer and penitence "against the evil and laxity of a 'paganized' world" (Polman 1955: 9). A pilgrimage tour with the Maastricht original statue of Mary Star of the Sea was planned for the province of Limburg in 1950 (Polman 1955). It took Bishop Lemmens no fewer than five years to accompany the statue and visit every parish, hospital and institution in the diocese.[27] This mass missionary movement received a special recommendation from Pius XII (Polman 1955: 4). Inevitably, as Marian event, the tour was

24 It was one of the pilgrim statues, but differently sculpted as the US copy, with only one single creased mantle (image 4.4 like, see the categorization in David Morgan's chapter, this volume).

25 Pope Pius XII endorsed the congress in a special radio message "C'est avec joi," September 5, 1947, in which he praised the faith of Dutch Catholics, which was admired across the world, and its Catholic school system, and called upon the Star of the Sea as a protectress, see: Tondini 1954: 543-549. Russia and Satan were especially addressed during the congress: J. Tesser, "Op welke grond en in welke zin noemen wij Maria tegenstandster van satan?" in Anon. 1948: 158-169; 167-168 mentions the teaching of atheist communism at the time.

26 In the article "Maria, Moeder der Mensen," *Gazet van Limburg*, September 4, 1947, 1.

27 Archive Dutch Provincialate SMM, no. 1131, dossier on the project; see also *Standaard van Maria* 26 (1950): 259-276. In 1992 the tour, in a limited form, was repeated as a re-evangelization project.

organized by the Montfort Missionaries, who even considered replicating the pilgrimage also on a national scale. In the meantime, near the city of Weert, in relation to the international apparitional boom, the first public postwar Marian apparition took place in the Netherlands, three days after the bishop blessed a Fátima statue, on October 13, 1949, but soon hushed up by the diocese.

An idiosyncratic antidote: the Pentagon

Against this (inter)national geopolitical and devotional backdrop, one ambitious and dedicated Dutch Montfortian priest showed a strong willingness in the early 1950s to personally follow up on Pius XI's call in *Divini Redemptoris*. This priest, Lambert J.M. Terstroet (1912-2003),[28] felt increasingly called to take responsibility for the defense of the Catholic faith.[29] His mission to employ Mary as an instrument for this goal was closely connected with his religious career.

As an adolescent Terstroet was already fascinated by Russia and its great writers. He reflected on becoming a missionary priest in revolutionary Russia, but hearing of the crimes executed on Christians he changed his mind and dreamt of a future in Iceland, a place well out of reach of communism. At the age of twenty he had however joined the Jesuits as a novice in his hometown of The Hague. Despite his zeal and his desire to become a priest, he did not pass the first year's evaluation and he was dismissed from this strict order. Having been inspired by the Virgin Mary from an early age, it was not an irrational choice for him to apply next to the Company of Mary. This order's focus on Montfort entailed the stipulation that its priests must commit themselves to carrying out "missions and retreats under the standard and protection of the Blessed Virgin" among the people.

Lambert Terstroet was a good match with the Dutch province of the Montfort Missionaries, as this province actively propagated Marian devotionalism. The *Standard of Mary* had been a highly regarded publication of the order's since the 1920s, and Terstroet would later become its editor-in-chief. The journal was fully dedicated to the study of the legacy of the order's founder and to the cultic aspects of Mary in general. It fitted him: in a personal evaluation his superior described him as intelligent and erudite for his age, but also enthusiast and temperamental, bit fanatical, in combination with idealism, a strong imagination and deep piety.[30]

28 See on Terstroet his personal dossier in the archive of the Dutch Provincialate SMM, no. 5670.

29 The encyclical of 1937, article 81, places the anticommunistic action of the Church under the protection of Church patron St. Joseph (that was also Terstroet's second name), but mentions not yet any protective role for Mary.

30 Archive of the Dutch Provincialate SMM, no. 5670.

After entering the Company in August 1934, initially in the Meerssen house and after 1940 in the seminary in Oirschot, Terstroet devoted himself fully to Mary, and this became evident at his ordination to the priesthood on March 23, 1941, when he vowed to situate Her in the center of the world. He decided to continue his theological formation and went to study Mariology at the Belgian university of Leuven. He spent four years at the theological faculty in Leuven to write a thesis on Mary and on the founder of the order Louis-Marie Grignion de Montfort and learned in the meantime Russian as well.[31] He received his doctorate on November 30, 1946, *magna cum laude*. Academically he was now formed and molded according to the Mariological pattern of his order. It would define his life.

Leuven was also the home of the Belgian provincialate of the Monfort Missionaries, where his confrère Hubert Jongen launched an intense propaganda campaign for Fátima with a series of books on the apparitions in 1943. Terstroet was thus in a position to acquire ample information on Fátima and, more importantly, about the new anti-Russian interpretation of its messages.

The young Dr. Terstroet seemed an excellent new recruit for the *Montfortanen*, as the Montfort Missionaries are usually called in the Netherlands. Not only did he firmly believe in Montfort's militant perceptions of missionary work and the role of Mary therein, he also personalized his own missionary venture by performing a prayer ritual of empowerment and confirmation by solemnly depositing a copy of his dissertation upon Montfort's tomb in the Loire village of Saint-Laurent-sur-Sèvre.[32] In line with his order and due to this ritual impetus, Terstroet devoted himself to a more militant form of Marianism. His conviction that Mary was a powerful instrument of protection for the Church and the new world order brought him under the lifelong spell of the Blessed Virgin.

When Terstroet emerged from his scholarly seclusion again in 1945, the world had radically changed, and he found himself once more in a peaceful Europe, which was at the same time facing the dangers of a new ideological conflict. The new politics and power relations between east and west, metaphorically described as a 'cold' conflict without violent confrontations, was increasingly being perceived as an existential threat to Christianity. Russia's active program of exporting communist ideology brought rapid changes in the postwar power relations among the former allies. At the Dutch grassroots level, too, the deteriorating situation caused people to take action, as Terstroet

31 A summary of his thesis *Maria en de Glorie van God volgens den Zal. Louis-Marie Grignion de Montfort 1673-1716* was published in *Standaard van Maria* 22 (1946): 65-70, 97-103, 129-135. His supervisor was Jozef J.C. Bittremieux, founder of the renowned Marian Days in Tongerlo. A full copy of his thesis can be found in the Montfort Missionaries Provincial archive in Valkenburg, no. 1819 and 2637.

32 Archive Dutch Provincialate SMM, no. 2637.

did by taking the Virgin Mary as the central weapon in his spiritual defense plan.

Forty years later, in a retrospective autobiographical note, Terstroet reflected on the roots of his defense plan.[33] He recalled having had a sort of vision during his Jesuit novitiate year in November 1933. While meditating as a seminarian, he saw himself sitting in a luxury car together with three Jesuits saints, among them the patron of students, Saint John Berchmans. They drove him to a beautiful palace where there were various female saints, and he was led into in a huge ballroom. There, bathing in light, Terstroet suddenly found himself in the presence of the Queen of Heaven. That very moment, he was blessed by the imposition of Mary's hands: "it was a feeling of bliss, of being in seventh heaven." This visionary vocational experience would guide him a year later to join the Montfort Missionaries and letting him discover the beauty and power of Mary.[34]

Fifteen years after that vision, in February 1948, during an educational retreat in Rotterdam, Terstroet again sensed the supernatural. This time, it was an inner voice telling him "Be for Me on earth what St. Joseph is for Me in heaven."[35] It was Mary speaking to him, he felt he had to obey and wanted to become her earthly husband. He was called upon to be a "workman" and help Her create an empire and a proper palace. The providential sign to take action eventually came in the fall of 1951, when he happened to hear about the plans for a centenary celebration for the definition of the dogma of the Immaculate Conception in 1954. Meditation in the Fátima chapel in the Dutch village of Berg en Dal finally gave him the specific inspiration to set up a five-year plan of reparation for the harm Russia had caused Christ and the Church.[36] When he participated some weeks later in an open-air celebration of the international Holy Year in Fátima on October 12-13, 1951, in the undulating landscape of that area, surrounded by approximately one million Marian pilgrims, he was completely overwhelmed by the power of Mary through her Immaculate Heart. Standing at the shrine he sensed the heavenly validation of his plan. He became convinced that the Immaculate Heart as Mary had revealed it in Fátima would triumph and would ultimately bring about the conversion of Russia to Christianity (Terstroet 1953a: 3-4).

33 Unsigned biographic document of Lambert Terstroet, entitled "21 november 1973: Feest van O.L. Vrouw Presentatie." Archive Dutch Provincialate SMM, no. 2626-7, 1.

34 Archive of the Dutch Provincialate SMM, no. 5670: Roepingsgeschiedenis, 2-3.

35 Unsigned biographic document of Lambert Terstroet, entitled "21 november 1973: Feest van O.L. Vrouw Presentatie." Archive Dutch Provincialate SMM, no. 2626-7, 2.

36 In an epilog to his book, Terstroet states that it was only later, in 1953, that he was informed about a similar idea of setting up spiritual five-year plans by the Reparation Society of the Immaculate Heart of Mary in Baltimore (USA), see Terstroet 1953a: 99; cf. Massam 1991: 424, for the society's 1947 five-year plan in Australia.

Back at the Montfort house in the village of Oirschot, he began to work out his ideas in the form of a devotional movement which would serve as a counterbalance to the Russian-Marxist economical five-year plans: Marian spirituality as a counterweight to the ideology of materialism. His anticommunism was fed not only by Russia's policies, but also by the significance of the United States as the "champion of freedom." Taking up this theme, he decided to name his battle plan the "Pentagon of the Empire of Mary" (*Pentagoon van het Rijk van Maria*) – a title inspired by the military headquarters of the US Department of Defense in Washington DC that had been opened in 1943.[37]

Terstroet's aim was to realize a protective devotional movement for the "Empire of Mary," a concept connected to the empire or Kingdom of Christ, taken from the writings of Grignion de Montfort. He viewed the Oirschot house as the headquarters of spiritual resistance and struggle against atheism. Together with a number of fellow Montfortian priests, and supported by the lay administrative center of the order in nearby Geldrop, the project began in late 1951. A few weeks later, the plan was fully developed and the official start date was announced for March 25, 1952. As the 1954 centenary was approaching, this implied that his five-year plan would have two separate halves: two and a half years before, and two and a half years after the jubilee date of December 8, 1954, concluding on March 25, 1957.

The basic idea was to make atonement and reparation through acts of love and gratitude for everything that had been ruined in the world by Russia. In practice, it was expressed as a "Eucharistic gift" in the form of daily Masses of Reparation, and it involved religious activism in the form of meetings in private houses of Catholics across the country, and especially initiatives to educate schoolchildren in a Catholic, anticommunist mindset and instrumentalize them as "innocent weapons" (cf. Peacock 2014). The whole plan pivoted around the idea of setting up a national system of daily intentions and Masses to be said by priests during those five years. Catholics were asked to pay three guilders for every Mass; Masses said for Mary's "most intimate intentions, those of her deepest nature". The empire therefore required a formalized organization, for which he created a 'diplomatic corps' of Mary's empire, comprising consuls and ambassadors. The highest body was made up of "Empire mediators" within the Pentagon, a group of twelve or more religious from orders and congregations in the Netherlands. There were also Departments of Finance and Information, and there was even a postal service to provide for the costs of postage. Terstroet was able to attract religious priests and brothers, nurses, teachers, parish pastors and some higher clergy for the various groups and departments. In addition to this army of Catholic civilians, he

37 However, it was not before the start of the Korean War in 1950 and the US policy of repression of communism, that the building became known in the Netherlands as a symbol of political and military strategy against communism and its dissemination.

set up a Marian Underground Movement (the "M.O.") to organize all Catholic schoolchildren.[38] Every school class had to make provision for an annual Mass and had to do 'deeds' that would have an impact on Russia: make maps of Russia and work on hidden action for the conversion of Russia. Children could also do their bit by shortening their playing time at school and saying Hail Marys instead in compensation for Stalin's "evil works", or "to repair what Stalin had corrupted" (Terstroet 1952 and 1953: 54). Each class got a new name derived from the Russian *Magnificat*, a hymn shared by both the Catholic and Orthodox Churches, a song that could unite people, also called the Song of Mary. Due to his previous school retreats in the Netherlands, Terstroet had easy access to the national Catholic school system.[39] This advantage, in combination with his "restless" character, ensured that the project soon gathered speed. He traveled the nation as a true wandering missionary.

The first Pentagon Mass was said in St. Lawrence's church in Ginneken (Breda) on March 25, 1952, and as soon as October 13, 1952, the feast of the apparitions of Fátima, the initial main goal for the country, 5000 paid Masses, was reached.[40] The idea to offer Mary the gift of Masses said in her honor every day for five years was quickly achieved. There were additional series of Masses as also offerings from Belgium and Germany came flooding in. Terstroet received enthusiastic letters from across the world in support of his initiative. He wrote project summaries in Latin and French as the Pentagon plan seemed to have the potential of reaching the international stage.

But it was not long after the successful start that his movement began to attract criticism. It was due to the scrupulosity, and to a certain degree of envy, of Anthony Schenk, pastor of the small village of Sappemeer in the north of the Netherlands, a much less Mariophile region, that things quickly began to shift. Schenk's criticism was related to the fact that the Netherlands had a longstanding tradition of competition in pastoral ministry between diocesan priests and religious. The many intentions for (and the money required for these) Masses to be said for Mary's Empire made this secular parish priest wary. He criticized the project in a letter to the bishop of 's-Hertogenbosch, the diocese in which the Pentagon office was established.[41] His parishioners received brochures about the movement and Schenk disagreed with their con-

38 He was probably inspired by Gretta Palmers' account *God's Underground*, about a Christian Fifth Column in Russia, a book that already was translated into Dutch in 1948. The fact that over those years in neither of the two Dutch Monfortian journals (*Standaard van Maria* and *In Slagorde*) there was any mention of the movement, confirms a certain covert character.

39 For the practical distribution of the necessary materials, he worked with a friendly educational publisher: Bertus van de Westelaken in Geldrop, director of the Lecturis publisher and printing house in Eindhoven.

40 Utrecht, Archdiocese of Utrecht, Archive Bishops Conference, minutes of January 12-13, 1953: Letter of the diocese's official J. Geerdink, December 1, 1952.

41 Letter of L.L. Terstroet to P.J. Margry, September 16, 1994.

12.2 Map of the Netherlands with pins, indicating the number of members (each pin up to 30) and the number of schools participating in the Empire of Mary project.
[Collection of Peter Jan Margry]

tent; he saw it as a covert way of collecting money which would only benefit the Montfort Missionaries: “a religious priests’ business”, in short.[42] He feared the immediate diminution of income for his and other local parishes.

The issue was brought before the archbishop of Utrecht, Cardinal Jan de Jong, who in turn asked his judicial vicar for advice. Vicar J. Geerdink’s report was placed on the agenda of the next bishops’ conference meeting in early 1953.[43] His principal objection was that the project “lacked taste” and infringed on the existing “sound devotions” to Mary.[44] In his report he just stressed, but without further explanation, that Mary did not have any “most intimate intentions,” as Terstroet had written. Possibly he tasted an erotic subtext in the phrasing. He also branded the name of the organization, “Pentagon,” as a secular invention. Moreover, the whole idea of having an empire of Mary in addition to the Kingdom of God was, wrongly, regarded as heretical. This concept derived from Montfort’s teaching about Mary’s co-redemptive role in salvation, a phrasing or teaching that also was in use outside the Montfortian spirituality (Schoffeleers 2006: 212-213).[45] For Terstroet personally the whole idea of Mary as *co-redemptrix* was already well-internalized, and he believed it had even been endorsed because a heavenly message received during an apparition – not recognized by the Church – of the Lady of All Nations in Amsterdam in April 1951 had announced the impending definition of Mary’s status as co-redemptrix as a new, fifth Marian dogma (Anon. 1999: 96-99).[46]

The Dutch bishops in fact adopted Schenk’s criticism, and characterized the Pentagon project and its context as a ‘muddleheaded’ initiative: a typical example of the often idiosyncratic actions of individual religious priests. The bishops intended to protect their clergy and flock, and stick to doctrinal purity.[47] But it was also remarkable that no formal reaction from the Dutch Church Province had been forthcoming, while the project had the full support of the provincial of the Montfort Missionaries and of Bishop Lemmens of Roermond, who strongly backed Terstroet.

Terstroet was informed directly after the bishops’ meeting that his plan had been deemed unacceptable. He was perplexed that his successful spiritual project had simply been condemned without consultation (Terstroet 1953a: 96-

42 Archdiocese of Utrecht, Archive Bishops’ Conference, Letter of November 26, 1952.

43 The conference took place in Utrecht on January 12-13, 1953.

44 Archdiocese of Utrecht, Archive Bishops’ Conference, Conference January 12-13, 1953: Letter of J. Geerdink to B.J. Alfrink, December 1, 1952.

45 Montfort wrote that the Empire of Christ will be preceded by an Empire of Mary. The idea of an empire of Mary was not uncommon in the 1950s, contrary to what the vicar reported.

46 Although the Amsterdam cult did not became publicly known in the media before 1954, the content of the messages were already circulating widely via an underground network of devotees.

47 Archdiocese of Utrecht, Archive Bishops’ Conference, Conference January 12-13, 1953: Letter of J. Geerdink to B.J. Alfrink, December 1, 1952.

98). His protectors, Bishop Lemmens and the Montfortian provincial C.M. Heiligers, made personal visits to the various bishops to try to save the plan, as well as their own faces. The bishop of Haarlem appeared not to have any insurmountable objections to the project, and Bishop Baeten of Breda also gave his permission to continue. But Bishop Mutsaerts of 's-Hertogenbosch did not budge. He demanded that there should be no further propaganda, fearing that his flock might be confused by the initiative as it existed in addition to earlier movements like the Legion of Mary, the Sodality of Our Lady, and the "Rue du Bac" popular association, the "Enfants de Marie Immaculée".

To be on the safe side and to formulate to a sound judgement after their premature verdict, the Dutch bishops' conference asked Terstroet to submit full documentation and an evaluation of his Pentagon project. This material was directly forwarded to the Holy Office in Rome for further doctrinal scrutiny. In the meantime he was instructed not to take any further action. What he did do, however, was to invoke Mary herself: "She now had to show she loved Her Empire" (Terstroet 1953a: 50-51).

Even the Mariophile Terstroet was astonished by the great variety of apparitions happening in the world in those years. For him, the connection with the rise of communism was beyond question. He therefore wrote an article that brought these phenomena together into one systemic explanation with the Immaculate (Terstroet 1953b). He traced the contemporary boom of transcendental phenomena down to Montfort and his ideas about Mary's role in the redemption of the world. This corresponded perfectly with the messages which the visionary Peerdeman was receiving at the time in Amsterdam. A new Marian figure, the mentioned Lady of All Nations, had been appearing to her since March 1945. The Lady's messages were anticommunist but also included new revelations about Mary Herself. In her sixth message of January 3, 1946, the Lady referred to rising tensions and the new threats to the world: "There will be a fight all over Europe and beyond." She further spoke about a spiritual or ideological battle, in which the Christian cross was being threatened by other crosses or symbols, from Nazism and Communism (Anon. 1999: 35). Follow-up messages reflected the new political tensions in the world: growing communism in Italy, or the first nuclear bomb to be detonated in the Soviet Union (Anon. 1999: 57-58). Knowledge of the apparitions began to spread in circles surrounding the visionary, and Terstroet was one of the first people to mention them publicly (Terstroet 1953b).[48]

48 For example, we know that the later bishop of Haarlem, Jozef Punt, born on January 10, 1946 in Alkmaar was specifically named after Mary as she appeared in this apparition; his mother was familiar with the visionary's spiritual director Mathias Frehe, who was then also pastor of Alkmaar. One of the first media appearances seems to be the mention of the apparitions in *Het Amsterdamsche Weekblad* of December 24, 1954.

In March 1951 Peerdeman received a vision of Rome and the Vatican being under threat; the Lady said the following:

> Rome must know her task in this time. Does Rome realize which enemy is lying in wait and creeping like a snake throughout the world? And by this I do not mean communism alone; other prophets will come - false prophets (Anon. 1999: 93).

On March 20, 1953 the Lady stated that the nations of Europe should unite to defeat the enemy and that Rome must seize the opportunity to battle "humanism, realism, socialism and communism which have the world in their grip" (Anon. 1999: 133-134); somewhat later she said that a "false spirit is ruling the world", a spirit that was giving rise to modern paganism and atheism (Anon. 1999: 136-137). The Lady regarded Amsterdam as the focal point from which unity had to be recreated. Her cult was only known to a limited number of people at the time, but in December 1954 a Catholic journal ran a story about it just a few days after a painting of the apparition was hung in public in an Amsterdam church in order to make the Lady and Her messages known to the world.[49]

In the meantime the Holy Office had read the Pentagon papers. On June 9, 1953, the Vatican nuncio to the Netherlands, Paolo Giobbe, informed Archbishop De Jong that there had been a supreme decision by the Holy Office to the effect that the "Empire of Mary" and the "Pentagon" to defend that empire could not be approved, neither in their title nor in their organization, and that all measures should be taken to stop the movement as soon as possible. The general of the Montfort Missionaries in Rome, Alexandre Josselin, wrote in a similar vein to the Dutch provincial Heiligers: the project must be stopped and its secretariat dissolved immediately, and all further propaganda should cease. While Heiligers had given Terstroet full permission a year earlier, he now had to call him back in and ensure to eliminate his plan with all its objectionable issues.[50] Josselin added that Terstroet's activities should be directed in other directions with immediate effect, and that he should remain under supervision. On June 8, Terstroet stopped the project he had started, and shifted his spiritual-pastoral focus to the regular religious and devotional activities associated with the 1954 Marian jubilee. "This priest has shown a magnificent example of submission" and has always been of "good will," Heiligers wrote to the Holy Office. Saying this also amounted to damage control for himself and for his order.

49 *Het Amsterdamse Nieuwsblad*, December 24, 1954, was the first newspaper to write on it.
50 Archdiocese of Utrecht, Archive Bishops' Conference, Letter of C.M. Heiligers to A. Josselin, June 6, 1953.

Interestingly, it transpired that the Holy Office did not object so much to the notion of an Empire of Mary, to any doctrinal inconsistencies, or to the financial aspects. The Holy Office was much more concerned about its possible effects on Dutch society and about possibly provoking the large Protestant community than with the atheistic threats from behind the Iron Curtain. Rome's reasoning was that they were afraid that Protestants would "ironically" criticize Catholic devotion to the Blessed Virgin in general.[51] This would then also be harmful to the fragile improvements made within the wider ecumenical movement of those years. A fortiori it was thought that such a project could undermine the position of the Catholic Church in the religiously divided Netherlands. In this way the anticommunist politics to which Pius XI had called the Church and which had been so strongly stimulated under Pius XII, were subordinated to and even sacrificed for the sake of another culture war: the delicate relations between Catholics and the other Christian denominations in the world. Reconciliation and collaboration with these other denominations were regarded as increasingly desirable and necessary in a secularizing world.

In a personal text, Terstroet explained what he regarded as Mary's "most intimate intention" (Terstroet 1953b). If the bishops' conference had realized this at the time, it might have made matters even more complicated. In hindsight, Terstroet was able to devise a synthesis of the things that had happened. It was now clear to him that Her "most intimate intention" had been ecclesiastical recognition of Mary as co-redemptrix. This was the message that Montfort had supposedly advocated already two centuries before, and it was the reason why Terstroet himself was chosen as an "earthly Joseph." When the apparitions of the Amsterdam Lady of All Nations were brought to public attention at the end of the Marian year 1954, Terstroet prayed before the image of the Lady that had recently been hung in St. Thomas' Church in Amsterdam. Before this extraordinary image of Mary depicted as "crucified," he suddenly felt fully enlightened and he once again experienced a deep feeling of bliss. At that very moment he realized that he was indeed "the man [Joseph] in the background, who ensures that Mary can feel safe."[52] Here his mission and person became in a bigoted way one. Having immersed himself in mystic love of Mary for so many years, he had become an immediate adherent of the first modern Dutch Marian apparition; none of this was a coincidence in his eyes, and he started to write about those apparitions (Terstroet 1953b, 1955). Again he backed the wrong horse, and in 1955 he was ordered to abstain from any dealings with the cult of the Lady, as it was rejected and forbidden by the bishop of Haarlem. Again, Terstroet obeyed, although not fully this time. He stayed

51 Archdiocese of Utrecht, Archive Bishops' Conference: Letter A. Josselin to C.M. Heiligers, May 31, 1953.

52 Unsigned document by Terstroet, entitled "21 November 1973: Feest van O.L. Vrouw Presentatie." Archive Dutch Provincialate SMM, no. 2626-7, 2.

in touch with the underground continuation of the cult and remained a quiet devotee for the rest of his life.

Thus the whole Pentagon project was abandoned and the whole affair hushed up in the summer of 1953. No one ever wrote anything further about it. The copies of Terstroet's book and all the project's files had to be retrieved and shredded or burned. The Montfort Missionaries involved did this all with the same dedication they had applied to the creation of their Pentagon. Terstroet even left his Pentagon-project out of his own vocational biography which was written down in 1986 as part of an oral history project on Dutch missionaries. The whole movement was retracted from or kept out of the collective memory. Just a single copy of the book seems to have survived: the copy I found back in 1994 in a second-hand bookshop in Breda.[53] This, and the later retrieval of some remaining documents in the archive now permitted me to save the movement from oblivion, as the project was not mentioned or left out in the history of the order (cf. Schoffeleers 2006: 249-257).

Amazed by the content of his book, I tried then to find out if Terstroet was still alive, and if he would be prepared to give me some background information or documentation on the project. After the demise of the Pentagon project he had been assigned to the work of organizing the pilgrimages of the Nijmegen Holy Land foundation, and from 1973 onwards he was sent to far-off Catholic missionary countries, where he taught and worked in pastoral ministry, all activities that would prevent him from becoming engaged in any further Mary mania. After being sent to the missions in various countries in the Global South, he ended up in an exile of sorts in the decidedly 'un-Marian' country of Iceland. When I contacted him there, I received two letters from the then 82-year old Montfortian priest. He was very surprised that anyone had even found out about his Pentagon project. He did not have documents anymore, as the cover-up had been rigorous. But as memories returned, the subject came to life again in his mind. He reflected that, despite "the cross of opposition," his current evaluation of the project was that the Pentagon project had actually been a success, given the large number of Mass stipends that Dutch Catholics had donated, more than enough to give Mary Masses until the last day of his five-year plan. So, despite the fact he was forced to stop the practical execution of the plan, the spiritual execution seemed to have continued until the very end, March 25, 1957. His submission to the judgement of his superiors had not been total.

He wrote to me that the experience had been "unforgettable," and that he was still impressed by the results, and he drew a parallel with his spiritual master Grignion de Montfort, who likewise had had to face strong opposition to his works of grace. For Terstroet, the "painful" prohibition by the bishop of

53 During my later research another copy of the book was found in the order's archive: Valkenburg, Archive Dutch Provincialate SMM, no. 940.

’s-Hertogenbosch had frustrated him most. He still regarded the many Masses for Our Lady and her “most intimate intentions” as a “Chalet de Paix” for Mary, the powerful, “unique Immaculate One.”[54] However, I must add, Terstroet did not make any retrospective claims regarding the fall of the Berlin Wall or Russian perestroika ...

Echoes of the past

The red scare had of course not fully disappeared from the Netherlands when Terstroet was removed from his project. In the Marian jubilee year itself, 1954, the Dutch bishops even issued a controversial pastoral letter to the faithful of their church province. This letter, still known as *Mandament*, contained instructions for the private lives of Dutch Catholics. First of all the text reflected a strong echo of the past as the bishops asked for strict obedience and rejected a separation between religion and the personal life. Despite their repudiation of Terstroet, they continued to profess that communism was anti-Christian and they described Catholics who adhered to communist principles as apostates (De Jong 1954: 43). Membership of socialist and communist unions, broadcast associations and political parties remained dissuaded, all Catholics were urged to participate in Catholic organizations and to close the Catholic ranks. In retrospect, it was an ultimate attempt to keep modernity at a distance and to preserve Catholic unity. The text was mainly the work of the traditionalist bishop Lemmens, who was influenced by his fear of societal change and the threats of the Cold War, but who was also still engaged in his missionary pilgrimages with the statue of Our Lady, Star of the Sea. The pastoral letter created a political crisis, but more seriously it was the start of an alienation process of the flock from the conservative Church and stimulated modernization precisely by trying to keep it back. This did not mean that Marian devotionalism was yet a thing of the past. Mary remained popular among Dutch Catholics, but the popularity of Fátima was mixed. The sanctuary itself was too far away for it to become a popular destination, but her message was still well received.

In an echo of the international Fátima pilgrimage of 1947 and the Star of the Sea tour in Limburg, new missionary tours with a Fátima statue were organized by the Montfort Missionaries in the south of the Netherlands around the Marian year (De Graauw 1955).[55] Bishop Baeten of Breda, one of the few who had supported Terstroet, received a copy of the statue from the bishop of

54 Letters of L.L. Terstroet to P.J. Margry, September 16 and November 1, 1994.

55 Also other missionary and protective Fátima statues traveled in those years along private houses, where they could remain for one of more days and sometimes stayed in every house of the village, like in Achthuizen on Overflakkee. *Katholieke Illustratie* 83 (1949): 686-687.

12.3 Special travel cases existed for touring statues of Our Lady of Fátima visiting private homes. Here in the house of the Stadhouders family in Oosterhout, October 18, 1954.
[Amsterdam, Meertens Institute]

Leiria through the intervention of the SMM. From May 1, 1955 to July 23, 1957 it made a 'Grand Retour' *Peregrinatio* through the diocese of Breda in order to bring people back to God and halt the advance of atheism through this pilgrimaging army in battle order ("acies ordinata") under the protection of Our Lady of Fátima (De Graauw 1955: 65). Every parish of the diocese was visited, and a parish mission organized during the visit. After the tour the statue was donated to the parish of Moerdijk, where it became a symbolic gatekeeper, as this village was the place where the main motorway from the Protestant north of the country entered the diocese. The place soon became a place of pilgrimage for Our Lady of Fátima (Margry & Caspers 1998: 613-617). Similarly, the Montfort Missionaries persuaded Bishop Lemmens of Roermond in 1956 to obtain a copy of the Fátima statue for the parish of Herkenbosch, turning this parish into a second new satellite shrine (Margry & Caspers 2000: 296-298).

When the Russians invaded Hungary in the same year on November 4, the Dutch reacted promptly with massive political and religious protests throughout the country. Silent protest marches, some of them consisting of tens of thousands of participants, were immediately initiated by the leaders of a number of major Dutch Marian and Eucharistic places of pilgrimage after the archbishop had issued a call to organize these (Caspers & Margry 2006: 61-63). It was the last major action of Dutch Catholicism against communism and Russian aggression in the Cold War. Neither the 1963 Cuban Missile Crisis nor the 1968 Prague Spring provoked any specific Catholic anticommunist actions. As Dutch Catholicism slowly crumbled and détente became noticeable in international relations, the Dutch got used to the status quo of the Iron Curtain and the Cold War-related scenarios of a Russian invasion with or without a nuclear attack, and they began to build their welfare state (Traa 2009).

Conclusion

This case study has attempted to draw attention to national and local Catholic initiatives related to the Cold War and the struggle against communism. It shows that in postwar Europe, at least in "Maryland" the Netherlands, various activities were organized at grassroots level to mobilize Catholics for the protection of the faith against atheist ideologies, in particular communism. Despite the presence of a multitude of Marian organizations, there was no coordination on a (supra) national level of how to relate to communism in practice and to Pius XI's call of action against it. The lack of a standing central policy or guidelines gave scope to individual initiatives. With the exception of the coordination of the pan-European Fátima pilgrimages, initiatives taken in the Netherlands to fight communism or to protest against it remained self-contained movements. In the Terstroet example, one religious priest proved able in a rather personal way to organize a nationwide mobilization of Catholic believers and donors. While his movement must have had at least a psychological impact on Dutch Catholics, increasing anticommunist sentiment – but private voices are scarcely documented – it remained isolated from global Cold War politics. Nonetheless it caught the attention of the Holy Office, and this led to the swift suppression of his "Empire of Mary".

Remarkably, this case shows that, despite the universal call by the pope for action against communism, the Catholic hierarchy in the Netherlands and the Vatican were not inclined to stimulate grassroots initiatives. At the time they were more concerned about religious issues and interconfessional relations in the Netherlands than about the threat from behind the Iron Curtain. In the case of the Pentagon project, the Dutch bishops' conference was more disturbed by its doctrinal inconsistencies, while the Holy Office worried about the denominational stability in the Netherlands due to the possible effects of the project on the Protestant part of Dutch society. Stressing the role of Mary in the work of redemption remained a delicate issue, especially in the context of the building up of an ecumenical movement at the time, and it was precisely this aspect that was explicitly present in the 'Dutch' Empire of Mary and its relations with the "coredemptrix", the Lady of All Nations of Amsterdam. The instrumentalization of the Virgin Mary in Cold War politics and for anticommunist action was not as unambiguous and uncomplicated as it seems.

BIBLIOGRAPHY

Anon. 1939. *Regels en oefeningen voor de Mariacongregaties in Nederland*. The Hague: Algemeen Secretariaat der Mariacongregaties / Nijmegen: Dekker & Van de Vegt.

Anon. 1946a. *Pius-Almanak. Jaarboek voor de Katholieken van Nederland*. Amsterdam: 't Kasteel van Aemstel.

Anon. 1946b. *Mariagarde*. The Hague: Landelijk Secretariaat der Mariacongregaties.

Anon. 1948. *Verslagboek van het Maria-Congres gehouden te Maastricht op 3, 4, 5, 6 en 7 september 1947*. Maastricht: Bestuur Maria-Congres.

Anon. 1949. *Katholieke Wereldkruistocht*. Nijmegen: Nationaal Bureau van het Apostolaat des Gebeds.

Anon. 1999. *The Messages of The Lady of All Nations. New Edition*. Amsterdam: Foundation The Lady of All Nations.

Barthas, Casimir. 1944. *De kinderen van Fatima die Maria zagen. Het inwendige en verstorven leven der zieners van Fatima*. Haarlem: J.H. Gottmer & Co.

Bekkers, Th.M.P. 1944. *De openbaring van Fatima*. S.l.: s.n.

Caspers, Charles, and Peter Jan Margry. 2006. *Identiteit en spiritualiteit van de Amsterdamse Stille Omgang*. Hilversum: Verloren.

Chadwick, Owen. 1993. *The Christian Church in the Cold War*. London: Penguin Books.

Christiaens, Kim, Frank Gerits, Idesbald Goddeeris and Giles Scott-Smith. 2015. "The Low Countries and Eastern Europe during the Cold War: Introduction." *Dutch Crossing. Journal of Low Countries Studies* 39 (3): 187-197.

Christiaens, Kim, Frank Gerits, Idesbald Goddeeris and Giles Scott-Smith. 2016. "The Benelux and the Cold War: Re-interpreting West-West Relations." *Dutch Crossing. Journal of Low Countries Studies* 40 (1): 1-9.

Coenen, Jos. 1945. *Fatima voor en na de onthullingen van Zuster Dolorata*. Maaseik: J.J. Romen.

De Graauw, A. 1955. "De Pelgrimstocht van O.L. Vrouw van Fatima." *Sancta Maria. Kerkelijk weekblad voor het Bisdom Breda* 29: 49, 61, 63, 69, 73, 77, 81, 85, 89, 94, 97-98, 101, 105, 111, 113, 117, 121, 125, 129, 133, 137, 141, 145, 149, 153, 157, 161, 165.

De Jong, Johannes, et al. 1954. *De katholiek in het openbare leven van deze tijd. Bisschoppelijk Mandement*. Utrecht: Bishops' Conference.

De Kadt, Jacques. 1947. *Rusland en wij. Hoe redden wij de vrede?* Amsterdam: Van Oorschot.

Dhanis, Edouard. 1944. "Bij de verschijningen en voorzeggingen van Fatima." *Streven* 11: 129-149, 193-215.

Dhanis, Edouard. 1945, *Bij de verschijningen en het geheim van Fatima: een critische bijdrage*. Bruges: De Kinkhoren.

Frijns, W.M. 1939. "Het Marialegioen: 'De Katholieke Actie bij uitnemendheid.'" *De Maasbode*, May 14, 1939: 13.

Geertman, Hendrik. 1946. *Mijn bezoek aan Fatima*. Heerlen: Joh. Roosenboom.

Gonzaga da Fonseca, Luiz. 1943. *Fatima. De boodschap van Maria aan de moderne wereld: verschijningen, vereering, wonderen*. S.l.: s.n.

Haimon, Paul. 1947. *Zo was het Mariacongres. Een foto-album over het Mariacongres 1947 te Maastricht*. Heerlen: Winants.

Hellema, Duco. 1995. "The Relevance and Irrelevance of Dutch Anti-Communism. The Netherlands and the Hungarian Revolution, 1956-57." *Journal of Contemporary History* 30 (1): 169-186.

Hellema, Duco. 2011. "De Koude Oorlog in Nederland. Een fijne tijd." *Historisch Nieuwsblad* 5. <https://www.historischnieuwsblad.nl/nl/artikel/27608/de-koude-oorlog-in-nederland.html>.

Herraets, C.J. 1945. *Fatima*. Tilburg: Bergmans.

Jongen, Hubert. 1944. *O.L. Vrouw van Fatima. Missionaris van God*. Leuven: Secretariaat O.L.V. Middelares.

Julien, Paul. 1945. "Dr. Paul Julien over Fatima. Indrukken van een Portugeesche reis." *De Maasbode*, October 13: 1.

Lippmann, Walter. 1947. *The Cold War: A Study in U.S. Foreign Policy*. New York: Harper & Brother Publishers.

Luykx, Paul. 1978. *De Actie "Voor God" 1936-1941. Een katholieke elite in het offensief.* Nijmegen: KDC.

Margry, Peter Jan, and Charles Caspers (eds.). 1996-2004. *Bedevaartplaatsen in Nederland*, 4 vols. Hilversum: Verloren.

Martel, C. 1944. *De wonderen van Fatima.* Utrecht: Het Spectrum.

Massam, Katharine. 1991. "The Blue Army and the Cold War: Anti-communist Devotion to the Blessed Virgin Mary in Australia." *Australian Historical Studies* 24 (97): 420-428.

Metz, Andreas. 1931. "Onze Lieve Vrouwe van Fátima. Het Portugeesche Lourdes." *Katholieke Illustratie* 65: 768-769.

Noyons, J. 1935. *Maria's Eerewacht. De Mariacongregatie en haar betekenis.* The Hague: Algemeen Secretariaat der Mariacongregaties.

Peacock, Margaret. 2014. *Innocent Weapons: The Soviet and American Politics of Childhood in the Cold War.* Chapel Hill: The University of North Carolina Press.

Perouas, Louis. 1983. "Le Grand Retour de Notre-Dame de Boulogne à travers la France (1943-1948). Essai d'interprétation." *Archives de Sciences Sociales des Religions* 56 (1): 37-53.

Pius XI. 1937. *Divini Redemptoris. Over het goddeloze communisme.* Utrecht: Het Spectrum.

Pius XII. 1946. *Sommamente gradita. Toespraak van Z.H. Paus Pius XII van 20 september 1942, met twee andere documenten, juli-december 1942. Radiorede [Mais de uma vez] van 31 october 1942 tot de geloovigen van Portugal bij gelegenheid der plechtige feestelijkheden ter eere der H. Maagd die in Fatima vereerd wordt. Radioboodschap door den paus op de vigilie van het geboortefeest van onzen Heer Jesus Christus, 24 december 1942, tot heel de wereld gericht.* Hilversum: Gooi & Sticht.

Pizarro. G. 1931. *Fatima het nieuwe Lourdes.* Averbode: Abdij.

Polman, H.J.M. 1948. "Nederland – Marialand." *Standaard van Maria* 24: 355-365.

Polman, H.J.M. 1955. *Limburg rond de 'Sterre der Zee', 1950-1955.* Heerlen: Joh. Roosenboom.

Ribbens, Kees. 1992. "Het rode gevaar. Victor Kravtsjenko en het Ruslandbeeld van de Nederlandse katholieken, 1946-1948." *Ex Tempore* 11: 103-110.

Robroek, Fr. 1952. "Tien jaar Maria-Legioen in Nederland." *Standaard van Maria* 28: 135-141.

Sassen, J. et al. (eds.). 1934. *De Katholieke Encyclopaedie*, vol. 7. Amsterdam: Uitgeverij J. van den Vondel.

Schoffeleers, Jan Mathijs. 2006. *Montfortanen in de Lage Landen: "een klein en arm gezelschap", 1881-2006.* Tilburg: Gianotten.

Spauwen, Victor, 1944. *De verschijningen van de H. Maagd Maria te Fatima.* Maastricht: s.n.

Terstroet, Lambert L. 1945. *Maria en de Glorie van God volgens den Zal. Louis-Marie Grignion de Montfort 1673-1716.* Diss. Doct. Leuven: Katholieke Universiteit.

Terstroet, Lambert L. 1953a. *Pentagoon van het Rijk van Maria. Een kort verslag ter oriëntatie voor het Doorluchtig Episcopaat van Nederland.* Oirschot-Eindhoven: SMM/Lecturis.

Terstroet, Lambert L. 1953b. "Het Gods-teken van deze eeuw: Maria, de Onbevlekte." *Verovering. Weekblad voor het katholieke gezin*, December 1953 [also published in *In Slagorde*, January/February 1954].

Terstroet, Lambert L. 1955. "Een boodschap van de Vrouwe van alle Volkeren." *De Standaard van Maria. Tijdschrift voor Marialeer en Mariaal leven* 31 (4): 1-11.

Thiers, Ottie. 2005. *'t Putje van Heiloo. Bedevaarten naar O.L. Vrouw ter Nood.* Hilversum: Verloren.

Tondini, Amleto (ed.). 1954. *Le Encicliche Mariane.* Rome: A. Belardetti.

Traa, Mark. 2009. *De Russen komen! Nederland in de Koude Oorlog.* Amsterdam: Athenaeum-Polak & Van Gennep.

Van der Scheer, Petrus. 1944. *O. L. Vrouw van Fatima.* Rotterdam: Vox Romana.

Van der Velden, P. 1948. *Fatima. Een boodschap voor deze tijd.* Tilburg: Henri Bergmans.

Vande Vijvere, J.M. 1931. *De Verschijningen van Onze Lieve Vrouw te Fatima en het Geheim eraan verbonden.* Ghent: J. Debruyne.

Van Driel, J.W. 1956. "La gloire de Marie aux Pays Bas." *Maria. Études sur la Sainte Vierge*, vol. 4, edited by Hubert du Manoir, 469-491. Paris: Beauchesne.

Van Es, Marinus M. 1944. *De verschijningen en de boodschap van O.L. Vrouw van Fatima.* Uden: Missiehuis 'St. Willibrordus'.

Verrips, Ger. 1995. *Dwars, duivels en dromend. De geschiedenis van de CPN 1938-1991.* Amsterdam: Balans.

Voets, Bert. 1981. *Bewaar het toevertrouwde pand. Het verhaal van het bisdom Haarlem.* Hilversum: Gooi & Sticht.

Wiebes, Cees, and Bert Zeeman. 1994. "Benelux." In *The Origins of the Cold War in Europe. International Perspectives*, edited by David Reynolds, 167-193. New Haven: Yale University Press.

13
MARY'S MEDIA IN THE COLD WAR PHILIPPINES

DEIRDRE DE LA CRUZ

As one of the world's predominantly Catholic countries with deep ties to the United States, the Philippines was wholly affected by the movements and ideologies of global Catholic anticommunism, particularly from the 1940s through the second half of the 1960s. The Second World War left the country in shambles, legally independent of American colonial rule but still wholly dependent on American economic aid. As in other countries of Southeast Asia, fledgling democracies contended with discontented groups across classes that agitated for changes in the political and economic status quo. Even before the war, in the earlier part of the twentieth century, sweeping transformations in the culture and political economy of land tenure brought about by American colonialism forged the matrix from which workers and peasants organized and communism found ideological purchase among labor leaders. By the early 1940s, the Hukbalahap, a contraction of Hukbo ng Bayan Laban sa Hapon (People's Army Against the Japanese) was founded as a guerrilla organization that mobilized some of the peasantry to fight alongside Filipinos and Americans against Japan. The "Huks," as they came to be called, continued their struggle against oppression by transforming into the Hukbo Mapagpalaya ng Bayan (People's Liberation Army) after the war, taking on an identity more explicitly affiliated with communism. For a time, the Huks were front and center in the proxy war fought by the United States against communism in Southeast Asia. The "Huk Rebellion," as it is known, reached its peak in the late 1940s, with approximately twenty thousand combatant rebels actively fighting against the Philippine Constabulary and countless thousands more providing them with various kinds of support in the countryside (Lanzona 2009: 7). Their movement had effectively diminished by the mid-1950s, although the perceived threat of communism remained. In the late 1960s, a new and protracted struggle began with the formation of the New People's Army (NPA), the armed wing of the official Communist Party of the Philippines (CPP).

In this context, Catholics throughout the country participated in and propagated devotions to Mary that for the first time operated on a distinctly transnational scale, owing in part to the coordinated fight against communism worldwide. This chapter examines two cases where we see the close alignment of Marian devotion with anticommunist politics in the Cold War Philippines: the Family Rosary Crusades and the alleged apparitions of Mary in Lipa, Batangas.[1] It will place special emphasis on how these practices and phenomena spread through a variety of media, attempting the dissemination of anticommunist sentiment and practice along a variety of scales, from the most intimate of domestic and religious spaces, to a national Filipino public. The key word here, however, is "attempting," and an important question this article pursues is the extent to which these ideologically aligned efforts between Catholic devotionalism and global anticommunism took root in the Philippine context, among whom, and to what end. This chapter is thus as much a study of the localization and attenuation of Cold War Mary as it is a documentation of the ways in which Marian devotion and Catholic anticommunism were inextricably intertwined in this part of the world.

The Family Rosary Crusade, global and local

The Family Rosary Crusade (henceforth referred to as the FRC) was an American apostolate founded by Fr. Patrick Peyton, an Irish immigrant to the United States who believed that the Virgin Mary miraculously interceded to cure him of tuberculosis. What began as an occasional reminder on American Catholic radio programs to pray the rosary in the mid-1940s soon grew into a full-fledged, global media ministry using mass rallies, television, and films to propagate devotion to the Virgin Mary through rosary prayer. That the FRC's heyday coincided with the consolidation of United States military, political, and economic dominance after World War II is no accident, and its spread would greatly benefit from the Marian devotion of the pre-Vatican II Church of Pope Pius XII and the strong association of rosary prayer with anticommunism through the revised messages of Our Lady of Fátima in the 1930s (Kselman 1986: 409). Indeed, the Family Rosary Crusade, a movement whose founder

1 For a much longer treatment of these cases, differently framed, see my book *Mother Figured: Marian Apparitions and the Making of a Filipino Universal* (2015).

overtly analogized their campaigns to a military assault, could only be born at the intersections of mid-century Catholic conservatism, the Cold War, and the popularization of mass media technologies that could make the battle against communism one to be fought on the most public, and private, of fronts.

But what would happen when the FRC went abroad? How effectively could their methods and messages translate to different contexts? A history of the FRC's localization in the Philippine context will demonstrate several ways in which the universal aspirations and ideological agendas of the Crusades sometimes fell short of, and sometimes exceeded, the organization's intentions. Despite its fixed modular scheme (which the FRC deployed worldwide), the deputizing of Filipino Catholics – be they priests, volunteers, teachers, or heads of household – to carry out the Crusades program of regular rosary prayer often resulted in the creation and resolution of local interests and concerns.

The "Crusades" in plan and practice

A general overview of what exactly comprised these "crusades" as conceived will serve as our point of departure. Wholly modular in structure, that is, designed to be implemented in any given context, the Rosary Crusades were made up of three distinct phases of activity. The first phase was the utilization of the mass media for advertising, likened by Peyton, per his penchant for military metaphors, to an aerial bombardment (Gribble 2005: 107). Radio, TV where available, billboards, newspapers, magazines, film trailers, even stamp cancels were used to herald the impending arrival of the crusades to one's city, town, or diocese. During this period, Peyton or one of his proxies met with local clergy teachers, charity leaders, and other religious and lay constituencies to explain the crusade and enlist participation by circulating information about the upcoming events in their parishes, schools, and community organizations.[2]

The second phase, which Peyton saw as the "movement of troops to capture the objective," was the crusade itself, which lasted approximately six weeks (Gribble 2005: 107). On the first Sunday or Monday of the program, each participating bishop issued a pastoral letter formally announcing the crusade to all parishes in the diocese. On the following five Sundays, the priests would preach a series of homilies that Peyton had authored, bearing themes such as "basic reasons for devotion to Mary," how to pray the rosary, the importance of

2 For an outline of the Crusades as proposed for the Philippines see North Easton, Massachusetts, Archives of the Holy Cross Family Ministries (AHCFM), Fr. Peyton's Visit to the Philippines: Fr. Patrick Peyton to archbishop of Manila Gabriel Reyes, January 13, 1952. The first crusade in the Philippines was held in 1959; for an outline of that crusade see AHCFM, Reports, 1961-1962: "Family Rosary Crusade, Archdiocese of Manila."

13.1 Family Rosary Crusade Rally, Luneta park, Manila in 1959. Father Patrick Peyton is standing in black on stage.
[Photo Holy Cross Family Ministries]

the rosary to family life, and others.[3] On these Sundays bulletins produced by the FRC headquarters in the United States were distributed among all families in the parish. Little by little over the weeks, parishioners would receive more and more information about the rally that would mark the crusade's climax, at the center of which was the charismatic founder of the movement, Fr. Patrick Peyton himself. Details such as where the rally was to be held, how to caravan or find transportation, and so forth, were gradually disclosed as local organizers of the event accomplished what often were impressive logistical feats of successfully negotiating with municipal leaders, transportation officials, and prominent businessmen, as well as some corporate sponsors.[4]

If all went as planned, these few weeks generated considerable buzz throughout the diocese or district: teachers told their students, who told their parents; hospital workers told their patients, who told their families; seminarians told their cohort; and so on, thus building anticipation for the rallies. The sheer amount of religious publicity for the rallies was extraordinary, and perhaps unprecedented. All forms of the mass media were used to achieve full saturations of visual space, via posters and bumper stickers, billboards, and newspaper ads, as well as radio announcements and, for those who had access to it, television.[5]

In the Philippines, the first major rally was held in 1959, in Manila, where an estimated 1.5 million people filled the Luneta, an enormous public park that sits adjacent to Manila Bay and is a site of great historical significance.

3 AHCFM, Publicity and Outdoor Advertising, 1959-1962: "Family Rosary Crusade Souvenir Program, Diocese of San Fernando, January 1, 1962, to February 11, 1961."

4 *Ibid.*: "Crusader for Prayer Coming to S.F. [San Fernando, Pampanga]," "Archbishop Santos Writes on Crusade," November 1, 1959; "Information for Newsmen Regarding Family Rosary Rally," "Bus Companies," and "Contract for Aerial Services."

5 AHCFM, Reports, 1961-1962: "Suggested Plan for the Celebration of the 1959 Family Week," Annex B.

The rally was deemed such a success that Peyton returned to conduct a nationwide series of crusades in 1962. All told, the two campaigns and their climactic rallies involved more than thirty cities and were attended by at least three million Filipinos – a remarkable number considering the entire population of the country at the time had not yet reached thirty million.[6]

The extraordinary participation of millions of Filipinos in the 1960s rallies begs the question: who were they who gathered to hear Fr. Peyton speak and what exactly motivated them? FRC reports, the press's assignation of types, and visual evidence provided by the numerous photos taken of the rallies reveal people from all walks of society: religious sodalities, families, society matrons, vendors, people with disabilities, ordinary folk, farmers, and youth. There were those who planned their journey to the rally site for days, and those whose curiosity was piqued moments before by a radio announcement giving the blow-by-blow of a giant American dressed all in black alighting from a small prop plane at an airstrip near their town.[7] And what took place at these rallies, aside from the crowd?

6 The cities were: Manila; Balanga City (Bataan); San Fernando (Pampanga); Cabanatuan (Nueva Ecija); Daet (Camarines Norte); Naga City (Camarines Sur); Masbate City, Sorsogon, Legaspi, Virac (Bicol); Calbayog, Borongan (Samar); Maasin, Palo, Tacloban (Leyte); San Jose (Antique), Jaro (Iloilo), Dumaguete (Negros Oriental), Tagbilaran (Bohol), Cebu City; Bacolod (Negros Oriental); Kalibo (Aklan); Roxas (Capiz); Butuan (Agusan del Norte); Tagum (Davao del Norte); Digos (Davao del Sur); Dipolog (Zamboanga del Norte); Cagayan de Oro (Misamis); Marbel (South Cotabato); Jolo (Sulu); and Ozamis (Misamis Occidental). Manila, Family Rosary Crusades Philippines Archives: "Family Rosary Crusades in the Philippines" (1962); and "The 50th Anniversary of the Family Rosary Crusades in the Philippines, 1951-2001" (2001).

7 In order to best convey the sense of spectacle of the Philippine Crusades, I have opted in this section to present a composite picture. Sources I've drawn on include: AHCFM, Reports, 1961-1962: "Family Rosary Rally," Lilia J. de Jesus, "A Knight and His Crusade – In Retrospect," "Iloilo Rally, Feb. 4, 1962," "Extract from Father Peyton's Letter of February 7, 1962," and "Family Rosary Crusade (Cavite, Bulacan, and Rizal Province)"; AHCFM, Publicity and Outdoor Advertising, 1959-1962: "Family Rosary Crusade Souvenir Program, Diocese of San Fernando (January 1, 1962 to February 11, 1961)," "One Million Attend Family Rosary Rally in Manila on December 6 (1959)," "1,500,000 Join Family Rosary Crusade Rally," and "Information for Newsmen Regarding Family Rosary Rally"; AHCFM, Reports, 1959: "Gran concentracion de la Cruzada del Rosario en Familia en Antique, Filipinas," and Fr. Patrick Peyton, "Diary of the Great Blessings of God and Our Lady on the Family Rosary Crusade in the Archdiocese of Manila," December 8th, 1959; Family Rosary Crusades Philippines Archives: "Family Rosary Crusades in the Philippines" (1962); Pasig, Lopez Memorial Library, "Peyton, Patrick" clippings file: "Big Bataan crowd hears Fr. Peyton talk on prayer," *Daily Mirror*, January 23, 1962, "Rosary Padre arrives in Tagbilaran tomorrow," *Manila Times*, January 23, 1962, "40,000 hear Father Peyton in Bataan rosary rally," *Manila Times*, January 24, 1962, "200,000 devotees hear Peyton in Pampanga," *Manila Times*, January 30, 1962, "Peyton in Ecija crusade," *Manila Times*, January 30, 1962, "Political forum caps Bohol rosary rally," *Manila Times*, October 24, 1963, and "Father Peyton arrives for Imus rally," n.d.

Imagine a town, large enough to be the provincial capital, small enough to be shut down for the day. The movie house and cockpits are closed and banners bearing the slogan "The Family That Prays Together, Stays together" canopy the streets. Not even the biggest church could accommodate the people who came. Narrow roads and building walls groan with the weight of congestion as buses, cars, and *calesas* (horse-drawn carriages) get as close as they can to the open field, which belongs to the local high school or university or to the capitol building's grounds. Imagine even more people spilling from the vehicles when Trafcon – short for Traffic Control, an ad hoc formation of members of the Philippine Constabulary and the local chapter of the Knights of Columbus – turns their drivers back. First-aid stations that dot the field are slowly swallowed up by the crowd. And toward one end of the grassy arena, there is a makeshift stage, covered with white and blue (colors most associated with Mary), appearing now like an island in a black sea, or as one spectator from the stage describes it, "a huge mosaic of cobblestones," (*Manila Times* 1962). On the stage, in a neat row that stands notably in contrast to the throng, dignitaries – the provincial governor or town mayor, select members of the local elite, perhaps even someone from the U.S. military, the bishop – preside over the scene. And there, finally, center stage, is the man everyone has come to see and hear: Fr. Patrick Peyton.

Certain protocols of ceremony are observed. The pre-rally commentary segues into an opening hymn to the Blessed Mother, which is followed by a welcome address, predictable oratory that is less predictably registered in any number of languages: Cebuano, English, Tagalog, Kapampangan, with all the pomp deemed necessary to herald the significance of the event. Then comes the collective recitation of the rosary, but only five of the fifteen mysteries. At times a few of the dignitaries would lead the prayer; at other times the leaders would be a carefully selected assembly of representatives from various social classes. There would be one more round of introductions before the "Rosary Padre" finally took the stage. In his notable brogue, Peyton might tell the story of how he founded the FRC in gratitude to the Blessed Virgin, who saved him from tuberculosis. He would tell of the other crusades that brought him into contact with people throughout the world. He would speak of prayer in general, and the rosary in particular, as the panacea for everything from the smallest of family conflicts to the greatest of global strife. And he might leave the audience with clever metaphors, such as "Group prayer serves as a spiritual megaphone," and "[Faith] is something like radio. God is there for everyone but He only comes to those who turn the dial of Faith" (Peyton 1962). Then he would descend from the stage into the crowd and, towering over it with his height, bless the rosaries thrust forward by anonymous limbs.

Peyton was a charismatic figure with classically Weberian characteristics. Those who witnessed Peyton in action testified to his power in rapturous terms: One letter to the *Manila Times* describes him at the 1962 rally in Sorsogon as follows:

> Fr. Peyton keeps the crowd spellbound; lifts his hearers above the ground; regales their hearts with soothing mysticism. As he speaks, one feels that he lives in a supernatural sphere (...) Fr. Peyton, through the Blessed Virgin, or better still, the Blessed Virgin through Fr. Peyton, did the impossible, the unbelievable. A crowd estimated at 140,000 attended (...) Fr. Peyton was a fountain that brought to Sorsogon the Biblical water springing up into everlasting life. He was a heavenly fire that came down to enkindle the hearts of men for God (Yllana n.d.).

For rally attendees, Peyton, and not the rosary, was Mary's instrument. To listen to him was to venerate, if not exactly pray, to Her. But localizing the rosary rallies in the Philippine context often entailed a curious and notable disconnect. Speaking of a rally in Surigao, one Filipino FRC volunteer I interviewed confessed:

> So I was joking with this old person. While Fr. Peyton was speaking, I said, "tita [or "aunty," an informal term of address], do you understand what the priest is saying?" "No." "Er, do you believe what's being said?" "Absolutely!" He he, that was the best. She can't understand what's being said, but she believes! And the majority were like that.[8]

This was not the only time I heard this story or one like it, as it surfaced in other interviews I did with Filipino FRC volunteers, suggesting that this was a common experience; after all, the majority of Filipino attendees would not have commanded the English needed to understand what Peyton was saying – much less understand it through his thick Irish accent. At these rallies, Peyton's charismatic aura and the force of the crowd alone sufficed to rivet attendees, and compel their belief. When it came to these rallies, the medium was the message. But this revival-like experience of the crowd and its potential excesses were immediately contained by the crusades' third phase, which Peyton depicted as "occupation forces to maintain the victory" (Gribble 2005: 107).

Localizing the pledge drives

Immediately upon completion of the rally, where and whenever it was held, the "pledge week" phase of the crusades would begin. Parish volunteers known as "crusade leaders" would be dispatched, in pairs, to go house to house in their community, collecting promises from the families to practice the Family

8 Interview with Larry Ersuela, Manila, October 8, 2001.

Rosary. Armed with a *Handbook for Crusade Leaders* and a worker's badge, these volunteers would prepare to "be spiritual salesmen of the Family Rosary (...) know [their] product thoroughly[,] (...) and plan in advance various methods of effective approach" (Gribble 2005: 107). The handbook presented volunteers with a variety of possible objections they might encounter and suggestions for how to deal with them.

The main instrument of the pledge drive was an index card, inscribed on the front as follows: "To obtain peace for the nations of the world, and the love and protection of God and Mary for myself and the members of my family, I solemnly pledge the daily Family Rosary."[9]

On the back were lines to list the name of the head of the family, the street address, and a series of spaces to be filled out by the crusade leaders upon visiting homes. These included the following:

1. Total number (Catholics and non-Catholics) who signed pledge in this family.
2. Number of non-Catholics who signed.
3. Number of Catholics who refused.
4. Reason for refusal.
5. Space for additional signatures.[10]

Pledge week was essentially a form of census taking, a point that then Archbishop of Manila Rufino Santos himself made.[11] In a memo from his office to all vicars forane for the Manila crusade of 1959, he urged 100 percent compliance by recommending that the vicars meet personally with each parish priest under their jurisdiction, that each priest urge his parishioners to be at home during the pledge gathering days, and that results be promptly submitted to the archbishop at the end of the pledge drive.[12]

Where families might fall through the cracks, Archbishop Santos recommended "the simple, practical, possible, and in fact, easy method" of using the children of the parish.[13] In a letter addressing public and private school teachers as the "second line of defense for the Family Rosary Crusade," Santos suggested that during pledge week, teachers "from day to day question their students to ensure that their homes have been visited by the two laymen [crusade workers], and if their family signed the pledge. The teachers can help enormously," he continued, "by getting the students to report on the progress

9 AHCFM, Reports, 1961-1962: "Our Family Rosary Pledge" (pledge card).

10 *Ibid.*

11 AHCFM, Reports 1959: Most Rev. Rufino Santos to Teachers of Public and Private Schools, October 21, 1959.

12 *Ibid.*: Most Rev. Rufino Santos, "Family Rosary Crusade – Pledge Gathering: Plan of Action for Vicar Forains [*sic*]."

13 *Ibid.*

of the house to house visitations (...) with regards to relatives, neighbors, and friends."[14]

The archbishop's recommendations to teachers did not fall on deaf ears. The high school students at St. Scholastica's, for example, one of Manila's most prestigious girls schools, produced an 80-page souvenir bulletin, in which their reflections and actions during the six-week crusade were meticulously recorded.[15] The students even innovated on some of the procedures of the pledge drive, generating their own individual reports that went beyond the information requested on the official pledge cards to include: the number of brothers and sisters seven years and older, the number of maids and houseboys, other relatives, and any other people residing in the house.[16] Here it is quite clear that at least one of the issues encountered in the implementation of the FRC in the Philippine context was the fundamental difference in how kinship – or the "family" – itself was defined, and that the schoolchildren innovated on the drive's methods to better capture what their families actually looked like. Fine-tuning these innovations further, the reports attempted to account more clearly for individuals' religiosity, measure their fidelity to the reception of the sacraments and to the Family Rosary, and assess their willingness to sign the pledge and attend the rally. The students even generated and monitored summary reports as the crusade and pledge week went on.[17]

That the pledge drive generated an enthusiasm for surveillance seems beyond doubt. But to what end? There is no evidence that any of the specific information collected on the cards went beyond the parish level, as Santos requested only the number of pledges from the parish reports, data that was forwarded in turn to FRC headquarters and were the measuring stick for the success of the crusades. In a letter dated January 18, 1960, about a month after the Manila crusade was held, a secretary for the office of FRC Manila wrote to Fr. Quinn, Peyton's right-hand man, to report that thus far, the pledge drive had yielded a total of 1,170,875 individuals signing, including 5,032 non-Catholics and 6,375 sick people. The secretary does go on to note that no communists had signed – but neither, she writes in the same sentence, had any lepers.[18]

On the one hand, this disclosure seems to indicate awareness of an overarching agenda to be vigilant and identify anyone of communist persuasion. On the other hand, it suggests that by this time communists existed as just one category of individuals, perhaps outcast, among many – including lepers.

14 AHCFM, Reports 1959: Most Rev. Rufino Santos to Teachers of Public and Private Schools, October 21, 1959.

15 *Ibid.*: "The Family Rosary Crusade Souvenir Bulletin."

16 *Ibid.*: "FRC Newsettes," in "The Family Rosary Crusade Souvenir Bulletin."

17 *Ibid.*

18 AHCFM, Correspondence, 1951-1962: Family Rosary Crusade Archdiocese of Manila to Reverend Joseph M. Quinn, January 18, 1960.

Furthermore, although Archbishop Santos desired to launch a second campaign immediately, he gave directions simply to gather an additional one million signatures. In other words, there were no specific directives to target or even follow up with the families and individuals who may not have signed the pledges the first time around. We might thus think of the census-like pledge drive as a campaign of surveillance without a clear objective apart from the obvious: to make sure everyone was pledging to pray. Although we cannot neglect the discourse of anticommunism and the military metaphors that percolated through the Filipino crusades via the directives of its American founding organization, we would also be wrong to conclude that this was first and foremost what the volunteers and participants at all levels had in mind as they went about their tasks.

Indeed, a closer look at some of the correspondence and volunteer reports reveals that concerns addressed or resolved by the crusades were often much more local or idiosyncratic in nature. For some, like one nun in Cebu who "worried about conditions in the remote barrios where the Protestant missionaries are making great progress," the rosary crusade was the "saving plank for real true Catholicism."[19] For others, like one sister of the Good Shepherd Convent and Orphanage in Baguio City, the practice of the Family Rosary was quite effective in preventing orphans from running away.[20] For yet others, women especially, the pledge for family prayer was about keeping their men. One woman, speaking of the effects of the crusade on her community in Jaro, Iloilo, wrote: "We thank the Blessed Virgin for thawing the hearts of the menfolks in our crusade," one of whom had expressed that, now, "he has something to come home for."[21]

It may seem rather obvious to point out, even if only by its name, that the Family Rosary Crusade also had at its ideological core the re-entrenchment of conservative domesticity and gender roles that one saw not only in American Cold War culture but also in the postwar period of the Philippines and well into the 1960s. Still, how this FRC-dictated re-entrenchment played out or was articulated in the Philippine context often left room for surprising ambiguities. Only men, for instance, could be the pledge collectors. And while this was justified under the rubric of the *pater familias* and the predominant stereotype that women were "naturally" more pious, it sometimes had to be explicated in peculiar terms. In the final sermon of the crusades, for example, the priests were instructed to prepare the congregation for pledge week by making the following comparison: "In the story of the First Christmas, there

19 Cited in AHCFM, Correspondence, Manhasset, 1959-1962: Fr. Patrick Peyton to Rev. Joseph M. Quinn, March 3, 1962.

20 AHCFM, Correspondence, 1960-1965: Sr. Mary of St. Rose Virginia to Fr. Patrick Peyton, February 5, 1961.

21 *Ibid.*: Mrs. Esperanza T. Buenconsejo to Fr. Patrick Peyton, February 5, 1961.

was no room for Mary and Joseph because the innkeepers only saw a pale, tired young girl accompanied by a strong, handsome, man. This week, when Mary comes to your doorstep, you will see only two men. They are her ambassadors. She wants to dwell in your home."[22] Once again, in context, the image projected by this comparison appears rather unorthodox, and perhaps even a little queer. The idiom of the Holy Family – with its "strong, handsome man" – suddenly morphs into two men, alone, seeking space in your home for the Blessed Mother. In a place where spectacular festivals of public devotion to Mary, as well as the dressing, maintenance, and trade in Marian images have long been a domain occupied by gay or effeminate men, it may not be so farfetched to see these "ambassadors" as attenuating, if not undermining, the masculinity of the *pater familias* that the FRC desired to project. At the very least it points to some of the more homosocial engagements generated by the pledge drives.

Filipina women, meanwhile, though prohibited from collecting pledges, performed a range of roles in the FRC. It was a coalition of women's groups that in the early 1960s spearheaded the formation of the FRC Auxiliary, and took charge of much of the fund raising for the various missions.[23] Usually belonging to the class of society matrons, these women organized fundraising events that included everything from can recycling to rummage sales, to mahjong tournaments, and gave money of their own. It was owing to the Auxiliary that the millions of pledge cards, hundreds of thousands of handbooks and posters, and other materials used for the FRC rallies were made available.

However, just as the male pledge collectors asserted an ambiguous masculinity as both heads of households *and* submissive sons of Mary in the homosocial formation of volunteer brigades, so too did women find in the FRC channels to assert their individual, albeit prudent, desires. These channels often took the form of correspondence between Auxiliary women and Fr. Peyton himself, letters that overwhelm the FRC Philippine archive.

> Dear Father Peyton: Reading your letter was just like talking to you in person (...) thank you very much for that beautiful and blessed bracelet that you are sending (...) I shall always wear them as my rosary beads (...) as a reminder of your good and wonderful self.[24]

> Dear Father: there have been so many changes in people since your wonderful crusade – we call it A.P. – after Peyton.[25]

22 AHCFM, Publicity and Outdoor Advertising, 1959-1962: Family Rosary Crusade Souvenir Program, diocese of San Fernando, January 1, 1962 – February 11, 1961.

23 AHCFM Correspondence, Ladies Auxiliaries, 1961-1969: First Anniversary Family Rosary Crusade Auxiliaries Souvenir Program.

24 AHCFM, Correspondence, 1951-1962: Nestora L. Benetua to Father Patrick Peyton, March 2, 1960.

25 *Ibid.*: Betty Velhagen to Father Patrick Peyton, February 28, 1960.

> Dear Father: please know that I could never forget your kindness (...) and your words of encouragement (...) to which I cling (...) with my most honest desire to live up to your beautiful expectations and hopes for mankind.[26]

Some of the womens' writings to and about Fr. Peyton were downright blush-worthy, such as the report filed to FRC headquarters about the Crusade in Caceres, Camarines Norte that reads: "The look in those blue Irish eyes seemed to heal wounds and scars in the soul. The slightest brush with his cassock lightened seemingly unbearable trials and earthly cares! A light touch of his hand blotted out pains and heartaches!! How else can one write about him but to say that he is divine?"[27]

These are love letters of a certain sort, they trace epistolary relationships that Peyton seemed only too willing to enter into, as they were important to keeping his mission alive and fostering support on the ground. But from the perspective of the FRC women these were chances for intimacy at a distance, opportunities legitimated by the long Catholic tradition of the relationship between priest confessors and pious women, yet potentially disruptive of the commitments that women were expected to make as mothers and wives in the Cold War re-entrenchment of domesticity.

An Asian Fátima

As other chapters in this volume have demonstrated, devotion to Our Lady of Fátima figures centrally in Catholic Cold War culture and politics. Populations worldwide, including in the Philippines, took up the injunction to acts of piety delivered through Sister Lucia's revised account of Mary's messages. But the Fátima phenomenon influenced more than just devotional practice; it provided the lens through which other apparition events were interpreted. Such was the case with the alleged apparitions of Our Lady in the small city of Lipa (Batangas province), fifty miles south of Manila, in the late 1940s Philippines.

In 1948, a young novitiate of the Order of Discalced Carmelites named Teresita Castillo claimed that the Virgin Mary appeared to her in the cloister on no fewer than fifteen occasions, proclaiming on the last of these to be "Mary, Mediatrix of All Grace" (Castillo n.d.). Castillo's description of her visions in testimonies she wrote decades after the fact reveal motifs and narrative features of other apparition events, in particular that of Mary's appearances at Lourdes. For example, Teresita's visions of Mary occurred serially, that is, over a number of consecutive days. The first of these visions readily resembled the

26 AHCFM, Correspondence, 1951-1962: Melba Oliver to Father Patrick Peyton, February 25, 1960.

27 AHCFM, Reports, 1961-1962: Lilia J. de Jesus, "A Knight and his Crusade – In Retrospect."

scene described by the visionary Bernadette Soubirous nearly a century past and many thousand kilometers away:

> At about 5:00 in the afternoon, I was walking in the garden (not much of a garden because it was a new foundation) and started to pray the rosary. When I reached the third mystery, I noticed that a vine I was passing by shook to the extent that I could not help but look at it. Since there was no wind, I thought perhaps a big lizard or snake was passing through the vine because of the way the vine was shaking. Suddenly I heard a woman's voice that said: "Fear not my child." Recognizing the voice, I immediately knelt down, turning my head from left to right, expecting to see someone. Then the voice continued: "Kiss the ground and whatever I shall tell you to do, you must do. Eat some grass, my child." (Perhaps this command was to test my obedience and simplicity.) "I want you to come to visit me here in this spot for fifteen consecutive days" (Castillo n.d.).

Anyone familiar with the apparitions of Mary at Lourdes would find the similarities between Teresita's and Bernadette's visions striking: the references to wind and praying the rosary at the time of the apparitions; the instruction to kiss the ground and eat grass; the request that the young Carmelite return for fifteen consecutive days. Perhaps the most significant similarity between the two serial visions of Mary is how they culminate in Mary's revelation of her name. Towards the end of appearances at Lourdes Mary declares "Que soy era Immaculada Councepciou" ("I am the Immaculate Conception"). On the last of her apparitions at Lipa Mary is reported to have likewise declared with equal command: "I AM MARY, MEDIATRIX OF ALL GRACE."

It is not only the similarities of Teresita's visions to those of Bernadette's at Lourdes that situate these Philippine apparitions in relation to apparitions of Mary the world over. Several aspects of Teresita's visions conform to patterns seen as far back as the late medieval and early modern period, such as the request to make the site of Mary's appearance sacred by performing a blessing at that spot (Castillo n.d.; Christian 1982: 105). In a related message, Mary asks Teresita to describe her physical features to the convent's chaplain, so that a statue may be made in the likeness of her apparition to the young novice, stating that it "look as you see me and [be] as big as that of Our Lady of Lourdes which stands inside the cloister" (Castillo n.d.). Again, and despite the features of Teresita's visions that seem "typical" of Marian apparitions elsewhere, it is Mary's appearance at Lourdes, and not at Fátima, that the young novice references the most.

The one exception to this in Teresita's testimony comes through Mary's message delivered to her on November 12, 1948, when she implores:

13.2 Devotional leaflet of Our Lady of Lipa.
[Collection of William A. Christian Jr.]

> Pray, my child. The people do not heed my words. Tell my daughters that there will be persecutions, unrest, and bloodshed in your country. The enemy of the Church will try to destroy the faith which Jesus established and died for. The Church will suffer much. Pray for the conversion of sinners throughout the world. Pray for those who rejected me, and those who do not believe my messages in different parts of the world. I am really sad, but consoled by those who believe and trust me. Spread the meaning of the rosary because this will be the instrument for peace throughout the world (...) But be not afraid for the love of my Son will soften the hardest of hearts and my motherly love will be their strength to crush the enemies of God. What I ask here is the same as in Fatima (Castillo n.d.).

Although this message might prove that the Mary of Teresita's visions was too a Cold War Marian figure, it is the only direct reference to the Catholic anticommunist milieu of the late 1940s in all of Teresita's writings. We will recall, furthermore, that Teresita penned her testimony in the early 1990s, a full four decades after her experiences, raising the possibility that hindsight afforded her a clearer lens through which to understand the full timeliness of the apparitions, that is, their appositeness to context. This does not mean, however, that other characters in the saga of the Lipa apparitions did not seize upon the relationship between Fátima, anticommunism, and Mary Mediatrix of All

Grace at the time of their occurrence. Indeed, once the news of the apparitions of Mary circulated beyond the cloister walls – and moreover, when the private apparitions yielded a very public and equally mysterious phenomenon – the link between Mary's apparitions at Lipa and the Catholic Cold War became crystal – or better put, materially – clear.

Showers of rose petals

The day before Mary allegedly made reference to Fátima in her message to Teresita, something marvelous happened. On November 11, 1948, rose petals fell outside of the Carmelite convent in Lipa. The first news of the showering petals appeared almost a week later, on November 17, in the newly resurrected daily *The Manila Times*. Jim Austria, the newspaper's society editor, wrote a first-person account of the marvel, describing the petals that "fell in graceful swirls straight down, almost like a drizzle, to a single spot" before him (Austria 1948: 1). As if keeping in lockstep with the broadening circulation of news about the petals, the showers themselves increased in frequency over the following several days. A corresponding swell of pilgrims started arrive, many of whom too became witnesses providing testimony to the "miracle of the roses" (*The Manila Times* 1948: 14). Soon the phenomenon spread further, as if to expand the supernatural force field well beyond the convent grounds: reports streamed in of petals falling in a nearby garden, at a local market, in a classroom, even in Manila. Reports came in of people claiming that single petals miraculously appeared on their persons or among their belongings after they left the convent.

As the phenomenon of the showers of petals grew, *The Manila Times* became more than just a source of information but a forum for witnesses, skeptics, and advocates. In this forum we see the kind of reflexive discourse that Michael Warner claims is the hallmark of a public as engendered by the circulation of texts (Warner 2002: 49-90). It is this public, I would argue, that was most responsible for framing the Lipa miracles in relation to Our Lady of Fátima and the Catholic Cold War. For one, the *Times* was an English-language daily in a linguistically plural society; that is to say, it was a publication that primarily represented the urban, cosmopolitan, and elite voices in the Philippines at that time. Indeed, many of the people mentioned and contributing to the newspaper coverage were members of the country's wealthiest families and political elite. The observations articulated by this particular public were thus specific to their own concerns and interests, among which was the threat currently posed by the Communist Hukbalahap. Not surprisingly, then, participants in this reflexive discourse emphasized what they interpreted as the anticommunist message of the miracles and apparitions. The article "Chief Justice and Noted Scientist Convinced Petal Shower a Miracle," claims that

13.3 Crowd witnessing a shower of rose petals in Lipa, c. 1948.
[From Keithley, "The Petals of Lipa"]

Dr. Manual L. Roxas, described as a "well-known Filipino scientist," believed that "the apparition is a warning or a message to the people to beware of communism," that the "enemy of God and the people is rapidly approaching our shores," and that this was comparable to the "similar ideology" that threatened Europe during the times of Mary's appearances at Lourdes and Fátima (*Manila Times* 1949: 1, 4). Others, like the United States-trained Filipino professor of political science Maximo Kalaw drew on Cold War rhetorics of axes of power, calling the miracle the first of its kind in a "brown world" (*Manila Times* 1949: 1, 4).

The particular public delineated by the mainstream English newspaper bore an enthusiasm for the Lipa miracles that was less religious than ideological. This public's participants advocated an anticommunist platform that drew from the Catholic Cold War as propagated on a global scale but devised primarily among followers in the United States, much like we saw with the Crusades for the Family Rosary. Indeed, the American press also covered the apparitions and miracles of Lipa, deploying a Cold War framework through and through, yoking the phenomenon to the divine sanctions at Fátima to take up the fight against communism. In fact, in 1949 and 1950 the Lipa miracles became a favorite topic for anticommunist crusaders on the American Catholic talk circuit from Biloxi, Mississippi to Santa Fe, New Mexico, with local newspapers and the Catholic press announcing and covering their speeches nationwide.

Casting the Lipa miracles beneath the rubric of anticommunism was only one way in which the phenomena were understood, however. The events taking place in the provincial town captured the attention of many others apart from the Philippines' political and social elite concerned with the threat of communism. Less socially and politically prominent people also arrived at the scene in doves, coming by the busloads. Students, aid workers, families, as well as parish, civic, and other groups organized themselves to travel from as far away as the central Visayan archipelago to make up what on some occasions amounted to upward of 30,000 eager observers on the convent grounds. For most of these ordinary Filipinos, a visit to Lipa was as much about the experience of pilgrimage and being present as the spectacle unfolded.

For example, and in contrast to the reportage in *The Manila Times*, the popular Tagalog-language magazine *Liwayway* covered the miracles in a way that spoke to the interests and sensibilities of its mass audience, rather than give platform to anticommunist rhetoric. In addition to providing more of a sense of what it was like to be there than the *Times* coverage had, *Liwayway*'s reporters took great care to provide details about the physical conditions surrounding the events, from the position of the convent windows, to the direction of the breeze. The lengthy feature in *Liwayway*, "Himala ng mga talulot ng rosas" (The Miracle of the Rose Petals), took care to appeal to their readership: in addition to opening the feature in a manner somewhat resembling true crime, they dedicated considerable space to a profile of the young novice Teresita Castillo, inquiring after her social standing and what kind of student she was, talking about her love for playing piano, and even musing at one point on the significance of the fact that she was born on the fourth of July (Independence Day in the United States) (D'Alarcon & La Vida 1948: 66).

In other words, the coverage of the Lipa miracles in the vernacular press focused less, if at all, on the events' anticommunist meanings. This is not to say, however, that *Liwayway* and other Tagalog-language publications focused only on the local, or even national, scene. In the fourth installment of "Himala ng mga talulot ng rosas" authors Rafael D'Alarcon and Dominador La Vida situated Lipa Carmel in a much longer genealogy of the Order of Carmelites. They talked about the significance of Carmel and the supposed vision of the Prophet Elijah, who having climbed the mountain to pray for rain, saw rise out of the ocean an enormous cloud that took the shape of Mary. They talked about the establishment of the formidable order and the main figures behind its reform in the sixteenth century, Teresa de Jesus and John of the Cross. In the final chapter of the article the authors linked the apparitions and miracles of Lipa to the appearance of Mary at Fátima, but instead of the strong anti-communist agenda advanced in *The Manila Times*, the authors wrote at length about the humble background of the three child shepherds (D'Alarcon & La Vida 1949: 30), the apparitions of the Angel of Peace (*Anghel na Kapayapaan*) that heralded the apparitions of Mary, and Mary's own appearance (which, comparatively speaking, is only briefly represented!). While the article references the numerous injunctions to pray, there is not one mention of the most famous message of Our Lady of Fátima to consecrate Russia to Mary's Immaculate Heart. Most surprisingly, there is not even mention, in this or any other coverage I have read of Lipa, of the reported appearance of showering rose petals at Fátima in 1917 and their possible connections (McGlynn 2017: 43-45)! In fact, the biggest take-away from the long feature "Himala ng mga talulot ng rosas" comes at the conclusion, with a section titled *Paulit-ulit ang lahat ng kasasayan* (History Repeats Itself). Here, the authors' ultimate interpretation of the Lipa phenomena draws on the authority of sanctioned apparitions of Mary worldwide in order to suggest that the Mary of Lipa is just one manifestation of a universal Mary, one whose purpose in appearing is to "awaken the hearts of all people so that they may bring their everyday lives into harmony with their souls and with the divine" (D'Alarcon & La Vida 1949: 44).

Situating the Lipa phenomena in a much broader history of Marian apparitions, miracles, and devotion, as the *Liwayway* article does, served to legitimate (if only popularly, since the official work of approbation lies with the Catholic Church) the phenomenon itself. Lipa may be an "Asian Fátima," but it is also an Asian Lourdes, an Asian Guadalupe, and so on. Popular interpretations did not limit themselves to culturally or geographically local comprehensions; on the contrary, their frames of reference were often significantly global, transhistorical, and even transpiritual (if you consider the relationship drawn, for instance, between the Prophet Elijah, the reformation of the Carmelite order, and the folk piety that typifies many modern visionaries). In sum, vernacular interpretations of Lipa not only served to attenuate the ideological imperative of Catholic anticommunism that characterized elite perspectives, they also, ironically, provincialized its singular and narrow focus.

Conclusion

It is all too easy to assume that Catholic anticommunism moved through the Philippines with imperialist unidirectionality, and to equate the religious aspects of the Philippines cum Cold War proxy with its political and military aspects. But as scholars of the Cold War have recently demonstrated, the historical picture is far more complicated than that on all fronts: religiously as much as politically and militarily. As was the case earlier in the twentieth century, when the Philippines was in actuality a colonial territory of the United States, the Cold War period saw the archipelago nation serve yet again as a laboratory for developing discourse and strategies in the battle against its ostensible enemies. A great variety of actors, both Filipino and American, took part in this experimentation, producing, in effect, the *global* Cold War (Woods 2012). Another way of putting this is to say that the Philippines was not just a theater of the U.S.-led Cold War, it was instrumental in defining that war's very global nature, where "global" is understood to be an ideological, as much as a spatial, construct.

On the ground, this production of the "global" in the global Cold War derived from the dialectical interaction between the local and the transnational. Models for political reform and economic development, for instance, were generated out of locally-specific structures of power and agricultural practices. Exportable counter-insurgency strategies were devised vis-à-vis Filipino guerilla tactics sedimented and forged over centuries under foreign rule. And Filipino Catholics took up with agency and enthusiasm the propagation of their own devotions and miracles, as seen when petals claimed to have fallen from the heavens in Lipa were dispatched throughout the world through letters and traveling Filipinos, causing mysterious occurrences on their own and making the "Wonders of Lipa" a global phenomenon (ABC 1949: 15; Villanueva 1949; Marcial 1949a: 39-42; Marcial 1949b: 42-43).

This chapter offers a perspective from the Global South on what our volume's editor has pithily termed "Cold War Mary." I have sketched out two cases where anticommunist messages or interpretations of Marian phenomena or practices were only as strong or as weak as was the perceived threat of communism by different groups across regions and social classes, and where other interpretations or agendas often asserted themselves. This calls into question whether the association of Mary with anticommunism in this period was ever a comprehensive phenomenon. Ever elusive, and perhaps even, excessive, the figure of Mary can always mean so much more to the people devoted to her, no matter how aggressively some groups attempt to harness her iconography, appearances, and injunctions to a single political agenda. The historical record does reveal one clear outcome, however, and that is that it is in the postwar/Cold War period of Marian devotion in the Philippines that the transnational promise of Filipino Marianism was engendered, that Filipino devotional publics situated and extended their purview to a world well beyond the Philippines, and that this set the stage for a later era when the country, along with so many postcolonial others, became the new centers of Christianity worldwide.

BIBLIOGRAPHY

ABC. 1949. "Suceso Prodigioso." March 30: 15.

Austria, Jim. 1948. "Miracle of Rose Showers Drawing Crowds of Devotees." *The Manila Times*, November 17: 1, 14.

Castillo, Teresita. n.d. (ca. 1990). Original Testimony.

Christian Jr., William A. 1982. *Local Religion in Sixteenth-Century Spain*. Princeton, NJ: Princeton University Press.

Cruz, Deirdre de la. 2015. *Mother Figured: Marian Apparitions and the Making of a Filipino Universal*. Chicago: University of Chicago Press.

D'Alarcon, Rafael, and Dominador La Vida. 1948. "Himala ng mga Talulot ng Rosas." *Liwayway*, December 20: 46-49.

D'Alarcon, Rafael, and Dominador La Vida. 1949. "Himala ng mga Talulot ng Rosas." *Liwayway*, January 3: 30-44.

Gribble, Richard. 2005. *American Apostle of the Family Rosary: The Life of Patrick J. Peyton*. New York: Crossroad Publishing.

Kselman, Thomas A. 1986. "Marian Piety and the Cold War in the United States." *Catholic Historical Review* 72 (3): 403-424.

Lanzona, Vina. 2009. *Amazons of the Huk Rebellion: Gender, Sex, and Revolution in the Philippines*. Madison, WI: University of Wisconsin Press.

The Manila Times. 1948. "Notables in Throng Brave Rain to See Miracle of Roses." November 22: 1, 14.

The Manila Times. 1949. "Chief Justice and Noted Scientist Convinced Petal Shower a Miracle." January 24: 1, 4.

The Manila Times. 1962. "40,000 Hear Father Peyton in Bataan Rosary Rally." January 24.

Marcial, Andres R. 1949a. "Lipa-Vadillo." *Santo Rosario*, 4 (5): 39-42.

Marcial, Andres R. 1949b. "Lipa-Vadillo." *Santo Rosario*, 4 (8): 42-43.

McGlynn, Thomas. 2017 [1943]. *Vision of Fatima*. Manchester NH: Sophia Institute Press.

Peyton, Patrick. 1962. "Family Fortress." *Daily Mirror*, January 13.

Villanueva, Francisco Jr. 1949. *The Wonders of Lipa*. Manila: Francisco Villanueva Jr.

Warner, Michael. 2002. "Publics and Counterpublics." *Public Culture* 14 (1): 49-90.

Woods, Colleen. 2012. *Bombs, Bureaucrats, and Rosary Beads: The United States, the Philippines, and the Making of Global Anti-Communism, 1945-1960*. Ph.D. dissertation. Ann Arbor, MI: The University of Michigan.

Yllana, Florencio. n.d. "Father Peyton's Grand Family Rosary Rallies." *The Manila Times* (reprinted in "Family Rosary Crusades in the Philippines" (1962), Manila, Family Rosary Crusades Philippines Archives).

14
"NO CONSECRATION, NO PEACE!"
THE FATIMA CENTER AND THE RUSSIAN ANNEXATION OF CRIMEA

MICHAEL AGNEW

During the third debate of the 2012 US Presidential Campaign, focused on foreign policy, sitting President Barack Obama challenged his Republican opponent Governor Mitt Romney on his foreign policy credentials, honing his focus on Governor Romney's past statements on the security threat posed by President Vladimir Putin's Russia, stating:

> Governor Romney, I'm glad that you recognize that al-Qaeda is a threat, because a few months ago when you were asked what's the biggest geopolitical threat facing America, you said Russia, not al-Qaeda; you said Russia. And the 1980s are now calling to ask for their foreign policy back, because the Cold War has been over for twenty years.[1]

While President Obama's quip featured prominently in highlight reels of the debate, in hindsight his argument that the Cold War had been consigned to the history books for more than twenty years has not aged well in light of more recent events. These include Russia's efforts toward advancing a neo-imperialist expansion into the former Soviet republics, its intervention in the Syrian Civil War, and allegations of collusion between the Russian government and members of President Donald Trump's campaign team during the 2016 U.S. presidential election. President Obama's dismissive stance toward Governor Romney's preoccupation with the security threat posed by Russia was in line

1 "October 22, 2012 Debate Transcript," Commission on Presidential Debates, <www.debates.org/index.php?page=october-22-2012-the-third-obama-romney-presidential-debate.>

however with several international relations scholars in the years following the collapse of the Soviet Union (Grigas 2016; Kalb 2015; Pleshakov 2017; Toal 2016). The end of the Cold War and the perceived triumph of democracy and capitalism marked a decline of interest in Russia and the post-Soviet republics. As American political scientist Agnia Grigas observes, the so-called 'end of history' posited by her American colleague Francis Fukuyama in 1989 gained popularity among international relations scholars and policymakers, and influenced the study of Russia and the former Soviet republics (Grigas 2016: 6). Indeed, there was at the time justifiable cause for optimism. Yet with tensions over the post-Cold War order and post-Soviet borders reemerging, it was clear by the mid-2000s, particularly as President Vladimir Putin consolidated his authority within Russia, that the apparent rapprochement between the Russian Federation and the United States and its allies, however tenuous it might have been, would not last. Revolutions in Ukraine and Georgia would be flashpoints in the relationship between Russia and the United States during the presidency of George W. Bush. Succeeded by President Barack Obama in 2009, the new administration's initial attempts (led by former U.S. Secretary of State Hillary Clinton) at a diplomatic "reset" with Russia during its first term would have limited success, as Russia continued its advance into the post-Soviet states. This push culminated with the annexation of the Crimea region in March of 2014 shortly after Russia hosted the Sochi Winter Olympic Games, as well as the amassing of Russian troops on Ukraine's eastern border. This seriously alarmed NATO members and led to Russia's indefinite suspension from the G8. NATO leaders and several international relations scholars now concur that the Russian government led by Vladimir Putin has emerged as a significant threat to European and American interests (Gardner 2015: 76), and the annexation of Crimea in 2014 has come to serve as a harbinger of the current geopolitical climate.

I provide this very brief overview of perceptions of the threat posed by the Russian Federation in the post-Cold War period, leading up to the 2014 annexation of Crimea, in order to illustrate that while sustained interest in Russia as a geopolitical player and the potential threat it posed to Western liberal democracy might have initially diminished in the years following the collapse of the Soviet Union, this is not true of The Fatima Center, a conservative Catholic organization devoted to the apparitions of the Virgin Mary at Fátima, Portugal in 1917. In the last years of the Cold War, much of the Fatima Center's appeal in the United States stemmed from its fusion of Catholic ultramontanism and American exceptionalism, which were then translated into a Marian apocalyptic historical vision, one that was grounded in the warnings of the Virgin at Fátima regarding the existential threat posed by Soviet Communism. Convinced that the Virgin Mary's request for the consecration of Russia in her messages at Fátima has not been appropriately fulfilled by the pope, the Fatima Center continues (even after the collapse of Soviet Communism in 1991) to demand that the Virgin's warnings regarding Russia be heeded in the pages of its quarterly publication, *The Fatima Crusader*. This has become even more acute as tensions between Russia and Ukraine, and by extension the NATO alliance, have mounted significantly in recent years, particularly with the annexation of the Crimea region by the Russian Federation.

This chapter will examine how this escalation in hostilities, particularly since the annexation of Crimea in 2014, has been interpreted by the Fatima Center as confirmation that the Virgin's message has not been fulfilled, and that the risks presented by the polarization of the Cold War era continue into the early twenty-first century. Surprisingly however given its history, much of the Fatima Center's recent coverage of the topic has stressed that Russia's actions have come from a posture of self-defense, in response to aggressive incursions by the United States and Western Europe into the affairs of Russia and the post-Soviet states. In this chapter I trace how a conservative Catholic publication, once known as the premiere textual body of anti-Soviet polemic in the North American Catholic milieu during the latter half of the Cold War period, has demonstrated itself to be particularly adept in marrying its message to the contemporary geopolitical climate, in this case by increasingly advancing a form of pro-Russian apologetics, particularly in regard to the Russian-Ukrainian conflict.

Fr. Nicholas Gruner and the Fatima Center

Born into an affluent Catholic family in Montreal, Quebec in 1942, Nicholas Gruner graduated with a Bachelor of Commerce from McGill University before deciding to enter the priesthood. Moving his studies to the Pontifical University of St. Thomas Aquinas in Rome, he was eventually ordained in the diocese of Avellino in 1976, and granted permission by the bishop to seek out a diocese in North America to take him on. In the meantime, Gruner, an intense devotee of the Virgin Mary, was offered the opportunity to take charge of the Canadian Pilgrim Virgin statue, one of seventy of Our Lady of Fátima blessed by Pope Paul VI in 1967,[2] and Gruner began touring North America in a van with the statue in order to promote devotion to Fátima (Cuneo 1997: 137). The International Fatima Rosary Crusade was founded by Gruner in 1978, evolving from the Committee for the National Pilgrim Virgin of Canada, although the new apostolate continued with the Pilgrim Virgin tours throughout Canada and the United States. Its headquarters were established at the Fatima Center on a quiet side road in Fort Erie, Ontario near the border between Canada and the

2 For more on the Pilgrim Virgin statues see Morgan 2009.

United States,[3] and over the subsequent forty years expanded with a network of offices in Brazil, India, Ireland, Italy, the Philippines, Spain, and in Coimbra, Portugal, where the last surviving seer, Sr. Lucia, resided in the Carmelite convent.

With its founding the Fatima Center began publishing a free quarterly magazine, *The Fatima Crusader*, billed as "the largest and most influential publication on Fátima in the world."[4] It began as an eight-page black and white newsletter detailing developments on the Pilgrim Virgin tour, accounts of the apparitions at Fátima, and traditional Catholic devotional material, eventually moving to a 64-page color magazine format with the mission of fostering devotion to the Virgin Mary and disseminating the urgent warnings of Our Lady of Fátima. The number of copies of the *Crusader* that the Fatima Centre reports are printed for each issue has fluctuated during the forty years of its publication, from a modest 30,000 in 1982, then sky-rocketing to 500,000 in the mid-1980s during the height of the controversy over the consecration of Russia, then declining significantly to 330,000 by 2010, and now 125,000 as of 2018.[5] The overarching apocalyptic tone that would nourish the publication in the decades to come was made evident in the very first issue in 1978, where, in his inaugural letter to fellow devotees of Our Lady, Fr. Gruner wrote:

> But since the hour is critical She also came to warn us that we must listen to Her, if not out of filial love for Our Mother, then at least out of prudent self-interest. If we ignore Her we do so at our own collective and individual peril. Human history is not only subject to the free will of men but also to God's providence. Through Fátima God is warning us, despite what our press and T.V. may tell us, that the world is in a serious crisis and we are on the brink of destruction. Let us therefore heed Fátima before it is too late.[6]

Fr. Gruner's Fatima Center may be understood as an *audience cult*, according to the criteria established by Stark and Bainbridge, in which members take part primarily through the consumption and patronage of mass media such as television, magazines, and books (Stark & Bainbridge 1985: 209). In the late 1980s the Fatima Center sought to utilize more fully the various media forms at its disposal and extend its reach. In the spring of 1987 Gruner began

3 Although Fr. Gruner is a Canadian citizen and his ministry is based in Ontario, he estimates that over 70% of his supporters are in the United States (Cuneo 1997: 205).

4 *What is the International Fatima Rosary Crusade?* 1998: 3.

5 Nicholas Gruner, "Dear Friends of Our Lady," *The Fatima Crusader* 9 (October-December 1982): l; *Id.*, "You Must Help Break the Plot to Silence Our Lady," *The Fatima Crusader* 21 (November-December 1986): 2; "Help Make a Difference," *The Fatima Crusader* 94 (Spring 2010): 63; and *The Fatima Crusader* 122 (Summer 2018): 31.

6 Nicholas Gruner, "Letter from the Executive Director," *The Fatima Crusader* 1 (Summer 1978): 1.

14.1 Father Nicholas Gruner (right) beside a statue of Our Lady of Fátima blessed by Pope Paul VI, ca 1968.
[The Fatima Center]

broadcasting *Heaven's Peace Plan*, a daily radio program carried by stations in the United States and Canada. He followed this program in September 1989 with the launch of *Fatima: The Moment Has Come*, a half-hour weekly television series featuring conversations with guests on a host of subjects also reflected in the pages of the *Crusader*. Greater accessibility to the Internet in the mid-1990s allowed Fr. Gruner's Fátima ministry to broaden its outreach even further, with their website www.fatima.org emerging as the go-to site for all things Fátima. Since establishing the website in 1996, the Fatima Center has demonstrated significant technological savvy, extensively utilizing social media platforms such as Facebook, Twitter, and YouTube. In the past forty years Fr. Gruner's Center has gradually developed into a significant Marian mass media apostolate on the subject of Fátima, notable by virtue of its militant anticommunism which dovetails with a Marian apocalyptic worldview, and its contestation with the hierarchy of the Catholic Church over varying interpretations of the import of Fátima.

The consecration of Russia

Fr. Gruner and his Fatima Center are perhaps best known for their emphasis on the act of consecration of Russia to the Immaculate Heart of Mary, which was requested as part of the 'Secret of Fátima' during Our Lady of Fátima's apparition to three children at Fátima, Portugal on July 13, 1917. Pope John Paul II first performed a public consecration of Russia and the entire world to Mary on May 13, 1982, at the shrine at Fátima on the sixty-fifth anniversary of the first apparition. At the time this act satisfied Gruner, who in fact praised the consecration as fulfilling Our Lady of Fátima's request that it be performed collegially in spiritual union with all the bishops of the world, whereas an earlier attempt by Pius XII, Gruner argued, was not sufficient in that it was performed by the pope alone.[7] However, Fr. Gruner's stance on the fulfillment of the Virgin's request, in order to stave off quite literally the utter annihilation of the world, began to shift by the spring of 1983. He argued that the collegial consecration of Russia must include every member of the Catholic episcopate, joining with the pope in a simultaneous ceremony on a specific day, and that the pope's 1982 consecration did not meet this stipulation, given the fact that not *every* single bishop in the Catholic Church had joined the pope in the consecration at the same time. As a result, Gruner cautioned, the fate of the entire free world hung in the balance, remaining vulnerable to the militant, atheistic Soviet communists, who would continue unabated to spread hatred, war, persecution, and death, and to accumulate massive stockpiles of nuclear armaments. The solution to the impending nuclear catastrophe from Gruner's perspective, " (...) is not in seeking unilateral disarmament but rather in praying and working so that the Catholic bishops obey Our Lady of Fátima"[8] by consecrating Russia according to the prescription set out in the apparitions. The same issue of the *Crusader* also included the first salvo in what would become an insistent campaign to petition the pope to sufficiently enact the consecration, with a template provided for those wishing to write the pope.[9]

Whether or not this petition campaign had any discernible impact is unclear, but on December 8, 1983, the Catholic feast day of the Immaculate Conception, John Paul II wrote to the bishops requesting their participation in a collegial consecration of the world to Mary on March 25, 1984. Yet in the first issue of *The Fatima Crusader* published following the March 1984 consecration, Fr. Gruner insisted the consecration requested by the Virgin still was not satisfied. Although the 1984 consecration was a step in the right direction, Gruner asserted that given its failure to mention Russia by name, and the belief that

7 Nicholas Gruner, "Dear Friends of Our Lady," *The Fatima Crusader* 9 (October-December 1982): 1.

8 *Id.*, "World Peace Depends on the Catholic Bishops and You," *The Fatima Crusader* 11 (May-July 1983): 4.

9 "What You Must Do," *The Fatima Crusader* 11 (May-July 1983): 24.

not all bishops had participated in the ceremony at the same precise moment, the consecration still waited to be accomplished.[10] Despite every assurance from the Vatican that the Virgin's request for the consecration of Russia had indeed been met, Fr. Gruner continued his one-man quest to broadcast his certain insistence that the consecration had not been realized. He appealed to the pope himself to acknowledge this and perform the consecration again, this time referring to Russia specifically, and compelling the bishops by a papal order to perform the consecration in collegial union with him. A decade later on July 12, 1995 the Center took out an ad in the Roman daily *Il Messaggero*, in order to publish an open letter to John Paul II calling publicly for the consecration according to their interpretation of the request. At the Third Fatima Congress convened by the Center in Rome in November 1996, a formal resolution was passed calling on a date to be set for the proper consecration (naming Russia and in union with the bishops at precisely the same hour) to occur.[11] These demands would continue into the twenty-first century and after the end of John Paul II's papacy, with one issue of the *Crusader* expressing the wish that " (...) Pope Benedict XVI will be the one who finally consecrates Russia to the Immaculate Heart of Mary exactly according to the request of Our Lady of Fátima"[12] upon his election to succeed John Paul II as pope.[13]

The urgency of Fr. Gruner and those who support his Fátima apostolate regarding the consecration of Russia is quite understandable given their highly apocalyptic reading of the messages of Fátima, particularly the second part of the three-part Secret. According to this Secret, if the consecration was not enacted Russia would continue to spread her errors throughout the world, causing more wars, the persecution of the Church, and the annihilation of whole nations. North America and the United States specifically were viewed as particularly vulnerable to this threat due to the perceived marked divergence between the two solitudes, with militantly atheistic Soviet Communism on one end of the spectrum, and Western liberal democracy, informed by a Judeo-Christian ethical framework, on the other. One only needed to look at

10 Nicholas Gruner, "The Pope Moves a Step Closer," *The Fatima Crusader* 15 (April-June 1984): 4.

11 "Fatima 2000: The Third Fatima Congress Resolutions," *The Fatima Crusader* 54 (Winter 1997): 49.

12 "Prayers Urged for Pope Benedict XVI," *The Fatima Crusader* 80 (Summer 2005): 7.

13 For selected additional articles representing the Fatima Center's denial that the consecration has been accomplished (there are indeed many), see: Joseph de Sainte-Marie, "Our Lady of Fatima's Demands Concerning Russia Not Yet Fulfilled," *The Fatima Crusader* 13 (October-December 1983): 10-13; Robert Sullivan, "Russia ls Not Yet Properly Consecrated," *The Fatima Crusader* 24 (March-May 1988): 9; Nicholas Gruner, "We Must Love the Pope, We Must Love the Bishops," *The Fatima Crusader* 33 (Summer 1990): 5-9; Augustine Smith, "News Update on Consecration of Russia," *The Fatima Crusader* 56 (Winter 1998): 44; and "But Wasn't the Consecration Already Done?" *The Fatima Crusader* 91 (February 2009): 23-26.

political developments in the 1980s (from the perspective of the Fatima Center), to be convinced that the consecration of Russia had not been fulfilled and that communism continued unabated to wield its malevolent influence in the world. Stoking anticommunist sentiment amongst its readers in the earliest issues of the *Crusader*, one article claims privileged access to the Red plan to spark revolution in the United States:

> Flying squads of Communists are to seize control of the water supply and shut it off; also the electrical power and gas. This means that no elevators or street cars are to be running. Homes would be without water, fuel or light. It would be impossible to communicate with friends or loved ones, even in another part of the city. Goon squads of professional murderers are to round up the people in business districts. Men are to be held as hostages in some of the larger buildings (...) These are exactly the methods used in Russia, Spain and other places where the Communist Party has been allowed to organize and come to fruition. They finally expect to do the same thing in the United States.[14]

This form of discourse is only a foretaste of the ratcheted up anticommunist rhetoric that follows in issue after issue, imbued with increasingly apocalyptic tones. *The Fatima Crusader* itself is trumpeted as worthy of one's financial support, as it is the only publication disseminating the full and accurate message of Our Lady of Fátima, and the privileged information it offers is needed to insure the faithful against otherwise inevitable communist enslavement.[15] The facts supporting the threat of communist enslavement are understood to be clear. If Russia had been consecrated as requested long ago, the Center maintains, the world would not have witnessed the Second World War, and the hundreds of millions of deaths and persecutions of the Church occurring behind the iron and "bamboo" curtains would have been prevented.[16] The antidote to all this cataclysm is devotion to Mary and the consecration of Russia, and if this is not undertaken immediately, the entire world (most notably the United States and Canada given its primarily North American audience) will be enslaved by Russia.[17]

14 Edward A. Newman, "Has the Crusade of Fatima Failed?" *The Fatima Crusader* 5 (Spring-Summer 1980): 9.

15 "*The Fatima Crusader* Needs Your Help," *The Fatima Crusader* 11 (May-July 1983): 31.

16 Running through many issues of the *Crusader* is a preoccupation with the status of Catholics and their persecution in communist countries, understood as a fulfillment of the Virgin's prophecy at Fatima that the Church would be persecuted if Russia was not converted. For examples, see: "The Continuing Soviet Persecution of Christians," *The Fatima Crusader* (Spring 1981): 19-20; "Communism is Coming Closer to Home," *The Fatima Crusader* 21 (November-December 1986): 7; and "Persecution Towards Catholics in Cuba," *The Fatima Crusader* 66 (Winter 2001): 14.

17 "Ignore the Message of Fatima... At the Cost of Your Enslavement and Nuclear Destruction," *The Fatima Crusader* 15 (April-June 1984): 16.

Most importantly for our purposes here however, the malleability of interpretation rendered possible by apparitions acting as an open plane of meaning not only leads to divergent interpretations, but in some instances, to heated contestation over their orthodoxy or lack thereof. Elements of this contestation have been highlighted, such as the conflicting interpretations over whether or not the consecration of Russia prescribed by the Virgin in the July, 1917 apparition had indeed been fulfilled. What began initially as a rather subdued yet persistent call on the Church by the Fatima Center to finally and sufficiently consecrate Russia to the Immaculate Heart of Mary, would soon balloon into a full-blown contest between Fr. Gruner and Church officials at the highest levels of the Roman Curia (the administrative body of the Church) over the interpretation and fulfillment of the Fátima message.

This rhetorical back and forth between Vatican officials and Gruner's apostolate took place with questions over Gruner's status as a Roman Catholic priest in the backdrop. By 1989, Gruner had yet to submit himself to the authority of a Canadian bishop, functioning as the Catholic equivalent of a "free agent" (Cuneo 1997: 141). As early as 1990, the *Toronto Star* reported that the Roman Catholic Archdiocese of Toronto had cautioned parishioners against donating money to the Fatima Center. It cited a statement from the Archdiocese, which advised the faithful: "In consideration of his present standing and his attitude toward the Church, it is completely inappropriate for members of the faithful to give any money to Father Gruner, his private organization, or his television program."[18] It is important to note here the emphasis on Gruner's Fátima mission as a private organization, presumably outside the purview of the Catholic Church and thus not in communion with it. In the same article it is reported that the Canadian interfaith television network VisionTV had pulled Gruner's television program *Fatima: The Moment Has Come* from its schedule, citing numerous violations of the network's code of ethics including controversial comments on women in the Church and members of the LGBTQ community. A heated tug-of-war between the Church and Gruner over his status continued through the 1990s until September 2001, when the Vatican's Congregation for Clergy announced that Gruner had been suspended by the Avellino, Italy diocese where he was originally ordained. This suspension was then confirmed by a sentence of the Supreme Tribunal of the Apostolic Signatura, barring Gruner from performing the functions of a Catholic priest.[19] In the first issue of the *Crusader* following his suspension, Gruner insisted that due to the intricacies of Canon Law the suspension was invalid and that he was in fact still a Catholic priest in good-standing, and that the announcement by the Congregation for Clergy was a ruse with the principal aim of undermin-

18 "Archdiocese Warns Against Fringe Group," *Toronto Star*, June 17, 1990: 10.

19 "Controversial Fatima Priest Suspended by Vatican," *National Catholic Reporter*, September 28, 2001: 11.

ing the credibility of the true message of Fátima by attacking its most vocal champion.[20]

Marian apparitions, as unbound and complex phenomena lacking self-evident meaning, by their very nature encourage a polyvocal range of discourse. The life and mission of Fr. Gruner's Fatima Center has been marked by claims of possessing ownership over *the* authoritative discourse concerning the message of Fátima and its full and accurate interpretation. Apparition narratives, analogous to Eade and Sallnow's observation regarding Christian pilgrimage, are above all an arena for competing discourses, a site for conflict between orthodoxies, sects, and confessional groups (Eade & Sallnow 1991: 15). The intrigue surrounding such elements of the Fátima apparitions as the release of the Third Secret, and the very prophetic and historical nature of the events associated with the Fátima message, encourage this contestation between rival religious groups. Debates about its Catholic orthodoxy aside,[21] the Fatima Center is a liminal entity occupying the margins of Catholic discourse, contesting the Church hierarchy on the question of Fátima. Today, the Center still possesses an extensive media network through which it solidifies its base of support and broadcasts its competing reading of the Fátima message.

The Fatima Center after the Cold War

The lowering of the hammer and sickle for the last time over the Kremlin compound on December 25, 1991 supposedly heralded the victory of Western liberal democracy over Soviet Communism. The Cold War, it seemed to many, had finally concluded on generally peaceful terms, with the cataclysmic annihilation of nations forewarned by such Marian apocalyptic groups as Fr. Nicholas Gruner's Fatima Center having been prevented. Through arms treaties committing to a significant reduction in nuclear stockpiles and an overall thaw in diplomatic relations between the two principle state actors in the Cold War conflict, the United States and the Soviet Union, the predicted great chastisement with Russia serving as its instrument had been averted. The Catholic Church played a significant role in eroding Soviet influence in several Eastern

20 Coralie Graham, "Don't Shoot the Messenger," *The Fatima Crusader* 69 (Winter 2002): 16.

21 In his study of the ecclesiastical politics surrounding the Marian apparition cult of the Lady of all Nations in Amsterdam, Peter Jan Margry argues that some of the depictions of the Virgin Mary by the cult conflict with Catholic dogma by portraying the Virgin as co-redemptress with Christ. This designation has been the subject of great debate and is not supported by Church teaching. While the Fatima Crusade vehemently contests the Vatican line on the message of Fatima, its rhetoric has not reached the extent of challenging official Church dogma directly (Margry 2009: 249).

bloc countries in the late 1980s, before the Soviet Union itself dissolved, most notably by providing spiritual sustenance to the Solidarity movement in Poland led by Lech Walesa.

Yet for an organization like the Fatima Center, which offered a fervent brand of anticommunism wedded to a Marian apocalyptic cosmology that occupied the locus of its mission and worldview, the historical developments surrounding the ultimate disintegration of the Soviet Union presented a significant dilemma. In the face of this new development, how could the particular form of anticommunist polemic which had nourished their readers over the preceding decade be maintained? Another Catholic organization centered on devotion to Our Lady of Fátima, the New Jersey-based Blue Army, interpreted the collapse of the Soviet Union to underscore the efficacy of the consecration of Russia by John Paul II in 1984, and the relevance of the message of Fátima to Cold War events (Cuneo 1997: 143). For the Fatima Center to adopt a similar position however, would have been to undermine their insistence throughout the 1980s that the consecration of Russia had in fact not been enacted according to the Virgin's prescribed formula at Fátima, thus continuing to expose the Church and the entire world to communist enslavement. Instead, from the early 1990s to the present, Fr. Gruner and his Crusade have insisted that the entire collapse of the Soviet Union and the adoption of liberal democracy and open markets in its former spheres of influence, is a manufactured ploy instigated by the communists. This strategy is intended to deceive the West and assuage its concerns regarding Soviet hostility, lulling it into a state of complacency, before the now-clandestine Soviets ultimately strike.

Prior to the USSR's final dissolution in December 1991, the Fatima Center acknowledged the necessity of repudiating at every turn each historical development pointing toward the gradual closing of the Cold War period. Perestroika (Gorbachev's package of political and economic reforms) was declared by the Fatima Center to be a hoax to appease the West.[22] Rather than eroding, the strength of the Soviet state apparatus was "(...) restructuring, rearranging, reorganizing, and rearming preparatory to its final thrust for world domination in the next five to ten years. Communism is not dead, as long as the Marxist-Leninist religion and dream of world conquest lives on in the minds of its leaders in the Kremlin."[23] The reforms initiated by Gorbachev were viewed, as one headline in *The Fatima Crusader* states, as "perversion, not conversion."[24] This perspective rejected the historical reading of the Blue Army and other groups devoted to Fátima that developments in the USSR and Eastern Europe

22 "Gorbachev's Perestroika is a Hoax," *The Fatima Crusader* 29 (September-November 1989): 2.

23 Donald S. McAivany, "Mesmerized by the Bear: The Great Soviet Deception," *The Fatima Crusader* 33 (Summer 1990): 25.

24 John Cotter, "The Changes by Russia Mean Perversion, Not Conversion," *The Fatima Crusader* 36 (Spring 1991): 13.

were the fruits borne out of the 1984 consecration and general adherence to Our Lady of Fátima's message. In subsequent issues, Fr. Gruner and his Fatima Center continued to steadfastly deny that Soviet Communism had indeed collapsed and no longer posed a clear and present danger to Catholicism and to the West in the manner it once had.[25] Current Russian President Vladimir Putin was accused in the early 2000s of being "the new Stalin," reassembling the neverquite-dismantled authoritarianism of the Soviet period and silencing dissent. The role of Putin in Russian public life was pointed to by the Fatima Center as evidence that the consecration of Russia has not been fulfilled and that Russia is about to embark on a reinvigorated quest to enslave the world.[26]

The Fatima Center's insistence on the continuing menace posed by Soviet Communism in the post-Cold War period is not unique to this organization. Rather, it is shared by other apocalyptic movements in North America as well, both religious and secular. Daniel Wojcik helpfully provides a larger context for this denial of Soviet Communism's collapse in his study of apocalyptic beliefs in the United States in the twentieth century. He notes that many of those from across the spectrum of religious belief and secular conviction, who hold apocalyptic worldviews that include a role for the Soviet Union in ushering in the end times, similarly view US-Russian relations after 1991 as a "false peace" before the end of the world. Rather than a refutation of their apocalyptic vision of the Cold War, the collapse of the Soviet Union is only the latest fulfillment of God's eschatological plan (Wojcik 1997: 153).

Although the Fatima Center maintains a Marian apocalyptic worldview that denies the collapse of Soviet Communism and insists that Russia will serve as the instrument of chastisement, inevitably the progression of historical events necessitate a re-evaluation of that world view. Regarding the adaptability of apocalyptic narratives, Wojcik notes: "Interpreters of apocalyptic prophecy are masterful *bricoleurs*, skillfully recasting elements and themes within the constraints of their respective traditions and reconfiguring them to formulate new, meaningful end times scenarios" (Wojcik 1997: 148). Fr. Gruner and the Fatima Center likewise have demonstrated a certain degree of malleability in altering the focus of their rhetoric to cohere with larger contemporary social concerns. Since 1991 they have revealed the core interpretation of the message of Fátima they had developed up to that point to possess a wide panoply of meanings, addressing not only the cosmic consequences

25 For additional *Crusader* articles on the continuing communist menace, see: Donald S. McAlvany, "America Disarms While Russia Still Prepares for War," *The Fatima Crusader* 39 (Winter 1992): 10-12; Paul Kramer, "Paving the Way for Antichrist: The Fatima Consecration Hoax Continues," *The Fatima Crusader* 41 (Summer 1992): 18-23; Augustine Smith, "Communism is Dead... Again," *The Fatima Crusader* 61 (Autumn 1999): 28-39; and "The Ongoing Threat from Russia," *The Fatima Crusader* 71 (Autumn 2002): special supplement.

26 *Fatima* 2008: 45.

of the struggle between Judeo-Christian liberal democracy and atheistic Soviet Communism during much of the twentieth century, but also containing more tangible social implications. The Center has broadened its apocalyptic rhetoric in order to acknowledge a great range of social ills, while still clinging to an anticommunist stance as the locus through which all other issues are interpreted. A broad spectrum of social evils are incorporated into the pre-existing discourse of the Crusade as consequences of the refusal of many to adhere to the Virgin's requests at Fátima, and as the first signs of the impending cataclysm to fall upon humanity if Russia is not consecrated and the reign of Christ restored. Essentially, every possible threat is melded into the Crusade's anticommunist apocalyptic vision, in order to ensure its continuing relevance during the so-called "culture wars."

Throughout the 1990s and beyond the Fatima Center tapped with greater frequency into the social conservative public discourse concerning such topics as abortion, homosexuality, sex education, and the erosion of the nuclear family. In concert with these primarily domestic moral threats, new international institutional threats would also enter the ring allied with communism and indeed springing from it, including the UN and the supposed construction of a New World Order, both seen as additional fulfillments of apocalyptic prophecy. This multitude of social ills, still linked to the errors of communism and viewed as the tangible consequences of ignoring the Virgin's prophetic warnings at Fátima, could not in and of themselves legitimate the continuing relevance of the Center's interpretation of the Fátima message as the twentieth century gave way to the twenty-first. The rhetoric lining the pages of the *Crusader* continued to hammer away at the threat of communism post-1991, a threat remaining unchecked as a result of the inability of the pope to sufficiently consecrate Russia to Mary. Nevertheless, there is a discernible acknowledgment on the part of Gruner and the Fatima Center that not only did the moral threats which typically occupied the minds of Catholic conservatives need to be incorporated into the preexisting apocalyptic cosmological framework of the Crusade to supplement its anticommunist focus, but so too did new monolithic international organizations need to be raised up as strawmen, as the latest fulfillments of the Virgin's warnings.

The Fatima Center's turn toward a greater emphasis on social issues and moral questions I suggest has aligned it more closely with mainstream Catholic conservatives and to some degree with official Church teaching. Similarly, the Crusade's increasing focus on the threats posed by the United Nations and the development of a New World Order parallels the convictions of other non-Catholic religious and secular apocalyptic discourses. As Wojcik notes, post-Cold War apocalyptic prophecy has generally become increasingly preoccupied with the dangers of political and economic unification. Many contemporary groups that adhere to this apocalyptic vision see the UN, the

New World Order, the signing of the North American Free Trade Agreement (NAFTA), the reunification of Germany, the creation of the European Union, the International Monetary Fund (IMF) and the World Bank all as signs of the coming one-world economy and one-world government overseen by the Antichrist (Wojcik 1997: 160). Viewed in this context, the malleable rhetoric of the Fatima Center's apocalyptic discourse following the end of the Cold War era is an extreme Catholic articulation of larger, more general apocalyptic trends in North American conservative worldviews.

Through its ability to fuse apocalyptic polemics with a religiously-informed social conservatism, which finds greater expression in the *Crusader* beginning in the early 1990s, the Fatima Center also taps into and in fact coheres closely with existing apocalyptic and socially conservative discourses formulated by Protestant Christian fundamentalist groups in the United States during the latter half of the twentieth century. Some of the most visible conservative Protestant leaders and their associated movements, such as Jerry Falwell and his political Moral Majority coalition,[27] and host of the Christian television program *The 700 Club* Pat Robertson, among others, share much of the same worldview and ethos as the Fatima Center, without the Catholic Marian gloss.

Although the Fatima Center and Protestant fundamentalist groups do share an apocalyptic vision of the Cold War period, their alignment is much clearer in regard to their apocalyptic rhetoric which interprets social ills (perceived from a religious and socially conservative vantage-point) and disasters as divine chastisements for not adhering to the will of God. Falwell's Moral Majority movement was founded in 1979, and was certainly more politically insistent than Gruner's Fatima Center in its public advocacy on socially conservative issues, such as opposition to abortion, promotion of the traditional family, opposition to homosexuality, and the call for the inclusion of prayer in the rhythm of the public school system (Bruce 1987: 184). Paralleling the Fatima Center's consequential reading of the HIV/AIDS epidemic,[28] a 1989 study of popular support for the platform of the Moral Majority found that many of its supporters held the belief that AIDS was God's punishment for homosexuality (Wilcox 1992: 212).

A generally congruent religiously-informed understanding of the September 11th attacks is held by Gruner and his Fatima Center. The key difference between the Protestant rhetoric and that of the Fatima Center is that the same type of narrative espoused by Falwell and Robertson was neatly folded into the Center's pre-existing Marian apocalyptic paradigm founded upon the apparitions of the Virgin Mary at Fátima. In an article leaving little room for ambiguity regarding the *Crusader*'s reading of the attacks, entitled "A Taste of Annihila-

27 For an ethnographic account of Falwell and his ministry, see Harding 2000.
28 *Heaven's Peace Plan*, Episode #130, 1987.

tion," September 11 is placed within the *Crusader*'s larger historical frame, as the latest evidence that the Virgin's messages have not been adhered to:

> Ground Zero also gives us a foretaste of hell. The raging fires, the intense heat, the loss of thousands of lives with no warning, and perhaps for some, little time to adequately prepare themselves to meet God (...) God does not want even one of His children to go to Hell. It is out of His love and compassion for us, that He allows this foretaste of Hell to happen, so that upon seeing and experiencing the Hell on earth, we will take heed and repent in time to avoid the Hell of eternity (...) Ground Zero is only the beginning. Our Lady warned us of annihilation of entire nations if we do not obey her Fátima requests.[29]

Note that this selection does not include a laundry list of sinful lifestyles and liberal interest groups calling for God's retribution, as Falwell and Robertson suggested in the days following the attacks (Lincoln 2003: 110), framing September 11 as an act of divine retributive justice. Given the Fatima Center's incorporation of a socially conservative agenda beginning in the early 1990s however, the same message of divine retribution is certainly implied by the call for repentance and obedience to the Virgin's requests. At the most basic level, the Fatima Center shares with conservative Protestant groups the view that September 11 was a cataclysmic event with significance that extends far beyond geopolitical concerns. More importantly from this shared perspective, September 11 was a sign of God's displeasure with the world, particularly America. Within the specific framework of the Fatima Center's Marian apocalyptic discourse, September 11 was an urgent reminder that the consecration of Russia must be fulfilled lest similar events of even greater magnitude rain down upon the earth.

Consistent with its view of a whole host of social ills as the "errors of Communism" spreading throughout the world unchecked, the Center did not hesitate to expose the supposed Russian involvement in the September 11 attacks. The *Crusader* charged that Russian criminal organizations supplied Osama bin Laden and Al-Qaeda with the necessary components for chemical, biological and even nuclear weapons, and that this connection constitutes unimpeachable evidence that the consecration of Russia was never fully enacted by the pope, allowing Russia to enable terrorists to attack the United States.[30]

29 Coralie Graham, "A Taste of Annihilation," *The Fatima Crusader* 69 (Winter 2002): 5.

30 Christopher A. Ferrara, "The Russian Connection to bin Laden: More Evidence Surfaces," *The Fatima Crusader* 69 (Winter 2002): 9.

2014 annexation of Crimea

Although in the months following the September 11 attacks Fr. Gruner and the Fatima Center alleged that the terrorist strike bore all the hallmarks of Russian involvement, and that Vladimir Putin constituted a "new Stalin," the organization has demonstrated a certain degree of malleability in altering the focus of its rhetoric to cohere with contemporary geopolitical preoccupations. Nowhere is this more evident than in the Center's treatment of the 2014 Russian annexation of Crimea in the pages of the *Fatima Crusader*. What is most interesting however in the Center's analysis is that while Russia still serves as the instrument of global chastisement, according to Fr. Gruner and the *Crusader* it is the United States and its NATO allies, and Ukraine itself, which have backed Russia into a corner, isolating, weakening, and humiliating it in the years following the collapse of the Soviet Union, provoking it to lash out in justified retaliation. The Fatima Center's Spring 2014 issue of the *Crusader*, released just weeks after the Russian annexation of the Crimean peninsula was entitled "Emergency Issue: Only She Can Save You!" and made clear from the outset that while Russia continued to spread its errors across the globe, it only did so in response to provocation from the West, which it saw as driving the world toward disaster by its exceptionalism and its unauthorized military interventions in other nations. The Center accused the CIA, the US State Department, and George Soros among others of orchestrating the Euromaidan protests[31] in Western Ukraine that led to the ouster of Ukrainian President Viktor Yanukovych, who sought closer ties with Russia.[32] One article in particular is worth quoting at length, for even prior to the current climate where accusations of fake news proliferate, the *Crusader* cautioned its readers that they were being sold a false narrative by the media and their own government regarding the annexation of Crimea:

> The same script (...) has been handed to all of Washington's puppets, and everywhere in the West the message is the same. "Putin invaded and annexed Crimea, Putin is determined to rebuild the Soviet Empire, Putin must be stopped..." The transparent lie that Russia sent an army into Ukraine and annexed Crimea is now accepted as fact everywhere in the West, even among critics of U.S. policy toward Russia (...) Obama says that Western ideals are challenged by self-determination in Crimea. Russia, Obama says, must be punished by the West for permitting Crimeans to exercise

31 The Euromaidan protests refer to a series of demonstrations in Kiev, Ukraine beginning in November 2013, which protested the government of President Viktor Yanukovych and its decision to suspend the movement toward greater association with the European Union, in favour of Russia. It culminated in February-March 2014 with the ouster of President Yanukovych and the annexation of Crimea by the Russian Federation.

32 "War 2014? Russia, Ukraine and the Third Secret of Fatima," *The Fatima Crusader* 109 (Summer 2014): 40-41.

> self-determination. The return of a Russian province on its own volition to its mother country where it existed for 200 years is presented by Obama as a dictatorial, anti-democratic act of tyranny.[33]

While the Fatima Center's Marian apocalypticism during and after the Cold War period certainly stressed that, in the polarity between American democracy and Soviet atheistic communism during the Cold War, God clearly possessed a preferential option for the former, it certainly did not shield it from condemnation, particularly on social issues such as abortion and gay rights. What is notable here however is that, in clear contradistinction to its traditional anticommunist rhetoric, Vladimir Putin and the Russian Federation are vociferously defended against the 'fake news' of the Western powers and the mainstream media establishment.

In recent years, this has now extended beyond the annexation of Crimea to include a defense of Russia's support for the regime of President Bashar al-Assad in Syria,[34] as well as celebrating the Kremlin's domestic policies placing strict limitations on the provision and advertising of abortion services, the criminalization of so-called homosexual propaganda, and laws enshrining the primacy of the Russian Orthodox Church in the cultural life of the nation.[35] Most strikingly perhaps given the history of the Fatima Center, the heading in an article from the Summer 2014 issue of the *Crusader* asks "Are the Errors of Russia Now More Our Own than Russia's?" and proceeds to list a litany of intrinsic moral evils now pervading the United States and the West more broadly. Subsequent passages from the article encapsulate well the Fatima Center's current interpretation of the geopolitical machinations between Putin's Russia and the West:

> The stench of Western corruption seems now to have already more than satisfied those who orchestrated the great fall of our once Christian society. We have fallen so far, in fact, that Russia itself is able to claim a moral high-ground (comparatively speaking) while reproaching the West for its own apparently greater decadence. Russia, the Bear – the monster, whose brutality and atrocities against Hungary in 1956 and against Czechoslovakia in 1968 will never be forgotten – is today rather easily able to justify its actions in Crimea (where virtually not a shot was fired in expelling the Ukrainian military from the peninsula, and where Russia's vital interests were threatened by the West's reckless pursuit of its own strategic interests).
>
> President Putin himself, whose public demeanor speaks of self-discipline and stern common sense, stands in stark contrast to the hapless U.S. Presi-

33 *Ibid.*, 53-54.

34 James Hanisch, "Has World War III Begun?" *The Fatima Crusader* 106 (Summer 2013): 59.

35 "Our Lady's E-Newsletter: March 2014," *The Fatima Center*, <http://archive.fatima.org/news/enlarchive/enl0314.asp>.

> dents of recent years – from the brazen adulteries of draft-dodger Bill Clinton, to the practically self-admitted warmongering of George W. Bush and the shameless immorality and entitlement championed by Barrack Obama.
>
> The United States' godless domestic and foreign policies have been reshaping America's image in the rest of the world's eyes for many years now. International polling consistently reveals a growing popular sentiment that the United States is the greatest threat to world peace today. President Obama's determination to launch a military strike against Syria in September of last year was a case in point for President Putin, who rightly pointed out that it is the U.S. which is driving the world toward disaster by its notion of exceptionalism and its unauthorized military interventions in other nations.[36]

Nevertheless, it should be noted that while more recent issues of the *Crusader* have framed Putin and the Russian government in a softer light vis-à-vis the decadence of the West, it remains adamant that world peace will not be fully realized until the Virgin Mary's request for the consecration of Russia to Her Immaculate Heart is finally fulfilled, and continues to advocate for the current pope, Francis, to do so.

I wish to conclude by highlighting that while the Fatima Center is often viewed as a marginal, if not extreme element of Catholic life in North America, its marriage of political and religious concerns in the Cold War era, and its treatment of more recent geopolitical flashpoints such as the Russian annexation of Crimea, continues to appeal to a significant constituency, and thus represents the latest articulation of a distinct and long-standing stream of apocalyptic discourse within the Catholic cult of the Virgin Mary. Perhaps most significantly given the concerns of this chapter, Marian apparitions in nearly every case occur and proliferate during times of great social, political, and economic upheaval, when the Church in particular is understood to be threatened by malevolent forces within and without. Since the Reformation the Virgin Mary has been promoted by the Church as a spiritual weapon against the Protestant Reformers, rationalists, Masons, secular humanists, up to socialists and communists more recently (Kane 2004: 101), at times descending from heaven herself to reassure, caution, and instruct the faithful. William Christian notes in his analysis of the incredible proliferation of apparitions in Southern Europe in the mid-twentieth century the particular efficacy of these apparitions in times of crisis. Christian writes that their value is:

> (...) that it is much simpler, if the visionaries can be believed, to hear what God has to say through his messengers about such-and-such a place right now, than to try to extrapolate correct conduct from what Christ said two thousand years ago and the accumulated wisdom of the Church (Christian 1984: 249).

36 James Hanisch, "Has World War III Begun?" *The Fatima Crusader* 106 (Summer 2013): 57.

The Virgin Mary has long been associated with apocalyptic imagery and cosmological narrative, and especially since the mid-nineteenth century, Marian apparitions have been perceived by Catholics as the primary vehicle for divine communications admonishing the world for its sins, comforting the Church in the face of social and political unrest, and delivering prophetic warnings regarding cataclysmic events that will occur if the heavenly warnings are not heeded. Thus, while there are indeed points of correlation between Protestant and Marian forms of apocalypticism, the latter, by virtue of its long history within the Catholic tradition and the fact that the cult of the Virgin Mary is a significant feature of the historical divergence between the two branches of Christianity, constitutes a distinct form of apocalyptic discourse. The Fatima Center is only the latest articulation of this distinctly Marian form of apocalypticism.

Following Christian, I contend that Fr. Nicholas Gruner's Fatima Center, marked by its apocalyptic Marianism, conservative Catholicism, and its particular socio-political context, provides a privileged vantage-point from which to examine the process by which a religious message communicated during an encounter with a vision becomes an anticommunist polemic which conforms to the social and political climate of the time. But it also allows us to examine the ways in which such mediums and their message can be particularly adept in marrying their cosmological vision to the contemporary geopolitical climate, in this case as I have outlined in this chapter, by increasingly advancing a form of pro-Russian apologetics, particularly in regard to the 2014 annexation of Crimea and the broader and ongoing Russian-Ukrainian conflict.

The visions at Ezkioga, Spain, in 1931 documented by Christian allowed concerned Catholics to make sense of the political unrest surrounding the formation of the Second Spanish Republic. The earlier apparitions of the Virgin Mary to Bernadette Soubirous at Lourdes punctuated the French transition to a secular republican style of governance. And so too, the visions and messages associated with the Virgin Mary at Fátima in 1917 have provided a framework within which concerned Catholics in the United States and Canada during the Cold War and onward have been able to make sense of the modern world. The apparitions have enabled Fr. Nicholas Gruner and supporters of his Fatima Center to construct a Marian apocalyptic worldview uniquely suited to the task of making the Cold War polarity between the United States and the Soviet Union conform to a historically interpreted cosmology. The Center fomented Catholic anticommunism in the face of the Soviet threat, and when this threat diminished, proved itself adaptable to the broader social concerns of Christian conservatives. In the development and dissemination of its apocalyptic worldview, the Fatima Center has seemingly relished its status occupying the margins of the Church, as a liminal entity often straddling the line between conservative Catholicism and outright defiance of ecclesiastical authority. With its continuing ability to adapt the core tenets of its worldview to the pressing crises of the day, such as the 2014 annexation of Crimea, and to exploit the latest communication tools to further broadcast its interpretation of the full message of Fátima, the Fatima Center constitutes a significant, albeit extreme example, of apocalyptic belief within the Catholic cult of the Virgin Mary.

BIBLIOGRAPHY

Agnew, Michael. 2010. *"Russia Will Be Converted": The Fatima Crusade's Marian Apocalyptic Discourse During and After the Cold War*. Unpublished master's thesis, McMaster University, Hamilton, Canada.

Bruce, Steve. 1987. "The Moral Majority: The Politics of Fundamentalism in Secular Society." In *Studies in Religious Fundamentalism*, edited by Lionel Caplan, 177-194. Albany, NY: State University of New York Press.

Christian Jr., William. 1984. "Religious Apparitions and the Cold War in Southern Europe." In *Religion, Power and Protest in Local Communities: The Northern Shore of the Mediterranean*, edited by Eric R. Wolf, 239-266. Berlin: Mouton.

Cuneo, Michael. 1997. *The Smoke of Satan: Conservative and Traditionalist Dissent in Modern American Catholicism*. New York: Oxford University Press.

Eade, John, and Michael J. Sallnow. 1991. *Contesting the Sacred: The Anthropology of Christian Pilgrimage*. London: Routledge.

Fatima: Only Way to World Peace. Fort Erie, ON: The Fatima Center, 2008.

Gardner, Hall. 2015. *Crimea, Global Rivalry, and the Vengeance of History*. New York: Palgrave Macmillan.

Grigas, Agnia. 2016. *Beyond Crimea: The New Russian Empire*. New Haven, CT: Yale University Press.

Harding, Susan Friend. 2000. *The Book of Jerry Falwell: Fundamentalist Language and Politics*. Princeton, NJ: Princeton University Press.

Kalb, Marvin. 2015. *Imperial Gamble: Putin, Ukraine, and the New Cold War*. Washington: Brookings Institution Press.

Kane, Paula M. 2004. "Marian Devotion Since 1940: Continuity or Casualty?" In *Habits of Devotion: Catholic Religious Practice in Twentieth-Century America*, edited by James M. O'Toole, 89-129. Ithaca, NY: Cornell University Press.

Lincoln, Bruce. 2003. *Holy Terrors: Thinking About Religion after September 11th*. Chicago: University of Chicago Press.

Margry, Peter Jan. 2009. "Paradoxes of Marian Apparitional Contestation: Networks, Ideology, Gender, and The Lady of All Nations." In *Moved by Mary: The Power of Pilgrimage in the Modern World*, edited by Anna-Karina Hermkens, Willy Jansen and Catrien Notermans, 182-199. Aldershot, UK: Ashgate.

Morgan, David. 2009. "Aura and the Inversion of Marian Pilgrimage: Fatima and Her Statues." In *Moved by Mary: The Power of Pilgrimage in the Modern World*, edited by Anna-Karina Hermkens, Willy Jansen and Catrien Notermans, 49-65. Aldershot, UK: Ashgate.

Pleshakov, Constantine. 2017. *The Crimean Nexus: Putin's War and the Clash of Civilizations*. New Haven, CT: Yale University Press.

Stark, Rodney, and William Sims Bainbridge. 1985. *The Future of Religion: Secularization, Revival, and Cult Formation*. Berkeley, CA: University of California Press.

Toal, Gerard. 2017. *Near Abroad: Putin, the West, and the Contest over Ukraine and the Caucasus*. Oxford: Oxford University Press.

What is the International Fatima Rosary Crusade? Fort Erie, ON: The Fatima Centre, 1998.

Wilcox, Clyde. 1992. *God's Warriors: The Christian Right in Twentieth-Century America*. Baltimore, MD: Johns Hopkins University Press.

Wojcik, Daniel. 1997. *The End of the World as We Know It: Faith, Fatalism, and Apocalypse in America*. New York: New York University Press.

15
CONCLUSION AND OUTLOOK

PETER JAN MARGRY

When historian Dianne Kirby called for greater scholarly interest in the role of religion during the Cold War in 2002, her focus was on Christianity in the West.[1] But as the Cold War was a worldwide phenomenon, Philip Muehlenbeck (2012) advocated a shift to a global outlook, including a pluri-religious perspective. In contrast with Kirby, he also warned against overemphasizing the influence of religion during that period. *Cold War Mary* mediates between and synthesizes these two views. It adopts a broad global scope, but at the same time, from the religious perspective, it interrogates the issue of militant (Catholic) Marianism and the instrumentalization of the spiritual and the supernatural. The results confirm the respective roles played by religion, devotionalism and Church politics during the Cold War, especially the role of Catholicism. Its scope is mainly on one single specific expression of the broader Cold War drive: the fight against communism. It shows how the cult of a saint, specifically of the Virgin Mary, was instrumentalized and positioned as a Cold War stronghold within the wider anti-atheist politics of Catholicism. Mary, and popular devotion to her, were the best means to connect and mobilize ordinary believers against the threats of communism. Her role as *protectrix* and warrior was performed on the local level, but also played out in interaction with the institutional Church, both the center, the pope and the Vatican, and the dioceses or national churches.

1 Kirby concluded that religion "mattered a great deal" during the Cold War (2013 [2002]: 20).

The combative role of Mary during the Cold War was embedded in and constructed on the basis of a long Christian tradition of fighting atheism. In reaction to the institutionalization of socialism and communism in nation states, in particular since the Russian revolution (1917), the Catholic Church had begun to create a new anticommunist narrative for the world community of Catholics. *Cold War Mary* shows how Our Lady was recast and used in various ways and in different national settings, from as early as the 1930s on. Later, during the Second Word War, Mary was transformed from a solitary, traditional representation of popular religion and devotionalism into a political and even militant instrument for protecting the faith. The adaptation and manipulation of the messages of Our Lady of Fátima in 1942 proved to be a crucial step in the creation of Mary as a Cold War warrior. The research presented here asserts that these new prophecies, and the symbols and visualization of the new Mary of Fátima, were pivotal to realizing Catholicism's anticommunist potential during the Cold War. The new strategy was mainly forged on the basis of the later Fátima revelations, and Fátima is therefore the major thread in this book. Mary was the spiritual weapon that could be wielded without violence and without immediately endangering the precarious status quo of various Christian communities in the new world order of those years. Nevertheless, although Marianism was applied only as a spiritual weapon, it did have transnational effects in the geopolitical sphere. As the contributions in this volume demonstrate, Mary's impact, whether through individual devotion or Church policies, on Catholic communities in the 'free world' and in the communist countries proved surprisingly strong. This has necessitated a revision of the scholarly view on how 'Catholicism', with its devotional strategies under the aegis of Mary, influenced the Church's anticommunist strategy (cf. Goubert & Cristiani 1952: 225).

With regard to the institutional Church, as a universal institution, the Vatican actively tried to protect its flock from destabilization by propaganda for or the forced imposition of atheism. The pope, especially Pius XII, was the principal agent of the Church in this respect. The Holy See in fact worked mainly through diplomacy and public letters and encyclicals, and was fearful of offending Russia and thus jeopardizing the interests of Catholics in the Soviet Union and its satellite states. However, strongly influenced as they were by their personal experiences of communism and their deep personal piety toward the Mother of God, both Pius XII and, later, John Paul II reposed exceptional trust in the power of Mary. Mary inspired and apparently supported them in their public stance against atheism. At the same time, the paradox of the Vatican, which encouraged its followers to fight against communism while restraining its own hand, flowed from the Vatican's diplomatic and political role on the world stage, a role that was too important to endanger.

The strongest measure the Vatican took was its 1949 decree excommunicating Catholics who defended or spread communist ideas, which was intended to prevent people from becoming atheists. Later, in 1955, Pius XII unilaterally proclaimed a 'ceasefire', stopping the organization of anti-atheist crusades. It was only under John Paul II, with his revival of anticommunist sentiments, that the Vatican engaged in direct action against communist rule. His drive for religious freedom played "a major political role" in bringing down communism in Eastern Europe.[2] Whether the ultimate fall of the USSR in 1991 was due to the influence of Our Lady of Fátima and the proper consecration of Russia to her Immaculate Heart is a long and ongoing debate among devotees. In any case, the anticommunist politics within Catholicism played a significant part.

In everyday practice, lay involvement and the lay Catholic Action movement played major roles at grassroots level in the Western world. The most effective way of combating communism was the "exemplary experience of a healthy and powerful Christendom" that every Catholic should have. This principle left no room for doubt and was meant to drive out the 'communist devil' through prayer and self-abnegation.[3] In other cases it was necessary to use the available spiritual armory: devotional exercises or practices such as prayer, the invocation of Mary, and rituals and events. This message did not fall on deaf ears among Catholics, quite a few of whom successfully prayed to Mary or organized events and pilgrimages to hold communism at bay.

A second result of the refashioning of Fátima was that these Portuguese apparitions assumed an exemplary function as a 'template' upon which many subsequent Marian apparitions and messages were based, even to the present day. This explains why, in Spain for example, Mary's active warning interventions predate the usual beginning of the Cold War. In a way this is also true for Belgium, where a wave of apparitions during the interwar years was initially linked to the rise of right-wing Belgian politics and of Nazism, but they were reframed by the local bishops after 1942 in the wake of the emergence of the new anticommunist Fátima.

The Vatican's formal position of restraint made it difficult to give official endorsement to lay and grassroots public protests against persecution, or to approve militantly anti-atheist campaigns related to the Fátima movement. Successful movements that operated internationally, such as the Blue Army or the Legion of Mary, with their mass anticommunist events, acted with an ambiguous mandate from Rome. Although the Vatican in fact favored these movements as forms of Catholic action, it was also wary of expressing its support publicly. Nevertheless, the explicit and implicit anticommunism manifested

2 Both scholars and contemporary leaders such as Michael Gorbachev endorse this view (Coppa 2010: 348-349).

3 Final answer in the brochure "A Hundred questions and answers on Russian Communism" by Catholic Action (Van Son 1936: 31-32).

by local Marian movements and actions, for instance the popular *Peregrinatio Mariae* processions with the statue of Our Lady of Fátima, demonstrated their influence east of the Iron curtain, and the regimes there were on their guard against such "counterrevolutionary" initiatives and their destabilizing effects. These movements, including the Family Rosary Crusade, were not just anti-Russian, but sent an equally strong message to Western Catholics themselves not to fall into the temptation of socialist ideas or secularization.

Apart from the Vatican's own international policy, this volume's findings show that there was no formal orchestration of or directive policy on anticommunist activities in the various dioceses. None of the contributors to this volume have observed any signs of coordination, either on a national, supranational, or international level, of the Catholic response to communism after Pius XI's call or during the Cold War. Protective initiatives or the monitoring of Catholic communities were left in the hands of the autonomous national hierarchies and of individual bishops or religious orders. Among the latter category, individual religious sometimes developed their own personal mission within the great endeavor. The creation of the Dutch *Pentagon* is one example of such a grassroots initiative, taken to mobilize Catholics across the nation to help protect their faith and their Church. Just as with the postwar apparitional wave in Germany, such initiatives were regularly ignored or suppressed by the Church itself, for fear that they might undermine the position of the local Church or obstruct the European ecumenical movement. Religious were also involved in organizing the international Marian lay crusades and the Legion of Mary.

The militant ideas in Grignion de Montfort's book *True Devotion to Mary* proved to be an important source of inspiration not only for the Montfort Missionaries but also for many lay believers. Prior to Fátima and again during the Cold War, this book served as a motivational source for people who regarded Mary as the leading protagonist in a society under threat from secularism. This popular text can also explain why Mary became so successful and why she continued to inspire visionaries, devotees and clergy so deeply from the late 1800s onward.

With the possible exception of Ireland and Portugal, where Catholicism or Marianism was strongly interwoven with national politics, Catholic grassroots initiatives received no support from, and were not connected with governments or their national politics. But the reverse – reactions to national politics – did occur, as the anti-right-wing apparitions in prewar Belgium show for example.

From a geographical perspective, it is obvious that deploying the 'Marian weapon' was not just a European strategy, as an equally militant role was ascribed to Mary in the Americas, in Africa, and in Asia. However, in terms of numbers and impact, the principal area of Mary's interventional presence lay in the West rather than in communist countries. The religiously divided Eastern Bloc and, as the chapter on Poland demonstrates, the suppression of Catholic practice and devotionalism in the Catholic countries there, made it difficult to instrumentalize Mary more widely, although more research is needed here to obtain the full picture.

For the most part, Mary's personal interventions and appearances occurred in the West. On the one hand, they warned Church leadership and national governments not to underestimate the communist threat and to be aware of unrest in society, and on the other, they reminded or warned ordinary Catholics not to believe communist propaganda, not to give in to the temptation to adopt communist ideas, and not to lapse into secularism.

Events surrounding apparitions of the Virgin created mass mobilization movements in countries such as Belgium, Italy, Spain, the Philippines, and the United States, with an even larger mediatized audience at a distance. The mass character of these events underlines the importance of modern apparitions as meaningful interventions. Devotionally and psychologically, Mary's presence influenced an important part of the faithful in their daily views of society. Admonished by Mary, believers gathered collectively in prayer. During the Cold War years, Mary became more expressive, articulating more substantial messages. She no longer uttered only a few words about prayer and penance, or gave single-sentence theological messages, as she had once done in Lourdes, but instead delivered elaborate instructions on how to act, and how to correct others who no longer practiced the faith properly, while threatening doom if they were to fall back into apostasy. The postwar boom made the communist regimes even warier of new such supernatural events within their borders. Despite the fact that these rarely contained specifically anticommunist references, these governments took measures to prevent or suppress new apparitional shrines that contested the ideology of the state as they belonged to the strongest agents of popular Marian religiosity.

The power of apparitions sometimes caused also concern to the Church itself, which was occasionally more apprehensive about internal disturbance and the deviant influence which the visions might exert through the actions of the Church's own believers than about the threat of Russia. The paradox points at the practical objections to participation in world politics while trying to uphold high principles and religiously inspired goals. The power of the apparitions lies mainly in their political symbolic value: a critique of the communist regimes, and a support and example for Catholics east of the Iron Curtain. Moreover, to a large extent they were a strong signal to Catholics in the West against losing the faith.

The various initiatives and events described in this volume support Powers's thesis (1995) on the plurality of anticommunism. Catholic anticommunisms were extremely varied, sprang from different motives, and various differences on a regional and national level can be distinguished. A focus on the local and grassroots levels, based on local archives and new types of sources, has made it possible to discover that 'the Catholic Church's' anticommunism was indeed pluralist in its forms of expression and idiosyncratic in its individual manifestations. The case of the Philippines adds yet another kind of pluralism. Research of the localization and adaptation of Cold War Marian events shows that these could be interpreted differently by different ethnic groups and in different cultural contexts, depending on the local, national or international perspective. It is not the only case that shows the importance of research in local archives.

Religious or Marian anticommunism seemed to have perished with the fall of communism and the end of the Cold War in 1989/1991. But although communist rule may have come to an end in Eastern Europe, totalitarianism seems to have remained, under a seemingly democratic cloak, while communism itself was never fully eradicated. The ideology remained dominant in countries such as China, Vietnam, Cuba, Laos, and North Korea. A new world order did arise, however, in which the binary theist-atheist frame was replaced by a multifocal one with various ethnic and religious alliances and nationalisms.

Initially, the collapse of the Soviet Union deprived most Marian devotees of their universal enemy and energizing adversary. Moreover, the role of Fátima appeared to have run its course when Mary appeared again in Medjugorje in 1981, an apparition which was later interpreted as the fulfillment of Fátima due to the fact that it occurred during the twilight of communism (Varghese 2000: 189). However, the example of the Baysiders movement and other apparitional cults shows that Fátima has remained a source of inspiration during the waning of the Cold War, and has also partially shifted to new enemies.

The centennial of Fátima was celebrated across the globe in 2017. Coincidentally, this was the same year in which newspapers again started to write about a new or revived Cold War. Russian aggression in Ukraine, Russia's annexation of the Crimea, and the United States' withdrawal from the 1987 INF treaty which limited the proliferation of intermediate-range missiles in the United States and the USSR all added to the idea that the Cold War had not yet come to an end. In any case the conservative Fatima Crusade never ceased its activities, regardless of the political climate. With Russia 'converted', new meanings for Fátima could be found. The Crusade viewed perestroika and its results as a hoax, and eventually turned its religious condemnations against the West and its moral decay. This bears out the point made by Mark Juergensmeyer that the Cold War enemy had changed: the 'new' common enemy was the loss of faith due to Western secular nationalism (1993: 1-41). This stimulated a fundamentalist religious revival against the popular secular ideology and the threat posed to traditional marriage and family values.

Mary was thrust to the fore once again. More visions with a conservative message were received across the globe, while a new international movement surfaced that organized protective recitation of the rosary at the borders of individual countries against religious and moral decay, in a clear reference to the *peregrinations* of the early Cold War.[4] In Poland, where this decay was perceived very strongly, it resulted in a nationalist mass Rosary Crusade for the 'homeland' in 2012 (Balcerzak 2018). The Fátima centennial was the incentive for the "Rosary to the borders" movement, a network of prayer groups across the world, under the guidance of Our Lady of Fátima. The rally was launched in October 2017 and once again mobilized hundreds of thousands to pray at 4,000 'prayer zones' along the 2,000-mile Polish border for the survival of Christianity in Poland.[5] In Italy a similar prayer campaign occurred on October 13, the intention there being to save the country from "Islamic nihilism and the denial of the Christian faith".[6] Devotees in Ireland, the United Kingdom, and Belgium followed suit with similar rallies. In 2018, the pope added his voice to the chorus, asking Catholics to pray the rosary because of spiritual unrest in the world and to bring the Church under Mary's protective mantle, especially in view of the crimes of sexual abuse in the Church.[7]

The Cold War period was a heyday for metaphors, which were rhetorically highly effective in controlling people through fear and threats of damnation, and to promote reductive binary worldviews and ideologies: for God or against God. This corresponded perfectly with the 'totalitarian' character of Catholicism, and it was a successful way of mobilizing Catholics to fight atheism in a religious way under the aegis of a Marian warrior. In sum, we can state that the role of Mary during the Cold War, instrumentalized in various ways by the actors involved, was substantial. Her interventions, messages, and warrior-like image influenced and affected the war in significant ways. It made the Cold War in part also a religious war, in its cause and goals as well as in its nature as a battle against atheism and secularism as representations of the Antichrist. The struggle was fought mainly with religious weapons, ranging from propaganda and prayer to devotional inspiration and divine intervention. During the long Cold War, Marian militancy partly also became a struggle of the Catholic world community against itself, as part of the Church and its flock started to drift away into modernism and secularism, democratic socialism, post-Vatican II liberalizing views, or felt under threat from competing religions. The Virgin Mary showed her flexibility and was convincingly engaged once more in this new culture war. In view also of what appears to be a current Cold War revival, it is obvious that her role as warrior and protectress of the faith is far from over.

4 For example: <www.rosaireauxfrontieres.be>.
5 <www.nytimes.com/2017/10/07/world/europe/poland-rosary-border-prayer.html>.
6 <www.churchmilitant.com/news/article/italians-pray-rosary-at-the-border>.
7 <https://donate.catholicaction.org/campaign/faith-defender-family/c155441>.

BIBLIOGRAPHY

Balcerzak, Agnieszka. 2018. "The Rosary Crusade for the Homeland. Poland's Controversial New Religious Movement" (paper presentation).

Coppa, Frank J. 2010. "Cold War and the Papacy." In *New Catholic Encyclopedia Supplement*. Volume 1, 342-349. Farmington Hills, MI: Gale.

Goubert, Joseph, and L. Cristiani. 1952. *Apparitions et messages de la Sainte Vierge de 1830 à nos jours*. Paris: La Colombe.

Haffert, John M. 1982. *Dear Bishop! Memoirs of the Author Concerning the History of the Blue Army*. Washington, NJ: AMI International Press.

Juergensmeyer, Mark. 1993. *The New Cold War? Religious Nationalism Confronts the Secular State*. Berkeley: University of California Press.

Kirby, Dianne (ed.). 2013 [2002]. *Religion and the Cold War*. Basingstoke: Palgrave Macmillan.

Laurentin, René, and Patrick Sbalchiero. 2007. *Dictionnaire des 'apparitions' de la Vierge Marie. Inventaire des origines à nos jours. Méthodologie, bilan interdisciplinaires, prospective*. Paris: Fayard.

Muehlenbeck, Philip E. 2012. *Religion and the Cold War. A Global Perspective*. Nashville: Vanderbilt UP.

Park, Karen E. 2017. "'Citadel of Orthodoxy': Meaning, Message, and Pilgrimage at Our Lady of Guadelupe Shrine in La Crosse, Wiscounsin." *American Catholic Studies* 128 (1):1-16.

Powers, Richard Gid. 1995. *Not Without Honor: The History of American Anticommunism*. New York: The Free Press.

Van Son, H.J.A. 1936. *Honderd vragen en antwoorden over het Russisch Communisme. Wat de wereld te verwachten heeft van het Communisme*. Tilburg: Comité Katholieke Actie 'Voor God'.

Varghese, Roy A. 2000. *God-Sent: A History of the Accredited Apparitions of Mary*. New York: Crossroad Publishing Company.

Wallace, James C. 2013. "A Religious War? The Cold War and Religion." *Journal of Cold War Studies* 15: 162-180.

TIMELINE

1905, June 11	encyclical of Pius X, *Il Fermo Proposito*, incentive to Catholic Action
1910, Oct. 5 1910, Nov. 20	overthrow of the Portuguese government Mexican Revolution
1917, March 8 (Old Style: Feb. 23) 1917, May 13 1917, May 13 1917, Oct. 13 1917, Oct. 16 1917, Nov. 7 (Old Style: Oct. 25)	February Revolution in Russia first apparition in Fátima: messages on the Immaculate Heart, penance, prayer Eugenio Pacelli (later Pope Pius XII) consecrated bishop in Rome final apparition in Fátima: miracle of the sun founding of the Militia of the Immaculata, for the conversion of enemies of the Church, by Father M. Kolbe in Rome October Revolution in Russia
1920, Aug. 15	Miracle on the Vistula, victory of Poland over the Red Army
1921, Sept. 7	Legion of Mary founded by Frank Duff in Dublin
1922, Feb. 6- 1939, Feb. 10	reign of Pope Pius XI
1929, June 13	Tuy (Spain) new apparition of Our Lady of Fátima to Lúcia: "consecrate Russia to my Immaculate Heart"
1930, Oct. 13	Fátima apparitions recognized by the bishop of Leiria
1931, May 13 1931, May 15	first national (Portuguese) pilgrimage to Fátima *Quadragesimo Anno*, encyclical by Pius XI on the dangers of totalitarianism for the social order; introduction Catholic social teaching
1932, Nov.- 1933, Jan.	apparitions in Beauraing (Belgium)
1933, Jan.-March	apparitions in Banneux (Belgium)
1934, Sept. 18	Soviet Union admitted to the League of Nations
1935	Exhumation and reburial of Fátima visionary Jacinta reminds Lúcia of the Russian conversion message

1936, July 17-1939, April 1	Spanish Civil War
1936, Sept.10-1947, Dec. 22	Dutch anticommunist action “For God”
1937, March 19	*Divini Redemptoris*, encyclical letter by Pius XI on the dangers of communism
1938, Sept. 15 - 1955, Oct. 1	apparitions in Kérizinen (France); publicly known since 1947
1938, May 13	Portuguese bishops visit Fátima in fulfilment of vow (made in October 1936) that they would do so if Our Lady were to protect the country from communism and civil war
1939, March 12-1958, Oct. 9	reign of Pope Pius XII
1941, August	Lúcia records three secrets given to her by Our Lady of Fátima and gives them to the Church
1942, April 7-8	statue of Our Lady of Fátima on pilgrimage from Cova da Iria to Lisbon
1942, May 13	25th anniversary of the Fátima apparitions
1942, May 13	25th anniversary of episcopal ordination of Eugenio Pacelli, Pope Pius XII
1942, Oct. 31	Pope Pius XII consecrates the world to the Immaculate Heart in a radio message for Portugal
1942, Dec. 8	Pope Pius XII invites all the bishops of the world to consecrate their dioceses to the Immaculate Heart
1943, June 2	film *El Milagro de Fátima* (*Fátima, Terra de Fé*) released in Portugal
1943, March 28-1948, Aug. 29	*Grand Retour* missionary pilgrimages of the statue of Our Lady of Boulogne throughout France
1945, Feb. 4-11	Yalta Conference on the postwar world and the division of Europe
1945, March 25-1959, May 31	apparitions of the Lady of All Nations in Amsterdam; the messages become public in 1954
1945, May 7-8	the end of the Second World War in Europe
1946, May 13	crowning of Our Lady of Fátima statue in Fátima; papal message on Our Lady of Fátima as the source of mercy and miraculous protectress of the whole world
1947, Jan. 25	(Family) Rosary Crusade founded by Patrick Peyton, CSC, in Albany (New York)
1947, March 12	Truman Doctrine speech in United States Congress (‘beginning’ of the Cold War)
1947, April 12	apparitions at Tre Fontane (Rome); conversion of anti-Catholic Bruno Cornacchiola
1947, May	foundation of the Blue Army of (Our Lady of) Fátima by priests Harold V. Colgan and John M. Haffert, OCarm (renamed World Apostolate of Fatima in 2005)
1947, May 13	start of a pilgrimage with a statue of Our Lady of Fátima through Europe, Africa, Asia, and Australia
1947, July 20	canonization of Louis-Marie Grignion de Montfort
1947, Sept.	first references to a ‘Cold War’ in *New York Herald Tribune*
1947, Sept. 2-8	Marian Congress in Maastricht
1947, Oct. 5-1956, April 17	Information Bureau of the Communist and Workers’ Parties (Cominform)
1947, Nov. 15	start visions of Cuevas de Vinromá (Spain)
1947, Dec. 8	start of a pilgrimage with a statue of Our Lady of Fátima through the United States
1947, Dec. 25	the “Bacon Priest” Werenfried van Straaten, OPraem, plans the foundation of ‘Aid to the Church in Need’ in Tongerlo (Belgium), an organization to aid oppressed or persecuted Christians in Central and Eastern Europe

1948, Feb.	communist coup in Czechoslovakia
1948, Feb. 10	vision of moving Marian statue in Assisi
1948, April 3	President Truman signs the Marshall Plan
1948, April 18	general elections in Italy
1948, June 24-1949, May 12	Berlin blockade by the Russians
1948, Sept. 12	apparitions of Our Lady in Lipa (Philippines)
1948, Dec. 26	arrest of Cardinal Mindszenty in Hungary
1949, April 4	the North Atlantic Treaty Organization (NATO) treaty signed
1949, June 6	start of the Mazury (Poland) apparitions
1949, July 1	papal decree *Responsa ad dubia de communismo* stating that Catholics who defend or spread communist ideas risk excommunication
1949, Aug. 29	detonation of first Russian atomic bomb
1949, Oct. 1	'fall' of China to communism under Mao Zedong
1949, Nov.	start of the Necedah (US) apparitions
1950	the Holy Year or Jubilee
1950, Nov. 1	declaration of the Assumption of Mary as a dogma
1950-1954	Stella Maris processions through the Dutch diocese of Roermond
1950, June 25-1953, July 27	Korean War (invasion of the South)
1951	film *La Señora de Fátima* released
1951	pilgrimage with statue of Our Lady of Banneux through the diocese of Liège
1951, Jan.-Oct.	pilgrimage with statue of Our Lady of Fátima through Australia; founding of the Legion of Mary in Australia in August
1951, April 29	apparition of the Lady of All Nations in Amsterdam raises issue of 'final' Marian dogma of Mary as co-redemptrix
1952, March 25	start of the Dutch 'Pentagon project' and the creation of an Empire of Mary
1952, July 7	Pius XII consecrates the peoples of Russia to the Immaculate Heart
1952, July 14	'We have learned', encyclical by Pope Pius XII on the Rosary Crusade
1952, Aug. 20	film *The Miracle of Our Lady of Fatima* released, on Fátima's anti-Russian messages
1953	*Peregrinatio Mariae* with the statue of Our Lady of Fátima through the diocese of Münster
1953, March 5	death of Stalin
1953, August 29	weeping Madonna of Syracuse
1954, (Dec. 8, 1853-Dec. 8, 1954)	first Marian Holy Year: centenary of the dogma of the Immaculate Conception
1954, March-May	Dien Bien Phu (Indochina): communist Vietminh defeat the French
1954, May 30	pastoral letter to the Dutch Church Province, with antisocialist/anticommunist content
1954, May-Dec.	*Peregrinatio Mariae* with the statue of Our Lady of Fátima through the German diocese of Cologne
1955, May 1-1957, July 23	*Peregrinatio Mariae* with the statue of Our Lady of Fátima through the diocese of Breda, Netherlands
1955, May 14	start of the Warsaw Pact

1956, Oct. 23- Nov. 10	Hungarian Revolution
1957, Aug. 26- 1980, Oct. 12	Polish *Peregrinatio Mariae* with icon of Our Lady of Częstochowa
1958, Feb. 11 1958	centenary of the Lourdes apparitions Second Berlin Crisis; Khrushchev's ultimatum to Western powers to withdraw from Berlin
1959, April 23 1959, Dec. 8	start of *Peregrinatio Mariae* with the statue of Our Lady of Fátima through Italy first Rosary Crusade in Manila (Philippines)
1960 1960, Dec. 18 1960, Sept. 29- Oct. 12	call from Portugal to all bishops to hold prayer campaigns to Our Lady of Fátima day of prayer and penance for all victims of communist persecution announced by the bishops of the United States second *Peregrinatio Mariae* through the diocese of Breda
1961, April 17 1961, Aug. 13	Bay of Pigs invasion in Cuba start of the building of the Berlin Wall
1962 1962, Oct. 14	Second Rosary Crusade in the Philippines Cuban Missile crisis
1963, Aug. 5	Nuclear Test Ban Treaty
1964, Nov. 21	Pope Paul VI renews consecration of Russia to the Immaculate Heart
1965 1965, Dec. 8	statue of Our Lady of Fátima travels to Vietnam closing of the Second Vatican Council
1966, June 6 and 20	*peregrinatio* of Our Lady of Częstochowa stopped by authorities and icon 'arrested'; *peregrinatio* continued with 'empty frame'
1968	founding of the Fátima-inspired Pro Deo et Fratribus, Famiglia di Maria Association by Slovak bishop Pavol Hnilica at Sessa Aurunca (Italy)
1970, April 7- 1995, Aug. 3	apparitions in Bayside (New York)
1971	Blue Army brings seventy pilgrimaging statues of Our Lady of Fátima to individual nations
1975, Aug. 1	Helsinki Accords reduce Cold War tensions
1978	the anticommunist international Fatima Rosary Crusade founded by Father Nicholas Gruner in Fort Erie, Ontario
1981, May 13	Turkish militant Ali Ağca, ordered by the Iranian government and/or the KGB, tries to assassinate John Paul II on St Peter's Square
1982, May 13	John Paul II, together with many bishops across the world, consecrates the world - including Russia - to the Immaculate Heart

1983, March 8	Soviet Union as "Evil empire", speech by Ronald Reagan
1984, March 25	John Paul II, together with all the bishops of the world, consecrates Russia and the world to the Immaculate Heart
1986, Feb. 25	Gorbachev introduces *glasnost* and *perestroika* in the Soviet Union
1989, June 4 1989, Oct. 7 1989, Nov. 9 1989, Dec. 1	victory of the Solidarity coalition in Poland Hungary abandons communism fall of the Berlin Wall restauration of diplomatic relations between the Holy See and Russia
1991, Juli 1 1991, Dec. 25	The Dissolution of the Warsaw Pact dissolution of the Soviet Union
2000, May 13 2000, Oct. 7-8	disclosure of the Third Secret of Fátima by the Vatican visit of the statue of Our Lady of Fátima to Rome for the Great Jubilee and the "Millennium of Mary"
2001, Sept. 11 2001, Sept.	terrorist attacks on New York and Washington DC Father Nicholas Gruner, founder of the Fatima Crusade suspended by the Vatican
2005, Oct. 7	creation of the World Apostolate of Fatima (successor to the Fatima Crusade)
2014, March	annexation of Crimea by Russia
2019, Aug. 2	President Trump withdrawal from the 1987 Intermediate-range Nuclear Forces Treaty with Russia, after violations of the treaty by Russia
2020	Coronavirus (Covid 19) crisis

AUTHORS

Michael Agnew is a Research Coordinator at Conestoga College in Kitchener, Canada. He received his doctorate in religious studies from McMaster University in 2015, based on his research of contemporary pilgrimage to the Catholic healing shrine at Lourdes, France. His research interests include modern Catholic devotions and pilgrimage, material religion, Marian apparitions, and religious accommodation policy. His work has recently been published in *Studies in Religion*, as well as the edited volumes *Religious Diversity Today: Experiencing Religion in the Contemporary World* and *Sacred Waters: A Cross-Cultural Compendium of Hallowed Springs and Holy Wells.*

William A. Christian Jr. writes mainly about Catholicism in Spain and Southern Europe. His central concern has been the relationship of individuals and groups with the saints, Mary, and God. His studies involve fieldwork in contemporary communities and archival work covering the medieval and early-modern periods. He teaches graduate courses in anthropology at the Universitat Autònoma de Barcelona, and has been a visiting professor in Paris, Pécs, Berkeley, and Santa Barbara. His books include *Person and God in a Spanish Valley* (1972, 1989), *Local Religion in Sixteenth-Century Spain* (1981), *Apparitions in Late Medieval and Renaissance Spain* (1981), *Moving Crucifixes in Modern Spain* (1992), *Visionaries: The Spanish Republic and the Reign of Christ* (1996), and *The Stranger, the Tears, the Photograph, the Touch; Divine Presence in Spain and Europe since 1500* (2017).

Deirdre de la Cruz is Associate Professor in the Departments of History and Asian Languages and Cultures, and Director of the Doctoral Program in Anthropology and History at the University of Michigan. Her research focuses on Filipino popular and religious cultures as they instantiate major concepts in the study of religion, Southeast Asian studies, and the theoretical and methodological intersections of anthropology and history. She is the author of *Mother Figured: Marian Apparitions and the Making of a Filipino Universal* (2015) and several articles on material religion, visual culture, and the occult.

Agnieszka Halemba (PhD 2003 Cambridge) is a social anthropologist currently working at the Institute of Archaeology and Ethnology of the Polish Academy of Sciences and teaching at the University of Potsdam in Germany. She focuses on the anthropology of religion, with long-term field research conducted in southern Siberia and Transcarpathian Ukraine. Since 2016, she conducts research on the significance of religious architecture in secular contexts based on fieldwork in North-Eastern Germany. She is also a head of the Anthropology Undisciplined Research Unit, which focuses on development of innovative methodologies for interdisciplinary research and an author of two ethnography-based monographs: *Negotiating Marian Apparitions: The Politics of Religion in Transcarpathian Ukraine* (Central European University Press 2015) and *The Telengits of Southern Siberia: Landscape, Religion and Knowledge in Motion* (Routledge 2006).

Thomas Kselman is Professor Emeritus in the Department of History at the University of Notre Dame. He was president of the American Catholic Historical Association in 2005, and a Guggenheim Fellow in 1989. Kselman is the author of *Conscience and Conversion: Religious Liberty in Post-Revolutionary France* (2018), *Death and the Afterlife in Modern France* (1993) and *Miracles and Prophecies in Nineteenth-Century France* (1983), which won the Shea prize of the American Catholic Historical Association. He is the editor of *Belief in History: Innovative Approaches to European and American Religion* (1991).

Peter Jan Margry is Professor of European Ethnology at the University of Amsterdam and senior fellow at the Meertens Institute, a research center of the Royal Netherlands Academy of Arts and Sciences in Amsterdam. His research focus is on modern and contemporary religious cultures, alternative healing practices, cultural memory and cultural heritage. He has published various monographs and edited volumes, among them *Shrines and Pilgrimage in the Modern World: New Itineraries into the Sacred* (2008); *Grassroots Memorials: The Politics of Memorializing Traumatic Death* (2011; with C. Sánchez-Carretero); *Spiritualizing the City. Agency and Resilience of the Urban and Urbanesque Habitat* (2017; with V. Hegner); *The Amsterdam Miracle: A Biography of a Contested Devotion* (2019; with C. Caspers).

Katharine Massam is Academic Dean and Associate Professor at Pilgrim Theological College within the University of Divinity in Melbourne, Australia, where she also leads the university's strategic goal in Gender and Theology. Her writing focuses on the intersections of theology and wider culture, particularly in postcolonial settler societies with an emphasis on the lived experience of religious belief. Her publications include *Sacred Threads: Catholic Spirituality in Australia* (1996), and *A Bridge Between: Spanish Benedictine Missionary Women in Australia* (2020). She was elected as a member of the Australian Institute of Aboriginal and Torres Strait Islander Studies (AIATIS) in 2017.

David Morgan is Professor of Religion at Duke University. He also holds an appointment in the Department of Art, Art History, and Visual Studies at Duke. Morgan received a PhD in art history at the University of Chicago (1990). He is author of several books, including *The Forge of Vision: A Visual History of Modern Christianity* (2015), *The Sacred Gaze* (2005), and *Visual Piety* (1998). Morgan is an elected member of Clare Hall, University of Cambridge, and of the American Antiquarian Society. He is co-founder and co-editor of the journal *Material Religion*, and co-edits a book series on Research in Material Religion, published by Bloomsbury. Morgan's work focuses on the history of Christian visual culture, mass-mediated imagery, art theory, and material culture. In 2018 he published *Images at Work: The Material Culture of Enchantment*.

Marina Sanahuja Beltran is a practising architect in Barcelona with a Master's Degree in Social Anthropology from the Universitat Autònoma de Barcelona. Her master thesis, on the social aspects of the architecture of rural habitats in the province of Castelló, is entitled "Tirant del fil. Construcció de l'entramat sociocultural del Mas de la Creu."

Monique Scheer is Professor of Historical and Cultural Anthropology at the University of Tübingen, where she also serves as Vice-President for International Affairs. Her research interests include historical and anthropological approaches to emotions, religion and the secular. Most recently, she has co-edited *Secular Bodies, Affects and Emotions: European Perspectives* (2019) with Birgitte Schepelern Johansen and Nadia Fadil and *The Public Work of Christmas: Difference and Belonging in Multicultural Societies* (2019) with Pamela E. Klassen. She has also just published a monograph titled *Enthusiasm: Emotional Practices of Conviction in Modern Germany* (2020).

Konrad Siekierski holds an M.A. in cultural anthropology from the University of Warsaw. Currently, he is a Ph.D. candidate at the Department of Theology and Religious Studies, King's College London. His research interests include the religious situation in the post-Soviet Republic of Armenia (with special focus on the Armenian Apostolic Church, Armenian Catholic Church and neopaganism), identity formation in the Armenian diaspora, and contemporary Catholicism in Poland. He is co-editor of *Armenia: Kultura współczesna w ujęciu antropologicznym* (2014) and *Armenians in Post-Socialist Europe* (2016), co-author of *Ormianie katolicy w Armenii i Gruzji. Historia, pamięć, tożsamość* (2019), and author of several journal articles and book chapters.

Tine Van Osselaer is Research Professor in the history of spirituality, devotion and mysticism at the Ruusbroec Institute of the University of Antwerp. In the last years, she has published on gender and religion (*The Pious Sex: Catholic Constructions of Masculinity and Femininity in Belgium, c.1800-1940*, 2013); and edited volumes on religion and medicine (*Sign or Symptom? Exceptional Corporeal Phenomena in Religion and Medicine in the Nineteenth and Twentieth Centuries*, 2017), religion and the family (*Christian Homes: Religion, Family and Domesticity in the 19th and 20th centuries*, 2014), religion in the Great War (themed issue of *Trajecta. Religion, Culture and Society in the Low Countries* 23 (2014) 2). She was the principal investigator of STIGMATICS: "Between saints and celebrities. The devotion and promotion of stigmatics in Europe, c.1800-1950", a project sponsored by the European Research Council. See https://brill.com/view/title/55448 (open access).

Robert Ventresca is Associate Professor of history at King's University College at Western University in London, Ontario (Canada). His research and teaching explore the role of religion in European fascism, as well as religious involvement in the Holocaust with a special focus on the Catholic Church. He is the author of *Soldier of Christ: The Life of Pope Pius XII* (2013) which was awarded the American Catholic Historical Association's 2014 Koenig Prize for Catholic biography, and of *From Fascism to Democracy: Culture and Politics in the Italian Election of 1948* (2004) which received an honorable mention for the Canadian Historical Association's Wallace K. Ferguson Prize.

Daniel Wojcik is Professor of English and Folklore Studies, and affiliate faculty in Religious Studies at the University of Oregon. His books include *The End of the World As We Know It: Faith, Fatalism, and Apocalypse in America* (1997); *Punk and Neo-Tribal Body Art* (1995) and *Outsider Art: Visionary Worlds and Trauma* (2016), and he has published widely on the topics of apocalyptic belief, alternative spiritualities, visionary culture, sacred place-making, subcultures, and vernacular artistic expression.

Sandra L. Zimdars-Swartz is Professor Emerita at the University of Kansas. She is the author of *Encountering Mary: From La Salette to Medjugorje* (1991) and numerous articles on apparitions of the Virgin Mary. She has recently published the chapter "Fatima and the Politics of Devotion" in *Marian Devotion, Political Mobilization and Nationalism in Europe and America*, edited by Roberto di Stefano and Francisco Javier Ramón Solans (2016), and the article "Lipa Comes to Necedah: Personal Experiences, Signs, and a Confluence of Imagery at an American Cold War Apparition," in *Nova Religio: The Journal of Alternative and Emergent Religions* 21:2 (2017): 100-110.

INDEX OF NAMES AND PLACES

COLOPHON

FINAL EDITING
Luc Vints

COPY EDITING
Lieve Claes

LAY-OUT
Alexis Vermeylen

KADOC
Documentation and Research Centre on Religion, Culture and Society
Vlamingenstraat 39
B - 3000 Leuven
www.kadoc.kuleuven.be

Leuven University Press
Minderbroedersstraat 4
B - 3000 Leuven
www.lup.be